introduction to
MANAGEMENT

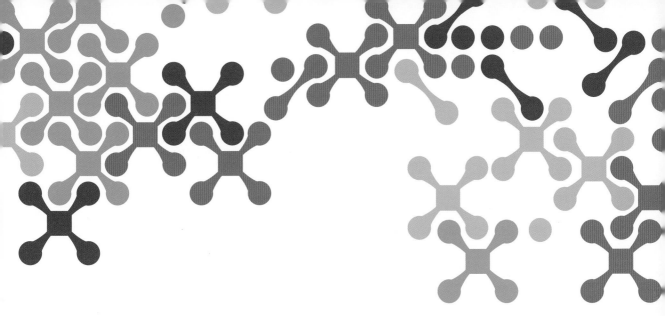

introduction to
MANAGEMENT

GEORGE GREEN LIBRARY OF
SCIENCE AND ENGINEERING

Colin Combe

OXFORD
UNIVERSITY PRESS

OXFORD
UNIVERSITY PRESS

Great Clarendon Street, Oxford, OX2 6DP,
United Kingdom

Oxford University Press is a department of the University of Oxford.
It furthers the University's objective of excellence in research, scholarship,
and education by publishing worldwide. Oxford is a registered trade mark of
Oxford University Press in the UK and in certain other countries

Published in the United States of America by Oxford University Press
198 Madison Avenue, New York, NY 10016, United States of America

British Library Cataloguing in Publication Data
Data available

Library of Congress Control Number: 2013951691

ISBN 978-0-19-964299-1

Printed in Great Britain by
Bell & Bain Ltd, Glasgow

Acknowledgements

A number of people have helped in the compilation of this book including members of the Department of Management at the Glasgow School *for* Business and Society at Glasgow Caledonian University. In particular, I am grateful to Dr Peter Duncan for providing a number of invaluable skillsets for the book. Thanks also to the management practitioners who contributed their valuable time and expertise to the practitioner case studies including Fernando Mendez Navia (Dex Europe), Alison Keir (NHS Forth Valley), Claire Carpenter (The Melting Pot), and James Bowes (Bowes Consulting). I have also benefited from the valuable guidance and support of the editorial team at Oxford University Press including Francesca Griffin, Benjamin Pettitt, Nicola Hartley, and Siân Jenkins. Thanks also to Sacha Cook for helping to maintain the momentum of the project at critical stages of the work.

I am also grateful to the reviewers for their wise counsel and invaluable guidance and recommendations. I have tried wherever possible to incorporate their suggestions to improve the quality of the book. Personal acknowledgements go to Debbie and Richard Combe for their patience and understanding during the long hours of researching and writing the book and to Robert and Catriona Brown for providing some welcome relief from the computer screen. I also acknowledge the inspirational legacy of Keith Thurley of the London School of Economics.

Guide to the Book

Identifying and defining

Clear, concise learning outcomes begin each chapter and help to contextualise the chapter's objectives. These outcomes are then revisited in the chapter summaries.

Each introduction explains the relevance of each chapter topic to managers. A clear, succinct overview of how the chapter will develop is also given.

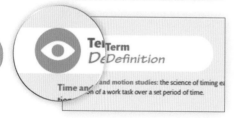

Clear definitions are provided throughout the text to help all students who are new to management get to grips with key terms. All definitions are also consolidated in a glossary at the end of the book for easy reference.

Management in practice

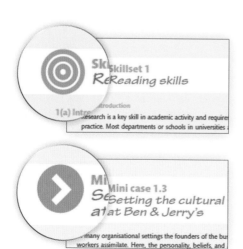

The skillsets provide insightful demonstrations of what skills are needed, how to apply them, and why they are relevant to both academic study and the professional workplace. The skillsets are cross referenced to each other throughout the text and are designed to be used as a package to provide a holistic skills base.

Management theories are played out in the real world every day. Contemporary examples from a truly international range of sources help you make the link from theory to reality. They also come equipped with QR codes to take you directly to the relevant organisation's website.

Each chapter includes an in-depth and elongated case study of a chosen organisation or individual manager from a wide range of both service and manufacturing organisations from around the globe. The case study focuses on particular key themes linked to the chapter and is followed by discussion points, questions and tasks.

Testing and applying your understanding

At the end of every case study, discussion points and questions help you assess your understanding of the central themes and your readiness to progress to the next part of the topic.

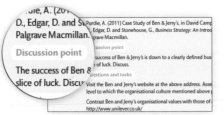

Each chapter concludes with a set of questions and tasks aimed at consolidating the main theories, approaches, and case study examples to prepare you for assessment.

Model answers to all questions in the book can be found on the Online Resource Centre (ORC). These provide the opportunity to see different ways of answering such questions and to check you are on the right track.

Test yourself on each chapter of the textbook and receive instant feedback on your answers through the MCQs on the Online Resource Centre (ORC).

The flashcard glossary will help you to memorise the key terms in the book; they can be viewed on portable devices such as iPhones. These can be found on the Online Resource Centre (ORC).

Reflecting and summarising

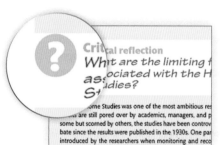

The critical reflection boxes focus on limitations of theory, new and different perspectives or schools of thought, or a viewpoint different from that expressed in the main text. They also provide an opportunity to reflect on the evolution of thinking around key themes.

At the end of each chapter you will find a summary of the key points covered as well as a brief paragraph explaining why each is important to academic study, or the workplace. These points revisit those outlined in the learning outcomes at the beginning of the chapter so you can check your understanding of key themes.

Taking your learning further

To take your learning further, reading lists have been provided as guides to finding out more about the issues raised within each chapter, and to help you locate the useful academic literature in the field.

A series of annotated web links, organised by chapter, has been provided to point you in the direction of important material on the principles of management.

QR Code images are used throughout this book. QR Code is a registered trademark of DENSO WAVE INCORPORATED. If your mobile device does not have a QR Code reader try this website for advice: www.mobile-barcodes.com/qr-code-software

Guide to the Online Resource Centre

The Online Resource Centre that accompanies this book provides students and registered adopters of the textbook with ready-to-use teaching and learning materials. These resources are free of charge and designed to maximise the learning experience.

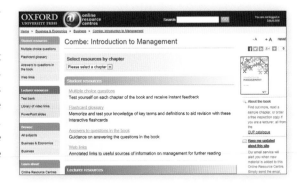

Lecturer resources

These resources are password protected. Access is available to adopters of the book. Please contact your local sales representative.

Library of video links

Annotated links to a range of useful videos demonstrate various aspects of management in practice with accompanying teaching notes.

PowerPoint slides

Customisable PowerPoint slides have been included for use in lecture presentations. Arranged by chapter theme, the slides may also be used as handouts in class.

Test bank

The test bank is a fully customisable resource containing interactive questions, such as multiple choice, true/false, and fill in the blank, accompanied by answers and feedback with which to test your students.

Contents in Brief

Detailed Contents

xiv

XV

xvii

xviii

xix

List of Figures and Tables

Preface

Introduction

This book provides a valuable introduction to key issues, concepts, ideas, and theoretical perspectives on management for students, teachers, and practitioners. The book is primarily aimed at undergraduate and postgraduate students who are new to the study of management. The contents have been designed, and the writing styled, in a way that deliberately appeals to those who seek an accessible, flexible, and fully supported introductory text on management. Although the book necessarily adopts the 'language' of business and management, the ideas, theories, and concepts are all clearly explained and supported by definitions and a glossary of terms where appropriate. The book is flexible in the sense that it supports a number of different learning approaches including text-based analysis and discussion, critical reflection, and case study discussion points, questions, and tasks. The Online Resource Centre (ORC) adds a further learning support facility and includes answers to the case study questions, multiple-choice questions (MCQs) and answers, PowerPoint slides linked to each chapter topic, and a series of test bank questions and answers for teachers.

Contents

The book comprises four main parts. Part One covers Management Principles and Functions including a treatment of what management is and the functions and roles of managers; and the development and application of management theory in different sectors and international contexts. Part One offers clear explanations and examples of the management process in action including key functions of planning, organising, leading, and controlling. Although these functions are presented in stages, it is clear that they overlap each other and are usually undertaken simultaneously. Thus, the sequence in which they are presented is simply a matter of choice. Part One also covers the important decision-making skill of management and adopts a critical view of the theoretical models devised to help the decision making process.

Part Two comprises elements relating to Managing People and Communications by first addressing the role, aims, and importance of human resource management (HRM) within common themes of managing equality and diversity in a global economy. This part of the book also features an explanation and critical evaluation of theoretical perspectives on motivation of workers and addresses key issues of empowerment and rewards in the modern business environment. The management of groups and teams is linked to this and is the focus of further explanation and critical scrutiny.

Part Three focuses on Management and Organisations with an emphasis on organisational structures (including modern iterations such as virtual organisations), organisational culture, and ethics. Issues of corporate social responsibility (CSR) and an ethical stance in business are important contemporary issues facing managers as they seek trust-forming relationships with consumers and other stakeholders. The analysis of these key concepts relates the evolution of thinking in CSR and business ethics and delivers a valuable insight into why these ideas and concepts have become an important element in managing organisations in the modern era.

Part Four features Managing Strategy, Change, and Innovation. This part begins with an overview of the strategy process before going on to apply theoretical models that help managers formulate and implement strategy. The discussion also extends to the evaluation of strategy. Each part of the strategic process is subject to a detailed explanation and also a critique of the limitations of each model applied. The analysis then turns to that of change. Here, the discussion begins with a rationale for the reasons why change is necessary in modern organisations. Detailed accounts of types of organisational change are outlined as are the management issues relating to the change process. This discussion leads on to the treatment of the culture of innovation and creativity with an emphasis on managing and influencing the development of innovation. A deeper discussion of information systems and knowledge management as catalysts for change and innovation is also included.

Key theme: Skillsets

A key added value to students using the book is the enhancement of skills that the content helps to deliver. The learning processes in the main body of the text, which are followed and supplemented by the Skillsets, provide students with insightful demonstrations of how to apply key skills to improve the quality of their academic performance and, ultimately, their employability. In the main body of the text these include the ability to choose and apply appropriate theoretical models; make effective decisions; design work schedules; motivate workers; understand the need for an ethical dimension to business; analyse internal and external environments as part of a strategy process; and many others.

The Skillsets provide a practical guide to applying many of the techniques that underpin academic work. These include essay writing skills; exam techniques; presentation skills; reading skills; personal development planning; time management; referencing techniques; critical analysis; sourcing materials; and analysing and using case studies. This section also gives examples of typical exam questions and guidance to model answers, and an example of an academic essay. These skills are not only a vital part of students' portfolio of technical abilities that help them to navigate their way through their academic career, but are also transferable to the workplace and help improve employability prospects.

XXV

Key theme: International in scope

The book has a distinct international flavour with case studies featuring examples of contemporary management issues and challenges in different contexts. These include the emerging economic powerhouses of Brazil, Russia, India, and China (the so-called BRIC nations); fast-developing nations of strategic significance such as Malaysia and Mexico; an example of a supra-national entity, the European Union (EU); and other distinct and diverse examples such as the rise and fall of Toyota in Japan; the organisation of police forces in Nigeria; the introduction of Total Quality Management techniques in Botswana; and the charismatic leadership style of former Venezuelan President Hugo Chávez.

The international tenor of the narrative content and examples used is designed to reflect the truly multi-ethnic and global characteristics of the modern student body. The content and design of the book provides clear and concise explanations and mini case studies, chapter case studies, question and answer sections, glossaries and additional web-based materials that will be of practical help to both domestic UK and international students. The content offers an insight into management techniques and practices evident in a broad range of regions and countries, whilst recognising the integrated characteristics of global management.

The book enhances learning and understanding in an international context by illustrating comparisons of management practice between different regions as well as highlighting the key social and cultural differences that influence management practice in different contexts and countries. The discussion covers many different sectors including service, knowledge economy, digital economy, pharmaceuticals, agriculture, retailing, public sector, social enterprise, and renewables among others. The regions and countries selected span the globe and range from a publicly owned organisation in the UK (BBC), to private enterprises in Europe and the USA (Nokia, IKEA, Procter & Gamble, Ford); a family run business in Australia (Visy) to a public body in Germany (European Patent Office). The role of multinationals in developing nations such as Guatemala (Starbucks) and Puerto Rico (Pfizer) are also included. The book features discussion on some recent trends in management such as the challenge of managing a social enterprise (The Melting Pot) and the management techniques for supporting innovation and creativity among small and medium sized enterprises (Dex Europe).

Key theme: Critical reflection

A key feature of the book is the critical dimension to much of the discussion. Although the book provides a comprehensive account of key introductory concepts of management, knowledge and understanding cannot ever be complete. Not all information is available at any given time, environments change (sometimes quickly and without warning), attitudes and beliefs change, technology changes rapidly, and so on. What we are dealing with is a dynamic environment in which management takes place. What is relevant, useful, and appropriate in one timeframe may become less relevant, of limited practical use, and inappropriate in the next. Also, different writers and contributors to management may come from different schools of thought, different cultures, or different political and economic environments. These cannot help but colour the way they see the world, and in particular the role and practice of management within that environment.

To account for these dynamic and diverse features of the environment in which the study of management takes place, the book pauses occasionally for what is called 'critical reflection'. The boxes containing critical reflections provide an opportunity to take note of some of the limitations associated with the approach to explaining and discussing key topics on management. They provide an opportunity to remind ourselves that other perspectives on the same topic exist and that they too have something to contribute to our understanding of management. Critical reflection also helps us to evaluate the true contribution to knowledge and understanding of a chosen approach by comparing it to other approaches or perspectives. Critical reflection is a skill that needs to be developed over time so that we are able to make balanced judgements regarding the quality, rigour, and robustness of analysis, discussion, and findings of the work we produce. It is a key emotional intelligence asset that is highly valued by employers and reflects the intellectual maturity of students and workers.

Teaching support

The book is also a valuable resource for teachers of management as it provides a systematic approach to key management issues and concepts; demonstrates how to apply a range of appropriate models to help enhance knowledge and insight into both management and the environment in which management practice takes place; provides a critical evaluation of models and frameworks; and gives access to a set of new case studies. The book aligns the syllabus of management teaching in many universities and colleges and can be used as a core text or supplementary reading for courses and modules on management. The Online Resource Centre (ORC) provides a range of additional support materials for teachers including:

- PowerPoint slides relating to each chapter with added hyperlinks to podcasts, YouTube videos and other sources of information;
- outline answers for the mini and main case studies in the book;
- test bank questions with 10 multiple-choice questions per chapter;
- a video library of clips to YouTube and other sites.

Management Principles and Functions

1

Introduction to Management

Learning outcomes

- Understand the meaning of management as a concept

- Recognise and explain the functions and roles of managers

- Identify and analyse management skills and competencies in different organisational settings

- Appreciate management practices and competencies in the contemporary global environment

- Evaluate the challenges facing modern managers

Bill Gates is probably one of the most successful and high-profile managers of a major corporation in the modern era. The former CEO and co-founder of *Microsoft* has put into practice his management philosophy and principles to good effect over a number of decades. Today, Microsoft remains one of the world's most successful corporate giants. Much of the success can be put down to some simple but effective management principles. In the context of the business where Microsoft operates, Bill Gates firmly believes that effective managers must have an understanding of what it is they are expecting their workers to do. So, programme managers must understand programming, marketing managers must understand marketing, and so on. Only by possessing a measure of technical competence can managers earn the respect of subordinates and make good decisions (Thielen, 1999). Unlike many other organisations who hire generalist managers, Microsoft primarily focuses on the level of specialist expertise candidates have before putting them into management positions. In contrast to other management protocols practised elsewhere (such as in Japan where seniority or 'next in line' characterises promotion criteria, *The Economist*, 3 January 2008), Microsoft only promote those who have demonstrated that they are the best person for the job rather than being influenced by extraneous factors such as internal politics, networking, or even luck. The analogy with Charles Darwin's 'natural selection' in the animal kingdom is a suitable metaphor for the guiding principles under which Bill Gates exercised his judgement on his managerial team. Thus, at Microsoft, those who perform well in one timeframe cannot rest on their laurels because they will quickly be out-performed by others. And those who cannot maintain the highest level of performance get replaced as they are no longer an asset to the business. Managers have to demonstrate an ability to adapt to changes in the environment whilst maintaining high levels of performance. This regime may appear brutal, but it accounts for the excellence that has maintained a competitive advantage for the company over four decades. The case is an illustration of a distinct management style in action underpinned by guiding principles. There are many different management styles and principles of management, some of which are discussed in this book. There is no generic model of management that guarantees effectiveness in all situations so managers need to find the style and methods that work for them in the environment in which they operate. It is this diversity within an unpredictable and changing environment that makes the study of management so compelling.

Skillset 1
Reading skills

At the end of this chapter you will find the first in the series of Skillset sections. These sections highlight the skills you will need in the course of your academic study but also many skills which will be invaluable in the business world beyond university.

This chapter's Skillset covers reading skills.

Managers rely on accurate, relevant, and timely information to help them make decisions. Very often this will entail a research effort by designated workers who are tasked with generating the type of information managers need. Deciding what information is needed, how to access it, and making sense of what it means are among the key research skills evident among workers in organisations. Some organisations have research as their core activity, such as research institutions or universities, most have someone in a designated role where research is carried out, such as a Knowledge Transfer Coordinator. Students will also have to acquire research skills in order to meet the challenges presented in their academic careers, such as writing essays, reports, dissertations, or theses. Among the important research skills lies the discipline of reading.

Accessing and engaging with the topics, cases, tasks, and other content requires the application of some research skills such as sourcing information, case analysis, literature searches and reviews, and managing workloads. This opening chapter will introduce management as a concept and a function where a broad range of skills and competencies are required. Reading skills form part of management skills and Skillset 1 is designed to offer an overview of what comprises reading skills and how they can be used effectively.

Definition

There are many definitions of management but most coalesce around common themes to offer a general explanation. Management is the organisation and coordination of the activities of a business (or some other formal organisational setting) in order to achieve defined aims and objectives.

Introduction

Management has a long history and dates back to well before it became a subject of formal study. As societies developed so too did the need for management in organising and deploying resources for the needs of society. Empires were built on effective management of resources and the technologies used to protect those civilisations. The Incas in South America, the ancient Egyptians, and the Romans in Europe are good examples of empires built on some form of management process.

By the eighteenth century feudal forms of society were giving way to more industrially based structures where small-scale and craft-based production was replaced by mass production. This involved a different form of management from that which had previously characterised the workplace. Instead of small-scale agrarian-based economies, many societies in Western Europe and the USA developed productive capacities that required a high level of control over large numbers of employees. The factory system ushered in a form of management based on control, authority, discipline, and strict rules and regulations. In many respects this was simply an extension of the way that such societies were structured; the class system ensured that the landed gentry or capital owning classes dominated the mass ranks of the workforce gleaned from the lower working class. The dawn of the wage labourer had arrived and with it a draconian form of management. Typical of this was the advent of scientific management proposed by Frederick Taylor in the late nineteenth century. Taylor (1911) believed that it was possible to measure in great detail the amount of work that each worker should perform as his or her daily duty and that wage rates (he believed that workers were not motivated by anything other than economic reward) could be set accordingly. This gave rise to the development of time and motion studies—a system that is still in evidence in some forms today. Chapter 2 discusses scientific management in more detail.

In the aftermath of the First World War (1914–18) workers in Europe started agitating for a new deal and a new social structure that was based on fairness and social welfare rather than one dominated by privilege for the few. Management practices reflected this change by initiating a trend towards more humane characteristics. The human relations school of management emerged as a counterbalance to the more rigid and process-driven management practices applied in the factory system. Protagonists of this approach included the industrial philanthropist Seebohm Rowntree (1901), Mary Parker Follett (1920), Elton Mayo (1933), and later the so-called neo-human relations school that included McGregor (1960) and Herzberg et al. (1959).

By the 1960s and 1970s the emphasis of management had evolved to an extent that writers such as Robert Greenleaf (creator of the servant leadership model) put forward radical ideas that saw a directive form of management (getting people to do things) replaced by a stewardship form of management (helping people to do things). The late twentieth century was characterised by concepts around 'best practice' management which included excellence and total quality management, reengineering, systems thinking, cross-functional teams, empowerment, delayering and flat organisation charts, learning organisation, dialogue, reinventing work, and diversity (Goetsche and Davis, 2011). The advent of the internet as a disruptive technology also changed management practices with a greater emphasis emerging on how to manage the advantages of speed and increased access to information and knowledge. This coincided with renewed interest in management thinking around the concepts of the learning organisation and diversity. All of these characteristics, concepts, and issues are addressed at some stage in this book, but for now attention turns to providing an introduction to management.

This opening chapter begins with a description of what management is. There are many different definitions of management according to different writers but for the purposes of clarity the definitions presented here call on the thinking of three key writers in the field: Peter Drucker, Henry Mintzberg, and Henri Fayol. This is followed by an outline and explanation of the main functions and roles of managers and includes a discussion around the different layers of management typically observed in organisations. The changing role of management in the public sector is recognised by an overview of the development of the new public management model. Analysis then extends to cover key management skills and competencies applied in the modern global environment. The chapter concludes with a critical evaluation of the challenges facing modern managers.

What is management?

Many writers have contributed to the understanding of what management is including such luminary names in the field as Peter Drucker, Henry Mintzberg, and Henri Fayol among many others. Drucker (2001) outlined a five point guide that encapsulates the essence of what management is. These are:

1 Making people's strengths effective and their weaknesses irrelevant.

2 Enhancing the ability of people to contribute.

3 Integrating people in a common venture by thinking through, setting, and exemplifying the organisational objectives, values, and goals.

4 Enabling the enterprise and its members to grow and develop through training, developing, and teaching.

5 Ensuring everyone knows what needs to be accomplished, what they can expect of managers, and what is expected of them.

Term
Definition

Management: the organisation and coordination of activities to achieve stated aims and objectives.

Fundamentally, Drucker viewed management as a means by which it is possible to coordinate hundreds or thousands of people with different skills and knowledge to achieve common goals.

Mintzberg (1989) defines management as having the following basic principles:
- to ensure the efficient production of goods and services;
- to design and maintain the stability of organisational operations;
- to adapt the organisation, in a controlled way, to the changing environment;
- to ensure that the organisation serves the ends of those persons who control it;
- to serve as the key information link between the organisation and its environment;
- to operate the organisation's status system.

Frenchman Henri Fayol was a trained mining engineer who spent most of his career in general management. From 1888 to 1918 he was Managing Director of the French mining and metal-lurgical combine *Commentry-Fourchamboult Decazerville*. Fayol's main contribution to management thought was his 1916 text, which appeared in an English version in 1949 as 'General and Industrial Management'. This translation from the French has resulted in some discussion of the use of the word 'management' (with its industrial connotations) as a translation or expression of the French word *'administration'*. However, Fayol clearly states that management plays a very important part in the government of all undertakings: large or small, industrial, commercial, political, religious, or any other. Fayol wrote that to manage is to forecast and plan, to organise, to command, to coordinate, and to control (Cunningham-Wood and Wood, 2001). This analysis still forms the basis of one of the most frequently adopted views of management. Fayol was one of the first theorists to stress the key position of the formal organisation chart and job descriptions. He also firmly advocated the belief that management could, and should, be taught.

7

Critical reflection
Is management a science or an art?

Since management first became a subject for study there has been a debate as to whether it constitutes an art or a science, or both. No definitive answer to this has been forthcoming, nor is it likely to as it tends to polarise opinion. There are elements of both art and science in the practice of management. If art is defined as a function that effects change and achieves stated aims through a systematic and deliberate course of action, then it clearly displays those characteristics. In this regard, management can be deemed an art from the perspective that it is an aspect of human behaviour that delivers knowledge and know-how as a means of achieving stated aims. In effect the art of management delivers the 'how' aspect of human behaviour. Science, on the other hand, represents a systematic body of knowledge linked to a particular area of study. Fundamentally, science is concerned with cause and effect relationships between different variables. The body of knowledge consists of concepts, principles, and theoretical perspectives that help an understanding of past events and inform predictions about the outcomes of future actions. Again, these are evident in the practice of management. Essentially, science explains the 'why'.

Protagonists of the 'management as an art' camp point to the fact that management involves the use of skills, knowledge, and techniques; that effective management relies on the application of these in many different settings and contexts. There is also a creative aspect to management such as employing different approaches to interpersonal relationships, problem solving, or innovative means of motivating workers. Influencing people's behaviour so that they help achieve stated aims is an art form. Alternatively, those who believe management is a science point to the fact that it exhibits all the characteristics of what constitutes a science. That is, it contains a body of knowledge based on widely accepted principles that are applied in many different organisational settings and environments. These principles cover a wide range of different management functions including delegating authority, decision making, business analysis, motivating workers, and so on. These principles continue to be used because they have been robustly tested through continuous observation and verified through empirical evidence. So, most likely, management is a combination of both art and science and the most successful managers are the ones who can deploy elements of both when and where appropriate.

Functions of managers

The main functions of managers involve forecasting and planning, organising, commanding and leading, coordinating and controlling. These key functions are of sufficient importance to merit dedicated individual chapters but it is useful to offer an overview of them here.

Forecasting and planning

Forecasting and planning involves assessing the future and making provision for it. The problems of forecasting and planning are many, but managers should ensure that within the organisation there is unity of direction, continuity, flexibility, and precision (Fayol, 1949). Planning is the process used by managers to identify and select appropriate goals and courses of action for an organisation. The planning function determines how effective and efficient the organisation is and determines the strategy of the organisation. Forecasting and planning are undertaken within a fast-moving and changing environment but are essential tools for gaining a better understanding of that environment so that more effective and informed decisions can be made. All organisations undertake some form of forward planning and forecasting of how the future will look. Forecasting is an essential part of planning for public sector organisations such as the police, health services, local authorities, and transport agencies as they need to match income with expected demand stretching well into the future. For example, the proposed high speed train line (HS2) linking London with Manchester and Leeds has to take into account future demand for rail travel, the expected business benefits, and the overall cost of the project. The planning also assesses the costs in terms of finance and the effects on the environment. A close understanding of these variables helps to inform decisions on large-scale infrastructure projects that have inordinately large social, economic, and environmental impacts.

Organising

Organising ensures that the organisation has the necessary resources in terms of staff, money, and materials and that they are brought together in the correct balance. Organising also involves managers creating structures of working relationships between employees that encourages collaboration and helps to achieve their goals. Managers will group people into departments according to the tasks performed and will also establish lines of authority and responsibility for members. An organisational structure is the outcome of organising. This structure coordinates and motivates employees so that they work together to achieve the identified goals (Jones and George, 2007).

Commanding and leading

Commanding involves maintaining activity among employees by making decisions and communicating them to subordinates. Leadership involves setting a clear direction for the organisation; creating and communicating a vision that employees can follow; and ensuring that employees understand their role in achieving goals. Thus, a leader is a person who exercises influence over other people (Huczynski and Buchanan, 2003). In his leadership role as chairman of London 2012, Lord Coe was able to use a combination of these attributes to help deliver a successful Olympic Games and smooth over some of the problematic issues such as the failure of the private sector security firm *G4S* to fulfil its remit and the ineffective ticket allocation system for some events (Hopkins, 2012).

The ideal outcome of the leading function is a high level of motivation and commitment from employees to the organisation (Stum, 1999). Although leadership is different from management, the two are interlinked. Management necessarily requires some form of leadership as, by implication, to manage is to accept responsibility for influencing the behaviour of others. There have been a number of theoretical frameworks developed over the decades and Bolden et al. (2003) provide a useful review of those that have been most influential. Of course, it is often the case that managers undertake leadership responsibilities without much leadership style being in evidence. The work carried out may be process oriented and managers only issue directives that are acted upon. However, for the most part, modern organisations require managers to lead in order to achieve the stated aims and objectives.

Coordinating

Coordinating involves the manager liaising with others in the organisation to ensure that activities occur at the right time and place and to ensure that they do not adversely affect other areas of organisational activity. This can only be attained by a two-way flow of information between workers and managers. The achievement of aims and objectives relies on effective coordination between different levels of management and workers. It is also reliant on the ability of managers to devise work schedules and outcomes based on the resources and capabilities within the organisation.

Control

The control function requires managers to effectively assess the extent to which the organisation is achieving its goals and to initiate corrective action to improve performance if necessary. Control and the monitoring of performance feature at all levels of the organisation from individuals, to teams of workers, departments, and the organisation as a whole. Control allows performance to be measured and regulates the efficiency and effectiveness of the organisation's activities (Hales, 1986). Levels of control will vary according to the organisational setting and context. For example, in process-driven industries the control function is high due to the continuous production line characteristics of the working environment. Alternatively, in many creative industries the control function is low as freedom of expression and movement is part of creating an environment and organisational culture that is conducive to creativity. In some cases there will be a mixture of both. For example, award winning Japanese architect Tadao Ando emphasises the need for freedom in exploring possibilities mixing the intuitive and illogical with the discipline that engineering and structural design requires (Royal Academy of Arts, 2013).

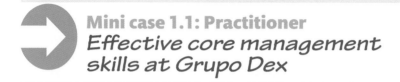

Mini case 1.1: Practitioner
Effective core management skills at Grupo Dex

10

Grupo Dex is an international consultancy specialising in the provision of services on European affairs, strategic planning, local development, and international economic and institutional relationships to private enterprises and public administrations. Founded in 1997, the company is based in Gijon in the Asturias region of northern Spain and has a presence in five other countries. The company is loosely structured to help maximise competitiveness through the expertise and knowledge sharing of a multidisciplinary team specialising in economics, law, and international relations. The group consists of four main divisions including *Dex, I + Dex, Dex Europe*, and *Dex Central Europe*.

Founding partner and chief executive officer (CEO) Fernando Mendez Navia has been involved in setting the strategic direction of the company as well as managing the deployment of staff in the myriad different projects in the portfolio. Fernando highlights his core skills as negotiation skills, cultural understanding, innovative approaches to problem solving, flexibility, and adaptability. He says 'It is necessary to have competence in many different aspects of business and relationship building in the modern environment. Flexibility is key to so many problem solving situations and opportunities that emerge as a normal part of running a business like ours. We think about flexibility when recruiting staff so that we can deploy their skills in many different ways'. It is these skills that have leveraged an advantage for *Grupo Dex* in the competitive arena of international cooperation projects and EU funded projects. In the industry in which *Grupo Dex* competes, it is necessary for staff to possess and be able to deploy all of these skills and attributes. Fernando gives examples of why flexibility is important by stating that 'in the management of an EU funded project there are typically numerous international partners that comprise the project team, each with their own ways of doing business, cultural norms, languages, and expectations of outcomes. It is important for Dex and our partners and clients that we are able to meet the challenges that these present'. One of the key roles of *Grupo Dex* staff

http://www.
grupodex.com
http://www.
grupodex.com

is to manage the cultural diversity of the team so that the partners' skills and experience can be brought to bear on the successful running of the project and problems of misunderstandings, interpretations, and expectations can be solved in a manner that ensures continuity of work and progress towards successful completion.

The cultural awareness attributes need to be complemented by technical skills in understanding the mechanisms of funding bodies—their regulations, guidelines, and procedures. Fernando recognises the importance of knowledge and insight to the organisation. He says 'we need to be able to demonstrate superior knowledge and expertise in our specialist field to maintain the confidence of partners and clients. That is what drives the value for an organisation such as Dex'. Partners often rely on *Grupo Dex* staff for guidance on tasks such as budget spending, financial audits, partnership agreements, administration, and others. It is this technical aspect of the company's service provision that adds real value to their partners and clients and the expertise they provide accounts for the growth of the business in the last decade or so. Much of this success is down to the ability of *Grupo Dex* management to effectively control and coordinate current projects (operational) whilst simultaneously planning for the future (strategic). This latter attribute involves using experience and judgement to interpret the way in which the EU as a trading and economic entity is likely to be shaped in future and what opportunities will become available going forward. To gain an insight into these developments, *Grupo Dex* staff deploys effective interpersonal skills to network on a pan-European basis, build strategic partnerships, and establish a presence in key decision making institutions across Europe.

Source: www.grupodex.com

Discussion point

Is it possible to identify the core skills that managers need to be successful?

Questions and tasks

Visit the Grupo Dex website, select a project from their portfolio, and evaluate how the functions of managers previously discussed in this chapter would be applicable. Would some functions be more central than others?

Give an example of an operational management activity and a strategic management activity at Grupo Dex.

 Online Resource Centre
Author commentary on this discussion point and questions can be found on the Online Resource Centre at: www.oxfordtextbooks.co.uk/orc/combe1e/

Management roles

As described by Mintzberg (1989) a role is a set of specific tasks a person performs linked to the position they hold. Roles are directed inside as well as outside the organisation. There are three broad role categories:

1 interpersonal;
2 informational;
3 decisional.

Interpersonal roles

Managers have interpersonal roles to coordinate and interact with employees and provide direction to the organisation. Three main roles include being the organisation's figurehead, leader, and liaison link to others.

Figurehead role

The figurehead symbolises the organisation and what it is trying to achieve. This role requires managers to be highly visible so that stakeholders come to recognise the manager as a symbol of the organisation. Sometimes the figurehead role extends to the marketing and promotion of the organisation and/or its products or services. The figurehead uses human and communications skills to carry out this function (Lussier, 2008). For example, the role that Richard Branson plays as head of the *Virgin* group extends beyond the boardroom to incorporate roles within the marketing and advertising function of the organisation. The Branson image and persona is used as a symbol of what the organisation stands for and how it views itself. In other cases the figurehead may assume a position of authority that extends to the wider community. For example, many chairmen try to influence government policy or regulation or even the industry in which they operate as part of their role as the figurehead of an organisation.

Leader role

Leadership can involve a wide range of roles as it incorporates many different activities. Acclaimed writer on leadership John Adair (2006) states that the leader role may involve providing motivation, inspiration, and encouragement to others. Leaders have to demonstrate qualities that others admire or seek to emulate or who, through force of character and personality, can get people to accept and support their views regarding the vision and mission of the organisation they represent. As noted previously, leadership differs from management. There is no consensus on what makes an effective leader in terms of the skills and attributes needed to engage and influence followers, but it is true that a measure of leadership is the extent to which they can gather a following to support their ideas and aspirations. Whilst it may be possible to teach management practices, it is not possible to teach someone to be a leader as it invariably involves some attributes that are determined at birth, or during early life development, such as charisma and personality. All organisations need some form of leadership whether it is a patriarchal figure in a small-scale family business, or head of a large-scale multinational. Failure to provide effective leadership can seriously undermine the credibility of an organisation. The crisis that engulfed the BBC in 2012 is a case in point: newly appointed Director General George Entwistle was unable to control events surrounding poor editorial control of news stories featuring child abuse allegations (Batty and Mitchell, 2012). Such high-profile organisations require strong leadership to navigate the myriad different, complex, and politically sensitive situations that are a common feature of their activities.

Liaison role

Managers also have a liaison role which is used to link and coordinate people inside and outside the organisation to help achieve goals (Mintzberg, 1989). This role is very much related to skills in communication, networking, interpersonal skills, and so on. Managers must understand the types of relationships they need to foster in order to help their organisation achieve its aims and objectives. This may involve communicating with a diverse range of people representing many different groups such as government, trade unions, consumer groups, suppliers, partners, industry regulators, and so on. The role of liaison between government and media has become a high profile and sometimes controversial position. Former UK Prime Minister Margaret

Thatcher relied on her press secretary Sir Bernard Ingham as a conduit for expressing her style of government and how it was presented to the wider world. Alistair Campbell held a similar position in the Blair government and his account of the role and his relationship with the prime minister and press is outlined in his diaries (Campbell, 2007). Both exhibited an understanding of how to present policy and the work of government in a positive light even though their combative style often had the opposite effect. In a liaison role, different approaches will be required to deal with the myriad of different people involved and managers need to develop an understanding of the subtle nuances that define the relevant communication style that is appropriate to each group or individual. The more effective managers are at utilising that skill, the greater the benefits to the organisation through the application of the liaison role.

Mini case 1.2
Managing with style and charisma: the case of Lee Iacocca

Acting as a figurehead of an organisation is one of the key roles of top management and requires attributes beyond the technical knowledge of the processes that transform inputs into outputs in the organisation. Rather, the effectiveness of a figurehead is the manner in which he represents the organisation, provides advocacy and guidance, develops and communicates the vision and strategy, and demonstrates leadership. This may require a combination of different attributes such as analytical skills, strategic thinking, intellect, charisma, drive, courage, communications skills, and so on. Few managers possess all of these qualities but some have been able to harness a select few to make a radical difference to the organisation they represent.

The lack of leadership qualities across modern corporate America forms the basis of Lee Iacocca's own withering critique of why the United States has suffered economic decline in the 2000s (Iacocca, 2008).

Perhaps one of the most celebrated figureheads of a major corporation is that of former chief executive officer (CEO) of US car maker Chrysler Corporation, Lee Iacocca. The car industry in the USA was in crisis in the late 1970s as it struggled with rising fuel prices, structural inefficiencies, and intense competition from Germany and Japan. Iacocca used his strategic thinking skills and a powerful personality to turn around the fortunes of Chrysler from a position where its future existence was in doubt. These two attributes combined to great effect as he set about dismantling the thirty-five business units that comprised the organisational structure to one that was leaner and fit for purpose. This was also designed to reinvigorate the culture within the organisation. This latter aspect was helped along by the figurehead duties of Iacocca himself as his powerful ego ensured that he was highly visible and vocal and therefore listened to. Although his authoritarian style of leadership may not have been appropriate in all circumstances and settings, in the context of Chrysler at that time it was the perfect antidote for the general malaise sweeping the organisation. An illustration of his willingness to act is outlined in his autobiography where he recalls that he sacked some thirty vice-presidents in his first three years at the helm (Iacocca, 1986). Iacocca sought managers who could set an example of demonstrable good leadership so that the trickle-down effects would instil a new and positive culture among workers. He also reached out to people, for example he persuaded key personnel in rival companies to join him at Chrysler and drive forward his change agenda and he gave a seat on the

13

http://www.
leeiacocca.com/
http://www.
leeiacocca.com/

board to a labour union representative. Importantly, he used his influencing skills and power to negotiate a Congress approved loan to stave off bankruptcy when Chrysler hit its worst financial crisis early into his reign as CEO. Iacocca is one of numerous examples of effective leaders and figureheads within organisations whose presence, charisma, and business acumen have defined an era. Others such as John D. Rockefeller (Standard Oil), Jack Welch (General Electric), and Steve Jobs (Apple) had similar transformational effects on the organisations they represented.

Sources:

Iacocca, L. (2008) *Where Have All The Leaders Gone*, New York, NY, Pocket Books.

Iacocca, L. (1986) *Iacocca: An Autobiography*, New York, NY, Bantam USA.

Discussion point

Do organisational figureheads always need to possess a dominant personality type?

Questions and tasks

Lee Iacocca, while lauded for his managerial skills, has also been critiqued by some commentators. Investigate Iacocca's career and assess the situations in which Iacocca's judgement has been called into question. Do you agree with the critique?

Visit the Lee Iacocca website, and review his Leadership Scorecard (http://www.leeiacocca.com/scorecard/scorecard.pdf). Select a contemporary business person and evaluate their leadership skills and style against these criteria.

Online Resource Centre

Author commentary on this discussion point and questions can be found on the Online Resource Centre at: www.oxfordtextbooks.co.uk/orc/combe1e/

14

Informational roles

Informational roles are associated with the tasks needed to obtain and transmit information for the management of the organisation. Three main roles are monitor, disseminator, and spokesperson roles.

Monitor role

The monitor role requires managers to analyse information from both the internal and external environment as a means of making better informed decisions (Mintzberg, 1979). Managers should acquire attributes of knowing what information to look for that is relevant to their organisation and industry in terms of influencing performance. They should also be able to apply techniques for helping make sense of information and contextualise it to the environment in which their organisation operates. In many instances effective monitoring by management can lead to a competitive advantage as the outcomes can offer better insights into what opportunities can be exploited as well as predicting the emergence of threats so that contingencies can be put in place to deal with them.

Disseminator role

The disseminator role refers to how managers transmit information to influence the attitudes and behaviour of employees. In many ways this may be rightly viewed as the most important management skill of all (Adair, 2009). This role requires superior communications skills that may include oral and written skills and even body language. Here, it is important that managers understand the correct media to use to disseminate information. For example, there are some communications that are best suited to face-to-face conversation rather than via electronic media. Telephone conversations may be useful for speeding up the exchange of information, but the lack of visible body language may mean that the manager is left unaware of the reaction of the recipient to the communication. Social media are increasingly used in the workplace but whilst some workers are used to this form of media, for others it may be an alien system that they do not feel comfortable using (Bennett et al., 2010). Developments in information and communication technologies (ICTs) have broadened the scope of possible media through which managers can disseminate information and many have greatly improved the presentation of key information to individuals or groups of workers. For example, e-mail is a ubiquitous and effective tool for disseminating information where there is no requirement for formality or visual references between sender and receiver. Effective dissemination requires an understanding of the appropriate media and the balance, tone, and nuance of the communication sent.

Spokesperson role

Organisations do not exist in isolation from the wider community and therefore it is necessary for the figurehead to act as a spokesperson on behalf of the organisation. This is closely linked to the liaison role outlined above. This usually involves speaking to the media, customer representative groups, industry and trade bodies, governments, universities and other educational and training institutions, and many others. The role relies on superior communications skills which can be honed over time through experience and training (Hartvigsen, 2007). It is vital that managers are able to communicate the mission and aims of the organisation they represent and to present it in a positive but also realistic light. It is likely that managers will be confronted with situations or events that require a response from the organisation, such as in cases of industrial dispute, or health and safety concerns of consumers. Here, the spokesperson is the main conduit for information from the organisation to the outside world. Not all managers are adept at this aspect of the job, however, and very often there are staff members whose remit includes that of media spokesperson.

Decisional roles

Decisional roles are associated with the methods managers use to plan strategy and utilise resources to achieve goals. Decision making is discussed in more detail in Chapter 7 but it is useful to note here that this role forms one of the most important aspects of management. Managers will be confronted with decision making duties on a daily basis and they require a range of skills and attributes to be effective. To deal with the potentially complex factors influencing decision making, Teale et al. (2003) emphasise the integrative approach. Some decisions will be operational in nature and may only be informed by past precedent, procedure, or experience. Others will have a strategic dimension to them that requires more analytical and intuitive skills alongside experience and knowledge. Either way, managers need to exude confidence in decision making so that others around them feel a sense that they are in command of their environment and showing leadership (Boyatzis, 1982).

The style of decision making differs markedly between managers. Some may take an egalitarian approach whereby they allow subordinates a say in the process, others may be more authoritative and make decisions entirely on their own. Very often the effectiveness of decision making depends on the way it is communicated as much as the nature of it. If those affected by the decision understand why it has been made and how to transfer it into action then it is more likely to be positively received. Poor communication of decision making can alienate workers, lead to poor execution of the actions required, and compromise performance. It also has an eroding effect on the trust and confidence that workers look for in their managers.

Entrepreneur role

In the private sector managers need to be able to decide on what new projects or activities to initiate and invest in with a view to making profits. Entrepreneurial acumen plays a key role in the success or otherwise of companies. Schumpeter (1949) viewed the entrepreneurial function as that of a change agent who brings into existence a new combination of the means of production. Stevenson and Jarillo (1990) set out a useful paradigm of entrepreneurship that identifies key factors driving this important aspect of management. These include the strategic, resource, and growth orientation of the organisation, rewards, entrepreneurial culture, and the management structure. Even in the public sector there is an increasing need for managers to innovate and be entrepreneurial in the way they utilise resources, build capabilities, and exploit opportunities for improving services and efficiencies (Kearney et al., 2010). An ability to understand, process, and assess risks lies at the heart of entrepreneurial behaviour and managers need to be able to evaluate the expected returns on investment in many different aspects of the business including finance, human resources, relationship building, marketing, logistics, and so on. In many ways it is the entrepreneurial flair of managers that makes the difference between gaining a competitive advantage or not. This book gives a number of examples and cases where entrepreneurial flair underlies the activities of managers. People such as Steve Jobs, Bill Gates, Sir Alan Sugar, Sir Richard Branson, and others have built their success on entrepreneurship.

Disturbance handler role

Organisations operate within dynamic and sometimes unpredictable environments. The constant changes require managers to assume responsibility for navigating a way through various forms of disturbances affecting the organisation. These can range from industrial disputes to political change in countries where they source supply; technical problems in production; the impact of proposed new industry regulations; or reputational damage from customer complaints. Fearn-Banks (2010) examines a number of cases of crisis management in action. Managers need to be able to deal with these and many more events that threaten business continuity. In most cases the disturbances have short-term effects that require managers to take action designed to remedy the situation (mechanics should be able to fix production line problems, for example). Where the effect has an impact on the strategic aims of the organisation then managers need to take action to mitigate the worst effects whilst maintaining strategic direction. It would take an event of seismic proportions to induce managers to abandon a strategy, usually it means that some aspects of the strategy may have to be adapted to cope with the effects of disturbance. The case of the World Trade Center in Chapter 3 illustrates the point by explaining how many organisations directly affected by the 9/11 terrorist attacks on the twin towers were able to continue trading and maintained their strategic focus due to contingency planning.

Resource allocator role

One of the most politically charged roles facing managers is that of resource allocator where financial, human, capital, and other resources are distributed to functional areas of the organisation. Here, there are likely to be competing demands for resources which can lead to tension and conflict (Kramer, 1989). Consequently, the manager needs to be part diplomat and part politician to manage the distribution of resources. Whilst seeking to be fair to all parties, it is essential that managers take a strategic view of resources and channel them to areas that best support the tactical aims of the organisation. This may prove unpopular in certain functions in the short term but will better ensure the long-term viability and performance of the organisation. Again, effective communications can smooth the process of resource allocation by providing a clear rationale for the decisions that underpin it.

Negotiator role

The resource allocator and disturbance handler roles both require an element of negotiation between managers and stakeholders including unions, workers, suppliers, industry representatives, regulators, partners, and so on. Managers need to have negotiation skills appropriate to each stakeholder group and to work towards a solution that does not compromise the long-term aims and objectives of the organisation. Cohen (2002) provides a useful insight into key negotiation skills for managers. In some instances managers may feel it is appropriate to yield to demands, in others they stand firm. The key to negotiating as a manager is to listen to the demands being made but to ensure that a solution is arrived at that does not cause harm to the ability of the organisation to achieve its performance targets, or undermine the existing relationships that help achieve those targets. Negotiation is required to ensure that a certain level of harmony is achieved so that workers remain committed to what the organisation is trying to achieve (Laborde, 1995). This can be difficult when there are competing and conflicting factions aiming to achieve different outcomes. Nevertheless, the impact of these should not have a detrimental effect on the organisation if managers have been able to build good working relationships and can deploy the correct communications and negotiating skills, as Mini case 1.2 of Lee Iacocca illustrated.

Levels of management

17

Organisations of different sizes and structures will have different layers of management (Smith, 2007). Traditionally, organisations were structured in a hierarchy with well-defined layers of management, each with their own span of control, authority, and roles. In many modern organisations this structure has been replaced by flatter designs with fewer layers of management and a more egalitarian approach to decision making across functional areas. Organisational structure is discussed in more detail in Chapter 11. Here, it is only necessary to highlight the three layers of management that are typically evident in a large number of organisations. The three main levels of managers are illustrated in Figure 1.1.

Top management

At the apex of the organisation is the top or executive level of management. Managers at this level are responsible for the performance of all departments and have cross-departmental responsibility. They establish organisational long-term goals, create strategies to achieve those goals, and liaise with middle managers.

Middle management

Middle managers act as a conduit between the top or executive managers and those at operational level. Middle managers need to be able to communicate the strategies devised by top management to those who have to implement them. Middle managers have a supervisory role

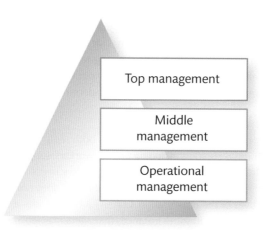

Figure 1.1 Levels of management in organisations

overseeing the work of first-line managers. They are also responsible for finding the best way to use departmental resources to achieve set goals.

Operational management

Operational or functional managers are responsible for the day-to-day running and operations of the organisation. They supervise the people performing the activities required to produce the good or service. Operational managers have no strategic responsibilities other than to communicate the actions required to implement strategy as directed by middle managers. The core function of operational managers is to ensure that the productive capacity of the organisation is maintained on an on-going basis and that short-term aims and targets are met.

? Critical reflection
*Are management roles clearly
defined and understood?*

Management is characterised by changing attitudes and trends. What passes for insightful and wise in one era is deemed inappropriate and ineffective in another. Many fads and phases have come and gone through the decades. In fact, the role of manager has also been subject to change over the years with some eras defined by strict and authoritarian rule (such as that witnessed throughout most of the Industrial Revolution in the eighteenth and nineteenth centuries) to ones where the workforce play an integral part in decision making (innovative and creative industries in the twenty-first century). Even the traditional layers of management have been subject to change. For example, the 1990s was characterised by a trend in some companies to disband the role of middle management to save on costs. Whilst some achieved short-term cost savings, many quickly realised that the gulf between top management and workers at the operational level was too great for the strategies devised and the role that workers were to play in achieving strategic aims to be effectively communicated. The real value of middle managers as a key link between top and operational management became evident thereby leading to a race to reintroduce this layer of management.

Even the role of top management becomes blurred under certain circumstances. Normally, top management is concerned with the strategic direction of the organisation and devising a plan of action to achieve long-term aims and objectives. However, during times of economic downturn when profits are shrinking and the returns on investment for shareholders are being squeezed, attention often turns to short-term survival rather than strategic aims. This is a mistake because only through devising a suitable and achievable set of long-term aims can an organisation ensure its long-term survival and prosperity. There may be some pressing short- or medium-term issues to deal with, but that is the role of middle managers rather than the executives at the top of the organisation. Top managers who concern themselves with short- or medium-term issues are not utilising their own skills and knowledge in a way that most benefits the organisation. Thus, one of the key characteristics of effective top management is to remain focused on the bigger picture rather than becoming embroiled in operational or middle management issues. This is not to say that they should detach themselves from these different levels of management as it is also a characteristic of effective top management that they be visible to and approachable by staff. A failure to be accessible creates tension throughout the organisation and alienates workers—'arrogance through detachment' as Mintzberg (2011) calls it. Nevertherless, the primary function of top management is to provide direction for the organisation as a whole through leadership and a well-defined strategy for achieving long-term aims.

Over the decades there have been different approaches and variations of the construct of layers of management. The private sector has been flexible in the way in which management is structured and the roles assigned to the different levels. The public sector is much slower to change but has been subject to reform as traditional models of management have come under scrutiny for the level of performance they deliver. One such attempt at reform was the emergence of New Public Management.

New Public Management

New Public Management (NPM) is a management philosophy of the 1980s that came to prominence in response to the need for reform in the public sector. It stems from a neo-liberal ideology that places an emphasis on the market over state intervention in the way economies are managed. Although NPM is a broad-ranging term and can mean different things to different people and groups, the basic principles are based on managerial schools of thought that seek to improve efficiencies in the public sector and the level of control exerted by government on the public sector. In effect, NPM advocated reform through a greater market-oriented public sector as the core philosophy. The idea behind this was to generate the benefits that private sector business practices could yield whilst maintaining wide-ranging service delivery. The advantages of NPM were cost savings gained by disaggregating departments (dismantling large bureaucracies into smaller, more fragmented units), and increased efficiency and quality derived through introducing competition between public and private sector organisations for service delivery contracts.

Rather than being a single philosophical approach to management, NPM can be viewed as a grouping of various management techniques and approaches. Many of the techniques were simply taken from private sector practices and transposed into the public sector (Pollitt, 1995). Critics, such as Argyriades (2002) argue that there is nothing new about NPM as the techniques and approaches that define it have been applied over many decades. Farazmand (2002) goes further by stating that NPM is simply an attempt by government to undermine the core values of the public sector. Whatever the perception of NPM, it is clear that it ushered in a new and changed role of the state in the way public services are administered and delivered.

The impetus for implementing NPM was the growing realisation that traditional models of public management were ineffective and costly. For example, large-scale, bureaucratic, and hierarchical organisations such as the NHS, local authorities, and the civil service were deemed incapable of delivering on their goals within the constraints of slow moving and standardised working practices. Many public sector organisations had a 'one best way' of thinking in their management approach that was antiquated, lacking in accountability, lacking in transparency, and lacking in quality. Proponents of NPM believed that only radical reform leading to innovative new ways of managing could deliver services based not only on need but also on public choice. Thus, it was argued, that much in the same way that the consumer is free to make choices in the demand for goods and services provided by the private sector, so they should be offered the same choice in the delivery of public services. NPM informed much of the public-sector reforms of the 1990s under the Blair government in the UK, but many critics point to the lack of any new form of management at the heart of the philosophy.

? Critical reflection
Should a 'business-like' management approach be implemented in the public sector?

The business-oriented approach to the management of public sector organisations believes that public managers should become more business-like in their approach to decision making. This involves considering the 'Es' of economy, efficiency, excellence, and effectiveness. The economic dimension is principally achieved by making savings in actual resource inputs relative to planned resource inputs, which may occur as a result of implementing cost-cutting exercises. Efficiency refers to the ratio between outputs and inputs. Improvements in efficiency may be achieved by increasing outputs in relation to inputs; reducing inputs in relation to outputs; or, ideally, doing both at the same time. Excellence is reaching for and achieving high standards of excellence, and effectiveness is increased by achieving a better ratio between desired objectives and actual outputs. If full effectiveness were achieved, then all the desired objectives would have been realised.

Much of the so-called business-like management practices in the public sector relate to cost savings or efficiency drives. What has been lacking is the emphasis on innovation and creative ways of solving problems relating to the delivery of public services. The greater emphasis on social enterprises or public–social partnerships indicates a move towards greater involvement in communities and the private sector in solving some of the pressing service delivery needs in this context. These types of enterprises and organisations, and the distinct management practices within them, form an important part of policies for public sector reform alongside cost and efficiency savings.

Managerial skills and competencies in the modern global environment

There are a number of skills that managers need to acquire and be able to perform in a modern global environment. Stonehouse et al. (2004) provide a useful insight into management in the global and transnational business environment. Most prominent among the necessary attributes are conceptual and analytical skills, human skills, technical skills, and cultural awareness.

Conceptual skills

Conceptual skills refer to the ability to analyse and diagnose a situation and find the cause and effect (Boyatzis, 1982). Analytical skills refer to the ability to make sense of the environment and to use the knowledge to inform decisions and judgements. The globalised economy in which most organisations compete is fast changing and complex, thereby increasing the need for good conceptual skills in managers who are charged with the duty of understanding the environment and making sense of it based on the knowledge gleaned from their analysis. It is not sufficient to simply learn the mechanics of conceptual skills as it also comprises elements of learning and experience. Formal education can help managers acquire the necessary understanding of the models and frameworks that help identify and diagnose a situation, but the ability to transform that into effective analysis to better understand cause and effect requires a range of attributes including intelligence, analytical skills, experience, and intuitive skills. Nevertheless, conceptual and analytical skills form a key component of the tools that managers have for understanding complexity in the global economy and are developed in conjunction with critical thinking. Critical thinking is a key element of the learning process and something that graduates need to be adept at. French and Tracey (2010) provide a useful insight into how graduates can enhance their capabilities through embedding critical thinking skills that underpin conceptual and analytical skills.

Human skills

Human skills are to be seen in an ability to understand, alter, lead, and control people's behaviour (Katz, 1974). In a global context these skills also incorporate understanding the characteristics and etiquette of doing business with people from different cultures. In many cases managers have to offer direction and leadership to workers from ethnically diverse backgrounds and this requires a heightened sense of awareness of the needs and expectations of those workers. Such an environment demands excellent interpersonal skills combined with a high level of cultural awareness. These attributes can help to motivate workers and provides the type of incentive that can lead to superior performance. Milne (2007) focuses attention on the link between motivation, incentives, and the creation of a positive organisational culture.

Human skills also extend to the relationship building aspect of management. Each organisation has to work in partnership with numerous other organisations to smooth the process of production and create brand loyalty among customers. The networking and relational capital employed by managers is an important means of ensuring that key relationships are acquired and maintained. In many ways this type of human skill can be the means of creating a

21

competitive advantage. For example, in the electronics industry many of the key distribution channels have been guaranteed by agreements reached by industry leaders in each part of the supply chain. This is as a result of effective and on-going business relationships between the parties involved. Prospective newcomers to the industry would find it difficult to break through this barrier to entry thereby ensuring a competitive advantage to incumbents. In other settings the human skills play out in the form of creating a following around ideology or a particular movement. For example, in the political arena, Martin Luther King, Jr. used his human skills to communicate to a broad constituency of people about the need for change regarding race relations in the USA as exemplified in his famous 'I have a dream...' speech in 1963. Social enterprise guru and Nobel peace prize winner Muhammad Yunus created a following for his vision for tackling poverty through access to micro-finance for the poor by extolling the virtues of social innovation in a series of academic publications, conference speeches, and effective networking with key decision makers such as ex-US President Bill Clinton. In Greece, relatively unknown political activist Alexis Tsipras galvanised support for his anti-austerity Radical Left Coalition Party in response to the economic crisis that crippled the country. His human skill in being able to communicate ideas to disaffected citizens was used to good effect to gather support for opposing the severe economic cuts imposed by the Greek government.

Technical skills

In some industries managers have to demonstrate a superior understanding of the technical aspects of the work carried out. Industries around the fields of engineering and science often require managers to possess technical understanding, skills, and job-specific knowledge in order to make informed decisions and to acquire the respect of workers who do possess those attributes (Gillard, 2009). In a global context there are many cultures where a superior understanding of the processes involved in the work carried out is a prerequisite for positions of power and leadership. In others, technical skills may be secondary to other attributes such as human and motivational skills or organisational and conceptual skills (VanIngen, 2007). However, in some settings it is a clear advantage. For example, Sir James Dyson possesses a high degree of technical competence that has been used to design a range of innovative home appliances. This competence is used not only as a means of creating a competitive advantage for the firm that bears his name, but also acts as a motivator for those employees who aspire to his level of achievement. Dyson discusses the role of technical skills alongside entrepreneurial flair in his autobiography (Dyson, 2000).

Cultural awareness

In a global economy cultural awareness is an essential part of modern management and has been the focus of academic attention. Chen et al. (2011) discuss the relationship between multicultural and management strategy issues. This is linked to the human skills whereby managers demonstrate an ability to communicate ideas and concepts, and offer leadership to a broad range of workers from different backgrounds. Sometimes those workers will be dislocated from the centre where managers have to use different forms of media to communicate. In other cases the workforce on-site will be comprised of people from diverse ethnic backgrounds. For example, most modern universities are a truly multi-ethnic and international setting comprising people from vastly different cultures. Managers need to be sensitive to the needs and demands of their cohorts of students. Examples may include revising teaching times around Ramadan for Muslim students, catering for the dietary needs of Jewish students, providing extra English language tuition for overseas students, and so on.

Mini case 1.3
Setting the cultural tone at Ben & Jerry's

In many organisational settings the founders of the business set the cultural tone to which workers assimilate. Here, the personality, beliefs, and attitudes of the founders permeate throughout the organisation to inform the prevailing culture. Although the culture is likely to change over time, or sub-cultures may emerge, the core values and beliefs instilled by the founders can resonate throughout the organisation long after they have gone. Thus, organisational culture is shaped very early in the development of the organisation and can be difficult to change, if indeed, change is what is desired. In the case of ice cream makes *Ben & Jerry's* a very distinct set of values and beliefs set the tone of the organisation's culture (Purdie, 2011). Ben Cohen and Jerry Greenfield established *Ben & Jerry's* as a small-scale venture in the late 1970s with the aim of supplying home-made ice cream to their local community. Ben and Jerry were two products of the hippie era of the 1960s in the USA who held idealistic convictions on a range of issues such as ecology, sustainability, social activism, and others. These beliefs and values played out in the way they ran their business and the expectations they had of workers as the business grew throughout the 1980s. The core values defined the organisational culture even though the company experienced huge growth on a global scale and found itself part of the firmament of large-scale corporate bodies with a global brand presence. The company was sold to *Unilever* in 2000 but one of the attractions that drove the purchase was the added value that the organisational culture brought to the sustainability of the business and is an asset that Unilever are keen to preserve and nurture (Hays, 2000).

Sources:

Hays, C. L. (2000) Ben & Jerry's to Unilever, With Attitude, *New York Times*, April. http://www.nytimes.com/2000/04/13/business/ben-jerry-s-to-unilever-with-attitude. html?pagewanted=2&src=pm

Purdie, A. (2011) Case Study of Ben & Jerry's, in Campbell, D., Edgar, D. and Stonehouse, G., *Business Strategy: An Introduction* (3rd edn), Basingstoke, Palgrave Macmillan.

Discussion point

The success of Ben & Jerry's is down to a clearly defined business plan and strategy and a large slice of luck. Discuss.

Questions and tasks

Visit the Ben and Jerry's website. Assess the brand's core values and the level to which the organisational culture mentioned above pervades the site.

Contrast Ben and Jerry's organisational values with those of another brand owned by Unilever. http://www.unilever.co.uk/

Online Resource Centre

Author commentary on this discussion point and questions can be found on the Online Resource Centre at: www.oxfordtextbooks.co.uk/orc/combe1e/

23

http://www.
benjerry.co.uk/

http://www.
benjerry.co.uk/

Challenges facing managers in the modern business environment

The twenty-first century places challenges and pressures on managers like no other era in history. Not only do managers now operate in a global economy but they are also confronted with an environment that is dynamic and constantly changing (Lewis et al., 2000). Although change has always been a feature of the environment in which managers operate, the modern business environment is characterised by a fast pace, increased access to information and knowledge, global competition, rapid changes in technology, diverse and multi-ethnic societies, empowered consumers, intense economic and business pressures, environmental challenges such as climate change, and a radically different type of workforce even from that which characterised the late twentieth century.

Within this environment managers need to coordinate activities, motivate the workforce, control processes and people, build and exploit relationships, manage technological change (often without fully understanding its application themselves), make business and strategic decisions, ensure good corporate governance and compliance with regulatory bodies, and display leadership. These are just some of the myriad expectations placed on modern managers across industry sectors that are increasingly defined by the need for innovation and creativity as catalysts for growth and competitive advantage. One of the biggest challenges facing managers in the twenty-first century is to be able to define and shape the new types of relationships in the workplace, both internal and external to the organisation. In particular, four key elements define the types of management suited to the modern era. These are illustrated in Figure 1.2.

Inclusive management

Access to education and learning opportunities (both formal and informal), information, and knowledge will blur the distinction between management and workers. Managers need to be

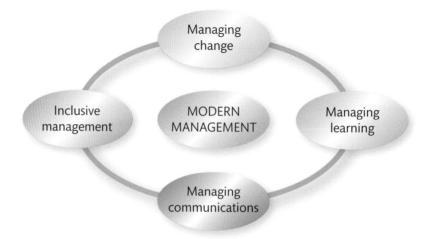

Figure 1.2 Types of modern management

able to build effective relationships with workers as partners in achieving organisational aims and objectives. Responsibility will be spread throughout organisations and each worker will have a stakeholding and vested interest in the performance of the organisation and the community and culture that exists within (Feldman et al., 2002). In effect, each worker will have some level of management role that allows them to contribute more meaningfully to drivers of competitive advantage such as innovation, networking, or problem-solving.

Managing the learning organisation

The concept of the learning organisation is not new but has become increasingly important in the modern business environment due to the ease of access to the vast array of information and knowledge that permeates all aspects of business. The concept of the learning organisation has been around for some time but really only firmly embedded itself as a means of adding value after a seminal work by Peter Senge (1990b) raised the profile of this approach. Shipton (2006) provides a useful typology for organisational learning research, although the ideas are not universally embraced (Grieves, 2008).

Making sense of this wealth of information and knowledge has become an important managerial task which can only be achieved with the collaboration of others throughout an organisation. Senge (1990b) notes that a learning organisation requires the formation of a culture of knowledge generation and sharing that demonstrably adds to the ability of staff to improve processes; innovate for the development and commercialisation of new products (or services in the case of the public sector); coordinate activities along the supply chain; communicate with stakeholders; or effect improvements in internal practices. Key to managing the learning organisation is the ability of managers to communicate the benefits of creating a learning-based environment where those outcomes can be better achieved. In effect, managers need to be able to promote and support learning throughout the organisation.

Management through communication

Communication has always been an important aspect of effective management but in the twenty-first century it has become an essential tool for a wide range of activities such as planning, controlling, strategising, decision making, coordinating, problem solving, conflict handling, and relationship building among others. It has often been said that managers display a range of different attributes but that few possess all the attributes necessary to be the complete manager. This is a dubious notion as different skills and attributes can combine to produce effective managers in different settings and different contexts. Thus, skills and attributes such as intelligence, judgement, interpersonal skills, analytical skills, intuitive skills, technical skills, and organisational skills are important to some degree (Banai and Tulimieri, 2013). However, a constant is the ability to communicate effectively with a broad range of people from diverse backgrounds and cultures. Management is essentially about influencing the behaviour of others to help achieve aims and objectives. As modern management practices trends point to more inclusive forms of relationship, the means by which managers communicate ideas and objectives is key to creating a culture that is both collaborative and productive.

Managing change

In similar fashion to managing learning, the concept of managing change has been around for a long time. However, it is of particular importance in the modern business environment as change now happens at a much faster pace and with much greater intensity. The catalysts for change have already been noted, but it is important to recognise that managing change is a complex, uncertain, and risk-bearing activity that managers need to understand and implement. Knowing the correct tools to use for this purpose is just one of the key skills of management, but the demands go further than that. Managers need to know when to implement change, to what degree, and what outcomes can be expected. All within a rapidly changing environment when the factors that influenced the decision in the first place may already have been subject to change themselves. Change management forms the basis of a deeper discussion in Chapter 16 but it is important to note here that managers must continue to be change agents into the future.

Management
words of wisdom

This book comprises sixteen chapters covering a wide range of management topics. A great deal has been written and said about management throughout the centuries by academics, politicians, practitioners, philosophers, journalists, and other commentators. It is a subject that generates many different views and perspectives, debates and discussion, argument and sometimes rancour. Perhaps the reason why few are ambivalent about management is because it plays such an important role in our lives. We all, at some stage in life, are required to undertake management functions, whether it be to organise family holidays, manage finances, oversee projects as part of work tasks, motivate people as part of a team, plan for weddings, or make life decisions such as buying a house, applying for a job, or persuading people to support your favourite cause. All of these and many more comprise elements of management and throughout a lifetime most people become accustomed to meeting the challenges it represents. We are all subject to management too. Whether it be in the work environment, church, sports club, school, or any other formal setting, it is likely that there is a distinct management structure and delegated roles and authority from which we take direction and guidance. Thus, management pervades all parts of our lives and influences how we perceive the world and take control of events that affect our lives.

The other chapters in this book comprise a main case study as a key feature. However, for this opening chapter it is worthwhile highlighting some quotes from influential people on management down through the ages. This gives an insight into the perspectives that people from diverse backgrounds and areas of expertise have on the myriad different issues pertinent to the art/science/practice of management in all its different forms.

Management

Management is, above all, a practice where art, science and craft meet.
Henry Mintzberg (Management writer and academic)

Determine that the thing can and shall be done, and then we shall find the way.
Abraham Lincoln (Former President of the United States of America)

Management theory

You cannot plough a field by turning it over in your mind.
Chinese proverb

Planning

There is time for everything.
Thomas Edison (American inventor)

Tell me and I'll forget, show me and I may remember, involve me and I will understand.
Chinese proverb

Organising

Take care of the minutes and the hours will take care of themselves.
Lord Chesterfield (British aristocrat)

Make use of time, let not advantage slip.
William Shakespeare, *Venus and Adonis* (Playwright)

Leading

Rank does not confer privilege or power. It imposes responsibility.
Peter Drucker (Management writer)

Controlling

There are some things I can't control, and that's just the way it is.
Susane Colasante (Author)

Decision making

The one word that makes a good manager—decisiveness.
Lee Iacocca (Former chief executive officer of Ford)

Human Resource Management

Every time I appoint someone for a vacant position I make one hundred unhappy and one ungrateful.
King Louis XIV of France

The best executive is one who has sense enough to pick good people to do what he wants them to do, and self-restraint enough to keep from meddling with them while they do it.
Theodore Roosevelt (Former President of the United States of America)

Motivation

True motivation comes from achievement, personal development, job satisfaction and recognition.
Frederick Herzberg (American psychologist)

Managing groups and teams

No man is an island.
John Donne (English poet)

Organisational structure

It is not the strongest of the species that survives, nor the most intelligent that survives. It is the one that is most adaptable to change.
Charles Darwin (Naturalist)

Ethics and corporate social responsibility

A man without ethics is a wild beast loosed upon this world.
Albert Camus (Philosopher)

Ethics is in origin the art of recommending to others the sacrifice required for cooperation with oneself.
Bertrand Russell (Philosopher)

Strategy

Do not repeat the tactics which have gained you one victory, but let your methods be regulated by the infinite variety of circumstances.
Sun Tzu (Chinese military strategist)

Marketing

Either write something worth reading or do something worth writing about.
Benjamin Franklin (Former President of the United States of America)

Many a small thing has been made large by the right kind of advertising.
Mark Twain (Author)

Change management and innovation

The power of imagination makes us infinite.
John Muir (Naturalist)

Knowing is not enough, we must apply. Willing is not enough, we must do.
Johann Wolfgang von Goethe (German writer, artist, and politician)

Summary

● **Understand the meaning of management as a concept**

The chapter gave a definition of management and an overview of the development of management in its historical context before going on to outline the nature of management according to some of the key writers in the field such as Peter Drucker, Henry Mintzberg, and Henri Fayol. The different perspectives on management led to a critical reflection around the question of whether management should be considered a science or an art.

● **Recognise and explain the functions and roles of managers**

The key functions of management were identified as forecasting and planning; organising, commanding and leading, and coordinating and controlling. The importance of each function is reflected in the dedicated chapters afforded to them in this book. A number of roles were identified around the headings of interpersonal, informational, and decisional roles. Interpersonal roles were linked to communications including figurehead, liaison, and leadership roles. Informational roles feature skills of monitoring situations and disseminating key information. Decisional roles involve risk-taking activities, entrepreneurship, and issuing directives to achieve stated aims.

● **Identify and analyse management skills and competencies in different organisational settings**

Management skills link to many of the roles they are expected to carry out. Managers need to be able to make decisions, analyse the environment using information and data, negotiate, liaise with stakeholders, and so on. Effective management relies on a combination of analytical, conceptual, and communications skills in public, private, and voluntary sectors. The benefits and challenges associated with transferring skills, competencies, and techniques from the private commercial sector to the public sector were discussed using the New Public Management model.

● **Appreciate management practices and competencies in the contemporary global environment**

Managers in the contemporary global environment require conceptual and analytical skills, human skills, technical skills, and cultural awareness. Demands may not require these in equal measure but there are aspects of each which managers have to possess to operate effectively in a global environment. The environment is dynamic, unpredictable, and diverse and managers need to be able to analyse opportunities and threats to help the organisation achieve aims and objectives. Networking and stakeholder relationships also feature prominently in modern management practices as they seek to exploit opportunities in new markets characterised by different cultures and expectations.

● **Evaluate the challenges facing modern managers**

Modern managers face an unprecedented array of challenges ranging from managing cultural diversity to integrating new technologies. The evaluation of the challenges in this chapter focused on the inclusion of stakeholders, communications, and creating a learning organisation. These help managers form partnerships internally and externally that mitigate the risks associated with complex and changeable environments. Managing change is also a key challenge as organisations seek to create a competitive advantage in this fast paced and dynamic environment.

Academics with an interest in management have created theoretical models and frameworks as a means to help managers distil and synthesise information and guide their analysis. Various theories of management have emerged since it became a formal subject for study at the beginning of the Industrial Revolution. The next chapter focuses attention on some of those theories and offers an insight into their component parts and a critique of their effectiveness in the context of the era in which they were developed.

Test your knowledge

1 Creating a vision for the organisation is a part of which management function?

2 Describe the figurehead role in an organisation.

3 What level of management has a responsibility for ensuring that production is maintained at a satisfactory level in a factory?

4 Interpersonal relationships feature as part of what management skill?

5 Knowledge generation and sharing underpins what aspect of management?

Apply your knowledge

1 Read the critical reflection on whether management is a science or an art. Draw your own conclusions on the debate and offer a rationale for your position.

2 Choose an organisation that you have had experience with (school, college, club, university, work, etc.) and identify the control functions that operate within it.

Further reading

● Alvesson, M. and Willmott, H. (2012) *Making Sense of Management: A Critical Introduction* (2nd edn), London, Sage Publications.
   The authors deliver a clear and systematic understanding of contemporary perspectives on management that addresses some of the assumptions that characterise the discourse in mainstream management.

● Flynn, N. (2012) *Public Sector Management* (6th edn), London, Sage Publications.
   This book is a useful contribution to the reading for students seeking a greater insight and knowledge of the distinct characteristics and techniques for managing in a public sector environment.

● Law, J. (2009) *A Dictionary of Business and Management* (5th edn), Oxford, Oxford University Press.
   This dictionary is a useful source of reference to help students get to grips with established and contemporary terminology typically employed by writers and practitioners of management. With over 7000 entries the dictionary is a comprehensive and easy-to-use source of definitions of the vocabulary of management covering marketing, decision making, internet business, human resources, and many more.

● Leahy, T. (2012) *Management in 10 Words*, London, Random House Business.
   To balance the overwhelmingly academic output on management, this book offers a valuable insight from the perspective of a practitioner. Terry Leahy is the former CEO of Tesco and brings his experience to bear by highlighting, explaining, and discussing the ten most vital attributes that he views as being behind managerial success. Leahy's guiding principles form around the notions that success often follows failure, and that the core values of the organisation are what drive profits in the long term.

● Van Assen, M., Van den Berg, G., and Pietersma, P. (2008) *Key Management Models: The 60 + Models Every Manager Needs to Know (Financial Times Series)*, Harlow, Prentice Hall.
   This book provides a series of frameworks for improving business performance and offers a clear and concise outline of what the models have been designed for and how to apply them. Students will benefit from having easy access to appropriate models linked to key concepts and theories relating to a wide range of management issues.

 Online Resource Centre
For more information, updates, and multiple-choice questions, please visit the Online Resource Centre at: www.oxfordtextbooks.co.uk/orc/combe1e/

Skillset 1
Reading skills

1(a) Introduction

Research is a key skill in academic activity and requires some effective learning to put it into practice. Most departments or schools in universities and colleges provide learning services around key research skills. The ability to carry out effective research relies on a series of skills that have to be learned and applied. These include a number of skills that will feature throughout the Skillset series in this book including sourcing materials, compiling a literature review, or avoiding plagiarism. Among the important research skills lies the discipline of reading. Reading is the basis around which much of the information needed to compile essays, reports, research papers and articles, reviews and exam papers, revolves. It is an important discipline to embed and even to enjoy. The acquisition of knowledge and the understanding of different perspectives, historical contexts, techniques for learning, and so many other skills result from effective reading.

1(b) Effective reading

Like so many academic skills, reading is something that has to be learned and applied. Most university and college libraries offer guidance and support to students in the skill of effective reading. These may include being able to source appropriate materials, access to reading in many different media such as e-books or traditional book form, operating search facilities, or understanding how to broaden the search for appropriate materials. Once the searching skills have been attained, it is then necessary to put into effect reading skills. Reading requires discipline, time, patience, and, of course, an interest in the subject matter. There are a number of key aspects of reading that have to be determined prior to its application.

1(c) Key issues around reading

Why read?

In the first instance a student needs to know why reading is necessary. This may be for an understanding of how learning and teaching schedules work and what the key learning outcomes of a chosen course will be. It may be as research to compile an assessed piece of work such as an essay or report. It may be for a better understanding of the activities and aims of an organisation prior to a job interview. The reasons for undertaking reading are varied and each will require access to particular types of reading materials. Thus, it is important to be able to understand why the reading is necessary, what types of reading materials are appropriate to support the learning required, the choice of media for accessing the reading material, and where to find it. Much of this understanding will be acquired through experience but it is also useful to seek advice and guidance from tutors and librarians as they will already have valuable knowledge they can pass on to help in this process. In particular, library staff can help save time and effort by pointing out where to find relevant reading materials.

As noted previously, the reasons for reading vary according to the type of learning, activity, or challenge that has been presented. There may be specific reasons why reading is necessary. For example, it may be to acquire a deep and comprehensive understanding of a particular topic. This will require extensive reading from multiple sources over a period of time. Undertaking a dissertation at Masters level or a PhD will involve extensive reading around a well-defined theme or topic. Alternatively, the reading may be to gain a general understanding of a topic in which case an introductory text may suffice. Reading is essential for undertaking critical reviews or analysing a specific issue. Literature reviews can only be compiled after undertaking reading from various different perspectives. Being able to offer a critique relies on a good understanding of a subject, much of which will be gained through reading. In some instances, reading will be for the purpose of gaining facts or specific information. As the skills and discipline of reading become firmly embedded, the joy of reading starts to emerge. Reading can be a pleasurable experience and something that enriches people's lives.

What to read?
Tutors should give recommended reading lists linked to each area of study in a module or programme of learning. Check the choice of core text and the recommended reading covering textbooks, journal articles, study guides, and other materials. Ensure that the core and recommended texts are available in the library or from electronic media. Always keep a record of the materials you use. This will save you time and effort in future if you need to access or reference the material again. The main things to record are:

- Author, title, date, publisher, place of publication (and page number) of all sources. These are needed for references
- Key terms and their definitions
- Key theorists, their theories, and dates
- Main aims, objectives, findings, and conclusions of papers and reports
- Main arguments/ideas for and against
- Important quotes
- Good ideas/thoughts

Activity 1:
Choose a book from a recommended reading list that is relevant to your subject. Read three chapters of the book and record each of the criteria outlined above.

Always acknowledge the source of any material you use. It is worth noting that most reading material around a specific topic is linked. That is, one book will recognise the contribution of other authors in the same or related field and this leads to one source opening up other complementary or even contradictory works. The reference lists and bibliographies in each text will highlight other relevant sources of information. It is necessary to broaden your reading around a subject to gain a better insight and knowledge gleaned from different viewpoints and perspectives.

Quick and efficient reading
One of the skills that students need is to be able to source, access, and read materials quickly. Time is often pressing when assessments are due, or a viva is scheduled, or when a chapter of a dissertation or thesis needs to be submitted for review. It is not always possible to undertake reading at a leisurely pace. Speed and efficiency are key, but without losing the requisite level of understanding. Some useful guidance can help. First, you need to determine if what you have sourced is actually worth reading in the context of what you need to know. You need to make an assessment of the value of the work in the context of what you need. A quick check of the material contents will inform the decision whether or not to invest the time and effort reading the material. For this purpose it is useful to check:

- title
- contents

- index
- abstract/summary
- date of publication

1(d) Speed reading

With limited time available for reading, being able to speed read is a useful skill. Speed reading strikes a balance between quick and efficient reading of material and being able to absorb the information needed. Everyone has their own comfortable reading speed and much depends on the type of material being read, the complexity of it, and prior knowledge and understanding. Where it is possible to speed read through literature, it is always advisable to take notes at the same time as points of reference to key issues or facts. Two techniques that support speed reading are:

- scanning: take a chapter or article and scan it for a piece of information as you would a telephone directory or dictionary;
- skimming: to get an overall understanding of the text, skim (don't read) every page looking for the 'signposts', for example, summary/abstracts, introductions/headings/boxes, diagrams/tables.

The **SQ3R** approach highlights the techniques that support speed reading:

- **Survey:** use surface reading techniques (scan, skim, as above) to find out if the material is relevant.
- **Question:** 'What topics does this chapter cover?'
- **Read** the selected material carefully to find meaning and to make sure you understand all the important ideas.
- **Recall/Write:** test your knowledge of what you have read. Summarise it in your own words.
- **Review:** look back at the text to see how well you remembered.

Be aware of, and try to overcome, some of the barriers to effective speed reading such as:

- unfamiliarity with topic/concepts;
- slow recognition of material;
- low attention span;
- word by word reading;
- lack of focus—inability to identify the relevant material;
- the effort to remember everything rather than to remember selectively;
- density and complexity of the text.

2 Management Theory

Learning outcomes

- Appreciate the nature of theory as an academic practice

- Understand the different theoretical perspectives on management

- Place theoretical models of management in their chronological and organisational contexts

- Assess the value of management theories and their use in understanding management in the modern era

In all academic work it is important to understand the role and purpose of theory. Theoretical perspectives help to conceptualise new ideas about phenomena around us and provide the basis for transforming an idea into a practical solution to a problem or a product innovation. However, there is sometimes a tension between academics and practitioners of management regarding the relevance of theoretical models and frameworks. Some practitioners take a sceptical view of academic output and fail to see what value it brings. Academics counter that many of the techniques routinely practised in organisations stem from academic enquiry and experimentation. Perhaps one of the most high-profile critics of management theorists is UK business tycoon Sir Alan Sugar. In his popular television series *The Apprentice* he has often remarked that academic qualifications are not always a candidate's most important attribute in the business environment. 'Many of the most qualified don't work well and they get fired. Academic qualifications can mean nothing when it comes to business acumen and getting the job done. I sometimes knock them down a peg if they wave their qualifications in front of me, or try to display an air of superiority over their colleagues. I don't like that' (*The Sun*, March, 2008). Rather, Sir Alan views the attributes for success as good judgement, entrepreneurial flair, and an 'eye for a sale'. However, what some business people perhaps overlook is that the work of academics extends beyond gaining qualifications and status. Many of the world's transformational innovations started with the development of academic theory. The development of the world wide web interlinking computers and creating the internet (Sir Tim Berners-Lee at the European Organization for Nuclear Research—CERN), DNA fingerprinting (Sir Alec Jeffreys at the University of Leicester), and the development of the concept of microcredit and microfinance for the poor (Professor Muhammad Yunus at Chittagong University in Bangladesh) are a few examples. Academic enquiry through research is the foundation of knowledge that drives innovation and the numerous practical applications that deliver added value to the wider community. Academic research and the development of theory adds to the stock of global knowledge by providing a valuable source of concepts, ideas, methods, techniques, and innovations across a wide range of disciplines.

Skillset 2
Referencing

This chapter's Skillset section covers referencing skills.

At the end of this book you will find a references section that lists the books, articles, and other source material referred to in the main body of the text. Referencing is of key importance as it offers readers an insight into the type of sources that have been used in the compilation of any written work. Referencing also ensures that the author adheres to copyright law by giving due recognition to other authors' works.

Student study skills

Skillset 2 offers a valuable guide to effective and proper referencing by outlining what referencing is, why it is important, and how to reference properly. You can also undertake an activity exercise to put into practice these referencing skills.

Definition

There are many different definitions of theory but most are variations around the same theme; theory is a set of principles around which the practice of an activity is based. Theoretical perspectives are developed to help us understand the world around us and the phenomena that make up that world. The complexity and dynamic nature of the world means that the same phenomena can be viewed from different perspectives. For example, differences in language, culture, climate, education, history, and tradition are just some of the many factors that inform perspectives on different phenomena. Theory helps to create a construct or set of parameters within which a particular phenomenon or area of study can be investigated and analysed in more detail to elicit a greater understanding. All academic subjects have evolved over time as knowledge on the subject matter is increased. Each has its own body of knowledge and theoretical models or frameworks around which that knowledge has been generated. Some theories are transferable across different disciplines whilst others are designed for a specific purpose within a specific discipline or area of investigation. Management theory is relatively new compared to that of the arts or sciences. Management only emerged as a recognised academic discipline in the mid-eighteenth century, thanks largely to the Industrial Revolution that spawned a number of studies into how best to manage resources in a mass production setting. Although management as a practice has been around for many centuries, for the purposes of this chapter the discussion focuses on the development of theory from the time of the Industrial Revolution.

Introduction

This chapter offers a chronological account of the evolution of management thinking and the development of theory starting from the work of Adam Smith in the eighteenth century. The chapter continues by presenting an overview of the key theoretical perspectives using the

Term
Definition

Theory: a set of principles designed to help explain a group of facts or phenomena.

competing values framework including internal processes, the rational goal model, human relations, and the open systems model. The discussion addresses the question of the extent to which management theory can further the effectiveness of management in the modern era. Much of this latter analysis is informed by contingency approaches to management. A common theme throughout the chapter is the critical analysis of the relevance of each of the theoretical perspectives to modern managers. To aid this analysis, examples of the different perspectives in different organisational settings and timeframes are used. The chapter concludes with a discussion on integrating different approaches to management.

Origins of management thought

As noted in Chapter 1, management as a concept has been around for a long time. The emergence of great civilisations such as the ancient Egyptians, Incas, and Aztecs, among others, would not have been possible without some form of management (Wood, 2005). The Roman Empire flourished as a result of strict command structures, division of labour, specialisation, and so on. They may not have turned the practice into a theoretical perspective or model, but nevertheless many of these approaches remain evident in the workplace today. As a formal academic subject the study of management started to take root in the late eighteenth century as the Industrial Revolution marked a move away from cottage industries and an agrarian economy to one characterised by mass production in a formal organisational setting—the factory. One of the most influential writers of the eighteenth century was Scottish economist Adam Smith who used the analogy of a pin manufacturer to highlight the environmental change. He noted in his classic 1776 book *The Wealth of Nations* that under the old craft system, one worker carried out all the stages of production towards the end product, whereas under the factory system each worker specialised and repeatedly undertook only one of those steps. With the latter system, the workers were able to produce more pins, more efficiently. Thus, modern management thinking was born from the need to think of ways in which to optimise the use of resources.

The work of Smith was followed by others who sought to find ways and means of introducing even more efficiency into the factory system. Very often the earliest and formative attempts to derive theoretical models in any discipline or area of study are referred to as the 'classical school' and management is no different. The classical school of management is characterised by the common theme of determining the 'one best way' to achieve the stated outcomes with a particular emphasis on the purpose of the organisation and its structure. The writing of Adam Smith proved to be a catalyst for increasing attention being paid to management for optimal effect.

As technology improved so the nature of work and the working environment changed. The expansion of the railways in the nineteenth century and later, the development of telegraph communications and other infrastructure radically altered the way work was done, the types of products produced, and the types of management systems put in place to ensure optimal levels of output (Crump, 2010). Interest in developing models of management and theoretical frameworks started to increase as academics, industrialists, and innovators sought ever more sophisticated ways of maximising output. This was given added impetus by the spread of the

British Empire which led to new markets and resources being exploited in Africa, India, and other regions around the globe (Griffin, 2010). By the early twentieth century distinct schools of thought started to emerge and compete with each other for dominance. Brought together this is often referred to as the competing values model. The main approaches include:

- the rational goal models of management;
- the internal process model;
- the human relations school;
- systems theory; and
- contingency theories.

Competing values framework

The goal of achieving organisational effectiveness in an environment characterised by rapid change is one of the fundamental challenges facing managers. Quinn et al. (2003) note that the development of different theoretical models of management, whilst exhibiting differences in construct and perspective, share this common goal. They outline four philosophical perspectives (or competing values) of management within which theoretical models are developed. These include the rational goal model, the internal process model, the human relations model, and the open systems model. Each model contributes to our understanding of the roles and challenges facing management, and each presents a theoretical means by which the management of organisations can be carried out for optimal effect. However, rather than viewing them as separate and isolated models, Quinn et al. (2003) provide the competing values model that seeks to integrate them by highlighting the value that each contributes to knowledge and understanding. Figure 2.1 illustrates the competing values model.

One of the key challenges facing management in organisations is to balance the need for flexibility whilst maintaining an element of control. This is represented by the vertical axis in Figure 2.1. The dilemma revolves around the need for managers to build in flexibility to deal with change, whilst ensuring that sufficient control is exercised to ensure that activities are carried out in an optimal manner. The tension between these two competing values presents a challenge for managers, especially since there can be no prescribed solution. Managers deal with the flexibility/control dichotomy in different ways according to how they view the most efficient means of achieving optimal effectiveness.

A further dimension is provided by the horizontal axis which highlights the extent to which managers focus on either the internal environment or the external environment. Again, managers will maintain a focus along the spectrum depending on their view of what balance best contributes to the organisation's aims. The segments linked to each model consist of the key criteria for achieving optimal effectiveness. For example, the rational goal model emphasises criteria geared towards maximising output such as productivity, accomplishment, direction, and goal clarity. Contrast this with the human relations model that emphasises the development of human resources through issues relating to workers' morale, commitment, participation, and the openness of the organisational culture. The open systems model is geared towards expansion and growth through innovation, adaptation, growth, and the acquisition of resources. Finally, the internal process model focuses on consolidation and continuity through documentation and information management with the emphasis on stability and control. The

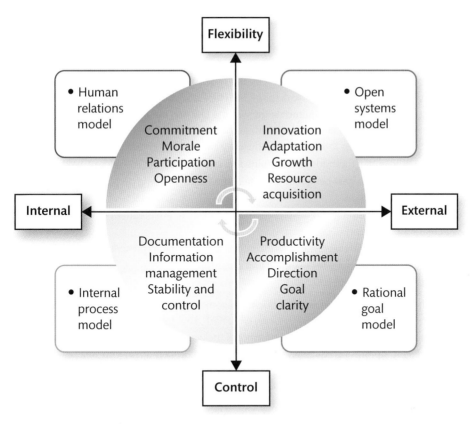

Figure 2.1 Competing values model

competing values framework highlights the many and varied factors that influence the management of organisations and, therefore, it is worth exploring the theoretical models that stem from it in more detail.

Rational goal models of management

The importance of the work of Adam Smith in the development of management thinking has already been noted in this chapter. In many ways, Smith set in train a philosophy around which managers could build models for the optimal use of resources in organisations. In an era of transformational change due to the Industrial Revolution it can be argued that the origins of the rational goal model began with the output of Smith. By the late 1800s the rational goal model was reaching its zenith in terms of its application in a global economy defined by powerful empires run by countries such as Great Britain and France (Bryan, 2010). In particular, the development of scientific management played a significant role in defining the type of management to be found in the large-scale factory systems around the globe during the late nineteenth and early twentieth centuries.

Scientific management

The most high-profile champion of the scientific management approach was Frederick Taylor (1856–1915). The essence of scientific management is described by Taylor in his seminal work *The Principles of Scientific Management* (1911) as 'the systematic study of the relationships between people and tasks to redesign the work for higher efficiency'. Taylor sought to reduce the time a worker spent on each task by optimising the way the task was done. Scientific methods were to be adopted as a means of achieving this rather than traditional 'rule of thumb' approaches. He highlighted five principles through which efficiency could be optimised. These include:

- the use of scientific methods to determine the 'one best way' to complete a task;
- the selection of the best person to undertake the task depending on physical and mental capabilities;
- the provision of training and development for workers to enable them to follow clearly defined procedures;
- the provision of financial rewards as incentives for adhering to prescribed methods; and
- shifting the responsibility for planning and organising work schedules from the worker to the manager.

The underlying principle behind scientific management was that tasks would be completed more efficiently if each worker knew exactly what had to be done within a specified timeframe. Routines and predictability were characteristics of the working environment that Taylor viewed as being key to optimising efficiency. Thus, all work was broken down into small manageable units that were capable of being timed. Each unit of work would then have its own routine set of actions or tasks ascribed to it and a timeframe for completion. In scientific management it is the responsibility of managers to ensure the work is carried out as prescribed through the constant monitoring and recording of outcomes. Thus, scientific management is characterised by a high level of control and discipline and an authoritarian style of management. Surhone et al. (2010) provide a deeper understanding of the components of scientific management.

It is worth noting that this form of management reflected the type of society that existed in the late nineteenth century in countries such as the UK and the USA. In the UK the class system informed the social structure with the owners of capital or landed gentry forming a small but powerful and wealthy elite. The majority of the population consisted of either skilled or non-skilled workers who were powerless and lived a wage/labour existence to survive. Although scientific management in its purest form may seem harsh and draconian by modern standards, the thinking behind it was very much in keeping with the economic and social structures in which its protagonists lived (Wrege and Greenwood, 1991). Through his writings, it is clear that

Term
Definition

Scientific management: science-based approach to optimising output in a production process.

Taylor possessed a rather jaundiced attitude towards the basic values of workers. One typical quote asserts that '. . . in a majority of cases the man deliberately plans to do as little as he possibly can, to turn out far less work than he is well able to do, in many instances to do no more than one-third to one-half of a proper day's work . . . this constitutes the greatest evil with which the working people of England and America are now afflicted' (Taylor, 1911).

One of the most high-profile adopters of scientific management was Henry Ford, who introduced the technique into his car manufacturing production lines in the early twentieth century. Ford believed that the production system was ideal for the implementation of the scientific management approach as a means of maximising efficiency and ensuring that workers delivered a guaranteed minimum level of productive input (Levinson, 2002). The constant monitoring and recording of activities along the production line underpinned by an authoritarian management style underscored the culture of the organisation. Ford pointed to the ever-increasing productivity and performance indicators as vindication of his decision to introduce scientific management in his car plants. However, economic statistics masked the reality of what was happening in his factories. By the 1920s it was clear that all was not as it seemed.

Problems of scientific management

The fact that many factories around the globe improved performance by adopting scientific management techniques proved to be a mirage when set against the growing discontent among the workforce. One of the problems of this approach is that it involves workers carrying out the same tasks day after day in the same section of the production line over a set period of time. Inevitably, feelings of boredom and alienation started to emerge among the workforce. The workers suffered from the tedium of the monotonous working experience and felt that they were just another cog in the wheel of production. Feelings of alienation from the company's objectives only served to exacerbate the negative culture that pervaded many factories, a state of affairs brilliantly satirised in Charlie Chaplin's film comedy *Modern Times* (1936).

A fundamental flaw in the scientific management approach is the lack of a human touch. Workers were expected to perform to the same standard every time they entered the working environment, regardless of their personal well-being or psychological state. For example, a key element of scientific management principles is to choose the best person do the job. However, the best person to do the job is not a constant, it will vary according to the condition of the worker on any given day. It would simply be unworkable to undertake a test on each and every worker on a daily basis to determine the best man or woman for the job. Economist Alfred Marshall pinpointed the key issue by stating that 'The value of a machine to a business can be calculated on the basis of its efficiency for its immediate work. But the value of an employee must be estimated . . .' (Marshall, 1919: 350). The complexity of the human condition was entirely ignored by proponents of scientific management which, ultimately, led to its demise as a dominant form of management.

Modern examples of scientific management

Despite the shortcomings of scientific management, it is possible to discern elements of it in many modern business settings. Where traditional production lines operate, scientific management techniques remain relevant if only to ensure the effective division of labour and a constant level of output. Of course, in many companies, such as Nissan, Toyota, Fiat, and other car manufacturers, many of the tasks formerly undertaken by people are now completed using robotics (Weimer, 2001). Nevertheless, there remain a number of tasks in assembly and

http://corporate.
ford.com/
our-company/
heritage

http://corporate.
ford.com/
our-company/
heritage

42

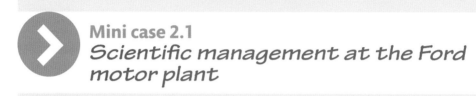

Mini case 2.1
Scientific management at the Ford motor plant

Henry Ford (1863–1947) founded the famous Ford Motor Company in Detroit, USA in the early twentieth century. As an industrialist, Ford was a champion of the assembly line production system that allowed the mass manufacture of his cars, most famously the Model T, which was to become a trademark product in the first two decades of the twentieth century. Ford's approach to business and his strategies for success are outlined in his re-published autobiography (Ford, 2009). Ford adopted the scientific management techniques extolled by his contemporary Frederick Taylor. Vindication of the introduction of this technique was the ever-expanding production and sales figures that Ford recorded. Underpinning the success of the management approach was the discipline that Ford instilled in workers. He firmly believed that the authoritarian style of management evident in his car plants was the bedrock of ensuring that the production line met stringent targets, that his workers would not be compromised into what Taylor referred to as 'soldiering'—that is, operating below the level of their capabilities. Like Taylor, Ford had a somewhat bleak perception of the average worker whereby, given the opportunity, he believed they would simply do the bare minimum. Hence, the need for time and motion studies to determine the optimum level of activity that could be expected of workers. Clearly, the scientific management approach produced results in the initial phase of its adoption. However, Ford neglected to address the effect that such a rigid form of management would have on the physical and psychological well-being of his workforce, some of which are highlighted in the work of Firsht (2012). Symptoms of worker discontent manifested in the form of high rates of worker turnover, absenteeism, increasing amounts of sick leave, and, in some instances, sabotage and vandalism of the production line. Eventually, the negative effects of implementing scientific management started to affect the performance of organisation, forcing a rethink by Ford on its long-term effectiveness.

Sources:

Firsht, H. (2012) 'Assemby Line Americanization, Henry Ford's Progressive Politics', *Michigan Journal of History* (Fall), pp. 1–18.

Ford, H. (2009) *My Life and Work—An Autobiography of Henry Ford*, Thousand Oaks, CA, BN Publishing.

Discussion point

Why was Henry Ford so blind to the negative effects of scientific management on his workforce?

Questions and task

How would you propose to adapt scientific management to deal with the needs of workers?

Highlight six physical or psychological effects of working under conditions of scientific management.

What are the likely symptoms of worker discontent under scientific management?

 Online Resource Centre
Author commentary on this discussion point and questions can be found on the Online Resource Centre at: www.oxfordtextbooks.co.uk/orc/combe1e/

components that are undertaken by humans and this is where some elements of scientific management are evident. Workers in some business sectors are paid according to whether their output matches set targets over a set period of time. In the clothes manufacturing industry teams of workers are given set targets for the completion of a prescribed group of tasks. For example, at Laura Ashley factories teams of workers collaborate on tasks that combine to produce a whole dress. The tasks are allocated to those workers best suited to complete the task efficiently and to a set standard. The reward system is purely economic with the trade-off being the time, effort, and skill of workers for monetary reward. Teams of workers compete against each other to win bonuses for producing the highest output over a defined period. Possibilities for social interaction are limited to break times as each worker is fully engrossed in their allocated tasks during production time (Campbell et al., 1999).

Other examples where scientific management is evident in the modern business environment are fast food restaurants such as McDonald's and KFC. Here, each task is clearly defined and targets are set for completing a transaction with customers. Workers require little training but are expected to quickly pick up the necessary skills to keep the fast delivery of food to customers at an optimal level. Call centres also have similar elements of scientific management where workers are constantly monitored and their output is recorded (Desai, 2010). Again, there is a trade-off between time and effort for monetary reward. Very often workers are paid for the number of calls they field in one shift. In this case some training is given to workers as they have to follow set procedures and scripts when dealing with clients. This will vary according to the type of businesses that the call centre is geared to serve but the purpose of it is to ensure that workers are able to deal with calls in the best and most effective manner possible.

The limited scope for advancement or job satisfaction in industries such as fast food outlets or call centres means that they typically have a high level of staff turnover. Managers need to monitor the flow of workers in and out in order to determine if it is having a negative effect on their output targets. In some instances, managers have introduced initiatives to alleviate some of the boredom and monotony of such jobs by introducing job rotation or extended breaks. Nevertheless, the understanding that such working environments are characterised by low skills, repetitive tasks, long hours, and low pay ensures the continuation of a high level of staff turnover (Hutton, 2002). Very often it is the temporary nature of the employment that makes it tolerable for workers, who tend to be of the younger generation. This phenomenon is a feature of such businesses around the world, especially among global brands such as McDonald's, KFC, or Starbucks (Klein, 2000). However, there are some settings where workers have little choice but to suffer the effects of scientific management as they are unwilling victims of an economic model that locks them into the wage/labour dichotomy. This is especially evident in fast developing countries such as China, Vietnam, Thailand, and India where labour is cheap and plentiful.

The Gilbreths

Two contemporaries of Frederick Taylor were Frank (1868–1924) and Lillian Gilbreth (1878–1972), a husband and wife team who refined Taylor's methods and made many improvements to time and motion studies (Gilbreth and Gilbreth, 1917). Basic time and motion studies had three elements, which were to:

1 Break down each action into components.

2 Find better ways to perform it.

3 Reorganise each action to be more efficient.

? **Critical reflection**
Is scientific management relevant in the modern business environment?

The advantages of applying scientific management techniques relate mostly to productivity and output in working environments where activities can be easily measured and the tasks prescribed. Time and motion studies were a common feature in factory systems throughout much of the twentieth century. However, the application of scientific management in the modern era has been consigned to the margins of management practice. The suitability of the practice has diminished as organisations have embedded more flexibility into their working practices and the relationships that underpin them. There is also a good legal reason why scientific management, at least in its purest form, is absent from the modern workplace. For example, at both the European and domestic levels, there are employment laws that protect workers from some of the excesses witnessed under the rigid and draconian working practices that characterise scientific management. The well-being of workers is a guiding principle underpinned by legislation. This means that workers are entitled to certain rights such as work breaks, freedom of association, safe and healthy working environments, and access to educational and personal development opportunities. Equal opportunities in the workplace have become a common feature underpinned by law. This makes choosing the 'one best person' to do the task problematic. Under equal opportunities doctrines, it would be necessary to constantly update what constitutes the 'one best person' and then to allow all employees the opportunity to apply for the position. This is clearly anathema to the thinking of pioneers such as Frederick Taylor, who lived in an era when managers dictated such things and their authority was unquestioned by subordinates.

Frank Gilbreth used his knowledge as a former bricklayer to study the reasons why work was often slow and inefficient. By filming bricklayers at work he was able to break down the work to single movements such that an optimal number of movements could be determined for the successful completion of the task. He also emphasised the need for employers to provide the correct materials and tools so that the workers could successfully complete the tasks in the time allocated. The aim of this approach was to ensure that the minimum number of actions were undertaken to complete the task, thereby simultaneously minimising fatigue and optimising productivity. Time and motion studies were a common feature of working environments (especially ones that required manual labour) throughout the early to mid-twentieth century and still exist in some organisations to this day. Nevertheless, the significance of this approach has diminished greatly in the modern era as the working environment (and the employment law that governs it) has changed dramatically. For example, many modern outputs rely on creativity, innovation, and the generation of ideas that are not reliant on specific physical actions and, therefore, cannot be measured and timed easily.

Perhaps of even greater significance than the time and motion studies was the work carried out by Lillian Gilbreth into issues of worker fatigue and the physical work environment. At first glance it may seem as if there is a contradiction in the philosophy of Lillian Gilbreth as her writings advocate scientific management whilst simultaneously being concerned with improvements to

Term
Definition

Time and motion studies: the science of timing each action that contributes to the completion of a work task over a set period of time.

workers' welfare. Previously it has been noted how injurious scientific management techniques were to the well-being of workers, both physically and psychologically. Lillian Gilbreth attempted to square this circle by concluding that 'through careful development of systems, careful selection, clearly planned training and proper equipment, workers would build their self respect and pride' (Gilbreth, 1914). Gilbreth argued that the key to successfully implementing scientific management in general, and time and motion studies in particular, was the ability of management to explain to workers the reasons for the prescribed work processes. Critics have subsequently argued that this grossly understates the complexity of the human condition in the workplace.

Internal process model

As noted above, the internal process model emphasises stability and control. To achieve this, bureaucratic models were developed to ensure that every aspect of activity within an organisation was prescribed, measured, recorded, and controlled. The model places a great deal of importance on the production of documentation that records information on the transformation process between inputs and outputs in an organisation. Thus, administration forms a major part of the control function within such organisations.

Bureaucracy

Bureaucracy represents perhaps the most systematic analysis of organisations as rational structure. German sociologist Max Weber (1864–1920) was one of the pioneers of bureaucratic organisational structures designed to create a type of organisation that maximises efficiency and effectiveness. The concept of Weber's vision of a bureaucratic structure is well articulated in his *The Theory of Social and Economic Organizations* (1947), where it is argued that this approach is the most efficient form of organisation and that it creates speedy, predictable, fair, and skilful management.

Key characteristics of bureaucracy

There are a number of key characteristics that define a bureaucracy. Foremost among these is the underpinning authority that controls activities in the organisation. Authority is dealt with in more detail in later chapters on leadership and human resource management. Here, it is sufficient to note that authority can be defined as the power to issue commands and hold people accountable for their actions. This is a key factor in ensuring the cohesiveness of a

45

Bureaucracy: an organisational system tightly controlled through the application of strict rules, regulations, and procedures.

46

bureaucratic structure where rules, regulations, and discipline are maintained through the exercise of authority. Other key characteristics flow from the authoritarian approach where lines of authority are clearly set out and workers know who to report to. Others include the principle that positions held within the organisation should be awarded on merit and not social contacts. These positions should be clearly defined to ensure that all personnel know exactly what is expected of them.

As the Industrial Revolution gathered pace in the nineteenth century the attraction of the bureaucratic structure within a process driven, mass manufacturing setting is clear to see. In this organisational form efficiency is gained by the organisational structure rather than being constrained by the influence of its leaders. That is, management teams have clearly defined rules, regulations, procedures, and definitions of their authority within the hierarchy. The structure still allows worker specialisation, but it is expressed within a highly formalised system.

Protagonists of bureaucracies point to the evidence of increases in efficiency and output in many industrial settings as vindication of their approach. However, by the twentieth century the lack of a human dimension to this structure featured prominently in critical assessments of bureaucracies. For example, Merton (1940) describes the ways in which certain features of bureaucracy may be affected by the personalities of organisational members. There is a reduction in personalised relationships, an over-internalisation of organisational rules and an emphasis on control which restricts discretion in decision making. Collectively these constitute dysfunctional consequences of bureaucracy and are referred to as 'red-tape'.

The rise of bureaucratic structures as a dominant force in the twentieth century encouraged a number of studies into their effects. Gouldner (1954) studied the ways in which organisational members reacted to the key characteristics of bureaucracy. In his study of a gypsum mine, he identified that the control strategies arising from the organisation structure varied markedly depending on the spectrum of formalisation: from the highly formalised organisation (punishment-centred bureaucracy) through to very informal settings (this latter extreme is sometimes referred to as mock-bureaucracy). The manner in which these different levels of control strategies play out are dependent on the perception of management of the organisational context. Representative bureaucracy is based on universal adherence to prescribed rules or where the rules are justified by a technical factor, as in a production line format. Punishment-centred bureaucracy is characterised by the rules being imposed by those in positions of authority in the organisation.

Although many modern businesses have adopted organisational structures that are less rigid and regimented than those with bureaucratic features, there remain some institutions where this approach is still evident. In particular, organisations that are process driven and rely on stability and control feature bureaucratic structures (Ritzer, 2004). In many countries the civil service is operated on bureaucratic doctrines to ensure that the process of delivering public service benefits to large numbers of people is achieved as efficiently as possible. The armed services and prisons often have bureaucratic structures to instil discipline and to underscore authority. In the UK, the National Health Service has traditionally been characterised by bureaucratic structures, although since the mid-1990s successive governments have attempted to introduce more flexible arrangements that more closely resemble structures seen in the private sector. The effects of this transformation are the subject of Lord Crisp's book *24 Hours to Save the NHS* (2011). The reasons for this move away from bureaucracies relate to the limitations of the approach, including:

- the slowness of activities and communication due to the hierarchical structure;
- the lack of innovation due to the prescribed work activities and schedules;
- the inability to change quickly to changes in the environment;
- inefficiencies caused by an over-emphasis on information and documentation;
- impersonal working relationships due to an emphasis on rules and regulations and the centralisation of authority and control.

The suitability of bureaucratic structures depends on what managers are trying to achieve for their organisations. Some may point to the certainty that a closely controlled environment brings as a means of motivating workers. It cannot be assumed that all workers enjoy or seek responsibility for innovation or creativity, or that they relish the prospect of assuming leadership roles. In some organisational settings, workers may be motivated by the very characteristics that define bureaucracies (Malone, 2004).

47

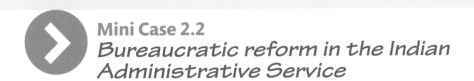

Mini Case 2.2
Bureaucratic reform in the Indian Administrative Service

India has a population of 1.15 billion people and is comprised of twenty-eight states. Although there are sixteen official languages it is known that many others are widely spoken in rural areas. The civil service in India is responsible for organising the administration of public services across this vast and diverse landscape. The Indian Administrative Service (IAS) is the key organisation overseeing the delivery of a wide range of services to the Indian public (jts Institute, 2013). Based on the bureaucratic model of the UK civil service during colonial rule, the ISA has come under pressure to continue the reforms that began in the mid-2000s, after the publication of findings from the Central Vigilance Commission (2001), so that it is fit for purpose in the twenty-first century. This is likely to prove difficult as the organisational culture of the ISA is firmly set around the guiding principles that have informed internal governance since partition in 1947.

Whilst some structural reform has been implemented, and new forms of working put in place (such as the increasing use of technology for delivering e-government solutions), one of the barriers to reform has been the relationship between civil servants and their political pay-masters. The traditional roles were defined by the imperative that politicians would debate policy and then legislate to introduce it. Civil servants were charged with the duty of executing the policy implementation. However, since the 1990s there has been an increasing trend for politicians to

www.civilservice.in
www.civilservice.in

become involved in the execution of policy, leading to an increase in corruption, lack of account-ability and transparency, and less effective delivery of services to the public (Appu, 2005).

Beyond political interference, there have been other external factors that have influenced the drive for reform. In particular, the trend towards a decentralisation of government brought about by an increase in social activism as people demand more control over the political, social, and economic factors governing their lives. The advance of technology has also played a part in bringing more democracy and debate into the public domain. This has had the effect of building a critical mass of public demand for reform. The Right to Information Act (2005) also had a significant effect on public opinion as the extent of the corrupt practices by those in positions of power became clear.

The bureaucratic structure of the IAS has been partly responsible for the way in which power has been abused. However, other symptoms of bureaucratic malaise have been evident, in-cluding the lack of professionalism and capacity building; ineffective reward systems; out-moded rules and regulations; a lack of accountability and transparency; and the erosion of core values and ethics (Venkataratnam, 2005).

Taking all these into account the government of India set out a reform package designed to maintain the benefits of a bureaucratic structure (stability, efficiency, control, etc.) whilst building in the new types of management that would re-orientate the organisation to meet the higher expectations of the public by delivering a dynamic, efficient, and accountable ap-paratus for public service delivery. Thus, the key elements of the reform of the bureaucracy involved organisational structure, mechanisms for ensuring accountability, capacity building, increased professionalism and modernity, implementation of a new recruitment system; and a more meritocratic performance and promotion system. It is likely to be some time before the results of the reforms become evident but those charged with the duty of delivering them are under scrutiny like never before in India.

Sources:

Appu, P.S. (2005) 'All India services: decline, debasement and destruction', *Economic and Political Weekly*, Vol. 40 , No. 9, pp. 826–832.

Central Vigilance Commission, Government of India (2001) *A study of the current state of punitive and preventative vigilance mechanisms*, New Delhi, Sarakata Bhawan.

jts Institute (2013) Indian Administrative Services, Bangalore. http://www.jtsinstitute.com/all-about-ias

Venkataratnam, V. (2005) 'All India Services: time to disband', *Economic and Political Weekly*, Vol. 40 , No. 17, p. 1791.

Discussion points

Are public sector bureaucratic organisations open to corrupt practices?

Are bureaucracies relevant in the twenty-first century?

Questions and tasks

List six characteristics of a bureaucracy.

Identify possible areas of resistance to reform at the IAS.

Identify and explain the meaning of the key elements of the reform of the IAS.

What are the advantages of a bureaucratic structure?

Online Resource Centre

Author commentary on this discussion point and questions can be found on the Online Resource Centre at: www.oxfordtextbooks.co.uk/orc/combe1e/

Term
Definition

Administrative management: ordered principles that guide activities throughout an organisation.

Administrative management

One of the most influential contributors to the internal processes model was French engineer Henri Fayol (1841–1925) who developed a theory of business administration that suggested that all activities undertaken in organisations can be divided into the following groups:

Technical activities:	production, manufacturing, and adaptation
Commercial activities:	buying, selling, and exchange
Financial activities:	the search for and optimum use of capital
Security activities:	the protection of property and persons
Accounting activities:	stocktaking, balance sheet, costs, and statistics
Managerial activities:	planning, organising, commanding, coordinating. and controlling

Table 2.1 lists Fayol's fourteen principles of good management (Fayol, 1949).

Importantly, Fayol stressed that the principles reflected his own rules and did not assume either universal application or permanence. Of particular significance is his recognition of the dynamic nature of the environment in which managers operate (Cunningham-Wood and Wood, 2001). As well as highlighting the principles of good management, Fayol also emphasised the limitations of management due to what he called 'changing circumstances'. As a means of dealing with uncertainty he stressed the need for adaptation as a key attribute of management. This type of thinking was to prove the basis of the contingency theories that became prominent in the 1960s and which still remain relevant in modern management. In that sense it can be seen that Fayol was ahead of his time.

Human relations models

By the beginning of the twentieth century there were already signs that the dominant scientific management approach had reached its peak. The tensions it created in the workplace have already been highlighted, but it was at the societal level that the appetite for change was most evident. Johnson (2007) notes that the first two decades of the twentieth century witnessed significant social change due to factors such as the rise of organised labour in the form of the growing influence of trade unions and their political voice through the UK Labour Party and other socialist organisations; the high-profile protests of the suffragettes campaigning for equal rights for women; and the

49

Table 2.1 Fayol's fourteen principles of good management

Division of work	Specialisation builds expertise and makes individuals more productive.
Authority	The right to issue commands and assume responsibility for their execution.
Discipline	Management leadership resulting in employees obeying orders.
Unity of command	One boss for employees, with no other conflicting lines of command.
Unity of direction	Members of the organisation must have the same objectives in a single plan.
Subordination of individual interest to general interest	Management must ensure that the goals of the organisation take priority over the interests of its individual members.
Remuneration	Payments and rewards must be designed to motivate workers.
Centralisation or decentralisation	Managers must decide on the appropriate balance between the two, depending on the state of the organisation and the quality of its personnel.
Scalar chain	A hierarchy of authority is necessary for unity of direction but there must be communication between people at the same level in the organisation structure.
Order	Both social order and orderly purchasing and usage of materials are important.
Equity	Fair treatment for all employees.
Stability of tenure	Procure a stable group of managers.
Initiative	All employees should be encouraged to exercise initiative.
Esprit de corps	Management must promote high levels of motivation among subordinates.

aftermath of the First World War when surviving conscripts demanded better working conditions after enduring the horrors of the first truly industrialised conflict. Wider and better access to education and healthcare were also key demands that reflected the spirit of the age.

Management thinking reflected these changes by focusing on the human condition in the working environment. This gave rise to the human relations approach which had social processes in the workplace as the source of interest. One of the early advocates of human relations was Mary Parker Follett (1868–1933). After starting a career as a social worker, Follett was soon in demand from the business community for her work on the creative potential of groups within organisational settings. In particular, Follett (1920) extolled the benefits of allowing self-managed groups to identify and solve problems relevant to their sphere of activity

Term
Definition

Human relations: system of management that places emphasis on social processes in the workplace.

and for which they accept a level of responsibility. This philosophy strikes a resonance with many modern businesses, such as in hi-tech industries, the business service sector, design agencies, and social enterprises, where small groups of people work together on projects and are empowered to take decisions that help to achieve the aims and objectives. Her recommendation that workers be part of a network to facilitate communications and knowledge sharing is striking in its relevance to the type of management thinking that exists in the twenty-first century, as is well explained in Graham (1995). As if to underline the demise of scientific management, Follett used her influence to encourage managers to turn away from the division of labour as the means of optimising production in favour of empowering workers to make decisions, accept responsibility, and contribute creatively to the working process. Although the human relations approach was deemed radical at the time, it initiated change in the mindset of managers that was subsequently reflected in the ways and means of achieving aims within organisations. The early work of Follett was to prove a catalyst for many studies into the physiological and psychological welfare of workers in the workplace and the effect it had on production. One of the most famous studies was that carried out by Harvard University researcher Elton Mayo in the 1920s at an electrical plant in Chicago.

The Hawthorne Studies (1924–1932)

These studies focused attention on worker efficiency at the Hawthorne Works of the Western Electric Company over an eight-year period. The company had decided to conduct an investigation into productivity levels. Worker productivity was measured at various levels of light illumination. Interestingly, the researchers discovered that regardless of whether the light levels were raised or lowered, productivity rose. After further investigation the researchers concluded that the workers 'enjoyed' the attention they received as part of the study and that this accounted for the continuous increase in production (Mayo, 1939)—a phenomenon thereafter known as the Hawthorne Effect. Over time, however, this effect dissipated and the researchers were able to attain more accurate readings of how the workers reacted to changes in their physical working environment. Later, the research was extended to test responses to psychological stimuli including the effects of working in teams and levels of association between workers. The most significant outcome of the Hawthorne Studies was the greater recognition of the importance of the workplace as a social environment where workers' interaction, collaboration, and participation influenced motivation, morale, and, ultimately, productivity (Gillespie, 1993). However, in other studies where many of the attributes of human relations approaches have been evident within a chosen organisation, no resultant increase in productivity was evident. Thus, it is clear that the effects of the human relations approaches are context specific, meaning that no generic conclusions can be drawn on the likely impact of its application. Nevertheless, the results from these studies have encouraged the application of psychology and sociology to the context of management in organisations. The human relations studies identified the importance of the informal organisation and the complexity of workers' needs and motivation.

The work of Follett, Mayo, and others has had a considerable impact on shaping the way the modern workplace is organised and built and the types of interpersonal relationships that exist within them. Much of the rights that are taken for granted in the workplace in the modern era relate back to the pioneering work of the early protagonists of the human relations school. Issues of freedom of association, regular work breaks, acceptable levels of heating and lighting, worker participation in decision making, and so on, are common features of the modern working environment (some underpinned by employment law). Even so, human relations based studies continue to be relevant as the working environment continues to change and evolve (see Chapter 4 for a more detailed discussion of these changes).

? Critical reflection
What are the limiting factors associated with the Hawthorne Studies?

The Hawthorne Studies was one of the most ambitious research projects of its kind and the results are still pored over by academics, managers, and practitioners to this day. Hailed by some but scorned by others, the studies have been controversial and subject to on-going debate since the results were published in the 1930s. One particular criticism is the level of bias introduced by the researchers when monitoring and recording the output of workers. The Hawthorne Effect—whereby behaviour is altered under conditions of scrutiny—has been well documented, but there was also the added dimension of feedback being issued to workers on their performance. Critics point to the unnatural responses by workers to this feedback and suggest it undermines the credibility of the results. Parsons (1974) argued that the introduction of prescribed rest breaks offered the workers an opportunity for learning that was not factored in when subsequent output rates were analysed. In some experiments the workers had access to information on how they were performing courtesy of the researchers who were monitoring their output, something previously unknown to them. This inevitably raised concerns that the experiment did not match the normal reality of the working practices in the factory. Mayo countered these criticisms by emphasising that the overall effect was of primary interest rather than any one experiment. In particular, he stressed that the purpose of the research was to determine how managers can induce better performance from workers as a result of those workers having different perceptions and feelings about their working environment. What is clear is that Mayo and his team of researchers ensured that the human relations approach gained in prominence and was the catalyst for managers taking a greater interest in workers as a social entity in the workplace, rather than seeing them purely from an economic perspective.

Mini case 2.3
The fashion industry

There are some industries where the output is dependent on the imagination, creativity, and innovation of workers. The fashion industry and many of the related areas that go to support it (advertising, events, photography, etc.) is an example of this. Many of the most successful brands in fashion, such as Dior, Versace, and Chanel, have staked their reputation on the risk associated with giving key workers the freedom to explore new opportunities and to experiment with new designs and concepts. The dominant culture of such fashion houses is one that reflects the liberal attitude of the leading lights in the industry (Godart, 2012). Strict adherence to rules and regulations within rigid working practices would be doomed to failure in an artistic and creative industry such as fashion. And yet, the industry is highly competitive and demands extraordinary levels of commitment from its staff to succeed, whether working for a high-end label or starting a fashion business (Burke, 2008). Invariably this is achieved by the energy and personalities of those at the top of the organisation driving forward the message underpinning the brand. Workers take the lead from this and are recruited in particular for their desire and drive to succeed. Fundamentally, the most successful fashion houses are built on the foundation of a shared belief and a willingness for sacrifice by the workers that is difficult to replicate in other settings. For example the Italian fashion label Diesel was set up by Renzo Rocco in 1978 with the purpose of shaking up the industry through risk taking and a working environment that has been variously described as 'unconventional'. Rocco surrounded himself with like-minded, cosmopolitan people from across the creative arts and hired the inspirational Wilbert Das as Creative Director. Key to the company's success was the open-minded and innovate design team. To maximise their impact Rocco gave them broad stylistic freedom and emphasised individuality. This created a unique working environment that paved the way for the emergence of one of the most successful and compelling brands in fashion.

Sources:

Adams, S. (December 9, 2012) Apple's New Foxconn Embarrassment, Forbes.com

Burke, S. (2008) *Fashion Entrepreneur: Starting Your Own Fashion Business*, Norwich, Burke Publishing.

Godart, F. (2012) *Unveiling Fashion: Business, Culture and Identity in the Most Glamorous Industry*, Basingstoke, Palgrave Macmillan.

Discussion point

How easy would it be to transfer the open-minded and liberal approach of the fashion industry to that of an organisation in the manufacturing sector?

Questions and task

What, if any, management theory does the case of Diesel adhere to?

What are the main risks associated with the 'unconventional' management approach that Diesel adopted?

Research and identify another example of an 'unconventional' approach to management in a formal organisational setting.

Online Resource Centre

Author commentary on this discussion point and questions can be found on the Online Resource Centre at: www.oxfordtextbooks.co.uk/orc/combe1e/

Open systems

A systems approach considers relationships inside and outside the organisation. The environment consists of the forces, conditions, and influences on the organisation. Systems theory considers the impact of three stages:

1 Input: acquire external resources.

2 Transformation: inputs are processed into products and services.

3 Output: finished products are released into the environment.

This is referred to as the transformation process, the component parts of which are illustrated in Figure 2.3. If the process was linear and did not involve feedback or the external environment, this would be termed a 'closed system'. However, a closed system relies on a very stable external environment, something that is rare. Open systems take into account the influence of the external environment.

A distinction has to be made between a general system and an open system. A general system refers to a set of interrelated parts brought together to achieve a stated outcome or aim. Katz and Khan (1978) identify two key components of an Open System as:

- links between the interrelated internal parts of a system;
- links between the entire system and the external environment.

Open systems rely on resources from the external environment (raw materials, human resources, etc.), which are then subject to the transformation process to create outputs that subsequently leave the system for distributors, retailers, and buyers. The key issue relating to open systems is the reliance on the external environment for the inputs from which added value can then be derived (Gray, 1991). However, the challenge to management is to identify the component parts that comprise the system, and all the key elements that comprise the environment in which they exist. The environment is complex and unpredictable and managers can only ever possess a fraction of the knowledge required to fully understand it. Here, it is necessary for managers to possess high quality analytical skills allied to a strategic perspective of which factors will determine the environment over an elongated period of time. For example, much has been written about global warming in recent years, but exactly how it is likely to affect business in ten years' time or even longer is largely unknown. Nevertheless, it is necessary for managers to think about how this issue will play out in the future and the likely impact it may have on their organisation. Greater understanding helps managers to be proactive in their business solutions rather than reactive to events that shape the environment, which is always going to be a less advantageous position.

Term
Definition

Open system: a system that interacts with the environment in which it exists.

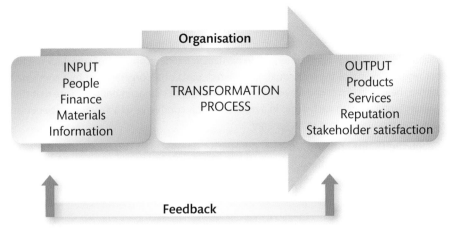

Figure 2.2 The transformation process

In order to be more proactive, managers rely on knowledge and learning from the experiences and outcomes of activities within an organisation. Pritchard et al. (2000) explain that organisational learning occurs as a result of a feedback loop from identifying and recording outcomes of activities and relaying that information back into the system to aid the future deployment of inputs in the transformation process. This is why information is a key input variable as illustrated in Figure 2.2. This process facilitates much closer interaction with the external environment and accounts for outputs that go beyond delivering products and services, but also includes factors such as stakeholder satisfaction and reputation. The complexity facing managers in the modern business environment becomes evident when one considers that the process outlined in Figure 2.2 only represents a small fraction of the number of influential factors that comprise the external environment. In reality there are many hundreds of factors that may have an impact in an open systems model. Figure 2.3 illustrates the complexity of open systems.

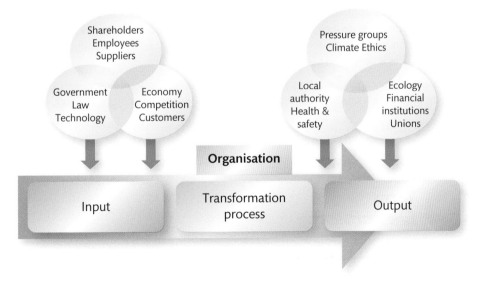

Figure 2.3 Complexity and an open system

The open systems model found favour throughout the 1950s and 1960s and can be seen as a natural extension of the human relations approach where greater emphasis on human and social aspects of work formed the dominant paradigm of thinking. As open systems thinking evolved, so greater insights emerged. In particular, the development of subsystems gave a better understanding of the individual, but related, parts of an organisation that combine to comprise the whole (Scott and Davis, 2006). It is the role of management to ensure that these subsystems interact with each other in a manner that is conducive to achieving efficiency and quality; this is often referred to as 'synergy'.

Although the failure of one subsystem will not be responsible for the failure of the whole system, it is necessary for management to ensure that maximum synergy exists between the subsystems as this underpins the principle that 'the whole is greater than the sum of its parts'. That is, greater benefits accrue to organisations where interrelationships between subsystems are at an optimal level.

Amagoh (2008) provides a valuable critique of different perspectives on systems theory, some of which highlight the benefits associated with an open systems approach. The benefits of adopting such an approach are wide ranging but perhaps the most significant is the enhanced knowledge and understanding that derives from the process of continuous feedback. This applies as much to the internal environment as it does to the external environment. Better understanding of the interactive dynamics of internal processes informs decision making and, ultimately, improves planning, coordination, efficiency, and quality. This helps an organisation cope with the vagaries of the external environment, which is itself better understood through the organisational learning that comes from continuous feedback.

Contingency

Even whilst the open systems approach was being widely adopted by managers throughout the 1960s, there already existed a view by many influential writers (Woodward, 1958; Burns and Stalker, 1961; Lawrence and Lorsch, 1967) that the environment in which organisations operated was too complex and unpredictable to advocate any one particular theory. This gave rise to contingency approaches that emphasise the need for managers to create and shape the organisation based on their understanding of the environment in which they operate. The underlying principle of contingency theory has it that firms must be flexible enough to adopt different stances according to need.

Contingency theory applies management principles and processes according to the particular characteristics of each situation such as the external environment, technology, structure, and so

Term
Definition

Contingencies: key factors that reflect the situation of an organisation.

on. Contrary to the rational goal school, contingency theorists do not believe in the guiding principle of 'one best way' to achieve a task. Rather, they emphasise that organisations should strive to be flexible, even to the extent that they are capable of operating both open and closed systems simultaneously. One subsystem (possibly a department within the organisation) may operate a closed system whilst others have open systems. For example, the marketing and sales departments in a hi-tech company may operate an open system that allows them to interact with operations and logistics departments as well as external stakeholders. However, it may be pragmatic for the research and development (R&D) department to operate a closed system to protect their innovative processes and intellectual property that forms the basis of developing new products. Innovative companies such as Hewlett Packard (computing and electronics), GlaxoSmithKline (pharmaceuticals), and Heinz International (food) constantly review the balance between open and closed systems across their organisations. Indeed, the spectrum between open and closed systems is one along which organisations constantly move depending on their operational requirements and their strategic aims. Thus, a chosen system is not a given that cannot be altered but rather a set of interrelationships that are capable of change. Contingency theory fits into this dynamic by creating organisational characteristics, such as its structure or level of interdependence, that can accommodate flexibility in a rapidly changing environment (Pugh et al., 1969).

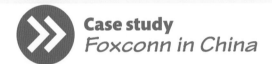

Case study
Foxconn in China

57

http://www.
foxconn.com/

http://www.
foxconn.com/

http://www.
foxconn.com/

It has been noted previously that the application of scientific management in its purest form is restricted in the modern era due to employment laws and the types of work practices and relationships that have evolved in organisations. However, there are parts of the world where labour rights and employment laws are almost non-existent. Many of the products we take for granted, such as Nike trainers, Apple iPads, mobile phones, toys, and gifts are manufactured in countries where mass production can take place at low cost. Many large global companies either set up wholly owned subsidiary manufacturing plants or outsource manufacturing to countries that can offer cheap labour. IT has been an area of great controversy in the last two decades as human rights pressure groups have sought to highlight the poor working conditions associated with some of the factories in developing countries such as India, Bangladesh, Indonesia, the Philippines, and Vietnam. In fact, there have been some high-profile cases where companies such as Nike and Next have had to act in order to restore their reputation as evidence of exploitation of workers (some as young as 10 years old) has emerged in factories producing their products (Knight and Greenberg, 2002). In many of these factories the working regime is governed by an authoritarian management who implement rigid work practices that exhibit many of the traits of scientific management. One of the most notorious examples is the Foxconn factory system in China run by the *Hon Hai Precision Industry Company*.

Foxconn was founded in 1974 to service the growing electronics industry in the USA. Soon afterwards, the company expanded globally and now has many plants in areas such as Mexico, Brazil, India, and Eastern Europe. Foxconn has also invested heavily in China where in 2010 they operated thirteen factories across nine cities. The company specialises in the design, development, manufacture, and assembly of the 3Cs: computers, communications, and consumer electronics. In

China the factories specialise in the manufacture and assembly of electronic components and circuit boards. One of their biggest clients is Apple who outsource this work for their leading brands the iPhone and iPad. The attraction of Foxconn to companies such as Apple is their commitment to the 'lowest total cost solution' as highlighted in their corporate vision (http://www.foxconn.com/GroupProfile_En/GroupProfile.html). The factories are designed and managed to deliver on the company promise of speed, quality, flexibility, and monetary cost saving. Nevertheless, Apple has been embarrassed by some of the worker abuses reported at the Foxconn factories and has been forced to act to avoid damage to their own reputation (Adams, 2012).

The Foxconn vision and strategy

Foxconn has a commitment to delivering high quality components for a range of industries. The vision of the company is to ensure that clients receive the highest quality service at a low total cost. The strategic aims of the organisation reflect this vision by emphasising the development of strategic relationships with top-tier PC and electronics companies such as Apple, Hewlett Packard, and Sony. Also part of the strategy is to develop global logistics capabilities and to maintain technologically advanced and flexible production capabilities. These align to the aim of further expanding production capacity. The main focus of the company strategy is economic performance leading to expansion and growth. However, the vision also focuses attention on stakeholders. The vision confirms a 'devotion to greater social harmony and higher ethical standards to achieve a win-win model for all stakeholders including shareholders, employees, community and management' (Foxconn, CSR Report 2010).

Scientific management at Foxconn

In 1988 Foxconn built one of the world's biggest factory complexes in the Chinese city of Shenzhen, eventually housing some 300,000 workers. Undercover journalist Jemima Kiss was able to provide eye-witness accounts of working conditions in the factory. The work mainly involved the assembly of components for the electronics and computing industries. The management principles adopted closely mirror those of scientific management with all decisions and responsibilities firmly placed on the shoulders of line managers to maintain discipline and order in an authoritarian culture. The workers each undertake a small prescribed task along the production line where there is no scope for interaction with other workers. Every step of the production process is monitored to ensure that the tasks are completed within strict time and motion standards. New workers have to learn how to perform the tasks quickly in order to maintain their place on the production line. The reward system is purely economic with workers receiving a standard rate for a shift which can last up to sixteen hours with overtime. The workers are afforded two short meal breaks in a typical shift. It is the role of management to ensure that output targets are met and this means controlling the workers' activities from the moment they clock in for work. Little attention has been paid to the physical working conditions with workers housed in warehouse style structures with strip lights and variable temperatures. Most workers have to stand throughout their shift as performing the prescribed tasks from a seated position would compromise speed. Many critics point to these working conditions as an example of worker exploitation and some reporters have gone undercover in the factories to confirm the accounts of workers (Kiss, 2012).

Much in the way that Henry Ford justified the introduction of scientific management techniques in his car plant a hundred years earlier, the management of Foxconn point to the $102 billion revenues generated in 2009/10 as evidence of the success of the approach. However, like Ford, the management have neglected the human cost of operating such a draconian set of working practices. Workers have been known to suffer both physical and psychological stress leading to a number of suicides. In 2010 fourteen workers ended their lives by jumping from high levels in the factory. The response of the company was to introduce anti-suicide netting and increase the number of counsellors. There was even a wage increase to placate the increasing sense of frustration among workers. Nevertheless, an investigation by twenty Chinese universities reported widespread abuse of workers and described the factory system as a labour camp (Tam, 2012).

The evidence of the abuse of workers and the poor working conditions provided by ex-workers and academic researchers, as well as undercover reporters, suggests that Foxconn have successfully implemented scientific management techniques to improve productivity, but have neglected the social aspects of the workplace, sometimes with dire consequences for the welfare of workers. Although some efforts have been made to address the issues (especially after clients such as Apple put pressure on the company to initiate reform) the reality still fails to live up to the rhetoric. A response from the General Manager in 2009 reveals how the company recognised the problems: 'Even in a tough economy, Foxconn did not waver on its commitment to employees and the culture that kept them challenged and provided a work–life balance. Foxconn worked vigorously to reduce the societal impact on the younger generation by way of employee welfare initiative in combatting psychological and work-related stress' (Foxconn, CSR Report, 2009). Given the fact that suicide rates at the factory peaked in the following year, the efforts made by management to alleviate the work-related stress proved insufficient. Table 2.2 outlines the match between scientific management principles and the techniques evident at the Foxconn factory in Shenzhen.

Table 2.2 Scientific management at Foxconn in Shenzhen

The use of scientific methods to determine the 'one best way' to complete a task.	A large number of tasks are broken down into a series of small actions along a production line. There is a prescribed method for undertaking each task.
The selection of the best person to undertake the task depending on physical and mental capabilities.	As the tasks are low skilled the scope for recruitment is wide. However, the majority of workers at the factory are under 30 years of age due to the physical demands of working up to 16 hours each day in a standing position.
The provision of training and development of workers to enable them to follow clearly defined procedures.	The low skills requirement means that training is at a minimal level. New recruits have to learn to complete their allocated tasks quickly to ensure that production targets are maintained.
The provision of financial rewards as incentives for adhering to prescribed methods.	The only reward offered to workers is economic. The workers receive payment for the shifts they complete.
Shifting the responsibility for planning and organising work schedules from the worker to the manager.	Managers set work schedules and production targets.

Sources:

Adams, S. (9 December 2012) Apple's New Foxconn Embarrassment, Forbes.

Foxconn (2009) CSR Report.

Foxconn (2010) CSR Report.

Kiss, J. (13 September 2012) 'The real price of an iphone: Life in the Foxconn factory', *Guardian*. http://www.guardian.co.uk/technology/2012/sep/13/cost-iphone-5-foxconn-factory

Knight, G. and Greenberg, J.D. (2002) 'Promotionalism and Subpolitics: Nike and its Labor Critics', *Management Communications Quarterly*, Vol.15, pp. 541–70.

Tam F. (2002) 'Foxconn factories are labor camps: report', *South China Morning Post*.

Questions and tasks

Is management theory of any use to the workers at Foxconn in Shenzhen?

By what criteria should management be judged in a factory setting such as that of Foxconn?

Is the factory at Foxconn in Shenzhen an example of an open or closed system?

Highlight four possible solutions to help the workers cope with the demands of the working environment at Foxconn in Shenzhen.

Online Resource Centre
Author commentary on these questions can be found on the Online Resource Centre at: www.oxfordtextbooks.co.uk/orc/combe1e/

Summary

● **Appreciate the nature of theory as an academic practice**

This chapter presented the nature of theory as a set of principles around which the practice of an activity is based. As an academic practice, theories are developed to aid an understanding of the world around us and the phenomena that make up the environment.

● **Understand the different theoretical perspectives on management**

Many different theories have been created over time to help managers achieve aims and objectives within an organisational setting. Theories have been designed to help achieve specific aims in different organisational settings and each is a product of the era and historical context in which they were developed. Thus, understanding theories requires an appreciation of the social, political, economic, and cultural dimensions that helped inform thinking at the time of their development.

● **Place theoretical models of management in their chronological and organisational contexts**

The chapter presented an evolution of thinking in management theory starting in the late nineteenth century with the rational goal school of Frederick Taylor's scientific management and Max Weber's bureaucratic models. This was followed by the human relations school and the work of Elton Mayo and the Hawthorne Studies. Human relations approaches emphasise the development of human resources through commitment, participation, and morale. The open systems model was discussed in the context of expansion and growth through innovation, adaptation, and the acquisition of resources. Finally, the internal process model was developed as a means of helping managers deal with complexity and change in the environment and, therefore, is characterised by issues relating to consolidation and continuity through documentation and information management with the emphasis on stability and control.

● **Assess the value of management theories and their use in understanding management in the modern era**

The value and limitations of each perspective has been a feature of the evaluation of theory in this chapter. This led to the discussion around contingency theory that emerged as a response to the increasingly dynamic and unpredictable environment in which managers have to operate. It was noted that no one particular theory was capable of accounting for all the variables in the environment and, therefore, contingency approaches were a pragmatic way of dealing with the myriad different situations faced by managers at any given time.

Conclusion

It is important to remember that the theoretical perspectives on management highlighted in this chapter are a product of the times in which the contributors lived. So, for example, scientific management techniques may seem out-dated and even anachronistic in a modern business environment; in the context of the world as it existed at the height of the Industrial Revolution it had merit and was deemed rational. It is also necessary to remain vigilant against generalisations when assessing the merits of the various theories put forward. For example, there is a temptation to think of the human relations school as being conducive to a more harmonious and collegiate working environment, and indeed it has made some contribution towards that aim. However, even under human relations types of management it is evident that tension, conflict, and worker alienation can emerge. Other factors play a key role in determining the effectiveness of human relations approaches, such as power, decision making, the dynamic between formal and informal relations, access to networks, and so on.

Increasing complexity in the business environment gave rise to the development of contingency theories. These focused on the key aspects of the environment that managers have to consider when designing and shaping their organisation in a way that helps deal with uncertainty in a rapidly changing environment. This is particularly relevant in the modern era where planning for change has become a necessary part of the management of organisations. Chapter 3 addresses the issue of planning alongside that of operations, logistics, marketing, and so on as functions of management.

Chapter questions and task

What are the problems commonly associated with Scientific Management?

What were the key findings of the human relations theorists?

What is the 'contingency' approach to management?

Choose a modern commercial business and explain the transformation process evident in the organisation.

Online Resource Centre
Author commentary on these questions can be found on the Online Resource Centre at: www.oxfordtextbooks.co.uk/orc/combe1e/

Further reading

● Cole, G. A. and Kelly, P. (2011) *Management: Theory and Practice* (7th edn), Basingstoke, Cengage Learning.

This textbook gives a lucid insight into the theory and practice of management and covers many of the key topics required for undergraduate study including historical and modern organisational and management theories. The content is contemporary and addresses issues such as gender, sustainability, and globalisation. The book provides a good starting point for undergraduates with a need to understand the basic issues relating to management.

● Donaldson, L. (2001) *The Contingency Theory of Organizations* (Foundations for Organisational Science), Sydney, Sage Publications.

The author is a leading contributor of articles on management theory and this textbook brings some of them together to explore the construct of contingency theory in organisational settings. The book offers a coherent account of the components of contingency theory and goes on to critically assess the value and limitations of the approach. Theoretical models are used as a basis for addressing some of the limitations of the contingency approach and to make it more robust. The book is of particular use to students with a basic understanding of management theory but who seek a critical evaluation of one of the more contemporary theories in management.

● Williams, K. (2006) *Introducing Management: A Development Guide* (3rd edn), Oxford, Butterworth-Heinemann.

For students new to management, the text by Williams offers a coherent and understandable introduction to the basic themes of management including innovations in management thinking as well as the principles behind management in practice. The text offers additional materials that help the review of learning, case studies, examples, and insights into the practical application of management techniques.

● Witzel, M. (2011) *A History of Management Thought*, London, Routledge.

This book presents an evolutionary guide to the development of management thinking from the early civilisations to the modern era. The author charts the changing economic, social, and political environment as a basis for explaining how management thinking has changed and helped to define certain eras. In some instances the author highlights the world-changing significance of the work of great management thinkers such as Frederick Taylor and the emergence of scientific management at the height of the Industrial Revolution. An interesting read that places many of the management theories into historical context.

● Wren, D. A. (2007) *The History of Management Thought* (5th edn), London, John Wiley & Sons.

Wren's updated version charts the development of management thought to help the understanding of modern management concepts and practice. The book highlights the key writers and thinkers throughout the period from the pre-industrial age to the contemporary business environment. The author identifies and discusses the significance of specific eras and analyses trends and movements through the ages. The book is a useful contribution to knowledge of the evolution of management thinking.

Online Resource Centre

For more information, updates, and multiple-choice questions, please visit the Online Resource Centre at: www.oxfordtextbooks.co.uk/orc/com7e1e/

Skillset 2
Referencing

2(a) Introduction

Chapter 2 takes a historical perspective to the evolution of management thinking and the development of theories that have accompanied it. The works of key writers in management from the eighteenth century onwards are reviewed. Each author has to be properly referenced for the purposes of sourcing material, adhering to copyright law and giving due recognition to contributors. 'Referencing', and the ability to follow good practice when referencing, is a key academic skill which you will require throughout your studies. Referencing is a skill that can also be transferred into the workplace as it can be used to add rigour to the compilation of reports, articles, project plans, strategic plans, and other written documents created for both internal and external use.

This Skillset explains why good practice in referencing is important, outlines different referencing styles, and provides a number of 'tips of the trade' to help ensure your referencing skills are first-class.

2(b) What is 'referencing'?

'Referencing' is a commonplace term for providing *citations* in the main body of your work to indicate the source(s) of other people's ideas/work; along with a *list of references* at the end of your work that provides bibliographic details which would enable the reader to source the materials you used/cited.

A citation is where you acknowledge whose ideas/work you are reporting. There are particular rules for when a quotation is used (i.e. you use the exact words taken from a particular source). Similarly there are number of rules for what bibliographic information is presented in the list of references.

2(c) Why bother with references?

The following comments (or something similar) are ones you might receive at some point in your studies as feedback on, for example, a coursework or report you submit:

'You need to work on referencing.'	'Citation required!'
'Where is the evidence for the points you make?'	'Who said this?'
'Needs to pay more attention to good academic practice in acknowledging sources.'	'Where do these ideas come from? Are they yours? Plagiarised?'

So why is referencing so important?

Referencing as 'honesty'

You must be diligent in acknowledging the work and thoughts of others by appropriately referencing throughout your work. Referencing enables you to show a clear distinction between your thoughts and the thoughts of others, to avoid charges of plagiarism. See Skillset 10 for a more detailed discussion of plagiarism—what it is and how to avoid it.

Referencing as 'evidence'

Citations are very important in providing a 'chain of evidence' by highlighting that you are reporting the ideas, industry statistics, and frameworks (and so on) of others to support your own arguments. An analogy could be a legal case where the lawyers would base their arguments on statute law (citing what law was broken), case law (citing cases to note the result in similar cases in the past), as well as the facts of the case. It would not be enough just to say 'I think that person is guilty'.

Referencing as 'I have done the reading'

Your list and use of referencing conventions, in combination with your arguments, provides evidence to show you have read widely and understood the key literature including where authors agree, and where they differ (see also Skillset 12 on analysis and evaluation).

Referencing as 'attention to detail'

Referencing is not difficult, but it requires attention to detail. Good practice in referencing can win the 'hearts and minds' of your readers, demonstrating you have command of the literature and can follow good academic practice. It says to the reader 'I have mastered a key academic skill, and I take care and attention over my work to get things right'.

Taking the last two points together. When marking assessments, one of the first things both the authors of this textbook will do is look at the reference list to judge: the range of sources used (demonstrates wide-ranging reading and a grasp of the literature?); how current are the sources listed (keeping up with the literature?); the types of sources listed (relying on textbooks/sources tutors have given you, or have you proactively found additional sources such as academic journal articles on your own?); and finally, are the references accurately and consistently presented (showing attention to detail). If all seems well with this, then we look forward to reading what is more likely to be a satisfactory piece of work.

Referencing as 'gaining marks'

Referencing is not difficult once you have a process/template to follow. As already noted, good referencing may enhance the perceived quality of your work so you can attract a higher mark. In some cases there may be explicit marks given for referencing and you would be needlessly 'giving marks away' if you do not follow good practice.

2(d) How to reference

There are a number of different referencing systems such as Harvard, APA (American Psychological Association), Vancouver, and so on. This section outlines some key principles for good referencing practice. The section is not intended to be comprehensive or a detailed review of each system—there are a number of sources listed at the end of this Skillset where more specific details can be found.

Referencing styles can be divided into two types:

Name (author), date styles such as Harvard or APA. Using these styles involves citing the *name(s)* of the author(s) and the *date* (year) of publication in the main body of your work. You then provide bibliographic details in a list of references at the end of the work. For example:

Citation in body of your work	List of References at the end of your work
Combe, 2014	Combe, C.A. (2014) *Introduction to Management*. Oxford: Oxford University Press.

Numeric styles such as the Vancouver referencing style indicate the citation via a number in the main body of the work. The number may be in brackets (for example [1]) or in superscript (for example [1]). This number cross references to bibliographic details at the end of the work (endnote) or in a footnote. For example:

Citation in body of your work	List of References at the end of your work or Footnote
For example [1] or [1]	**1.** Combe, C.A. (2014) *Introduction to Management*. Oxford: Oxford University Press.

Management and business writing typically uses the name, date style. Numeric styles tend to be used by legal (footnotes) or medical/science publications (endnotes).

The following are examples of how to reference some of the most commonly used types of sources you may use (based on the Pears and Shields, 2010 version of Harvard style).

Textbook
Notice the requirement for details of the publisher when listing a textbook.

Citation in body of your work	List of References at the end of your work
Combe, 2014	Combe, C.A. (2014) *Introduction to Management*. Oxford: Oxford University Press.

Journal article
Unlike a textbook, a publisher is not required. Instead the volume and issue of the journal in which the article was published is required; as well as the page numbers for the article. In this case the volume/issue are shown as '14(1)'. Note that there are variations on this practice, such as 'Vol. 14, Iss. 1'.

Citation in body of your work	List of References at the end of your work
Pugh et al., 1969	Pugh, D.S., Hickson, D.J. and Hinings, C.R. (1969), 'The context of organization structures' *Administrative Science Quarterly*, 14(1), pp. 115–126.

In the body of your work 'Pugh et al.' is used rather than Pugh, Dickson, and Hinings. 'Et al.' is a shortened version for 'et alia', a Latin phrase meaning 'and others'. So the citation in the text is really 'Pugh and others'. You only use 'et al.' when there are three or more authors.

Direct quotation from textbook/journal article

Citation in body of your work	List of References at the end of your work
Combe (2014, p. 36) notes that: 'Theoretical perspectives are developed to help us understand the world around us and the phenomena that comprise that world.'	Combe, C.A. (2014) *Introduction to Management*. Oxford: Oxford University Press.

There are particular conventions where you use a direct quotation in your work (i.e. where you use the exact words from someone else's work). Points to note are:

- The citation takes the form of the name, date convention with the addition of the page number(s) where the direct quote occurred in the original source. This enables the reader, if they wish, to confirm that you have accurately quoted your source—the example above would have an entirely different meaning if 'understand' became 'misunderstand' (only three more letters).
- In addition, quotation marks are put around the words of the quotation itself.

- Where the quotation is longer than around a dozen words, or more than a line (conventions vary), then (as well as the name, date, page number(s)) present the quote as a separate paragraph and indent it from both sides. Change the text to single line spacing even if the rest of the text is in (for example) double line spacing. The quotation marks/indentation/line spacing make the quotation stand out as not your own words and important enough to be 'highlighted'.

Website

There are particular standards for the referencing of internet/web-based resources. A list containing 'www.website.org' is not acceptable, if only because the website may have dozens of pages so having the address of the 'home page' is not helpful in indicating where the material came from. In the list of references you should disclose: the author, the year the source was published on the web (it is good practice for websites to note this), the name of the actual page, the URL, and the date when you accessed the source.

Citation in body of your work	List of References at the end of your work
Glasgow Caledonian University, 2008	Glasgow Caledonian University, 2008, *Citing and Referencing*. from: http://www.gcu.ac.uk/student/coursework/referencing/index.html [Last accessed 1 May 2012]

Note that providing the author as a 'name' (an organisation in this case) rather than as a web address (URL) means that the author can be incorporated into your standard alphabetical list of references, and referred to in the text using the normal name, date convention as 'Glasgow Caledonian University, 2008'.

See the sources at the end of the Skillset for a much wider range of examples than are given here.

2(e) Advice and guidance

Make a reference list at the start of doing a piece of coursework of those sources you know you will cite in the body of your report (for example, this textbook!). This will save time later on when deadlines approach, and allow you to work on using the correct format at an early stage. Once you have a number of examples of the standard format (such as a textbook, a journal article, and a website) then it is largely down to you to accurately and consistently follow these examples.

There can be differences between what is required by particular modules/tutors, universities, or academic disciplines (for example, management or law students). It is worth checking with your tutors what their expectations are regarding referencing style. Perhaps even confirming what they mean/expect for 'Harvard Style', as there can be variations! For example, sometimes the date in the list of references is presented *without* brackets (see Pears and Shields, 2010) and sometimes *with* brackets (see Bournemouth University (2011)). Does your tutor require *one* list, in alphabetical order, of all references (books, journal articles, online sources and so on)? Or do they ask for *separate* lists for each category of source?

Whatever style you use, you should provide comprehensive disclosure of the appropriate bibliographic details such as author(s), date of publication, publisher and place of publication, volume, issue, page numbers, the URL, the date accessed; and so on.

A reference list is different from a bibliography. A bibliography is a list of all the resources you consulted whether you cited/referenced them in the main body of your work or not. A list of references has only those sources you referred to in the body of your work. If you are not required to submit a bibliography; then do not include one.

Before you submit your assessment, check that all the authors you cite in the text are present in the list of references at the end. In particular, make sure the first few references in each section/ chapter are correct (in both text and list), as the reader may be particularly likely to sample these ones. If all is well with these, the reader will relax and expect good work. If they are not correct, the reader may keep checking and find more errors—diverting their attention and their 'belief' in your work. If the reader checks the authors cited in the text against the list at the end and some are missing (from the main body or the list)—what will they think of the quality of your work? Was this just poor proofreading? Has the author put references in the text/list that they did not actually consult?

2(f) Practical tips and activity

Develop the habit, when reading academic journals and textbooks (in particular), of noting how the author(s) incorporate citations into their writing (and more generally how they approach academic writing). This can enable you to develop and enhance your own effective academic writing style.

Possibly the most common convention is to end the sentence with the citation. For example (extract from Chapter 2 of this book):

> "The expansion of the railways in the nineteenth century and later, the development of telegraph communications and other infrastructure radically altered the way work was done, the types of products produced and the types of management systems put in place to ensure optimal levels of output (Crump, 2010)."

Alternatively, the sentence might begin with the citation (extract from Chapter 2):

> "For example, Merton (1940) describes the ways in which certain features of bureaucracy may be affected by the personalities of organisational members."

Activity

Choose a piece of your own academic writing or someone else's (such as a journal article) and evaluate whether:

1 Citations are given to acknowledge others' work at appropriate places. In general terms the test is to read the material and ask 'says who?' for each statement. If this is something which is clearly the author's own thoughts, then perhaps a citation is not required. However, in many cases there will be a requirement for a citation to acknowledge the source(s) of the ideas, facts, statistics; and so on.

2 Does the author adopt good practice in citing their sources? If not, why not? For example, the citation of direct quotations may be missing page number(s).

3 Do all the sources cited in the body of the work appear in the list of references? Are they in the correct place in the list (i.e. in alphabetical order)?

4 Does the list of references incorporate all the relevant information, presented appropriately?

5 Is a consistent approach taken to how both the citations and list of references are presented?

6 If there are any shortcomings, what could be done to make sure good practice is followed?

Over time you can develop a good 'eye' for citation/referencing which will enable you to enhance your work.

2(g) Summary of the Skillset

Good practice regarding citation and referencing is a key skill that can enhance the quality of your academic work throughout your studies. It is worth spending time developing your ability to provide citations/lists of references in an appropriate place/manner at an early stage in your academic career—it is not difficult though it does require (and demonstrates) attention to detail. Although there are a number of common principles, there is no one best way beyond accurately and consistently applying whichever style you have chosen to adopt. Referencing skills can also enhance report writing in a workplace situation, providing an evidence base for the facts used or points made. This Skillset was concerned with the citation of sources in the body of your work and the presentation of a list of references at the end of your work. Other Skillsets consider the related processes of sourcing materials (Skillset 4), reviewing literature including assessing the 'quality' of sources (Skillset 7), and what plagiarism is (and how to avoid it) (Skillset 10).

References/Further reading/Resources

American Psychological Association, 2012, *APA Style*. [Online.] Available from: http://www.apastyle.org/

Bournemouth University, 2011, *BU Guide to Citation in the Harvard Style*, Student and Academic Services: Library and Learning Support, Bournemouth University, Bournemouth, UK. [Online.] Available from: http://www.bournemouth.ac.uk/library/citing_references/docs/Citing_Refs.pdf [Gives a good range of examples of how to cite and list sources.]

Glasgow Caledonian University, 2008, *Citing and Referencing*. [Online.] Available from: http://www.gcu.ac.uk/student/coursework/referencing/index.html [A series of web pages exploring this topic.]

McMillan, K. and Weyers, J., 2009, *The Smarter Study Skills Companion*, 2nd edition, Pearson Education, Harlow, UK.

Pears, R. and Shields, G., 2010, *Cite Them Right: the essential referencing guide*, 8th edition, Palgrave Study Skills, Palgrave Macmillan, Houndsmill, UK.

3

Planning

Learning outcomes

- Understand the planning process

- Evaluate the advantages and limitations of planning

- Comprehend the role of planning in setting goals and objectives

- Recognise the different types of plans

- Understand the required skills of management in the planning process

Planning is such an important part of modern organisations that a great deal of effort and resources are allocated to it. Planning has become a specialised discipline in many industries and is supported by specialist consultancies. The more complex the processes are in organisations the greater is the need for effective planning. The National Health Service (NHS) in Scotland is a case in point. Such is the complexity of organising work schedules for healthcare staff that a specialist internal website has been developed to help improve efficiency in planning. In fact, workforce planning has become a key strategic issue in the sector as managers seek to match changing demand conditions with resources. The aim is to create a workforce planning capability across the entire NHS Scotland to support a wide range of activities including service redesign, workforce projections, and supply/demand forecasting. The NHS in Scotland is on target to deliver key goals such as the development of technical workforce planning skills, improve awareness and understanding of the wider strategic context of workforce planning, and the creation of an integrated approach to planning especially around finance and service planning. The case of NHS Scotland illustrates the importance of planning to ensure effective service delivery into the future in an environment characterised by significant social, economic, and demographic change.

Skillset 3
Time management

This chapter's Skillset section covers time management.
Time management is an important element of planning in business and it is expected that students will be able to make a clear link between the time management of their own workload and the key issues that have been discussed in this chapter, such as understanding the advantages of time management as part of a plan, and building goals and objectives around a timeframe in order to achieve them.

Student study skills
Students need to be able to manage their time effectively in order to keep pace with the learning process, assessment deadlines, and the work/life balance. This Skillset provides a practical insight into how to manage time by providing a template and example of a typical semester and the various activities that have to be managed within that timeframe.

Workplace skills
Time management is a vital skill in the workplace. With multi-tasking and multi-skilling key features of modern workplaces, time management techniques have taken on extra importance. This Skillset is designed to deliver techniques that help to embed time management into the everyday discipline required of workers.

Definitions

A plan is a formal statement of intent that identifies goals and objectives and how they are to be achieved. A goal is an identified outcome that has been chosen and an objective is an aim that can be measured and achieved within a stated timeframe. Planning is the process of defining and setting goals, identifying the means and coordinating the activities by which those goals are to be achieved.

Introduction

Planning is one of the four main functions of management, the others being organising, controlling, and commanding and leading (Fayol, 1946). Planning is important as the environment in which organisations operate is characterised by uncertainty and change. Managers have to develop and implement plans in order to chart a pathway to achieving the many goals within an organisation. The goals may include improving performance, enhancing the skills and competencies of staff, marketing a new product, communicating with customers and suppliers, or reconfiguring production schedules for anticipated changes in demand. These are just some of the many reasons why managers have to plan for the future.

Different types of plans will be chosen according to the types of goals set by managers. Some plans are short-term with prescribed outcomes such as monthly production output targets, others are medium- or long-term and require a significant redeployment of resources. Short-term plans (weekly or monthly) are usually undertaken at the operational or functional level of an organisation and are devised, controlled, and implemented by functional managers such as production or sales managers. Medium-term goals (every six months or annually) are set by middle managers who act as intermediaries between strategic managers and the workers and operational managers. Middle managers give direction and allocate resources to the functional areas of the organisation such as production, sales, customer service, marketing, etc. (Gomez-Mejia et al., 2008). Long-term plans (between one and ten years) are developed by strategic managers who are executives within the organisation. These plans are designed to achieve long-term goals such as becoming a leading competitor in an industry, building market share in key regions of the globe, or becoming technological leader in the industry over a set period of time.

All plans involve managers making choices regarding resource allocation, what opportunities to pursue, and the means by which set goals are to be achieved. Again, these choices are made in an uncertain environment that is subject to rapid change. This ensures that decision making is a balance of risk against perceived benefits. Plans are designed to minimise the risk and maximise the benefits to the organisation as it seeks to achieve its goals. However, it is important to recognise that not all events, scenarios and changes to the environment can be accounted for and, therefore, any plan is necessarily limited in its effect. Managers need to weigh the advantages of devising and implementing plans against the limitations associated with them.

The planning process

To help achieve goals, planning is integrated with other functions such as organising, control, and leading. Planning sets the direction that guides the organisation towards achieving goals. This function works in alignment with the way resources are organised (human, financial, capital resources), activities are measured and controlled, and how workers respond to the direction of managers in the pursuit of goal achievement. The functions of organising, controlling, and leading are discussed in later chapters. However, it is important to think of them as integrated functions

Term
Definitions

Short term: from one day to six months.
Medium term: from six months to one year.
Long term: one year or more.

rather than isolated aspects of management. Planning and control functions are most closely aligned and form what can be identified as the planning process. This is illustrated in Figure 3.1.

The first step in this process is the formulation of plans where the goals are identified and the means by which those goals are to be achieved are decided. Also, the timeframe for achieving the goals is determined at this stage. The second stage involves the actual implementation of the plans. Here it is necessary for managers to delegate tasks and activities that transform the plans into action. The third stage is evaluation of the progress that is being made as the plans begin to be implemented. Control measures are used to determine the match between the expected outcomes and the actual outcomes recorded as the actions start to yield results. At this stage it may be necessary for managers to take remedial action to correct any discrepancies between outcomes and targets. This may involve changing the types of actions being undertaken, the targets set, or the plan itself. Much depends on the reasons why there is a discrepancy between outcomes and set targets. Managers must be able to use the planning process to revise and review assumptions under which they make decisions, check and monitor trends in outcomes and performance, and evaluate progress towards goals.

Figure 3.1 The planning process

Goals and objectives of organisations

The terms 'goals' and 'objectives' are used frequently in discussions on management, sometimes they are used interchangeably to mean the same thing. However, there is a subtle but important difference between them. An objective is a clearly defined and measurable outcome that has to be achieved within a given timeframe. Goals relate to a specified position that the organisation seeks to attain. Goals and objectives are so closely related that they are invariably discussed together. Hannagan (2008) provides a useful account of the key differences between goals and objectives. Whilst objectives can be quantified and a timescale linked to their achievement, very often goals are more imprecise and broad ranging. An organisation's goal may be to become a leading player in an industry sector, or to deliver 'world-class' service. Both of these are often cited as goals of organisations but do not always lend themselves to precise measures which allow it to be stated unequivocally that they have been achieved.

There will be a different set of goals and objectives linked to different levels in the organisation— operational, business, and corporate. These are discussed in more detail later in this chapter. Other goals and objectives may relate to relationship outcomes (building the brand loyalty of customers or forming partnerships with suppliers), reputation enhancing outcomes (accreditation or recognition of quality), or ethical standards (awards for corporate social responsibility or the attainment of sustainability standards). Whatever the desired outcome, a plan will need to be devised to help achieve it. Typically, such plans are a combination of clearly defined targets and imprecise targets. The SMART model is a commonly used format for setting out targets.

Specific: identifying key aspects of performance that can be measured.

Measurable: identifying key aspects of performance that can be quantified.

Achievable: specified outcome that is capable of being met.

Rewarded: specified rewards for achieving set targets.

Timely: timeframe set for achieving stated outcomes.

The SMART model is a useful one for guiding the formation of a plan (Doran, 1981). However, this model, as well as other types of approach, needs to be designed for the purposes of identified groups or individuals in an organisation. A generic plan would not necessarily contain outcomes that specifically relate to the activities of certain groups or individuals. So,

Term
Definitions

Goal: specified position the organisation seeks to attain.

Objective: clearly defined and measurable outcome to be achieved within a specified timeframe.

although time consuming, it is necessary to customise a plan for the purposes of groups or individuals. For example, there may be a SMART plan for a team of workers developing a new product, or one that relates to the performance of the sales team.

The nature of the work and the characteristics of the activities undertaken will inform the way in which the plan is designed for each context. This is significant because the internal activities will have different levels of importance or priority attached to them. For example, in hi-tech companies such as *Hewlett Packard* or *Sony*, research and development (R&D) is typically given a high priority and will be reflected in the plans for expected outcomes. Alternatively, some support activities, such as routine administrative work, may be given a lesser priority. Much will depend on how the activity fits into the strategic plan for the organisation. The importance of the activity will most likely be reflected in the resource allocation directed towards it in terms of finance, time, personnel, technology, and so on. For example, there are likely to be some activities that are time bound, such as logistics (the process of getting raw materials into the organisation and finished products distributed to retailers or customers), and this will be reflected in the expected outcomes in the plan. Others may rely on collaboration with external third parties (possibly a licensing agreement to transfer technology to an outsourced supplier). This can make the timeline for achieving outcomes less certain as it entails less control over the management of the activity. Thus, plans need to be devised in line with the characteristics of the tasks and activities undertaken.

Mini case 3.1
Revising performance plans at Hitachi

Japanese electronics giant *Hitachi Ltd.* set up a subsidiary called *Hitachi Plant Technologies Ltd* in 2006 with the aim of creating a global enterprise that supports industrial plants in various sectors such as pharmaceuticals, pumps and compressors, air conditioning, and power plant construction. The company formulated a long-term plan for the period 2006–2010 with the goal of bolstering the competitiveness of the business by taking advantage of synergies between the business units that comprised the company (Hitachi Appliances Inc. Business Strategy, 2010). Synergies are advantages that accrue from the sharing of resources, knowledge, relationships, expertise, and experience between different businesses. In the case of *Hitachi Plant Technologies Ltd* these synergies led to higher than expected sales for 2006/7. However, the managers at the company revised the expected earnings for 2007/8 downwards due to increased competition in the industry and a lack of profitability in some of their plants. This is an example of a management team monitoring the external business environment and the internal performance of the multiple business units that comprise their company. By evaluating the information received, they were able to revise their targets to reflect the new business reality they faced. Action was taken to address the reasons for the expected short-term downturn in earnings and new targets devised. However, the plan to achieve the long-term goal of the company remained the same. The case highlights the requirement of managers to be able to distinguish between the need for short-term remedial action with revised targets and the need for radical change to established plans. This difference is clearly set out in the work of Mckeown (2012).

Sources:

Hitachi Appliances Inc. (2010) Business Strategy. Business Conditions and Key Strategies 2006–2009. http://www.hitachi.com/New/cnews/100609/20100609e_9_AP_fin.pdf.

Mckeown, M. (2012) *The Strategy Book*, Harlow, FT/Prentice-Hall.

Discussion points

Is it possible to assign specific timeframes to what are termed short-, medium-, and long-term plans?

Should executive managers get involved in short-term operational planning?

Questions and tasks

What are synergies? Give examples from your own experience.

Identify some key factors in the external environment that can affect business performance.

Why is it important to sometimes revise performance targets?

 Online Resource Centre

Author commentary on these discussion points and questions can be found on the Online Resource Centre at: www.oxfordtextbooks.co.uk/orc/combe1e/

Advantages of planning

Planning is an important function in all organisations as it contributes directly to the achievement of goals and objectives. Planning is integrated with other functions such as organising and control, where issues of resource allocation and the monitoring and evaluation of performance form important factors in determining the achievement of goals and objectives.

Planning and control

Planning is an essential part of the control function in organisations as it sets the standards of performance and targets for output. This allows managers to determine whether or not current practices are delivering the performance aimed for and to take appropriate action to rectify any shortfall or to find new and better ways of improving performance. This latter advantage can be the basis for innovation and creativity in the organisation and become a source of competitive advantage (Wong and Chin, 2007). It is clear that planning and control functions are inextricably linked.

Planning and actions

Planning helps managers to take a systematic approach to achieving goals and objectives. In the first instance it helps to focus attention on the types of activities that need to be undertaken to achieve the goals and objectives. This, in turn, helps to clarify the extent to which those goals and objectives are realistic, appropriate, and achievable. This is as equally relevant to employees as it is to managers because workers need to be able to put into action the plans devised by managers in an integrated manner. The plan acts as a guide to the types of activities that need to be carried out in the organisation and, therefore, contributes to an ordered, coordinated, and rational approach to achieving the goals and objectives.

Planning and risk

The rational approach to management has a number of merits, most notably, it helps deal with uncertainty. Planning is a means by which managers can help to mitigate risk by introducing a measure of control on future events. Although there are many factors that are outside the control of management, it is possible to make contingency plans to deal with the effects of those factors. Planning provides an opportunity for managers to minimise the effects that uncertainty and ambiguity bring, especially in areas affecting business continuity such as the supply chain (Zsidisin, 2000). Previous experience plays an important part in helping managers draw up plans in this context. For example, scenario planning is a method of systematically putting in place courses of action in response to events that have an impact on the organisation both internally and externally. Mietzner and Reger (2005) lucidly discuss the advantages and disadvantages of scenario approaches.

Planning and resource allocation

There are also sound economic and competitive reasons for planning. In particular, it helps to allocate resources efficiently to those areas of activity that are going to deliver the goals and objectives. As part of an operational plan, managers can determine the optimal use of resources in each activity and allocate them accordingly. This is important for the sustainability of the business as it provides the organisational intelligence required to minimise costs, reduce waste, and achieve maximum returns from resources. These advantages can form the basis of a competitive advantage. Hughes (2005) examines the role of organisational intelligence in creating a competitive advantage in more detail. Competitive advantage can be gained when planning delivers economic benefits derived from more coordinated and efficient working practices, the ability to respond to or withstand the impact of any negative effects from the external environment, and a well-motivated and disciplined workforce who can understand the transformation process between planning and action. Workers perform better when they know what is expected of them, have targets which are challenging but achievable, and are appropriately rewarded for their efforts. Time management is an important factor in achieving this and something that all workers need to consider and build into their work activities. A well-set-out plan that adds detail to these factors can create a positive organisational culture that may be the catalyst for competitive advantage.

Types of plans

There are many different types of plans that managers can develop and use to help achieve goals. Some plans are designed for specific purposes such as production or financial plans, others are more broad ranging and have a strategic aspect to them, such as long-term plans for growth in the business. Plans can be divided into three broad types that include:

- Operational plans
- Business plans
- Strategic plans

Each level of planning entails its own level of risk, resource allocation, and timeframe (Ansoff, 1968). These are illustrated in Figure 3.2.

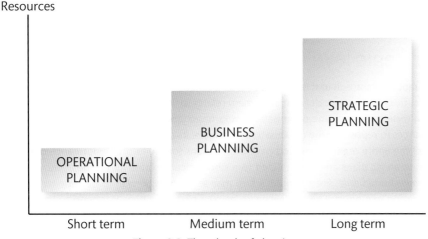

Figure 3.2 Three levels of planning

Operational plans

Operational plans are clearly defined plans that detail how the goals of an organisation are to be achieved. These plans are typically concerned with the short-term goals of the organisation, those which relate to everyday operations such as output, scheduling, logistics, sales, and so on. Managers may set weekly or monthly targets around these operational functions and plan, design, and monitor activities to ensure that they are achieved. Operational plans usually feature on-going and routine activities that form the basis of the transformation process from inputs to outputs. Sometimes referred to as standing plans, these are characterised by rules, regulations, and well-defined processes. Workers at the operational level are typically distant from the strategic plans devised by executive managers. Nevertheless, it is at this level that the conceptual strategic plan has to be transformed into actions. Consequently, it is necessary for strategic planners to be able to communicate their strategy in a way that is comprehensible and relevant to those at operational level.

Business level plans

Business level plans relate to a longer timeframe and feature aspects of strategy for achieving the stated aims of the organisation. Managers of business plans typically set targets for six months or a year ahead. Often, business level plans are not as detailed as operational level plans. Business level managers may set targets within a range of acceptability, such as an increase in sales of 6–8 per cent or improving supply chain logistics within a given time range. These medium-term plans link into the strategic aims of the organisation more closely than operational plans and have more flexibility built into expected outcomes.

Business level managers act as an important conduit between strategic managers and those who are expected to implement strategy-based actions at the operational level (Zabriskie, 1989). Indeed, the effectiveness with which the strategic vision is communicated throughout the organisation is a vital element that will determine the success of a chosen strategy. In the 1990s many organisations started the process of removing business level managers from their organisational structure, principally for cost reasons. This gave rise to the term 'downsizing' and followed a strategy of cost efficiency in many organisations. However, the real value of this level of management quickly became apparent when strategic managers found it difficult to articulate their strategic plans to the workers at operational level. Soon the race was on to refill the business level with managers who possessed the necessary skills to plug this communications gap (*The Economist*, 2011).

Strategic level plans

Strategic plans are characterised by a much longer timeframe, sometimes encompassing years. This is because strategic management relates to the long-term aims of the organisation, the direction in which the organisation seeks to go, and how managers intend to reallocate resources to reposition the organisation to achieve its stated aims (Porter, 1996). These plans affect the entire organisation and have implications for the future performance of the business. Strategic plans are often related to a single, clearly stated aim to be achieved over an elongated timeframe. For example, a firm may set a strategic plan to become technological leaders in their industry within five years, or, over perhaps a two-year period, a public sector organisation may plan to restructure internally to achieve better and more efficient communications systems.

Planning at the strategic level has traditionally been the preserve of a select few people at the apex of the organisation. These individuals set the scene by highlighting the vision of the organisation. Practices vary considerably between different organisations, industries, and regions. This is reflected in the broad range of writing on the subject. For example, Elbanna (2009) offers an insight into the determinants of planning in the cultural context of the Middle East. The vision sets out what the organisation stands for and its philosophy. Strategic planning stems from this vision and adds detail to what the long-term goals of the organisation are and how it is intended that the organisation will achieve them. However, the traditional model of strategic planning has been subject to challenge and many commentators now believe that access to the strategic decision making process needs to be broadened to include those charged with the challenge of managing its implementation (Sinofsky and Iansiti, 2009). The rise of teamworking in modern organisations has raised the possibility of introducing more inclusiveness into the strategic planning process. Danish brewer *Carlsberg* have introduced structures that expand the concept of inclusivity in the strategic planning process as a means of ensuring that new ideas and innovations can flourish. Managers have to weigh the advantages of this against the risk of slowing the decision making process.

?

Critical reflection
Does planning stifle creativity and change in organisations?

One of the most compelling critical assessments of planning was delivered by Henry Mintzberg (1994) in his article for the *Harvard Business Review* entitled 'The Fall and Rise of Strategic Planning'. Mintzberg argues that strategic planning impedes strategic thinking because the former is about analysis (a step-by-step approach to achieving stated goals) whereas the latter is about synthesis (the use of intuition and creativity to determine the direction of the organisation). Mintzberg articulates the difference between protagonists of the formal approach and his own view. In particular, he argues that the formal sequence of procedures leading to action that characterises strategic analysis does not recognise the need for experimentation as the basis for learning and the formation of better-informed strategies. In essence, he views strategic planning as the expression of existing strategies based on formal analysis, whereas he advocates synthesising learning from a wide range of sources and experiences as the basis for determining the strategic direction of the organisation. This does not exclude planners, but necessarily involves a host of other influential players who contribute to organisational learning and strategic thinking. Mintzberg clarifies the different roles that planners and managers play in strategic thinking. Although planners can dedicate more time and effort to analysis, they seldom have decision making powers at the strategic level. Hence, their main role according to Mintzberg is to pose questions rather than to answer them. Thus planners should use their analytical skills to encourage managers to develop strategies in new and creative ways, to challenge the status quo, and to innovate to achieve organisational goals and objectives.

The business plan

Planning is also necessary for those who seek to set up and manage their own business venture or who have already done so but seek to expand their business. In these cases a business plan is a necessary document for detailing how the business is to be created, developed, and grown over a period of time. Many books have been produced illustrating how to devise a business plan. The Harvard pocket guide (Harvard Business School, 2007) is a well-crafted and readable version. A business plan has a number of main attributes that help to formalise key criteria in this process. These include identifying:

- barriers to setting up or growing a business;
- those whom you need to collaborate with and their level of commitment;
- a specific pathway for achieving set targets and aims;
- how to attain profitability and growth;
- where you can acquire finance and investment funds;
- how to minimise the risk of failure and limit liability;
- how to build in flexibility to contend with a dynamic environment;
- how to align goals and objectives with strategy.

Business plans vary markedly according to the type of business concerned, the target audience (banks, investors, partners, suppliers, etc.) and the scale of ambition for the business. However, most business plans include sections that cover the business characteristics, market and competitor intelligence, management, action plans and contingencies.

Business characteristics

The business characteristics require details of why the organisation is in business, what it does, and what it sells. This is where the manager has to describe the purpose of the organisation and add detail to the activities to be undertaken to transform inputs into outputs. The marketing and sales of the products or services are included as are the finances of the business. This latter criterion is of vital importance as it will determine the economic viability of the business.

Market and competitor intelligence

Market and competitor intelligence is another important element of the business plan as it highlights exactly how an identified gap in the market is to filled by the business. Investors and financiers of the business will require market intelligence as evidence of unfulfilled need before they can fully analyse the risk associated with supporting the business. This intelligence will include but is not limited to:

- the size and characteristics of the market segment or segments to be targeted;
- the potential spending power of the target market;
- the scope for repeat business and growth of the target market;
- the level of competition;
- the pricing strategies of rivals;
- the profitability of competitors and within the industry generally.

Roles and responsibilities

The business plan must also identify who the key managers will be and clearly define their roles and responsibilities. The roles may include general management duties or specific areas of responsibility such as within the functions of sales and marketing, production, customer service, logistics, etc. The plan must include details of how the skills, experiences, and qualifications of management personnel align with the requirements of the business. Previous work experience must be outlined in detail. The business plan is used for both internal and external purposes. Internally it helps to formally record all relevant information for the purposes of setting up and growing the business. Externally, the plan must be designed to inform potential backers, and stakeholders (such as key customers or suppliers). It is crucial that the personal qualities and character profiles of the management team are disclosed in a comprehensive and honest manner in order to gain the confidence and trust of third parties.

Implementation and contingency

The business plan needs to outline how the plan can be transformed into action. That is, the implementation stage of the plan has to offer a detailed insight into how the business is to be set up and what activities need to be undertaken in order to achieve the stated aims. Implementation usually involves adding specific activities to the functions outlined in the business characteristics section. For example, the finances of the business will include set-up costs, marketing costs, staff costs, loan repayment schedules, break-even analysis, revenue turnover, and profit projections over a two- or three-year period, and so on. Finally, contingency plans need to be included to highlight the actions that would be implemented should specified problems emerge in the course of setting up and running the business. These may include actions to deal with changes in interest rates, a shift in consumer demand, change to industry regulation or accreditation, loss of key personnel, and so on.

The business plan is a document that needs to persuade people to believe in the business to the extent that they will invest money or be prepared to collaborate in its activities. The plan has to be detailed and yet concise and understandable (Friend and Zehle, 2009). It has to be a true reflection of reality and be capable of being transformed into actions. Most importantly, it has to be realistic and achievable. There are many different templates for producing a business plan; each is designed to achieve outcomes in the context in which they are created, whether that be for a new venture, an established business seeking growth, a voluntary organisation, or a social enterprise. For example, research shows that business planning for social enterprises requires a different approach to that of commercial businesses (Conway, 2008).

Components of a business plan

Executive summary: an overview of the whole concept or business

Business profile: a description of your business

Product/service/market analysis: chosen market and position in the market

Marketing plan: strategies to attract and keep clients

Legal and risk management plan: business protection planning

Operating plan: how the business works

Management and personnel plan: skills and experience

Finance plan: investment, expected turnover and profit, cash flow projections

The action plan: what you will do and when

Appendices: This section includes information to support or expand any of the above, such as business references, client testimonials, qualifications, detailed product information, consumer research data, environmental audit procedures, financial projections and statements, contracts and legal documents.

Business continuity planning

81

It is essential that managers put in place plans to ensure that the business will survive and prosper into the future. There are many factors that can conspire to threaten the viability of a company beyond competitive pressures from rivals (Lindstrom et al., 2010). These may include technical failures, loss of key personnel, a breakdown of relations with key stakeholders, political change, terrorism, changes to industry regulation, industrial disputes, and so on. For example, the *Bank of Japan* continually revises business continuity plans for functions such as the circulation of currency and the operation of payment and settlement systems in order to be able to carry out its functions during times of emergency such as during and after the 2011 tsunami (Bank of Japan, 2013). Bank staff are trained to deal with different scenarios to ensure a timely and effective response to disasters. Business continuity planning is an attempt by managers to mitigate the risk associated with the myriad different scenarios that may threaten the existence or future of the organisation. This may involve:

- contingency planning;
- scenario planning;
- succession planning.

Contingency planning

The world in which organisations operate is not always predictable and therefore contingencies have to be put in place to deal with situations that either directly or indirectly affect the operations and objectives of the business. Managers should have the underlying philosophy that 'if it can go wrong, then it will go wrong'. This is because the environment in which organisations operate is typically dynamic, changeable, and often unpredictable. Contingencies

Term
Definition

Contingency: something that might happen.

constitute a 'Plan B' for when 'Plan A' fails. Bowman (2008) provides an invaluable insight into how organisations build strategies to protect their data and information systems and ensure business continuity in the face of potentially catastrophic events.

Contingency planning can involve a wide range of activities that are key to business continuity. They can be broad ranging or specific, complex or simple, quick to install, or applied over a protracted period of time. Much depends on the nature of the business, the resources used, the types of personnel, and the business goals and objectives. For example, many companies will have an emergency fund for resourcing activities during unexpected changes in the environment. Thus, a department may require extra resources to deal with the sudden departure of a supplier. This may allow them to seek a suitable replacement or to access other sources of supply until a suitable long-term supplier can be found. Most contingency plans are implemented at the operational level due to the frequency with which day-to-day events unfold. Thus, production schedules can change quickly as demand fluctuates; personnel arrive and leave in short order; distribution may be affected by weather conditions; and so on. French company *Danone*, which produces the water brand *Volvic*, and chocolate makers *Cadbury* are among many producers that have well-established procedures to deal with sudden changes in demand such as fast-track human resource recruitment systems and flexible work schedules (Times 100 Business Case Studies, 2013).

However, contingencies have to be built into the strategic plans of organisations. Factors that affect the strategic direction of a company will have more severe consequences than those affecting operations. This is because strategy involves higher risks, considerable reallocation of resources, and is over a longer timeframe. This latter point is significant because it is much more difficult to predict events and scenarios over an elongated timeframe, thereby increasing the exposure to risk. As Childs (2009) emphasises, firms should 'prepare for the worst, and plan for the best'.

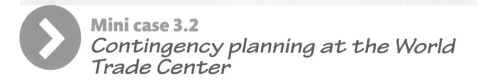

Mini case 3.2
Contingency planning at the World Trade Center

Many of the businesses affected by the terror attacks on the World Trade Center buildings in 2001 had already put into place contingencies for ensuring that business information was stored in data warehouses in case of a catastrophic event. Although the attacks had huge political, social, and human consequences, many of the affected businesses were able to resume normal trading relatively quickly because of the contingencies they had made for disruption to operations. EMC Corp is a data storage company that had some 76 client companies in and around the World Trade Center on the day of 9/11 including many such as *Commerzbank* that had a carefully thought-through data security contingency plan (SearchStorage.TechTarget.com, 2013). Senior Vice President Joseph Walton noted that the largest and most technologically sophisticated companies were able to survive because of the contingency plans that had been put into action. In particular, the plans for systems that supported real-time data backup at secondary data centres proved prescient as this allowed normal trading business to resume very quickly.

The systems critical to the operations of major financial institutions housed in, or in the vicinity of, the World Trade Center recovered very quickly as the contingency plans played out in the aftermath of the catastrophe. In some cases business was automatically transferred to backup locations and in others repairs were quickly undertaken at the affected sites. Many managers had learned lessons from a previous attack on the World Trade Center in 1993 and had invested in contingency planning around IT systems, making it one of the best prepared set of offices in terms of systems and data recovery capability.

If the contingency plans for IT support worked well, it was in contrast to those put in place for the loss of key personnel. In some instances, businesses lost their entire disaster recovery management team in the attack, leaving them completely exposed through lack of leadership and expertise. Work space for staff became extremely scarce and it quickly became evident that most contingency planning had focused mainly on back-office operations at the expense of either customer facing or personnel intensive activities. Contingencies for ensuring the on-going command and control of staff who suddenly find themselves dislocated from their normal business environment was an important lesson learned, as was the need to ensure work space for staff in another location. Although the cost of ensuring that backup space is available may be considered an unnecessary expense, the events of 9/11 prove that the unthinkable can become a reality.

One other important lesson learned from 9/11 is the risk associated with having a high concentration of businesses in a compact geographical area. Many companies had their backup systems located in the same area of Manhattan and found them to be disabled by events (ComputerWeekly.com, 2013). Contingency planners have subsequently been working with infrastructure planners to assess the weaknesses in the telecommunications cable systems. Whilst the scale of the damage done to the system was relatively small compared to the overall network, the effect on business continuity was considerable due to the intensity of use in the constricted environment of Manhattan Island. Nevertheless, despite being tested to the limit, many businesses managed to return to some form of trading relatively quickly in the aftermath of the attacks, largely thanks to effective contingency planning.

Sources:
Computer Weekly.com (7 September 2013) Disaster planning and business continuity after 9/11. http://www.computerweekly.com/news/2240082860/Disaster-planning-and-business-continuity-after-9-11

SearchStorage: Tech Target (2013) Banks avoid data disaster on Sept. 11. http://searchstorage.techtarget.com/tip/Bank-avoids-data-disaster-on-Sept-11

Discussion points

Is it realistic to expect most businesses to incur expense by preparing for potentially catastrophic events?

In contingency planning should managers 'think the unthinkable'?

83

Questions and tasks

What is the function of a data warehouse?

In financial services, what activities or functions are most essential for business continuity?

Identify two key lessons learnt from the World Trade Center catastrophe from a business continuity perspective.

Online Resource Centre

Author commentary on these discussion points and questions can be found on the Online Resource Centre at: www.oxfordtextbooks.co.uk/orc/combe1e/

Scenario planning

In order to mitigate risk many managers undertake scenario planning whereby key personnel think through or enact events that are likely to have an effect on the business. Again, scenarios may be aligned to operations or they may have strategic significance. Mietzner and Reger (2005) provide a valuable insight into the advantages and disadvantages of scenario planning for strategic foresight. Either way they are designed to inform managers of the possible events that may affect the organisation and threaten its ability to achieve the goals and objectives, or, in worst case scenarios, its very existence. Key characteristics of scenario planning include the:

- description of the possible future business environment;
- identification of possible outcomes that challenge the status quo;
- ability to be thought-provoking, informative, challenging, and plausible;
- evidence-based, logical, and rational analysis of future possibilities.

Before embarking on scenario planning, managers need to determine the parameters of the exercise. These include:

- the time horizon for the plan;
- the geographical scope of the plan;
- the business units or products affected by the plan;
- any identified constraints in the compilation of the plan;
- the expected outcomes and deliverables associated with the plan.

The scenario planning should be part of a wider process that helps managers to make decisions that will protect the organisation from negative influences from the external environment,

Term
Definition

Scenario: imagined sequence of future events.

Figure 3.3 Scenario planning process

improve internal operations, and position the business to achieve its strategic aims and objectives in the future (Wright and Cairns, 2011). Managers have to first set clear objectives before identifying the key issues to be analysed. Scenarios are built around the identified key issues. The analysis reveals what options are available in terms of response to the scenarios. Further analysis refines the options available. All learning that takes place in the process should contribute to future planning and analysis. Figure 3.3 illustrates the process of scenario planning.

Scenario planning is closely linked to forecasting but the two approaches have different aims. Forecasting is a feature of most organisations, whether it be market intelligence, resource needs, supply conditions, or any other unknown variable, and is often used to underpin scenario planning with details of specific issues (Hanke and Wichern, 2008). Forecasting is typically used to measure the performance of the business plan in each identified scenario. It also helps to inform managers of the value attached to various operational and strategic choices and options available. Forecasting is usually undertaken within scope and time horizons that make prediction easier. Ringland (2006) emphasises the fact that scenario planning focuses on issues beyond the time horizon where events can be accurately predicted. Figure 3.4 illustrates the difference between forecasting and scenario planning. Scenario planning was developed as a means of dealing with increasing uncertainty in environments that are subject to increasing complexity and rapid change. In such environments it is not possible to draw any definitive conclusions as to how these will affect the organisation. Consequently, managers will seek a range of views from different sources regarding the effect that possible changes to the business environment will have on the organisation. These views will typically provide managers with different scenarios, each with their own level of impact on the operations, goals, and objectives

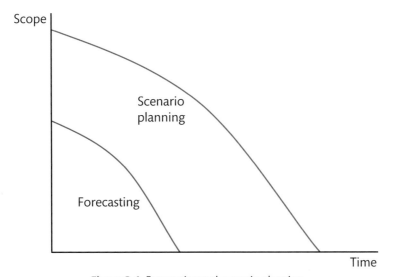

Figure 3.4 Forecasting and scenario planning

of the organisation. Crucially, they help to focus the minds of managers on a broader range of possibilities rather than on just a few obvious ones.

A core element of scenario planning is the identification of the key drivers of the industry in which the organisation competes. These may involve technology, human resources, economic factors, social trends, legislation and regulation, the political environment, and so on. Thus, scenarios are built around the key driver (or in some instances drivers) that is identified as having the biggest influence on the prosperity of the organisation. For example, in the UK, industry regulation is an important driver in the financial services and banking industry.

Banks seek less regulation to ensure greater freedom in their operating and strategic decision making. However, they have to develop scenarios based on the possibility of ever tighter regulation of the sector in the wake of the so-called credit crunch. The effect of this economic event was that many financial institutions suffered huge losses having previously taken excessive risks in lending, partly due to the liberal regulatory regimes that have characterised the industry since the mid-1980s. In this case other scenarios may be built around issues of political stability, macroeconomic indicators (inflation, unemployment, interest rates, etc.), or changes in demand conditions and levels of disposable income. Each will have an influence on the others as they are clearly interrelated and, therefore, effective scenario planning must attempt to integrate key factors to arrive at a plausible outcome. Managers can benefit from sharing views on different scenarios as such discussion informs and improves the analytical skills and enables them to better understand the environment in which their organisation competes.

❓ Critical reflection
What are the risks of scenario planning?

It can be seen that scenario planning has a number of advantages associated with it and has been applied in a wide range of different organisational settings as a means of dealing with uncertainty. Scenarios help to open up people's minds to the way the future may play out and provide a focus for leveraging expertise and experience in making judgements about what the future will look like. However, there are some pitfalls that managers need to be aware of before subscribing fully to the scenario planning approach. First, scenarios tend to be developed around distinct structures. As Davis et al. (2007) note, there is a risk that people become constrained by the very conceptual structure that has been designed to open up possibilities. Also, once a stream of consciousness is set in train around a particular scenario, there is a risk that a sense of inevitability prevails regarding the outcome. Whether this is doom-laden or overly optimistic, the outcome may have been derived from a psychological desire to embrace it from an early stage. It may be that only a few dimensions of uncertainty have been analysed as part of a scenario and others neglected. Often there is an ad hoc feel to scenario planning whereby only a few dimensions feature and those are often reduced to manageable variables to facilitate an outcome. For example, a scenario of the future may be viewed as a choice between two outcomes—things either go one way or another. In reality the environment is subject to constant change and increasing complexity thereby limiting the relevance of scenario planning. Although scenario planning continues to play a role in strategic thinking in many organisations, it is important to understand the risks associated with the approach and the limits of its potency in dealing with uncertainty.

Succession planning

Succession planning refers to a process undertaken by managers that ensures each role within the organisation is filled at all times. This can be achieved by redeploying staff internally (perhaps after a period of training) or recruiting a new staff member from the open market. Succession planning is vital for business continuity when key personnel leave their employment with the organisation. The succession plan can be for any level in the organisation and for any specific job. Plans will have to be devised to replace managerial positions at executive, business, and operational level. Small-scale and micro businesses are faced with succession issues just as much as large-scale and corporate enterprises (Motwani et al., 2006). Some may have strategic decision making powers, others supervisory duties. All will perform a function in the business but will have varying levels of 'hard-to-replace' competencies attached to them. Some positions may be deemed critical and, therefore, will require more detailed and fast-response succession plans. Mostly, these positions will be filled by incumbents in the organisation either permanently or as a stop-gap whilst a permanent replacement can be recruited. The aim is to ensure a seamless transition between the departing employee and the person who takes over the role.

The succession planning process

Succession planning has to be undertaken in a systematic manner to ensure that roles critical to the organisation are identified and plans made to fill them when existing incumbents leave. Four main stages of succession planning can be identified. These are illustrated in Figure 3.5.

Stage 1 involves identifying those positions in the organisation that are considered critical to ensuring business continuity in the event of the loss of key personnel. There are various criteria involved in determining what constitutes a critical role. These may include the position within the organisational structure and the contribution made to the vision and mission of the organisation. The role may be linked to a specific task within the organisation. In the case where the task undertaken would be considered a vital component of the core function of the organisation, if left unfulfilled it would prevent the organisation from achieving its goals and objectives.

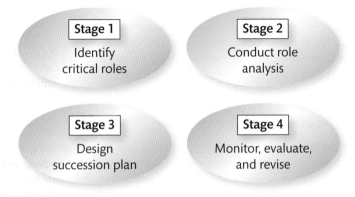

Figure 3.5 Stages of succession planning

> **Table 3.1** Identifying critical roles in an organisation
>
> | Department | Job title | Grade | Line manager | Retirement date* | Critical role |
> |---|---|---|---|---|---|
> | | | | | | |
> | | | | | | |
> | | | | | | |
> | | | | | | |
>
> *The reason for succession planning may be due to natural turnover of staff as well as retirement.

Some highly valued mechanical or engineering skills that are difficult to replace may also come into this category. Similarly, there may be leadership roles within the organisation that require distinct skills, expertise, or attributes that are difficult to acquire from the labour market. Succession planning should also identify those workers with considerable tacit knowledge and experience who may be nearing retirement. When valuable human resources leave employment, a great deal of wisdom and knowledge leaves with them. Stage 1 needs to identify where that potential loss resides and initiate plans to fill the gap. Table 3.1 illustrates an example of a format showing the key criteria needed to identify critical roles in an organisation.

Stage 2 involves undertaking an analysis of those roles considered critical to the organisation. Here, the specific skillsets and distinct competencies associated with them are identified and used as a basis for determining the existing capabilities and competencies of the workforce within the organisation. The analysis will seek to determine why certain identified positions are considered critical; what external and internal factors affect the role; how the role will be deployed in the future and the associated capabilities and competencies required; the existing level of capabilities and competencies; where gaps exist in current capabilities and competencies and the appropriate strategies needed to fill them. Table 3.2 illustrates a role analysis format.

Stage 3 is the actual design of the succession plan. This stage represents the outcome of Stages 1 and 2. The plan should incorporate the outcomes of the analysis into a single document that provides the basis for a succession planning strategy. Typically, these strategies should highlight where gaps exist, how they are to be filled, the timeline for completion, the resources to be allocated to the task, and the personnel responsible for ensuring the strategy is achieved. Table 3.3 illustrates an example of a succession plan.

Stage 4 is an example of good corporate governance as it features ongoing organisational learning which informs better and more efficient decision making in the future. Typically a succession plan will cover an elongated timeframe (sometimes as long as four or five years ahead), but it is essential that it is monitored and reviewed regularly, perhaps on an annual basis. This will ensure that it remains relevant, robust, and workable in the changing

Table 3.2	Role analysis form		
Critical role:		**Job title:**	
Reason for critical role status:		Retirement date:	
External factors:		Internal factors:	Future role specification:
1		1	
2		2	
3		3	
4		4	
5		5	
(i) Capabilities and competencies required:			
(ii) Existing capabilities and competencies:			
Identified gaps between (i) and (ii):			
Strategy for filling the identified gaps:			

environment in which organisations operate. For example, some jobs that were assigned the status of 'critical role' in one time period may not be so assigned in another as circumstances change. Alternatively, other new roles may emerge where 'critical role' status is appropriate. The issue of succession is dynamic and sometimes complex and requires constant monitoring, evaluation, and revision.

Table 3.3	Succession plan						
	Critical role	**Identified gaps**	**Strategy**	**Completion date**	**Line manager**	**Resource allocation**	**Status**

Critical reflection
What forms of bias may exist in the succession planning process?

One of the problems associated with succession planning when the incumbent is still with the organisation and is party to the succession process is the risk of so-called corporate cloning. That is, the incumbent has a particular view of the skills and experience needed to carry out the job that may soon be falling vacant. The incumbent is likely to support a candidate with a similar background, outlook, qualifications, and values. Either consciously or sub-consciously, the incumbent may have a bias towards a certain type of replacement, one that very much resembles his or her own profile. Moreover, it is highly likely that the chosen successor may be someone to whom the incumbent is familiar and may have worked with. These forms of bias can lead to the wrong candidate being appointed as a successor and it is particularly prevalent in family-run businesses where the emotional link to siblings or relatives may obscure the rational analysis of what is the best outcome for the business.

Mini case 3.3
Succession planning at Visy

Richard Pratt was born in the Polish city of Danzig (now Gdansk) in 1934 but arrived in Australia with his parents five years later to escape the Nazi invasion of his homeland that led to the outbreak of the Second World War. His father Leon started a box-making firm to supply the fruit growing industry in the state of Victoria. Spurning an acting career, son Richard took over the business in the early 1960s. The company, named *Visy*, grew to be the world's largest privately owned paper and packaging firm with Pratt's personal wealth being estimated at over A\$5 billion at the time of his death in April 2009.

The Visy business had become synonymous with Pratt's personality and management style. Variously described as driven, direct, and blunt, there was little that escaped his attention in his business empire that eventually included six divisions of the company. In many ways he typified the energetic spirit of entrepreneurship and hard work that characterised immigrants to Australia in the postwar period. However, by the mid-2000s he had been diagnosed with prostate cancer. The news brought into stark reality the need for a succession plan if the business was to survive the loss of its central player (Thomson, 2009).

From 2005 until his death in 2009, Pratt carefully planned his succession whilst simultaneously easing himself out of the day-to-day role of managing the business. A more detailed account of the process of succession planning at Visy is provided by Kirby and Myer (2009). Of utmost importance was keeping the business under family control and, therefore, he set about appointing his children to key positions within the business. In particular, Pratt appointed his son Anthony to the position of Chief Executive of the entire Visy empire although control of the divisions was split equally between

http://www.visy.com.au/

http://www.visy.com.au/

all three of his children, including daughters Heloise and Fiona. Thus, Pratt Industries based in the USA was given to Anthony; the family investment business Thornley Holdings went to Heloise and her husband; and Visy Industrial Packaging went to Fiona and her husband. Crucially, each family member had time to build experience of running these business arms whilst Pratt remained alive and able to proffer advice and guidance where necessary. The A$3 billion Visy manufacturing group was divided equally between the three children. To support the transition Pratt also brought in trusted non-family board members to help manage the business but also to improve the company's corporate governance after a highly damaging price fixing scandal rocked the business in the 2000s.

The systematic and carefully laid succession plan has ensured that those charged with the responsibility of taking the business forward have the best possible platform for making a success of it. For many of the world's leading corporate bosses, business continuity is compromised by neglecting this important, but highly personal, aspect of planning.

Sources:

Kirby, J. and Myer, R. (2009) *Richard Pratt: One Out of the Box: The Secrets of an Australian Billionaire*, Milton, Queensland, John Wiley & Sons.

Thomson, J. (April 28, 2009) Richard Pratt's strong succession plan, Smartcompany.com. http://www.smartcompany.com.au/strategy/20090422-richard-pratts-strong-succession-plan.html

Discussion points

When is the best time to start preparing for succession to leadership in an organisation?

Should family businesses always try to keep leadership positions in the family?

Questions and tasks

Why is succession planning important?

What are the key issues that have to be addressed when undertaking succession planning?

Identify an organisation where succession is a problem that needs to be addressed. Outline what measures the organisation has taken to put in place succession plans.

Online Resource Centre

Author commentary on these discussion points and questions can be found on the Online Resource Centre at: www.oxfordtextbooks.co.uk/orc/combe1e/

Management skills in the planning process

Management plays a key role in all forms of planning in organisations. Planning requires the full commitment of management as it invariably involves decision making about strategy; reallocation of resources; delegation of power; setting of performance indicators and targets; internal and external relationships and so on. The scale of management involvement will depend on the level at which the planning takes place in the organisation. For example, executive managers will not be fully involved in day-to-day operational types of planning but will be kept informed of decisions. It is unlikely that operational managers will be involved in strategic planning. Nevertheless, all the managers in an organisation need to be involved in planning at the appropriate level and all need to understand the strategic aims and objectives of the organisation. In his seminal work, Katz (1974) identified the key management skills needed to achieve these aims and objectives. As Peterson and Van Fleet (2004) note, the relevance of Katz's typology is enduring in the modern era. Key management skills were introduced in Chapter 1, but it is worth exploring these in more detail in the context of planning. Relevant key skills include:

- organisational skills;
- technical skills;
- analytical skills;
- conceptual skills;
- communications skills.

Organisational skills

The roles carried out by managers in the planning process are many and varied. They include organising resources and controlling activities to achieve specified outcomes. These roles are explored in more detail in later chapters. Effective planning requires managers to coordinate activities between individuals or groups both internally and externally. For example, planning the development of a new product or service will require coordination and communications skills to facilitate the collaboration between marketing and sales staff with those of product design or production staff. It may also require the coordination of activities between internal staff and external partners such as distributors, advertising agencies, retailers, and others. Many of these skills deployed by managers are of a practical nature and involve good organisational abilities.

Technical skills

Managers at the operational and business levels often require technical skills in order to fully understand the competencies and proficiencies required to achieve stated outcomes and targets. Technical skills may include knowledge or practical skills in specialised activities such as production and manufacturing, logistics, accounting and finance, engineering, computing, and so on. Managers may require these skills (or at least a highly developed understanding of them) as they will be putting in place plans to leverage maximum advantage of their deployment in the operations and business activities of the organisation. Very often, managers at these levels of the organisation have technical qualifications and

Term
Definition

Organisational skills: ability to coordinate resources and activities.

Technical skills: knowledge or practical skills in specialised activities.

Analytical skills: ability to separate a whole into its component parts for study and interpretation.

Conceptual skills: problem solving by understanding complex environments.

practical work experience in the area of specialisation that allows them to make informed decisions around planning.

Analytical skills

Managers need to have a feel for the environment in which their organisation exists. Very often the planning process requires managers to pre-empt changes in the environment. Here, managers deploy their analytical skills to anticipate changes in key variables such as supply and demand conditions; technological developments; production capabilities; the intensity of rivalry; political and regulatory changes; changes to tastes and fashions; the availability of key skills; and many more. Analytical skills are developed through experience, but also from an intuitive grasp of the environment in which the organisation exists. It is very difficult to teach analytical skills, as much depends on a host of intangible factors such as personality, intelligence, intuition, perception, and other psychological factors that combine to underpin the analytical skills deployed by managers. Analytical skills refer to the process whereby managers scrutinise a wide range of information (statistical, verbal, graphical, etc.) and use it to inform their decision making. The aims, outcomes, and targets set around the different types of plan rely on effective analytical skills as managers try to make sense of the existing environment and make informed judgements about how that environment will change and evolve over time. This role is of utmost importance because it informs the types of decision making that determines whether or not the organisation will achieve its stated aims and objectives.

Conceptual skills

Planning is often viewed as a technical process where coordinated activities are identified and undertaken to achieve specified outcomes. However, planning also plays a role in solving business problems or as part of a strategy for innovation. Effective planning requires the selection of relevant information from the huge amount that is normally generated within an organisation; it often requires an understanding of the organisation as a whole as well as the relationships between its divisions or departments and how they fit into the wider business environment. As Katz (1974) outlined, planning around these variables requires conceptual skills when managers have to think in abstract terms around complex situations. These skills are usually deployed at executive level where long-term strategic planning takes place.

Term
Definition

Communications skills: ability to connect with people through various media to achieve aims and objectives, to motivate and lead.

Communications skills

One of the most important skills of management is to be able to communicate aims and objectives, strategies, ideas, concepts, and plans to the workforce. Plans need to be implemented effectively and part of that process is to communicate the reasons for the plan, the expected outcomes and targets, the timeframe for achieving set targets, and the activities that need to take place to ensure their success. The challenge of communicating plans will vary according to the level in which they are to be implemented in the organisation. Operational plans will be communicated by managers who most likely have day-to-day close contact with those charged with carrying out the activities. Alternatively, strategic managers are usually quite distant from those who will have to undertake actions implement the chosen strategy. As noted previously, very often it is the role of business level managers to act as a conduit between strategic managers and operational level workers to communicate the strategy and the activities required to ensure its success.

Communications skills vary in type and effect. Some managers may adopt one-to-one communication to get their message across to workers, others may use different types of media channels (e-mail, memos, newsletters, etc.), some may prefer to speak to the workforce as a group. Whatever method is adopted, managers need to understand the most effective means of communicating in the myriad different contexts and settings in which plans are to be implemented. Communications skills are of such importance to effective management that we will return to the subject with more detailed analysis and discussion in Chapter 9.

Managers may utilise some or all of the key skills in the process of planning. The ability of managers to employ these skills effectively will go some way to determining how well a plan is developed and implemented and whether or not it is successful in achieving its aims. Different types of plans will require different mixes of management skills. For example, contingency planning requires good analytical skills to determine where the key threats to the business reside; scenario planning requires conceptual skills to derive a wide range of possible outcomes that may affect business continuity; operational planning has a greater emphasis on technical skills where managers possess a specialist knowledge of key tasks; strategic planning combines analytical and conceptual skills to determine the best long-term direction for the organisation.

Planning has been a feature of management for many years and can provide a basis for influencing and controlling events. However, planning is no panacea for dealing with rapid change and unexpected events that characterise the modern business environment in all its complex manifestations. Caution has to be exercised so that a false sense of security does not emerge around the planning process. That is, just because an event has been planned for does not mean that its effect can be coped with. For example, Japanese engineers designed and built some of the world's most robust infrastructure to cope with earthquakes. However, the magnitude of the March 2011 earthquake and resultant tsunami was beyond the scope of what could be absorbed, leading to unprecedented devastation. Managers have to realise the limitations of planning as well as the advantages.

Limitations of planning

All organisations need to engage in the planning function in order to function properly and achieve goals and objectives. However, it needs to be recognised that plans have certain limitations and that sometimes they can stifle knowledge sharing (Puddicombe, 2006), innovation and creativity, present barriers to achieving goals and objectives, and constrain risk taking and entrepreneurship. Perhaps the most common criticism of the planning function is the emphasis it places on rules, regulations, procedures, and other administrative processes. This can often lead to rigidities as personnel stick firmly to the set plan rather than taking risks or building in flexibility to facilitate the pursuit of new and better ways of operating or seeking and exploiting opportunities in the market. Some managers may introduce some measure of flexibility into their planning processes but the actual function of planning necessarily involves setting out guidelines for action that are expected to be adhered to. In many modern industrial and business settings, the route to competitive advantage often resides in taking risks, changing direction quickly, and having the organisational agility and flexibility to exploit opportunities. Rigid adherence to set plans can run counter to these attributes. Indeed, research shows that often there is no discernible link between formal planning and business performance (Falshaw et al., 2006), thereby adding weight to the perspective offered by Mintzberg as outlined earlier in the chapter in the discussion of strategic level plans.

Bias

Another significant limitation associated with planning is the risk of introducing bias in its compilation. The design, content, and expected outcomes of a plan will inevitably reflect the perceptions, beliefs, and attitudes of those charged with delivering it. Consequently, plans may be designed (either knowingly or inadvertently) that suit the interests of some to the detriment of others in the organisation. This is especially the case when there are resources to be allocated as part of a plan. In some instances, a plan may advantage a particular group at the expense of the organisation as a whole. Some individuals or groups within organisations may have excessive power to influence the setting of plans that support their interests rather than the interests of the whole organisation. Bias is a natural by-product of any planning process that involves human subjective judgement, but it has to be controlled so that it does not undermine the achievement of goals and objectives.

Over-reliance

Over-reliance on the capability of plans to deliver outcomes can be a problem for managers. The more elaborate the effort that goes into the planning, the more danger there is of an overriding sense of security among managers and workers. That is, there can be a perception that all angles have been covered and that every possible scenario has been analysed and contingencies built in, leading to a greater sense of security pervading the culture in the organisation. This can prove to be no more than a 'chimera', an illusion of comfort that masks some internal weaknesses that have gone undetected. Planning is often based on forecasts of future events but those events may manifest themselves in myriad different ways that can often take managers by surprise in their character and scale of influence. In an influential article, economist Paul Schoemaker (1991) highlighted the danger of excessive reliance on the perceived scenario rather than building in flexibility to reflect the dynamics of uncertainty in planning. Employees may similarly be affected by a false sense of security that planning can engender. Excessive attention to fulfilling the targets set out in detailed plans may not be the most efficient or optimal use of human resources. Workers may miss opportunities to extend themselves, to achieve wider goals, and to pursue other value adding activities because they are psychologically 'locked-in' to achieving the set targets in the plan.

The false sense of security that plans often generate is further undermined by the fact that the environment is typically dynamic and subject to rapid change. Even the most sophisticated and detailed plans may become redundant as internal and external events conspire to undermine their relevance. Managers have little control over external events that may affect their plans, for example changes to industry regulation, shifts in macroeconomic variables such as inflation or employment rates, and political, social, and environmental change. Plans are designed with current knowledge and future expectations in mind. Current knowledge may be incomplete and future expectations are notoriously unreliable. Consequently, plans may not reflect the reality of the situation facing the organisation. It is for this reason that an over-reliance on plans is a dangerous pursuit, meaning managers have to build in a level of flexibility that recognises the impact that uncertainty brings.

Costs

Finally, there is a cost of planning to be borne in terms of time and money. The more complex the plan, the more time consuming it will be to devise. Even once the plan is compiled there is an on-going cost of monitoring and evaluating its set performance targets against actual outcomes. Where many alternatives exist, there may be high costs incurred as each is analysed and tested before a decision is made regarding which one to adopt. Here, there may be a danger of the costs exceeding the benefits of the plan. Both the advantages and the limitations of planning were evident in the run up to London hosting the Olympic Games in 2012. This major global event has offered an opportunity to identify and assess the types of planning that took place to deliver a successful Games. Of particular interest is the fact that the planning process not only had to deliver the event successfully, but also to leave a lasting legacy for the region in terms of sustainable development, ecological protection, active lifestyles, and a host of other key objectives that formed part of the successful bid document.

Case study
London 2012 Sustainability Plan

Introduction

On 6 July 2005 International Olympic Committee (IOC) president Jacques Rogge announced in Singapore that London would host the 2012 Olympic Games. Almost immediately the formal planning for delivering the games got under way. Two main organisations were established with a remit to oversee the successful delivery of what became known as the 2012

Games. The London Organising Committee of the Olympic and Paralympic Games (LOCOG) was responsible for planning and staging the games. The Olympic Delivery Authority (ODA) was responsible for building the stadiums and other infrastructure for the games, and for delivering a lasting and viable legacy of use. Delivering the 2012 Games on budget, on time, and under unprecedented public scrutiny was an immense challenge to the organisers and was made possible by highly effective planning throughout the process.

Beyond 2012

A key factor for being awarded the games was the legacy once the main event was over. The London bid team emphasised the lasting benefits that would continue long after the Olympic flame had been extinguished on the last day of competition. The location of the games in east London was the biggest regeneration project in Europe. Collaboration between the ODA, the London Development Agency (LDA) (the mayor's agency for sustainable economic development), and local authorities ensured that the legacy included the building of thousands of new houses, extended parkland, transport links, and the retention of some sports venues. The location was specifically chosen for its regeneration potential and its sustainability. Thus legacy was a common theme running through both the bid proposal and the plans for delivery and extended beyond the site location to include benefits to communities across the UK in terms of employment opportunities, business development, volunteering opportunities, training and education, and health and well-being.

Guiding principles for the sustainability aspect of the 2012 Games were articulated in the 'Towards a one planet 2012' theme. This theme was closely related to the 'One Planet Living' concept developed by the World Wildlife Fund/BioRegional which provided the evidence to support the view that as a global community we are living beyond the regenerative capacity of the planet. In effect, we are consuming more resources at a rate in excess of the planet's capacity to replenish them. It also highlighted the huge discrepancies in consumption of Earth's resources between different countries. The principles of 'Towards a one planet 2012' were formed with a view to addressing the sustainability issues highlighted in the WWF/BioRegional document (www.oneplanetliving.org).

Sustainability Policy

A Sustainability Policy document was produced by the Olympic Board in June 2006 and then later updated in November 2009 and finally in February 2010 (London 2012, Sustainability plan summary). The policy identified five priority themes which could best contribute to achieving legacy aims. The themes formed the basis for the sustainability plan and included the following five key areas.

Climate change

The delivery of the 2012 Games was to provide a platform for demonstrating long-term solutions in terms of energy and water resource management, infrastructure development, transport, local, seasonal food production, and carbon impact mitigation and adaptation. A stated aim included a commitment to minimise the carbon footprint of the Games and legacy development through optimising energy efficiency, energy demand, and use of low-carbon and renewable energy sources.

Waste

The 2012 Games were to be a catalyst for new waste management infrastructure in east London and around other venues by minimising waste at source, diverting construction waste where feasible and all Games-time waste away from landfill. Influencing behavioural change towards environmental sustainability would be addressed by promoting the waste hierarchy of 'reduce, reuse, recycle' as a means of influencing behavioural change.

Biodiversity

This priority consisted of a commitment to enhance the ecology of the region around the Olympics main site in Stratford, east London as well as other venues. In particular, there was to be a greater contribution by the sports sector to nature conservation.

Inclusion

The aim was to deliver the most socially inclusive Games ever held by promoting access, celebrating diversity, and facilitating the physical, economic, and social regeneration of the area and surrounding communities.

Healthy living

This priority was designed to inspire people across the country to participate in sport and develop active, healthy, and sustainable lifestyles.

Sustainability Plan

A key feature of the 2012 Games delivery plan was to maximise sustainability. Sustainability refers to new methods and technologies that can be deployed to maximise social and economic benefits and reduce the environmental impacts associated with delivering the games and the legacy thereafter. The London 2012 Sustainability Plan was published in December 2009 and covered the three main phases of preparation, event staging, and building a lasting and sustainable legacy.

Preparation

The Olympic Park hosted the main venues including the Olympic Stadium, the swimming pool, and velodrome. Sustainability was an integral part of the planning and design of the venues as well as the support infrastructure such as transport and communications links. The preparation process included environmentally sensitive issues of demolition, clearance, waste disposal, remediation, and construction with each presenting different challenges to meeting sustainability targets. New methods and technologies have been developed and implemented to raise the standard of design and delivery of regeneration projects—a legacy that has redefined 'best practice' for future projects. For example, new types of construction materials such as ceramics and glass that are strong and long-lasting and designed, produced, and delivered within exacting environmental standards have proved a catalyst for innovation in those producing industries.

Event staging

London 2012 was a unique event from a sustainability perspective. No other previous Olympics had a sustainability plan of such scope and ambition. London 2012 was truly groundbreaking as so many of the sustainability activities had never been implemented before. In many ways the games set new standards in a number of different industry sectors so that it can be viewed as a catalyst for innovation in the UK and beyond. As no previous benchmarks were available, planners developed new methods of measuring and evaluating sustainability outputs and targets. The principle of knowledge sharing under which all 2012 Games activities were undertaken has ensured that the added value of these new methods was disseminated into the public domain. Thus, stakeholders involved in current and future projects have benefited from applying the knowledge and experience of those involved in delivering the sustainability targets for the 2012 Games.

Building a lasting and sustainable legacy

The legacy of the 2012 Games featured both physical and social dimensions not just for the immediate locale but across the UK. The main venues and the Olympic Park have been used as the platform for environmentally friendly regeneration projects. Stringent targets for reducing carbon emissions and action plans for dealing with climate change are just two examples of the lead that the 'Towards a one planet 2012' has given to subsequent proposals for regeneration. In many respects the sustainability targets relate to changing behaviours as much as actions. In essence, it was designed to be a catalyst for changing the mindset of stakeholders towards the issue of sustainability. In particular, the Olympic Park was designed to act as a 'blueprint' for sustainable living that could then be replicated or improved upon in communities across the country. The impact that large-scale events such as the 2012 Games has on influencing environmental awareness and behavioural change is the subject of research that will further the understanding of sustainability issues. This aspect helps to underline the fact that sustainability is about people and lifestyle as well as technology and policy. The Sustainability Plan features the three phases: the timeframe for action, the identification of the designated lead partner for each phase, and examples of sustainability considerations. These are highlighted in Table 3.4.

The priority themes underpinned the planning around the issue of sustainability for the 2012 Games and beyond. The plan informed the promises made by government and the Mayor of London regarding the legacy of the Games. The challenges in meeting the promises were immense, risky, and complex. For example, some of the promises on waste treatment were made before the facilities and technology for providing it were available. The application of new and untested event management methods had to be robust enough to cope with the sheer scale of the Olympics whilst meeting strict deadlines and adhering to contractual obligations. Targets for sustainability were made without any previous benchmarks as a guide to feasibility. There was high risk associated with planning for outcomes that had never been achieved before. All

Table 3.4 Responsibilities for sustainability for London 2012

Phase	Period	Lead	Example of sustainability considerations
Planning and construction Olympic Park and new permanent installations at other Games venues; some temporary facilities and new or upgraded transport infrastructure; development of skills, jobs, and business opportunities; legacy planning and transition works.	2006–11 and 2013–14	ODA LDA	Design of buildings Sourcing of building materials Construction impacts Equalities and diversity in construction employment Community relations and consultation Local benefits from construction Inclusive design Health and safety on site Biodiversity impacts Waste management Support programmes for skills development and business opportunities

Table 3.4 (Continued)

Phase	Period	Lead	Example of sustainability considerations
Staging the Games Cultural Olympiad ceremonies, torch relays, test events, pre-Games overlay and fit-out of venues (bump-in), event operations, Olympic–Paralympic transition, and post-games break down (bump-out)	2008–12	LOCOG	Construction, methods and materials for temporary venues and overlay
			Travel for athletes, spectators, and workforce
			Catering and healthy food
			Health and safety at venues and for workforce
			Inclusion and diversity policies for workforce
			Cultural Olympiad with celebration of diversity
			Power supply and consumption during Games
			Sourcing and performance of equipment, merchandise, and clothing
			Games-time waste management
			Bio-diversity conservation
			Volunteering
			Public education programmes
			Outreach projects to promote sustainability and engage stakeholders and commercial partners
Realising the legacy	2006–2020	UK govt.	Energy and waste infrastructure
			Healthy lifestyles and sport promotion
		Mayor of London	Legacy park design and function
		OPLC	Building performance
		LDA	Promoting healthier, more sustainable lifestyles
			Use of legacy sporting facilities
		Local authorities	Increased sports participation, healthier living, cohesive communities, and volunteering
			Raised international profile of London and UK
			Supporting sustainable growth of London and UK economy

Source: London 2012 (December, 2009) *Sustainability Plan* (2nd edn), Towards a One Planet 2012, London.

the commitments made had to be delivered within sound economic models and budgets. It may be some time before a definitively accurate evaluation of how the sustainability plan for the games played out in reality.

Sources:

London 2012 (February, 2010) Sustainability plan summary, London. http://www.london2012. com/mm/Document/Publications/Sustainability/01/24/08/07/london-2012-sustainability-plan-summary.pdf

London *Sustainability Plan* (2nd edn) Towards a one planet 2012, London.

Discussion points

Is legacy planning for an Olympic Games a cosmetic exercise, or does it actually deliver tangible benefits to the wider community?

How effective can planning be for achieving outcomes that are based on behavioural and cultural change?

Questions and tasks

Identify a major legacy promise highlighted in the 2012 Games bid document and undertake research to determine if there is any evidence of it being met.

What types of planning were undertaken in the process of delivering the 2012 Games?

Identify four external factors that had an impact on the planning targets of the 2012 Games.

Online Resource Centre

Author commentary on these discussion points and questions can be found on the Online Resource Centre at: www.oxfordtextbooks.co.uk/orc/combe1e/

Summary

● **Understand the planning process**

The planning process follows a systematic journey through formulation, implementation, and evaluation. The learning that takes place throughout this process feeds back to help better inform future planning or to adapt current plans.

● **Evaluate the advantages and limitations of planning**

Planning involves a systematic process of implementing actions that help to achieve goals and objectives. Planning is important for the effective allocation of resources and to measure and control activities that contribute to the achievement of goals and objectives. The limitations of planning have to be recognised by managers including the potential stifling of creativity, innovation, and experimentation.

● **Comprehend the role of planning in setting goals and objectives**

Planning helps to focus the minds of managers on what goals and objectives need to be achieved, what resources are required to achieve them, and how best to deploy them.

● **Recognise the different types of plans**

This chapter has outlined just some of the many plans that have been devised to achieve different goals and objectives. These have included business plans, scenario planning, succession planning, and so on. Different plans are devised according to different levels of management in organisations such as operational, business, and strategic planning. Each have their own characteristics and design format according to what managers intend to achieve. The analysis highlighted the different levels of complexity linked to different types of plans.

● **Understand the required skills of management in the planning process**

Planning requires a range of different but complementary skills such as organisational, technical, analytical, conceptual, and communications skills. Depending on the type of planning necessary to achieve stated goals and objectives, the level of reliance on these skills will vary but, in the modern business environment, it is necessary for managers to excel at some and display competence in others.

Conclusion

Planning is a process that helps to provide clarity about the appropriate actions that need to be taken to achieve stated aims.

Planning is flexible and variable in complexity and scope. In some instances, it may provide the basis for a proposal such as a business plan, in others it may involve trying to understand the future and be shrouded in uncertainty, such as in scenario planning. Some plans may be laden with quantitative measures whilst others rely wholly on the analytical and conceptual skills of managers or workers. The prevalence of planning as a function of management would suggest that there is a high added value attached to the activity. However, critics of planning point to the fact that the modern world is far too dynamic, changeable, and unpredictable to lend any credibility to carefully laid-out plans.

Planning and organising are management functions that are closely linked as both have a role to play in the way work is organised and resources allocated. As a logical progression of ideas and concepts, Chapter 4 explores the management function of organising in some detail.

Chapter questions and tasks

Define planning and outline some of the advantages it offers.

Highlight the key components of a typical business plan.

Why do managers value the outcomes of scenario planning?

What is the biggest threat to business continuity for a large-scale toy manufacturing company in China?

Identify the four main stages of succession planning.

Online Resource Centre
Author commentary on these questions can be found on the Online Resource Centre at: www. oxfordtextbooks.co.uk/orc/combe1e/

Further reading

- Chapman, S. N. (2005) *Fundamentals of Production Planning and Control*, Harlow, Prentice-Hall.

  This book provides a concise, practical, survey-based approach to explaining the production planning process and the control function within the productive process. The explanations are clear and follow systematic approaches to the planning process which makes the narrative content easily accessible to those with limited knowledge of this important function of management.

- Finch, B. (2010) *How to Write a Business Plan* (Creating Success Series) (3rd edn), Kogan Page, London.

  A practical guide to creating a business plan with key elements clearly outlined and delivered in a systematic and coherent manner. An effective guide for anyone wishing to understand how to set up a business or students seeking an insight into the compilation of a business plan.

- Lindgren, M. and Bandhold, H. (2009) *Scenario Planning: The Link between Future and Strategy*, Palgrave Macmillan, Basingstoke.

  The most valuable aspect of this book is the insights offered around the thinking behind scenario planning with effective discussion of concepts, ideas, models, and tools for practical application in companies. The authors demonstrate how strategic flexibility can be achieved through scenario planning for long-term competition and performance. The premise is that scenario planning is as much an art form as a practical management tool.

- Nolan, T. N., Goodstein, L. D. and Goodstein, J. (2008) *Applied Strategic Planning* (2nd edn), Jossey Bass, Chichester.

  The book delivers an overview of the applied strategic planning process and is aimed at planners and other participants in the process. Of most value are the key questions identified for further discussion and the systematic way the book helps organisations identify their ideal future, as well as delivering guidance on how to develop a plan to achieve it using tools, techniques, and processes.

- Patterson, S. J. and Radtke, J. M. (2009) *Strategic Communications for Nonprofit Organization: Seven Steps to Creating a Successful Plan*, John Wiley & Sons, Chichester.

  The book provides a good example of how planning plays an important role in non profit organisational settings by defining issues and policies and discussing how they are perceived by the public in terms of effectiveness. The authors have designed worksheets, forms, surveys, and self-assessment tools to create a total communications plan for practitioners and students interested in understanding the role of planning for effective public relations in this distinctive sector.

- Poynter, G. and MacRury, I. (2009) *Olympic Cities: 2012 and the Remaking of London* (Design and the Built Environment), Ashgate, Farnham.

  To align with the case study of London 2012 this book delivers an invaluable insight into the planning for redesigning the urban landscape in and around the Olympic site. Of particular interest is the treatment of the planning process underpinning many of the urban regeneration programmes directly linked to the delivery of the 2012 Games.

- Rothwell, W. J. (2010) *Effective Succession Planning: Ensuring Leadership Continuity and Building Talent from Within* (4th edn), Amacom.

The book sets out a complete and systematic succession planning programme and incorporates latest trends and best practices for recruitment and retention using worksheets and effective assessment tools.

● Sahlman, W. A. (1997) 'How to write a great business plan', *Harvard Business Review*, Vol. 75, No. 4, pp. 98–108.

The author sets out a step by step guide to compiling an effective business plan with all the key topics covered and explanations as to why they are important in communicating how the business is to be developed and managed.

Online Resource Centre

For more information, updates, and multiple-choice questions, please visit the Online Resource Centre at: www.oxfordtextbooks.co.uk/orc/combe1e/

Skillset 3
Time management

3(a) Introduction

As a student, you will need to be able to manage your time effectively in order to keep pace with the learning process, assessment deadlines, and your work/life balance. In your working life, time management is an important element of planning in business at all levels: operational, business, and corporate (see Chapter 3). With multi-tasking and multi-skilling key features of modern workplaces, having time management skills/techniques you can use have taken on extra importance. This Skillset delivers techniques that help you embed time management into your everyday discipline for study/work. There are several activities to complete.

3(b) Start with 'SMART'

As noted in Chapter 3, a starting point for planning is to clearly identify what you want to achieve with the acronym 'SMART' being a useful way of helping you to clearly articulate your targets/objectives.

Before starting the activity below, you may wish to reread the relevant part of Chapter 3 to remind yourself about 'SMART' targets/objectives. Note that sometimes the 'R' in SMART also stands for 'relevant' or 'realistic'. The important thing is to use the tool in a way that is useful and makes sense for you.

Activity 1

Use the following table to identify the key targets/objectives you wish to achieve over the next few months. Evaluate them and note in each of the 'SMART' columns (where relevant) whether it is, for example, 'Specific'; and perhaps give a comment to justify your answer. The comment provides an opportunity for some reflection about where difficulties might arise either in specifying the objective, or in attempting to achieve it.

'How do you eat an elephant? One bite at a time.' Rather than 'I want to pass all my modules', perhaps consider having separate objectives (sub-objectives) for each assessment you have to undertake.

Target/Objective/Goal	Specific	Measurable	Achievable	Rewarded	Timely
Achieve a mark of 60% or more in my first assessment for Module 1 by submitting my best work on [a particular date]	Yes.	Yes by (1) meeting submission date and (2) by achieving a mark of 60% or more.	Yes. However, there is another assessment due the same week so I have to balance my time well.	Yes. A mark of 60% or more will help me achieve the degree classification I want.	Yes. Date chosen is before final submission date to allow me to visit my parents for the weekend.

105

3(c) Prioritising

With your SMART targets/objectives, you know what you want to do, and why (e.g. reward) and when you have to complete the task(s). However, with your busy life you may be overwhelmed by the variety of competing tasks you have to undertake: studies, work, family, social life; and so on. Which tasks are the ones you should focus on today/this week? Stephen Covey (author of the best-selling book on the 7 *Habits of Highly Effective People*) has a simple but effective tool for helping you put 'first things first' (the title of another of Covey's books; Covey and Merrill, 1994). In other words, this tool will help you *prioritise* your tasks.

Covey (1994) suggests that tasks/objectives can be categorised according to two dimensions:

> First, their **Urgency**—are your tasks/objectives **Urgent** or **Not Urgent**?
> Secondly, their **Importance**—are your tasks/objectives **Important** or **Not Important** to achieving your objectives/goals?

From these two dimensions, we can generate four categories of activities:

1 **Important/Urgent:** for example an imminent assessment deadline or deadline for a job application. These are activities demanding your current focus and time/attention.

2 **Important/Not Urgent:** for example backing up your files, thinking about your long-term career goals or building your 'network' of contacts. Here, although there may not be

immediate deadlines and pressure, over a longer time, there are potential consequences of not giving time to these elements.

3 **Not Important/Urgent:** for example, taking a phone call from a friend while working on your assessment. One test as to whether you are driven by 'urgency' might be to ask yourself the question—'when I receive a text message on my mobile phone do I usually stop what I am doing and read the text' (regardless of whether I am expecting the text or not). If the answer is 'yes' then you may be overly driven by the 'urgency' dimension even when importance is not an issue. In a work situation, you can quite easily fall into a pattern of answering e-mails as soon as they come in regardless of their importance; and other more important tasks are put to one side. One way to manage your e-mails/texts is only to look at them at particular times of the day; leaving the rest of the day free to push on with tasks without their 'distraction'. Of course, this may not be appropriate if you are expecting an important message.

4 **Not Important/Not Urgent:** for example, watching a movie you have already seen which fills up your time with seemingly purposeful activities. You should strongly question the value of these activities in the context of their contribution to achieving your objectives.

There are no universal definitions of urgent/important and you must make your own judgements. These calibrations/judgements of what is urgent or important may change over time. There may be occasions (for example in the final year of your studies) when your studies gain an urgency/importance that, for a time, overshadows other parts of your life. More generally, as you near a deadline something may move from being Not Urgent to Urgent. Not all important tasks are urgent; and not all urgent tasks are important. Categories 3 and 4 may be 'displacement' activity that you are 'allowing' to fill your time rather than focusing on more important/urgent matters. This is not to say that, for example, some relaxation may not be important—but a sense of proportionality is required.

How often you complete/modify the table would be up to you. McMillan and Weyers (2009) suggest writing a list each day to help you prioritise your *future* activities; for example by working on Category 1 activities first. In Chapter 3, as well as deciding what to do, planning also included implementation (attempting to carry out the plan); evaluation (by which you judge the extent to which you achieved what you set out to do); and reflection on what worked and what didn't (in order to learn from your experiences and amend your future plans). Activity 1 allowed you to reflect on what you did in the *past* and possibly learn from your experiences.

106

Activity 2

(a) Write a list of the key study/work/other tasks you carried out over the last week. Making lists are a key time management tool. However, without a sense of the importance/urgency of the items on the list, you may focus your time and effort on the wrong things.

(b) Then, based on the descriptions of the four categories of activity given above, allocate the tasks in the table below. Note that rather than a table, the categories can be portrayed as a two-by-two matrix (e.g. Covey and Merrill, 1994; MacMillan and Weyers, 2009).

Time Period: From ...To ...

	1	2	3	4
	Important/ urgent	Important/ not urgent	Not important/ urgent	Not important/ not urgent
Tasks/ activities				

(c) Within Columns labelled 1 to 4 (re)arrange the tasks/activities in order of priority (or rank them with, in Category 1, '1' being the most important/urgent task; and so on). This can be useful, as even within the Important/Urgent column there may have been particularly pressing tasks to be completed first.

(d) The table can now be used to reflect on what you did over the last week. Where did you put your focus/efforts? Was the emphasis on Categories 1 and 2? Alternatively, Categories 3 and 4? In some cases, what was Important/Urgent may not have been something you could plan for—it arose out of a need to react to current events. However, with hindsight, did you make best use of your time?

3(d) In-tray exercises

Beyond your studies, time management and the ability to prioritise your work are key skills that employers are looking for in their employees. As part of a selection process, potential employees may be asked to undertake an '**In-tray exercise**'. As the name suggests, you would be given a number of documents in various formats in your In-tray (for example, the printout of an e-mail, a handwritten note, a letter, and so on). You are then asked to: (1) evaluate the documents to decide the order in which you would deal with them (in other words identify the key issues and evaluate their importance/urgency; see Section 3(c) above); (2) compose replies if appropriate, or at least identify what actions you would carry out to deal with the various documents. You are given a time limit for the exercise so you have to plan your work and manage your time effectively.

The website AssessmentDay has links to a free example of an In-tray exercise (and answers). You may wish to try this. See: http://www.assessmentday.co.uk/in-tray-exercise.htm [Last accessed 19 January 2012].

3(e) Career planning

Chapter 3 outlined three broad types of planning ranging from short-term (operational) through to long-term (strategic planning). As part of your programme of studies, you may undertake Personal Development Planning (PDP; the terminology used may vary), defined as:

> a structured and supported process undertaken by an individual to reflect upon their own learning, performance and/or achievement and to plan for their personal, educational and career development (Higher Education Academy, 2012).

Alternatively, in your workplace, you may have Personal Development reviews or requirements for continuing professional development (CPD); the terminology can vary. Some of the time management, objective setting, and prioritisation techniques covered in this Skillset may also be applied to this long-term planning for your career development, for example, in developing SMART objectives; or creating a Gantt chart to map your planned activities across several years.

3(f) Tools for time management

There are a number of tools available which can help you with your time management, many of which are electronic in nature, so you can have them on your computer or mobile phone. Electronic diaries allow you to, for example: make appointments (sending an invitation to others to arrange meetings), categorise activities, set reminders in advance of deadlines for tasks; share your diary with friends/colleagues; and so on. Remember to back up your diary if possible, as the more we come to rely on an electronic diary, the more we miss it if anything goes wrong (flat battery, software malfunction, etc.).

Although discussing it in detail is beyond the scope of this Skillset, project management software (e.g. Microsoft Project) is available to help you plan and manage your projects. Gaining experience in using such software will also give you another skill you can 'sell' at an interview.

3(g) Other tips for time management

You may have a number of sub-goals as stepping-stones to reach your longer-term objectives. For example, some people deliberately seek out job interview opportunities with companies/roles they do not particularly want to work for or with whom they are not likely to have a successful interview. Rather than these failed interviews being a waste of time, they are regarded as crucial to becoming an experienced interviewee for the occasion when the person is being interviewed for their 'dream job'.

Everyone wants to do his or her very best work every time. However, sometimes that is not possible. You may be able to save time by acknowledging that, on this particular occasion, you will do a 'good job' but not your 'best job' so that you can use time gained on other objectives. From a management decision making perspective, this is known as 'satisficing', in other words, satisfactory rather than optimising/perfection is the goal.

We have covered some tools which can help you plan, but remember not to suffer from 'paralysis by planning'. Planning by drawing up lists and so on can be very useful, but (usually) this is not the endpoint—you must act on your plan to achieve your objectives. Planning itself may become a Category 3 or 4 activity (see Section 3(c) above).

There is a traditional military maxim that says 'No plan survives contact with the enemy'. Alternatively, the Scottish poet Robert Burns wrote 'The best-laid schemes o' mice and men Gang aft a-gley'. Both quotes are different ways of saying that, when implementing them, plans may require revision, abandonment, or replacement. Consider having windows of time for the completion of tasks, for example an optimal deadline (Monday) and an absolute deadline (Wednesday). If you work towards the optimal deadline then you may have a buffer of time for when/if things go wrong. For example, if an assessment is due for submission at 16.00 then finishing your document at 15.45 may make you vulnerable to the printer malfunctioning or running out of paper.

In terms of your studies, you may wish to consider your expertise and enthusiasm for particular subjects. It may be that you have to give priority early in the term to those subjects you are not as expert in, or not as keen on, in order to avoid having to rush later on to complete something you are not particularly comfortable with. Remember, Olympic athletes work on their weaknesses as much as, or even more than, their strengths.

3(h) Summary of the Skillset

Effective time management, as part of a wider planning process, is of value to you for both your studies and working life. This Skillset introduced several tools (for example SMART objectives and Gantt charts) which can make your planning and, in particular, time management more effective. There were several activities for you to undertake to help enhance (and reflect on) your time management skills.

References/Further reading/Resources

AssessmentDay, 2011, *In Tray Exercise*. [Online resource.] Available at: http://www.assessmentday.co.uk/in-tray-exercise.htm [Last accessed 19 January 2012].

Covey S. R. and Merrill A. R., 1994, *First Things First*, Simon and Schuster, London.

Higher Education Academy (HEA), 2012, *PDP–Personal Development Planning*. [Online resource.] Available at: http://www.heacademy.ac.uk/resources/detail/pdp/pdp [Last accessed 19 January 2012].

McMillan, K. and Weyers, J., 2009, *The Smarter Study Skills Companion* (2nd edn), Pearson Education, Harlow.

Open University (2012) *2.4 Planning with Gantt charts* [online] Available from:IR http://openlearn.open.ac.uk/mod/oucontent/view.php?id=398576&section=1.10.4 [Last accessed 22 January 2012; Includes a link to a Gantt chart template].

Time Management That Works [Online resource.] Available at: http://www.timemanagement.com/ [A resource offering advice on time management and a free Time Management e-course (registration required)].

4 Organising

All formal organisations require a structure and chain of command that underpins authority. This helps managers organise and deploy resources in ways that help achieve stated aims. Nowhere is this more evident than in the armed forces where authority is formally and rigidly recognised through rank. Modern armies in developed nations have large inventories of equipment in the form of weapons, vehicles, communications, buildings, and so on. However, the most important asset is the personnel. In striving to achieve the mission of defending the nation, soldiers and officers must work closely together. However, this closeness is bounded by formal recognition of rank so that when orders are given they are carried out without question. Most armies are organised in a way that enables a common understanding of the chain of command so that, under combat conditions, complex and dangerous manoeuvres can take place with maximum efficiency. Three key elements underpin the discharge of orders. First, the rank system reflects a person's authority, responsibilities, and experience. Secondly, the organisational structure reflects the delegation of responsibilities, and thirdly, military customs and traditions serve as a bonding mechanism that enhances group cohesiveness. Former US Army General George Patton summed up the ethos of the formal organisation of a military force by saying 'If you can't get them to salute when they should and wear the clothes you tell them to wear, how are you going to get them to die for their country?' (Thinkexist.com, 2013)

Skillset 4
Sourcing materials

This chapter's Skillset section covers sourcing materials.
Sourcing materials is a key skill that all managers need to master. This Skillset outlines a process of sourcing including guidance on identifying the purpose of sourcing, deciding on boundaries, identifying sources, creating a search strategy, and evaluating the search. Knowing when to stop is also a feature of this process.

Student study skills
Students will benefit from taking a formal approach to sourcing materials by adopting the simple techniques outlined in this Skillset. Proper search techniques can save time, aid the quality of output, and underpin the discipline that students require to navigate their way through the various academic challenges they are going to face.

Workplace skills
Being able to source materials that support work tasks is an important skill in many occupations and professions. The plethora of information sources available through new technologies has made this skill ever more important. Organisations have high expectations that graduates will have a good understanding of how to work with new media technologies that support the sourcing of materials. This Skillset helps students prepare for work without the need for additional training by the employer, thereby adding value to their overall employability.

Definition

Organising is a management function that involves making decisions about what activities and tasks have to be undertaken; who is to undertake them; and how they are to be grouped and scheduled. Organising also entails putting in place a reporting structure that features a chain of command so that decision making authority can be formally recognised.

Introduction

This chapter on organising is a logical progression from the issues and concepts discussed in the previous chapter on planning. Effective planning requires the organisation of resources to help define goals and objectives, and to formulate strategies for achieving them and for integrating activities and tasks. Organising is a skill that entails arranging work activities and schedules in a way that helps the organisation achieve its stated goals and objectives. These activities can be broad ranging, diverse, and feature many different types of skills and know-how. To maximise efficiency and effectiveness, it is necessary for managers to be able to understand these characteristics within their organisation so that they can make informed decisions about what activities and tasks are to be carried out, by whom, and when. This process requires decisions to be made about the reporting structure within the organisation and the chain of command for the exercise of authority. These are essential for ensuring that work is supervised and carried out to an expected standard. The issues of authority, chain of command, and span of control are discussed in more detail later in the chapter, but it is recognised here that all formal organisations have an established mechanism in place to underpin the organisation of work.

There are a number of important factors that influence decisions about the organisation of work. Much will depend on whether the organisation is mechanistic or organic in design. Also, issues of authority, chain of command, and span of control are all dependent on the organisational structure that is designed and implemented by management. The different types of organisational structures, and the rationale for their implementation, are covered in more detail in Chapter 11. However, it is necessary to set the scene for this by addressing the underpinning concepts of authority, chain of command, and span of control as well as understanding the choice of centralising or decentralising decision making powers within the organisation.

At the core of organising activity is the deployment of human resources. It is easy to forget that the purpose of management is to facilitate the achievement of stated goals and objectives by organising resources in the most effective way possible. Human resources play a pivotal role in this process and, therefore, managers have to ensure that the organisational structures, work support mechanisms, and control features are designed in a way that is conducive to achieving goals and objectives at the operational, business, and strategic levels of the organisation.

Formalising the organisation of work

All organisations require some level of formal control over the organisation of work to be carried out (Dwyer, 2005). The control function is discussed in greater detail in Chapter 6 but here it useful to set the scene for analysis of the key aspects of organising. Formalising the organisation of work refers to the extent to which work tasks are subject to guidelines and the behaviour of employees controlled through rules, procedures, and regulations. In highly formalised working environments, the employee is expected to undertake activities and tasks in a pre-ordained manner, set by guidelines and strict procedures. Workers in factories producing mass market, standardised products are most likely to operate under such conditions. The scope for employee initiative or decision making in such an environment is limited, verging on zero. A high level of formalisation is the preferred approach in such working environments because the top priority for managers is to ensure output targets are met. At the other extreme, some organisations allow workers extensive latitude to make decisions that affect the way they carry out their tasks and activities. Thus, in many creative industries there is no discernible formalisation but rather a liberal regime better suited to supporting a culture of innovation.

Levels of formalisation vary markedly between organisations, and even within the same organisation. In some businesses it is necessary for some tasks to be controlled by strict rules whereas in other parts of the business a different function may be subject to only minimal control. For example, in universities in many western countries the academic staff are given a great deal of freedom to organise their non-teaching activities as they see fit. The working environment for academics is liberal with no formal codes of conduct or regulations that clearly set out what work has to be done, when, and how. Many academic staff organise their research activities around their work/life balance. However, administrative and support staff within universities are subject to much greater rigour when it comes to formalising work. Those staff members are more likely to have their work schedules clearly set out along with the rules and regulations, timescales, and procedures relating to their tasks and activities. The extent to which formalisaton exists within any organisation is reflected in the type and level of authority exercised, the chain of command, and span of control. In turn, these will determine whether decision making powers are centralised (restricted to a privileged few) or decentralised (delegated to a wider number of people down the chain of command). These all remain important aspects of organising in the twenty-first century (Drucker, 2001) and form the basis of much of the discussion in this chapter.

Term
Definition

Formalisation: the level to which an organisation sets formal rules, procedures, and regulations for work tasks and activities.

Organising authority, chain of command, and span of control

Three important characteristics of formal organisational design are the level of authority, the chain of command, and the span of control that is delegated to key personnel.

Authority

Authority refers to the power to command and direct people within the context of the formal work setting. Authority is a right conferred on key personnel to tell people what to do. The recognition of authority facilitates the carrying out of activities and tasks. In some organisational settings, such as the armed forces outlined above, authority is formal and recognised by rank, hierarchy, and strict obedience. In others, the authority is more informal and implied, such as in the creative industries where no formal hierarchy may be evident but where authority is expressed in more subtle and nuanced ways.

Authority is an important factor in ensuring that activities and tasks are carried out. Pettinger (2007) describes it as the legitimisation of the capability to exercise influence and the relationship by which that influence is exercised. As authority is inextricably linked to power, there has to be some form of sanction available if authority is not recognised. Very often sanctions may only be implied, but in most organisations a formal set of rules, regulations, and procedures are designed to ensure that authority is recognised and the list of sanctions available should personnel fail to react in an appropriate manner to reasonable and agreed commands from those in positions of authority. Here, a fine line has to be drawn between those in the organisation who may seek to challenge the status quo and seek new and better ways of achieving stated goals and objectives (a laudable, often encouraged attitude) and outright disregard for established lines of authority. This latter attitude may manifest itself in a challenge to authority or a failure to meet obligations to perform assigned duties. Barnard (1938) outlined key conditions that determine whether or not authority is accepted. These include situations where the worker:

- understands the command or directive being communicated;
- believes the order is consistent with the purpose of the organisation.

Term
Definition

Authority: power to command or control others.

- perceives the command or directive as compatible with his or her personal interests and aligns to their job specification;
- possesses the physical and intellectual capabilities to comply with the order.

There are different types of authority evident within organisations and each is exercised with a view to enabling workers to carry out their duties effectively. Of course, the most effective type of authority is one that does not require close management and supervision of workers as the level of respect for authority and the motivation to deliver high quality outputs is already firmly embedded in the values and beliefs of workers. Nevertheless, even in such organisations, lines of authority need to be established. Three of the main types of authority are:

- line authority;
- staff authority;
- functional authority.

Line authority

Line management authority is the common and basic form of command structure and clearly demarcates superiors from subordinates. Typically, a line manager has authority to issue orders and directives to workers at the operational or business level and is invariably concerned with the functions carried out in the organisation such as production, storage, distribution, sales, customer service, etc.

Staff authority

The next level of authority consists of those who have the right to support, advise, and assist those with line authority. These are staff authority positions and are designed to support the effectiveness of those with line management responsibilities. There needs to be a close working relationship between line and staff authority personnel to ensure high levels of efficiency and effectiveness. A shared understanding of the organisation's mission, vision, and strategic direction underpins the relationship. Staff authority is a level of management that is normally associated with larger organisations where a wide range of diversified functions are undertaken and there are significant numbers of personnel to manage. For small and medium sized enterprises (SMEs) it is unlikely that the organisation would require an extra layer of authority such as a legal department or a training and development department.

Functional authority

Functional authority gives certain staff members the power to initiate actions (or to stop actions taking place) in a designated area of expertise. The purpose of this type of authority is to allow managers to make decisions quickly and prevent disruption to the productive process. For example, production managers can make decisions to help maintain flow of output based on their experience and knowledge of the production process without referring to a higher authority.

Key criteria for the effective deployment of authority include:
- the use of formal communications channels;
- the use of direct lines of communication between managers and subordinates;
- the use of the complete chain of command for giving orders;
- the use of effective communication skills by managers;
- the use of formal lines of communication for organisational business purposes;
- that the order is authenticated as being issued from a recognised manager.

Information gathering is an important aspect of management as it helps to inform decision making, such as the delegation of authority. The plethora of information available means that managers have to create an information sourcing strategy so that time, effort, and resources are deployed in the best possible way when gathering, storing, and disseminating information.

It is the role of management to delegate levels of authority to key personnel with a view to ensuring that activities and tasks are carried out effectively and efficiently. It is a key skill to determine the extent to which authority should be delegated and the appropriate level of power assigned to each authority in the organisation. Any misalignment of authority and power may lead to inefficiency, confusion, tension and/or conflict. To avoid these there has to be a distinct and fully recognised chain of command.

Chain of command

A formal chain of command has been a feature of organisational structure since the earliest forms of mass production as part of the Industrial Revolution in the eighteenth century. Although less prevalent in a formal sense in the twenty-first century a chain of command continues to play a role in many organisations. It is possible to have multiple chains of command in the same organisation (Alberts and Nissen, 2009); however, it is more common for there to be one recognised chain of command. A chain of command is built into an organisational structure design to allow authority to be passed down from the top. Thus, each person in the chain is directly responsible to the authority above. In essence, a chain of command is a reporting mechanism that brings clarity to the issue of who gives orders, and to whom. To further clarify lines of authority, a general principle is that each worker should report to only one manager—this is termed the unity of command. This principle underpins the linear relationship that links the layers of authority from top to bottom in the organisation. Thus, each worker will know whom they should approach if they wish to discuss any issue regarding their duties.

Some of the most celebrated writers on management have been protagonists of the formal approach to organisational structure and the rigid adherence to concepts of authority, chain of command, and responsibility that flows from it. For example, as noted in Chapter 2, Max Weber emphasised the importance of the chain of command in underpinning his ideal of a bureaucracy defined by impersonality, authoritarian rule, and rationality. Frederick Taylor viewed the chain of command as a key element for ensuring that responsibility was firmly placed on managers. Henri Fayol included chain of command in his fourteen management principles. However, in the modern era, changes in attitudes, social relations in the workplace, organisational goals and objectives, access to and use of information technologies, types of products and services produced among other factors have resulted in a radical rethink of the relevance

Term
Definition

Chain of command: line of authority that extends from top to bottom in an organisation.

Critical reflection
Do modern businesses need a formal chain of command?

For many decades a formal chain of command was standard for the design of organisational structures. However, by the late twentieth century this paradigm had begun to be challenged by new approaches to organisational structure. In particular, it can be seen that a chain of command relies on some form of hierarchy within the organisation, one that has distinct layers of authority and power. This was effective in organisations where issues of efficiency and control were paramount. Firms producing a standardised product for the mass market found hierarchical structures with a formal chain of command conducive to their goals and objectives. However, many modern businesses rely on a different set of criteria for success. For example, very often it is the sharing of knowledge between workers that drives innovation as the source of competitive advantage. To facilitate this firms have abandoned hierarchical structures in favour of flatter, more egalitarian structures where more workers are brought into the decision making process and where power is distributed more equally. This makes a formal chain of command less relevant as workers collaborate together to solve problems and generate new ideas. So, although the concept of the chain of command is very much part of management, its primacy as a dominant approach has been undermined by more informal and free-flowing types of organisational structure. The linear relationship between different levels of authority has given way to more network orientated relationships within organisations, unencumbered by the rigidities of hierarchy.

117

of the role that a formal chain of command has in organisational structure. Kassing (2009) provides valuable observations on why employees might break the chain of command. These may include ethical reasons, competency reasons, matters of discipline, or safety considerations.

Span of control

The span of control in an organisation refers to the number of employees that any one manager is responsible for. Key to determining the span of control is the extent to which managerial responsibility can extend before it becomes too unwieldy and difficult to control. It is important to match the span of control with the managers' ability to effectively and efficiently manage the workforce within their range of responsibility. This decision will determine the number of managers required in the organisation and the level of authority and power needed to carry out their duties.

Importantly, the span of control has an influence on how effectively the organisation and coordination of activities and tasks are carried out (Daft, 2003). Responsibility for too many subordinates may result in an excessive management burden, a lack of effective control, and may ultimately lead to inefficiencies. Moreover, the acceptance of authority can be compromised by a lack of effective communication between managers and workers as they become increasingly distant from each other due to the sheer number of subordinates the manager has to deal with. Alternatively, too few subordinates may not be utilising the available management skills and capabilities to their fullest extent which, again, leads to inefficiencies. Supermarket giant *Tesco* continually review their

Term
Definition

Span of control: the number of employees that a manager is responsible for.

organisational structure with the aim of optimising the span of control. With typically six layers of management in each supermarket, it is the duty of the human resource (HR) manager to find the correct ratio between management and staff (Egremont, 2007). So, if the current ratio is 1:5 the HR manager will explore ways and means of making it 1:6 without any loss of efficiency, quality of customer service, or negative effect on staff/management relations.

Critical reflection
Is there an optimum number of workers for an effective span of control?

Experiments have been carried out to determine the optimum number of subordinates that should be allocated to a single manager. One of the early attempts to do this was by management consultant A. V. Graicumas (1933), who used mathematical formulae to help work out the optimal number of subordinates a manager should be allocated. The outcome revealed that the number of potential interactions with subordinates increases exponentially in relation to the manager's increasing span of control. Thus, adding a fifth subordinate to a manager's responsibilities raises potential interactions from 44 to 100; adding an eighth increases potential interactions from 490 to 1080, and so on. Graicumas concluded that the optimal number of subordinates was six, beyond which management becomes increasingly problematic and less effective. The work attracted the attention of renowned scholars including L. E. Urwick of Oxford University. In an article for the *Harvard Business Review* in 1956, Urwick concurs with many of the views expressed by Graicumas, although he stops short of endorsing his figure of six as being optimal. Of the span of control Urwick notes that 'there is nothing that rots morale more quickly and more completely than poor communication and indecisiveness-the feeling that those in authority do not know their own mind, and there is no condition which more quickly produces a sense of indecision among subordinates or more effectively hampers communication than being responsible to a superior who has too wide a span of control' (1956: 43). However, the outcomes of the experiments were never entirely convincing as the number of subordinates invariably changes according to factor variables such as the type of work, the culture and structure of the organisation, control systems, style of management, and so on. In reality, the appropriate span of control has to be determined by managers in the context of their own organisational setting.

In many modern businesses the span of control is determined by the nature and scope of the roles that exist within the organisation. In some instances, the functional activity is narrowly defined (such as warehousing) whereby the span of control is necessarily limited. Alternatively, there may be a diverse range of functions, meaning that the manager could have responsibility for subordinates in marketing, finance, and sales, thereby extending the span of control significantly. Daft (2003) links larger spans of control to situations where work performed by subordinates is stable, routine, and concentrated in a single location. Also, the complexity of the work has a role to play in determining the span of control. In organisations where activities are largely routine and standardised, the span of control can be extended as the burden of managing a relatively simple process is low. For example, on factory production lines managers can be responsible for a large number of workers engaged in routine tasks. Even so, there are some production companies that seek to broaden the span of control depending on the changing strategies. *Toyota*, a company renowned for lean production, announced in June 2010 that they intended to expand the number of front line managers and reduce the span of control as a means of improving quality assurance (Miller, 2010).

Where managers assume responsibility for a range of different and highly complex set of processes, the burden becomes much greater. In this case the span of control may be narrowed to allow better quality management over a smaller range of activities but ones which contribute greatly to the quality of outputs and help achieve a competitive advantage. For example, in genetic engineering, managers may have responsibility for a small number of highly skilled workers whose output is vital to the organisation's pursuit of strategic aims. Often, this may mean taking on more managers overall, but executive decision makers would have to weigh the benefits and costs of this human resource issue.

119

Span of control in the modern organisation

In much the same way that concepts of authority and chain of command have been subject to review and change in recent years, new ideas around the span of control have marked business transformation processes since the late 1990s. In particular, it is clear that the span of control for managers has increased as a result of technology where new channels of communication have opened up possibilities for liaising with the workforce through different forms of media including mobile telephony, social networking, and e-mail. Although these methods of communication cannot replace one-to-one contact, they do provide a mechanism for a dialogue that ensures that managers have some form of contact with workers at all times during a normal working day (exactly what constitutes a normal working day is a topic for more detailed discussion in Chapter 8 covering human resource management). Another reason for expanding the span of control stems from the nature of the workforce in modern businesses. Many workers are now part of small teams that are often self-managed and controlled. A great deal of autonomy is afforded to workers who are collaborating on projects, solving problems, creating new ideas, and sharing knowledge. Managers can be given a much greater span of control in such environments because the role is more about monitoring team performance than micro-managing individuals. This makes responsibility for a greater number of employees more manageable. Invariably workers who are afforded this greater freedom to self-manage are highly qualified, trained, motivated, and feel that they have a stakeholder position in the organisation. The extent to which authority and decision making is delegated throughout an organisation depends on the level to which these powers are centralised or decentralised. Trends in this issue tend to ebb and flow over time but as it is a key management decision it is worthy of further discussion.

Mini case 4.1
Chain of command in the Nigerian Police Force

The Nigerian Police Force (NPF) has been subject to a great deal of scrutiny and subsequent criticism for endemic corruption, abuse of power, and even extra-judicial killings (Uwaifo, 2012). These matters have been the subject of investigative reports that have been the catalyst for reform. A key factor in creating a culture where such abuses can flourish is the centralised control and command structure that has been a characteristic of the organisation. For example, all budgetary and fiscal control within the force resides with one person in the form of the Inspector General of Police (IGP). Such a concentration of power has resulted in endemic corruption, unaccountable patronage, and widespread financial mismanagement. The effect has been to diminish the ability of those in lower levels of command to resource the activities that they were responsible for such as riot control, robbery, and general policing. The second Presidential Committee on Police Reform (2008) highlighted the 'gross inadequacies of human, material and technological resources made available to the Nigerian Police', a criticism backed by the findings of researcher Aluyor (2005). One of the aspects of the NPF that came under review was the levels of authority and chain of command that underpinned the structure of the organisation.

In 2010 the NPF comprised over 380,000 personnel making it the largest institution in the country and the largest single employer. The ranking structure of the NPF is illustrated in Figure 4.1.

Each level of command within the NPF has its own span of control over a number of subordinates lower down. They must also report upwards to their line managers in the chain of command. The span of control expands with movement upwards through the ranks. Ultimately, the Inspector General of Police is responsible for all officers serving under his command. This ranking system

Figure 4.1 Ranking system in the Nigerian Police Force

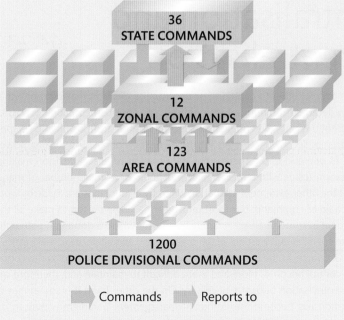

Figure 4.2 Command structure in the Nigerian Police Force

operates across all forces in the country. The country is divided into 36 state commands; 12 zonal commands; 123 area commands; and 1,200 police divisional commands as illustrated in Figure 4.2.

The structure of the organisation and the ranking system is very similar to other police forces around the world, particularly that of the UK. Indeed the structure of the NPF is a legacy of British colonial rule which formally ended in 1960. Although the structure, authority, and chain of command is potentially effective, the root cause of the problems associated with the NPF is the concentration of power at the top of the structure and the culture of patronage and corruption that has blighted attempts to reform the country's police and other national institutions.

Sources:

Aluyor, G. B. O. (2005), Performance evaluation of the Nigerian Police in crime prevention in urban areas', *Journal of Land Use and Development Studies*, Vol. 1, No. 1, pp 1–7.

Uwaifo, G. (28 October 2012) Restructuring of the Nigerian Police Force, *NigeriaWorld*. http://www.lafarge.com/wps/portal/1_6_1-Dates-cles

Discussion points

What are the main problems associated with centralising power and decision making in an organisation such as the NPF?

Is decentralising the NPF the answer to the problems of corruption and financial mismanagement?

Questions

Identify the advantages of the ranking system in the NPF.

What types of authority are evident in the NPF?

Is the span of control at each level of the NPF structure conducive to effective management of policing functions?

 Online Resource Centre
Author commentary on these discussion points and questions can be found on the Online Resource Centre at: www.oxfordtextbooks.co.uk/orc/combe1e/

121

Centralisation and decentralisation

The debate over whether to centralise or decentralise decision making is one that has raged on for many decades (Cummings, 1995). Although no conclusive outcome is possible, it is possible to present the issue of centralisation/decentralisation from a polemic perspective where the two extremes set the parameters for the delegation of decision making powers in an organisation. At one end of the spectrum is the situation where all decision making powers in the organisation reside with either a single individual or a small number of managers at the top level. At the other extreme is a situation whereby all decisions are made by workers further down the chain of command. It is most unusual for a single person to make all the decisions, but it is evident in some small-scale family businesses where a dominant patriarchal or matriarchal figure oversees every aspect of the organisation and all decision making flows from that individual. Of course, as the business grows and becomes more complex this concentration of power and control becomes more and more difficult to maintain and, therefore, an increasing level of decentralisation becomes necessary. On the other hand it is sometimes evident that decentralisation has become the dominant management paradigm within an organisation. Chandler and Ingrassia (1991) provide an overview of such trends among US firms in the early 1990s. For the most part, the level of delegation of decision making in most organisations resides somewhere between these two extremes and it is necessary to understand the merits and limitations of each approach. First, though, it is useful to set out the factors that influence decisions about the level of centralisation or decentralisation.

Influencing factors

The level of concentration of decision making power is dependent on a number of factors. These may include:

- history;
- size;
- products and services;
- structure;

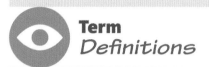

Term
Definitions

Centralisation: level to which decision making powers are concentrated among a few people at the top level of an organisation.

Decentralisation: level to which decision making powers are delegated to lower levels within an organisation.

- control;
- management style;
- trust.

History

Precedent may play a role as there may have been an elongated period of centralisation of control that has defined the management style and structure of the organisation and has stood the test of time. In this case, management may be reluctant to change what has become a defining characteristic of the organisation. Fast food retailers *Pizza Hut* and *Burger King* have always had a centralised structure as a means of maintaining control over the many thousands of outlets they own.

Size

The size and complexity of the organisation may have an influence because as the organisation grows and extends the number and type of activities engaged in, the more difficult it is to manage. This is especially the case when expansion entails subsidiaries abroad with both workers and functions dislocated from the headquarters. Franchising is a method of retaining control but taking advantage of local knowledge as the business expands globally. This was the preferred method that proved so successful for *The Body Shop*. Alternatively, small-scale businesses offer the opportunity for much greater centralisation of control as all aspects of the business are within the management sphere of a select few decision makers.

Products and services

The types of products and services produced have an influence on the delegation of decision making. In some organisations, such as hi-tech industries, the specialised nature of operations often requires superior technical understanding and, therefore, may result in a more decentralised form of decision making that matches capabilities with management power. In organisations delivering a more standardised product, the scope for centralising decision making is greater. In the service sector the delegation of decision making is variable according to the type of service being delivered but also on what the client expects. In many situations, clients require quick solutions which may require a greater degree of autonomy for workers in their decision making powers. In this instance, centralisation would simply slow down the process of delivering added value to clients.

Structure

Chapter 11 deals with organisational structure in some detail but, in the context of the centralisation/decentralisation debate, it is clear that structures are designed to facilitate one in favour of the other. Flatter structures tend to allow greater involvement in the decision making process with workers operating at a similar level in terms of power and authority; whereas tall, hierarchical structures tend to favour certain groups over others and power is vested in the few at the top of the organisation.

Control

Linked into the structure of the organisation is the level of control that is exercised by those in power over subordinates. Centralisation of decision making suggests a greater level of control compared to decentralisation where a more liberal regime is the norm. Although it is never easy to make hard and fast rules regarding the link between control and structure, clearly there are reasons why those structures are designed in the way they are. Part of the reason has to do with the company's policy on delegating power and decision making. Thus, the control function is a key factor when putting in place mechanisms to support either greater or lesser control. Control as a function of management is covered in more depth in Chapter 6.

Management style

The style of management is also key to understanding the level of centralisation or decentralisation. In some industries, the management style is characterised by close working relationships with workers, consensus, discussion, debate, and collaboration. Certainly in many creative industries, such as advertising and design, this forms an integral part of the dominant culture. In fact, a liberal regime may be seen as essential for driving innovation and stimulating new ideas. Here, decentralisation may be evident with key personnel throughout the organisation being given the freedom to explore opportunities and make decisions that support the pursuit of innovative suggestions. In this context, management style becomes an important strategic issue as it has a direct influence on creating a competitive advantage. Indeed, talent management has become a distinct area of study in itself with Aston and Morton (2005) and Collings and Mellahi (2009) providing some interesting reviews and investigations into the subject. In other organisational settings the management style may be one where the control function is a priority. In organisations such as call centres, production line factories, and fast food restaurants, decision making among workers at the operational level is likely to be limited as the nature of the work determines that processes and output are the dominant themes.

Trust

Delegating rights to decision making entails placing trust in workers to respond positively and responsibly to the power that has been bestowed upon them. Trust is a human construct that is dynamic, changeable, and subject to constant review based on experience. Decentralising decision making represents a leap of faith by managers and an increased level of risk. However, trust can be extended as well as reined in depending on outcomes. Pirson and Malhorta (2007) examine the management of trust across multiple stakeholder groups including employees while Mayer and Gavin (2005) offer a valuable assessment of the dynamics of trust between managers and employees and how it influences performance. Clearly, it is the role of those in positions of power to monitor and evaluate the returns on investment in trust that is forthcoming from workers over a period of time. In many ways, levels of centralisation or decentralisation reveal a lot about the level of trust between managers and workers in an organisation.

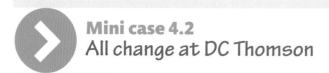

Mini case 4.2
All change at DC Thomson

DC Thomson is a major UK publisher of newspapers, magazines, and comics and was established in 1905 in Dundee. The organisation now has additional offices in Glasgow and London making it one of Europe's largest family-owned media businesses. In 2010 DC Thomson produced over 200 million print media products including the famous *Beano* and *Dandy* comics. Underpinning much of the success of the business is the legacy left by founder David Couper Thomson from whom the company takes its name. A strict Presbyterian, Thomson not only barred trade unions from his premises but also refused to employ Catholics, something that would be illegal in the modern era on the grounds of discrimination (Bell et al., 1999). Thomson prided himself on the discipline and regard for authority shown by his workers. How much of this was down to fear is open to conjecture. Nevertheless, the emphasis on command and control, authority, and rigid forms of work schedules were instrumental in the company's success throughout the twentieth century (Bell et al., 1999).

By the 1990s much of the strict management style displayed by Thomson and subsequent managers had been diluted as a combination of social, economic, and technological change brought in new forms of relationships between managers and workers. Technology in particular determined that new working relationships had to be instilled in order to get the best out of creative personnel. This was emphasised in the restructuring the company undertook in 2005 with the aim of improving business processes relating to subscription marketing and management. This also entailed introducing new working practices designed to drive volume sales and increase profitability.

The centralised control and rigid chain of command was relaxed, although not abandoned. Importantly, staff at all levels were consulted on the proposed changes, something DC Thomson himself would have found unthinkable. One key outcome of the restructuring was the creation of a 'direct-to-customer' sales department that has autonomous decision making powers and is viewed as a stand-alone profit centre. Thus, the company has undergone a transformation since the early 2000s that is designed to help meet the challenges of the media industry in the twenty-first century. The most radical change was the closure of the UK's oldest comic, the *Dandy*, in 2012 (Sweney, 2012). The case illustrates how some firms need to grasp change even though they may be tempted to cling to historical precedent. The decision to decentralise aspects of the business was a courageous one as it entailed formally ending the management style that had been responsible for the company's success in previous years. Nevertheless, it was a decision that had to be made to ensure that the company remained competitive in the modern era.

Sources:

Bell, A., Bradley, M. and Kemp, A. (15 August 1999) 'New nation, old bigotry', *Guardian*.

Sweney, J. (13 August 2012) 'Oldest comic, the Dandy, faces closure', *Guardian*.

Discussion points

Does history influence the way in which resources are organised and deployed in organisations?

Do workers benefit from the decentralisation of decision making in an organisation?

Questions and tasks

What was DC Thomson trying to achieve by decentralising parts of the organisation?

Research the history of DC Thomson and briefly outline the management philosophy underpinning the running of the business up to the 1990s.

Global media corporations are invariably run by powerful individuals (e.g. Rupert Murdoch, Silvio Berlusconi, Ted Turner). Why is this the case?

Online Resource Centre

Author commentary on these discussion points and questions can be found on the Online Resource Centre at: www.oxfordtextbooks.co.uk/orc/combe1e/

Centralisation

Centralisation refers to the extent to which decision making power is concentrated at a single point in an organisation. That point may be a small group of people at a particular level in the organisation. Either way, the power to make decisions is very much the preserve of the minority. Usually, the centralisation of decision making is concentrated in the top management level.

Advantages of centralisation

It would be wrong to assume that the centralisation of decision making in an organisation suggests a lack of trust between managers and employees, or that top management are autocratic and protective of their power. Very often there are sound economic, operational, or strategic reasons for centralisation. For example, it may be more cost effective to manage from the centre when standardised procedures underpin activities and the transformation of inputs into outputs. If such procedures have been tried and tested over time, and continue to deliver the strategic aims of the organisation, then there is little motivation to alter the status quo. Only when new advantages can be derived from change would it be necessary to look again at the decision making structure within the organisation. Of particular significance is the overall management of the organisation. Centralised decision making is undertaken to benefit the entire organisation. This may be in contrast to delegating decision making to particular departments where there is a risk that managers at departmental level will favour those within their sphere of influence. This may disadvantage other departments, lessen organisational cohesiveness, potentially lead to conflict, and risk the misalignment of strategy with stated aims.

Centralising decision making at the top level of an organisation may be beneficial as it taps into the human resources where executive skills reside. Experience, conceptual and analytical skills, or communications abilities may be key attributes possessed by top managers and, therefore, it is logical to concentrate decision making at that level. It is also the level at which leadership abilities are often most evident. Most workers expect to see leadership from the executive level to maintain confidence in the running of the organisation and to look to when the trading environment becomes challenging.

Advantages of decentralisation

Perhaps the most compelling reason for decentralising decision making is that it frees up time for senior management to concentrate on the strategic direction of the organisation. Many operational or business level decisions can be made lower down the hierarchy of an organisation, especially where the standardisation of procedures is a characteristic of the organisation (Ezigbo, 2012). In fact, it is probably unwise for senior managers to get involved in operational decision making as managers at that level are better placed to understand and act on what changes need to be undertaken. For example, marketing managers will have a better understanding of the firm's customers than executive level managers as they work with them on a daily basis. Similarly, production managers have the skills and expertise to know what the productive capacity of the organisation is, and the capability to change output and attend to issues of quality. These attributes are unlikely to be possessed by executive managers whose skills and experience lie in other areas. More importantly, if top managers become immersed in short- or medium-term decision making, it lessens the time and intensity of effort they can dedicate to strategy. As top managers are responsible for the long-term prospects of the organisation, it is rational to allow them to concentrate on strategic issues and delegate other matters to lower level management.

Decentralising decision making entails empowering workers further down the chain of command. This can have important morale boosting effects on those managers who feel they are being valued and trusted by senior managers. The further down the chain of command these decision making powers are delegated, the more workers will feel they have a greater stakeholding in the welfare and performance of the organisation (Leana, 1986). A highly motivated workforce is more likely to improve performance and create a positive organisational culture. For example, workers will be able to respond much more quickly to changes in the environment if they are able to make quick decisions. This increase in flexibility and speed are hallmarks of many modern businesses who seek competitive advantage by seizing the opportunities that emerge in the market but require fast responses. The more adept the organisation is at exploiting such opportunities, the better they perform against rivals. Thus, empowering workers through decentralisation is one way of achieving a competitive advantage.

Mini case 4.3
To centralise or decentralise? Procter & Gamble

Procter & Gamble is an American multinational corporation producing a wide range of consumer products, most notably soaps and detergents, but with a vast array of other products in their portfolio. The company operates extensively on all continents and had, until the mid-1990s, a decentralised structure whereby local managers had a great deal of autonomy to make decisions relating to the business units within their area. However, by 1995 the company was suffering a downturn in demand for their products in various regions and new competitors were threatening their market dominance. As part of a strategy for growth and enhanced performance, the company began the process of centralising decision making towards the headquarters based in Cincinnati, Ohio. One of the reasons cited for this move was evidence that global managers were no longer cooperating with each other. In fact, the structure of the organisation was viewed as an impediment to cooperation (Tomkins, 2000).

A restructuring divided global operations into geographical divisions in North America, Europe, the Middle East, and Asia, with a vice president assigned to oversee operations in each area, and cooperation with other areas. With the power balance more towards the centre, the company sought to control costs and make better use of resources. However, by the 2000s the centralised structure came under review as the trading environment changed, leading to losses at P&G and the abrupt departure of CEO Durk Jager (CNNMoney.com, 2000). Key to competitiveness was the ability to respond quickly to customer needs. Part of this process was the need for innovation in order to remain a leading player in a highly competitive industry. Thus, the strategy of centralisation was reversed to one of decentralisation whereby local managers were assigned greater authority to make on-the-spot decisions. This strategy was designed to make the company more flexible, agile, and responsive to changes in the environment, and ultimately, to improve competitiveness through innovation (Business Development Strategies, 2012). The case of Procter & Gamble illustrates the point that the issue of whether to centralise or decentralise decision making is subject to change depending on environmental conditions.

Sources:

Business Development Strategies (2012) The Strategic Development of Procter & Gamble into a Global Giant. http://wearedevelopment.net/2012/04/29/the-strategic-development-of-proctor-and-gamble-into-a-global-giant/

CNNMoney.com (2000) P&G CEO quits amid woes. http://money.cnn.com/2000/06/08/companies/procter/

Tomkins, R. (12 June 2000) 'Revenge of the Proctoids', *Financial Times*.

127

http://www.pg.com/

http://www.pg.com/

Discussion points

Is it suitable to centralise decision making when a corporation operates in many hundreds of product and market areas?

What environmental factors influence the decision to centralise or decentralise decision making in global corporations?

Questions

Identify the reasons for centralisation at Procter & Gamble in the mid-1990s.

Identify the reasons for decentralisation in the 2000s at the company.

Does the change in strategy signify flexibility to changes in the environment, or indecision regarding which approach is appropriate?

Online Resource Centre

Author commentary on these discussion points and questions can be found on the Online Resource Centre at: www.oxfordtextbooks.co.uk/orc/combe1e/

Limitations of centralisation and decentralisation

The limitation of one level of delegated decision making tends to be the corollary of the other. That is, the advantages of centralisation reveal the disadvantages of decentralisation and vice versa. For example, the centralisation of decision making is best suited to stable environments, whereas decentralisation is more appropriate in fast-moving, complex, and changeable environments. While centralisation is more likely in organisations where lower level managers are not skilled or experienced enough to assume that level of power, in decentralised organisations the prevailing assumption is that lower level workers seek, accept, and thrive on the responsibility bestowed upon them in the form of greater decision making power. The extent to which workers seek greater autonomy of decision making will depend on the organisational culture. Decentralised organisations need to have a culture where empowerment is a key feature of the working environment. This is less important in centralised organisations where the dominant culture is likely to be informed by processes, regulations, procedures, and formality.

Other key factors place limitations on the extent to which decision making is delegated throughout an organisation. The geographical spread of activities plays a role, as the more widely dispersed the organisation is the more difficult it is to manage from the centre, hence, decentralisation may be a rational choice. Also, the level of risk attached to decision making powers is significant. Where decisions have strategic significance the risk of decentralisation becomes increasingly problematic as failure may have disastrous consequences. Alternatively, relatively minor decisions will bear a smaller risk and are more likely to encourage decentralisation. Thus, the scope of decision making power plays a role in determining the extent of centralisation or decentralisation. Either way, it is the choice of top managers to determine the extent to which they wish to empower workers.

Organising human resources

Human resource management is discussed in more detail in Chapter 8. However, it is useful to recognise the organisation of human resources in this chapter as it plays an important part in decisions regarding authority, chain of command, and span of control. Key issues in the organisation of human resources include determining what work needs to be done and by whom, work specialisation, work schedules, and timeframes for completion. A distinction is made here between organising human resources, that entails setting out work specialisation and work schedules, and human resource management, which deals with recruitment and retention, employment contracts, conflict resolution, and strategic issues relating to personnel. Before going on to discuss work specialisation and schedules in more detail, it is worth pausing to gain the benefits that theory can bring to our understanding of the organisation of work design.

Theories of work design

Many theoretical perspectives have been taken to analyse and explain work design in many different settings. These include different organisational types (public, private, voluntary, etc.), under different political ideologies (capitalism, communism, mixed economy), and different types of working environments (heavy industry, service sector, creative, etc.). Four main theoretical perspectives have emerged that have spawned the most compelling arguments to reflect the diverse settings under which work is designed. These are outlined in Figure 4.3.

Process improvement

Process improvement theory recognises that work is completed through a series of phases or processes each of which delivers added value. Work processes are viewed as a key part of organisational functions and structure and a key element of work design (Davenport, 1992). Mostly suited to manufacturing or production line settings, this approach emphasises a structured, measured set of activities that are designed to produce a specified output for a particular customer or market. The main value of process improvement is that it concentrates the minds of managers on understanding how work processes evolve through the different phases such that improvements in quality can be derived.

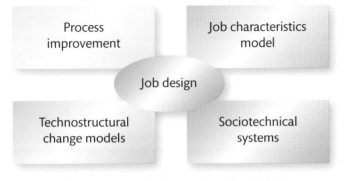

Figure 4.3 Theoretical perspectives of work design

Sociotechnical systems theory

The focus of sociotechnical systems theory (STS) is the enhancement of job satisfaction and improved productivity through the development of an effective work design process. Key to achieving these is the emphasis placed on interdependencies between, and among, people, technology, and the working environment. Thus, as protagonists of the theory Emery and Trist (1969) note, sociotechnical theory recognises that production processes are systems composed of human and technical elements and that understanding this relationship forms the basis of work designs that are responsive to both task requirements of the technology and the social and psychological needs of workers. The theory has inspired numerous studies including empirically based evidence in the field (Passmore et al., 1982; Parker and Wall, 1998). It also gave rise to related theoretical perspectives including the job characteristics model.

Job characteristics model

The job characteristics model is one of the most widely used theories for explaining work design in relation to worker motivation. The theory sets five core dimensions around which any job can be described. These include:

- skill variety;
- task identity;
- task significance;
- autonomy;
- feedback.

A central tenet of the theory is that the five core dimensions play a role in influencing and determining the psychology of workers when tasked to perform duties within a work environment and that this can be managed to deliver better outcomes. The theory has spawned a great many research investigations where the measurement of the potential of jobs to enhance worker satisfaction forms the basis of investigation. Many different aspects characterise the output, for example, some have focused on cross-cultural factors (Welsh et al., 1993), whereas others assess the extent to which workers are empowered to play a role in job design (Wrzesniewski and Dutton, 2001). It has also resulted in a huge output of different types of diagnostic survey methods to determine the effectiveness of job design (Johns et al., 1992).

Technostructural change models

Technostructural change models refer to change through the reconfiguration of the organisation's technology and structure. The purpose of this approach is to introduce change that enhances technical specialisation, expertise, and the decentralisation of authority away from headquarters. This approach is very much aligned with trends toward empowering highly skilled workers to take control of their outputs and to problem solve in their own working domain (Adler, 1992; Cummings and Worley, 2001). The technostructural change model features the development of network-based structures in organisations which is a key feature of many modern business environments.

Managing the organisation of work

Organising human resources serves a number of important purposes in an organisation and ensures that stated aims relating to functional activities are carried out effectively and efficiently (Daft et al., 2010). Three main managerial inputs are required for this. The first is to determine what work needs to be done and which department, division, or group within the organisation is responsible for its completion. There may be clusters of tasks to be carried out and it is the role of the manager to coordinate these tasks so that intended outcomes are achieved as efficiently as possible. The second managerial input is to assign work to particular individuals or groups of workers along with the appropriate level of responsibility for its completion. Here, it is necessary to address the issue of work specialisation, also known as the division of labour. Thirdly, managers need to schedule workloads so that there is on-going activity of workers leading to successful outcomes over a stated period of time. Work schedules help workers understand their duties and responsibilities according to their employment contract and the expectations of managers. They also help workers to organise their working days effectively so that they know what they have to do, when and how.

Identifying activities and assigning responsibility

Each organisation exists for a purpose; usually this is outlined in the mission statement. However, more detailed accounts of what activities are to be undertaken in order to achieve the mission of the organisation have to be formally stated. This is where the actual jobs or cluster of jobs are identified. Each organisation may have several clusters of jobs that, combined, comprise the activities that transform inputs into outputs. Lam (2005) asserts that innovative approaches to organising jobs can lead to improved performance and effectiveness. To achieve this it is essential that jobs are properly assigned to particular functions within the organisation such as marketing, sales, production, finance, etc. Some jobs may straddle two different functional areas and, therefore, it is necessary to assign responsibility and clearly set out the chain of command and line management for those jobs in order to avoid confusion and potential conflict and to smooth decision making.

One way to ensure that jobs are assigned to clearly identified workers is to create departments, divisions, or groups of workers where the jobs are grouped together. There are many different ways to classify different activities and jobs, but the purpose of creating a formal grouping is to set boundaries, demarcate tasks, and formally assign authority, chain of command, and span of control. Departments or divisions can be further sub-divided into areas of specialisation such as functional departments (marketing, sales, production, finance) or product departments (design, assembly, packaging, storage) where all activities support the delivery of products. Others may be based on geography (where jobs are grouped according to location), processes (where jobs are grouped according to the flow of activities that leads to output), or customer-orientated (where jobs are grouped to support customer service). The size of an organisation will determine the extent to which departmentalisation takes place: large organisations may feature several different types of departments, whereas small-scale businesses may only have one or two. Whatever the reason for introducing these groupings, they all provide a structure around which work activities can be identified and scheduled and responsibilities assigned.

Work specialisation

Work specialisation refers to the extent to which identified tasks in an organisation are divided into separate and discrete tasks. The purpose of work specialisation is to ensure that no one individual has the burden of undertaking the entire work task, but rather it is sub-divided into a series of smaller tasks that are undertaken by other workers assigned to the tasks.

As seen in Chapter 2 on management theory, the concept of work specialisation has a long history in formal working environments. When deployed properly it can help deliver increases

Work specialisation: the extent to which tasks and activities within an organisation are broken down into separate jobs.

in production and improved efficiency as workers know exactly what they have to do and in what order. Work specialisation was ideally suited to the factory systems that the likes of Adam Smith, Frederick Taylor, and Max Weber built their ideas of management around. However, work specialisation can only go so far before diseconomies of human resources kick in. This is where adding more workers to the tasks assigned actually incurs more costs than benefits. It may take longer to coordinate increasing numbers of workers, they may require more supervision as more diverse personalities are added to the mix, and issues of boredom, fatigue, low morale, etc. may manifest themselves in the form of decreases in output or poor quality products (Robbins and Coulter, 2012). Thus, work specialisation needs careful management to determine the optimal number of employees assigned to tasks and to check for signs of negative responses to the working environment. In modern businesses where production lines still feature, managers have introduced a range of measures to circumvent the negative aspects of work specialisation such as job rotation, extending the job design, greater freedom of association, access to training and education, and better physical working conditions.

Work schedules

It is the role of managers to organise the work schedules so that subordinates understand exactly what is required of them. Work schedules outline:

- what tasks need to be done;
- the order in which they are to be carried out;
- who is assigned to complete each task (individuals or groups);
- the timeframe for completion.

Work schedules: detailed account of what work tasks need to be undertaken, the order in which they are to be completed, who is to undertake the tasks, and the timeframe for completion.

Work schedule designs have been a feature of formal working environments since the emergence of the Industrial Revolution. They vary in format and complexity but they are all designed to underpin the outcomes detailed above. One of the earliest and most widely used formats is the Gantt Chart. Henry Gantt was a close colleague of Frederick Taylor and his work schedule design was very much aligned to the concept of scientific management that Taylor pioneered. The longevity of the Gantt Chart as a work schedule template owes much to its simplicity and effectiveness. Simply put, it shows actual and planned output over a period of time. Figure 4.4 illustrates the Gantt Chart. On the horizontal axis is the time dimension and on the vertical axis are the work activities to be scheduled. The chart offers a visual representation of what work has to be done, when it is to be completed, and progress towards its completion. For managers it allows them to monitor progress and helps them make decisions on how to complete tasks satisfactorily within a given timeframe (Gantt, 1919). A quick glance at a Gantt Chart informs a manager as to whether a task is ahead, behind, or on schedule for completion.

Managing the successful completion of the task requires planning and organising. In the Gantt Chart in Figure 4.4 the planning details the work activities needed to complete the task, the order in which they are to be undertaken (listed in the first column), and the timeframe for completion (months). The planned sequence is illustrated by a box located within a timeframe, represented by the green shaded boxes. The orange shaded boxes represent actual progress towards completion of the work activity. A quick glance at the chart reveals any deviations from planned schedule. Thus, it can be seen that Activities 6 and 7 have fallen behind schedule (by around 2 and 4 weeks respectively) and will require remedial action from managers to bring them up to speed if the planned timeframe for completion is to be met.

Gantt Charts and others of a similar nature have stood the test of time and are still widely used in many industry sectors, especially those featuring production lines or systematic work rotas. However, the working environment has undergone some transformation in the last two decades or so, such that new technology, new types of products and services, and the effects of globalisation and the rise of the service sector have all contributed to the need for managers

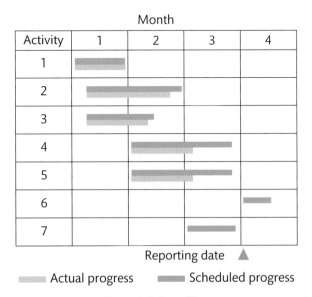

Figure 4.4 Gantt Chart

to think more closely about designing appropriate work schedules for their workforce. In particular, whilst the eight hour working day lasting from 9.00am to 5.00pm still remains prevalent, many other types of work schedules have emerged to better reflect the needs of business. For example, service sector workers such as business consultants and IT specialists often work flexible hours to accommodate the needs of their clients. Many workers operate remotely from a central headquarters or physical building where most functions are carried out. In some instances, workers can negotiate their work schedules around their other commitments or leisure time. This is often referred to as the work/life balance and has been the focus of much academic investigation and discussion (Bond, 2004; Facer and Wadsworth, 2008). These new forms of work arrangements have posed challenges as well as opportunities for managers as they seek to organise their human resources effectively.

The extent to which flexibility is built into employment contracts is dependent on a number of factors. First, the type of work has to be able to accommodate flexibility. Production processes may preclude this form of work schedule as it requires the physical presence of the worker at a particular location over a set period of time. Flexibility is also dependent on a certain level of trust. If workers are being allowed time away from the main location of employment (perhaps being allowed to work from home), then there has to be some means of ensuring that the worker is in fact being productive during those hours which comprise the working day. As the 'normal working day' is sometimes difficult to determine, this makes the issue of trust even more important. One area of contention is the extent to which employers should be able to monitor and control the activities of workers when they are physically dislocated from the main workplace. Some workers may feel that their right to privacy is being violated, whereas employers may argue that they have a duty to ensure that tasks are being carried out satisfactorily.

Types of flexible work schedules

There are many types of flexible working arrangements, some are limited in scope whereas others entail taking extended periods of time away from the working environment. The most common forms of flexible working include the following:

Flexitime

A system that allows employees to choose their start and finish times within set parameters. These typically involve extending the timeframe for work beyond the core hours when most business takes place.

Term
Definition

Flexible work schedules: the ability to design work schedules that operate across a broader time dimension.

Compressed working week

This form of flexible working entails compressing the work that would usually take place over five days into a more limited number of days, usually two or three. The number of hours completed in those days is increased to match those that would have been covered during the full five-day period.

Telecommuting

A system that allows workers to operate from home (or some other non-office location) during a pre-arranged time during the working week.

Job sharing

An agreement where two people share the same job.

Expanded leave

A system that allows employees the right to take extended periods of time away from work without losing any of their employment rights. This can be granted for a number of reasons such as academics taking a sabbatical, staff who have caring duties for family, medical reasons, or to expand skills and education.

Advantages of flexible work schedules

There are some distinct advantages to building flexibility into work schedules. Managers may seek to use flexibility as a means of boosting morale and motivation of workers as it offers workers more control over their working lives. Research by Kelliher and Anderson (2010) pointed to a correlation between flexible working arrangements and greater intensity of work effort by employees. The trust invested in workers by management may result in them being more committed to the goals and aims of the organisation and contribute to creating a positive organisational culture. This is especially the case for workers who are able to produce their best at certain times of the day. Some workers may schedule their workloads around other daily life commitments but still deliver a good quality output by the end of the day. Flexibility can be used as a means of attracting high quality employees who value the freedom it offers to self-manage their working lives. It can also help retain valued staff (Kalleberg, 2001).

There are direct economic benefits for employers who adopt a flexible work schedule and welfare benefits for employees (Osterman, 2000). The organisation may incur less overhead costs as workers share office space and equipment. Work schedules can be designed to maximise the capacity of the workspace. There may also be an opportunity to enhance customer service by ensuring that someone is always on duty to field their calls and deal with any issues that may arise. Access to high quality service encourages the brand loyalty of customers which is an important source of competitive advantage. In the public sector, stakeholders very often seek access to services outside normal working hours and flexible work schedules allow extended delivery of these.

Careful thought has to go into the design of flexible work schedules. Systems that are poorly thought through or poorly managed can have negative consequences for organisations. For example, flexibility may only be appropriate for certain workers. Those who are afforded the freedom to work from home may abuse the trust by not putting in a full day's work as other temptations or commitments pose challenges for their time. Also, those workers who need to be *in situ* may resent the freedom given to those who are allowed to take advantage of flexibility. In effect, to introduce a flexible system often entails managers treating workers differently, with all the potential for conflict that can arise from that. There are also the costs of travel and time associated with working in a defined location. This may cause economic disadvantage over a period of time that may further stoke resentment and feelings of discrimination.

Some systems may be well meaning but can lead to problems as it becomes the norm in the psyche of workers. For example, workers may be allowed flexitime on an ad hoc basis whereby they arrive sometime between 09.00 and 10.00 and make up any lost time at the end of the working day. If the organisation relies on those workers to offer customer service or support clients or suppliers during the hour of 09.00–10.00 then this arrangement will pose problems. Managers have to ensure that all angles are covered and that the core business functions do not suffer as a result of introducing more flexible arrangements.

? Critical reflection
Why have flexible working patterns become so prevalent in modern organisations?

Flexible working arrangements have become the norm in many business settings and in large part reflect the changes that are evident both in the business environment and society. The extensive use of software applications in information and communications technologies (ICTs) has facilitated more diverse forms of working arrangements including telecommuting (Potter, 2003). The globalisation of business has put pressure on companies to be 'open for business' around the clock (this is especially the case in e-commerce-based industries) as they try to deal with the effects of hypercompetition (Volberd, 1998). Changes in society in the last few decades have also been significant with more women taking up full-time employment. In future, it is likely that the workforce will comprise greater numbers of elderly people. All these changes require managers to think more creatively about the work schedules they can offer workers. However, such flexibility is not without some risks. Some critics have cited the fact that flexibility has blurred the lines between work and non-work activities to the detriment of both employers and employees (Bridges, 1994; Smith, 1997). The demarcation line between work and non-work life is a fine balance that some view as essential to the order of things. Friedman et al. (1998) view flexibility as a challenge to what they term 'the mutually reinforcing balance' of the work/life dichotomy.

Case study
Organising work schedules at Lafarge

Introduction

Lafarge is a Paris-based industrial company specialising in cement production, construction aggregates, concrete, and gypsum. It is the world's second largest producer behind the Swiss-based Holcim Group. Lafarge was established in 1833 by Joseph-Auguste Pavin de Lafarge in the Ardeche region of France, an area rich in limestone rock which is the raw material for cement. One of the firm's most significant early contracts was to supply lime for the building of the Suez Canal in 1864. Later, the company pioneered the production of white Portland cement, a product still in high demand today (Lafarge, 2013).

Lafarge expanded both its operations and product portfolio throughout the twentieth century. Key strategic developments included diversification into related industries, such as the 1980 merger with Coppee, the Belgian coal, coke, and fertiliser company, to form Lafarge Coppee. Key acquisitions followed including that of the UK quarry operator Redland in 1997, Hima Cement (Uganda) two years later, and in 2001 the purchase of the famous Blue Circle brand, making Lafarge one of the world's two biggest cement manufacturers. The company operates in many dozens of countries around the world with significant investments in fast developing nations such as India and Brazil.

The cement production process

Cement is manufactured using a combination of limestone and clay. Limestone is a sedimentary rock comprised mostly of calcite. The calcite is mostly comprised of the remains of organisms such as shellfish and corals. As generations of these organisms die they accumulate on the sea bed and over millennia form limestone rock. Although some limestone comprises pure calcite, most contains other elements such as sand or silt and is referred to as 'dirty limestone'.

Wherever significant deposits of limestone are to be found, then the potential for exploiting it for cement production exists. Typically, the limestone is quarried and then crushed into a fine powder material before being blended in the correct proportions. The blended raw material is termed 'kiln feed' or 'raw feed' and is heated to very high temperatures (around 1500°C) in kilns. The raw material enters the kiln cool and is then transferred through the heat to emerge as material called 'clinker' which resembles round nodules of around 25 millimetres in diameter. Once cooled the clinker is stored temporarily before being transferred to the cement mills where the material is ground into a fine powder. Gypsum (calcium sulphate) is added to the mix as an important binding agent along with water. The end product is a fine powder cement, either grey or white in colour, which is then transferred to silos to await packing. Once packed the cement is ready for distribution to construction sites around the world.

Work schedules

The production of cement is a process that requires a sequence of activities and functions. One of the main processes is the work of the kiln that transforms the raw material into clinker. The kiln has to be maintained within certain temperature ranges to ensure good quality clinker. Consequently, the only time the kilns are stopped is for major maintenance work. In fact, all the processes involved in producing cement run almost constantly not only to ensure high quality and high volume output, but also to keep the sequence of activities and functions

137

running in harmony with each other. This requires management to arrange work schedules for employees around the continuous process of the factory. Although technology has made many jobs in the cement factories redundant, there is still a great deal of human input required, ranging from quarry work to monitoring and managing the kilns and cement mills, to laboratory work to test quality levels. In most cement factories these activities go on around the clock with workers operating in shifts to ensure continuous production.

To ensure that production continues around the clock all year round Lafarge operate shift systems for workers. However, the system is not uniform in all plants and can vary even within operating plants. A number of different systems have been put into place according to the particular needs of the plant managers and the working habits of workers in different jobs in different countries. For example, quarry workers usually work a three-shift system with the first shift being 06.00 to 14.00; the second from 14.00 to 22.00; and the third from 22.00 to 06.00. This system operates over a five-day week, although workers normally have their days off on different days to ensure continuous production. Workers will change shifts over a set period of time. Table 4.1 outlines the three-shift system.

In the UK and USA a four-on/four-off system is evident within the cement factory such as the kiln or cement mills. In this system an employee works four days (normally on 12-hour shifts 06.00 to 18.00), and then has four days off. This gives the employee a 48-hour working week but compresses it into four days, followed by four days off. In the same way that the three-shift system fills a working week, similarly the four-on/four-off system is organised to ensure that all working days are filled for continuous production. Table 4.2 outlines a typical example of how this system is organised. Note that in this system the 'working week' effectively covers eight days as the shift pattern rolls out.

In some areas of the factory where most of the workers' duties entail non-physical work (such as monitoring instrumentation reading, evaluation, and report writing) a four-on/two-off system operates. In a normal seven-day working week this amounts to 60 hours worked through

Table 4.1

Three-shift system

Time		Sat	Sun	Mon	Tues	Wed	Thu	Fri
06.00	14.00	**Shift 1**	**Shift 1**	**Shift 1**	**Shift 1**	**Off**	**Off**
14.00	22.00	**Shift 2**	**Shift 2**	**Shift 2**	**Shift 2**	**Off**	**Off**
22.00	06.00	**Shift 3**	**Shift 3**	**Shift 3**	**Shift 3**	**Off**	**Off**

Table 4.2

Four-on/four-off system

Time	Sat	Sun	Mon	Tues	Wed	Thu	Fri	Sat
06.00–06.00								
06.00–18.00	**Day 1**	**Off**	**Off**	**Day 4**	**Off**	**Off**	**Off**	**Off**
19.00–07.00	**Off**	**Day 2**	**Day 3**	**Off**	**Off**	**Off**	**Off**	**Off**

Table 4.3	Four-on/two-off system							
Time	Sat	Sun	Mon	Tues	Wed	Thu	Fri
07.00–19.00	Day 1	Day 2	Day 3	Day 4	Off	Off	Day 5

the completion of four 12-hour shifts (although in some plants this is reduced to 48 hours for four eight-hour shifts with one day off). In this case another shift would cover the hours 19.00 to 07.00 to ensure continuous production. Sometimes workers work permanent night shifts in certain factories, in others the shift patterns switch after a period of time. Table 4.3 outlines how this system is organised.

It can be seen that Lafarge operate a range of different work schedules that are designed to offer flexibility to workers, suitable rest periods and ensure continuous production. There is also scope for workers to swap shifts or days on and off with each other as long as line management permission is sought and secured. From the company's perspective the shift systems work effectively as they ensure that the process of manufacturing cement continues uninterrupted.

Source:

Lafarge (2013) www.lafarge.com http://www.lafarge.com/wps/portal/1_6_1-Dates-cles

Questions and tasks

Research the Lafarge company and comment on the chain of command evident in a typical cement factory.

Why does Lafarge operate different work schedules in different factories and even within the same factory?

Are there any risks associated with operating a shift system?

The economic recession of 2010/11 led to a slump in the construction industry. What should management at Lafarge do to deal with the downturn in demand for their products?

In a process-driven organisation such as a cement factory, what can managers do to avoid monotony and boredom among the workforce?

Online Resource Centre

Author commentary on these questions can be found on the Online Resource Centre at: www.oxfordtextbooks.co.uk/orc/combe1e/

Summary

● **Understand the key components of organising**

The key components of organising comprise identifying work activities that need to be carried out and the schedule for their completion over a set period of time. Organising refers to the allocation of resources—the type, quantity, and manner of deployment to achieve stated goals and objectives.

● **Recognise formal approaches to the organisation of work**

Formal approaches to the organisation of work refers to the set rules, regulations, and procedures put in place to ensure that work is carried out as specified and scheduled and in a manner that is most conducive to achieving goals and objectives. Different organisations take different approaches to formalisation with some having clearly defined processes (e.g. production lines in factory systems) whereas others are less formal (e.g. some creative industries).

● **Appreciate the concepts of authority, chain of command, and span of control**

Three important characteristics of formal organisational designs were identified as authority, chain of command, and span of control. Authority is the power to command or control others; chain of command refers to the line authority from the top of the organisation to the bottom; and span of control is the number of subordinates a manager is responsible for. These concepts are necessary to underpin a formal organisational design but will vary according to the type of organisation, the products or services produced, and the organisational culture in relation to control.

● **Critically evaluate the advantages and limitations of the centralisation and decentralisation of decision making**

The formal organisational design reflects the management approach to organising resources. The issue of whether to centralise or decentralise decision making is further evidence of the prevailing view of management with regard to the type of management regime operated. The identified merits and limitations of each were identified and discussed in the context of different organisational settings and influencing factors such as organisational structure, history, size, and management style among others.

● **Comprehend key issues in the organisation of human resources**

Theoretical models were presented as a basis for discussing the diverse settings under which work is designed. Similarly, models for work specialisation and work schedules help managers plan and control work design. The discussion recognised that new forms of working arrangements, such as flexitime, have added to the complexity of organising human resources and thrown up as many challenges as opportunities. The twenty-first century workplace is a vastly different environment to that evident even as recently as the 1990s. Technology has played a key part in ensuring different forms of working arrangements are possible.

Conclusion

The organising of resources follows on from the planning process as a key function of management. Organising will be undertaken differently and in different ways according to the type of organisation, what it produces, its aims, the structure of the organisation, and the management style. Organising is a key management skill and is undertaken to ensure that resources are used effectively and efficiently. The trend towards globalisation and the opening up of new markets around the globe has altered the workplace irrevocably. These have created opportunities for organisations to compete on a global scale but raised the level of risk too. What is needed alongside planning and organising is strong leadership from managers as they strive to exploit the opportunities that the modern business world presents. Chapter 5 addresses leadership as an aspect of management. Importantly, it is necessary to think of leadership as a distinct attribute and skill that is different from management as a function. The reasons why this is so are outlined in more detail in the next chapter.

Chapter questions and tasks

Describe three types of authority.

What is the purpose of a Gantt chart?

Why is the formal work schedule still a prominent feature of organising modern working environments?

Is it possible to determine the optimal span of control for an organisation?

Online Resource Centre

Author commentary on these questions can be found on the Online Resource Centre at: www. oxfordtextbooks.co.uk/orc/combe1e/

Further reading

- Chokroverty, S. (2011) *20 Questions & Answers About: Shift Work Disorder*, Sudbury, MA, Jones and Bartlett.

  This book offers information and guidance for those facing the turmoil caused by shift work. The author provides useful responses to key questions relating to the negative effects of shift work. The physical and psychological effects of shift work are addressed and the author provides some guidance on the practical steps that workers can take to deal with them.

- Crosby, R. P. (1992) *Walking the Empowerment Tightrope: Balancing Management Authority and Employee Influence, Organization Design and Development*, New York, Incorporat.

  This book builds on the premise that without authority no one in an organisation is empowered. This theme is explored in detail and provides the basis for discussion around how to balance authority and power by empowering people and helping them to channel that power towards qualitative and productive ends. The book provides a valuable analysis of the delicate balance between authority and the need for workers to assume greater responsibilities.

- Gratton, L. (2011) *The Shift: The future of work is already here*, London, Collins.

  Gratton highlights the key factors that determine the significant changes currently impacting on working lives. In particular, the book examines five key forces that the author identifies as being central catalysts for changes to working lives. These include globalisation, society, demography, technology, and energy. The book provides a timely addition to discussions on this topic and updates the understanding of how the work environment is subject to change and what it means for workers in the twenty-first century.

- Kuehn, U. (2006) *Integrated Cost and Schedule Control in Project Management*, London, Management Concepts.

  Kuehn provides explanations of the tasks and techniques for effective project management. Among other issues addressed are the identification of work packages, budgets, and resource management. Useful insights are also provided on how to establish a cost/schedule performance measurement technique and the application of project control charts. The book offers an invaluable guide to the effective management of work schedules.

- Miller, D. P. (2008) *Building a Project Work Breakdown Structure: Visualizing Objectives, Deliverables, Activities and Schedules* (ESI International Project Management Series), Boca Raton, FL, Auerbach Publications.

  Miller employs the extensive use of diagrams to illustrate project planning and scheduling. The book gives a useful insight into how business professionals control and manage projects to ensure they are delivered on time and with targets achieved. The author explains the application of Work Breakdown Structure (WBS) in an eight-step process and applies it to different contexts including software development and events staging.

● Watson, T. (2006) *Organising and Managing Work* (2nd edn), Harlow, Financial Times/ Prentice Hall.

This book highlights the everyday practices of people at all levels in organisations as they manage their work. Watson calls on management theory to link into real-life practices and dilemmas to illustrate some approaches to dealing with conflict, ambiguity, and uncertainty in a range of different scenarios. The book delivers an examination of organisational events and issues through the use of case studies.

Online Resource Centre

For more information, updates, and multiple-choice questions, please visit the Online Resource Centre at: www.oxfordtextbooks.co.uk/orc/combe1e/

Skillset 4
Sourcing materials

4(a) Introduction

As discussed in Chapter 4, organising is a skill that entails arranging work activities and schedules in a way that helps the organisation to achieve its stated goals and objectives; likewise, as students you need to organise your resources to achieve your aims. One of these resources is the wealth of materials available to support your learning and assessment work. You will benefit from taking a formal approach to organising your resources to maximise the quality of materials you discover and use; and circumvent the disadvantages associated with information overload.

In the workplace, being able to source materials that support work tasks is an important skill in many occupations and professions. The plethora of information sources available through new technologies has made this skill even more important. Organisations have high expectations that graduates have a good understanding of how to work with new media technologies that support the sourcing of materials for writing reports and other documents.

This Skillset will help you search for appropriate materials for coursework/business reports and, consequently, save you time, enhance the quality of output; and underpins the type of discipline that you require to navigate your way through the various academic challenges you face. Finding sources is the initial, but important, part of the overall process of identifying sources, reading/evaluating them, and then using the sources to construct your arguments. This process is often called 'undertaking a literature review'. A literature review provides a coherently argued evaluation of a body of current knowledge relating to a particular topic (adapted from Machi and McEvoy, 2009).

The focus of this Skillset is on sourcing written/text-based materials but the principles also could be adapted to finding images and other media formats.

4(b) A process for sourcing materials

Imagine your tutor has given you a task relating to the topic of 'organising' in organisations. Part of this task is to review the current literature on the topic. It is tempting to 'jump in' and gather as much material as you can for your assessment or report. However, with easy access to what is an ever-increasing range of sources, many of them online and only a few clicks away, information overload (too many sources to deal with in a meaningful way) is a real possibility.

The following questions provide the basis for a simplified generic process for sourcing materials:

a What are you hoping to accomplish with the materials you find? In other words, 'what are you looking for'?

b Where will you look? Which of the sources that are available to you are best suited to your search?

c How will you look? What particular tactics will you use to search for materials?

d How will you evaluate what you find?

e How will you keep track of all the useful sources that you find?

Based on these questions a simplified process for sourcing materials is:

1 Identify the purpose of your search.
2 Decide on the boundaries of your search.
3 Identify the sources you will examine.
4 Create a search strategy.
5 Implement your search strategy.
6 Evaluate what you have found.
7 Capture bibliographic and other details of sources you regard as useful.

In practice, these stages may overlap. For example, you may not wait until you have completed all your searching (Stage 5) before capturing details of what you have already found to be useful (Stage 7). Each stage is discussed below.

4(c) Stage 1: Identify the purpose of your search

There is a saying 'begin with the end in mind'. What is the purpose of your search for relevant materials? This may be to define concepts; describe theories; identify examples to illustrate theories; discuss advantages and disadvantages; and so on.

It can be useful to have a 'research question'. For example, when is decentralised decision making most appropriate for an organisation? This question will guide your search. When you consider you have enough materials to 'answer' your question then it may be time to stop searching.

4(d) Stage 2: Decide on the boundaries of your search

Management topics, such as 'organising', can be broad in nature. Having identified the purpose of your search then it can be valuable to think about what the boundaries of the search may be. These boundaries may relate to (for example):

- **Time**—you may be interested in sources published on 'decentralisation' since the year 2000.
- **Geographical scope**—you may be interested in sources relating to 'decentralisation' and organisations in the United Kingdom (UK). Alternatively, you may be interested in particular countries such as the UK and China, perhaps to provide an element of comparison and contrast between the two.

- **Industry scope**—you may be interested in the automotive industry or the supermarket sector.

It can be useful to create a 'concept map' that outlines the key terms or concepts relating to your topic or question. These concepts, individually or in combination, can provide your search terms for Stages 4 and 5. You may wish to add to these as your search progresses. The concept map can be a key tool in deciding what the boundaries of your search will be.

Activity

The table below represents the start of a concept map for Chapter 4: Organising. The core concept, 'Organising' is in the centre and some of the key related concepts (for example Span of Control) are listed around the outside of the core concept. You could have as many or as few related concepts as you wish.

Task: Browse through Chapter 4 and identify what you regard as the key concepts around 'organising'. Then complete the concept map with what is appropriate for you. You may then wish to create a similar concept map for an assessment that you have to undertake.

Span of Control		
Chain of Command	**Organising**	

4(e) Stage 3: Identify the sources you will examine

Knowing where to look is important. Using the title of Chapter 4 'Organising' generated 7,070,000 hits from a search in the Google search engine. However as you are particularly interested in academic sources related to 'organising', using Google Scholar limited the number of hits to 360,000 hits. Google Scholar refines general searches to look at scholarly/academic sources.

Here are some generic sources of management-related literature (in alphabetical order rather than priority):

- Academic journal articles.
- Consultancy houses, for example articles published by McKinsey and Co in the *McKinsey Quarterly*.
- Electronic databases (for example Emerald) which provide access to a range of journals and other sources.
- Government (or their departments) reports or legislation, for example the Scottish Government.
- Market/industry reports, for example Keynote reports—Keynote are a UK-based provider of market intelligence.

- Newspapers ('quality' ones).
- Company websites (their 'official' websites that may have corporate information such as annual reports or recent news items).
- Professional/trade journals, for example *The Grocer* is a trade publication for the UK food and drink sector.
- Search engines such as Google or Google Scholar.
- Textbooks.

Many of the categories in this list (even those not identified as 'electronic') may be held electronically; for example, many textbooks are now available as e-books.

Where not to look? See the section below on the evaluation of sources, but remember that sites such as Wikipedia may not have been through the quality control/peer review process that other sources may have received.

It may be obvious, but your university librarians (who are experts in identifying sources and using search techniques) may be able to help you. Contact your librarian and you may be able to give them a list of key terms (see concept maps above), they will then use their expertise to suggest, or search, a range of sources on your behalf. Your librarians may have knowledge of, or access to, sources which you do not.

Some tips:

- Build up your own list of key sources on a topic.
- As a student (or staff member), you may require a special user ID and password to access the electronic resources your institution subscribes to. For example, if you are studying in the UK, it is important to know your Athens user ID and password.

The endpoint of this stage is a list of sources you wish to consult.

4(f) Stage 4: Create a search strategy

You now have a clear purpose in mind for your search and have a list of sources to consult. You still have some work to do. There may be variations in terminology or spelling used in different countries. For example the different spelling of 'centralisation' (UK) and 'centralization' (United States of America). Synonyms are words which, though different, have the same meaning. For example 'systematise' is a synonym for 'organise'. Depending on how inclusive and all encompassing you wish your final list of search terms to be, you may wish to extend the terms from your initial concept map.

Assuming that you wish to search for online resources, rather than typing in all the terms from your concept map (plus variations)—though that might be a starting point—you may wish to refine your search, using the advanced search options which are available for a number of online sources.

Operator	Outcome	Example
And	Results must combine both terms, so they *narrow* the range of potential results	Span of Control **AND** Decentralisation
Or	Results can combine either term, so they *broaden* the range of potential results	Centralisation **OR** Decentralisation
Not	Results disregard terms, so they *exclude* some potential results	Centralisation **NOT** Decentralisation

Typically, you can refine your search using what are called Boolean operators. These help you refine the logic and scope of your search. The most common terms are described in the table on page 145.

There may be other ways you can refine your search. Using the Google search engine, for example, you can use quotation marks to 'force' the search engine to look for exactly the phrase you have typed in: for example 'span of control'. It is worth spending time reading the Help Menu(s) for these resources. For example, there is an Advanced Scholar Search Tips page for some further advice on making effective use of Google Scholar (see http://scholar.google.co.uk/intl/en/scholar/refinesearch.html).

Another powerful way to search for materials is to identify specific sources such as academic journals and conduct a 'hand search'. In other words, sift through the Table of Contents and perhaps the abstracts of articles in each issue 'by hand' over a number of years—perhaps starting with the most recent issues. If available, it can be useful to browse print-based versions of the sources in this way. This is a powerful search technique, as it requires you to engage with key items from the range of potential sources in a deeper way than clicking from electronic source to source.

Some tips:

- It can be useful to find recent literature review articles on your topic. Other researchers or organisations may have also conducted a systematic search for materials relating to your topic. Try searching for your topic using the terms you are searching for and the term 'literature review'.
- Once you have identified a key author or topic, you could conduct a backwards or forwards search. A 'backwards' search follows, for example, a particular author or topic 'back' from the date of the publication you found. Alternatively a 'forwards' search looks for more recent work by the same author or on the same topic.

4(g) When to stop?

How do you know when you have found 'enough' information? This can be difficult to judge, as there will always be other sources to consider. This is where a clearly bounded objective and search strategy can help. A term used in the context of research is 'data saturation', referring to the situation where, although you could gather more data, you are not adding to your understanding of the issue or question you are examining. When looking for sources of information, consider stopping when you are not finding anything new that contributes to your task or review. For example, stop when the same articles are appearing as results from searches, or the same key authors are appearing. Some authors may publish widely based on similar material (over a comparatively short period) and they may not really have anything dramatically 'new' to say across a range of articles published over the same comparatively narrow timeframe.

4(h) Stage 6: Evaluate what you have found

By now, you may be feeling overwhelmed with the volume of potentially useful material you have found. Even using some of the operators and search techniques discussed above, you may still have a long list of sources. How do you evaluate which sources are most appropriate for you?

In evaluating the sources, there a number of interrelated questions you should ask yourself about the source(s) you have found. These include (adapted from material from the University of Berkeley Library, 2008):

- Does the source relate to your topic?
- Is the source too general or too specific for your needs?

- When was the source published? Typically, recently published sources are more useful. For websites, is there evidence of when the site was last updated? The lack of a date may indicate the site does not have appropriate authority or that the information is out of date.
- Do the contents of the source relate to the time period you are interested in? For example, you may be interested in the views of managers from the 1980s on centralisation versus decentralisation.
- Who was the intended audience of the source? For example, was it written for an academic reader, a practitioner/manager, or the public?
- Who is the author? What are their claims to being an expert in this area?
- What is the writing style adopted? Is it 'academic' in tone with references in the text and a list of references at the end? Does it adopt a balanced view or is it opinionated and/or biased? For example, does the writing clearly support a particular view, group or 'agenda'? More generally, does the writing seem 'rigorous' to you in presenting an evidence-based and balanced argument?

Based on the list above, there are a number of factors to consider. To narrow this down you should ask yourself two questions: Is this source suitable? Is this source authoritative? Your ability to make judgements about the sources you uncover is a skill worth developing.

Speed reading: Develop your skills in being able to speed read enough of a document to be able to identify whether it meets your needs or not. For an academic journal article, this may involve reading (in roughly this order) the abstract, introduction, and conclusions. If the author(s) has written the article well, then you should have a clear view from these three areas of the purpose of the paper, its scope, and the contribution to knowledge the authors were trying to achieve. Have a brief look at the reference list as it might suggest other articles worth looking for.

4(i) Stage 7: Capture bibliographic and other details of sources you regard as useful

Even using the strategies outlined above, you may have dozens or even hundreds of sources that are relevant/potentially relevant and useful. Your search may have been conducted over a number of days or weeks. How do you keep track of them all? Good practice is to keep a record of the bibliographic details of the sources you are going to investigate further/use, along with (initial) comments of what the papers contain and notes about what is most interesting/ useful about the paper.

You could do this via a table in a document or spreadsheet with appropriate headings for the bibliographic data (for example author(s) names, date of publication, title of source) and also your initial comments (for example: a survey of Nigerian managers' attitudes). You may wish to use/have access to bibliographic software applications such as Refworks or Endnote, which can help you manage the bibliographic details of the sources you find and wish to keep track of. Once stored in your database then these applications can generate a list of references for your work in a pre-set or user-specified format. Detailed discussion of these packages is beyond the scope of this Skillset. Consult the links to Refworks/Endnote websites given at the end of this Skillset for details regarding the functionality of these applications.

Tip: You may have made a mistake in entering text some weeks earlier. Remember to proof-read what the software generates, as it is only as good as the raw material entered (Garbage-in; Garbage-out).

4(j) Summary of the Skillset

This Skillset outlined some strategies for organising, in a systematic way, your approach to sourcing materials for undertaking assessments during your studies and for researching

147

reports in your workplace. This Skillset should be read in conjunction with Chapter 2's Skillset on referencing.

References/Further reading/Resources

Keynote Reports: http://www.keynote.co.uk/

Machi, L. A. and McEvoy, B. T. (2009) *The Literature Review: six steps to success*, Thousand Oaks, CA, Corwin Press.

McKinsey Quarterly: http://www.mckinseyquarterly.com/home.aspx

McMillan, K. and Weyers, J. (2009) *The Smarter Study Skills Companion* (2nd edn), Harlow, UK, Pearson Education.

Rowley, J. and Slack, F. (2004) 'Conducting a literature review', *Management Research News*, No. 6, pp. 31–9.

Bibliographic software

Endnote: http://www.endnote.com/

Refworks: http://www.refworks.com/

Evaluating sources

Massey University, APA Referencing: Electronic Sources: http://www.youtube.com/watch?feature=player_embedded&v=V6KZK4-SXfU [YouTube Video. The first part of this video focuses on evaluating online resources.]

University of California Berkeley Library (2008) Critical Evaluation of Resources: http://www.lib.berkeley.edu/instruct/guides/evaluation.html [See links at the foot of the page to other sources on evaluation.]

Help for using search engines

Google, Inside Search: http://support.google.com/websearch/?hl=en

5 Leading

Learning outcomes

- Understand the difference between leadership and management

- Relate theories of leadership to their application in different environments

- Evaluate the role of power and influence in different organisational settings

- Critically assess contingency theories of leadership

- Understand the concepts of, and differences between, transformational and transactional leadership

Winston Churchill was one of Britain's greatest ever leaders. Not only did he lead Britain to victory in the Second World War but he did so by raising spirits, motivating people, and mobilising the war effort. His communications skills were put to good use in a series of radio broadcasts when the outlook was at its bleakest. Churchill also possessed a ruthlessness and a focus on the bigger picture that was to prove decisive in turning the fortunes of war in the favour of Britain and her Allies. One of his many quotes on the issue of leadership was 'I see that a speaker at the week-end said that this was a time when leaders should keep their ears to the ground. All I can say is that the British nation will find it very hard to look up to leaders who are detected in that somewhat ungainly posture'. What Churchill was referring to was the requirement of leaders to understand and act in the long-term interests of the nation rather than to be distracted by endless minor issues that only affect short-term aims or operational issues. This is a maxim that applies equally to managers of organisations with a remit covering strategic aims. Managers at executive level need to look at the bigger picture, set long-term aims, and devise ways to reallocate resources to achieve those aims. Just as Churchill was able to call on the loyalty of followers during the war effort, so managers should strive to set out strategic aims that workers can understand and accept such that their leadership creates an effective following.

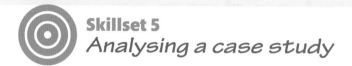

Skillset 5
Analysing a case study

Each chapter in this book has case studies to illustrate key issues and concepts. Case studies provide useful insights into the link between theory and practice. Skillset 5 provides guidance on techniques that help in the process of using case studies effectively.

Student study skills

Students will be presented with numerous case studies throughout their academic life. This Skillset outlines techniques for making the most of case studies by linking the structure and content to key learning outcomes.

Workplace skills

Students may have to take a leadership role in managing accounts, consultancy, research or other roles that require the articulation of case material as part of their work duties. This Skillset provides an insight into how to analyse case studies for maximum effect. It will also help students in the compilation of case studies which may form part of a report or summary article.

Definition

Leadership requires a following to be considered valid. Only when people accept the influencing power of a leader does it become an effective tool. Leadership is the ability to influence others to behave in ways that are conducive to achieving the aims and objectives set by a leader with managerial authority (Robbins and Coulter, 2012). In a business setting, leaders create the vision and mission of an organisation and determine its strategic direction and goals. To achieve

Leadership: the ability to influence a group in the attainment of goals or objectives.

these goals requires the workforce to respond positively to the direction given by the leader. Thus, leadership consists of a mix of different skills and attributes such as communication skills, analytical abilities, strategic thinking, inspirational and motivational personal traits, charisma and personality, intelligence, and so on. Leaders may specialise in just one of these and still be effective, or they may possess a mix of them that proves sufficient to create a following.

Introduction

Leadership has been a feature of academic enquiry ever since management became a formal subject of study in the eighteenth century. However, in similar fashion to management, leadership has been a characteristic of mankind since the dawn of civilisation. Stories of great leaders have formed the basis of legend. Some are inspirational and a force for good, whilst others have used their power for destructive means. Some examples include Genghis Khan (founder of the Mongol empire), Julius Caesar (Roman Emperor), Adolf Hitler (leader of the Nazi party), Mahatma Gandhi (father of modern India), and Nelson Mandela (anti-apartheid campaigner and President of South Africa). These leaders have achieved transformational leadership status through political ideologies that have influenced and gained the support of large numbers of followers. Without followers there can be no leadership.

The business world has also been a forum for the emergence of leaders. Although not as high profile as political leaders, business leaders have been able to use their power and influence in ways that can be viewed as transformational. For example, Henry Ford was instrumental in changing the way work was organised in order to facilitate the mass production of cars. Many of the techniques and principles that Ford introduced are still evident today. Whilst Ford's focus was on output and efficiency, other business leaders introduced a social welfare aspect to their philosophy. Seebohm Rowntree came from a family of chocolate makers in England that had its roots in the cathedral city of York. Following in the footsteps of his pioneering father Joseph, Seebohm set about creating a working environment that placed a high emphasis on worker welfare in an era defined by endemic social poverty (Rowntree, 1901). Here, it is possible to discern leadership characteristics that transcended business to incorporate issues of social reform. From the examples given, it is clear that leadership encapsulates many different characteristics of personality within a wide array of different settings. Motivations for leadership are often complex and determined by a wide range of influencing factors. This chapter on leadership works through this complexity by using theoretical models to shed light on a function of management that is an integral part of organisations but is very distinct from the other functions of planning, organising, and controlling.

The chapter opens with an explanation of the differences between management and leadership. This is necessary as it helps to place leadership in its appropriate context by articulating the difference between management as a function and leadership as a key skill or attribute of management. To aid an understanding of leadership, the chapter calls on theoretical models such as traits, situational, functional, behavioural and styles, transformational, and contingency approaches. Examples of leadership will be given throughout including those of transformational and transactional leadership in a business context. There will also be a treatment of power and influence within different organisational settings including the challenges of leading in a global context.

Management and leadership

Much of the discussion of management in this part of the book concerns the functions of management including planning, organising, and controlling. Leadership is also considered to be a function of management as it plays an important role in ensuring the effective running of an organisation. However, the attributes and characteristics of leadership are quite distinct from the other functions. For example, many of the skills required to plan and organise resources and to implement control mechanisms in an organisation can be considered tacit knowledge that can be transformed into written documents or passed on through knowledge sharing, education, or training. Management techniques are often based on tried and tested operational guidance that can be learnt and then communicated to others in the form of direction. Leadership as an attribute is an entirely different prospect and cannot easily be passed on in this manner. For example, some managers create a following by the force of their personality or charisma. Richard Branson is a high-profile champion of his company *Virgin* (as discussed in Chapter 1) and uses his personality as a means of communicating not just with his employees but with a wide range of stakeholders (Singai and Sriram, 2012).

Contrary to some of the modern day thinking around leadership, it is difficult to teach people how to project such a personality unless they already have that innate ability. Many of the traits required to be a leader are in the genes; people are born with character traits that allow them to assume leadership roles (De Neve et al., 2013). In some instances leaders emerge because of their technical or competence-based skills. In these cases the following emerges because of the inspirational effect their abilities have on others. For example, Steve Jobs of *Apple* had a worldwide following due to his strategic and innovative thinking around applications of technology. Nevertheless, he still had to communicate those ideas to a broad audience as a means of establishing that following.

Management and leadership are evident in organisations as they are inextricably linked. Kotter (1990) emphasised the order and efficiency that good management brings to an organisation whilst recognising that leadership is necessary to effect change and to provide motivation and inspiration to employees. Invariably, the manager and leader is one and the same person, as it is expected that the manager carries out functional duties whilst simultaneously displaying leadership qualities. The distinction between management and leadership can best be described as functions that create order and stability and ensure that processes are carried out efficiently (management), and attributes and skills that inspire, motivate, and effect change (leadership). Perhaps the most distinguishing feature of leadership is the attendant attribute of creating and communicating a vision for the organisation that inspires followers to want to contribute to its achievement.

Traits theory

A trait is an aspect of personality that influences behaviour in a particular direction. Personality traits are numerous and potentially complex as they consist of a range of innate characteristics formed by factors such genetic make-up, cognitive thinking, intelligence, culture, education, up-bringing, values and beliefs, morals, and so on (Kirkpatrick and Locke, 1991). The traits approach is the oldest in the study of leadership. It centres on the idea that there exists some quality in certain individuals which distinguishes them from others and marks them out as leaders. The 'great men' variant of this approach, first popularised by Thomas Carlyle (1888), assumed that these features were innate and qualities such as courage, willpower, flexibility of mind, knowledge, and integrity, were put forward as essential attributes. Judge et al. (2002) present some of the most common traits that have been identified, including:

- *Intelligence*: Should be above average but not of genius level. Particularly good at solving complex and abstract problems.
- *Initiative*: Independence and inventiveness, the capacity to perceive a need for action and the urge to do it.
- *Self-assurance*: Implies self-confidence, reasonably high self-ratings on competence and aspiration levels, and on perceived ultimate occupational level in society.
- *The helicopter factor*: The ability to rise above the particulars of a situation and perceive it in its relations to the overall environment.

Many different models have been developed over the years to test and assess personality types. Perhaps one of the most widely used is the Myers-Briggs Type Indicator (MBTI) that comprises 100 questions based on how respondents would feel or react to certain situations (Myers and McCaulley, 1985). The results from the test are used to classify respondents into one of four personality types including:

EI

Extroverted:	sociable, assertive and outgoing
Introverted:	quiet, unobtrusive, and shy

SN

Sensing:	practical and ordered, emphasis on routines
Intuitive:	reliant on subconscious processes, strategic in thinking

TF

Thinking:	use of reasoning, logic, and rational thought
Feeling:	emphasis on personal values and emotions

JP

Judging:	emphasis on control, order, and structure
Perceiving:	flexible with emphasis on spontaneity

Combinations of these classifications describe sixteen different personality types. For example, INTJ (introverted/intuitive/thinking/judging) are said to be visionary type personalities. Many organisations have used the Myers-Briggs Type Indicator as a means of trying to pre-determine the personality types of prospective employees as part of their human resources strategies. It is an indicator that is particularly attractive to employers operating in sectors where interpersonal relationships and emotional intelligence are considered premium assets. Typical users include firms in business management consultancy (KPMG, Deloittes), universities (Stanford, UCLA), hospitals (NHS), and retailers (Marks & Spencer). In such settings the personality traits of managers play a key role in setting the vision and culture of the organisation as well as providing strategic leadership.

Despite the fact that the MBTI has been widely adopted, it is not without its limitations. In particular, the framework requires personalities to be fitted into a given set of characteristics. Very often personalities are complex and changeable, making this process difficult and unreliable (Stricker and Ross, 1962). To address some of the shortcomings of the MBTI researchers focused attention on the key dimensions of personality that could be applicable to a broad range of people. In particular, the Five Factor Model has provided a basis for classifying human personality. Studies by Digman (1990), McCrea (1992), and Smith et al. (2001) have all contributed to understanding how to apply the model and its relative usefulness in different contexts. Table 5.1 gives an outline of the Five Factor Model.

Extraversion is the trait most associated with effective leadership due to their preponderance for dominating social situations through assertiveness. Here, the force of personality is as significant to leadership credentials as skills and experience. However, other traits are also evident in leaders such as high levels of emotional stability (similar to the helicopter effect when under intense pressure) and openness to experience that allows them to embrace or even effect change.

Contemporary perspectives of traits theory have placed less emphasis on innate characteristics in favour of ideas relating to socially acquired traits. Jung and Sosik (2006) focus attention on traits of self-monitoring, engagement in impression management, motivation to attain social power, and self-actualisation. Zacarro et al. (2004) emphasise the importance of self-awareness in leadership traits. The most contentious element of this is the attendant assumption that leadership as an attribute can be learned and that through certain forms of education or training managers can be imbued with the necessary traits of leadership. Although this idea is not new (the myth of the 'playing fields of Eton' as a producer of leaders has done much for the commercial success of public schools), it has gained in currency in the modern era. Many commercial training agencies base their programmes on the notion that leaders can be created (or existing managers made more effective) by subjecting them to outward-bound or commando-type courses. The idea of 'producing a leader' has also permeated some human resource departments of organisations where selection techniques have been designed to identify leadership traits in candidates.

Table 5.1   **Five Factor Model**

Personality type	Description
Extraversion	Gregarious, assertive, sociable
Agreeableness	Good-natured, cooperative, trusting
Conscientiousness	Responsible, dependable, persistent, organised
Emotional stability	Positive: calm, self-confident, secure Negative: nervous, depressed, insecure
Openness to experience	Imaginative, sensitive, curious

Critical reflection
Is it possible to define what makes an effective leader?

Attempts to establish clearly identifiable common factors that enable the compilation of a universal list of traits is problematic. As early as 1940 Bird investigated all the existing leadership traits and compiled a list of seventy-nine characteristics that differentiated leaders from non-leaders. However, the results showed that less than 5 per cent of these characteristics were common to four or more of the investigations. One of the several limitations of research into leadership is that the qualities that define effective leadership in one organisational setting may differ markedly from another. In some industries, such as engineering, leadership qualities are often linked to technical aptitude, whereas in the creative industries it is more often the force of personality and interpersonal skills that define effective leadership. In many cases it is the situation that defines an effective leader. For example, the qualities that made Winston Churchill a prime candidate for being a 'great leader' were effective only during times of war. In the aftermath of the Second World War he was defeated at the polls and his political career never recovered. Thus, leadership style can be seen to be effective in one situation but not in another.

Situational theory

Situational theory emerged as a different perspective to understanding leadership. Whereas proponents of trait theory believed that 'great men' found their place in history through effective leadership, social scientists believed that the contrary was the case. That is, events at important junctures in history produced the leaders who took command of the situation and achieved goals and objectives (Hersey and Blanchard, 1969). Importantly, situational theory assumes that different situations require different characteristics of personality or traits, that no one set of characteristics is deemed optimal. The work of Hersey and Blanchard is an example of the situational theory of leadership based on four leadership styles (from highly directive to laissez-faire) and four levels of follower (able, willing, unable, and unwilling). For effectiveness, Hersey and Blanchard assert that the leadership style must match the appropriate level of followership development. Thus, leadership behaviour becomes a function not only of the characteristics of the leader, but of the characteristics of followers as well.

 **Term**
Definition

Leadership traits: personal qualities or attributes that differentiate leaders from non-leaders.

Mini case 5.1
The charismatic Mr Chávez

The world of politics has been the crucible from which many leaders have emerged. There is no one set of traits that defines what a great leader is in this context. President Woodrow Wilson of the USA (1913–21) was notoriously introverted and found engaging with the public an ordeal. Nevertheless, through the power of his intellect and ability to mobilise people of influence around him, he attained the highest office in the land and led his country through the First World War. Nelson Mandela, on the other hand, exuded charisma and had a global following based on the transformational effect his communications skills had on political change in South Africa.

One of the most charismatic personalities in global politics in the early twenty-first century, until his untimely death in 2013, was the President of Venezuela, Hugo Chávez. Although Venezuela is an oil-rich state, there are pockets of extreme deprivation, social unrest (the country tops the league in murder rates per capita in South America), and political turmoil. However, Chávez managed to use the force of his personality to gather a following not just in Venezuela but internationally. Part of his appeal was the consistent manner in which he used the country's position as an important oil producer to wield influence and raise his political profile. In particular, he skilfully communicated the ideals of revolutionaries such as Che Guevara to challenge the US hegemony in the region (Marcano and Tyszka, 2008). Socialist principles have long been a feature of the Latin American psyche and he was able to tap into this mindset to create a considerable following. The romance of the under-dog taking on the giant neighbour is a common theme that finds favour among many people, especially those who are economically disadvantaged. Chávez used his charisma, intelligence, communications skills, and political know-how to gain the support of a sufficient number of people to maintain his power base in the country. The extent to which he was able to beguile many in his country was evident in the national outpouring of grief when he finally succumbed to cancer in February 2013. Carroll (2013) provides a valuable insight into the life and legacy of Chávez for Venezuela and its people.

Sources:

Carroll, R. (2013) *Comandante: Inside Hugo Chávez's Venezuela*, Edinburgh, Canongate Publishers.

Marcano, C. and Tyszka, A. B. (2008) *Hugo Chávez: The Definitive Biography of Venezuela's Controversial President*, New York, Random House.

Discussion point

Are charismatic leaders effective in politics?

Questions and tasks

Identify five personality traits that help to form a charismatic leader.

Is charisma necessary to become an effective leader?

Identify three charismatic leaders, one each from the world of business, politics, and sport.

Online Resource Centre

Author commentary on this discussion point and questions can be found on the Online Resource Centre at: www.oxfordtextbooks.co.uk/orc/combe1e/

Functional theory

Functional theory offers a useful insight into leadership by focusing attention on specific leader behaviours that are expected to deliver organisational effectiveness. Early work by McGrath (1962) and later Hackman and Walton (1986) emphasises the key role of the leader as one of facilitating the needs of workers to complete tasks. According to this view, leadership effectiveness is determined by the extent to which the leader has contributed to group effectiveness and group cohesion (Fleishman et al., 1991; Hackman and Wageman, 2005). Functional theory is flexible and can be applied not only to group leadership but also at the organisational leadership level (Zacarro et al., 2001). Klein et al. (2006) highlight five main functions of leadership for promoting group effectiveness. These include:

(i) environmental monitoring;

(ii) organising subordinate activities;

(iii) teaching and coaching subordinates;

(iv) motivating others;

(v) intervening actively in the work of the group.

A number of different leadership behaviours can be seen as facilitating these functions. For example, Fleishman (1953) used the categories previously developed by the Ohio Studies (these are discussed in some detail later in this chapter) of 'initiating structure' and 'consideration' as a basis for investigation. Initiating structure places the emphasis on task completion and involves role clarification, setting targets for performance and outcomes, and ensuring that subordinates understand their duty of achieving the set targets. Consideration is more concerned with relationship building and involves a range of emotional intelligence skills such as acts of support, guidance, and mentoring.

Styles and behavioural theories

A key characteristic of the styles approach to leadership is the recognition that any effective analysis has to include the followers as a factor. Leaders have to be adaptable in order to appeal to different types of followers. This adaptability will be most evident in the style of leadership they deploy. Very often the effectiveness of organisations is dependent on the choice of leadership style and how appropriate it is. Style theorists pursue a goal of determining the most appropriate style of leadership. Referring back to Chapter 2 on Management Theory, it can be seen that one of the early contributions to style theory was generated by the Hawthorne Studies, conducted between 1924 and 1932 by Elton Mayo and his team of researchers. The 'Hawthorne Effect' whereby output continued to rise despite changes to the physical working environment was explained by the fact that the social context of the work group had been altered, and the interest being displayed in the workers by the researchers was itself enough to generate greater productivity. The key finding was that the rise in output was caused by the style of supervision, and it was changed to a more human-relations oriented style that generated greater worker morale and increased output. Even though critics highlighted some significant weaknesses in the design and conduct of the studies, the outcomes radically changed the way managers and academics thought about leadership and management.

Mayo was just one of several influential writers and practitioners contributing to our understanding of leadership style in organisational settings. As a result many different styles of leadership have been identified and used as a basis for analysis, experimentation, and debate. The main types of leadership styles to have emerged from studies dating back to the early twentieth century are outlined in Table 5.2.

Table 5.2 Leadership styles

Style	Key writer	Description
Bureaucratic	Weber (1905)	Highly structured with clearly set procedures. Little or no scope for leaders to explore new problem solving techniques. Leaders adhere to set procedures before passing decision making to the next level in the hierarchy.
Charismatic	Weber (1905)	Leads by motivating workers through the force of personality and communications skills. Charismatic leaders are committed to the organisation and its goals.
Autocratic	Lewin, Lippett, and White (1939)	Autocratic leaders are bestowed power and authority to make decisions on their own. This style is effective where workers require close supervision but is less so in environments where innovation and creativity are key value adding activities.
Democratic	Lewin, Lippett, and White (1939)	Takes account of other opinions and ideas but, ultimately, makes the decision. Workers contribute to the final decision thereby increasing employee satisfaction. Capable of assimilating changes faster and more effectively by minimising resistance. Not effective when a quick decision is needed.
Laissez-faire	Lewin, Lippett, and White (1939)	Little guidance or feedback is given by the leader as workers are expected to be experienced and skilled enough to assume responsibility. Where this is not evident then the leaders are failing in their duty to lead.
People-orientated	Fiedler (1967)	Undertakes support, training, and development of workers, increasing loyalty and job satisfaction.
Task-orientated	Fiedler (1967)	Emphasis is on the task and its successful completion. Does not cater for the workers' emotional needs and requires the type of close supervision and control that some workers may resent. The leadership style is task and goal orientated.

Table 5.2	(Continued)		
	Style	**Key writer**	**Description**
	Servant leader	Greenleaf (1977)	The leader ensures that the workers have everything they need to be productive and complete the task. Workers perceive the leader as an instrument to be used in order to reach their goals rather than one who issues commands.
	Transactional	Burns (1978) Bass and Avolio (1991, 1993)	Empowered to perform certain tasks and to either reward or punish workers according to their performance. The manager leads workers and the workers consent to follow the leader.
	Transformational	Burns (1978) Bass and Avolio (1991, 1993)	Motivates workers to be effective and efficient. Superior communications skills form the basis of a relationship between leader and followers that focuses on goal attainment. Transformational leaders are strategic in their thinking and outlook.

Group dynamics and styles of leadership

Another major influence on thinking about leadership came from studies of group dynamics. This psychological perspective emanated from studies undertaken in the United States in the late 1930s and was concerned mainly with laboratory experiments aimed at ascertaining the dimensions and influences on small group behaviour, including the effect of leadership on the process whereby 'group norms' develop, and how 'conformity' may be induced in a group setting. A key writer in this aspect of leadership was Kurt Lewin, a German-Jewish Gestalt

Term Definitions

Behavioural theory: theoretical perspectives that support the view that particular behaviours separate leaders from followers.

Styles theories: theoretical perspectives that support the view that it is the style of management that separates leaders from followers.

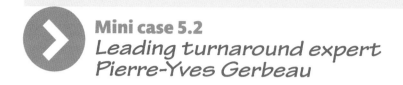

Mini case 5.2
Leading turnaround expert Pierre-Yves Gerbeau

Pierre-Yves Gerbeau is a French entrepreneur with a reputation for flair, dynamism, and the ability to turn his management skills to a multitude of different challenges. His leadership style is task-oriented with an emphasis on turning around organisations from positions of failure to success. Although not neglectful of workers' emotional needs, Gerbeau leads from the front by meeting challenges head-on. This style is conducive to getting things done as very often organisations are in dire need of rescue by the time he takes control and time is often a luxury. Thus, the leadership style involves hands-on control of managers assigned to tasks designed to transform the fortunes of the organisation.

Gerbeau has been involved in numerous turnaround strategies for organisations, most famously the controversial Millennium Dome in London that was originally built to be the centrepiece of the millennium celebrations in 2000. The project came in late and over budget, and was blighted by technical and reputational problems as an events venue. Gerbeau was hired for his turnaround skills which he had previously honed as executive manager at the ailing *Euro Disney*. As Chief Executive of the Millennium Dome his task-oriented skills allowed him to make quick decisions, follow them through, and ensure that each detail of what was decided was delivered. Gerbeau continues to believe in the guiding principle that business people, not politicians, should be in charge of large-scale projects (*Guardian*, 2000). His overriding management philosophy is one that emphasises the need for each tier of management to be made directly accountable, flexible, and able to understand risk. In particular, he believes that his leadership style has to be absorbed by other managers to ensure that decisions made are firm and consistent, rather than popular. Even so, his performance as Chief Executive won around many sceptics in both government and business circles (Walker, 2000). Underpinning this philosophy is a belief that leadership means leading by example and communicating the values of the organisation. In a few years Gerbeau and his team were able to turn around the fortunes of the Dome such that, by 2005, some six million visitors had passed through its doors. Now named the O2 Arena, the Dome is one of the foremost venues for entertainment in the UK.

Sources:

Guardian (16 Aaugust 2000) Live Chat.

Walker, A. (2000) PY Gerbeau: King of the Dome, BBC News Online, London.

> **Discussion point**

What motivates workers to follow a task-oriented leader?

> **Questions and tasks**

What is a 'turnaround' expert?

Research the profile of Pierre-Yves Gerbeau and highlight three other organisations (apart from the Dome and Disneyland Paris) that he has worked for.

Define the characteristics of a task-oriented leader.

Online Resource Centre

Author commentary on this discussion point and questions can be found on the Online Resource Centre at: www.oxfordtextbooks.co.uk/orc/combe1e/

psychologist who had escaped Nazi persecution in 1933. Lewin was influenced by his personal experiences during the Second World War, much of which proved to be a catalyst for his interest in perceptions of 'authoritarian' regimes. If the Hawthorne Studies had suggested that more permissive leadership appeared to generate greater organisational effectiveness, Lewin sought to discover why this was. His work set out to determine how various styles of leadership might influence the properties of groups and the behaviour of their members.

One important study was conducted with 10-year-old boys and sought to examine what factors induced different patterns of group behaviour, such as rebellion against authority or apathetic submissiveness to authoritarian domination. The study by Lewin, Lippitt, and White (1939) tried to answer the question 'Is not democratic group life more pleasant, but authoritarianism more efficient'? To answer this question the researchers created a basic design that involved four clubs of 10-year-old boys with each of the clubs being subjected to three different styles of adult leadership. The summary findings are outlined in Table 5.3.

Although the findings would come as no surprise to modern sociologists and psychologists, when they were published in the 1940s they marked a radical departure from the norms that

Table 5.3 **Summary of Lewin, Lippitt, and White study**

	Description	Findings
Authoritarian	The leader determined all strategy, dictated each step that was to be followed, decided what each member of the club was to do, and praised or criticized them personally.	Generated more hostility and aggression. Created 'scapegoats'. More discontent (some boys dropped out of the experiment). Greater dependence and less individuality.
Democratic	Policies and particular activities emerged from the discussion by the group, encouraged and assisted by the leader, with the division of tasks being left to the group and the leader being 'objective' rather than 'personal' in his praise and criticism.	More productive than laissez-faire, but less so than under authoritarian. Originality and motivation greater when leader was absent. Greater 'group-mindedness' and friendliness. More mutual praise and support.
Laissez-faire	Complete freedom for the group or individuals to decide what to do, without any involvement by the leader, who was willing only to supply information when asked and who commented very infrequently on any members' activity.	Less work was done. Work was of an inferior quality. Boys expressed a preference for a democratic leader.

were viewed as appropriate role behaviour for both teachers and managers. Lewin and his associates had taken the findings of the Hawthorne Studies a stage further by directly relating different leadership styles to the behaviour of small work groups in order to analyse both the social dimension and the effects on productivity. The study encouraged others to undertake further investigations designed to either validate or refute the findings in the context of the adult working environment and in the application of management techniques. Of the myriad different studies that followed, two of the most important were the studies into the effects of change in organisations by Coch and French (1948) and the effects of decision making roles in organisations by Morse and Reimer (1956).

Coch and French

The study by Coch and French (1948) into overcoming resistance to change considered the problems that arise when an industry is forced into change, leading to an alteration of the nature of the work which individuals are tasked to perform. The outcomes found that there was a close correlation between the need to change and higher levels of absenteeism, increased number of grievances, low efficiency and the restriction of output, and a marked increase in aggression towards management. The work focused on the reasons why change induced such strong emotions among workers and why it met with such high levels of resistance. The Coch and French study aimed to determine what leaders could do to overcome such resistance and for this they drew heavily on the work of Lewin et al. (1939), taking it further by examining both natural shifts in leadership patterns, when there was no stress in the organisation, and conditions where change was brought about by outside pressures. They found that both democratic and authoritarian leadership styles had roles to play, although in most circumstances, they concluded that the democratic style was the most suitable. However, much depends on the social cohesiveness of the group and the extent to which social pressure can be applied. This is most evident where goals are clearly stated, the pathway to achieving the goals are well defined, where individuals within the group can identify their own objective within the group objective, and where there is consensus in how to achieve the goals. Interestingly, the study found that when greater stress was applied with no clear goals stated, this resulted in a stronger compulsion among the group members to bestow power on a central person who would then assume responsibility for removing the ambiguity and reducing the stress.

Morse and Reimer

The study by Morse and Reimer (1956), carried out in a large industrial organisation, sought to examine two hypotheses:

(i) An increased role in the decision making process for rank and file groups increases their satisfaction, while a decreased role in decision making reduces satisfaction.

(ii) An increased role in the decision making process for rank and file groups increases their productivity, while a decreased role in decision making decreases productivity.

The results showed that the individual satisfactions of the members of the work groups increased significantly under the participative and employee-centred leadership programme, and significantly decreased in the authoritarian, non-participative control programme. However, although both the experimental and the control groups exhibited increased productivity, the authoritarian, production-oriented leaders in the control group were shown to have generated an even greater increase in productivity. The appearance of the 'Hawthorne effect' was discounted by the authors on the basis of the 'satisfaction findings' where they concluded that, had the experiment continued, the employee-centred leadership experimental groups would have produced the greater output in the long run. Subsequently a computer simulation substantiated this conclusion. By the mid-1950s the findings from such studies had been applied in the context of management and supervision in a number of large-scale organisations. The stage was now set for a theory of leadership and style which stressed participative management. The most important contributor to this school was Rensis Likert.

Table 5.4 summarises Rensis Likert's (1961) management style typology of four systems. According to Likert, System 4 management achieves high productivity, greater involvement of individuals, and better labour/management relationships. Likert also developed a sixty-four-item questionnaire, which was intended to measure employees' perceptions of the style of management they would prefer. Results usually showed that they would like a shift, but not a large one, towards the participative System 4. Likert believed that only when

Table 5.4 — **Likert's systems of management style**

System 1	System 2
• Exploitative and authoritarian	• Benevolent-authoritative
• Management use fear and threats	• Management uses rewards
• Communication is downward	• Attitudes to superiors are subservient; information flowing upward is restricted to 'what superiors want to hear'
• Superiors and subordinates are psychologically distant.	• Strategy decisions are taken at the top of the organisation.
• Majority of decisions are made at the top.	• Lesser decisions within a prescribed framework may be delegated downwards.

System 3	System 4
• Consultative	• Participative group management
• Management uses rewards and occasional punishment.	• Use of group participation and involvement in setting high performance goals and improving working methods; communication flows upwards, downwards, and laterally
• Some involvement of subordinates is sought.	• Communication is open.
• Communication is both up and down; upwards communication still tells superiors what they want to hear; subordinates can have a moderate amount of influence on the activities of their departments, since, although broad strategy decisions are taken at the top, more specific decisions are taken at lower level.	• Subordinates and superiors are psychologically close.
	• Decision making is spread throughout the organisation and is integrated into the formal structure through a series of overlapping groups with each group linked to the rest of the organisation by means of persons (called linking pins), who are members of more than one group.

Source: Based on Likert (1961).

Critical reflection
How robust is Likert's theory in helping us understand what makes an effective leader?

Although the work of Likert has been acclaimed and widely used, it is not without its critics. Some point to the fact that his theory is prescriptive and makes a number of assumptions which cannot be universally sustained. He assumed there to be complete harmony of interest across the organisation and he largely ignored the problems associated with role conflict among groups. Also, while it is possible for leaders to develop their subordinates into working teams with high levels of group loyalty, this is a scenario that may not always be necessary for effective action. To assume that work forms the focal point of life interest for all workers, or even for a large proportion of them in an organisation, ignores the distinct likelihood that, for a substantial number of people, work derives only instrumental value. That is, they work as a means to an end (mostly economic reward), rather than as a lifestyle choice. In fact, many people are indifferent or actively avoid jobs that proffer opportunities for roles that are difficult, important, or meaningful. Not all will strongly identify with their work and not all will necessarily prefer larger, more complex, or more interesting jobs.

leadership moved away from being 'task centred' to become 'employee centred' could the necessary supportive relationships develop. Employee-centred leadership would encourage a climate in which individuals would be self-motivated to strive for the achievement of organisational goals.

The Ohio Studies

An important contribution from behavioural theorists investigating leadership styles emerged from research at Ohio State University in the late 1940s. These constituted further developments on the work of Lewin, Lippitt, and White, who had identified the two polar opposite leadership styles of authoritarian and democratic, with the former being more related to concern for tasks and the latter more related to concern for people. The Ohio Studies identified two main dimensions of leadership. The first was related to task, and was termed 'initiating structure'. Stodgill (1948) describes this as reflecting the extent to which the leader restricts or facilitates the interactions of the group members towards goal attainment.

The second dimension was related to people, and was termed 'consideration' (Huczynski and Buchanan, 2007). This represents the extent to which the leader is considerate of the feelings of subordinates. The studies were carried out in a military setting where aircraft bomber crews had to complete a questionnaire evaluating the leadership style of their crew leader, with items related to the two dimensions. For example, in the 'initiating structure' dimension they analysed whether the leader normally made his own attitude clear to the crew, whereas on the 'consideration' dimension they examined whether he found time to listen to crew members. The following stage in the Ohio Studies was crucial in terms of revealing insights into leadership style. The initial task indicated how people differed in their style of leadership as perceived

Term Definitions

Initiating structure: extent to which the leader defines his/her role and those of subordinates to achieve goals and objectives.

Consideration: the extent to which a leader builds trust and respect of subordinates by considering their feelings.

by their subordinates. The subsequent step was to analyse how competent these leaders appeared to be in the eyes of their superiors. On the dimension 'initiating structure', the superiors' high ratings of the 'leader' correlated with the high ratings given by subordinates, but on 'consideration' there was either no correlation or a negative one. Thus the leaders who were judged competent by their own superiors tended to be high in 'initiating structure', but low on 'consideration'. Therefore, whilst superiors judged their leaders' competence mainly in terms of formal standards related to task, crew members claimed a higher degree of satisfaction under commanders who scored highly on consideration and who were judged by crew members, if anything, to be more competent.

The results of this part of the Ohio Studies appeared to suggest that the best choice of leader might be someone who could score above average on both dimensions, thus satisfying both his subordinates and those who gave him the task of leading. However, the Ohio Studies did not produce sufficiently consistent results to enable the researchers to relate the two dimensions to 'effectiveness' (Schriesheim et al., 1995). It is understandable that employees of any kind prefer those who manage them to show consideration, and perhaps this is especially true of bombing crews whose own lives could be in jeopardy if a commander put the performance of the task above all consideration for the crew. It became evident to a number of the Ohio researchers that something was missing from their analysis, and that was the situation.

The importance of the Ohio Studies, however, was that they enabled the leadership role to be conceptualised in a way that is manageable and which allows for some self-diagnosis and self-evaluation. Consequently, their approach of assessing leaders, in terms of task performance, came to be the basis of a number of techniques which were, and still are, widely used by consultants operating in the area of leadership and management training, and in the field of 'organisational development' (OD); which, although receiving minimal uptake as a means of pursuing organisation effectiveness in higher education, is more widely used in industry and, to a somewhat lesser extent, in the public services.

Contingency approaches

The research into leadership outlined previously has revealed that there is no one style which is best for all situations. One of the key writers on leadership, Fred Fiedler, made this notion axiomatic when developing what is termed a 'contingency' model of leadership style. Essentially,

Fiedler's theory proposed that effective group performance relied not only on the leadership style but also the degree to which the situation bestows control to the leader (Fiedler, 1967). Fiedler concentrated his efforts on the study of working groups whose members had to interact to achieve a common task. In an early experiment featuring schoolboy basketball teams, he expected to find that the most effective teams would also be the most close-knit in social terms. In fact he found that the teams with the best results were those whose leaders were the more psychologically distant. Follow-up studies to this led him to a conclusion which came to dominate all his later work. Fiedler concluded that

> a task-oriented leader performs best in situations at both extremes; those in which he has a great deal of influence and power, and also in situations where he has no influence and power over the other group members. Relationship-oriented leaders tend to perform best in mixed situations where they have only moderate influence over the group.

(Fiedler, 1967)

Of crucial importance to Fiedler's contingency model is the type of relationship that exists between the leader and the followers. Note that this is not the same thing as the style of leadership employed or even a product of that style; rather it could be determined by situational factors. The situation plays an influential role in determining the appropriateness of the leadership style and consequently its relative effectiveness. In situations where the leader is accepted, clear direction is preferred by followers. Where the leader is rejected, clear direction becomes imperative for the achievement of goals and objectives. On the other hand, where there was only a certain degree of acceptance, then the more relationship-oriented behaviour appeared to pay off in terms of better results. Based on his research, Fiedler (1967) presented two basic propositions:

(i) Leadership behaviour is distinguishable from leadership style; leadership behaviour may be altered, perhaps through skills training, but the leadership style of any individual is likely to remain essentially the same, because it derives from that individual's inner needs, which are unlikely to change.

(ii) The effectiveness of group performance depends on whether there is a match between the leadership style and the (favourable or unfavourable) characteristics of the situation.

Term
Definition

Contingency theory: that the effectiveness of groups depends on the fit between the leader's style of interactions with subordinates and the degree to which the situation bestows control on the leader.

The favourableness of the situation

Fiedler defined 'favourableness of the situation' as the degree to which the situation enables the leader to exert influence over the group. He identified the following three factors as being of major importance.

Position power

This relates to the degree to which the leader's position makes it likely that he or she will be supported. The General has more of this kind of power than the Lieutenant, and the head of department more than the senior lecturer.

Task structure

This relates to the extent to which the task can be clearly defined and structured. With a highly structured task, where individual members of the team have specific and detailed steps to perform, the situation favours the leader.

Leader–member relations

This relates to the extent to which the leader is accepted, respected, liked, and trusted. The leader who has such relations with his or her followers can influence them almost regardless of his or her position power. The one who does not have such relations depends on position power for influence.

Of the three factors referred to above in terms of favourableness, the most important proved to be the leader–member relations; position power came last, although it still mattered. Task-oriented leaders proved to be more effective in situations which were either highly favourable to them or relatively unfavourable. Relationship-oriented leaders tended to be more effective in situations which were moderately favourable to them. So, what are the implications of Fiedler's theory? If a leader's style is inappropriate to the situation, is it realistic to think that the style can be fundamentally changed? Fielder thought not. Might it be easier to get rid of the leader? Perhaps, but situations change, and it would not be feasible to appoint and dismiss leaders as frequently as there are new situations (Ashour, 1973).

167

Critical reflection
What is the bais of Fiedler's position on leadership performance?

Fiedler is suggesting that leadership performance can be improved by fitting the job to the leader. This is not as hard as it sounds, particularly if we think of leadership being exercised by a senior management team. If the members of the team have different styles, it is feasible to match the right leader to the particular task in hand. Although Fiedler's work has been subject to criticism, it remains an influential and useful model as it takes into account the situation when thinking about leadership style, something that previous studies tended to ignore.

Transformational and transactional leadership

The main theoretical models presented in the previous discussion in this chapter have featured forms of transactional leadership (Ohio Studies, Fiedler, etc.) where the individual leader directs, motivates, and influences followers to act in ways conducive to achieving stated goals and objectives. Here, the leader communicates the nature of the task(s) and the role(s) required to undertake them to the followers. There are a number of factors that characterise this form of leadership. First, there is normally a reward system in place that is underpinned by a formal contract (Robbins and Coulter, 2012). This is necessary to ensure that followers are suitably rewarded for their performance. The reward system may extend beyond economic rewards to include promotion, increased decision making powers, greater freedom to explore new ideas, leadership of a project team, and so on. Secondly, the style of management may include intervention when actions or outcome deviate from a previously agreed standard or pathway. The type of intervention will depend on the leadership style; some may be passive (only intervenes when there is evidence of deviation) or active (seeks evidence of deviation). However, it is worth noting that transactional forms of leadership can include the laissez-faire approach whereby the leader takes an inactive, passive, and non-interventionist stance. It can be argued that this barely constitutes leadership at all but much depends on the organisational culture and the reaction of workers to the environment that this style creates.

Transactional leadership is in stark contrast to transformational leadership where the individual leader uses force of personality and communication skills to inspire followers to undertake actions that are primarily in the interests of the organisation or the goal(s) set. In transformational leadership, self-interest takes a subordinate position to the achievement of the goal(s). Transformational leaders usually have a profound and powerful effect on those followers whose actions they seek to influence. Once followers 'buy-into' the goal or objective of the leader they become highly self-motivated in the tasks that help in the pursuit of the goal or objective. In politics, for example, Nelson Mandela was a globally recognised transformational leader who gathered a following in the pursuit of the goal of dismantling the racially discriminatory social and political structure of 'apartheid' in South Africa.

Ling et al. (2008) analyse the effect of transformational leadership on corporate entrepreneurship. In this environment, transformational leaders inspire followers to seek new and better ways of producing, marketing, and selling products and services. Or, they may motivate people to perform beyond their current capabilities by encouraging them to engage in developmental activities or improving their skillsets. The key to transformational leadership in business is to influence stakeholders in a way that makes them want to contribute to the organisation's goals. This is achieved by instilling a sense of greater purpose in the followers, perhaps by giving a sense of pride to be part of something bigger and more rewarding than simply undertaking an agreed set of tasks for a specified reward. Transformational leaders need to be able to communicate ideals and a vision that encourages followers to raise their performance and seek new and innovative ways of contributing to the organisation's goals and objectives. This may be expressed in a myriad of different ways including intellectual (such as problem solving), creative (new designs for products), innovative (new and better ways of producing the product), or emotional (mentoring subordinates) that contribute to the achievement of goals and objectives. The key characteristic of transformational leadership is that followers

Term
Definitions

Transactional leadership: leaders who guide, mentor, and motivate followers by clearly establishing roles and tasks for the achievement of the stated aims or goals.

Transformational leadership: leaders who inspire followers to act in ways that benefit the organisation or a wider cause other than their own self-interest.

willingly undertake actions that add value and contribute to goal achievement as a result of the respect, trust, and admiration they have for the leader and the ideals he or she promotes (Bono and Judge, 2003). Consequently, transformational leaders tend to instil greater ambition in the minds of followers.

Power and influence

Power and influence are very closely related to leadership. Power can be said to be a capacity that an individual or group has to influence the behaviour of others (Daft, 2008). The exercise of power means that others (followers) behave in a manner that the leader wants. It should be noted that power may not necessarily have to be exercised in order to achieve this outcome. The assumption that power exists may be sufficient to influence the behaviour of followers. Thus, it can be said that a dependency relationship forms between the individual or group with power and the followers. That is, the greater the dependency that followers have on the leader, the greater the level of power the leader has. However, dependency is not a static phenomenon but is subject to change (Mintzberg, 1983). Followers will constantly review their level of dependency and the outcome of this will, in turn, be reflected in revised levels of power and influence that the leader has. In effect, power derives from the ability of the holder of power to control something desired by followers (freedom, money, status, time, etc.).

Power is a key determinant of the type and style of leadership exercised. There are five main sources of power including coercive, reward, legitimate, expert, and referent (Daft, 2008). Table 5.5 describes these different sources. Leaders have been known to employ one or more of these sources of power as a means of influencing the behaviour of followers. For example, there is an element of coercive power in prisons as a means of maintaining control. Leaders in the prison service create an environment whereby their authority and control is underpinned by a climate of fear or enforced compliance with rules and regulations. Punishments such as solitary confinement or the denial of privileges are common forms of punishment dealt out to miscreants who step out of line.

Of course, long-term compliance in this environment may also result in rewards for prisoners, such as extended home visits or detention in lower security facilities. The combination of punishment and reward underscores the culture within the organisation and informs the type

Table 5.5	Sources of power	

Source of power	Definition
Coercive	Power is dependent on fear. People react out of the fear of the negative consequences of non-compliance.
Reward	Compliance is achieved through the ability to dispense rewards that followers perceive as valuable.
Legitimate	Power is derived from the status or position that a person holds within an organisation.
Expert	Power is derived from the possession of skills, experience, or expertise that others aspire to and may seek to emulate.
Referent	Power is derived from the possession of valuable resources or personal traits that are valued by others.

of leadership style. In terms of leadership style, this example can be seen to be bureaucratic and/or autocratic.

In other settings the reward system forms the major motivating factor and contributes to the evident leadership style. In the financial markets of London and New York the culture is one of aggressively pursuing performance targets. The leadership style is invariably determined by the expertise shown by those in positions of authority. That is, they have already proved themselves adept in the highly competitive arena and have exhibited a level of expertise that commands the respect of followers who seek to emulate their feats. This leadership style is one that is task-orientated or even transformational.

A legitimate source of power is derived from the acquisition of status that bestows a level of authority and control over others (Daft, 2008). As people are allocated tasks within an organisation, there is usually a level of responsibility and attendant authority that links to the status. Executive managers have more legitimate power to make decisions than middle managers; the Dean of a university has more legitimate power than a lecturer; an army general has more legitimate power than a corporal, and so on. Legitimate power is closely linked to leadership style as it bestows an authority on an individual that can then be used as a means of influencing the behaviour of subordinates. There is no particular style of leadership that links to legitimate power as much depends on the organisational setting, the level of authority, the personality of the leader, the attitudes of subordinates to the legitimate power holder, the culture of the organisation, and a host of other variables. Nevertheless, legitimate power is the most common and most highly visible form of power within organisations. In some cases legitimate power is symbolised by regalia and emblems such as in the number of stripes given to various ranks in the armed forces, the title of doctor or professor in universities, or the elaborate headwear of tribal chiefs in some traditional African communities. Although the link between power and influence and leadership is clear, the manner in which it plays out in different organisational settings makes generalisations unsatisfactory. Leadership style is dependent on a number of social, personality, emotional, and cultural factors that all play a part alongside the acquisition of power and the influence that comes with it.

Mini case 5.3
FIFA: Crisis? What crisis?

FIFA is the world governing body of football with over 200 member states (more than the United Nations) split into six confederations covering all continents around the globe. Based in Switzerland, the FIFA Congress elects a President, General Secretary, and the Executive Committee. The role of President is the most important leadership position and certainly the most high profile. Sepp Blatter became the 8th President of FIFA in 1998. His tenure has been characterised by his management of football into a truly global phenomenon and a multi-billion dollar industry. Alongside managing this huge transitional phase in football, Blatter has had to contend with allegations of corruption within the organisation he heads.

FIFA is essentially a bureaucracy with most of the power residing with the President. It has been Blatter's personal mission to ensure that the World Cup is held in locations that reflect the truly global appeal of the sport. Consequently, host nations have included Japan/South Korea and South Africa as well as traditional football strongholds such as Germany. Perhaps the most controversial decision of the FIFA executive was the choice of Qatar to host the 2022 World Cup, a country that has no real football tradition and where summer temperatures can reach 50°C.

In May 2011 Blatter addressed the world's media to answer questions about corruption and the handling of the World Cup host nation process. Adopting the management technique of underplaying the seriousness of the situation to defuse criticism, Blatter famously retorted 'Crisis? What is a crisis?' (Scott, 2011). However, there was a political astuteness to his response as he knew that his continued leadership relied not on the storm of controversy that the media would whip up, but rather to the power brokers of FIFA that are the executive members and the big sponsors such as Adidas and Nike. Blatter's leadership style is bureaucratic and controlling, both necessary elements in managing a sport that so often mixes politics and economics. For example, under his tenure FIFA has amassed some $1.85 billion in broadcast rights revenue and secured lucrative long-term contracts with leading brands such as sportswear leaders Adidas, Samsung electronics, and Budweiser beer among others (FIFA, 2012). Blatter has been able to use the commercial pulling power of FIFA to bolster his leadership credentials among the decision makers both internal and external to the organisation. Many of the member states of FIFA rely on the financial success of the organisation as they receive annual income from the governing body and this may account for some of Blatter's popularity among small nations with voting rights in FIFA elections.

Sources:

FIFA (2012) Finances, income. http://www.fifa.com/aboutfifa/finances/income.html

Scott, M. (21 May 2011) 'FIFA president Sepp Blatter to football world: "Crisis? What is a crisis?"', *Guardian*.

Discussion points

Do the structure and governance procedures of FIFA confer too much power on the leader?

Is there a crisis of leadership at FIFA?

http://www.fifa.com/

http://www.fifa.com/

Questions and tasks

Identify the source of power and the style of leadership of Sepp Blatter.

What style of leadership is most appropriate for a global organisation such as FIFA?

Identify five main sponsors of the FIFA World Cup.

 Online Resource Centre
Author commentary on this discussion point and questions can be found on the Online Resource Centre at: www.oxfordtextbooks.co.uk/orc/combe1e/

Leadership in a global environment

The modern business environment is characterised by increasing complexity, rapid change, and a great deal of uncertainty. The global economic downturn initiated by financial meltdown known as the 'credit crunch' of 2008 was compounded by Eurozone currency crises (most notably in Greece and Italy) and the human, environmental, and financial costs of the Japanese tsunami of 2011. This unstable and turbulent environment is the one in which modern managers have to hone their leadership skills. However, the main challenges remain the same: to lead the process of planning, organising, and controlling resources to achieve both the short- and long-term aims and objectives of their organisations. The nature of the environment makes these tasks much more challenging but nevertheless the key functions of managers remain relevant.

Saee (2005) analyses the leadership skills required in twenty-first-century organisations. Globalisation has presented a trading environment that is open 24 hours a day, with instant communications and dynamic and unpredictable markets. Consumer demand characteristics change more rapidly and supply chain expectations have been ratcheted upwards. These are just some of the pressures facing leaders in modern businesses. To cope with such complexity, leaders have had to become adept at understanding the strategic significance of human capital, knowledge, and the power of learning in organisations. The concept of continuous development is one that applies not only to staff but to managers and leaders too.

Organisational structures have become more diverse and flexible thereby requiring different forms of leadership. Delegation, trust, and empowerment are just some of the characteristics of modern businesses whereby leaders bestow greater power on how outcomes are achieved onto subordinates. In some instances, such as in network or virtual organisations, the leadership is dislocated from followers. This adds another dimension to the type of leadership style that is effective in a digital economy where technology plays a central role in facilitating relationships. Chapter 11 on Organisational Structure explores these concepts in more detail, but it is worth noting here that new forms of structure have had the effect of changing the type of leadership style in organisations where management is either 'horizontal' or part of a network rather than hierarchical in nature. This has necessarily required leaders to adopt a greater awareness of cross-cultural team working where the emphasis is on people-orientated leadership skills rather than task-driven ones.

Another significant challenge facing modern business leaders is to create institutions and corporate entities that the wider public can have confidence in (Kim et al., 2009). The ethical dimension to corporate governance has taken on a greater significance since the financial crisis of 2008 when consumers' confidence in the integrity of public and private institutions was seen as having been compromised. It is incumbent on the next generation of business leaders to re-engage with stakeholders by demonstrably raising the standards of corporate ethics and corporate social responsibility. The challenge to leaders is to achieve this in a global context, to think and act globally when shaping the corporate mission and vision, and back it up with actions. This requires a transformational type of leadership. Numerous writers have contributed ideas regarding the particular attributes required by transformational leaders including Bass (1985), Bass and Avolio (1990), Yukl (1981), and House (1996). Typical attributes of transformational leaders include:

- Sensitivity to the broad-based external factors that influence their decisions.
- Relational skills that allow them to integrate a more eclectic range of stakeholders in geographically dispersed and culturally diverse locations.
- Creativity and problem solving skills that inspire followers.
- Motivational skills to mobilise and channel human resources effectively.
- Strategic and tactical skills to exploit short-term opportunities and set a long-term path for success.
- Informational skills that enable them to deal with the complexity and scale of knowledge and data.

Clearly the nature of leadership in a global context requires a greater emphasis on development. This development may involve a more systematic approach to nurturing the next generation of leaders rather than the unstructured approach of waiting for leaders to emerge. In other words, the focus will be on ensuring that global leaders are made rather than born.

Case study
The inconspicuous Carlos Slim Helu

Introduction

Carlos Slim Helu is officially the richest man in the world according to respected monitor *Forbes Magazine*. Surprisingly, few outside the Americas have heard of a man who owns over 90 per cent of Mexico's telephone market and accounts for around 7.5 per cent of the country's gross domestic product (GDP). Part of the reason is the inherent modesty he believes is an ingredient of his success. Eschewing the usual ostentatious trappings of wealth, Slim prefers to operate his *Grupo Carso* organisation from a modest office complex on the outskirts of Mexico City from where he manages his expanding interests in telecommunications companies around the world. Not that he is without some indulgences, however, as one of the world's foremost collectors of Rodin sculptures, his interests covers many of the arts and sciences as well as philanthropy in numerous 'just causes'. Indeed, as the 69-year-old Slim has often remarked, he intends to take nothing with him when he dies (Martinez, 2013). This may take a spending spree of epic proportions as his wealth creation from his three Brazilian telecoms companies normally nets some $12 billion per annum alone. This is before considering similar or even larger returns from his interests in Mexico (*Telefonos de Mexico* controls over 90 per cent of the fixed telephony market) and the USA where his *America Movil* organisation owns eight more companies.

Of all of these the acquisition of the previously state-owned *Telmex* telephone company in 1990 is the most significant and the one that proved the catalyst for Slim's extraordinary accumulation of wealth and power. In total he controls around 200 companies in fields as diverse as

http://www.
carso.com.mx
http://www.
carso.com.mx

telecommunications, mining, food and restaurants, financial services, and internet service providers. Part of this success story is the leadership style that Slim adopts as a basis for influencing those around him who can deliver business success. That includes not just industry partners and members of the wider business community but also, crucially, those in decision making positions at governmental level (both in Mexico and abroad) whose patronage he needs to ensure that factors such as regulation are structured favourably for his companies.

Background

Carlos Slim Helu is of Lebanese descent, the son of an entrepreneurial father who arrived in Mexico in the early twentieth century. In contrast to many of his contemporary billionaires, Slim did not make his fortune from the new economy such as e-business or computing. Rather, he is a product of old economics, with interests predominantly in the infrastructure-led business sectors of telecommunications and mining. However, like many aspects of his personality there are contradictions, such as his investments in software companies when the focus of business attention was on hardware in the early 1990s. He has no personal interest in computing but surrounds himself with friends such as computing scientist Nicholas Negroponte and technology futurologist Alvin Toffler. Also, as a multi-billionaire in a country of extreme poverty, Slim sees no conflict by emphasising his belief that the new civilisation develops and thrives on welfare (by 2010 he had donated some $40 billion of his wealth to charity).

This mix of welfare and enterprise offers an insight into the leadership style and vision that Slim uses as a basis for his business philosophy. For example, an Internet Service Provider (ISP) company run by his son-in-law reported a meagre 90,000 customers in two years of trading in Mexico in the late 1990s. The reason put forward was that so few Mexicans owned a computer at that time. Slim established a financing scheme that allowed customers on low wages to pay for a computer alongside their telephone bill over a two-year period. By 1999 the company was the biggest seller of computers in the country with over 3000 sales per day.

The business model of Telmex

The key to understanding the rise of *Grupo Carso* from a very successful business empire to one of the foremost powerful enterprises in the world is the formulation and implementation of a very simple business model—that of pre-paid cell phone services. In the mid-1990s Slim called together his most important partners for a meeting where he presented his business model for the cell phone sector of the business. He termed it the *'Gillette Plan'* after the American razor company. The logic behind this choice was to transfer the hugely successful business model of *Gillette* to the telephony sector. Fundamentally *Gillette* sells the razors to customers and then follows that with selling razor blades, thereby keeping customers 'locked-in' to the business model. By requiring customers to sign up to the pre-paid cell phone service, the business is able to 'lock-in' customers to the business model. This simple but effective technique has ensured high levels of brand loyalty and huge market share for *Telmex* and has contributed to the exponential growth of the company in the intervening years. However, by 2013 the dominance of *Telmex* (and the title of the world's richest man) came under threat from new telecoms regulations and changes to the Mexican constitution that resulted in significant decreases in the share price of *Telmex* (Carlyle, 2013).

Leadership style

Much of the success of companies under the control of Carlos Slim Helu is attributable to his leadership style. Interestingly, it is difficult to pinpoint any one style that Slim adopts as there is evidence of task-oriented and autocratic styles in some instances and people-oriented and

174

transactional styles in others. Although he uses his network of influence effectively, it cannot be said that he is one of the most charismatic leaders in global business; as mentioned, many outside the Americas will not have heard of him. Part of the reason for this is his desire to remain 'under the radar' of public attention in a part of the world characterised by social instability brought about by drug wars. Underpinning Slim's leadership style is his adherence to management principles that he devised to help form a guide to his way of doing business. In the authorised biography, Martinez (2013) sets out the ten guiding principles of Carlos Slim Helu. These are:

- *Keep organisational structures simple.* Organisations that have minimal hierarchies are more flexible and quicker to respond to opportunities. Decision making is quicker and more effective.
- *Maintain austerity in times of plenty.* This principle helps to strengthen the company and offers scope for greater capitalisation of the business that contributes to accelerated growth.
- *Be proactive in seeking modernisation, simplification, and improvement in productive processes.* Modernisation, simplicity, and improvements help to reduce costs, increase efficiency, and maintain brand loyalty of customers.
- *Never limit the company to the parameters of the owner.* Expansion and growth can be initiated by managers as well as the owner.
- *Work together to achieve goals.* The collective will and active collaboration of workers helps to underpin the organisational culture that is goal oriented.
- *Money leaving the company evaporates.* The focus is on re-investing profits.
- *Creativity solves problems.* Creative minds help to solve problems not only for business but for countries too.
- *Remain optimistic.* A positive outlook from management permeates down through the organisation and shapes the organisational culture that has goal achievement at its core.
- *All times are good.* The philosophy that all times are good for those who have work and are able to carry it out further defines the organisational culture.
- *Nothing will be taken from here.* The businessman is a creator of wealth which he manages only temporarily.

These management principles give a hint as to the leadership style and philosophy of Slim. It is possible to discern a people-oriented approach to business. Those who work for Slim have noted his support through education, training, and development. But more than that, he emphasises the importance of teamwork, of the group ethic, and the role that each individual has in contributing to the collective goodwill. This is a leadership style that is informed by the understanding of the value of human capital. In many ways Slim underplays his position of power and influence to focus attention on what others are able to do and achieve within a wider workplace community. This explains his disdain at learning of his newfound position as the world's richest man (Martinez, 2013). Principle number four gives an insight into this approach but emphasising that it is not the leader who sets the parameters of what the company can achieve but rather the creativity, innovation, and drive of those in the 'collective'. Nevertheless, the influence that such power and economic wealth has on others cannot be underestimated. Much depends on how that power and influence is used and the impact it has on others. Here, it is possible to discern elements of transformational leadership as Slim has been able to communicate his guiding principles in a manner that helps to motivate workers to be creative and innovative and to solve problems. This stems from the formation of a relationship between himself as the leader and the workers as followers. The followers have been able to understand and 'buy-into' the strategic vision of the organisation which has goal attainment at its core. However, beyond that, the workers have recognised a certain referent power exuded by Slim that has had the effects of enhancing their loyalty and bolstering their 'buy-in' to the strategic vision. At the heart of Slim's leadership style is people. As he noted himself in an interview in 2007, 'It is people that make things possible, people who are interested, motivated, who wear the team's jersey proudly, as we say, and who know they are capable of facing every challenge that comes their way' (Caparelli, 2007).

Sources:

Caparelli, E. (2007) Interview for *Epoca Negocios* magazine, 6 August 2007.

Carlyle, E. (15 March 2013) 'Carlos Slim Perilously Close To Losing Title Of World's Richest As Fortunes Tumble', New York, Forbes.

Martinez, J. (2013) *Carlos Slim: The Richest Man In The World/The Authorized Biography*, Green Bay, WI, Titletown Publishing.

Questions and tasks

Are there pragmatic reasons for Carlos Slim Helu's philanthropy?

Explain the concept of customer 'lock-in' and give another example of a company that has adopted this model.

Identify the leadership styles most associated with Carlos Slim Helu.

What motivates workers to follow the leadership of Carlos Slim Helu?

What type of power does Carlos Slim Helu have? Explain your choice.

Online Resource Centre

Author commentary on this discussion point and questions can be found on the Online Resource Centre at: www.oxfordtextbooks.co.uk/orc/combe1e/

Summary

● **Understand the difference between leadership and management**

The difference between general management and leadership was explained by highlighting some of the unique characteristics that underpin leadership, such as personality, emotional intelligence, culture, communications skills, and so on. It was noted that many aspects of management can be taught or gained through experience, but leadership requires a set of attributes not available to all or capable of being taught in a formal way.

● **Relate theories of leadership to their application in different environments**

Theoretical perspectives of leadership, such as the situational, functional, styles and behavioural models, were used as a basis for understanding the application of leadership in different organisations and environments. From the discussion it is possible to distinguish different forms of leadership such as that linked to particular situations and circumstances or that which emerges from a particular type of personality.

● **Evaluate the role of power and influence in different organisational settings**

The evaluation of power and influence showed that they are very closely related to leadership. Power was identified as a capacity that an individual or group has to influence the behaviour of others. Power ensures that others (followers) behave in a manner that the leader wants. Power and influence have a key role to play in determining working relationships, authority, and the formation of a dominant organisational culture. The chapter highlighted examples of different types of power and the application of power in different organisational settings ranging from the highly formal (police or army) to the relatively liberal regimes seen in advertising agencies or other creative industries.

● **Critically assess contingency theories of leadership**

Much of the discussion around contingency theories focused on the work of Fiedler whose proposition was that effective group performance relies not only on the leadership style but also the degree to which the situation bestows control to the leader.

● **Understand the concepts of, and differences between, transformational and transactional leadership**

The chapter outlined examples of transactional and transformational leaders. The former guide, mentor, and motivate followers by clearly establishing roles and tasks for the achievement of stated aims or goals whereas transformational leaders inspire followers to act in ways that benefit the organisation or a wider cause other than their own self-interest.

Conclusions

The debate as to whether leaders are 'born' or 'made' is one that will go on into the future, but the discussion in this chapter has set out the various perspectives in a balanced and logical manner that allows readers to go on and form their own views on this topic. The trend in recent years has been for managers to delegate authority and decision making powers to groups of workers or project teams as a means of harnessing the skills and expertise of workers. The form of leadership evident in organisations has reflected this trend with the emphasis being on styles that inspire and motivate rather than ones that focus on the task. However, during times of economic downturn, leaders and managers often become more risk averse, and this can be reflected in the way in which control is reined in to those with executive power and authority. This and other key issues form the basis of the discussion in the following chapter where the focus of attention turns to the control function of management.

Chapter questions and tasks

According to Fiedler, what three factors are of major importance to the favourableness of the situation?

Identify situations where it would be appropriate to adopt the following leadership styles: authoritarian; democratic; and laissez-faire.

Identify an example of a charismatic and transformational leader. Explain your choice.

Using the Myers-Briggs typology identify your own personality type.

Give an example of each of the five sources of power.

Online Resource Centre
Author commentary on this discussion point and questions can be found on the Online Resource Centre at: www.oxfordtextbooks.co.uk/orc/combe1e/

177

Further reading

- Adair, J. (2010) *Effective Leadership: The Complete Guide to Strategic Management*, London, Pan.

  John Adair is a prolific writer on leadership and leadership training. He is also credited with introducing the concept of strategic leadership where the influence of the leader often extends to many thousands or even millions of people. This book explains the strategic dimension to leadership by highlighting the leader's role in responding to external events in a dynamic environment. Key issues discussed include creating an organisational structure, allocating resources, and communicating the strategic vision. The discussion on leadership skills focuses on how to make judgements quickly; making decisions with incomplete information; and how to choose effective 'second tier' leaders. A useful and insightful contribution that is of relevance to students, academics, and practitioners.

- Gifford, J. (2010) *History Lessons: What Business and Management can Learn from the Great Leaders of History*, London, Marshall Cavendish.

  The book examines the past as a means of providing lessons in leadership from some of the great practitioners of the past. Key figures include Winston Churchill, Martin Luther King, and George Washington. The book presents a description of the concept of leadership before going on to highlight the key characteristics and traits of personality possessed by great leaders that helped them to inspire and motivate others. Although set in a historical context, the work remains true to its objectives throughout by maintaining a focus on leadership skills.

- Giuliani, R. (2003) *Leadership*, New York, Chivers, Windsor, Paragon & Co.

  Mayor Giuliani was one of New York City's most high profile and popular mayors. His popularity reached its zenith during the 9/11 terrorist attacks when his leadership skills were put to the most extreme test. The book deals with Giuliani's management and leadership style before and after the attacks. The narrative is informative but also readable as the mayor takes the reader on the journey through his life and discusses the events and people that influenced his leadership style. Tough and uncompromising, but also capable of great warmth and humility, the ex-mayor reveals a complex set of traits that came together on 9/11 when the city most needed leadership.

- Radcliffe, S. (2009) *Leadership: Plain and Simple*, Harlow, Financial Times Series/Prentice Hall.

  This book offers a valuable and practical framework to help develop effective leadership skills. The work focuses on three leadership practices selected from real situations. The practices are explained and discussed around the themes of leaders being guided by the future; engaging with others for stimulating and productive relationships; and delivering results to move the business forward.

- Spanyi, A. (2010) *Operational Leadership* (Strategic Management Collection), Business Expert Press.

  This book attempts to redress the imbalance between functional managers (whom the author claims are abundant) and operational leaders (who are alleged to be few in number). The book discusses the evolution of leadership attitudes and behaviours to chosen operational activities such as product development, sales, production, customer service, human resources, information technology, and finance. The author presents a framework for assessing effective leadership in an operational setting.

 Online Resource Centre

For more information, updates, and multiple-choice questions, please visit the Online Resource Centre at: www.oxfordtextbooks.co.uk/orc/combe1e/

Skillset 5
Analysing a case study

5(a) Introduction

'Read the case study for next week's class' is a typical parting comment from your tutor at the end of a tutorial or seminar session. Case studies are a key teaching and learning tool and, throughout this book, chapters contain mini case studies and an elongated case at the end. You will be presented with numerous case studies throughout your academic life, so understanding how to analyse case studies is a key skill that you will benefit from as you progress with your learning. Some organisations may use case studies as part of their selection process—for example, leading management consultants McKinsey and Company (see McKinsey, 2012). In the workplace you may have to take a leadership role in managing accounts, consultancy, research, or other roles that require the review or articulation of case material as part of your duties.

This Skillset provides an insight into how to analyse case studies for maximum effect. It will also help you in the compilation of case studies which may form part of a report or summary article. Finally, the skills developed through this Skillset will be useful for all chapters of the book and will provide you with the ability to maximise your understanding and knowledge when accessing case studies.

5(b) What is a case study?

Case studies are, typically, narrative (story like) examples of real-life (or based on real life) examples of (in our case) management in practice. As can be seen in this textbook, the cases can be comparatively short (a paragraph or so) or more extended (running to a number of pages and possibly including supplementary data such as financial information). For our purposes we largely discuss text-based (written) case studies but there could be multi-media case studies which include video/audio files as well as text. For example, the Skillset for Chapter 12 includes an exercise where the material for the case study of Semco is from a YouTube video.

Case studies can refer to a range of (possibly interrelated) situations such as:

- a particular theoretical point;
- a particular issue, challenge, or decision;
- a particular individual, organisation, or industry sector.

5(c) Case studies as a learning tool

So why do we provide case studies in textbooks and use them as the basis for discussions in class?

Yin (a key author on conducting case studies for research purposes) notes three conditions where case studies can be an effective research strategy (adapted from Yin, 2009):

1 There is an interest in how and/or why things happen.
2 It is not possible/desirable to control events.
3 There is a focus on contemporary events.

Yin is using the term 'case study' in a different context (relating to undertaking research) from how we are using the term here. However, his conditions fit well with why case studies are also used for learning as, in general terms, they focus on understanding the deeper processes and interactions of the situation being described (effectively Yin's Condition 1); they provide

179

insight into individuals/organisations and so on which we cannot readily access ourselves (Condition 2); and they focus on contemporary events/issues or allow us to reflect on and learn from the past to inform the future (Condition 3).

At a simplistic level, case studies provide examples to illustrate points that are made regarding theory, in other words they link theory to practice to 'bring theory alive'. This is useful; however, there are more powerful reasons for using some forms of case studies:

- Case studies as tools allow you to engage with, and apply, theory to real-world situations.
- Case studies can allow you to integrate a range of different aspects of your learning. A lengthy case study (say 25 pages long) may have elements relating to the interplay between leadership, culture, planning, decision making, and ethics.
- Finally case studies as the basis for analysing and assessing real-world situations where there may be a number of different perspectives and no one perfect answer. They provide the basis for simulating the real world where you (or your group) have to decide . . . what would we have done (reflecting on the past)? Or . . . what would we do (reflecting on the future)? They represent a 'puzzle to solve' (after GTTP, undated).

In reality a case study may be used at different times for different purposes. As a teaching tool one of the benefits of the case study is their flexibility—the same case can be used in different ways depending on the purpose of the class.

As a critical element of learning and teaching, case studies are particularly associated with the Harvard Business School, one of the world's leading business schools. Key characteristics of the Harvard case study method include (from Harvard Business School, undated):

- Students read the case and play the role of the decision maker.
- Students analyse the case, consider alternatives, and make recommendations.
- Students come together in groups to discuss the case before the class.
- In class, the tutor's role is to question, guide, and facilitate discussion amongst the class—not give the answers! Eighty-five per cent of the class time is input from the students.
- In many courses 50 per cent of the mark relates to the quality of a student's participation in class.

5(d) How to analyse a case study

Given the range of uses of case studies in class, it is not possible to cover all eventualities and this section describes a general process which you may wish to customise depending on your particular needs. The process outlined is adapted and developed from material by Acadia University (2006) and Glasgow Caledonian University (2008). The assumption is that the task you have been given requires some recommendations/decisions to be made at the end based on your analysis of the case. For simplicity, we assume the task is carried out by you as an individual to feed into a group discussion at class. We can break the process of analysing a case study into six stages:

1 Preparation
2 Starting off
3 Analysis
4 Recommendations
5 Take stock
6 Afterwards

giving the acronym PSARTA. We will now look at each stage in turn.

Stage 1: Preparation

It may be an obvious point, but make sure that you have all the materials available before you start. This would include the case itself but possibly other reading materials such as journal articles, textbook, or lecture notes. Have you done any preparatory reading that is required? You may wish to (re)familiarise yourself with any of the key concepts/theories and so on which you may wish to use.

Stage 2: Starting off

There are two strategies here: one is to read the questions/task before reading the case itself (Option 1); the other is to have a first read through the case without any preconceptions about the questions/task (Option 2). Both options have their advantages and disadvantages. Option 1 gives you a focus for your reading; however, particularly for longer more complex cases, you may miss some important points as they were not your focus. Option 2 allows you to keep an open mind and give yourself a wider initial perspective on the case (remember the 'helicopter factor' leadership trait from Chapter 5); however, you may regard this option as more time-consuming as it lacks focus on the task set.

Regardless of whether Option 1 or 2 is chosen—now read the case material. Depending on your reading style you may wish to scan (read quickly) the case taking in, particularly, things like: the headings (for the overall development of the argument); the introductions/conclusions to sections (which should set up the material and end with the key points); and any tables or figures (these may summarise some key points; also read the text before/after these where their importance should be explained). Alternatively you may wish to read the case through more fully. Based on this initial reading consider:

- Who are the key stakeholders in the case? For example senior management, employees, shareholders, customers, suppliers, trade unions, local authorities, or central government.
- What are the main issues/themes emerging from the case?
- Is there any indication *why* the issues/themes have developed?
- How important do these issues appear to be in relation to each other? This can help give you focus later on.

Once this is complete you may want to do some more reading, either regarding theory or to find out more about the person, company, or industry sector.

Stage 3: Analysis

'Theory' can, and should, help you make sense of what may be a multi-faceted and complex case. So at this point consider which concepts or theoretical frameworks you wish to use; and how you will use them. For example, using a list of leadership traits may help to analyse a case on leadership in order to identify issues which have helped or hindered the effectiveness of a particular leader.

Reading Skillset 12 Critical Analysis may be of use in helping you decide how to apply theory to your case. Re-read the case again as often as required to identify the key issues and themes and organise them around the concepts and theoretical frameworks you have chosen.

As you move deeper into understanding the case, be sensitive to differences between symptoms and problems; or cause and effect. For example: poor morale of employees may be a symptom (indication) of poor leadership (the underlying problem). In the Carlos Slim Helu case study, the low customer base of the Internet Service Provider (effect) was due to low levels of computer ownership (cause). Establishing a financing scheme for those on low wages (cause) allowed many more customers to afford to buy computers (effect), which in turn impacted positively on the company's business. You could develop (on paper or electronically) a mapping of symptom/problem or cause/effect which would help you build your understanding of the case. Once you feel you have reached a plateau in terms of your analysis (in that no further insights are generated), then it is time to move on to the next stage.

The website of Glasgow Caledonian University (2008) has a link to a grid which may be useful to help you structure your thinking. It is a table with five columns: level (for example, operational or strategic), main issues, related problems, relevant theories, and possible solutions/recommendations.

Stage 4: Recommendations

Based on your understanding from the previous phase, you may have been asked to make a decision or recommendation(s); or more generally give an answer to a question where there is no right or wrong answer. Good practice would be to:

- Consider a range of options. The first recommendations (or answers) that come to mind may not be the best or most appropriate ones. Decision making theory suggests that the more options considered, the better the final decision is likely to be. Be clear whether the recommendations are to be at an operational or strategic level (for example). See Chapter 3 Planning for discussion of the distinctions between operational and strategic planning.
- Identify the key assumptions which underpin each option. What is the cause and effect chain which leads issues/problems and to the solution(s) you would recommend?
- Test the options against whether they are feasible. Could they actually be achieved/implemented in the real world? Are your proposed recommendations legal and ethical? What resources (time, money, staff, skills, etc.) would be required? And so on.
- You may wish to develop some criteria or ranking system against which to evaluate your options.
- Rank your options according to the criteria/ranking system.
- Make your choice(s)!
- Depending on the task set you may also have to give guidance on how your recommendations could be implemented.

Stage 5: Taking stock

'Taking stock' means revisiting and reflecting on what you have done and, in particular, the recommendations/answers/conclusions you intend to make. It is like stocktaking in a shop at the end of the year—do you actually have the goods you think you should have? Key questions to ask yourself at this stage include:

- What is the evidence base for what I recommend or conclude? For example, the final question in the Carlos Slim Helu case asks you to 'explain your choice'.
- Normally your answers or recommendations would be based on the data presented in the case study (to ensure a level playing field across all students). If you include other material: Is it appropriate/necessary to do so? (Was the answer in the case already?) Is the material valid in relation to the case? (For example, have you recommended a new technology which would not have been available at the time in which the case is set?)
- Revisit the arguments for what you recommend. Do the links between cause and effect make sense? Ask yourself 'Can I make a persuasive case based on theory and the evidence of the case which will be convincing and persuasive to others in my class?'
- It may also be worth briefly considering 'Am I sure that I have followed through on the task set?' In particular, remember to make recommendations which are clear and prioritised if

that is what is required. It is easy to become bound up in the analysis and forget to focus on the 'output' at the end.

- Ask 'Do my arguments present a balanced, realistic, and unbiased view of the case?'

Stage 6: Afterwards

After the class you could review what you learned from the case and take notes (if you have not already) on some of the other options, recommendations, points of view which emerged from the class discussions. Perhaps also reflect on the process you used, and whether you would do anything differently next time. This 'after-action review' process is used in many organisations and is a key part of becoming what is called a reflective practitioner.

5(e) Activity: Carlos Slim Helu

Chapter 5 ends with a case study on the world's current (2012) richest person, Carlos Slim Helu. This activity gives you the opportunity to apply some of the principles of case study analysis from the previous section. The activity is built around the PSARTA process outlined at the start of the Skillset but, in this case, rather than recommendations you have specific questions to answer.

1. **Preparation**—read Chapter 5 up to the start of the Carlos Slim Helu case.
2. **Starting off**—Read the Carlos Slim Helu case *without* reading the questions. What are the key themes or issues which you gain from the case? How does the case link to the theory you read about in the chapter?
3. **Analysis**—Read the specific questions. Decide what concepts/theory you will use and how. For example, an understanding of leadership styles may help you with Question 3. Reread the case and (where appropriate) use the theory to analyse the case and come up with your answers to the questions.
4. **Recommendations**—or in this case your answers to the questions set.
5. **Take stock**—review how you have used theory and the case to provide rigorous, logical, and persuasive answers to the questions set.
6. **Afterwards**—what did you learn about leadership from the case? What did you learn about undertaking case studies from carrying out this activity?

5(f) Summary of the Skillset

Case studies are a common and powerful teaching and learning tool. They take many forms ranging from short to long pieces of work; cases focused on particular themes to cases which integrate a number of themes to reflect the complexity of real-world management. This Skillset outlined a process for analysing case studies which will enhance your ability to obtain the most value from the cases in this textbook. Note that, given the variety of possible case study types, this process may have to be adapted to fit a particular case. This Skillset should be read in conjunction with Chapter 12's Skillset on critical analysis.

References/Further reading/Resources

Acadia University (2006) *An Approach to Case Analysis*. [Online resource] Available from: http://plato.acadiau.ca/courses/Busi/IntroBus/CaseMethod.html

Glasgow Caledonian University (2008) *How to Analyse a Case Study*. [Online resource] Available from: http://www.gcu.ac.uk/student/coursework/writing/casestudy.html

GTTP (Global Travel and Tourism Partnership), Undated, *How to Write a Good Case*. [Online Resource] Available from: http://www.gttp.org/docs/HowToWriteAGoodCase.pdf [This Skillset focused on analysing cases written by others. This article looks at the other side of things—how to *write* a good case for teaching purposes. Although specific to the context of travel and tourism, much of the advice could be adopted to a more general management context.]

Harvard Business School, Undated, *How the HBS Case Method Works*. [Online Resource] Available from: http://www.hbs.edu/mba/academics/howthecasemethodworks.html

McKinsey and Company (2012) *Interview tips*. [Online Resource] Available http://www.mckinsey.com/Careers/Apply/Interview_tips [In particular the section, and links, regarding what they call a 'case interview'.]

Yin R. K. (2009) *Case Study Research: design and methods* (4th edn), Thousand Oaks, CA: Sage Publications. [A different form of case study. This book is a leading text on case study research and is worth noting for when you undertake your project/dissertation.]

Further Resources

Harvard Business School, *Participant-Centred Learning and the Case Method: a Harvard Business School multimedia resource*: http://hbsp.harvard.edu/multimedia/pcl/pcl_index.html [With both text and video options, this resource gives you a 'behind the scenes' look at the preparation and delivery of case studies 'Harvard Business School style'.]

McKinsey and Company, Game: Team Leader—test your people skills: http://www.mckinsey.com/locations/swiss/career/team_leader/index.asp [An interactive problem-solving game.]

6 Controlling

Learning outcomes

- Understand the meaning of control in organisations and why it is necessary

- Recognise the different types of control mechanisms in organisations

- Contextualise control in different organisational settings

- Critically assess measures of control and their effectiveness

- Understand the limitations and barriers to control

Management is essentially about being able to influence other people's behaviour in order to achieve set aims and objectives. Necessarily, there is an element of control in this process that managers exercise in order to ensure that those behaviours are conducive to achieving outcomes. Car maker Henry Ford was legendary for his controlling style of management. An advocate and pioneer of so-called 'welfare capitalism', Ford had a vested interest in improving the lives of his employees and reducing the rate of employee turnover at his factories as research informed him that hiring and retaining workers reduced costs and increased efficiency (Bak, 2003). However, the control element of the relationship between employer and worker at the Ford plants extended well beyond the confines of the factories. Ford set up 'Sociological Departments' to monitor and manage the behaviour of workers. Thus, workers who demonstrated a clean life—no heavy drinking, gambling, or 'inappropriate relationships'—were rewarded with a higher rate of pay. This approach was condemned by many workers' organisations (formal unions were banned at the Ford plants) and over time the workforce rebelled against the intrusion into their private lives. Although hugely successful, the Ford plants were intermittently blighted by industrial unrest and worker alienation partly due to the excessive control practised by managers. Getting balance between control, freedom, and workers' rights is a challenge all managers have to deal with.

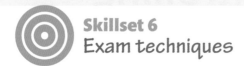

Skillset 6
Exam techniques

Educational institutions such as schools, colleges, and universities have a control mechanism for ensuring that students reach the required level of academic skill to merit certification of degrees or other qualifications. Professional organisations such as the Chartered Institute of Management Accountants similarly use exams to control standards. Successfully negotiating exams requires the application of techniques alongside the acquisition of knowledge on the subject to be examined.

Skillset 6 at the end of this chapter offers an insight into these techniques and helps to prepare students for the challenges presented by undertaking exams.

Definition

Control in the management process is concerned with guiding and regulating the activities of an organisation, or any constituent parts of the organisation, by means of management judgement, decision, and action, for the purpose of attaining agreed objectives (Merchant, 1982). In an organisation, control consists of verifying whether everything occurs in conformity with the plan adopted; commands issued; and the principles established. Controls are required to determine whether or not the organisation's action plans are being realised. Controls facilitate the identification of where deviations or shortfalls are occurring such that corrective action may be taken.

Introduction

This chapter opens with an overview of the types of control and an explanation as to why control is necessary. A control model is presented as a management control system and different types and levels of control are analysed in the context of different organisational settings. The focus of analysis will be on issues of production and quality, human resources, and finance. The issue of quality is one that has gained in prominence in recent decades and this is reflected in the chapter through analysis and discussion of control and Total Quality Management (TQM). Control systems for both strategic (long-term) and operational (short-term) objectives are presented as a means of highlighting the different forms of control relating to different types of management. Strategic controls are concerned with the overall performance of the organisation or a significant part of it, such as a major service department. Increasingly, organisations build in control mechanisms to ensure business continuity in the face of threats such as natural disasters, terrorism, or reputational damage (Vinas and Jusko, 2004). Operational controls measure activities within sub-sections of an organisation and usually cover a shorter time period than strategic controls. The chapter concludes with an outline of the key characteristics of an effective control system.

Types of control systems

There are three main approaches to implementing organisational control:

- bureaucratic control;
- market control;
- clan control.

Bureaucratic control is concerned with the implementation of rules, regulations, and procedures underpinned by formal authority as a guide to how employees should behave. The environment is characterised by practical activities such as budgeting, information gathering, performance targets and appraisals, and formal communications systems (Koontz and Weihrich, 2006). This form of control is typically associated with large-scale administrative centres such

Term Definitions

Control: monitoring of activities and functions to ensure that outcomes are in line with set targets or align with plans and then acting to rectify any deviations.

Control process: the activity of setting performance targets, measuring and recording outcomes, and matching them against set targets or standards.

as government departments and the civil service. Market control places a greater emphasis on economic criteria as a means of control. These may include pricing mechanisms, profit targets, returns on investment, and so on. These are typically seen in high performance financial organisations such as stock brokerages, money markets, or hedge fund operators. Clan control refers to functions or activities within an organisation that are the locus of workers' shared beliefs, values, goals, and/or expectations. Managers have to assess the nature of the dominant organisational culture before determining the appropriate control system to implement (Daft et al., 2010). In some settings control needs to be tightly monitored to ensure compliance (examples include the prison service, call centres, fast food restaurants) whereas in others the dominant culture may require a more liberal and 'light touch' approach (such as in the creative arts).

Purpose of control systems

Organisations implement control systems to determine if their goals are being met and to take corrective action if they are not. Control is regulation of the organisational activities that help keep performance within pre-determined acceptable limits. They help managers to reduce errors in the production process thereby minimising costs and improving efficiency. Control systems can also help the management of increasingly complex organisations (Abernethy and Stoelwinder, 1994). This is especially the case when one considers the challenges of new types of organisational structures where workers may be dislocated from the centre, or where many activities are outsourced to third parties. Virtual organisations present a number of control challenges. These organisations consist of a number of individuals or groups who contribute their own skills and expertise to the production process then leave the organisation. The work is controlled and coordinated by a central hub or contractor but the majority of contributors never actually meet physically. The group shares resource platforms, such as an intranet, for the purposes of communication. The Hollywood film industry is a good example whereby the process of making a film consists of hundreds or thousands of small and varied actions by an army of freelance workers such as designers, scriptwriters, actors, lighting, directors, producers, etc. Since the industry freed itself from the costly and restrictive studio system, this form of organisation has proved extremely effective (Finler, 1988). Control can help managers make decisions that allow the organisation to adapt to changes in their environment. Data and information gathered from control systems allow managers to monitor, record, anticipate, and respond to changes in the environment. Thus, control has a strategic as well as an operational dimension. Figure 6.1 outlines the key steps in a control process.

Setting standards is the first step in any control process. A control standard is a pre-determined target against which all following performance is measured and compared. Consequently, the control standard has to be measurable and be consistent with the aims and objectives of the organisation (Flamholtz, 1979). Once the standard has been set then the measurement of performance can

Term
Definition

Control system: the chosen design and combination of elements in a control process.

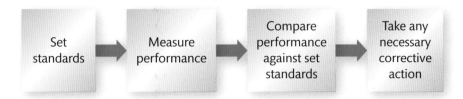

Figure 6.1 Key steps in a control process

take place. This is a continuous process and one that needs to be recorded and analysed. It is the role of management to identify and implement suitable performance indicators that are valid and are capable of revealing valuable insights into the performance of a range of activities undertaken both internally and externally. Evaluation and comparison of the data and information from the performance indicators will reveal if the set standards have been exceeded, matched, or if they have not been achieved. The outcome will determine if any corrective action has to be taken. Normally, managers will also be able to determine what type, where, when, and by whom corrective action should be taken. If standards are being matched or exceeded, it may be that the status quo is the preferred outcome and no corrective action is needed. In some instances it may be decided that the set standard has to change, that it may no longer best represent what constitutes a suitable level of performance. This may result from changes in the environment, technological advance, market intelligence, competitor performance, new industry regulations, and so on.

Timing of control

Control can take place before, during, or after, an event—the earlier the better, but many controls can only realistically be introduced after organisational activity has taken place. Pre-control is essentially pre-emptive, as in the scheduled maintenance of plant, machinery, and buildings which, it is hoped, prevents breakdowns and the need for major repairs. Concurrent control is exercised while an event is taking place. For example, status indicators inform engineers of the need to take corrective action before the machinery reaches a dangerous state. Post-control is the poorest form of control, as it is exercised after the event. In this instance it may be that a service has been delivered to clients and the control mechanism is designed to assess whether the organisation or department has achieved its objectives.

All organisations exhibit some forms of control systems that are implemented for a range of different purposes. Writers such as Ouchi (1979), Davila (2005), Sandino (2007), and Davila et al. (2009) have each contributed insights into control systems adoption in different organisational settings. Reasons for implementation include to:

- standardise performance, e.g. written procedures;
- safeguard assets, e.g. internal audit, authorization, and record keeping;
- check on output, e.g. quality assurance, inspection;
- clarify authority, e.g. job descriptions, organisation charts;
- monitor overall performance, e.g. reports, statistics, performance indicators;
- aid forward planning, e.g. budgets, forecasts, plans;
- improve network analysis;
- coordinate activity, e.g. meetings;
- control behaviour, e.g. disciplinary rules and procedures, grievance procedures, performance appraisal, and management by objectives.

Mini case 6.1
TATA Daewoo Commercial Vehicles

South Korea-based TATA Daewoo Commercial Vehicles is one of the world's largest heavy duty commercial vehicle manufacturers specialising in body assembly, paint, trim, chassis, frame, and final shops. The production capacity of the manufacturing plant is around 20,000 vehicles. The Manufacturing Automation and Control Systems (MACS) arm of TATA Technologies identified a control system that included production monitoring from start to finish; real-time information on production status for any vehicle; quality assurance at chosen locations; and collection of component data for vehicle tracking purposes (TATA Technologies, Case Studies, 2013). The result was the development of a customised manufacturing execution system (MES) designed to align with, and enhance, control throughout the production process. This included complete work-in-progress tracking along the production line; improved collection and analysis of production data; more accurate monitoring of actual work shift production; closer inspection of the production line by supervisors; and greater integration between the production line and other parts of the plant such as stores and distribution.

The control system delivered both operational and strategic advantages. Operationally, it enabled higher standards to be maintained, closer monitoring of performance, better quality inspection; and coordination of activities. At the strategic level, the system allows the company to compete more effectively by generating production data and information that helps managers make business decisions more quickly than rivals. TATA Technologies also leveraged advantages from its long association with Indian car manufacturer TATA Motors to access insights and knowledge on developing manufacturing control systems. In 2004 TATA Daewoo was acquired by TATA Motors as part of the latter's global ambitions. The takeover of TATA Daewoo made the company the fourth largest truck manufacturer in the world. The historic link to the TATA conglomerate clearly had strategic significance when choosing the partner to develop the system. Once the system was operational and demonstrated its worth, then TATA Motors made their move to acquire the company. However, the strategy has not been without its problems. In 2009 the South Korean authorities ordered the recall of 3000 Tata Daewoo trucks after faults in the steering system were detected (*Economic Times*, 2009). This demonstrates the fact that even in the most sophisticated control environments, problems can and do occur when producing complex manufactured products.

Sources:

Economic Times (18 October 2009) Tata Daewoo ordered to recall 3000 trucks in South Korea. http://articles.economictimes.indiatimes.com/2009-1018/news/28477852_1_tata-daewoo-commercial-vehicle-trucks-safety-defect

TATA Technologies Case Studies (2013) Tata Daewoo simplifies manufacturing operations with improved automation. http://www.tatatechnologies.com/global/Incat_CaseStudies_Summary.aspx?CaseStudyID=35&menucode=224

Discussion point

Can competitive advantage be sustained through the development and implementation of a control system?

The control model

The control model contains the four essential elements of the process as described in Figure 6.1. However, it is worth noting the role of planning in this process too. Planning involves the clarification of where you want to be (your goals) and how you intend to get there. Planning is the establishment of defined standards of performance against which the actual performance achieved can be compared. Control is a critical link back to planning in the process of management (Robbins and Coulter, 2012). Objectives, targets, and standards of performance need to be communicated to those concerned and to those who are subject to the operation of the control system (Dubrin, 2008). A monitoring system requires the creation of mechanisms which provide feedback on aspects of organisational performance. The points selected for these feedback mechanisms must be critical to the effective functioning of the organisation or department. The control points must accurately reflect the real status of the organisation. The ability to select critical control points is one of the arts of management, since sound control depends on them. Typically, in a manufacturing setting, a process engineer will be tasked with monitoring and assessing performance at different stages of the production process. In a departure from strict TQM principles that places responsibility with the person undertaking the task, at Korean car manufacturer *Hyundai* the corporate governance structure clearly delegates responsibility for this to assigned engineers rather than assembly workers.

The following questions provide a useful checklist for these control decisions:

- What will best reflect the goals of the department?
- What information will best highlight that the goals are not being met?
- What will best measure any deviations?
- What will best inform of the cause of the failure?
- Can control points be viably introduced economically?

In order to compare actual performance against desired performance, the information generated at the control points must be interpreted and evaluated in order to clarify progress, reveal deviations, and identify probable causes. This information should be fed back to decision takers.

The final element in the control system is the taking of corrective action to rectify the deviations (if any) from desired performance. Managers need to determine what needs to be done to improve performance and initiate appropriate actions to correct any deviations. The control

Critical reflection
Can creative people flourish in a highly controlled environment?

The control system of computer giant *IBM* has been the subject of much scrutiny and copying by rivals over the years. Much of the success of the company can be put down to the rigid codes that underpin the activities of workers in the factories. And yet, when developing the first personal computer the workers responsible for Research & Development were allowed to operate outside the restrictive codes of practice to purchase components from external sources. The tight deadlines and targets imposed upon the team led them to look for solutions outside the restrictive controls imposed by company policy. This case is often cited as an illustration of what can happen when strict controls are imposed on creative, talented and goal-oriented employees. Leavitt and Lipman-Blumen (1999) coined the term 'hot groups' to describe such high achieving groups. They argue that such workers add significant value to organisations but are often stifled by an overly controlled environment. They argue that the culture that pervades such groups cannot easily be controlled, nor should it be. In industries where competitive advantage is often achieved through creativity, innovation, risk taking, and challenging the status quo, such groups can prove invaluable if they are allowed to flourish in an environment that is open, flexible, people-oriented and encourages independence and autonomy. Creating such an environment is a major challenge for managers who may be used to operating within the boundaries of hierarchies or departments.

system adopted must also be reviewed and evaluated to assess whether or not it remains relevant to the monitoring of targets and objectives. Those targets and objectives also need reviewing to ascertain their appropriateness in a changing environment.

Controls should be flexible and remain workable in the face of changed plans, unforeseen circumstances or outright failure. Controls must be worth their cost. The end result of controls must be improved organisational performance, and the cost of the control system must be outweighed by its benefits, which should include the capability of presenting information that indicates when and where corrective action is needed. An adequate control system should disclose where failures are occurring, who is responsible for them, and what should be done to correct the failures.

Production and quality control

Production is part of operational control, which is designed to achieve short-term targets. Production targets may be set for a timeframe ranging from one day through to one year. They may be changed quickly to respond to changes in demand or for strategic reasons. Production control involves numerous different activities including materials handling, parts, and assemblies (and subassemblies) from their initial stage to the end product. Other related activities include planning, scheduling, routing, dispatch, and storage. Production control is designed to ensure that the process is carried out in an organised and efficient manner. Chiarini (2012) offers a valuable overview of production control systems in different manufacturing settings, including Toyota. Traditionally inspection of the production process was the dominant control system in place in most manufacturing settings. The main inspection points were:

(i) when raw materials are received prior to entering production;

(ii) when products are undergoing the productive process;

(iii) when products are finished and prior to despatch.

Although this system appears logical and easy to implement there are a number of flaws associated with it. Most fundamentally, this type of inspection process does not actually add value. That is, if it could be guaranteed that no defective outputs would be produced, then the need for inspection would become redundant. As it is, inspection is costly in terms of time and effort, as well as the negative perceptions it creates in the minds of consumers. Sometimes the inspection happens too late to prevent defective products entering the sales process, thereby further denting consumer confidence and goodwill.

Traditionally, inspection was carried out by a separate group of workers from those actually responsible for the output. This may lead to different perceptions of what constitutes 'quality' and result in the production control system becoming disjointed and incoherent. However, perhaps the most compelling reason for changing the traditional approach is that it is no longer in alignment with modern production techniques such as Just-In-Time (JIT) or TQM, see Table 6.1. Modern production control systems are geared towards quality assurance rather than inspection. Pioneering quality management guru Deming noted that 'Inspection with the aim of finding bad ones and throwing them out is too late, ineffective and costly. Quality comes not from inspection but from the improvement of the process' (Deming, 1982).

Quality management improves the functions and activities across the organisation by focusing attention on reducing errors and waste and cutting costs. Many of the techniques developed for quality management emanate from Japan where companies such as *Toyota* and *Sony* adopted them as a means of creating a strategic competitive advantage. These techniques have become prevalent in companies around the globe. In the pharmaceuticals industry, where quality is potentially of life or death importance, firms such as *Glaxo SmithKline* have introduced a range of techniques including TQM and Six Sigma to support a robust quality assurance system. Table 6.1 highlights some of the most commonly used methods.

Term
Definitions

Quality: output that conforms to a pre-determined set standard.

Quality management: the act of overseeing activities and tasks required to achieve and maintain a pre-determined level of quality. This includes creating and implementing quality planning and assurance, and quality control and improvement.

Table 6.1	Quality management systems		
Quality management system	**Origin**	**Description**	
Kaizen	Japan	First developed by Japanese electronics company *NEC*, Kaizen is a progressive method of improving quality through small, incremental improvements. The emphasis is on improving existing methods gradually.	
Total Quality Management	Japan	Total Quality Management (TQM) is a comprehensive and structured approach to organisational management that seeks to improve the quality of products and services through continuous refinements in response to continuous feedback.	
Six Sigma	USA	Six Sigma refers to acceptable defect rates in a factory and was invented by American multinational *Motorola*. The sigma is a measure equal to one standard deviation on a normal curve, or a bell curve. The aim is to reduce production of defective products by six standard deviations, that is, one defect for every 3.4 million products.	
Pareto diagram	Italy	One concept in the Pareto principle is that 20% of the work creates 80% of the results. It is a cost–benefit method used to focus a company's resources. A Pareto chart displays this concept in graphical form, showing columns of time and resources used to deal with an issue versus benefits gained.	
Balanced scorecard	USA	First developed in 1987 by American semi-conductor firm *Analog Devices*, the balanced scorecard is a report card for a business that reports a grade on individual features in key chosen areas. A survey filled out by customers, for example, can provide satisfaction grades for each area of service marked on the balanced scorecard.	
Just-in-Time	Japan	An inventory strategy designed to increase efficiency and decrease waste by receiving goods only as they are needed in the production process.	

Critical reflection

Are there dangers in relying too heavily on technology as a control mechanism?

One of the key areas of control in businesses of all sizes is that of inventory. Technology has played an important role in raising the quality of inventory control by allowing workers to track raw materials and products throughout the supply chain. Real-time estimates of stock availability, distribution times, production capacity, and so on all contribute to the bank of knowledge that maximises efficiency, minimises costs, and improves customer service and supplier relationships. However, there are some potential dangers that lurk in an environment that is so closely controlled. Foremost among these is the drift towards bureaucracy as installing the necessary infrastructure to support a controlled inventory system adds a layer of management and administration to the organisation.

So, although inventory control adds value, it also incurs a cost and this balance between them has to be monitored and managed. A second danger is that of placing too much trust on technology and ignoring the personal touch. When problems arise in the supply chain, clients and customers overwhelmingly prefer to deal with empowered personnel to solve their problem rather than rely on the robotic response of a machine. Adding a human touch to the process can lead to a competitive advantage by building valuable long-term relationships with customers that encourages brand loyalty. Finally, inventory control only focuses on the process along the supply chain and not the quality of the products or services along that chain. Often an effective inventory system masks problems elsewhere in the transformation process between inputs and outputs.

Control and Total Quality Management

Previously, in Chapter 4 on Organising, the management technique of the division of labour was highlighted. When Adam Smith formalised this approach to enhancing efficiency in the eighteenth century it was viewed as an innovative and practical means of improving production and the technique has been widely used ever since. However, the technique is not without some flaws. In particular, managers discovered that when work tasks are broken down into smaller units and performed by a small number of workers, no one person is wholly responsible for the quality of the output. Furthermore, the output was generally of a standard that was adequate rather than high. In effect, the craft of production that characterised the pre-industrial age had been lost in the relentless march towards mass production, efficiency, and cost minimisation. For products of relatively simple design that only required a standard level of quality (such as pins or bolts), the deployment of the division of labour made economic and operational sense. However, where a greater level of craftsmanship was required to produce a high quality product (such as bespoke furniture or tailoring) the division of labour often proved restrictive. Indeed, as time moved on, the traditional skills that delivered high quality products started to become less prevalent as mass production took over.

It would be well into the twentieth century before the problem of infusing quality throughout the production process was properly addressed by managers. However, it should be noted that 'quality' as a concept is often misconstrued as referring to high levels of craftsmanship or the use of the most expensive materials. In fact, quality in the context of manufacturing refers to the ability to deliver products in a manner that minimises waste and maximises added value. Thus, taking the previous example of pins and bolts, the production of those products would be deemed to be 'quality' if the process meets these criteria.

Although academics such as Feigenbaum (1956), Juran (1974), Deming (1982), and Garvin (1988) made significant contributions by developing methods designed to introduce quality

Figure 6.2 Components of a Total Quality Management system

into the productive process, it was the Japanese who applied them to best effect. The fundamental principle of ensuring quality in production according to Japanese industrialists was to place the responsibility for quality firmly on the shoulders of the individual who undertakes the productive task. This responsibility extended beyond simply performing the task, but also included the responsibility to seek new and better ways of achieving the outcome. Ishikawa (1985) provides an articulate insight into the Japanese interpretation of how to introduce the concept of total quality control into a manufacturing process.

As methods of ensuring quality developed, the whole culture of organisations started to reflect the new thinking. This gave rise to what is known as Total Quality Management (TQM) where customer needs and expectations are matched by a philosophy of continuous improvement in the work processes that combine to produce products and services. Figure 6.2 highlights the components of a TQM system. Continuous improvement includes finding ways to reduce waste as a means of adding value. Crosby (1979) articulated the concept by asserting that 'quality is free, it is waste that costs'. This involves analysing every activity within the organisation to identify waste, assess the value added, and take any necessary action based on outcomes. In essence, TQM focuses attention on identifying waste that does not add value to customers or other stakeholders and then taking appropriate action to rectify the situation. TQM became a prominent topic of investigation by academics and practitioners throughout the 1980s and 1990s with Crosby (1996) providing an updated account of his seminal work 'Quality is free' from the late 1970s. Hackman and Wageman (1995) provide a valuable insight into the empirical, conceptual, and practical issues relating to total quality management.

The application of TQM requires a system of control to be introduced as it has implications for organisational structure, functions that are carried out, levels of responsibility, power and authority, chain of command, and the procedures set in place to coordinate activities. TQM involves many different functions, but not in isolation. Rather, the key to its successful implementation is how effectively those functions can be integrated within the TQM principles. The

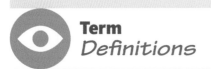

Term *Definitions*

Total Quality Management: a method of ensuring quality that focuses on customer needs and expectations by emphasising continuous improvement.

technique has been implemented in many different industries. For example, in the late 1990s dairies across the USA adopted TQM in an effort to manage antibiotics and prevent residues in meat and milk. The state-owned Indian Railways has also implemented TQM principles to address issues of over-crowding, timetabling, accident prevention, and improved quality of comfort for passengers. Table 6.2 identifies and describes the dimensions of TQM.

Control of TQM systems can emerge from different sources. Figure 6.3 outlines the locus of control typically seen in manufacturing settings.

The control of TQM includes:

Table 6.2	Dimensions of Total Quality Management	
	Dimensions of TQM	**Description**
	Top management	Top management support is one of the most important factors determining the success or otherwise of TQM. Top management must apply TQM principles consistently and accept full responsibility for the product and service offerings that follow its application.
	Customer relationships	The needs and expectations of customers is paramount and must inform the actions of all employees.
	Supplier relationships	The key principle is that quality is more important than price when selecting suppliers. TQM demands long-term relationships with suppliers such that they become partners in the process of continuous improvement.
	Workforce management	Workforce management must be guided by commitment to training and the empowerment of workers so that they possess the necessary skills and freedom of expression to contribute to continuous improvement.
	Employee attitudes	Managers need to stimulate, inspire, and motivate workers so that they fully engage with the principles underpinning TQM.
	Product design process	TQM demands that all departments are involved in the design process and collaborate to achieve customer satisfaction.
	Product flow management	Both quantitative and non-quantitative tools should be applied to help ensure processes contain no errors.
	Quality data and reporting	Records of quality indicators need to be maintained. Quality-related information needs to be constantly generated, stored, and disseminated to relevant participants for analysis and feedback and/or action.
	Role of quality department	The department responsible for quality needs to be able to access top management and given autonomy to act and communicate with other departments.
	Benchmarking	A benchmarking policy for key processes needs to be set up.

Figure 6.3 Sources of control of Total Quality Management systems

Setting targets

Quality is the key target to be set and must be determined with the customer needs and expectations as a guiding principle (Slack et al., 2007). Previous customer needs and expectations should not be used as a measure of quality but rather as a benchmark from which continuous improvement can help deliver new, innovative, added value products and services more efficiently. The targets will be set out in the quality manual compiled by managers that outlines the organisation's quality system, policy, and strategy.

Extending the scope of activities

The TQM system needs to be extended to incorporate the activities of other stakeholders such as suppliers and distributors. Control measures along the supply chain help to align quality throughout the sphere of influence of the organisation both internally and externally (McAdam and Henderson, 2004). Managers compile a procedures manual that sets out in detail the functions to be carried out by all those involved in the transformation process (inputs into outputs including distributors and retailers) as well as the attendant responsibilities assigned to each stakeholder (individual or group).

Establishing preventative measures against waste

The control function in TQM is not only linked to the quality of the finished product or service, but also includes establishing preventative measures against waste or inefficiencies prior to the productive process (Dahlgaard and Dahlgaard, 2002). Key tasks of managers include analysing the data and information generated for the purposes of tracking quality throughout the process so that remedial action can be taken quickly if targets look like being missed. The analysis also helps to pinpoint the reasons why quality is not being maintained such that resources can be deployed to remedy the situation quickly. To be effective, managers need to compile detailed work instructions, specifications, standards, and processes that support the process.

Factoring in and integrating the human dimension to the process

Ultimately, the effectiveness of TQM relies on the quality of the human resources that put it into action (Collard, 1993). Much depends on the qualifications, training, and competence of managers and workers in adding value to the activities they are involved in. However, there are other factors that play significant roles in determining the success or otherwise of a TQM system. These involve the attitudes, values, and beliefs of human resources and the organisational culture. At management level, TQM can only be successful if each manager 'buys-into' the concept and actively engages with the process in his or her everyday working experience. Similarly, workers are vested with the responsibility of adding quality to everything they do and this requires them to be fully engaged with the concept too. In other words, the process of TQM informs the dominant organisational culture such that it becomes a fully embedded characteristic of the working environment. This is arguably the most complex and difficult challenge facing managers with aspirations of applying TQM as illustrated in Mini case 6.2 below.

Creating an integrated organisation

Total Quality Management is a system that requires organisation-wide integration of activities and functions. This links to factoring in the human dimension as an integrated organisation requires group work and effective communications systems linking workers with middle and high level managers. Each person within the organisation needs to fully understand the duties assigned and have the ability to carry them out. However, beyond that there needs to be flexibility in the control system to facilitate knowledge sharing as a basis for continuous improvement. The level of control exerted (and where that control function stems from) is an area of contention among academics and practitioners (Godfrey et al., 1997). Research by Soltani (2007) suggests a close correlation between the application of TQM and increased levels of control over the workforce. Thus, it is the workers who are being controlled rather than the work processes. This has fundamental implications for the effective deployment of TQM systems as it requires workers to fully engage with the concept. Any perception that the system is designed as a monitoring and control mechanism over their input or activities is likely to be met with resistance and defeat the purpose of the exercise.

Total Quality Management has as a guiding principle that activities must be undertaken correctly from the beginning. This can only be achieved if managers and workers are equipped with the resources and skills to carry out their duties effectively. Failure to do so would constitute waste and undermine the quest for quality. Achieving the requisite level of skills may require investment in training and other forms of human resource development.

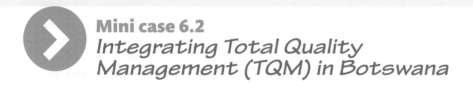

Mini case 6.2
Integrating Total Quality Management (TQM) in Botswana

This mini case focuses on the attempts to introduce the Japanese inspired TQM system into a developing country such as Botswana. Mitki and Shani (1995) provide some insights that help a better understanding of the cultural challenges of implementing TQM in different cultural contexts. The case highlights the barriers and difficulties that arise when attempting to transfer management control techniques across cultural boundaries.

Many management approaches are developed in line with the distinct national cultural characteristics such as that of TQM that emanated from Japan. TQM is a set of management practices that are geared towards meeting or exceeding customer expectations. It places an emphasis on process measurement and strong control mechanisms as a means of continuous improvement. TQM as a concept has been adopted by many organisations in diverse cultural settings. However, not all record the same level of success from its implementation. Ngowi (2000) noted that TQM is embedded in the cultural values and assumptions that are consistent with the culture of its origin. His research into one hundred construction firms in Botswana revealed some tensions in the process of implementing TQM in a culture very different from its cultural base. Although the values embedded in TQM could be transferred to the organisations, some of those values were resisted in the cultural context of the wider society.

Although the national cultural characteristics of Botswana are heavily laced with notions of tradition, this plays out differently from that seen in Japanese society. Whereas the Japanese link tradition with control and self-reliance, in Botswana there is a more fatalistic aspect to the national culture. The research by Ngowi revealed some interesting insights into how difficult it is to transfer management techniques across different cultures. For example, in the context of introducing TQM in the construction industry, Botswana workers do not tend to take responsibility for their own actions, rather they believe this to be the role of management. Similarly, Botswana workers leave the prevention of problems to management—a further contradiction of TQM principles. The social structure in Botswana also presents a problem when introducing management techniques where greater reliance on worker initiative is a prerequisite for success. For example, Ngowi (2000) found workers have a deeply embedded sense of where they belong in what remains a fundamentally tribal society. Consequently, Botswana society is more prescriptive than achievement orientated. Whereas TQM emphasises rewards for workers' contribution to improved outcomes, in Botswana few workers possess aspirations of this nature (Ngowi, 2000).

The implementation of TQM in the construction industry is further hampered by the itinerant nature of the workers who spend little time with the same company but rather transit from project to project. The attempt to integrate TQM into the working environment in Botswana in the early 2000s was marked by ambivalence in most cases, and outright resistance in others. Clearly it would take a closer alignment of organisational and national cultures for TQM to be successfully implemented in this context. On a more practical level, it is important for managers to adapt techniques to fit the cultural context into which they intend to apply them. Both government and business in Botswana are introducing initiatives to enable the introduction of new techniques. Business consultancies such as *Excelle* understand the national culture and the types of management techniques that can improve quality and efficiency. As a principle of understanding the context of managed development in Botswana the company designs training programmes to align cultural factors with new management techniques. The case study of *Toyota* in Chapter 12 illustrates the consequences of ignoring this principle.

Sources:

Mitki, Y. and Shani, A. B. (1995) 'Cultural challenges in TQM implementation: some learning from the Israeli experience', *Canadian Journal of Administrative Science*, Vol. 12, No. 2, pp. 161–70.

Ngowi, A. B. (2000) 'Impact of culture on the application of TQM in the construction industry in Botswana', *International Journal of Quality and Reliability Management*, Vol. 17, No. 4/5, pp. 442–52.

Discussion points

Is it suitable to attempt to introduce management techniques such as TQM into Botswana?

Should managers intervene to alter national cultures to suit their commercial interests?

Human resources control

Control systems are designed to influence human behaviour. That is, to alter their behaviour to remedy deficiencies or to monitor and analyse trends, or to align their behaviour to set standards that deliver acceptable levels of performance. It is easy to neglect the fact that underlying all control systems is the human condition with all its attendant complexity and variation, especially in the modern global context (Kramer and Syed, 2012). However, those charged with the duty of designing control systems have to bear in mind that their effectiveness is only as good as the willingness of people to engage with them. For example, it cannot be assumed that all employees understand or agree with the aims and objectives around which the control system is built. Individual employees may have personal aims and objectives that they perceive are being compromised by the implementation of a particular control system. Different departments may have different perceptions and reactions to control systems, either favourable or unfavourable. This compromises the goal of an integrated organisation that is one of the key characteristics of an effective control system. The risk and uncertainty associated with human resource control systems has to be carefully assessed before implementation (Verano-Tacoronte and Melian-Gonzalez, 2008).

Control is inextricably linked to political processes and power structures within organisations and much will depend on how this plays out in the working environment. Bloom and Van Reenen (2011) analyse trends in human resources and productivity from a range of perspectives including risk, competitiveness, ownership, and regulation. Clearly, there is much to be gained by pursuing control to further the aims and objectives of individuals or groups. For example, performance data and information may be presented in ways that make an individual or group look more productive and efficient than the reality suggests. Alternatively, others may stick rigidly to the procedures and regulations surrounding control systems in a way that is bureaucratic and stifling of innovation and change.

Cultural factors also play an important role in determining the type of control system that is appropriate in different environmental settings and contexts. There are some cultures that absorb and accept high levels of control both at organisational and societal level (Japan, China, Korea) whereas others are characterised by more individualism and free-will (USA, Sweden, the Netherlands). The cultural dimension to management is dealt with in more detail in Chapter 12 on Organisational Culture. Here, it is sufficient to recognise that it is not possible to implement a standard control system that is equally effective in all regions of the world. Each has to take account of the cultural nuances of the people whose behaviour it aims to influence.

The organisational culture and context is another determinant of the type of control system that is appropriate. For example, call centres operate in a highly controlled environment characterised by high levels of monitoring and recording of performance of employees and satisfaction rates of customers. In other settings, such as advertising agencies or other creative industries, the control system is barely discernible as the organisational culture demands a more free and liberal approach to achieving outcomes. Empirical research findings by Lund (2003) investigating marketing professionals in the USA found that job satisfaction was more closely aligned to organisational cultures around organic processes (featuring flexibility and spontaneity) than mechanistic processes (featuring stability and control). Previously, it has been noted that the armed forces or police operate tightly controlled systems to ensure compliance by personnel to set modes of behaviour. In such settings, resistance to control is likely to result in punishment. Resistance is a challenge to the successful implementation of control systems and is worthy of deeper discussion.

Resistance to control

Striking the correct balance between a control system that delivers both operational and strategic advantages and one that is perceived as oppressive to employees is a challenge facing managers charged with the duty of designing and implementing the system. In some cases the level of control exercised in an organisation will meet with resistance from employees. This is a potentially dangerous scenario as some controls will inform future decision making, or may have health and safety implications. Resistance to control manifests itself in many different ways, from lack of engagement through to insubordination. Bain and Taylor (2002) highlight worker resistance to overt control and monitoring in call centres.

The reasons for resistance may also be many and varied. Most commonly, workers feel that their freedom is being compromised by an overly intrusive control system. This is becoming increasingly prominent in organisations where the use of technology can reveal what workers are doing during working hours. Some workers perceive this as an invasion of privacy and resent the surveillance under which they perceive themselves to be. In the United States the *National Workrights Institute* advocate greater resistance to what they believe are the 'most violated principles in the American workplace'. They note that the majority of workers are unaware of how pervasive the lack of privacy is in the workplace. Typical examples include keyboard stroke monitoring, reviewing and storing workers' e-mails, monitoring time spent on the phone, video surveillance, drug testing, and out-of-hours contact such as pagers or cell phones.

When workers perceive that managers are trying to control their behaviour then resistance to the control system is likely to follow. Similarly, the quest for greater accountability and transparency in organisations may be a laudable one, but if it engenders a feeling of a lack of trust in employees then resistance may follow. Another factor leading to resistance is the focus of the control system. If the focus is on generating quantitative data and information, this may leave gaps that can only be filled by good quality analytical skills. These skills need to be used to understand the context in which the data and information are being generated.

The most effective way to overcome resistance is for managers to design a robust, appropriate, and relevant control system at the outset. Dialogue with workers in this process is often rewarded with greater levels of acceptance and engagement with the system. When workers understand how it works and what it is trying to achieve then the potential for resistance is reduced (Guttman, 2008). It is also important to build in verification procedures to ensure that the information gathered is accurate. This is especially important for performance indicators, with multiple standards and information systems being deployed for the necessary checks and balances that increase trust in the process.

Critical reflection
Should workers' activities in the workplace be constantly monitored?

The working environment has been subject to huge changes in the last two decades as factors such as demographics, technology, legislation, and social attitudes have forced change. The control of human resources in the working environment has had to keep pace with those changes leading to a raft of new working arrangements many of which were highlighted in Chapter 3 on Planning. One of the most controversial implications of the changing working environment has been the potential for increasing monitoring and surveillance of workers using technology. The widespread use of computers, mobile phones, SMS, internet, and so on has raised the possibility of employers being able to check exactly what workers have been doing and when. As so often happens when technology advances at a rapid pace, the ability to draw up new guidelines and legislation to deal with it is often subject to some time lag. As such, many working arrangements are based on trust. Trust is of course a two-way street and needs to be subject to constant review and updating.

One of the problems relating to the use of technology in the workplace is to determine exactly what type of activity is acceptable to both employer and employee. Employers can expect to exercise their right to ensure work is being carried out satisfactorily, whilst workers retain the right to a certain level of privacy in the workplace. The balance between these is still evolving in workplaces around the globe and is subject to a host of social, cultural, political, and legislative factors. In some instances workers have turned to the law to protect against excessive control and monitoring of activities using technology in the workplace. The case of *Copland v United Kingdom* (2007) lends illustration to how workers can have a measure of control over what information is gathered about them and how it is used. It also highlights how individuals can seek redress for invasion of privacy in the workplace using the existing legal mechanisms. The case involved a secretary in Wales who discovered that her employers had been secretly monitoring her private communications, including personal e-mails sent over the internet, in the workplace without her consent (Combe, 2009). After reporting the breach to the Information Commissioner, the case was sent to the European Court of Human Rights who found that her privacy had been violated and awarded her €3000 in damages. The verdict was reached in light of the Human Rights Act (1998) and the Regulation of Investigatory Powers Act (2000). The outcome was celebrated by unions but greeted with dismay by employers' representatives who viewed it as giving a 'green light' to employees to use company equipment and time for their own personal use.

Financial control

Financial resources that either flow into or out of the organisation require control systems. These are vital as they have implications for monitoring cash flow, meeting liabilities, managing creditors, monitoring performance, helping make investment decisions, and so on. The main type of control is budgetary. The two principal types of budgets are financial and operational. A financial budget focuses on the sources and uses of financial resources whereas an operational budget highlights what quantities of products or services are required to create outputs and the financial resources that contribute towards this. A budget is put in place as a plan to express different factors in financial terms such as units of output, time, supplies, transport, or any other factor relevant to the operations of the business. Budgets are important because they provide a system for measuring performance across many different activities that the organisation is engaged in and highlight where resources are being used (Pettinger, 2007). The main reasons for implementing budgetary controls are to help managers coordinate and manage resources effectively and efficiently; help establish expectations through benchmarks and standards; provide guidelines relating to the use of the organisation's resources; and to help assess performance.

It is important that managers apply and use budgets appropriately. Budgets instil a discipline into organisations but strict adherence to them may actually result in missed opportunities or lack of innovation. To gain a competitive advantage, managers of organisations need to take risks. A budget should set parameters and inform decision making but managers must beware of the dangers of becoming constrained by them. Other types of financial control can also add to the bank of knowledge that managers have regarding different aspects of the business and its performance. These include financial statements, ratio analysis, and financial audits.

Financial statements

Any profile of an organisation's financial position is termed a financial statement. The main types of financial statements are the balance sheet and the income statement. The balance sheet is a snapshot of the organisation's financial position at any given time. The income statement is a summary of the organisation's financial position over a period of time.

Ratio analysis

Financial ratios compare different elements of a balance sheet or income statement to one another. Ratio analysis calculates one or more financial ratios to enable evaluation and assessment of a chosen aspect of the finances of an organisation, such as cash flow (liquidity), level of debt (current liabilities), returns (return on capital employed), or operations (working capital).

Financial audits

Financial audits are a different form of control system from financial statements or ratio analysis as they are designed to check the robustness of the accounting, financial, and administrative procedures that are in place within an organisation. Financial audits can be undertaken within the organisation, whereby internal accountants evaluate the performance of the financial procedures currently in existence. However, for a more independent evaluation, external auditors are called in to undertake an investigation. This latter approach is designed to ensure the maximum accountability, transparency, and rigour of the audit. Financial audits must be sufficiently robust to reveal the effectiveness and accuracy of existing financial control systems in an organisation.

Mini case 6.3
A failure to control at Allied Irish Bank

Throughout most of the 1990s and 2000s many western economies experienced a long period of sustained economic growth. Much of the growth stemmed from unprecedented confidence in the ability of the global economy to maintain the high levels of demand that were the driving force behind jobs, investment, and wealth creation. The banking industry sought to fuel this boom by taking advantage of a 'light touch' regulatory regime to expand the amount of credit and lending provided to customers, both retail and commercial. Ireland was one of several economies riding the wave of optimism that characterised this era with the Anglo Irish Bank, Allied Irish Bank (AIB), and Irish Nationwide Building Society* being among the most prominent players in the financial whirlwind sweeping through the country. However, it was not to last. In 2008 the 'credit crunch' brought the Irish economy to its knees and the full extent of the reckless lending and poor risk assessment by banks became clear (McDonald, 2010). Too many had failed to put in place the sort of safeguards and controls that would have prevented or slowed the rush to lending in high risk markets.

The Allied Irish Bank was one of the country's most respected and trusted financial institutions. However, during the late 1990s the management of the bank started to explore opportunities in non-traditional markets including in the Far East and India, where previously their presence had been minimal. They also fuelled the Irish boom in the housing market by making available 100 per cent mortgages to customers without the financial means to sustain repayments. Other financial institutions did likewise in the headlong pursuit of profit and growth. In a report by Finnish financial expert Peter Nyberg, he noted that the cause of the financial crash was a combination of 'almost unbelievable' risk taking by banks and a 'complicit' public willing to take on ever-increasing amounts of debt (Nyberg, 2011). Crucially, though, he highlighted the lack of effective controls in banks as a major reason for the scale of the crisis that ensued.

One of the main criticisms of the AIB among others was the lack of basic risk assessment and even the maintenance of loan documentation. Nyberg noted an inability or unwillingness of bankers to understand that credit is not a sale, but a risky asset. Nyberg described a banking system in which loans were not properly classified and files often badly maintained and lacking in documentation. In short, there was a complete lack of effective controls. The situation was allowed to continue unchecked due to negligence on the part of the regulator who had identified areas of 'bad practice' but failed to act. By 2011 the Irish banks had received five bailouts by the taxpayer amounting to around €70 billion (£61 billion). The consequences of lack of effective controls will be felt for many years to come as the Irish economy (and others within the Eurozone) struggle to get to grips with the huge debts built up over the 'boom' years. Sadly, this scenario is one that has been mirrored in other countries, most notably in the UK where famous names such as the Royal Bank of Scotland and Lloyds TSB have had to be rescued by the taxpayer after they too failed to control their lending and investment policies.

*After the transfer of business from the Irish Nationwide Building Society to the Anglo Irish Bank the new company was called the Irish Bank Resolution Company Limited.

www.aib.ie
www.aib.ie

Sources:

McDonald, H. (30 March 2010) 'Allied Irish Bank crisis blamed on "special loans" to property developers', *Guardian*.

Nyberg, P. (2011) *Misjudging Risk: Causes of the Systemic Banking Failure in Ireland*, Dublin, The Stationery Office.

Discussion point

Is it possible to fully regulate the banking industry?

Questions and task

Explain what the 'credit crunch' is.

What were the main reasons for the Allied Irish Bank and others needing a bailout by the taxpayer?

What internal controls are needed by banks to guard against excessive risk taking?

Online Resource Centre

Author commentary on this discussion point and questions can be found on the Online Resource Centre at: www.oxfordtextbooks.co.uk/orc/combe1e/

Strategic control

Control has become an increasingly important aspect of management due to the formalisation of factors such as quality and safety across many industries. A high level of control may be necessary to acquire and retain safety certificates or accreditation that allows the organisation to operate. This is most evident in industries such as airlines, food processing, teaching, and healthcare. It is the responsibility of managers to ensure that control systems are in place to detect any deviation from acceptable standards such that remedial action can be taken. Failure to do so can lead to temporary suspension of operations, or in extreme cases the disqualification of the right to operate. In the healthcare sector in the UK some hospitals have had their trust status (a licence to operate independently) removed and responsibility placed in the hands of a third party because of poor operating standards. Also in the UK, the *Food Standards Agency* works in tandem with local authorities to ensure that all licensed restaurants and food processing or retailing outlets meet minimum levels of hygiene and quality. The *European Commission* in Brussels has been active in pursuing a policy of harmonisation of standards across a wide range of industries in Europe. All member states have to ensure that their industries are compliant with the standards set even if they already have stringent controls as part of their domestic legislation. There are various methods through which managers can build control into the organisation's strategy. Four basic types of strategic control are described below.

Premise control

Every strategy is based on certain planning premises—assumptions or predictions. Premise control is designed to check systematically and continuously whether the premises on which the strategy is based are still valid. Premises are concerned with environmental factors (economic trends, technology, interest rates, regulations, etc.) and industry factors (competition, markets, customers, etc.). An example of premise control is when organisations update their understanding and knowledge of key economic data such as levels of employment, interest rates, inflation, etc. to ensure that the premises under which they designed their strategy remains in alignment with the performance of the economy. Key questions for management are:

- Which premises should be monitored?
  Environmental factors—those over which the firm has no control but can influence strategy;
- How are premise controls enacted?
  The strategy's key premises should be identified and recorded during the planning process and responsibilities for monitoring those premises should be assigned to those with qualified sources of information.

Implementation control

Implementation control is designed to assess whether the overall strategy should be changed in light of results. For example, executive managers of an organisation may devise a strategy to achieve technological leadership in an industry. This is a long-term plan that will require the identification of activities and investments that combine to help achieve the aim over a protracted period of time. Measurable targets will be set to assess whether or not the strategy is working and key 'milestones' set to ensure that appropriate progress is being made. Pradtare (2011) outlines two types of implementation control:

- Monitoring strategic thrusts: projects that need to be done if the strategy is to be accomplished and information on the strategy's progress.
- Milestone reviews: critical events and resource allocations through time, and full-scale assessment to scrutinise the strategy.

Strategic surveillance

Strategic surveillance is designed to monitor a broad range of events inside and outside the firm that are likely to affect the course of its strategy. The basic idea behind strategic surveillance is that important yet unanticipated information may be uncovered by a general monitoring of multiple information sources such as trade magazines, industry conferences, business bulletins, online sources, etc.

Special alert control

A special alert control is the thorough, and often rapid, reconsideration of the firm's strategy because of a sudden, unexpected event. This may be because of natural disaster (the Japanese

Term *Definition*

Strategic controls: control systems designed and implemented to support the long-term aims and objectives of an organisation.

Term
Definition

Operational controls: control systems designed and implemented to support the organisation's short- to medium-term goals and objectives.

nuclear power agency had to radically alter its strategy after the catastrophic tsunami of 2011), terrorism (the strategic implications for businesses affected by the attack on the Twin Towers on 9/11 is discussed in Chapter 14 on Strategy), criminality (the aftermath of the widespread corruption at Enron included a radical change in regulatory strategy in the USA), or incompetence (banking bosses' inability to manage risk in the run up to the 2008 credit crunch led to strategy being imposed upon them by government).

Operational control systems

Operational control systems guide, monitor, and evaluate progress in meeting short-term objectives. While strategic controls attempt to steer the company over an extended period (usually five years or more), operational controls provide post action evaluation and control over short periods—usually from one month to one year. Three types of operational control system are budgets, schedules, and identifying critical success factors.

Budgets

As previously noted, budgetary control is an important aspect of any business or organisation. The budgetary process was the forerunner of strategic planning. A budget is a resource allocation plan that helps managers coordinate operations and facilitates managerial control of performance.

Scheduling

Timing is often a key factor in the success of a strategy. Scheduling considerations in allocating time-constrained resources and sequencing interdependent activities often determine the success of strategy implementation. Scheduling offers a mechanism with which to plan for, monitor, and control these dependencies.

Identifying critical success factors

Another useful way to effect operational control is to focus on 'critical success factors'. These factors identify the performance areas that are of greatest importance in implementing the company's strategies and, therefore, must receive continuous management attention. Each key success factor must have measurable performance indicators.

Characteristics of effective control systems

Effective control systems are closely integrated with planning and have a number of key characteristics including flexibility, accuracy, timeliness, and objectivity. In the first instance the alignment of control with the planning process will determine the effectiveness of the control system. These two factors are inextricably linked and, therefore, the control standards have to be designed as the planning process takes place. The control system also needs to be flexible enough to cope with change. If circumstances or the environment change, the control system needs to be able to reflect the impact of those changes in the way in which performance is measured. Rigid control systems would not be able to offer an insight into the effects of change on performance and would therefore be unreliable. Accuracy of information is another important characteristic of control systems. Managers rely on accurate data and information as a basis for decision making. The data and information should also be delivered in a timely manner to make them relevant, contemporary, and suitable for use. Finally, there needs to be an element of objectivity built into the system. Here, using just one set of indicators is often insufficient as it can lead to bias. In fact, it is good management practice to look beyond the numbers generated and to assess the overall performance of the organisation using a combination of statistical data, analytical skills, and experience.

209

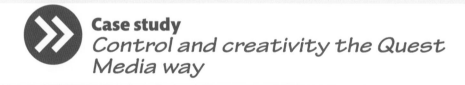

Case study
Control and creativity the Quest Media way

Introduction

The media industry in all its forms thrives on creativity and innovation. The generation of ideas for commentary, information, entertainment, and education form the bedrock of much of the output. The output is invariably the end result of various collaborations between workers with a range of skills and experiences including copy writing, design, analytical skills, technical skills, photography, and so on. Much of the added value stems from the freedom afforded to workers in the industry to explore new ideas, form new partnerships and relationships, or design their own work schedules as required to fulfil their obligations (Davies and Balkwill, 2011). The industry is wide ranging and includes broadcasting, publishing, internet services, music, theatre, arts, and so on. These industries invariably attract people who are creative, driven, and dedicated and who thrive in challenging and pressured environments. The concept of Leavitt and Lipman-Blumen's 'hot groups' (1999) is evident in parts of the media industry where notions of freedom and independence work in tandem with a level of control and self-discipline to ensure that new ideas are generated, deadlines are met, and performance is of a high quality.

The media industry has been revolutionised by technology in the last two decades as the advent of digital technology has offered new opportunities for improving the quality and range of products

www.quest.nl
www.quest.nl

and services over multiple platforms. The publishing industry is an example where old labour-intensive print technology has been replaced by new computer generated imaging and print facilities that has radically improved quality and efficiency. For example, teams of workers can collaborate remotely on page design using real-time imaging technology. Workers and managers can access production updates in real time and quality control has become standardised. This case study focuses on the implementation of a technology enabled control process introduced at magazine publishers *Quest Media* in the Netherlands. *Quest Media* is a publishing house formed by the amalgamation of Dutch firm *Quest Media* and the French media giant *Hachette Filipacchi Media* in 1986. Since then the company has published the prestigious *Quote* and *Elle* magazines aimed at women readers. Other titles followed including related magazines *Elle Girl, Elle Wonen*, and *Elle Eten* as well as a range of complementary magazines such as *Red* (women's lifestyle), *Sante* (women's health), and *Fiscalert* (finance). These titles had a good, loyal readership that generated a sizeable revenue stream for parent company *Hachette*. However, by the late 1990s the company started to explore ways in which new technology could improve workflow management and in-crease control in each stage of the publishing process across their three sites in Amsterdam. This was in response to an internal audit that highlighted the excessive amount of time being spent on routine planning and tasks that shifted resources from their core activity of publishing.

The workflow management specification

The move to integrate a workflow management system into the publishing and production pro-cess at *Quest Media* represented a risk as well as an opportunity. The risk came from not knowing how the workforce would react to the new process and the effects this would have on motivation and the quality of the end products. The opportunities came in the form of better management of resources and processes and the potential for freeing up more time on the creative aspects of publishing. It was determined by project coordinators that the best way of engaging workers in the process was for them to be fully integrated into the development and implementation of the system. Thus, dialogue with key staff was an important feature in determining exactly what specifi-cation the system needed and the overall aims of the project. The rationale of increasing control to free up creative inputs was the underlying principle communicated to workers by management.

The key feature of the workflow management system was the ability of the technology to inte-grate all stages of the production process in a seamless manner. That meant being able to deliver production updates in real time. Not only that, but the system also needed to be clear, ordered, logical, and transparent to all users across all editorial departments and should be able to be inte-grated into all existing systems across the company. Crucially, the system had to be user-friendly to allow staff to work with it quickly and effectively no matter what stage of production they operated from. This feature was important because it determined the extent to which workers could engage with the system and experience the benefits it could deliver. This was not only relevant to the 160 permanent staff located across the three sites in Amsterdam, but also to the many freelance work-ers that formed the network of skills available to the company. These allow the editors to pick and choose from a wide variety of different styles in design, layout, photography, and so on.

The workflow system facilitates integration between departments internally (for example, the marketing and advertising department could more easily communicate and collaborate with editorial departments) as well as providing access to external stakeholders (such as freelance workers). Each worker with access can clearly see the progress and status of work in any other department and use the knowledge to inform and guide activities. The transparency increases the level of monitoring of others' work, but the transparency adds value in integrating activities seamlessly to provide a more streamlined production process that results in greater efficiency and higher quality. The time saving can be used to concentrate attention on the creative pro-cesses rather than on manual production activities.

The company decided to adopt the *Van Gennep PlanSystem 3* as the workflow management system. The system has the capability to help workers create, plan, collect, and store a host of information and imagery relevant to each stage of production. Importantly, the software is compatible with existing information systems, thereby creating a customised solution that can be applied across the organisation. To the user it appears that a single system is in use no matter what function is being performed. For example, a photographer in the field can send real-time images to the editorial department via the system, receive feedback, and resume the task based on the new information. This process can continue until the editor gets the shot he or she wants. Others in the production process may also become involved, such as the person responsible for page layout and design. As workers become more familiar with the range of functions the system offers, and increase their experience of using it, then confidence in the technology increases. Thus, workers feel empowered rather than controlled by the system.

Operational control

The most significant advantage of introducing an effective workflow management system at the company has been the time saving that has allowed a greater focus on quality rather than production activities. For example, traditionally the publishing process started with a planning meeting involving managers from each stage of the production process. Editors would draw up the plan for each publication on paper and present it to other managers for approval. This was not only time consuming but also highly ineffective as the plan was reliant on a basic abstract drawing devised by an editor. Each time a change was proposed a new drawing had to be produced and presented for approval. The workflow system allows for a standardised plan to be presented that is capable of being altered, disseminated, and agreed upon in a matter of minutes. Relevant managers can be located anywhere in the world and contribute to the editorial plan in real time. In fact, change can happen right up to the last minute using the system. This is an invaluable asset as opportunities for advertising may emerge close to publication deadlines. The system allows change whilst maintaining quality control.

The workflow system has also allowed the company to build in more flexibility in the work schedules of staff. In particular, it facilitates more remote working. This raises the prospects of increasing their portfolio of freelance workers thereby accessing a wider range of skills, being more competitive in labour costs, and reducing overheads. There are also economies to be made from cross-fertilising ideas, applications, and solutions from one title to all titles. If a more efficient means of completing a task in one stage of production on one title can be transferred to others in the portfolio, cost and efficiency savings accrue across the organisation as each share the same standardised workflow system. By automating and streamlining production the workflow system has delivered a range of benefits including:

- standardised production across all titles;
- greater control of processes and activities;
- better communications integration between departments;
- improved transparency in the range of activities performed by workers;
- greater quality control;
- time, effort, and money savings;
- broader access to the skills and experience of freelance workers;
- increased possibilities for remote working.

Conclusion

The case of *Quest Media* has highlighted the challenges and benefits associated with introducing new technology into a production process. In particular, the case has shown how it is possible to increase the level of control whilst maintaining the creative inputs that determine the quality of the end product. Much depends on the reaction of workers to the introduction of the system, with dialogue, training, and hands-on experience of working with the system being vital components in its successful implementation. The benefits include greater transparency of activities and inputs from each stage of production. On the face of it, this may be perceived as a threat to workers who might resent the increased exposure it brings to their activities. However, resistance to the change was low as workers experienced the benefits of closer working relationships across the organisation and the increased amount of time they had to focus on the creative aspects of their work. The company ethos of 'creativity over technology' struck a chord with a workforce stimulated by creativity and innovation.

Sources:

Davies, G. and Balkwill, R. (2011) *The Professional's Guide to Publishing: A Practical Guide to Working in the Publishing Industry*, London, Kogan Page.

Leavitt, H. J. and Lipman-Blumen, J. (1999) *Hot Groups: Seeding Them, Feeding Them, and Using Them to Ignite your Organization*, New York, Oxford University Press.

Discussion points

Are creative workers more difficult to control than non-creative ones?

Do workers at Quest Media have to compromise their right to privacy to accommodate the new workflow system?

Questions and tasks

Identify and explain three main advantages of introducing a workflow management system at Quest media.

Give two examples of how the Van Gennep workflow system improves efficiency at Quest Media.

What strategic control factors are evident in the case?

 Online Resource Centre
Author commentary on these discussion points and questions can be found on the Online Resource Centre at: www.oxfordtextbooks.co.uk/orc/comb1e/

Summary

● **Understand the meaning of control in organisations and why it is necessary**

The control function relates to the process of guiding and regulating the activities of an organisation, or any constituent parts of the organisation. Control requires management judgement, decisions, and actions, for the purposes of attaining agreed objectives. Controls are necessary to determine whether or not the organisation's action plans are being realised. Controls help managers detect deviations or shortfalls in the expected outcomes of action plans such that corrective action may be taken.

● **Recognise the different types of control mechanisms in organisations**

There are many different types of control that can be applied to achieve different outcomes. The three main control types highlighted in the chapter were bureaucratic, market, and clan control. Bureaucratic control is underpinned by the application of rules and regulations and is often associated with large-scale public sector organisations, such as the civil service. Market control is where economic criteria are used as a basis of control, such as returns on investment. Clan control stems from shared beliefs or values held by workers. Here, it is important that managers understand how those shared beliefs and values help to form the dominant culture before setting in place control mechanisms.

- **Contextualise control in different organisational settings**

The discussion around control mechanisms featured different organisational settings such as the civil service, police, creative industries, and financial services among others. The type and suitability of control mechanisms has to align with the type of organisation, what it produces and what the stakeholder expectations are. Consequently, the choice of control type varies between industries and organisations within industries.

- **Critically assess measures of control and their effectiveness**

A number of different control mechanisms were identified and discussed such as production and quality control, financial control, and human resources control. Each has different types of control mechanisms and the reasons for their application vary. For example, the control of quality has many different approaches but is underpinned by a need to instil the concept of quality or continuous improvement into the dominant culture of the organisation to be effective. Some control mechanisms are measurable and effectiveness can be determined by quantified outcomes, such as the number of completed and successful transactions that have passed through various inspection stages. It was also noted that the effectiveness of control may be subjective when considering the effect it has on workers in different organisational settings.

- **Understand the limitations and barriers to control**

The limitations and barriers to control were discussed principally from the perspective of resistance to control. Workers will react to the application of control mechanisms in different ways ranging from acceptance through to rejection. Managers need to understand the limitations and barriers to implementing control mechanisms in the context of the organisation in which they manage as well as the external environment in which the organisation operates.

Conclusions

This chapter has highlighted some of the advantages associated with implementing an effective control system as well as some of the hazards and limitations of it. Foremost among the advantages are the potential costs savings from increased efficiency, better quality products, higher quality customer service, and a more integrated and cohesive workforce. The key challenge for managers is to be able to identify the appropriate type and level of control that is acceptable and understood by workers and that can help deliver the organisation's aims and objectives. An overly controlling environment can lead to hostility and conflict between management and workers, whereas an overly liberal regime may result in shoddy work, lack of respect for authority by ill-disciplined workers, and a downturn in employee productivity.

All formal organisations need leadership and it is the leader's role to communicate the reasons for and the benefits of the chosen control system. Whilst workers may be involved in the dialogue regarding the type and level of control that is appropriate, ultimately, it is the role of managers to decide on the one to be implemented. Good management practice will be evident when the correct balance is struck between control and a good working environment in which employees and the organisation can prosper. Another aspect of good management practice is the ability to make effective decisions. Much of the discussion in this chapter has revolved around managers' ability to evaluate the environment before deciding on the appropriate control system to implement. Decision making is an integral part of management and forms the basis of explanation, discussion, and analysis in the next chapter.

Chapter questions and tasks

Giving examples, outline some of the reasons for organisations to introduce formal control systems.

What are the sources of control in a TQM system?

What forms of resistance to a control system may be evident from workers?

What attributes does a control system require to be effective?

Online Resource Centre

Author commentary on these questions can be found on the Online Resource Centre at: www.oxfordtextbooks.co.uk/orc/combe1e/

Further reading

- Anthony, R. N. and Govindarajan, V. (2006) *Management Control Systems* (12th edn), New Jersey, McGraw-Hill Higher Education.

  This text is a more condensed version of previous editions but contains enough content to deliver useful insights into the different aspects that comprise management control systems. The value of the book lies in its clarity of exposition in explaining how managers design and implement control systems for business strategies. The book uses a number of examples and cases to contextualise different approaches to control in different organisational settings.

- Bowhill, B. (2008) *Business Planning and Control: Integrated Accounting, Strategy, and People*, London, John Wiley & Sons.

  This text gives a systematic and clear introduction to key areas of business planning and control by linking issues of strategy, management, and accounting information. The book goes on to describe how control systems are designed and for what purpose, using case study examples as illustrations. A useful text for both undergraduates and postgraduates seeking a basic insight into the development of control systems by managers.

- Merchant, K. and Van der Stede, W. (2011) *Management Control Systems: Performance Measurement, Evaluation and Incentives* (3rd edn), Harlow, Financial Times/Prentice Hall.

  This third edition of a well-regarded textbook has a number of new features that makes the work more contemporary and comprehensive. The book contains a wide range of international examples that place in context the myriad issues surrounding control systems, tools, and techniques. The book uses a combination of theory and practical examples to explain the complexities of management control systems. Among the new topics included are corporate regulation, risk management, the implications of the 2008 financial crisis, corporate governance and ethics, and the application of the balanced scorecard technique.

- Oakland, J. S. (2003) *TQM: Text with Cases* (3rd edn), Oxford, Butterworth-Heinemann.

  The issue of TQM is explained in a coherent and logical manner so that non-specialists can understand the concept and how it is applied. In particular, the book explains how TQM can be applied to achieve world-class performance and backs the theory with practical examples. Key aspects of the book include the Business Excellence Model, self-assessment, and benchmarking. The treatment of quality management systems provides students with a clear insight into how this aspect of management has emerged as a key route to competitive advantage in the 2000s and beyond.

- Streatfield, P. (2001) *The Paradox of Control in Organisations: Complexity and Emergence in Organisations*, London, Routledge.

  The author uses his experience in business to articulate how managers deal with the issue of control. The book departs from mainstream approaches to explaining control by focusing on aspects of management that are beyond the 'control' of managers. The text provides a useful insight into how managers deal with situations that normal control systems cannot.

Online Resource Centre

For more information, updates, and multiple-choice questions, please visit the Online Resource Centre at: www.oxfordtextbooks.co.uk/orc/combe1e/

Skillset 6
Exam techniques

215

6(a) Introduction

This chapter of the book represents the half way point of the learning process and presents a point where attention during a module turns to assessment in general and examinations ('exam(s)') in particular. This Skillset focuses on exams and exam technique. It provides you with examples of typical exam questions related to the topics in the book and is accompanied by model answers. You will be able to discern exam writing techniques that are conducive to passing this type of assessment instrument. These will include writing concise responses that provide sufficient depth of knowledge and analysis, use of cases for illustration purposes, structuring a response, and focusing on the question asked.

Students need to be able to pass exams to achieve the academic standard that contributes to their employability. This Skillset can be used as an aid to achieving the standards expected in this particular context. In addition, the characteristics tested by examination (for example, the ability to perform under time pressures) are also valued by employers.

6(b) Why do we still have exams?

Trends in what constitutes an appropriate assessment at university have changed over time. From examinations being the final and perhaps only assessment, many degree programmes moved to continuous assessment—a range of pieces of coursework or other assessments throughout the module. Exams were seen as little more than a test of memory/recall. However, it may be that exams are making a comeback. So, why do we still have exams? There are four main reasons:

- exams test your ability to (in many cases) respond to unseen questions;
- exams test your ability to create a coherent answer under the pressure of a time constraint;

- exams test your understanding of the topic the question relates to, and may also test your ability to analyse and evaluate;
- exams are 'proof' that you did the work. Written reports or essays can be plagiarised, or even purchased, but you have to be present for an exam and may have your identify verified.

6(c) Types of exams

For our purposes we will consider two types of exam:

- Closed book exam—the 'classic' exam where you revise but are not allowed to bring any notes, textbooks, and so on to help you with the exam itself;
- Open book exam—in this case you *are* allowed to bring notes, textbooks, and so on to help you with the exam. You are not normally allowed electronic sources.

Critics of closed book exams regard them as a memory test; however, the requirements to analyse and critically evaluate test more than just rote learning. Open book exams can be more difficult than closed book ones as you would not gain marks for just copying from a source.

Exam questions can take many different forms, such as multiple-choice, short answer, or essay formats. For our purposes we are considering the essay format in which you would write a paragraph or number of paragraphs/pages in response to the question.

It is important to develop the skill of being able to read the question(s) carefully and understand what is required. This means thinking about not only the topic (for example 'control') but also the other words which are very important such as:

- Critical evaluation—taking an evidence-based approach to weigh up different points of view;
- Analysis—a process of reasoning or thinking which, for example, may break a topic down into its constituent parts to examine the interrelationships between them.

See University of Manchester (undated) for more terms which can be used in exam questions.

6(d) A process for sitting exams

Why would someone who does not know the subject area as well as you do achieve a higher mark than you? It may be that their exam technique is better than yours. We can divide the process of preparing for, and sitting exams, into three broad phases:

- Phase 1: Beforehand—revision
- Phase 2: On the day (and during the exam)
- Phase 3: Afterwards—learning for the future

Each phase is discussed below.

6(e) Phase 1: Beforehand—revision

Preparation is crucial and should not be left to the last minute. Key aspects to think about include:

- **Review the material** you have gathered as part of the module (module handbook, lecture notes, articles, textbooks, and so on). What are the key themes you, or your tutors, have identified? Do any of the themes overlap with content of other modules? There may be an opportunity to revise one topic which helps you with more than one module. For example 'motivation' is a management topic but it might also form part of a module on human resource management. Similarly, some topics in this book cross chapters. For example, leadership (Chapter 5) can be an important influence on organisational culture (Chapter 12).

- **Resist the temptation to rely purely on lecture notes.** Study the module handbook, the lecture content, the directed reading, papers given out, and so on. You are given a range of material ('actual', e.g. handouts, and 'suggested', for you to follow up for yourselves) for a reason—to help you develop your understanding of the module content. You should also consider doing some wider reading of your own, and think about your own personal knowledge and (work) experiences and how they might fit with the module content. Giving lecturers 'our own' examples back to us is good; but giving us *your own* relevant and appropriate examples is even better.
- **Make revision notes.** A key aspect here is that the process of reading–revising–reading–revising will help you assimilate the material. Typically you will gradually condense your notes to a comparatively small kernel of knowledge which you can read quickly and that will 'spark' other associations with the material you are revising.
- If possible, **look at past papers** for your subject. These may help you identify key themes and also give you examples of the sort of wording used for questions.
- **Think about what the tutors said** at any revision session—were there any 'clues' about what topics are important? However, try and avoid 'question spotting' as that is a high risk strategy. For example, the syllabus may have changed from previous years so you cannot rely on a particular topic appearing. Make sure you are certain about: the topics covered (did the tutor say a particular topic will not be examined?). How long will the exam last? Where is the exam to be held? How many questions are you expected to attempt? Are there any compulsory questions?
- **Develop a plan** for your revision. Typically blocks of around one hour with five or ten minutes break can help you keep focused. It is important to spread the blocks out and not try and cram things into too short a time. See Skillset 3 on time management.
- If you can, try and sit a mock exam even if it is only one question. Marking might be by yourself, your fellow students, or perhaps it may be a more formal event marked by your tutors. In any case the realism (and possibly anxiety) of sitting down and writing your answer will be good practice for the real thing.
- You are **part of a learning community** with your fellow students. Remember to engage with them as they can offer advice and support you (and vice versa). Try and develop your own strategy for dealing with exams, though, and remember that what works for someone else may not work for you.

The following is a serious, but unconventional, exam revision tip: Write more Christmas cards/postcards/letters to friends and relatives.

As tutors we regularly hear comments after exams such as 'I could have written more if I had more time' or 'I ran out of time' or 'My hand was sore'.

When was the last time you took up a pen or pencil and wrote out, longhand, something which others could read and understand? In the exam you can expect to have to write fairly continuously for two hours (or more)! How fast can you write legibly and for how long? A *serious suggestion* is that you spend time (re)developing your ability/endurance at hand writing as this is a skill which most of us do not practise these days yet, clearly, it is a critical aspect of how much you can write during the exam (and hence the 'volume' of content that is available for tutors to mark). In the past students were used to hand-writing lecture notes; but were slow at typing. Now the opposite is true!

6(f) Thinking about how to answer the questions set

Before moving onto what to do on the day of the exam itself, part of your revision should be to consider carefully how you will approach actually sitting the exam. Not in any order of importance, there are a number of key principles.

217

Structure your answer—an introduction, middle (main part), and conclusion. The beginning is important as it helps you structure (for yourself and the reader) what is coming up instead of 'leaping in' ('look before you leap'). The conclusion is also important to draw your key points together.

Answer the number of questions required. If you have to answer three questions from six, answer three questions! This may be obvious, but some students only really answer two questions with, at best, some brief notes for a third one. This usually makes it difficult to achieve a pass mark—it is *much* harder to turn a mark of 19/25 into 24/25 than it is to turn a mark of 5/25 into 10/25. Good time management is crucial. You will already know the number of questions you are expected to answer and the length of the exam—so work out how long you have per question.

Theory and examples. A good answer will usually cover both the relevant 'theory' (including naming key authors/articles and discussing their work) *and* give some examples (for example from leading organisations) to illustrate the points made. This is a general principle, and getting the balance right in the context of a particular question is important, but not always easy—some questions may emphasise just the theory (but an example or two to illustrate the theory is good), other questions may specifically ask for examples to support the points you make (so you would lose marks if you covered the theory but had no examples). In general, 'theory' comes first, and an over-reliance on anecdotes/examples is unlikely to result in a good mark.

A common question asked is 'In the exam, do we need to reference material like we have to in our courseworks?' The short answer is 'no'. However, if you can indicate that you know who some of the key authors are, and when they wrote their key works, then it is only natural that tutors would wish to reward this additional knowledge/understanding.

Question for reflection

A simple and perhaps trivial example, but consider the following:

> There are five things you need to think about when looking at competition in an industry *[no author, no date]*

compared to

> Porter's Five Forces model identifies five 'forces' to consider when analysing competition within an industry *[author, no date]*

compared to

> Porter (1980) developed the Five Forces model which identifies five 'forces' to consider when analysing competition within an industry. Over 30 years old, Porter's model is . . . *[author and date]*.

Which version do you think should receive the highest mark (other things being equal)? Why?

6(g) On the day (and during the exam)

Make sure you had plenty of sleep before the examination. Have breakfast and set off for the exam location in plenty of time. Remember to bring pens, your student ID card, and a bottle of water (dehydration can reduce brain function and energy levels!). When you reach the venue, check that you are in the correct place. If possible enter your name, student ID, and so on, on the cover of the exam booklet before the exam starts.

Remind yourself of the number of questions you have to attempt (how many minutes each) and if there are any compulsory or choice sections of the paper. Know how many questions you have to do, how many minutes you have for each question, and which questions you want to do (if there is a choice).

'You may now turn the question paper over . . .'

Carefully read the question paper including the instructions (remember to check it is the right paper). Choose your questions and plan your time accordingly. Note down a plan for each of your questions (or you can do this at the start of each question as you go along). Conventional wisdom is that you do your best (the easiest?) question first. However, ensure you do not become carried away and lose track of the time as you have a lot of material to write about for this one question. Make sure you keep to your timings. In particular, make sure you leave enough time to adequately attempt the final question.

Ideally you have time left to reread your work and perhaps polish it a bit. However, if time is running out, write in note form to indicate what you would cover and any key points.

'You should now stop writing . . .'

6(h) Afterwards

You cannot change what you did for the exam just finished, but you can learn from the experience . . . for the next time.

There are two key points when you can reflect on your revision and the exam itself. First, a day or so after the exam. Secondly, once you have received your results and (perhaps) had an opportunity to see your exam script and the marker's comments.

A day or so after the exam can be a good time to consider your revision strategy. For example:

- Did you start early enough?
- Did you have all the relevant materials to hand?
- Did you spend enough time on each question or did you run out of time for the final question?
- What would you do differently next time?

Once you receive your results and can consider the marker's comments (which may be some weeks after the exam)—are there any lessons to be learnt?

6(i) Activity

This activity provides an opportunity to practise your 'exam technique'.

1 Overview
You will sit a closed book (see Section 6(c)) examination comprising one question. The examination will be based on the content of Chapter 2 of this textbook on management theory. You will have 40 minutes to write your answer. The question will be awarded a mark out of 100; the pass mark is 40. Fix a date/time for the exam now, so that you have a target you must work to.

2 Preparation
Based on the advice in Sections 6(f) and 6(g) read and revise the chapter as preparation for the examination. Depending on the time you have available this revision might be a day or so, or longer.

3 The examination
Put aside some time and quiet space so that you can sit the exam under appropriate conditions. As you will be hand-writing your answer, make sure you have the appropriate materials available.

4 The question

This is your question:

> Describe and compare the key underlying concepts of the classical approach to organisational theory with the human relations approach, and evaluate the extent to which these concepts are still relevant to modern day organisations.

Remembering the principles outlined in Section 6(h) . . . your 40 minutes starts now . . .

. . . Your 40 minutes are up . . . please stop writing . . .

5 Outline answer

The following is an outline answer.

You can use this answer to evaluate your own work. If you work closely with fellow students, you could ask them to 'mark' your answer (out of 100) from their own understanding of what

Text of Answer	Comment
The seeds of management theory were planted in the eighteenth century by such people as Adam Smith, Charles Babbage, and Robert Owen but modern management theories were developed from the early to mid-1900s and incorporated the classical, human relations (HR), and neo-HR systems and contingency approaches. The following will describe and compare the classical and the HR approaches and evaluate the continuing relevance of these ideas to modern day organisations.	● Introduction ● Last sentence sets up what the answer will cover using key words from the question.
Classical approach F. W. Taylor, principles of scientific management (1911), H. Fayol, general principles of management (1916), M. Weber, legitimate authority and bureaucracy (1924). Discuss the main principle of each of these authors and for each one, assess the continuing relevance for modern day organisations. Summarise the classical approach: based on universal prescriptions; one best way; formal structures of organisation; organisations as unitary entities with shared or mutual objectives; 'organisation as a machine'; 'economic' or 'rational' man. Human relations approach Elton Mayo—Hawthorne experiments (1880-1949); Mary Parker Follett (1868-1933). May include the neo-human relations theorists—Maslow, McGregor, Herzberg, and Likert. Briefly discuss their contributions and assess their continuing relevance. Summarise the HR approach: informal structures; group dynamics; other motives apart from money; leadership style an important influence; more psychological approach; what motivates and how to motivate; 'social' man. Compare the two approaches, e.g. 'rational' versus 'social' man.	● Main body ● An outline is given here—not the continuous prose expected. ● Remember to 'compare' the two approaches.
Summary of main points and general conclusion as to the relevance, or otherwise, of the theories to modern day organisations.	● Conclusion ● Clear end point to answer the question set regarding the relevance of theories

is required; then ask them to mark your answer using the model answer. This could be a good revision/learning opportunity for them too. If they have done the practice exam, you could return the favour for them.

Based on the advice in Section 6(h), what lessons might you learn from this activity which you can apply to your actual exams?

6(j) Summary of the Skillset

The ability to perform well in examinations is a core academic skill. The requirement to plan your revision and then effectively rise to the often stressful and pressured situation of the examination itself has its counterpart in performing to deadlines within the workplace. This Skillset distilled a range of advice on preparation for exams, performance during exams, and reflection after exams. In addition an activity provides the opportunity to put the advice into practice.

References/Further reading/Resources

Colorado State University (2012) *Look at each exam question to identify key words.* [Online.] Available from: http://writing.colostate.edu/guides/processes/exams/pop2b.cfm

Glasgow Caledonian University (2012) *Exams.* [Online.] Available from: http://www.gcu.ac.uk/student/exams/

McMillan, K. and Weyers, J. (2009) *The Smarter Study Skills Companion* (2nd edn), Harlow, Pearson Education.

University of Manchester *Glossary of Exam Terms.* [Online.] Available from: http://www.humanities.manchester.ac.uk/studyskills/assessment_evaluation/assessment/glossary.html [Part of a series of pages on Assessment and Evaluation.]

7 Decision Making

Learning outcomes

- Comprehend the nature and characteristics of decision making

- Understand the different types of decisions

- Understand the application of the decision making process

- Apply models of decision making

- Critically evaluate the limitations of decision making models

Decision making is an integral part of management and an activity that takes place every day at different levels, such as operational, functional, or strategic. Managers have to trust their judgement based on factors such as experience, knowledge, intuition, intelligence, analytical skills, and so on. Some of the most successful managers have reached the top of their profession because they are able to make the correct judgement calls more often than their rivals. Some view this as a product of experience and knowledge, others put it down to luck or being able to access the right people to help achieve their aims. Whatever the reason, the most successful managers all display an aptitude for understanding their environment and making critical decisions that give a competitive advantage. A prime example of this is George Soros who made his reputation (and money) speculating on currency markets. This requires judgement, nerve, and an understanding of the balance between risk and reward within a complex and highly changeable environment. He gained international notoriety when, in September 1992, he risked $10 billion on a single currency speculation when he predicted the shortened value of the British pound. His prediction came true and in one day of trading he generated a profit of $1 billion. Thereafter, Soros was known as the man who 'broke the Bank of England' (Litterick, 2002).

Skillset 7
Literature review

The choice of literature that comprises a review is dependent on informed decision making. Each decision taken is the outcome of a process of evaluating a range of variables that act as enablers or resistors to achieving set aims. This chapter on decision making presents students with models of decision making that can be transferred to the skill of undertaking a literature review.

Student study skills

A review of literature is a key element of students' project work, essays, dissertations, and other academic output. This Skillset provides students with clear guidance on how to compile a review that includes choices of which literature to include, how to make judgements about the value of literature to the understanding of a particular topic, and the importance of critique in the review.

Workplace skills

The skill of undertaking an evaluation of the quality of literature can be transferred to many workplaces where there is a requirement for making value judgements on the quality and usefulness of the vast array of written material available to support activities. This Skillset will enhance decision making about which literature adds value and how it can be articulated to stakeholders.

Definition

Decision making is a position or judgement reached after due consideration and a choice has been made between alternative courses of action. Decisions are reached using cognitive processes, memory, thinking, intelligence, analysis, and evaluation. Eisenfuhr (2011) refers to decision making as a process of making a choice from a number of alternatives to achieve a result.

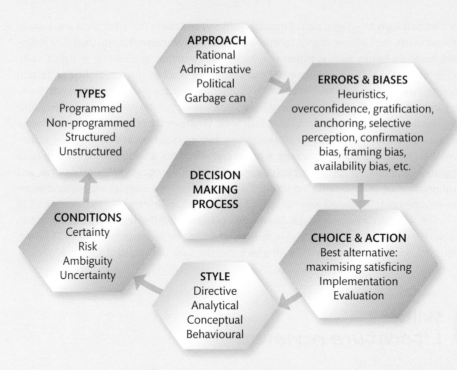

Figure 7.1 The decision making process

Introduction

The chapter begins with an explanation of the conditions that affect the decision making process such as uncertainty, risk, and ambiguity. This is followed by an outline of the nature of programmed and non-programmed decision making. Descriptions, analysis, and examples are given for models of decision making including the rational, administrative, intuitional, political, and garbage can models. Emphasis is on the processes, advantages, and limitations of the models. For example, issues of bounded rationality and satisficing are used as means of explaining the limitations of the administrative model. Factors leading to error or bias in decision making are highlighted and discussed. The chapter concludes with an analysis of the link between decision making and different styles of management. Figure 7.1 illustrates the key elements comprising the decision making process.

Conditions affecting decision making

Once a problem or opportunity has been identified it is necessary for managers to undertake the process of decision making. That process is affected by the prevailing conditions under which activities such as analysis, research, and evaluation take place. In particular, issues of certainty/uncertainty, risk, and ambiguity all have an influence on the ability of managers to make the correct decisions. As such it is worth exploring these three issues in some detail.

Certainty and uncertainty

The amount of information available to help inform a decision will be variable. In some instances managers will have access to all the information they need to make an informed decision. In that situation managers have a clear understanding of the relative merits of all the alternatives. Certainty is rare but can occur in situations where variables are measurable and a quantitative calculation provides information that informs the best decision. This is often the case in engineering and construction works where the parameters and targets are known. For example, the construction of the *Millau Viaduct* in southern France required structural engineers to slot two ends of the construction together over a 2.4 kilometre length with only a 25 millimetre deviation tolerance. All the engineering and construction decisions were governed by these exacting and fully calculated parameters (Saxton, 2007). For the most part decision making is undertaken in conditions of uncertainty whereby only some of the information needed is available. Uncertainty involves an element of risk as managers make decisions without having all the information when assessing alternatives. The role of the manager in this situation is to assess the risk and the benefits and make a decision based on the relative outcomes of the assessment. One of the problems of uncertainty is the risk of a distortion of beliefs that can affect managers when confronted with a lack of information (Sjoberg, 2007). Sometimes this manifests itself in the form of wishful thinking or unrealistic perceptions of the problem or solution.

Risk

Risk entails managers making judgements about the likely outcome of alternatives. Under conditions of uncertainty an element of risk will be attached to any decision. Risk management is the identification, analysis, assessment, control, and avoidance, minimisation, or elimination of unacceptable risks. At the strategic level, the risk factor becomes ever more acute and difficult to map as the timeframe for analysis is elongated. Sperandio and Girard (2010) offer a framework for decision making linked to risk assessment that focuses on the strategic level of management. Some industries thrive on risk and uncertainty, such as gambling, the stock markets, investment banking, and so on. Quah et al. (1994) analyse the intuitive aspect of hedging strategies in international currency markets. Other industries try to minimise risk such as insurance, health and safety, and business consultancies.

Ambiguity

Ambiguity refers to situations where goals are not clear or well understood or the means by which they are to be achieved are uncertain (Daft, 2008). Ambiguity increases the risk of decision making as those involved cannot be certain that they are pursuing the correct outcome let alone the means by which they get there. Ambiguity can lead to wasted resources, ineffective risk assessment, lack of coordination, and a lowering of staff morale. It is the role of management to minimise ambiguity by showing leadership and communicating exactly what the organisation is trying to achieve and how they intend to put in place actions to achieve clearly stated aims. The functions of management outlined in Chapters 3 to 6—including planning, organising, leading, and controlling—should come together to minimise ambiguity. However, it is worth noting that different cultures view ambiguity differently. In developed western nations much of the decision making process is governed by notions of rationality, whereas in China, for example, ambiguity is viewed as a natural phenomenon within the environment

225

(Fox and Tversky, 1995). Hsu and Chiu (2008) offer an interesting comparison on decision making models between the western and eastern hemispheres. The condition of certainty and level of uncertainty, risk and ambiguity have effects on the types of decisions made. Two main types of decisions are programmed and non-programmed decisions.

Programmed and non-programmed decisions

Decisions vary markedly in terms of the inputs and knowledge required to support them. In some instances decisions are routine and require little insight or extended knowledge to support them. This may be in situations where previous knowledge and experience reveal what the outcome will be and therefore a high level of certainty allows decisions to be arrived at relatively easily. In other situations the key factor variables are characterised by complexity and uncertainty. Numerous alternatives may be possible thereby adding to the ambiguity and risk attached to each decision. These two examples lend illustration to the difference between programmed and non-programmed decision making.

Programmed decision making

A programmed decision is one that is routine, non-complex, and with outcomes that are predictable (Kinicki and Williams, 2010). The information and knowledge required to make programmed decisions are likely to be easily identified, readily available, and well understood. Programmed decisions occur frequently and become part of routine procedures in many organisations. In supermarkets, managers in charge of logistics and supply chains make programmed decisions on a regular basis regarding the types and volumes of products to order. *Tesco* have become experts at predicting the volume of demand for a range of standard products such as milk and bread. This feeds into their decision making process relating to supply orders at particular times during the working week to fulfil demand and maintain a flow throughout the supply chain that maximises efficiency and reduces costs. Decisions are made routinely based on prior knowledge, experience, and detailed information on demand and supply. Thus, rules and procedures for undertaking decisions of this nature are firmly embedded in the operations of the company. This will include pinpointing who is able to make the decision at any given time. Increasingly, automated systems undertake the process of programmed decision making where the activities are systematic and routine.

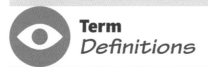

Term
Definitions

Programmed decision: a decision that is routine and repetitive.

Non-programmed decision: a decision that is unique to the situation and that requires a unique solution.

Non-programmed decision making

A non-programmed decision is one that is unstructured and unique to the situation (Kinicki and Williams, 2010). Normally these types of decisions arise from inadequate or unclear information, an environment characterised by uncertainty or ambiguity, and where several different interpretations of the situation and information are possible. Often these types of decision revolve around opportunities that emerge in the business environment and which require managers to assess whether or not to pursue them. The decision will be informed by inputs from personnel throughout the organisation as well as perhaps some external stakeholders. For strategic decisions managers may have to consult shareholders as part of a due diligence process before making a decision. Non-programmed decisions may be as a result of changes in the environment that were unforeseen, meaning managers need to react quickly to the evolving situation. Economic downturn may negatively affect demand for the product or service produced, meaning that managers have to make non-programmed decisions on how to deal with that. It may involve the rationalisation of staff, cutting back production, decreasing the product range, cutting the marketing budget, and so on. Non-programmed decisions are unique to the situation (although there might be some precedent from the past, no two situations are absolutely identical) and may not involve an optimal or ideal solution but rather one that serves its purpose. For example, if a company lowers the returns on investment for shareholders as a result of diminishing market share or a dip in profits, it may not be welcomed by investors but the decision to do so may help to secure the future of the business in the longer term. In 2010 Canadian IT and business process outsourcing company *CGI Group Inc.* announced that they would not be giving dividends to shareholders as a result of the downturn in the economy and in order to prioritise global growth for the future (Lasalle, 2010). This was a non-programmed decision based on an understanding of the current economic conditions and the long-term strategic aims of the company.

227

? Critical reflection
Are there appropriate steps that can be taken to ensure effective decision making?

Very often bad or inappropriate decisions are made because managers have not created the correct conditions or environment in which effective decision making can emerge. Most people in professional environments have had experience of meetings where participants engage in different conversations simultaneously or where one person dominates the proceedings. Sometimes there is no effective mechanism in place to put into action decisions that are made. In other instances the wrong personnel may be in the decision making positions. There are some valuable prerequisites for creating a positive and constructive environment for effective decision making.

Perhaps the most important first step is to clearly define what the objective is. This enables the correct people to be chosen to attend meetings or participate in whatever forum the decision making takes place. There also has to be a set process through which decisions can be reached. This may involve the final decision resting with an individual, or it may be through consensus, or some other format. Whatever the process chosen, it is necessary that each participant understands what it is from the outset. Involving the correct people is essential to effective decision making. Even in situations where the final decision rests with an individual, it is good practice to take proactive steps to involve stakeholders. Where the decision rests on a group, then that group should be representative of stakeholders. In the decision making forum it is important that all participants have an opportunity to contribute. This may require an effective chairman who controls the proceedings. Dissenting voices need to be heard even if it is a minority of one. This helps to avoid the phenomenon of groupthink (discussed later under 'Errors and biases in decision making'). The chairman should also ensure that the group do not drift towards adversarial point scoring but remain true to the objective. Finally, it is important to adopt a creative approach to decision making that may require participants to step out of their 'comfort zone' to explore new ways and means of reaching a decision. This might be brainstorming, role playing, or playing 'devil's advocate'. These techniques go some way to creating the type of environment in which better and more effective decision making can take place.

Types of decision making models

There are many different types of decision making models that have been devised to help managers analyse, evaluate, and implement decisions. Some use a systematic and process oriented approach, others incorporate some of the intangible factors that influence decision making, such as intuition. The models chosen for this chapter are inclusive of both these approaches and include:

- the rational model;
- the administrative model;
- the intuitional model;
- the political model;
- the garbage can model.

Rational decision making model

The rational decision making model assumes that people will seek to maximise their economic returns, and that by doing so they undertake rational and consistent courses of action to achieve that outcome. At the organisational level, managers seek to maximise economic returns for the company (the criteria for public sector or not-for-profit organisations are different as they are invariably based on issues of accountability, transparency, best value, or social welfare returns). Secchi (2010) provides an illuminating insight into how the concept of rationality can be extended within organisations' decision making processes. The rational decision making model assumes a number of key criteria including that:

- there is an agreed goal;
- the problem is structured;
- there is a high level of certainty regarding the environment;
- there is complete information;

7. IMPLEMENT DECISION

6. DECIDE

5. EVALUATE ALTERNATIVES

4. DEVELOP ALTERNATIVES

3. ANALYSE ALTERNATIVES

2. GATHER INFORMATION

1. IDENTIFY THE PROBLEM

Figure 7.2 Rational decision making model

- the outcomes of alternative solutions can be measured and understood;
- there is an economically optimal solution;
- decision makers are rational in their approach and assessment of alternatives.

Figure 7.2 highlights the stages that comprise the rational decision making process.

Stage 1 **Identifying the problem:** the first stage of the process entails identifying the problem (or the opportunity). The rational approach is most useful when confronted with relatively complex problems that require a decision to be made. The identification of a problem is an important first stage as it provides the necessary insight into the nature of the issue to be resolved. Analysis at this stage should determine whether or not there is a problem that requires a decision.

Stage 2 **Information gathering:** the second stage involves the information gathering process. This stage helps managers concentrate on acquiring the type of information that adds detail to the nature of the problem and creates the knowledge that informs decision making.

Stage 3 **Analysis of the situation:** analysis of the situation will reveal what alternative courses of action are available. Analysis may reveal different interpretations of the data and information gathered and present decision makers with options to consider. Analysis needs to be both broad-based and deep.

Stage 4 **Develop options:** once the analysis has taken place managers are in a position to develop options. Effective analysis should reveal what decisions are available. This stage often requires some creative thinking and a superior understanding of what is possible.

Stage 5 **Evaluate the options:** after the alternative decisions have been identified managers need to be able to *evaluate* them in terms of their appropriateness to achieving stated aims, their feasibility, and acceptability to stakeholders who affect the decision(s) or are affected by the decision(s). Managers need to determine appropriate criteria in order to fully and effectively evaluate the alternatives available. Sometimes evaluation can be based on quantitative data, others may be qualitatively based, and sometimes a mixture of the two is appropriate. In some instances managers may rely on their intuitive skills or knowledge and experience as much as on formal evaluation methods.

Term
Definition

Rational decision making: decisions based on consistent choices designed to maximise economic returns.

Stage 6 Select a decision: this is the critical phase whereby a preferred decision is selected. There is an analytical aspect to this phase as managers seek to understand what the consequences of the choice of decision may be. A risk assessment may be a feature of this stage to better understand the consequences of the choice.

Stage 7 Implement the decision: finally, managers have to implement their choice of decision. At this stage they should ensure that colleagues are fully committed to making the choice work even if some may harbour reservations about it.

The main advantage of applying the rational decision making model is that it provides a structure in which the decision making process can be undertaken. The systematic approach that underpins the structure focuses attention on the key factors that influence the decision making so that the process consists of a logical progression of ideas, analysis, and evaluation. The model helps decision makers arrive at an outcome in a disciplined and comprehensive manner having considered many key factors.

There are, however, some significant weaknesses associated with the rational approach. In the first instance the model assumes that human beings think and act rationally and, therefore, make rational decisions. Very often information is incomplete or distorted or there may be some emotional element involved in the decision making process that influences outcomes. Decision making involves a range of emotional and intellectual stimuli including values, beliefs, attitudes, judgement, intuition, and knowledge. These vary considerably between different people, especially when different cultural influences in the global environment are taken into consideration. Also, although it helps to highlight what needs to be done to arrive at a decision, the rational model offers no insight into how to enact a decision. Very often the time available to analyse the identified key factors is inadequate or has failed to include key stakeholders. Competitive pressures can limit the amount of time available to undertake effective research and analysis into a problem or opportunity, thereby forcing managers to make decisions without access to full information. Similarly, time or resource limitations may mean that insufficient time and effort are given to assessing alternatives. Li (2008) provides empirical evidence from research at Korean electronics giant *Samsung* that points to the first stage of the rational decision making model being unattainable because workers do not perceive a problem, or if they do, they do not understand the nature of it. In the case of Samsung the production managers perceived their product range to be aged but had no evidence to confirm it. Workers perceived no problem at all. Thus, the rational decision making model was ineffective in dealing with this scenario, leading to a search for alternative approaches by managers. The debate surrounding whether or not a rational decision making model is appropriate in certain situations and professions is one that has been going on for some time. Mini case 7.1 brings into focus the problems associated with this model when dealing with the diverse and complex nature of human behaviour.

Mini case 7.1
Ethical decision making model for social care provision in New Zealand

In 2004 the psychology profession in New Zealand, as part of a wider social care association, introduced a model of decision making as part of a code of ethics designed to enhance levels of trust with clients and other stakeholders, improve professionalism, and offer guidance for psychology professionals in decision making roles, especially in the area of social care provision. This has been subsequently updated under the 'Code of Ethics' for Aotearoa New Zealand Association of Social Workers (2012). The guide was welcomed by many within the profession as a timely support mechanism for psychologists dealing with complex and sensitive social and psychological problems. However, the move also sparked a debate into the wisdom of introducing a prescriptive set of guidelines into what is by definition a very complex, unique, dynamic, unpredictable, and rapidly changing set of circumstances that are common features of the case environments in which social psychologists operate. Introducing an ethical dimension to the mix further adds a layer of complexity and ambiguity that can sometimes make decision making more difficult. For example, perceptions of ethical behaviour can vary markedly between different social groups. Critics noted that ethical decisions are often made without access to full information, often within constricted timeframes, and sometimes without sufficient support and resourcing. These are the realities of delivering social care provision. However, proponents of the Code of Ethics countered with the claim that for the majority of cases decisions are made on a routine basis and require little deliberation. This view underpins the rationale for the design of the model of ethical decision making for New Zealand's psychologists working in social care. The attendant Code of Ethics necessarily demands cognitively explicit, linear, and rational decision making.

The main criticism of the rational approach is that it failed to significantly advance the ethical decision making process from that which had been in practice previously. Traditional approaches were founded on the principles first set out by Janis and Mann (1977) and involved the following linear process of decision making:

(i) canvas a wide range of courses of action;
(ii) survey a full range of objectives and values;
(iii) carefully weigh all known positive and negative consequences;
(iv) search for new information intensively;
(v) re-examine all alternatives and considerations before making a decision;
(vi) make detailed implementation plans and prepare potential contingencies.

This rational style of decision making has been a feature of health professions for many years but exhibits a number of weaknesses including the lack of recognition that most professional workloads are so intense that the scope for undertaking this process is limited. Indeed, the much cited failures of social care providers in high-profile cases has served only to remind the public of the impossibly high expectations placed on social care professionals. Ethical decision making is influenced by a wide range of social, economic, and psychological variables including personal characteristics relating to values, beliefs, culture, mood, emotions, and so on. External factors also play a role, such as the structure of the organisation, levels of authority and control, reporting processes, support mechanisms, and the transfer of knowledge. The most relevant tension between the designers and critics of the ethical decision making model implemented for New Zealand's psychologists working in social care is that the former sought a goal-assured or optimal decision, whereas the latter believe that no such model can exist in the context of their everyday working reality.

Sources:

Aotearoa New Zealand Association of Social Workers (2012) *Code of Ethics.* http://anzasw.org. nz/social_work_practice/topics/show/157-background-of-the-code-of-ethics

Janis, I. L. and Mann, L. (1977) *Decision-making: Making a psychological analysis of conflict, choice, and commitment*, New York, The Free Press.

Discussion point

Is it appropriate to formulate a Code of Ethics to inform decision making in a profession such as social psychology?

Questions

What are the main criticisms of the Code of Ethics for decision making designed for psychologists in New Zealand?

What types of decisions are psychologists most likely to make during the course of their work in the social care sector?

Are past decisions helpful as a guide to best practice in decision making by psychologists involved in the delivery of social care?

Online Resource Centre

Author commentary of this discussion point and questions can be found on the Online Resource Centre at: www.oxfordtextbooks.co.uk/orc/combe1e/

Administrative model

The administrative model of decision making developed by Simon (1960) is a rational model, but one that incorporates more realistic assumptions of uncertainty and ambiguity in the environment. It also assumes that not all information is available to decision makers and that very often the identified problems are unstructured and not measurable. These constraints align more closely to the reality of the environment in which managers undertake the decision making process (Cyert and March, 1992). Consequently, managers rely more on the attributes of intuition, experience, and judgement compared to the proponents of the rational model for whom decisions are derived from a process of undertaking systematic activities. Decisions under the administrative model tend to be of the non-programmed type where the problem is unstructured and unique to the situation. Two key elements define the administrative model, those of bounded rationality and satisficing.

Bounded rationality

The ability of humans to make decisions is limited by their capacity to absorb and analyse information. Although they may seek to take a rational approach to decision making, this limitation acts as a boundary or parameter beyond which they are unable to process information effectively (Simon, 1982). The diversity of environments and the rapidity with which they change make these limitations all the more acute as decision makers are required to process ever-increasing amounts of information that varies in importance and complexity. This makes strict adherence to the rational decision making model problematic.

Satisficing

To retain some level of rationality, the administrative model includes the concept of 'satisficing'. The word 'satisficing' was created from an amalgamation of the words 'satisfy' and 'suffice' and was designed to capture the essence of compromise in negotiations. Thus, satisficing is not the optimal position but one that is acceptable. This position may be the most pragmatic as there may be an opportunity cost associated with continuing a search for an optimal outcome. That is, the time and effort spent on further research and analysis of options may be a cost that outweighs the benefits (Nutt, 2004). Satisficing is a useful concept for moving forward and bringing closure to a situation or problem requiring a decision. Satisficing is a position often arrived at in negotiations whereby there is a recognition by all parties that no one party is going to achieve an optimal outcome at the expense of others. Satisficing is a position that allows all parties to leave the negotiations with a satisfactory outcome. The question then turns to—'satisfactory' for whom? As the Second World War was drawing to a close in 1945 the three leaders of the axis nations, Josef Stalin (Russia), Franklin D. Roosevelt (USA), and Winston Churchill (UK) met to determine the future shape of Europe. Each leader had his own idea of the preferred outcome but to reach agreement meant compromises on all sides. Ultimately, Europe was divided between east and west. Countries such as Poland, Czechoslovakia, Hungary, Romania, and Bulgaria found themselves on the communist-dominated Russian side of Europe, with the western nations retaining the democratic tradition. This gave rise to the term 'Iron Curtain' that demarcated the two sides until the fall of the Berlin Wall in 1989. So, although the 'satisficing' approach led to an agreement, the outcome was far from satisfactory for the millions of people living under the yoke of the Russians for decades thereafter.

Bounded rationality and satisficing are two concepts that bring a better level of realism to the administrative model compared to the strict doctrines of the rational model. Here, there is an element of heuristics employed where a 'rule of thumb' can help the decision maker find a solution in complex and uncertain situations (Moustakas, 1990). It also better recognises the limitations and flaws inherent in the human condition. For example, it recognises that managers often fail to clearly state goals and objectives; fail to effectively prioritise problems or opportunities; misjudge information; cut corners and fail to undertake effective research; and seek to find closure at the earliest opportunity. These are just some of the many human characteristics evident in managers and workers. The longevity of the administrative model as a means of understanding decision making owes much to its recognition of the human aspect of dealing with this important function of management.

Term *Definition*

Administrative model of decision making: a model that recognises the limitations of decision making in ambiguous and unclear situations when information is incomplete.

> **?** **Critical reflection**
>
> ## Is 'bounded rationality' a rational approach to understanding the human condition?
>
> In the early 1960s Herbert Simon defined bounded rationality in terms of human behaviour that is intended to be rational but is limited by what he termed 'cognitive defects'. The motivation for Simon's intervention was to encourage economists to incorporate a more realistic and human aspect to the development of theories and models. Simon's contribution was significant in generating academic interest in the role of human cognition into the discourse surrounding economics. However, as Foss (2001) points out, his definition was imprecise and led to assumptions around bounded rationality that failed to fully capture actual decision making processes. In an attempt to fill this gap in understanding, Weber and Mayer (2010) suggest two types of cognitive bounds on rationality. These are processing limitations which recognise restrictions on the quantity of information processed, and perceptual limitations that recognise the restrictions on perceptions of how the information is processed. Weber and Mayer note that most assumptions in bounded rationality only recognise processing limitations and largely ignore the ones relating to perceptions. This has led to a one-dimensional view of bounded rationality that makes the decision making process overly simplistic. This revelation initiated a debate regarding the efficacy of existing models of bounded rationality. Economist Oliver Williamson (2000), whilst recognising the absence of perceptions and cognitive biases in traditional economic theory, asserts that bounded rationality provides a strong foundation for decision making. Conversely, Foss (2003) believes the lack of acknowledgement of perceptual limitations is a significant weakness and advocates the incorporation of cognitive social psychology into the assumptions for bounded rationality to offer a more robust and realistic decision making model. The debate illustrates how different academic disciplines view their contributions to issues such as decision making and how those contributions shape our understanding of them.

Intuitional model

The administrative model takes account of some of the human aspects involved in decision making. One of the attributes of the human condition is the development of an intuitive characteristic to understanding the environment. Intuition is instinctive knowledge or insight without conscious reasoning, even though the conscious mind is used for rationalising and formulating outcomes. Simon (1987), as one of the early proponents of the administrative model, provides an articulate and convincing account of the role of intuition and emotion in the management decision making process. Decision making based on intuition is built on a combination of knowledge and judgement of past experiences that informs thoughts and behaviours. It also requires people to be more in touch with their emotions and to have the sensitivity to understand the world around them (Agor, 1990; Parikh, 1994). An intangible asset, intuition is something referred to when managers state that an option 'just does not feel right' or that they have a 'good feeling' about a decision. These 'feelings' derive from a heightened recognition of past experiences and their link to the new situation presented. Intuition can be thought of as an advanced form of pattern recognition

Term
Definition

Intuition: instinctive knowledge or insight without conscious reasoning.

that delivers an insight, sometimes referred to as an 'inner voice' or 'sixth sense'. Sometimes these can prove insightful and valuable, and at other times misguided and damaging. Myers (2002) discusses the power and perils associated with intuition in a management context.

Intuitive decision making is often evident in fast-moving and uncertain situations that require a decision quickly. Commanders in the Israeli Defence Force (IDF) in the field of battle are trained to react to different situations but in the 'fog of war' very often it is the intuitive skills that inform decision making. As such a great deal of time and training is given over to honing intuitive skills and forms part of the selection process for higher ranks in the Israeli army. Kahneman (2011) provides an insightful critique of this approach based on his own experience and research. In such situations there may be little or no time to undertake rational analysis. Very often the problem is unstructured to the extent that rational approaches become ineffective or there may be no past precedent to call on to inform decision making. Sometimes both the rational and intuitive approaches are adopted in dealing with situations. For example, doctors treating a patient in an emergency situation will follow a rational and systematic process to diagnose trauma or illness, but it is often in conjunction with their intuitive knowledge about what is happening to the patient. In many cases the intuitive knowledge fills the gap when insufficient information is available. Figure 7.3 outlines some of the ways in which intuition can be used to make decisions.

Experience-based decisions are a common feature of how managers arrive at a decision. Very often they look to past precedence for an answer to a problem. The rationale is that if a solution worked in the past then it can work again. Over time managers build a considerable bank

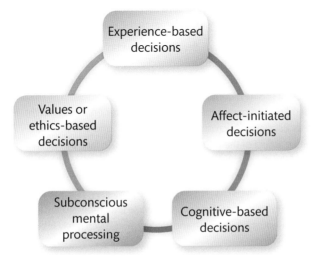

Figure 7.3 Intuition as a decision making support mechanism

of experience based on events and situations they have faced in the past. They may have made mistakes in the past and later rectified them by moderating their behaviour. They may have been lucky and hit on an effective solution to a problem by accident. They may have received training to help them make sense of the environment in which they operate and make decisions. No matter where the experience comes from or how it is derived, it all contributes to the bank of tacit knowledge that managers carry with them in their minds. Much of the decision making that takes place in organisations is as a result of knowledge gained from past experience. This experience can also contribute to a higher level of intuitive skill if managers recognise and embed the associated emotional element of the experience in the form of a memory. When faced with similar situations in future the memory triggers an emotional response that heightens awareness and understanding.

Another type of decision is the affect-initiated decision. These are highly influenced by intuitive processes as managers make decisions based on feelings or emotions (Agor, 1986). Intuition is enhanced when people are in touch with their emotions. Emotions are highly sensitive reactors to the environment that allow a heightened sense of awareness and understanding of situations and relationships that help inform appropriate responses. Emotional intelligence is a term often used to describe the extent to which people understand themselves and how they affect others in their environment. Managers can make decisions based on their values, or for cultural or ethical reasons. Fundamental to the ethical stance is an understanding or perception of what is 'right and wrong'. Although these perceptions change and are complex there are a wide range of behaviours that can be deemed as 'right' or 'wrong' by consensus. Identifying and placing in context ethical dimensions to decision making feeds into the intuitive part of the mind that helps inform appropriate behaviour. Thus, intuitively, managers know how the consequences of their actions and behaviours affect others' welfare. Over time these values based on ethics become embedded in the mind and inform a person's way of thinking such that ethical values always take precedence over non-ethical ones.

Subconscious mental processing is what the human brain does most of the time. The majority of actions undertaken by humans are completed without consciously thinking about them, such as walking the dog, talking to people, or even driving a car. Neuroscience research experiments confirm that the parts of the brain responsible for action show signs of activity before the conscious mind actually registers the action (Soon et al., 2013). Thus, subconscious mental processing completes the task before the conscious mind tells it to. This process is a skill that can be honed and utilised as a means of enhancing the intuitive parts of the mind.

Cognitive-based decisions derive from the field of psychology where cognition is seen as the process by which sensory input is transformed, reduced, elaborated, stored, recovered, and used (Neisser, 1967). Cognition is an everyday activity for humans as they interact with each other and their environment. In a business context, cognition works in tandem with intuition as the former enhances understanding and comprehension, and the latter enhances insight. High-profile business people such as Bill Gates (Microsoft), Donald Trump, and Oprah Winfrey have extolled the virtues of the intuitive aspect of their decision making skills. In fact, business history is replete with examples of successful entrepreneurs who have relied on their 'instincts' rather than formal training. Allison et al. (2000) argue that entrepreneurs tend to by-pass rigorous analytical endeavour in favour of a reliance on intuitive skills. Their cognitive processes inform them that it is rational to make decisions based on 'instinct' as they invariably view limitations on time as a constraint to their business activities. Consequently, in-depth and analytical research rarely features in their approach.

The debate regarding the most effective way of approaching decision making has been a feature of management discourse for many decades. Proponents of the rational model argue that the systematic and analytical approach yields superior results. However, it is clear that the intuitive aspects of decision making have found favour among many academics including Kleinmuntz (1990) who highlighted the fact that so many management problems have no formula for a solution. Mintzberg (1994b) addressed the weaknesses inherent in the rational model by taking a strategic management perspective. At the strategic planning level, Mintzberg asserts that the rational model of decision making is inappropriate because strategy cannot be planned. His argument is that planning is about analysis whereas strategy is about synthesis. Sometimes managers trust their instincts even though they may predominantly favour a scientific or analytical approach. This flexibility in thinking can reap rewards as Mini case 7.2 illustrates.

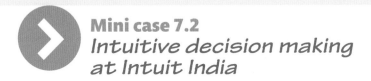

Mini case 7.2
Intuitive decision making at Intuit India

Intuit is an American software company founded by Scott Cook and Tom Proulx in 1983. The company produces products for individuals and small businesses including personal finance programmes *Quicken* and *TurboTax*. The *Quickbooks* range of accounting programmes for small businesses is a global seller. The company has several overseas sales offices and a number of semi-autonomous development sites including that of *Intuit India*. With revenues now regularly topping $3 billion annually the company is a Fortune 100 listed enterprise and one that has previously taken on and beaten industry giants Microsoft in their core business (Taylor, 2012).

Much of the decision making process at Intuit has traditionally been based on sound analytics and metrics. The company founders have taken a largely methodical route to company development and growth. Whether it be developing new products, building network relationships, partnering, or market development, the company has based decision making on careful analysis and risk assessment around its innovation strategy (Upbin, 2010). However, as the experience of key personnel within the company grew alongside that of the business, a more intuitive characteristic of the decision making style started to emerge. One example is the product launch by *Intuit India* that delivered a prototype in just seven weeks. Rather than relying on the time consuming rational approach to decision making the company took a more intuitive approach.

In line with the strategy of exploiting opportunities in all sectors of Indian industry the company focused their skills and experience on developing an SMS (Short Message Service) marketplace that would form a hub of information for Indian farmers seeking to identify the markets that would offer them the maximum price for their products. Rather than spending months creating and developing a platform, the company created a prototype in a matter of weeks. With no back-end technology the information was delivered manually. Only when the market was proven did the company set about building the *Intuit Fasal* platform. The approach was high risk and unproven but the management team of Cook and Proulx ran with their 'hunch' that things would work out. Eschewing the reliance on traditional analytics they took their cue from years of experience, a close understanding of the market dynamics, and the value of experimentation. In fact, the rationale for the approach taken was that it entailed less risk as the prototype could be tested and proven before a large-scale investment decision was necessary. Subsequently, the intuitive side of decision making has become a feature of the company's approach, not in place of analytical and rational approaches but complementary to them.

http://www.
intuit.co.uk

http://www.
intuit.co.uk

Sources:

Taylor, S. E. (2012) *How the Makers of Quicken Beat Microsoft and Revolutionised an Entire Industry*, Boston, MA, Harvard Business School Press.

Upbin, B. (April 9, 2010) 'Why Intuit Is More Innovative Than Your Company', Forbes.com. http://www.forbes.com/sites/bruceupbin/2012/09/04/intuit-the-30-year-old-startup/3/

Discussion point

Is reliance on intuition more risky than an analytical approach to decision making?

Questions

Why has it taken almost thirty years for the management of Intuit to introduce an intuitive aspect to their decision making?

What were the main risks associated with the Intuit venture into the Indian farming market?

Is intuition only valuable when considering issues that are culturally specific to experience?

 Online Resource Centre
Author commentary on this discussion point and questions can be found on the Online Resource Centre at: www.oxfordtextbooks.co.uk/orc/combe1e/

Political model

There is a political dimension to all formal organisations as they comprise people with varying interests, values, beliefs, and goals. People or groups will behave in ways that help them to maximise their influence on the management of the organisation through the acquisition of power and authority. Decisions made by managers very often enhance the position of one person or group at the expense of another. Pareto optimality (giving advantage to one without disadvantaging another) is very difficult to achieve in an organisational setting but can feature as part of strategic decision making (Tschappeler et al., 2011). The pursuit of goals within a political environment often leads to conflict as people seek coalitions and enact behaviours that are designed to help them achieve their own (or their sub-group's) goals. Figure 7.4 illustrates key elements of the political model. Like other models, the political model is built on a number of assumptions including that of the diverse range of interests, values, beliefs, and goals

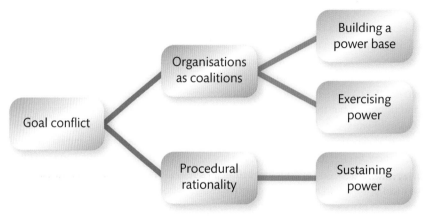

Figure 7.4 Political model of decision making

of individuals or groups within an organisation. This diversity often leads to conflicting views between managers on how best to deal with situations and how best to achieve goals.

Another assumption is that information is incomplete and ambiguous. Diversity of interests tends to make information more complex and difficult to 'read'. Consequently, a rational approach to making sense of the information is undermined by its complexity and range. A further assumption is that managers arrive at a decision after a period of discussion, analysis of alternatives, debate, and negotiation. Here, satisficing is a common outcome as managers seek closure on the issue at hand.

The political model illustrated in Figure 7.4 starts with the premise that there are conflicting views regarding the goals to be achieved by the organisation. This can be the catalyst for intensifying political activity internally as different individuals or factions manoeuvre themselves into positions that are advantageous to the pursuance of their aims. These aims may be multifarious in type and scope and may include personal ambition, departmental influence, resource allocation, strategic decision making, and so on. Pfeffer and Salancik (1974) provide an interesting case study of the political process in decision making around a university budget.

Two different perspectives underlie the manner in which political activity plays out in organisations and informs the decisions that underpin that activity. The first perspective views organisations as a series of unstructured coalitions where interpersonal relationships constantly form and disband according to the level of political advantage gained from each. People within organisations will seek and nurture relationships with others if they perceive the returns from that relationship will help them to achieve their aims. They will constantly update their view on this and make decisions based on their value judgement. In some instances that judgement will be to end or drift away from relationships that fail to deliver what they want.

The second perspective is that of a structured organisation where decisions are based on rationality and clearly set-out procedures. Here, the emphasis is on how to work politically within the boundaries of the system. Understanding and exploiting the procedures is the means by which decisions are made that help advance the cause of individuals or groups. The civil service is an example of procedural rationality where there is a clear promotional pathway that can be pursued. There is a political dimension to this too because individuals or groups need to position themselves favourably in order to achieve their aims. This may require the help and guidance of others as they try to make sense of the system within which they operate. Once goals are achieved, then procedural rationality helps to sustain the power base as there is a formal power structure and authority that underpins it.

Achieving goals by exploiting coalitions helps to build a power base and offers the possibility of exploiting that power base. Sustaining that power into the future depends on how adept

Term
Definition

Political model: a decision making model that recognises the influence of groups with different interests, aims, and beliefs within an organisation.

people are at continuing to identify and exploit relationships that help to maintain the power. Each of these perspectives requires a range of decision making capabilities, some short-term, others strategic in outlook. However, in each of them there is a heightened sense of the political environment in which individuals and groups operate. To succeed within a highly politicised environment requires a combination of interpersonal skills and an ability to build consensus. This is evident in Mini case 7.3 where an age-old tradition of decision making in the tribal lands of Afghanistan has stood the test of time.

Mini case 7.3
Decision making in the Loya Jirga of Afghanistan

Afghanistan is an ancient land with a long and deep-seated culture based on adherence to the Holy Quran. However, even pre-dating the time when the nation embraced Islam is the tradition of holding 'Jirga'—a gathering for consultation purposes. This process was subsumed into Islamic tradition whereby the Holy Quran commands Muslims to the Shura (consultation). The *Loya Jirga* is convened when an issue of high importance needs a decision based on the discussions and opinions of tribal leaders. Normally, the issue has high national or international importance, such as the form of relationships forged with international forces deployed within the country. In 2011 it was reported that the *Loya Jirga* national assembly was to meet to discuss peace proposals put forward by western allies (Farmer, 2011).

Jirga is seen as a reliable and authoritative decision making process that involves many layers of Afghan society (although women are conspicuous by their absence) including scholars, professionals, and religious leaders. Tribal leaders believe that the *Jirga* is an impartial forum where decisions are discussed in an open and rational manner and that it constitutes an important political dimension to decisions affecting civil society in the country. Noelle-Kimini (2002) provides a fascinating insight into the history, structure, and political influence of the *Jirga*. The *Jirgas* are notable for the length of discussions and the formulation of a process that eventually leads to consensus. Tribal leaders need to strike a balance between interests that serve their purpose and the valued cohesiveness of the society in which they live. The decision making process follows a distinct procedure that starts with the head of state inviting tribal leaders and others to attend the *Jirga*. The *Jirga* then agrees terms of reference and a framework for communication. There follows the official discussion and debates on agreed issues. The *Jirga* then sets a mechanism for a final decision. Consensus is achieved when all attendees agree on a position. This accounts for the sometimes lengthy discussions. Nevertheless, agreement must be reached before the *Jirga* can set up a committee to implement the actions agreed upon.

In many ways it can be seen that the *Jirga* follows the same decision making process as local and council authorities in western countries with key representatives of communities brought together to make decisions that affect the lives of the communities. A key difference is the democratic nature of western models compared to the method of representation at the *Jirga* which is based on heredity (tribal leaders), knowledge (scholars), status (religious leaders), or political prowess (the head of state). However, the longevity of this system owes much to the effectiveness with which it allows many different views to be expressed but ultimately reaches a conclusion through consensus. It also underpins Afghan culture by ensuring that tradition is valued and respected.

Sources:

Farmer, B. (15 November 2011) 'Afghan Loya Jirga National Assembly to Discuss Peace', *Telegraph*. http://www.telegraph.co.uk/news/worldnews/asia/afghanistan/8891152/Afghan-Loya-Jirga-national-assembly-to-discuss-peace.html

Noelle-Kimini, C. (2002) 'The Loya Jirga—An Effective Political Tool? A Historical Overview', in C. Noelle-Kimini, C. Schetter, and R. Schlangerweit. *Afghanistan—A Country Without A State?*, Franfurt, IKO-Verlag fur Interkulturelle Kommunikation.

Discussion point

Has the *Jirga* system more to do with maintaining an ancient tradition than operating an effective mechanism for decision making?

Questions

What are the main advantages of the *Loya Jirga* system of decision making?

Is the *Jirga* democratic in its decision making process? Explain your answer.

What type of management style is evident in the decision making processes of the *Jirga*?

 Online Resource Centre
Author commentary on this discussion point and questions can be found on the Online Resource Centre at: www.oxfordtextbooks.co.uk/orc/combe1e/

241

Garbage can model

The garbage can model is mostly linked with situations where cause and effect is ambiguous and where the key player or players do not know what their preferred outcome is. Here, the decision that is ultimately reached is separate from the decision making process. The previous sub-sections have clearly set out the process through which decision makers arrive at a decision. In the garbage can model, no such process can be used. Often the information that helps to frame a process is missing or only partially available. The inclusion of luck, chance, or accident into the equation is an important element in understanding this approach. March (1988) identified four key streams that coalesce to inform decision making in a highly ambiguous environment. These are:

Choice opportunities:	pre-set times when decisions have to be made (for example a promotion round)
Participants:	the people who have the influence to present opportunities (for example marketing managers who present challenges to production staff for adapting an existing product)
Problems:	problems that concern people (for example a service delivery expectation)
Solutions:	problems that require solutions (for example new ideas)

In this model the choice opportunities represent the garbage can containing the myriad different participants, problems, and solutions. Different combinations of these three elements determine the number of people interested in a solution to an identified problem leading to a decision. Different combinations of participants may have a different perspective of the problem and derive

Term
Definition

Garbage can model: a model of decision making based on the assumption that the environment is characterised by extreme uncertainty and that responses to that environment are neither rational nor predictable.

a different solution by arriving at a different decision. This unstructured and almost random set of interpersonal relationships may appear a rather haphazard way of arriving at decisions but is a feature of many fast-paced, flexible, and agile organisations where creativity and innovation are key drivers of competitive advantage. In creative industries such as publishing, advertising, and design the key to advantage often lies in the ability of key people to network, exchange ideas, and quickly transform them into new and innovative outputs. In this regard, the garbage can model more closely reflects the reality of decision making in many modern businesses.

Critical reflection
Why is decision making through consensus not universally accepted by managers?

Many of the decision making models assume a 'top-down' approach whereby power and authority bestowed on managers at the higher echelons of an organisation are given expression in the form of decision making. Decisions are made at the top and communicated downwards to subordinates who have to action them. It is, by design, exclusive and does not take into account the views of wider stakeholders. This approach is evident in organisational structures that are hierarchical with clearly defined levels of authority and span of control. The exclusion of stakeholders (some of whom may wield significant influence) can lead to disengagement with the company aims, lower morale, and insubordination. However, in many modern business settings this hierarchical structure has been replaced by flatter structures, network organisations, and even ones with no discernible form of formal power and authority.

The trend in many industry sectors has been to allow a greater number of people to contribute to the decision making process rather than relying on the decisions of a few to cascade down through the organisation. The intention is to access greater expertise, understand different perspectives, and expand inclusiveness by creating a more egalitarian route to decision making. The trend towards a more inclusive form of decision making changed the means by which decisions are arrived at in many organisations. As opposed to the traditional, non-collaborative approaches, there has been a trend towards that of consensus decision making processes. Supporters of the consensus approach believe that it fosters better decision making because it allows input from a wider constituency of stakeholders that addresses a greater number of concerns.

Although the consensus approach may appear more democratic and inclusive, this type of decision making process is not without its problems. Often the decision arrived at is through majority vote after a period of debate and discussion. It is a forum that is adversarial in nature as different factions do battle to air their views and persuade others to agree to their view. It encourages political activity which can manifest itself into a fractious and divided workforce rather than a united and cohesive one. Consensus decision making does not require full agreement to work but has all the potential for leaving a residual of discontent or even animosity in its wake. This may undermine the ability of the workers to cooperate fully in implementing the decision.

Errors and biases in decision making

Managers seek to maximise the returns from the decisions they make, or at least seek to satisfice to allow them to proceed towards their goals and objectives. Very often the ability of managers to make astute judgements that inform decision making is compromised by human failings. Errors and bias typically result from an inability to manage complexity or fully comprehend the issues. In some instances it follows from poor judgement, over-reliance on past experience, or an overly simplistic solution to a problem. Identifying common errors and sources of bias is a useful first step towards making better decisions. Table 7.1 outlines some typical types of errors and biases that can undermine effective decision making.

One of the biggest dangers facing decision makers is that of 'groupthink'. Groupthink is a way of thinking that evolves during the interaction of a close-knit group of people. The negative effect of such an intense and close group is the tendency to drift towards a position of unanimity rather than focusing on a full and deep analysis of the problem. A subconscious collective mood emerges that undermines the ability of individuals to dissent from the group's way of thinking. One of the most serious examples of the negative effects of 'groupthink' in recent times was in the lead up to the explosions and close meltdown of the *Daiichi Fukushima* nuclear plant in the aftermath of the 2011 tsunami in Japan. Officials underplayed the threat of tsunami when designing the plant as there had been no significant event for over a thousand years (World Nuclear Association, 2013). The National Institute for Advanced Industrial Science and Technology (NISA) was instructed to concentrate on the effects of earthquakes when modelling their risk assessment. The focus of officials in decision making positions was channelled towards a narrow set of scenarios that were deemed most likely to happen rather than the wider range of possibilities (Acton and Hibbs, 2012).

Part of the problem lay in the strong collective culture of Japanese society where stepping out of alignment with the group is seen as almost deviant behaviour. This culture is not conducive to challenging the majority view or those of superiors. It was within this collective mindset that the disaster unfolded. In the event, an undersea earthquake triggered a giant tsunami that overwhelmed the plant leading to almost catastrophic consequences. The 'groupthink' of officials meant that the destructive capability of a tsunami was never taken seriously enough to merit close attention when decisions on health, safety, and contingency planning took place during the commissioning phase of the plants by operators TEPCO.

Table 7.1	Errors and bias in decision making	
Type of error or bias	**Description**	
Heuristics	Using 'rule of thumb' to simplify decision making	
Over-confidence bias	Unrealistically positive views of performance or capability	
Gratification bias	Choosing an alternative that delivers immediate reward	
Anchoring effect	Concentrating mostly on initial information	
Selective-perception bias	Decision based on the decision maker's biased perception	
Confirmation bias	Seeking information that reaffirms past choices	
Framing bias	Focusing undue attention on certain aspects of a situation	
Availability bias	Compromising objectivity by focusing on recent events	
Randomness bias	Excessive influence of random events in the environment	
Representation bias	Adopting inappropriate analogies	
Sunk costs bias	Failure to see that current actions cannot change past events	
Self-serving bias	Taking credit for success but not responsibility for failure	
Hindsight bias	Thinks an event could have been predicted after the fact	

Decision making and cognitive styles of management

There are many different cognitive styles for decision-making. Myers (1962) (see Figure 7.5) presents a model that narrows the scope of these into four cognitive styles of management:

1 analytical;

2 conceptual;

3 behavioural;

4 directive.

The model is designed to link the different ways of thinking associated with these styles of management, to the level of ambiguity tolerance associated with each. The way of thinking has a spectrum ranging from the rational and procedural (linked to the analytical and directive styles) that emphasises the use of models, data, and 'rules of thumb' based on tried and tested techniques. Further along the spectrum the emphasis changes to that of intuition, abstraction, imagination, and other human traits and characteristics (linked to conceptual and behavioural styles).

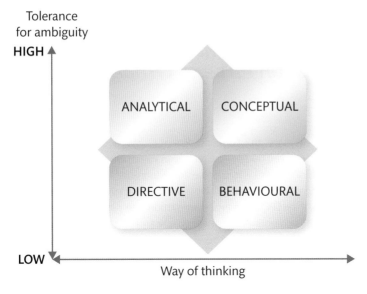

Figure 7.5 Decision making and cognitive styles of management

The analytical and directive styles

The analytical style is one characterised by careful consideration of information in unique situations. The analytical style of management is one that is a feature of engineering or science-based professions where theoretical models have been tried and tested to determine appropriate decisions. The analytical style is one that tries to minimise the risk associated with decision making in an uncertain environment. The quality of analysis based on minimal information means that this style has a high level of tolerance for ambiguity.

This is in contrast with the directive style that is based on rules, procedures, and regulations. These parameters are set within a preconceived notion of the environment in which they were designed. Any change in this environment places stress on the viability of the decision making process and is therefore characterised by a low tolerance for ambiguity. Consequently, the directive style tends to consider only a few alternatives. Further along the spectrum of ways of thinking are the conceptual and behavioural styles.

The conceptual and behavioural styles

The conceptual style maintains a broad outlook and considers many alternatives in making decisions. There is a high level of tolerance for ambiguity. This contrasts with the behavioural approach that has much less tolerance for ambiguity as it relies on being receptive to suggestions from others who have access to information and knowledge. A key characteristic of the behavioural style is the avoidance of conflict. This often arises through insufficient or inadequate information, hence the low tolerance for ambiguity.

In some instances, managers will exhibit elements of more than one style and implement them according to different situations and different goals. This flexibility is a feature of modern management where there is an expectation and value placed on the ability to adapt styles according to need.

http://www.
epo.org/
http://www.
epo.org/

Case study
The decision making process at the European Patent Office

Introduction

Situated in Munich, Germany, the European Patent Organisation was formally established in 1977 and comprises two main bodies—the European Patent Office (EPC) and the Administrative Council. The purpose of the EPO is to oversee and administer an agreed application procedure for innovators seeking patent protection across the forty signatory countries under the aegis of the EPO. The mission of the EPO is to support innovation, competitiveness, and economic growth across Europe through a commitment to high quality and efficient services delivered under the European Patent Convention of 1973. The executive of the EPO comprises the President, five Vice-Presidents, and four other members who sit on the Management Committee of the EPO. There is also an education and training aspect to the EPO's activities with patent-related training programmes for lawyers, patent office staff, judges, examiners, and others with an interest in patenting as an intellectual property right. However, the core activity is to examine patent applications and award the status of European patent. There is a close and on-going dialogue between the EPO and member states as well as non-European countries.

Patents

A patent is a formal intellectual property right that protects inventions. A patent protects the intellectual innovation that underpins how things work; what new inventions do; how they are applied; the materials they are made of; and how they are made. Patents for innovations awarded by the EPO must have some tangible and practical quality to them. The patent award process is outlined on the EPO website. Essentially, a patent bestows the right on the owner to prevent others from making, using, importing, or selling the invention without permission. Owners of patents can sell them, license them, or use them for their own commercial enterprise. Before being awarded a patent, an inventor must demonstrate that the invention meets certain criteria. The invention must:

● be new;
● demonstrate an inventive step (extends beyond that which already exists);
● be capable of being manufactured or used in some form of industry.

Patents are not awarded for scientific or mathematical discovery or theory. Nor do they cover works of art, literature, or musical production. In Europe, patents are not awarded for ideas or concepts or computer programs. The patent regime in the United States is more liberal and does allow for patents on such criteria, for example, the 'One-Click' software designed by e-commerce retailers Amazon.com was awarded a patent in the USA amid much controversy (Paul, 2010). This lack of harmonisation of criteria for awarding patents has made decision making problematic in the realm of intellectual property rights at the global level.

Main activities and procedures of the EPO

The EPO has a duty to carry out searches and undertake examinations on patent applications from innovators in any of the forty countries that they oversee. They do likewise for a number of international applications filed under a Patent Cooperation Treaty that involves non-European countries. As well as deciding on the award of patents, the office also deals with opposition to the award of European patents. The European patent system relies on the full

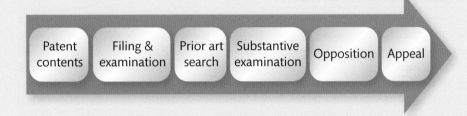

Figure 7.6 European patent procedure

disclosure of any invention through publication. The general public can then access details of all European patent documents through the EPO's European Publication Server. The European Patent Register provides details of the status of any patent application in the process of filing and examination. The EPO holds over 70 million patent documents that are available on the online *Espacenet* service.

The award of a patent requires a systematic and rational approach to decision making and this is reflected in the procedures put in place to arrive at an appropriate and fair decision. Figure 7.6 illustrates the European patent award procedure.

The patent application procedure begins with the formal submission whereby the basis upon which the patent application is submitted is presented. The second stage is the formal examination of the application. This is where the examiners check that the application meets all the primary criteria for consideration and present an examiners' report on the outcome. The third stage of the decision making process is the search for prior art. Prior art refers to all the information that is in the public domain in any form prior to the date of the patent submission that may have a bearing on the originality of the patent's claim. Any invention that is discovered to exhibit 'prior art' will not be considered valid for an award of a patent. At this stage the examiners study the application as a whole in terms of the claim, the description, and any drawings that support the application claim. This part of the process follows a distinctly rational process of decision making. That is, key concepts are identified, documents are searched, a technical classification is assigned to the invention, a more refined search is undertaken, and finally an evaluation report is given. Examiners then decide whether or not to proceed. If no prior art is revealed then the application goes forward for more substantive examination. If there are no substantive objections then the criteria of novelty (extending the state-of-the-art), non-discoveries (ensuring that there is a tangible and practical aspect to the invention), and inventive step (that it constitutes a distinctive advance on what already exists) are all satisfied. Figure 7.7 illustrates the procedure from search to substantive examination.

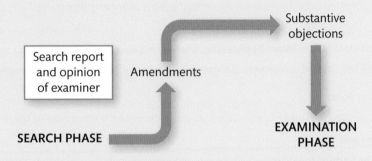

Figure 7.7 From search to substantive examination of a patent application

Understanding the decision makers

To be awarded a patent requires innovators to deliver a new invention that meets the criteria set out by the EPO. However, there are many inventions that sit on the margins of those criteria and, therefore, require an element of persuasion to convince the examiners of the worthiness of the patent application. This is where the decision making process evolves from the rational to the perceptual. That is, different examiners may perceive the same thing differently based on their understanding of the technical aspects of the invention, its application and use, and the extent to which it constitutes an inventive step. To increase the impact that the application has, innovators need to understand the decision making processes evident among examiners. For example, it is useful to know what the background of the decision maker is, such as his or her education, specialism, cultural influences, etc. Similarly, an insight into the decision maker's previous decisions can reveal the thought processes that lead to a particular outcome. In civil courts it is standard practice for lawyers to research the background and professional history of judges who are assigned to cases involving their clients.

A patent examiner is a key decision maker in the patent procedure. In the initial phase of enquiry the patent examiner is likely to follow a rational and systematic method of decision making regarding the formal application and its fit with the process. This approach is suitable for determining how many inventions are claimed in the application, if the application satisfies the formal criteria, and whether a patent is to be granted to cover any invention claimed in the application. For the most part, examiners will call on tried and tested techniques and experience to make these decisions. However, there is an element of subjectivity in the process as examiners are often required to make decisions based on their opinions. For example, there may be no past precedent for arriving at a decision regarding the scope of any patent to be awarded for something that is unique in its construct. Here, there has to be a persuasive aspect to the application that is designed to influence the examiner to make a favourable decision. The tension arises from the fact that the patent examination should be rational but the method by which they arrive at a decision is a mixture of different approaches. Thus, some aspects of the decision making process are routine and structured, whereas others are unique and unstructured. Add to this the right of applicants to request an interview with examiners and it is easy to see how the whole process moves on from a rational and structured process to one that involves advocacy, argument, and persuasion. Most of the arguments revolve around issues of what constitutes novelty, state-of-the-art, or inventive step. Many decisions are dependent on the opinion of a chosen person who is considered to be 'skilled in the art' of what the invention is designed to achieve. A skilled practitioner needs to be aware of what is considered common knowledge in a particular technical field and have access to everything that is currently state-of-the-art. This helps to reduce the reliance on the persuasive aspect of evaluating applications but cannot eradicate it completely. Indeed, many protagonists of the current patent system believe that it is healthy for there to be a persuasive aspect to the decision making process.

Sources:

European Patent Office, Patent Applications, Munich. http://www.epo.org/applying.html

Paul, R. (11 March 2010) Controversial Amazon 1-Click patent survives review, arstechnica.com.

Discussion point

Does the persuasive aspect of patent applications undermine the robustness of the process?

Questions and tasks

Identify the parts of the patent application process that align to the rational decision making model.

What other types of decision making are evident in the patent application process?

Why is there no global decision making system for patent applications?

 Online Resource Centre
Author commentary on this discussion point and questions can be found on the
Online Resource Centre at: www.oxfordtextbooks.co.uk/orc/combe1e/

Summary

- **Comprehend the nature and characteristics of decision making**

The nature of decision making requires a position or judgement to be reached after due consideration of all relevant factors. Essentially, decision making entails a choice being made between alternative courses of action. Decisions are reached using cognitive processes, memory, thinking, intelligence, analysis, and evaluation. There are numerous characteristics of decision making including the approach taken, the type of decision to be made, the influence of errors and biases, style of management, and the conditions under which decisions are made.

- **Understand the different types of decisions**

There are many different types of decision making models. The main types identified and discussed in the chapter were programmed, non-programmed, structured, and unstructured decisions. Programmed decisions are routine and non-complex, non-programmed decisions are made within an uncertain environment where information is ambiguous. Here, the decision is unique and requires a unique solution. Some decisions are structured and follow a process, others are non-structured and rely on experience or intuitive skills.

- **Understand the application of the decision making process**

Issues of certainty/uncertainty, risk, and ambiguity all have an influence on the ability of managers to make the correct decisions. A rational approach to decision making can be adopted in an effort to minimise uncertainty and risk. This process may include identifying the problem or issue, gathering and analysing information, developing and evaluating alternatives, and then making a choice. It was noted that the assumptions underpinning the rational approach have undermined its credibility and been the catalyst for other types of application of the decision making process to be developed.

- **Apply models of decision making**

A number of different models of decision making were presented and explained including the rational model, intuitive, administrative, political, and garbage can models. Each has its merits and limitations. Some were developed in an attempt to overcome some of the limitations exhibited by others. The chapter included a critical evaluation of the key characteristics of the models, their purpose, and how they can be applied.

- **Critically evaluate the limitations of decision making models**

Each of the models presented in the chapter has certain limitations that were identified and discussed. For example, the rational model is overladen with unrealistic assumptions, similarly the administrative model featuring 'bounded rationality' is based on assumptions that can prove to be misaligned to actual decision making processes. Some decisions are made using intuition rather than a rational approach. Sceptics point out that success using this approach is as much down to luck as judgement, whereas proponents believe that intuitive skills can be honed over time using a mix of experience and highly developed cognitive processes.

Conclusions

This chapter has set out the main approaches to decision making and offered a critical assessment of the value of each. It is impossible to identify one particular model or style of management that is capable of delivering an optimal solution for decision making as the nature of the task is governed by many different variables and types of situation. The role of management in the modern business environment has become an eclectic mix of the analytical, behavioural, and intuitive styles. Managers may find themselves having to make decisions on technology, human resource capabilities, networking arrangements, or ethics in a globalised and rapidly changing environment. It is unlikely that managers possess the requisite skills, knowledge, and understanding of all (or even many) of these but, nevertheless, they are required to make important decisions that feature them. More than ever managers need to harness the qualities of the people around them to help make the decisions that deliver the goals of organisations. Consequently, managing human resources has become an increasingly important role in modern businesses and forms the basis of the discussion and analysis in the next chapter.

Chapter questions and tasks

Identify and describe an occasion when you have decided to act on a 'hunch' or an intuitive feeling that it is the correct thing to do.

Outline the seven main steps in the rational decision making process.

Identify the main difference between the rational and administrative models of decision making.

Give three examples of politically motivated decisions in organisations.

Online Resource Centre

Author commentary on these questions can be found on the Online Resource Centre at: www. oxfordtextbooks.co.uk/orc/combe1e/

Further reading

- Adair, J. (2010) *Decision Making and Problem Solving Strategies: 66 (Creating Success)*, London, Kogan Page.

  An invaluable addition to the prolific output by Adair. The author sets the scene by outlining how the mind works before discussing what he terms the 'art of decision making'. Adair articulates the reasons why managers in organisations fail to make a decision or opt for the wrong one before setting out the processes that lead to effective decisions and problem solving. Key concepts are expressed in a lucid manner and the writing style is accessible to both undergraduate and postgraduate students.

- Gigerenzer, G. (2008) *Gut Feelings: Short Cuts to Better Decision Making*, London, Penguin.

  Gigerenzer focuses attention on the role of instinct and intuitive thinking in the decision making process. The work is from the perspective of a psychologist but offers valuable insights for practitioners and students of business by revealing the processes at work that help decision making through the application of techniques designed to enhance intuitive thought.

- Proctor, T. (2009) *Creative Problem Solving for Managers: Developing Skills for Decision Making and Innovation* (3rd edn), London, Routledge.

  Innovation is key to creating a competitive advantage in many modern industrial settings and this book focuses attention on the ideas and skills involved in problem solving creatively. The author analyses the types and reasons for blockages in the creative process and suggests some compelling techniques for overcoming barriers to innovative decision making.

- Spiegler, R. (2011) *Bounded Rationality and Industrial Organization*, New York, Oxford University Press.

  The key issue addressed by Spiegler is the assumption of managers in organisations that consumers are rational with well-defined preferences and an understanding of the market. In fact, the author reveals that consumers are characterised by inconsistencies and have context-dependent preferences. The book challenges the orthodoxy of traditional economic models based on conventional thought by analysing the theory of bounded rationality.

- Stone, D. (2012) *Policy Paradox: The Art of Political Decision Making*, London, W.W. Norton & Co.

  Stone addresses the political dimension to decision making by first setting out the premise that policy making is a political struggle over values and ideas. Of particular interest to students is the way in which the narrative reveals paradoxes in even the most simple policy decisions. The book offers a useful insight into the complexities of decision making and offers some compelling examples by way of illustration.

- Tschappeler, R. and Krogerus, K. (2011) *The Decision Book: Fifty Models for Strategic Thinking*, London, Profile Books.

  The book reveals fifty decision making models used on MBA courses and focuses on the key questions of 'What do I want?' and 'How do I get it?'. This compact and concise book is a useful aid to assessing decision making models and provides an accessory to more in-depth texts.

251

Online Resource Centre

For more information, updates, and multiple-choice questions, please visit the Online Resource Centre at: www.oxfordtextbooks.co.uk/orc/combe1e/

Skillset 7
Literature review

7(a) Introduction

A review of relevant literature is a key element of your project work, essays, dissertations, and other academic outputs. The choice of content that makes up a literature review is dependent on informed decision making. Each decision taken is the outcome of a process of evaluating a range of variables that act as enablers or resistors to achieving set aims. This Skillset provides you with clear guidance on how to compile a review that includes choices of which literature to include, how to make judgements about the value of literature to the understanding of a particular topic, and the importance of critique in the review.

The skill of undertaking an evaluation of the quality of literature can be transferred to many workplace situations where there is a requirement for making value judgements on the quality and usefulness of the vast array of written material available to support activities. This Skillset will enhance decision making about what literature adds value and how it can be articulated to stakeholders.

7(b) What is a literature review?

The term 'literature review' can be applied to both the *process* of reviewing the literature, as well as the label given to the *output* of such a process—the 'literature review' chapter(s) or section(s) in a document such as coursework, project, dissertation, or thesis. Combining the process and output views, a working definition of the term 'literature review' is that it is the appropriately structured and reasoned output of a systematic process of finding, reviewing, and evaluating the literature to meet a specific purpose relevant to a particular topic under investigation.

It is also worth considering what a literature review is not:

A literature review is not ...	Why not?
... the result of a brief interrogation of an Internet search engine.	Although internet sources may give good coverage of sources, there may be additional sources (such as textbooks) which are not online.
... a series of quotes copied and pasted from a range of sources (even if properly referenced).	Too many quotations are unlikely to have the depth of analysis and evaluation of a good literature review. It may become 'He said ...' ... 'She said ...'.
... a description of what several authors said.	Although there may be elements of description, a good literature review will have greater depth of analysis and evaluation.
... a summary of all that is written on a topic.	You are likely to have a word count to meet in your assessment—you must decide what constitutes the most relevant/appropriate material. So decision making is involved in making choices from a range of alternatives.
... a document which presents your side of the argument.	A good literature review will acknowledge and explore contradictions and tensions in what authors say.

So a literature review has several characteristics:

- there is a clear focus in terms of purpose/topic;
- a systematic process is undertaken;
- there is evaluation of the literature;
- it has an appropriately structured output.

A literature review should be: (1) comprehensive, at least in relation to the purpose and sources available (some sources may not be available to you as they are expensive to access, even for your university library; although inter-library loans may be possible); (2) methodical/systematic in that there is a clear and appropriate process which you follow which could be explained to others if required; and (3) a well-balanced evaluation of the literature beyond only describing what has been written on the topic.

7(c) Why undertake a literature review?

There are several reasons for undertaking a literature review. These include: *First*, to discover and make sense of what has gone before in relation to your topic. *Secondly*, to unpack, clarify, and understand the concepts, frameworks, and theories which underpin your topic. For example, the decision making process (Chapter 7) is a multi-faceted concept requiring an examination of types of decision, decision making approaches, and so on. By breaking down the decision making process into these different areas, and reviewing what different authors have said, we can create a much clearer picture of the concept. *Thirdly*, to understand the latest thinking and developments in your topic area. Or there may a combination of these.

7(d) A process for undertaking a literature review

A general process for undertaking a literature review is as follows (adapted from Machi and McEvoy, 2009; Saunders and Lewis, 2012):

1 Identify the purpose of your literature review.
2 Gather your literature.
3 Make sense of the literature you have found.
4 Evaluate your literature.
5 Add your critique.
6 Write your literature review.
7 Review your review.

This process is unpacked in the sections below.

7(e) Stage 1: Identify the purpose of your literature review

What is the purpose of your literature review? The answer to this question may have several dimensions.

What is the purpose in relation to the overall task you are undertaking (or are set)? Is the literature review the main purpose of the task? For example, you may be asked to 'critically evaluate the literature regarding the decision making processes managers adopt within organisations'. Alternatively, it may be that the literature review is part of a larger task. For example, when undertaking research (such as a project or dissertation) a literature review is one important (but not the only) element of the project as a whole. The literature review may be used to help identify a 'gap' in the literature which your research will then seek to 'close'.

This is an important decision to make as all the other steps follow from this.

7(f) Stage 2: Gather your literature

Having identified the purpose of your literature review, execute a well-thought-out search strategy to gather the relevant literature. This stage may require decisions related to the particular topic(s) which you have to focus on. There is more information on gathering/sourcing materials in Skillset 4, but the following table summarises the key points which relate to this Stage of our literature review process.

253

Stage of the process for sourcing materials	Brief overview (See Skillset 4 for more details)
1 Identify the purpose of your search	What is the purpose of your search—this should align to the purpose of the literature review as a whole.
2 Decide on the boundaries of your search	What are the key terms or concepts? Are there any limits in terms of (for example) time period or geographical/industry scope?
3 Identify the sources you will examine	Where will you look? For example: online databases (which ones?); particular academic journals; search engines such as Google Scholar; company/government sources.
4 Create a search strategy	What search terms will you use? What timeframe will you be looking at? And so on.
5 Implement your search strategy	Implement the strategy created in Stage 4.
6 Evaluate what you have found	You may generate a long list of resources and have to evaluate which sources are most appropriate for you.
7 Capture bibliographic and other details of sources you regard as useful	Capture appropriate details from those sources you regard as particularly useful.

Try not to rely on standard textbooks—recent Journal articles and so on are expected and evidence of a breadth of appropriate reading beyond the lectures, handouts, directed reading, and so on, will usually be rewarded. It is *not* good practice to cite your lecture notes, no matter how flattering this may be for the tutors(s) concerned.

7(g) Stage 3: Make sense of the literature you have found

The final part of the search strategy outlined in Section 7(f) was to capture bibliographic data from those sources which you regard as most relevant and useful to the literature search you are conducting. This stage of your literature review takes that process further.

One common way to help make sense of the literature you have found is to capture key aspects of each of the materials in a number of tables which provide summary information, insight, and perhaps even a notional 'grade' for the source. For example the following table could be used to capture bibliographic information and your overall impressions of the source.

Title	
Author(s)	
Publisher	

Date	
Web address	
Access	
Description	
Key issues or questions	
Methodology	
Key indicators	
Findings	
Rank	

Remember that it may be more effective to speed read (see Section 4(h) in Skillset 4) each source first. You may wish to consider giving the source a 'rank' or 'grade' (the final row in the table above) to help you quickly prioritise what material will be most useful and deserves greater attention later on. This rank/grade should 'make sense' for you and could, for example, be something like the following:

Rank	Meaning
A	Must read
B	Very useful
C	Useful
D	Background understanding
E	Limited added value
F	Not worth following up

7(h) Stage 4: Evaluate your literature

Having made sense of the sources you have found the next step is to provide a more detailed and in-depth evaluation of the sources you have found most useful and that are worth following up on. Once again, the use of a table can help you approach this in a systematic way. The dimensions of the table will depend on the nature and purpose of your review so the following example, although it may have some general application, is intended to be illustrative rather than comprehensive or universally applicable. The table below was developed by the author of this textbook in order to systematically evaluate literature relating to a European Union funded research project he was involved in.

	Key questions	Possible indicators	Evaluation	Score
Quality of analysis	How well has the approach to, and formulation of, the analysis been conveyed?	Clear rationale for choice of data or method adopted.	[Significantly shortened.] The rationale is well stated and logical.	3
Quality of findings	How credible are the findings?	Findings and conclusions are fully supported by data/evidence. Clear indication of how the researcher arrived at conclusions. Findings have coherent logic and are resonant with other knowledge and experience.	[Significantly shortened.] Lack of empirical evidence limits the findings but does not undermine claims made based on the in-depth interviews carried out. There is a rationale to how the researchers arrive at conclusions; outcomes are well articulated and strong in validity.	4
Policy recommendations	Are policy recommendations explicitly stated? If so, how robust are they in informing new practice?	Policy recommendations identify new methods, techniques, processes or theories to advance knowledge and/or practice. Reasons and rationale given for policy recommendations. Feasibility and suitability of the implementation of recommendations has been considered and assessed.	[Significantly shortened.] No explicit policy recommendations are articulated.	3
Transferability	How can the application of the frameworks/ methods inform the project or other projects?	Extent to which the design and methodology can be applied to this project or other projects.	[Significantly shortened.] The work adopts a broader methodology to previous research in the field. There is a high transferability value to this approach for future studies.	4
TOTAL SCORE				14

For this review the key dimensions (left hand column; Y axis) of the evaluation were:

- Quality of analysis.
- Quality of findings.
- Policy recommendations. This dimension was of particular interest given the nature of the research project.
- Transferability. This dimension related to the extent to which the frameworks/methods used in the paper being reviewed might be applied to the research project. So again, this dimension was of particular interest to this particular research project.

Across the X axis (top row of the table) the columns are as follows (with some examples given):

- Key questions which may guide your evaluation.
- Possible indicators which might indicate a particularly well-written paper.
- Evaluation—this would contain notes which provide your evaluation of the paper based on the dimension, the key questions, and possible indicators.
- A score to indicate the 'value' of that particular element. In this case the score rates from 1 to 5 where 1 = little value and 5 = high value.

Again—you could make your own table up based on what will be important for your work and your review.

7(i) Stage 5: Add your critique

You would now have comments on each of the sources you reviewed. The next stage would be to build up an evaluation or critique of the sources *as a whole*. Read Skillset 12 regarding analysis and critical evaluation to help you think about how to approach this.

7(j) Stage 6: Write your literature review

As a very general approach, your literature review could be constructed in three segments:

- Introduction;
- Main body;
- Conclusions.

Each of these is discussed in greater detail below.

Introduction: As there is a considerable volume of literature out there and different ways to structure your literature review, it is important to tell the reader, even briefly, what you are going to cover and how you will be structuring your review.

Main body: This may be one, or a number of, sections. This depends on how you structure your work and how long the review will be. The way the main body of your literature review is structured depends on the 'story' you wish to tell.

In terms of the overall structure of the review you could (after Writing Center, 2012) present your review in *chronological order*, starting from the oldest material and working up to the most recent. This may also give you the opportunity to: discuss how thinking around your topic has evolved; compare and contrast the beginning and end of the time periods; or highlight particular dramatic developments. An introduction to a literature review structured in this way might read:

'Taking Simon's (1960) rational model of decision making as a starting point, this literature review will review the development of decision making theory over time . . .' [structure based on chronological order of the material].

Alternatively you could present your review according to a number of *topics*, perhaps deconstructing a larger topic or concept into a number of sub-topics. This gives you some flexibility and choice, but be careful that you link all these sub-topics together in a meaningful way. An introduction to a literature review structured in this way might read:

> 'This literature review is based around three key themes: 1) the nature of decision making; 2) the decision making process; and 3) error and bias in decision making . . .'
> [structure based around particular themes].

Other options include:

- Organising your review around the *geographical focus* of the literature. For example starting with your own country then comparing and contrasting that with what has been found for other geo-political areas such as the European Union;
- Organising your review around the *methodological approach* adopted. For example grouping those articles which report surveys relating to your topic; then case studies; and so on;
- Organising your review around *key authors*. For example, by taking Simon's work on decision making as a starting point then weaving in others' work as a critique of Simon's work.
- And so on.

There may be some overlap between the various options—the most important point is to structure your review by whichever approach makes the most sense to you and the reader.

Conclusions: Draw the key points together. It is not necessary to repeat all the key points you make—think about what the key things are that you want the reader to know/remember from the review. If the literature section is part of a longer document (such as a research project) then end the conclusion by linking to the next section.

7(k) Stage 7: Review your review

As with any piece of written work there is always scope to proofread and revise your literature review. Later on in the process you may find additional material (such as when a new journal issue is released) which you can add to your review.

Tips for writing and reviewing your review:

- Make sure your introduction clearly states the purpose of the review and the structure of what follows; and that you follow through! As you write more, the shape and focus of your review may change without you knowing it.
- Avoid describing one piece of work after another. Look for opportunities to compare and contrast your material—where do sources agree; where do they disagree? What are the strengths, weaknesses, and gaps in the literature you have reviewed? And so on.
- Be pedantic about adopting good practice in accurately and consistently referencing your sources. This is particularly important for a literature review as it is a key place where you are examining others' ideas and work.

7(l) Summary of the Skillset

Conducting an effective literature review process and being able to write a persuasive literature review (as an output of that process) are key skills for your academic studies and the workplace. This Skillset outlined a process for conducting a literature review and each stage of the process can be linked to stages/decisions taken as part of the rational decision making model.

Table 7.2	**The rational decision making model applied to conducting a literature review (adapted from Figure 7.2)**	

Stage	Stages in the rational decision making model	Decisions/questions in conducting a literature review
1	Identify the problem	What is the purpose of your literature review?
2	Gather information	How (and where) will you gather your literature?
3	Analyse alternatives	What is the literature telling you?
4	Develop alternatives	What different interpretations of the literature might there be?
5	Evaluate alternatives	Adding your critique. Evaluate the sources/interpretations.
6	Decide	Decide how you will structure your literature review; what will be included; and what will be your key arguments.
7	Implement decision	Write your literature review; and review your review.

References/Further reading/Resources

Coughlan, M., Cronin, P. and Ryan, F. (2007) 'Step-by step guide to critiquing research. Part 1: quantitative research', *British Journal of Nursing*, Vol. 16, No. 11, pp. 658–63. [Although not written for a 'management' audience, this paper contains valuable information on what to ask yourself when evaluating literature. It is Part 1 of two.]

Hart, C. (1998) *Doing a Literature Review*, London, Sage.

Machi, L. A. and McEvoy, B. T. (2009) *The Literature Review: six steps to success*, Thousand Oaks, Corwin Press.

Ryan, F., Coughlan, M. and Cronin, P. (2007) 'Step-by step guide to critiquing research. Part 2: qualitative research', *British Journal of Nursing*, Vol. 16, No. 12, pp. 738–44. [Although not written for a 'management' audience, this paper contains valuable information on what to ask yourself when evaluating literature. It is Part 2 of two.]

Saunders, M. and Lewis, P. (2012) *Doing Research in Business and Management: An essential guide to planning your project*, Harlow, Pearson Education.

Wallace, M. and Wray, A. (2011) *Critical Reading and Writing for Postgraduates* (2nd edn), Sage Study Skills Series, London, Sage Publications.

Writing Center (The) (2012) *Literature Review*. [Online Resource] Available from: http://writingcenter.unc.edu/handouts/literature-reviews/

Part

2

Managing People and Communications

8

Human Resource Management

Managing diversity is one of the key challenges human resources managers face in a globalised economy. Many governments have become involved in setting equality frameworks through legislation to encourage organisations to recognise the benefits of a multi-ethnic and culturally diverse workforce. According to a study of fifty developed economies around the world carried out by Oxford Economics on behalf of Forbes Insights (2012), Norway has the most diverse workforce, followed by New Zealand and Iceland. The USA is ranked 9th, with the UK coming in at 17th. The main reason for Norway's lofty position is mainly down to the government's quota system that requires organisations to have a certain percentage of women on the board of publicly quoted companies. Ethnic diversity was not included in the study so the outcomes must be treated with some caution. Countries at the bottom of the rankings include the Czech Republic, Poland, and Hungary—all east European states in the early stages of developing legislative measures underpinning equality and diversity. Their membership of the EU has given a boost to their diversity credentials, however. The study also includes data on gender and ethnic diversity across more than 500 occupations in 300 different sectors in the United States and United Kingdom, thereby giving a unique insight into how diversity is being managed in those countries.

Skillset 8
Typical exam questions and answer guidance

One of the key criteria for recruitment used by HR managers is to determine the level of academic qualifications possessed by candidates for jobs. Exams are an inevitable part of a range of assessment instruments used by universities and colleges to test the knowledge, understanding, and critical skills of students. Skillset 6 focused on exam techniques. Skillset 8 provides some examples of typical exam questions and model answers. Students can cross reference the exam techniques with the approach to answering some typical exam questions on management.

Definition

Human resource management (HRM) is concerned with the management of the organisation's workforce. The key role of HRM in the organisation is to attract, select, train, evaluate, and reward employees as well as providing leadership that contributes to the formation of a positive organisational culture. HRM also involves conflict resolution and acts as a mediator between representatives of employees (mostly trade unions) and the executive management of the organisation.

Introduction

Human resources have become a key element of management as the range and diversity of skills and experiences required in the modern business environment has expanded rapidly in recent decades. This trend has been brought about by a wide range of different factors including:

- the impact of new technologies;
- changes to work schedules;
- the development of global economies;
- new and more flexible organisational structures;
- development and demand for new innovative products;
- the move away from traditional heavy industry to service and knowledge-based industries.

These and other changes have brought about new demands and challenges for the type of skills, expertise, and experience required to fulfil the needs of modern businesses. Effective human resource management is key to matching those demands with the supply of labour that can deliver added value and contribute to the strategic aims of organisations. Unlike the function of personnel (which focuses on the administrative aspects of managing the workforce), human resource management has a strategic aspect to it as managers seek new and innovative means of developing and deploying workers to achieve stated aims and objectives.

This chapter begins with a definition of human resource management (HRM) in organisations and goes on to identify the core activities of attraction, recruitment, and retention. The discussion goes on to explain key HRM strategies in the context of the recruitment and retention of staff and the implementation of reward systems. Attention then turns to the concept of equality and fairness in human resource management and the challenges of managing diversity in the modern global economy. This will include a section on how managers can improve their diversity awareness. The discussion reflects existing measures that support the principle of equal opportunities in the workplace. However, it is also recognised that these are not currently accepted or implemented by many countries and that this can pose significant challenges for managers operating in global markets. This is followed by an assessment of human resource processes featuring policy, recruitment, performance, and feedback evaluations. The chapter concludes with an overview of how management can develop workers as key assets and manage effective employee relations.

Core HRM activities: attraction, recruitment, and retention

The core functions of the human resource management department in any organisation are to attract, recruit, and retain staff.

Attraction

A number of factors will determine how successful managers are at achieving this. Some of them relate to the skills and experience managers have in terms of spotting and assessing talent. They may be reliant on effective marketing of what the organisation has to offer potential recruits. There are inevitably economic constraints on how much the organisation can offer in terms of rewards for new recruits, or the other types of incentives such as flexible working hours. Workers have a wide range of motivating factors that encourage them to seek employment with specific organisations. These may include pay and conditions, types of tasks, location, flexibility in work schedules, types of co-workers, and so on. Sometimes workers are attracted by the reputation of the organisation for producing high quality outputs, ethical standards, or customer service. Organisations such as *NASA*, *Microsoft*, *Rolls Royce*, and the *BBC* can attract high quality candidates due to their reputation for expertise, quality, creativity, style, or other attributes that set them apart from others. Some organisations devise and implement strategic plans to attract and nurture talent. *Specsavers* worked with company image specialists *Words and Pictures* to design a recruitment and development programme aimed at raising the organisation's profile among graduates to create a continuous flow of talent (Newby and Howarth, 2012). One of the key challenges facing human resource managers is to match the needs of the organisation with the motivations and expectations of the types of workers they seek to attract. Increasingly, employers are using social media and web-based technologies, such as *LinkedIn*, in the recruitment process as a means of accessing information about potential recruits, lowering the search costs, and increasing efficiencies. Allen et al. (2007) investigate web-based recruitment by analysing attitudes to a website on applicant attraction.

Recruitment

Human resource management also involves overseeing the process of recruitment. It is vital that the process is seen to be transparent and that it offers equal opportunities for all. The selection process has to be seen to be fair, open, and rigorously applied. From the organisation's perspective, it is important that the process delivers the best fit between candidates and the needs of the job. The few candidates chosen for interview should consist of those who have displayed or demonstrated the specific skills, attributes, and experience necessary to fit the criteria of the job. This can be a fairly complex challenge as some attributes are difficult to measure such as flair for creativity, or interpersonal or networking skills. Here, managers rely on historical evidence to build a picture of the added value that potential recruits may bring. HRM managers use a number of techniques to help form a judgement on the suitability of a candidate including psychometric testing, aptitude tests, presentations, role-playing exercises, and so on.

Information on the candidate usually comes from the curriculum vitae, references, and documents such as qualifications and accreditations. In many ways these sources are formal and the candidate has some measure of control over the information given. Increasingly employers are using social media as a source of information on candidates as sites such as *Facebook* or *Twitter* may reveal a truer picture of the personality and values of the candidate. Many users of social media adopt a cavalier attitude to the information they post about themselves without realising the potential consequences for compromising themselves. Ultimately, HR managers along with others in the decision making process have to use their experience and knowledge (as well as sometimes their intuitive skills) to arrive at a decision about who they want to recruit.

Retention

Once recruitment has taken place, the task of HRM is to ensure retention of staff. This is important as high staff turnover can prove to be time consuming and costly and may damage the reputation of the organisation. Key to retaining staff is to ensure that the factors that attracted them in the first place are evident in practice. Failure to make good on the promises made when attracting staff will have a negative effect on morale and, ultimately, result in key workers seeking employment elsewhere. The relationship building element of HRM has to be effective to ensure staff retention and this begins with induction and follows on through regular formal and informal settings where staff can communicate with managers. Beyond the formal terms and conditions of employment there needs to be a 'psychological contract' between employer and employee that underpins goodwill and trust. This form of relationship is not easily articulated in a formal contract, rather, it is an intangible asset that can be of benefit to workers, managers, and the organisation as a whole. The formation of this type of relationship is a key factor in retaining valuable workers. Here, it is important that managers and staff appreciate and understand their respective views on retention from this perspective (Vos and Meganck, 2009).

Other factors that boost retention include effective and progressive reward systems, recognition of high performance, greater freedom and decision making, opportunities for personal development and education, and the creation of an integrated, cohesive, and supportive workforce who work closely and collaboratively on shared aims and objectives. Retention becomes difficult when there are skills shortages in parts of the economy. For example, high quality IT specialists have been at a premium in many industry sectors, including telecommunications and engineering, leading to a higher emphasis being placed on specialist human resource strategies linked to organisational structures that are designed to attract and retain highly skilled workers (Holland et al., 2002; Dockel et al, 2006).

Releasing human resources

One other area that HRM covers is the shedding of employees. Whilst the majority of the work carried out by HRM staff relates to attraction, recruitment, and retention, there are times when organisations need to release staff from their employment. This is a notoriously sensitive and difficult task and one that requires great skill and knowledge. There are legal, moral, emotional, and logistical challenges with this process, all likely to be carried out under conditions of great

Term *Definitions*

Attraction: making the organisation the employer of choice for potential recruits.

Recruitment: the process of assessing candidates' suitability for employment.

Retention: implementation of activities to ensure that employees remain loyal and that their terms and conditions of employment are met.

pressure and negative feelings among the workforce. Nevertheless, it is a fact of life that some organisations need to shed employees to survive, change direction, restructure to remain competitive, or as part of a cost cutting exercise. How this is handled may have repercussions for the future prospects of the organisation and top managers will rely on HR managers to advise and guide the process effectively.

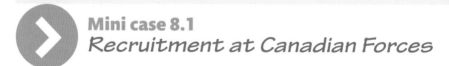

Mini case 8.1
Recruitment at Canadian Forces

The use of the internet and other electronic media has had a galvanising effect on the recruitment process of many organisations. For managers sifting through many hundreds of applications, the internet provides an efficiency saving by allowing candidates to access job information, check the criteria for recruitment, and undertake aptitude, psychometric, or other tests remotely. This process filters out those candidates with a realistic chance of recruitment who can then be called for interview. Online recruitment is quick and cost effective for organisations whilst maintaining the principle of open access to candidates. In some cases electronic media such as video conferencing allows candidates to be interviewed remotely. Increasingly, candidates are being recruited without ever meeting the interview panel face-to-face.

There are some organisations where the new media have limited application in the recruitment process. The *Canadian Forces* have an online application procedure that allows potential recruits to enter their details matched against a set of criteria (Canadian Forces, 2009). This approach was the result of a review of recruitment procedures and practices in 2006 (Canadian Forces Recruiting, 2006). The application can then be posted or e-mailed for processing. However, beyond that stage the process follows a traditional format whereby chosen applicants have to undertake a fitness test at an approved gym; pass an aptitude test at a *Canadian Forces Recruiting Centre* (CFRC); complete a medical examination at CFRC; and, finally, undertake an interview with recruitment officers. These require the physical attendance of candidates to assess the physical, mental, intellectual, and emotional character of potential recruits. The HR department at *Canadian Forces* ensures that the process is geared towards matching recruits to the demands of the various units they may be assigned to. Only by undertaking a rigorous selection procedure based on the physical participation of candidates can they make effective decisions on recruitment. Successful recruits are required to attend an enrolment session where they swear allegiance to the Queen and receive a certificate of employment.

Source:

Canadian Forces (2006) Review on Canadian Recruiting Process (Part 1). http://canadian-forces.blogspot.co.uk/2006/08/review-on-canadian-forces-recruiting_03.html

Canadian Forces (2009) Canadian Forces Employment Application. http://cdn.forces.ca/_PDF2010/CF_application_form_demande_emploi_FC.pdf

Discussion point

Is it possible to achieve a full understanding of a candidate's qualities solely by using online recruitment methods?

http://www.forces.ca/

http://www.forces.ca/

268

Human resource management strategies

They key aims of HRM are to effectively manage employees, employee relations, and all the processes and practices that support the needs of staff. Importantly, the strategic aim of HRM is to configure a match between the skills, experience, and expertise of employees and the needs of the organisation as it strives to achieve its wider strategic aims such as building market share, becoming technological leaders, expanding markets, achieving competitive advantage, etc. Thus, HRM involves seeking the ways and means of gaining an optimal return from the investment in staff. The design and implementation of strategies to achieve this is a vital role that human resource managers undertake. There are a number of different approaches to human resource strategy and Figure 8.1 highlights some of the main ones.

269

Figure 8.1 Approaches to human resource strategies

Unitarism

The unitarist approach is built on the assumption that all concerned parties in an organisation share the same aims and objectives relating to products, services, customers, suppliers, and other stakeholders. This approach requires a high level of conformity among employees who are expected to consistently meet set standards of output and performance based on distinct working practices. The Japanese car manufacturing industry is an example of a unitarist approach in action whereby workers follow a highly regimented and planned routine within a culture that is compliant.

Pluralism

In contrast to a unitarist approach, pluralism facilitates a number of aims and objectives, not all of which will be compatible with each other. Rules, regulations, and procedures are drawn up as a means of managing the potential conflict that can arise from different views and perspectives on organisational aims and objectives. The pluralist approach is prevalent in the public sector where different service providers operating in the same department may have radically different aims and objectives but have to work together to provide an integrated service.

Radicalism

The radical approach to human resources is to allow the staff to manage resources and make decisions on the deployment of staff in the productive process. The radical approach assumes that industrial harmony cannot be achieved until the employees are allowed to control the means of production and the processes that support it. This approach has its roots in a Marxist philosophy whereby the ownership of capital and productive capacity is transferred from the owners of capital to the workers. The case study on *Semco* in Chapter 9 offers an insight into the implementation of this approach, although it should be noted that replicating the success of that company has largely proved elusive for followers who adopted a similarly radical approach.

Conflict

The role of the HR managers in this approach is essentially to contain and deal with conflict. Here, the working environment is characterised by a lack of trust, no general consensus on the aims and objectives of the organisation, complexity and diversity in the types of skills and experiences possessed by the workforce which is spread across multiple work locations. The potential for conflict is heightened by the multiple different organisational cultures and the lack of a cohesive working unit. HR managers need to manage this situation by reconciling differences, encouraging harmony by implementing activities that encourage integration, and developing and applying methods to facilitate the formation of a positive organisational culture. This type of approach is often evident in the aftermath of a merger or takeover between two organisations when two or more sets of workers are brought under the same ownership but have no shared organisational culture, are dislocated from each other, and where an element of mistrust and uncertainty exists. The merger between *Time-Warner* and *AOL* in 2000 had all the ingredients for such a conflict as the two organisations had very different types of workers, different cultures and histories, and, ultimately, different ideas about what the merger was designed to achieve (Arango, 2010). In this case the conflict management of the HR managers failed to overcome the challenges posed by these tensions and the merger was a spectacular and expensive failure.

Term
Definition

HRM strategies: ways in which the skills, experience and expertise of employees can be matched to the long-term aims and objectives of the organisation.

Conformity

In contrast to the conflict scenario, conformity refers to a situation whereby workers disregard their differences and tensions to work in a cohesive manner for the greater good of the organisation. In this case, the HR managers display strong leadership and strategic qualities to firmly set out the standards required and performance targets for workers as a means of underpinning the development of an organisational culture of conformity rather than conflict. Conformity is closely aligned to unitarism whereby the workforce have a shared understanding and acceptance of organisational aims and objectives and then set about achieving them in an integrated and coordinated manner. In some cases conformity is managed through coercion, such as in the armed forces where insubordination is punished, in others it is through effective communications and a distinct organisational culture, such as in the civil service.

Consensus

Consensus refers to a scenario whereby full and complete unanimity of understanding and acceptance of the organisation's aims and objectives, processes, management style, rewards, etc. is achieved. Here, HR managers work in harmony with the workforce through an ethos of partnership. This approach is only ever achieved in very small-scale or micro-businesses where no complex human interactions are evident and where there is a common understanding of the aims and objectives and a shared organisational culture. Consequently, consensus is rarely, if ever, witnessed in reality. Even in the most close-knit organisations there will be some level of tension between managers and staff over some issues relating to the working environment.

Critical reflection
What key attributes do modern HR managers look for in workers?

It is difficult to assign any one approach to a particular area when discussing HR strategies. Different industry sectors exhibit different characteristics and this is reflected in the relationships between staff and management. For example, industries that are traditional, slow to change, and process driven tend to have stable relationships, whereas those where technology and working practices are subject to change tend to be more disruptive. Relationships change over time as new working practices become the norm. This was evident in the newspaper industry in the 1980s when the introduction of new technology led to widespread industrial disputes. The industry is now technologically driven with workers using digital media as the norm. HRM is about managing change as well as dealing with personnel issues. Change has become a necessary part of competitive strategies for many organisations and requires a different kind of workforce. Thus, the key attributes of modern workers are often cited as adaptability, flexibility, creativity, an innovative approach, team-orientated personality, problem solving ability and capable of taking responsibility. Increasingly, workers are in close contact with HR managers to help manage change and to pre-empt problems. The trend in many modern businesses is towards partnership, although much depends on the extent to which the aims and objectives of the organisation are commonly shared throughout the workforce.

Equality and fairness

In the modern era HRM is governed by the overarching principles of equality and fairness. This is a significant change in philosophy compared to the factory system that emerged at the beginning of the Industrial Revolution. As discussed in Chapter 2, the working environment of that era was dominated by the owners of capital who exercised complete power over the workforce in terms of recruitment, work tasks, working practices, and rewards. In the intervening period there have been significant changes to that relationship whereby collaboration, consensus, and dialogue between management and staff has replaced the draconian and authoritative approaches of the class-based system of the late nineteenth and early twentieth centuries.

The overriding principles of equality and fairness in the workplace have grown out of concerted efforts by workers and their representatives (mostly trade unions) to create an environment whereby workers' rights are respected and where every individual has an opportunity to participate and flourish. Now, the concept of equality and fairness is enshrined in law and every organisation has to adhere to the principles laid down in law. There is also an obligation to abide by the spirit of the law by taking active steps to encourage equality and fairness in the workplace. For example, a great deal of effort has been made by HR managers to link equality with work/life balance principles as a means of demonstrating fairness in access to employment opportunities and to recognise the competing demands on the key workers from multiple sources (Dickens, 2012).

Equality and fairness relate to the practice of treating workers in an equal and fair manner regardless of age, race, religion, status, disability, education, or other personal characteristics. Recruitment and retention of workers must be based on merit and the qualities that individuals possess in alignment with the requirements of the tasks they are expected to carry out. Basic human rights inform this position as it is a matter of common decency within a civil society that individuals are treated with equal respect and dignity. These guiding principles should be evident in the way in which organisations are managed including the style of management, communications, regulations, policies, procedures, and so on. These help to shape the attitudes, beliefs, and values of workers and staff in the organisation such that they develop a culture of respect for equality and fairness. Those who violate these guiding principles (through harassment, bullying, intimidation, discrimination, etc.) should be subject to agreed

Term
Definition

Equality and fairness: the formal and informal means of ensuring that each individual worker or potential recruit is treated with respect and dignity and that they are judged on merit and not on race, gender, age, or any other personal characteristic.

disciplinary measures. Training in equality and fairness and diversity is designed to raise the awareness of the requirement to adhere to guiding principles and to encourage compliance. There are also economic and competitive reasons why organisations need to effectively manage equality and fairness. It helps in the recruitment of high quality staff, enhances the organisation's reputation, and builds brand loyalty in customers.

Critical reflection
Are equality and fairness commonly shared characteristics of the modern global working environment?

273

The discussion so far has assumed that equality and fairness in the workplace are underpinned by law and fully observed by organisations. Whilst this is mostly the case in developed countries, there are many other countries where no employment rights exist for the majority of workers. The case study of Foxconn in Chapter 2 is an extreme example of this. In India, Pakistan, and Bangladesh many of the customs and practices carried out in the workplace have been unchanged for centuries. In farming communities a feudal system of ownership persists, meaning that dynastic families retain control of the land. In many sectors bonded labour is the norm, whereby impoverished families borrow money from factory- or land-owners to establish themselves in their employment. There is no prospect of the debt being fully repaid due to the interest charged and the low rates of pay, thereby locking the workers into a form of slave labour. This practice is prevalent in a number of industry sectors such as leather goods, textiles, manufacturing, brickworks, and quarrying. Most disturbingly a great many bonded labourers are known to be children. Here, the concept of HRM is alien and although there are specific laws in India to ban bonded labour, the practice still persists. The lack of effective law enforcement, public indifference (the caste system of social hierarchy exacerbates the problem), and lack of land reform has allowed this form of slavery to flourish. There are a number of organisations such as the *International Justice Mission* and the *National Coalition against Bonded Labour* who have lobbied government to act more robustly to eradicate the practice. Another approach has been to restructure the economics of the employment system. The *Grameen Bank* is Bangladeshi initiative established by Nobel prize winner Muhammad Yunus seeks to offer microcredit to workers to allow them to benefit from their labours without being perpetually indebted to landowners or factory owners (Yunus and Jolis, 2003). Finally, it should be remembered that it is not just owners of capital in developing or least developed countries who are responsible for labour exploitation. Some large and powerful western corporations have been accused of exploiting cheap labour in developing countries with clothing manufacturers Nike and Gap being two of the most high-profile examples. The negative publicity surrounding the disclosure of exploitative practices led both organisations to radically alter their working practices in factories in developing nations.

Managing diversity

As the development of the global economy has gathered pace in the last thirty years, so too has social mobility, resulting in much greater diversity in the demographics of many societies. Diversity refers not only to differences in factors such as age, gender, race, religion and so on, but also in issues relating to ethics, morals, social responsibility, and norms of behaviour. In the modern era, the dominant paradigm for governing this diversity is that of equality and human rights. That is, many countries have adopted the philosophical approach to governance of equality whereby each individual in society is afforded certain rights before the law. This also informs employment law and through the establishment of equal rights in the workplace relating to recruitment, working conditions, respect, and so on. There is the imperative that managers proactively support equality and afford all workers equal opportunities. Failure to follow this approach would be considered unethical and possibly illegal. There are also organisational benefits from adopting and implementing equal rights, such as better customer relations, improved reputation, better workforce relations, and so on (Tatli et al., 2007). Thus, equality and diversity have become enshrined in the doctrines governing many work-based relationships. This is evident in the way managers deal with notions of justice and inequality. For example, distributive justice dictates that workers should be treated fairly concerning pay, promotions, office space, and similar issues. These rewards should be assigned on merit and performance. Managers should also seek to avoid biases from occurring. These are systematic tendencies to use information in ways that result in inaccurate perceptions. For example, social

Term
Definition

Diversity: range of varied personal characteristics including age, race, gender, nationalities, religions, cultures, beliefs, values.

status is a type of bias conferred on people of differing social positions. Stereotyping is another form of bias that stems from inaccurate beliefs about a given individual or group. Much work has been done in recent years on understanding how best to manage diversity, but there has yet to emerge a dominant theoretical framework that encapsulates the dynamic and complex nature of managing this phenomenon. Yang (2011) advances understanding by analysing diversity management practices using institutional and resource-based theoretical models. He also proposes possible approaches for further research into diversity management.

There are a number of approaches that managers can adopt to help them deal with diversity in the workplace. Some of the most common include:
- increasing diversity awareness through equality and diversity training programmes;
- increasing workplace exposure to a diverse range of workers—these help managers to become aware of their own biases and to moderate their attitudes and behaviours to deal with them;
- increasing collaboration with workers from diverse backgrounds to help them better understand cultural differences and their impact on working styles;
- practising effective communication with diverse groups;
- ensuring top management is committed to diversity by involving them in working practices that expose them to workers from diverse backgrounds.

Effective management of diversity is important because the modern working environment is characterised by a wide range of people from different social, religious, and cultural backgrounds. Very often the success of the organisation is dependent on how well those people integrate and work collaboratively to achieve shared aims and objectives in a harmonious environment. The challenge for management is to accommodate the different needs and expectations of a diverse workforce whilst maintaining these critical success factors. In some instances it may require flexibility, tolerance, and understanding to maintain good relations. For example, many businesses have Muslim workers who have specific prayer times and need to fast during Ramadan. In some settings, such as factory production lines, this may require management to implement contingencies to ensure that the religious rights of workers are observed whilst maintaining productive capacity. Occasionally high-profile sporting events, such as important football matches, coincide with the normal working day. The rarity of the event means that in such circumstances management can accommodate a temporary relaxation of work schedules to allow most workers to view the event. The increase in goodwill this creates normally derives long-term benefits for the organisation.

Bigger challenges face management when there is a potential conflict of interests between groups of workers from different backgrounds. People from different backgrounds will have different work schedules, norms of doing business, styles of communication, and so on. This can lead to misunderstanding, mistrust, and a less than cohesive workforce unless it is managed effectively. Here, it is important for workers to be educated in the diverse ways and means by which different workers undertake tasks and manage their workloads in the modern business environment. Managers have to take the lead to demonstrate the type of cultural awareness and values that workers are expected to learn as part of the process of embracing diversity. Managers also have to decide how to manage diversity without compromising the organisation's core aims and objectives. This has to be achieved within the ethos of equality that is underpinned by employment law. Thus, diversity management has much to do with ensuring that equal rights and opportunities are afforded to all workers. The integration and cohesion of the workforce is enhanced when there is a general perception of equality and fairness in the way in which management deal with human resource issues. Another key advantage of effective diversity management is the freshness of ideas and creativity that people from different backgrounds bring to the working environment (Cox and Balke, 1991). In an era characterised by the need to be innovative and creative, organisations can gain a competitive advantage from exploiting these attributes of workers.

For the reasons outlined above, diversity management has become an important strategic issue in many organisations and has attracted a great deal of attention and investment. Diversity should be a feature of every aspect of the organisation, including succession planning, reengineering, employee development, performance management, reviews, and rewards (Cascio, 1995). The importance of ensuring that diversity is understood and accepted throughout the entire organisation cannot be understated. Top management has to work effectively within a diverse workforce every bit as much as those on the shop floor. Thus, the development of the organisation is inextricably linked with the effectiveness with which diversity is managed such that it contributes to the formation of the dominant organisational culture. This culture radiates outwards towards customers, suppliers, and other external stakeholders. These stakeholders are similarly comprised of people from diverse backgrounds, thereby ensuring a common purpose in the aims and objectives and underlying philosophy of this type of management. This can have important benefits for brand loyalty, business reputation, relationships, and so on. Reilly (2011) argues that one of the key trends in HRM is the shift towards managing diversity locally for global benefits. Organisations that have a truly global perspective need to understand diversity in the local context and apply their diversity management techniques in global markets. Australian airline *Qantas* provides a good illustration of this philosophy in action.

Mini case 8.2
Managing diversity at Qantas

Qantas is the national airline carrier for Australia and has a workforce comprising over ninety different nationalities and fifty-five different languages. Diversity management is key to the company's human resource strategic aims that include the development of an inclusive and integrated workforce. Further, the company believes it can leverage a competitive advantage by attracting the best quality recruits to deliver added value services to their global consumer base and achieve the strategic aim of becoming the world's best premium and low cost airline. The approach to managing diversity at Qantas is outlined in the company's diversity statement (Qantas Diversity Statement, 2012).

The recruitment process at Qantas has to reflect high ideals of equality and diversity and this is governed by strict adherence to Equal Employment Opportunity and anti-discrimination guidelines. Guidance for potential candidates is provided in a number of different languages and the selection process is closely monitored to ensure that hiring decisions are based on merit. The company is proactive in implementing tailored programmes to support equality and diversity such as the Women @Qantas Development Program, Graduate Program, and the Harvard Leadership Program. The company has also sought to engage, recruit, and retain staff from indigenous groups in Australia through School-based Traineeships and University Cadetships. Diversity also creates work/life balance challenges that the company has addressed by introducing flexible working arrangements and the establishment of child care centres. These

http://www.
qantas.com.au/
http://www.
qantas.com.au/

initiatives are all designed to encourage a wide range of people from different backgrounds to make the company an 'employer of choice'. They help to build loyalty and facilitate the integration of a diverse workforce. The Qantas diversity strategy is the responsibility of the Board Nominations Committee that ensure the establishment, monitoring, and reporting of measurable objectives. The outcomes inform future diversity strategies and their implementation.

Despite the many laudable efforts made by the company to maintain high standards of fairness and equality it has not been immune to disputes. In October 2011 baggage handlers, engineers, and pilots called a strike in protest at restructuring plans that they believed would cost many jobs. The strike cost the company around £9 million per day and caused huge damage to the reputation of the company (ABCNews, 2011). The Australian government even threatened to impose a settlement on the workers through existing but rarely used legislation. Although the dispute was ultimately resolved the residual discontent continues to rumble on with potential for further damaging disputes in the future. So, although diversity management can help to integrate workers and improve internal relations, it is no panacea for overcoming some of the wider tensions that habitually affect relations between management and staff.

Sources:

ABCNews.com (8 October 2011) Delays expected as Qantas engineers strike. http://www.abc.net.au/news/2011-10-06/qantas-workers-call-off-strike/3318244

QANTAS Diversity Statement (2012), Qantas, Mascot, NSW. http://www.qantas.com.au/infodetail/about/corporateGovernance/diversityStatement.pdf

Discussion point

Is it possible to achieve equality and fairness in the workplace?

Questions and tasks

Describe three methods that Qantas implements to develop an inclusive and integrated workforce.

Highlight some of the tensions that may arise at Qantas when managing equality and diversity policies.

Why is diversity management an important issue for the organisation?

Online Resource Centre

Author commentary on this discussion point and questions can be found on the Online Resource Centre at: www.oxfordtextbooks.co.uk/orc/combe1e/

Human resource management processes

The skills, experience, and expertise of staff employed by organisations are vital components of any strategy. Although technology can help smooth operations and facilitate the manufacture of new products or services, it is humans who have to initiate and develop new ideas and generate innovative ways of adding value to the organisation. The processes involved in managing human resources include assessing the human resource policy; the recruitment process in attracting and retaining key skills within the workforce; human resource performance in relation to set targets; and feedback on performance.

Human resource policy

Every organisation has to develop and implement a human resource policy. However, for many organisations human resources are an integral part of their strategic plans. It may mean that the firm aims to attract the top executive managers available in the industry or it may aim to become the organisation of first choice for university graduates in the industry over a particular timeframe. Human resource policies will incorporate the overriding criteria that determine the type of skills and experience the organisation needs to attract, the reward system, the training and staff development process, and the system for monitoring, assessing, and appraising staff performance. There are wide differences in approach to determining the types of skills and experience required. Much depends on the strategic aims of the organisation and the products and services produced. For example, in modern organisations teamwork, the empowerment of workers, and knowledge sharing form part of strategy implementation and the policies towards human resources reflect this. The reward system is likely to go well beyond simple financial inducements to include peer recognition of competence and increasing power in the decision making process (Combe, 2006).

The recruitment process

Firms need to be able to attract and retain skilled staff who possess the correct qualifications and experience to add value to the organisation and help achieve its strategic aims. Organisations have to put into place a recruitment policy that is designed to bring in the best people. For this there has to be a job analysis that involves formalising expected tasks, duties, and responsibilities. This is followed by the job description that summarises the specific knowledge, skills, qualifications, and experience required to perform the tasks, duties, and responsibilities to a minimum standard.

Human resource performance

When organisations recruit staff they expect a return on their investment. All staff should add value to the organisation and contribute to achieving strategic aims. Managers need to set targets and undertake periodic staff appraisals to ensure that standards of performance are being met. Of course, in many modern organisations, managers expect workers to go beyond the minimum set standards of performance and this is reflected in the culture whereby innovation, creativity, and knowledge sharing are all dominant themes. Although the modern trend is for workers to be empowered and to take on more autonomous decision making responsibilities for their work schedule, there still needs to be some control and evaluation process to ensure performance targets are being met.

Performance appraisal is a process of observation, evaluation, recording outcomes, and providing feedback to workers. This process has important strategic implications because it will determine, in large measure, the human resource strategy for the future. The rigour with which human resource appraisal is undertaken varies quite markedly between different businesses and between different industries. Some organisations have a high level of control and evaluation, such as call centres and manufacturing; others have a more relaxed and liberal regime, such as advertising agencies and other creative industries.

Feedback from human resources

One of the key characteristics of modern organisational structures is the development of self-directed teams with authority and power to make decisions relating to their own projects. Part of the responsibility offered to teams is to feed back all relevant information to senior managers to help in the process of making strategic decisions. This requires an effective communications system whereby workers can easily and efficiently feed back relevant information on a regular basis. Some organisations put in place formal systems that determine the timing and type of feedback to be delivered to senior managers, for example, feedback on how strategic decisions affect the workers' ability to achieve their objectives. From this, managers can make necessary adjustments or implement change as required. One way of gaining human resource feedback is through a company intranet. The intranet is an ideal mechanism for allowing staff from geographically dispersed parts of the organisation to communicate with each other and senior managers. Most organisations have a forum for discussion and feedback as part of their intranet. There are also specific software applications available that are designed to facilitate feedback. For example, *Amazon.com*, the online retailers, uses the *eePulse* software to electronically poll workers on a bi-weekly basis on their opinions and attitudes to specific strategic developments in the company. The poll allows workers to rate the effect that company developments have on their work duties. Responses range from 'no impact' to 'overwhelmed and need help'. Workers can also feed back general comments on their working environment. All the information is collected in real time and sent to managers for analysis (Combe, 2006).

Mini case 8.3: Practitioner
Healthcare provision for the elderly at NHS Forth Valley and Stirling Council

Alison Keir is an Occupational Therapist and North West Rural Project Leader with NHS Forth Valley in Scotland. Alison has undertaken research into the effectiveness of current policies regarding the assessment of elderly patients seeking to return to their home. This is a delicate and sensitive issue in which the physical and emotional needs of the patient need to be assessed by a team of specialists from a range of different departments. It is the role of HR managers to ensure that the multi-disciplinary team (MDT) possess the skills, competencies, emotional intelligence, and clinical abilities to deliver a service that is appropriate to the needs of the patients. The characteristics of an effective multi-disciplinary team have been set out in a document produced by the National Cancer Action Team (2010) and can be used as a guide for other specialist areas of the NHS. Crucially, the desire of the patient is also taken into account. Alison puts into context the underlying philosophy of the new thinking in healthcare provision by stating that 'this aligns to the neo-liberal approach that has informed recent government policy on the issue and has led to a trend in many more elderly patients being discharged from hospital to resume their lives at home, albeit with continuing care provision as appropriate'. Although the number of personnel involved in the service delivery can be extensive, some key roles can be identified. These include the geriatrician, physiotherapist, occupational therapist, nurse, and social worker. Each of these specialist skill areas requires a range of attributes and technical competencies. In particular, practitioners need to be able to make judgements based on the emotional, physical, and practical needs of patients. This entails a deep knowledge of the specialism balanced with an acute awareness of the emotional needs of patients. Each must complement the other when arriving at decisions affecting the welfare and emotional needs of elderly patients. It may be some time before specialists acquire the necessary all-round competencies required. It is mostly through a combination of experience, training, and support that this complex set of skills and attributes becomes honed and fully embedded in practitioner practice.

Geriatrician
The geriatrician will be a consultant with many years of experience and postgraduate training in the care of the elderly. They will review a patient's medical condition, prescribe and monitor medication, and seek any further medical investigations. In a rehabilitation setting, the geriatrician will liaise with the MDT and discuss their views with the patient. If there are concerns regarding a patient's capacity the geriatrician will liaise with a psychiatrist.

Physiotherapist
Physiotherapists working in a rehabilitation setting will be either junior staff who gain experience under the direction of a senior therapist, or a senior therapist who has chosen to specialise in the care of the elderly. Their role is to assess mobility and transfer skills and work with the patient and the team to develop treatment programmes to improve strength and mobility, and to provide walking aids or equipment, if required.

Occupational therapist
In care of the elderly the occupational therapist (OT) will either be a junior member of staff, on a rotational post, under the supervision of a senior OT, or a senior OT who has chosen to specialise in the care of the elderly after several years of postgraduate experience. The role of the OT is to help people maintain their independence. A comprehensive understanding of medical conditions and prognosis is required, combined with the ability to assess cognitive and physical skills in order to understand where functional difficulties lie.

Nurse
A nurse will work as part of a team comprising both junior and more experienced nurses. Posts tend to be fixed, rather than rotational. The nursing role is to care for the patient over a 24-hour period, and give consideration to safety and independence, day and night.

Social worker
The social worker is often based with the team and will become involved following a referral under the supervision of a senior social worker. The social worker's case load is likely to include a combination of people leaving hospital and people living in the community. The social worker will consider the support available to facilitate hospital discharge and will include the practical support which is available and the funding options to put this into practice. The social worker is likely to continue to be involved when the older person is first discharged from hospital.

Comment
The research carried out by Alison highlighted some of the challenges that managers face when adopting this approach to healthcare provision. She notes that 'HR managers at the NHS have to ensure that the correct personnel are brought together to deliver the services required. This can be problematic as they face a number of competing pressures including funding, logistics, timeframes, matching resources with need, sourcing qualified and able personnel, aligning delivery with policy requirements, assessing performance, and so on'. With an increasingly ageing population in the UK, these pressures are only likely to increase, thereby placing a greater emphasis on sourcing and recruiting the personnel who can deliver the distinct services needed for this particular demographic.

Sources:

Based on author interview with Alison Keir (2012).

National Cancer Action Team (2010) *The Characteristics of an Effective Multidisciplinary Team (MDT)*, London, NHS.

Should the desire of elderly patients be paramount in deciding whether to discharge from hospital?

Questions

Identify three key issues that HR managers have to consider when recruiting personnel to work in the treatment and care of the elderly in hospital.

What skills and competencies do HR managers look for in professionals in the treatment and care of the elderly?

What wider social, political, or economic factors do HR managers have to consider in the treatment and care of the elderly?

Online Resource Centre

Author commentary on this discussion point and questions can be found on the Online Resource Centre at: www.oxfordtextbooks.co.uk/orc/combe1e/

Developing workers as assets

One of the key aspects of HRM is to devise, implement, and evaluate methods of maximising returns from the investment in human resources. In similar fashion to the way organisations seek returns on investment in capital, machinery, infrastructure, and processes, so it is expected that human resources should contribute to the aims and objectives of the organisation. Developing workers as key assets in the organisation involves a number of different factors that combine to contribute to the aim of maximising returns from employees and to ensure that employees are given the support necessary to achieve their own aims and meet the standards expected of them. Some of the key elements of development are highlighted in Figure 8.2.

Health, safety, and well-being

The top priority for managers is to ensure that the working environment meets health and safety standards. Although these standards vary markedly around the world (in some places they are conspicuous by their absence) in developed and many developing countries organisations need to adhere to laws governing health and safety. Beyond compliance with legal obligations, managers have to take proactive steps to ensure the good health and safety of employees. These may include training programmes, accreditation from recognised health and safety bodies (such as the British Standards Association), health checks for workers, non-smoking policies and help for workers to quit (see Mini case 9.2 on *Azucarlito* in Chapter 9), the establishment of an occupational health department to support health and safety, stress-releasing activities, and so on. The issue of work-related stress is particularly acute in many modern businesses with

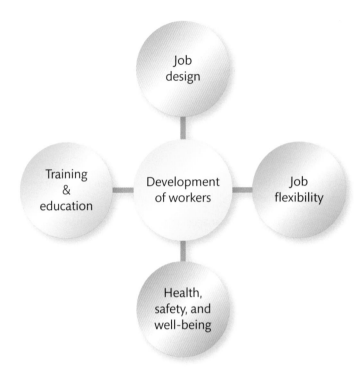

Figure 8.2 Key elements for developing workers as assets

pressure to perform consistently at a high standard within ever-increasing workloads being primarily responsible for stress-related illnesses. Organisations are known to lose many hours of working time through employees going absent due to stress. This has negative effects on morale, output, reputation, and relationships with stakeholders. Managers need to be able to recognise and treat the symptoms of work-related stress and deal with the underlying causes of stress. These causes may be multifarious in nature and complexity and may include over-work, staff tensions, poor working conditions, ineffective management, and dealing with technology, among others. Occupational health schemes play a crucial role in identifying problems early and dealing with them effectively through the implementation of specifically designed initia-tives such as access to exercise equipment, relaxation rooms, re-scheduling of workloads, time-out programmes, stress-releasing exercises, training on how to work safely with computers and other equipment, eye tests, psychological counselling, and others.

Job design

One of the roles of management is to create a job design that ensures outcomes are achieved. Job design is the process of matching the elements that comprise a job based on the needs of both the organisation and the workers. Health and safety considerations also feature in the job design. Essentially, job design is concerned with the way a set of tasks is organised and includes:

- identifying what tasks need to be carried out;
- deciding when and how those tasks are to be carried out;
- the number of tasks to be carried out;

- the order in which the tasks are sequenced;
- factors that affect the completion of the tasks;
- deciding who is to carry out the tasks;
- the timeframe for completion of the tasks;
- the expected outcome of the tasks.

The role of the HR manager in this process is to offer guidance and advice to operational and general managers regarding the best use of human resources in carrying out the tasks. This may include matching specific workers to specific tasks, ensuring that the outcomes are achievable, that health and safety obligations have been met, and that the tasks fit with the terms and conditions of employment contracts. Beyond that the HR managers may seek to liaise with other managers to improve workers' morale and sense of accomplishment by seeking ways of recognising achievement, providing further training opportunities, extending decision making authority, or empowering workers in the process of completing tasks.

Job flexibility

Job flexibility has become an important issue for both employers and employees in recent years as more and more people value a work/life balance. Demographic changes, attitudes to work, technology, and gender issues are just some of the factors that have ensured that a higher priority on flexibility has been a key feature of the modern workplace. For example, there are more women in the workplace in the UK than at any time in the past. This has required employers to be creative in the ways in which they can retain the key skills and experience that women workers bring whilst operating a flexible work schedule to allow for the caring responsibilities that are an important part of many women's lives. Changing attitudes have had an effect on men in the workplace with EU legislation underpinning rights to temporary leave after the birth of a child. Senior citizens are an increasing presence in the workplace, especially after legislation removed compulsory retirement. These are just some of the reasons why job flexibility has become an important issue for HR managers. Flexibility may mean allowing work from home, flexitime, extended leave during particular times of the year, part-time work, and so on.

Education, training, and development

Perhaps one of the most important tasks of the HR manager is to devise ways of maximising the returns from investment in human resources. Workers bring a range of skills, expertise, and experience with them when they are employed by an organisation. However, these attributes and value adding qualities are not static but can be added to over time through training and education. The concept of dynamic capabilities refers to the ability of an organisation to acquire ever-increasing value from existing workers. This has become a prominent theme in the thinking of strategic managers in recent times as the nature of work often demands that workers bring flexibility, creativity, innovation, and new ways of thinking and acting to add value in the competitive global economy.

Education refers to the formal approach to enhancing skills, experience, or knowledge and is normally carried out separately from the working environment, most usually at colleges or universities. Training, on the other hand, is the systematic development of skills, knowledge, values, and attitudes of individuals that are required to successfully carry out tasks. The development aspect of training refers to the growth of the individual regarding competencies, knowledge, and awareness.

Effective HRM brings together the three key elements of education, training, and development as a means of:

- developing the workforce to undertake added value activities;
- delivering the formal training and qualifications for new, young workers;
- improving efficiency and the standard of performance to remain competitive;
- adhering to health and safety regulations;
- informing workers of the organisational processes.

It is essential that HR managers work closely with other managers to identify where training, education, and/or development needs are required. For example, performance statistics may reveal a need for more or better training of staff in specific tasks; or when new technology is to be introduced; or where new industry regulation affects the way in which tasks are carried out. In some instances organisations can gain a competitive advantage by predicting what training needs will position the company in an advantageous position in future. HRM involves facilitating education, training, and development using a number of techniques including:

- placing workers in formal educational courses;
- creating learning opportunities from observing trained workers;
- facilitating participation in working parties, project groups, or specialist teams;
- introducing job rotation or job swaps both internally and externally to the organisation;
- giving access to self-learning facilities and materials.

Human resource managers need to oversee the effectiveness of programmes for education, training, and development to ensure that the investment is yielding returns. HR managers at *National Semiconductors* in Greenock, Scotland were able to identify improvements in skills, productivity, commitment, and communication after introducing a training programme that helped managers focus on practical leadership skills for increased engagement by the workforce (HRM International Digest, 2012). Evaluation also informs managers if current provision needs to be adapted or if new approaches are needed. Not all returns can be easily measured as some entail emotional factors such as attitudes, motivation, leadership skills, and so on. Here, the experience and knowledge of HR staff can help to evaluate how effective staff engagement has been on the programmes to which they have been assigned. A number of key indicators will emerge to give a general insight into the effectiveness of the organisation's education, training, and development provision. Key outcomes will relate to how the provision has affected efficiency and performance; knowledge generation and sharing; flexibility and adaptability of staff; engagement and use of technology; safety records; absences; morale and motivation; levels of qualifications of staff; and, of course, how they influence staff attraction, recruitment, and retention.

Managing employee relations

Another aspect of HRM is to oversee and regulate employee relations. As seen in the mini case study of *Qantas*, the effects of a breakdown in employee relations can be highly damaging both to the economic performance of an organisation and its reputation. Among the main issues that HRM is concerned with are managing communications between owners, managers, and staff; establishing procedures for negotiations, disputes, and discipline; contributing to the human resource element of organisational development; promoting good relationships between staff and management; problem solving employee-related issues; and managing internal employee-related processes such as promotion, conflict resolution, contract negotiations, and so on.

Much of the work of HR managers is guided by the employment legislation emanating from both the domestic government and bodies such as the EU. Organisations have to comply with the raft of legislation that underpins employees' rights as well as those covering issues such as health and safety, data protection, equal opportunities, and many others (Dickens and Hall, 2009). It is important that HR managers monitor the compliance of the organisation to ensure not only good governance but to promote good employee relations. Employee relations also includes dealing with their representatives, such as trade unions, to ensure the set standards of behaviour are being observed, that agreed standards of performance are being met, and that employees are being treated fairly and in accordance with the terms and conditions of their employment contracts. The relationship between workers, their trade unions, and management was traditionally adversarial in nature, with each faction fighting to secure the best deal. In the modern business environment the relationship has changed to one where dialogue, consensus, and even collaboration characterise the nature of the relationships. Although disputes still arise from time to time, the confrontational approach that characterised the 1970s and 1980s has given way to a more professional and collaborative approach. This can be seen in the way in which employee relations features as part of the wider organisational development (OD) remit where issues such as service delivery, implementation of technology, quality, and relationship building form part of the dialogue between employees and management.

Employee relations works in tandem with organisational development. OD is not an easily defined single concept but, rather, is a term used to encompass a collection of planned change interventions built on humanistic-democratic values that seek to improve organisational effectiveness and employee well-being. The OD paradigm values human and organisational growth, collaborative and participative processes, and a spirit of inquiry. OD has a strong emphasis on collaboration. Concepts such as power, authority, control, conflict, and coercion are held in relatively low esteem among workers. The key underlying values of OD in the context of employee relations include:

- Respect for people: individuals are perceived as being responsible, conscientious, and caring and should be treated with dignity and respect.
- Trust and support: the effective and healthy organisation is characterised by trust, authenticity, openness, and a supportive climate.
- Power equalisation: effective organisations de-emphasise hierarchical authority and control.
- Problem solving: problems need to be addressed rather than ignored but not in an antagonistic or confrontational manner.
- Participation: everyone is affected by organisational development issues. Participation in decision making processes should be inclusive.

Term
Definition

Employee relations: the process of maintaining effective dialogue and communications with employees (or their representatives) to maintain a harmonious working relationship between staff and managers.

285

? Critical reflection

Why are industrial disputes fewer in the twenty-first century compared to the 1970s?

Trade unions have traditionally been the main representatives for workers' rights, pay, conditions, and other employment-related issues. Union membership reached its zenith in the 1960s and 1970s but has been in decline ever since. There are numerous theories put forward for this ranging from the increase in home-ownership (people are less likely to take industrial action due to financial pressure) to the increase in the professional classes and less dependence on heavy industry such as steelmaking, coal mining, and shipbuilding—traditional hotbeds of trade union membership. Since the industrial strife that characterised the 1970s, many trade unions have changed the focus of their attention away from what was termed 'collective bargaining' (a method of leveraging negotiating power through collaboration with other unions) towards upholding the legal rights of individual members (Taylor, 2002). The employee relations climate in the twenty-first century is very different from the hostility that characterised much of the previous century. There is now a much clearer understanding by trade unions of the needs of corporate enterprises in the global economy and, similarly, there is much less hostility shown towards trade unions in corporate boardrooms. A significant trend has been the increase in the number of alternative dispute resolution initiatives that have emerged. ACAS (Advisory, Conciliation and Arbitration Service) is the standard bearer for dispute resolution but other bodies have started to provide specific services, for example in discrimination cases. HRM as a key service delivery in organisations has had to adapt to these changes and tailor solutions to employee-related issues within this new relationship between workers and management.

Human resource management in the modern workplace has become increasingly complex as issues of diversity, fairness, equality, flexibility, and so on have put pressure on managers to configure processes, procedures, and systems to cope with the demands brought by each of these issues, which need to be overtly and demonstrably managed in the working environment in a way that meets the organisation's legal and moral obligations whilst maintaining the focus on the core operational and strategic aims. Tensions arise when there is conflict between these two aspects of management. For example, the concept of positive discrimination is highly contentious. Positive discrimination refers to a situation where the HR managers have identified a gap in the number of recruits from a particular group such as women workers, an ethnic group, or disabled workers. It is lawful within the many developed countries to positively discriminate when an identified group is less well represented in the workplace. Some argue that this is discriminatory in itself: although there is no bar to anyone applying for the post (thus equal opportunities remain), identifying and encouraging people with specific characteristics to apply is often perceived as discriminatory by those applicants who do not possess those characteristics.

In other situations some employees may be able to negotiate flexible work schedules whilst others are not able to do so. Much depends on the nature of the tasks that workers are expected to carry out, the power and authority of workers, the level of responsibility, historical precedence in work arrangements, and other such factors. Clearly, these compromise the concept of equality in the workplace and can lead to tensions that the HR managers have to deal with. In some working environments the nature of the work itself and the environment in which workers operate is specialised and so unique that a different approach is required. One such case is in the security services where the imperative for secrecy pervades much of what happens within the organisations that are assigned the task of safeguarding national security. Whilst some aspects of management in the organisation closely resemble practices seen in public and private organisations, there are other aspects that reflect the unique nature of the working environment in which they operate.

Case study
Managing training and development at MI5

Introduction

The UK intelligence service known as MI5 has the remit of safeguarding national security against threats of terrorism, sabotage, espionage, and other activities designed to undermine the state and its security. Key to the work of MI5 operatives is the ability to obtain, collate, analyse, and assess secret intelligence on individuals or groups deemed to pose a national security threat. The organisation is also proactive in countering threats to national infrastructure and acts as a source of guidance and advice to government on matters of national security.

The complexity and range of activities that the organisation undertakes is broad ranging, as the nature of the threats posed by the nation's enemies has become more sophisticated and widespread. Although the threat of conventional terrorism persists, other threats have become pressing such as cyberwarfare and drug-related crime that undermines the fabric of society. The source of threats changes over time as well. For decades the service was engaged in countering the terrorist threat from the Provisional IRA in Northern Ireland and on the mainland. In more recent times the threat has emanated from Islamic terrorists linked to *Al Qaeda*. The sources of cyberwarfare attacks are more difficult to track down but nevertheless are becoming increasingly prevalent. To counter the welter of threats facing the nation, MI5 has to recruit able operatives who possess a range of intellectual, analytical, technical, and strategic skills deployed in a diverse range of roles. The career opportunities at MI5 are outlined on the organisation's website (www.sis.gov.uk/careers).

Roles and activities of MI5 operatives

The roles of MI5 operatives are broadly divided into 'generalists' and 'specialists'. The generalists move postings on a regular basis to gain experience and broaden their understanding and knowledge across a number of activities. Typically general operatives are involved in investigative work, evaluation and assessment, operations, or policy-related work. Invariably they move location every few years depending on the needs and requirements of the service. Other areas are much more specialist in nature, for example, surveillance work, language and communications, IT, or strategic planning. The shift in the main sources of national security threats (Islamic terrorists and cyberwarfare) has increased the need for operatives with language skills (mostly Arabic), IT expertise, and surveillance and analytical skills. Thus, the HRM aspect of the

https://www.
mi5.gov.uk/

https://www.
mi5.gov.uk/

service plays a pivotal role in determining just how effective the service is in fulfilling its aims and objectives.

Training and development

Human resource management at MI5 is highly committed to the training and development of operatives. This is a vital part of the strategy to ensure that the most able people are deployed in areas of need, and that their skills and expertise are constantly being updated to meet the challenges of a fast-changing environment. Although the selection process is rigorous, it is standard practice to allow all operatives the opportunity to access training and development. In keeping with many employers in the private and public sector, the service is accredited as an *Investors in People* employer and therefore has to demonstrate equal opportunities and fairness in their human resource practices. The organisation has been awarded Star Performing Network Status for its equal rights practices concerning Lesbian, Gay, Bisexual and Transgender (LGBT) people by campaign group Stonewall in 2009. In many ways the HRM practices relating to training and development mirror those seen in many other organisations in terms of design and content with an emphasis on leadership, communications, and processes. However, the training and development that is tailored to the specific needs of the organisation is provided by the in-house academy where the focus is on IT skills, investigative and analytical skills, or covert operational techniques. This is provided by a mix of in-house experts and externally sourced professional trainers and consultants. Of course, all staff and externally sourced service providers are closely vetted before becoming operational. Operatives will have to undergo a Developed Vetting (DV) procedure before acquiring the necessary security clearance.

Approaches to training and development

The initial training that operatives receive is the induction programme. This is an important first stage of training as it offers the opportunity to communicate the values, aims, and philosophy that underpin the work of the organisation. It provides new recruits with an insight into the history, culture, and legal framework of the organisation as well as the health and safety issues and procedures for ensuring security. Each department that comprises the organisation has an opportunity to communicate what they do and their contribution to the aims and objectives of the organisation. The assessment of recruits begins almost immediately as it is important to determine where best to deploy staff and to identify those with leadership potential. Leadership is a key attribute that the organisation seeks and those who aspire to, or are chosen for, leadership roles can access foundation courses in management and leadership.

The training and development provision at the organisation is based on a blended learning approach including class-based learning, mentoring by experienced staff, on the job training, coaching, modular courses, and specialist skills training. One of the main challenges facing HR managers is to ensure access, availability, and delivery of training programmes to operatives who are physically dispersed and who have a range of different work patterns. To deal with this the organisation has invested in developing e-learning tools that offer greater flexibility in access and delivery. A specialist Learning and Technologies group was established to support this initiative. Other learning opportunities include guest speakers, language training, enrolment in further education or university courses, and development days when staff can undertake studies or activities outside the normal workplace.

The role of HR managers at MI5 in the context of training and development is to monitor the effectiveness of training provision, manage the training and development processes, guide and advise management on the changes or adaptations required for the provision, and ensure that equal access to training and development is available to all staff. They will also decide which training and development activities are compulsory for all staff and those which are at the discretion of individuals. Operatives are subject to monitoring and evaluation by managers to determine their suitability for specific postings and activities and to appraise their response to the training and development provided. The HR managers will play a role in advising and guiding management as they carry out these duties and make decisions regarding the deployment and future training and development needs of operatives.

It is likely that the training and development needs of operatives at MI5 (and the other services, GCHQ and MI6) will become increasingly specialised as the range of threats becomes more sophisticated and the means of detecting and dealing with them becomes more complex. The HR managers will play a key role in determining which types of training and development will be needed into the future within a dynamic and uncertain environment that is characterised by rapid changes in technology, social and demographic changes, political and economic pressures, and legislative reform regarding issues of privacy, surveillance, and data sharing. Ultimately, the ability of the organisation to carry out its activities to achieve its core aims and objectives depends on people and it is the role of HRM to manage the investment in operatives to ensure that they can deliver the skills, knowledge, and experience for the safekeeping of UK citizens from both internal and external threats.

Sources:

Careers at the Secret Intelligence Services. https://www.sis.gov.uk/careers.html

MI5 careers (2009) https://www.mi5.gov.uk/files/Global/Careers/Stonewall_Guide.pdf

Discussion point

Is HRM at MI5 any different from any other organisation?

289

Questions and task

Identify the key skills and attributes that HR managers at MI5 are looking for in their recruits.

What main roles do HR managers at the organisation undertake?

Research and highlight the eligibility criteria for employment with MI5.

Online Resource Centre

Author commentary on this discussion point and questions can be found on the Online Resource Centre at: www.oxfordtextbooks.co.uk/orc/combe1e/

Summary

● **Understand the role, aims, and importance of human resource management**

The role of human resource management is to ensure that strategic aims relating to all aspects of human resource utilisation and development are achieved. The key aims are to attract, recruit, and retain staff that add value to the organisation and help achieve its stated aims and objectives.

● **Appreciate the different approaches to adopting human resource strategies**

The main human resource strategies were identified as being unitarism, pluralism, radicalism, conflict, conformity, and consensus. Each one displays its own characteristics and the discussion focused on the application of the different approaches in different organisational settings.

● **Identify the challenges of managing diversity**

Diversity brings opportunities for organisations but also presents a number of challenges such as how to avoid conflict of interests between groups of workers from different backgrounds; organising work schedules to accommodate the needs of certain types of workers (working mothers, Muslim workers during Ramadan, etc.), effective communications, promotion and status, working within the law, and so on. HR managers have to understand these challenges and find ways and means of dealing with them in a fair and equitable manner.

● **Understand the approaches to evaluating human resources**

Evaluation of human resources takes place throughout the processes of attraction, recruitment, and retention of workers. HR managers have to evaluate what skills and attributes are required and what rewards will attract the type of workers they need. Evaluation of potential recruits is a key feature of the process of assessing applications, interviews, testing, and other forms of determining whether or not candidates can be employed. Once recruited, HR managers have to design human resource performance targets for employees and assess the contribution of workers in line with agreed targets. Evaluation is a constant requirement of HR managers and forms a major part of their role.

● **Critically evaluate the means by which managers can develop workers as key assets and manage human relations**

A number of techniques were highlighted as means by which managers can develop workers as key assets. The critical evaluation of these focused on the merits and limitations evident in different organisational settings. The discussion featured job design, job flexibility, training and education, and the health, safety, and well-being of workers. In particular, the evaluation was based on contemporary developments in the workplace such as the increasing number of women in work, new health and safety directives, and the principle of lifelong learning and continuous professional development.

Conclusion

This chapter has highlighted the diverse and challenging nature of HRM in the modern working environment. HR managers have a wide range of issues that they need to contend with whilst maintaining a focus on the aims and objectives of the organisation. HR managers seek to optimise returns on human resource investment. One way to achieve this is to create harmonious working relationships and the chapter revealed the changes in attitudes between management and workers (and their representatives) over the last two decades that has led to a more understanding relationship. Motivation plays a key role in determining how competitive the organisation is, or how well it achieves its stated aims and objectives. HR managers will contribute to the ways and means adopted to improve worker motivation both as individuals and as part of a group. The next chapter explores this important area of management by focusing attention on the importance of motivation, the techniques for improving motivation, and the benefits that can accrue from a highly motivated workforce.

Chapter questions and task

Identify and describe the three main tasks of HRM.

Explain the concept of a 'psychological contract'.

What role does HRM play in managing effective employee relations?

What techniques can HR managers use to introduce job flexibility in the modern workplace?

Online Resource Centre

Author commentary on these questions can be found on the Online Resource Centre at: www.oxfordtextbooks.co.uk/orc/combe1e/

Further reading

- Kirton, G. and Greene, A. (2010) *The Dynamics of Managing Diversity* (3rd edn), Oxford, Butterworth-Heinemann.

  A coherent and lucid presentation of contexts, policies, and practices for developing a sustainable, high performing, and diverse workforce. The book explains the relevant laws pertaining to diversity in an understandable manner as well as exploring wider issues such as cultural differences.

- Pilbeam, S. and Corbridge, M. (2010) *People Resourcing and Talent Planning: HRM in practice* (4th edn), Harlow, Financial Times/Prentice Hall.

  The book focuses attention on the people resourcing of organisations and provides a balanced approach between academic and practitioner requirements that have been used in CIPD Professional Standards. The authors call on real-life examples to bring to life the various HRM issues and concepts. There is extensive use of case studies and effective application of theory to deliver a lucid and valuable account of HRM in practice.

- Saunders, M., Millmore, M., Lewis, P., Thornhill, A., and Morrow, T. (2010) *Human Resource Management: Contemporary issues*, Harlow, Financial Times/Prentice Hall.

  The book is aimed at honours, MBA, and/or Masters level students and provides a strategic dimension to HRM. The discussion follows an integrated approach linking HRM strategies to key concepts in competitive strategy such as leveraging advantage from capabilities. The book also explores the strategic aspects of reward systems and knowledge management in organisations.

Online Resource Centre

For more information, updates, and multiple-choice questions, please visit the Online Resource Centre at: www.oxfordtextbooks.co.uk/orc/combe1e/

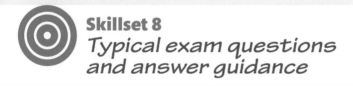

Skillset 8
Typical exam questions and answer guidance

1 Is scientific management an appropriate approach to the management of modern organisations? Discuss.

2 Discuss how managers can influence the formation of a positive organisational culture.

3 Using examples, discuss the decision making criteria that managers consider when determining whether or not to adopt a new technology for internal processes.

4 What are the limitations of the classical model of decisions making?

5 Critically assess the merits of decentralisation of control in an organisation. Why are so many managers reluctant to decentralise control?

6 Identify the key characteristics of the human relations school of management theory. Using examples, discuss the advantages of implementing a human relations approach to managing an organisation.

7 Draw an organisational structure evident in a modern organisation of your choice. Discuss the reasons for adopting such a structure.

8 Critically assess the contribution of trait theories to our understanding of leadership.

9 Outline the central elements of Total Quality Management and evaluate its importance in contemporary organisations.

Answer guidance

1 Is scientific management an appropriate approach to the management of modern organisations? Discuss.

Response should give a brief definition of Scientific Management. Scientific management still has a role to play in modern businesses and is very evident in manufacturing industry and call centres. Answers to this question should offer some modern examples of where SM is to be found. Some may refer to links with Japanese working practices such as Just-in-Time to illustrate SM in the modern era. High marks can be given to those who identify the types of industries where SM is both evident and desirable such as in call centres where the workforce have very proscribed tasks, there is constant monitoring and evaluation, and where the workforce accept the trade-off between freedom and economic reward. High marks too for recognising that in other industry sectors SM is inappropriate. In particular, the creative industries of media, publishing, and the arts would not incorporate SM because of the stifling effect it can have on innovation and creativity. There should be some recognition that legislation and union agreements combine to place limitations on the worst examples of SM whereby working conditions are closely monitored and are within the guidelines of acceptability. This includes both physical and intellectual labour. Thus, fast food restaurants, factories, and IT-based data in-putting jobs need to comply with European legislation on working hours, break times, and physical conditions. In reality, many low paid, low skilled jobs take place under conditions where SM is the norm. In some instances workers are happy to accept SM as part of their working practice. For example, car factory workers at Nissan in Sunderland have adopted Japanese working methods based on SM as the norm. Students should recognise that SM is very much part of the modern business environment.

2 Discuss how managers can influence the formation of a positive organisational culture.

Managers can influence the formation of a positive organisational culture by job rotation to multi-skill employees and to make workers aware of different aspects to the functions within the productive process. Managers can involve more people in the decision making process by altering the structure to a flatter, more cohesive set of units. Managers can form teams and offer incentives to groups to achieve aims, thereby circumventing the feelings of alienation among workers. Each worker will feel part of the mission and aims of the organisation. This may be underpinned by offering financial incentives such as shares in the company. This gives employees a vested interest in the performance of the company. Managers can also extend reward schemes beyond simple financial reward to incorporate greater freedom, more breaks, peer recognition, awards for good practice and performance. Managers can also improve the physical working conditions by investing in a state-of-the-art working environment including heating, ventilation, colour schemes, etc.

3 Using examples, discuss the decision making criteria that managers consider when determining whether or not to adopt a new technology for internal processes.

The main criteria that form the decision making process for managers contemplating intro-ducing new technology into their organisations include the cost of acquiring the technology, the cost of implementing the technology, the retraining of staff to utilise the technology, the scope the technology offers for delivering efficiencies or competitive advantage, the cost of disruption in the change-over period to adopting the new technology, the extent to which the technology is diffused across the industry sector, and the longevity of the use of the technol-ogy. There are many examples relating to each of these criteria. These may include a firm seek-ing competitive advantage in the pharmaceutical industry whereby companies traditionally take a long-term view of investing in both research and development of new drugs alongside that of investment in developing the types of technologies required to produce new drugs. Many firms will take a decision on investing in new information systems depending upon the types of skills required to operate the system effectively and the cost efficiencies it will bring to the organisation.

4 What are the limitations of the classical model of decision making?

Answers should highlight the key features of classical theory such as the identification of the issue requiring a decision; identification and generation of alternative courses of action and their consequences; evaluation and ranking of alternatives; selection of the alternative; and evaluation of the decision. Limitations should include: classical approaches do not recognise biases in the process such as representative bias, prior hypothesis bias, assumptions made by the model may not apply in certain cases, for example where there is incomplete information, or by limited capacity to process information. Classical models often do not recognise vari-ables like ambiguous information, time constraints.

5 Critically assess the merits of decentralisation of control in an organisation. Why are so many managers reluctant to decentralise control?

In many modern businesses the concept of empowerment of workers has been given impetus by the decentralisation of power from headquarters. This allows for teams of specialist workers to take charge of projects, make decisions, and complete the work more efficiently. Decentrali-sation makes communications within organisations smoother and limits bureaucratic prac-tices that stifle innovation and creativity. It also allows local managers the scope to negotiate contracts with suppliers that offer best value. Local managers are also better informed about their competitive environment and can make better judgements about the types of plans and decisions that result in the achievement of specified aims.

Many managers are, however, reluctant to decentralise control principally because they fear the effects of strategic drift. That is, local managers may take decisions that are in direct conflict with the desired and stated aims of the organisation. It may mean that the reputation and image of the organisation is compromised because of the increased power being exercised at the local level. The lack of strategic control from the centre may lead to the diminution of competitive advantage as the coherence of strategy is compromised. Many managers prefer to maintain a close control on operations to ensure accountability and to control spending.

6 Identify the key characteristics of the human relations school of management theory. Using examples, discuss the advantages of implementing a human relations approach to managing an organisation.

The characteristics of the human relations school should include workers' welfare, an emphasis on the working environment, teamwork, groups, worker interaction, physical conditions, wider set of rewards, social factors in the workplace. The advantages of implementing a human relations approach should cite the work of either Follett or Mayo. Human relations, according to Follett, facilitates the growth of both the individual and the group in the workplace and can boost productive efficiency by creating an environment that exploits human interaction for problem solving and conflict resolution. This approach allowed human creativity to flourish. Examples of human relations in modern organisations include the creative industries of fashion and advertising where the working environment is open, non-hierarchical, unstructured, and designed to encourage the free and open discussion and creation of ideas. Many modern businesses operate human relations by empowering small groups of workers to achieve aims in the way they see fit. Mayo highlights the physical as well as the social environment. Examples may include modern businesses that create a working environment that is conducive to achieving efficiency, improving staff morale and motivation, and meeting health and safety standards.

7 Draw an organisational structure evident in a modern organisation of your choice. Discuss the reasons for adopting such a structure.

Answers should include a graphical representation of both product and market areas in the structure. It should also represent any discernible hierarchy within the organisation. The reasons for adopting the structure should include ease of communication, flexibility, economies of scale in selling products globally, delegation of authority to geographically dispersed managers, and ability to communicate the corporate vision.

8 Critically assess the contribution of trait theories to our understanding of leadership.

The answer should recognise the limitations of trait theory in explaining what makes a successful leader. It should note the characteristics of trait theory and then give examples of where it is evident and where it is not. This should form the basis of a critical assessment of the weakness of the theory in fully explaining what makes successful leadership. Answers should determine that some traits are evident in a great many leaders while others are less prevalent. It should also recognise that other factors play a role in the development of leaders such as experiences and cultural dimensions.

9 **Outline the central elements of Total Quality Management and evaluate its importance in contemporary organisations.**

Central elements of TQM: definition of TQM, efficiency and effectiveness, total process, customer focus at every stage, identify internal and external customers, measures of quality, information collection and analysis. Identify goals and objectives of everyone in the organisation. Enhance teamwork. Understand costs of poor quality and remedies, inventory management, JIT, encourage creativity, vision, leadership training. Should stress the importance of creating a competitive advantage through increasing efficiency and customer satisfaction.

9 Motivation and Communications

Learning outcomes

- Understand the components of the job characteristics model and the role of job design in worker satisfaction and motivation

- Critically assess the theoretical perspectives on motivation

- Evaluate the effect of worker empowerment as a key motivator

- Understand and assess the different reward systems in terms of motivation

- Assess the information richness of communications media and understand the barriers to effective communication

Possibly one of the most famous names in the entertainment industry is that of Walt Disney. During his career he was able to build an entertainment empire that covered film, television, theme parks, studios, and many more. Key to his success was his ability to motivate others to perform to the highest standards, in some cases to standards the workers didn't even realise they had (Nelson, 1999). His genius lay in his ability to command the total loyalty of his workforce and to get them to 'buy into' the Disney philosophy that was all about bringing happiness to the people (Nelson, 1999). His mantra was 'we are in the happiness business' and this underpinned the purpose and strength of the Disneyland theme parks. It didn't matter if customers spent ten minutes or ten hours in the park, Disney motivated his workers to engage with them to spread the happiness theme. Disney's motivational abilities stemmed more from an understanding of human nature than from learned techniques. Much in the way his films transported viewers to a different world, so he believed that anything was possible in the real world if people were motivated to pursue their goals. As a manager, Disney could also be notoriously tough and he demanded high standards from all his staff. However, he made each staff member feel valued and part of something special. He allowed ideas to flow from whatever source and everyone had opportunities to express themselves (Niles, 2009).

Skillset 9
Presentation skills

This chapter will highlight the need for effective communications skills as a means of motivating workers. Communications is a vital part of the range of skills and attributes that management must possess in order to ensure that work is not only carried out properly, but that workers are motivated to undertake work tasks with an attitude that is conducive to delivering quality within a harmonious working environment. One aspect of communications skills is the ability to give effective presentations to a wide range of stakeholders including management superiors, workers, trade unions, suppliers, government bodies, etc.

Student study skills

Presentation skills form an important part of the learning process for students and this Skillset provides a valuable insight into some of the techniques that can be applied to help students understand what attributes and skills are required to produce effective presentations.

Workplace skills

Communications skills are one of the most valued assets that employers seek when recruiting staff. In the modern business environment it is likely that workers will be required to communicate effectively with a wide range of people both internal and external to the organisation. Whether operating at the functional, middle management or corporate level, communications skills are a vital part of the process of adding value in many modern organisations.

Definitions

Motivation refers to the influential impulses which encourage a person to sustain a commitment to a particular course of action. The impulses may emanate from within the person or be the result of external influential factors. Motivation can be viewed as an incentive to act in a particular manner. Communication is the transference of knowledge or information from sender to receiver.

Introduction

Motivating workers is a key management skill as it helps organisations to achieve their aims and objectives. Workers may be motivated by a range of different influencing factors including:

- economic reward;
- status;
- power;
- peer acceptance;
- the mission of the organisation;
- altruism;
- self-esteem;
- inspiring leadership.

Managers may need to employ a series of different motivational techniques for different groups of workers or even for individual workers depending on their understanding and knowledge of how the workers react to the stimuli. Some managers can motivate through force of personality, communication skills, or the ability to derive value from well-honed interpersonal skills. In others, it is the respect they command as leaders, their experience, skills, or expertise that has been demonstrated in the field. Motivation has a psychological dimension to it and is set within a social environment. Managers need to understand that environment and the nature and characteristics of the personnel who inhabit it.

Motivation can be the difference between gaining and sustaining a competitive advantage in highly competitive industries. In the modern business environment it is necessary for managers to employ effective motivational techniques to ensure that the organisation gets the best from their employees. Importantly, some of these techniques may be subtle and nuanced rather than regimented and contrived. Workers generally have a keen sense of knowing when they are being manipulated and controlled rather than being inspired and motivated. This chapter explores some of the key factors that determine motivation as a management skill and calls on theory to help the process of understanding how this important issue can be managed effectively.

The chapter begins with discussion of the job characteristics model and considers the role of job design and redesign as a means of improving job satisfaction and motivation. This is followed by a critical assessment of the theoretical perspectives relating to motivation including:

- the instrumental approach;
- Maslow's hierarchy of needs;
- McGregor's Theory X/Theory Y;
- Herzberg's hygiene factors and motivators;

- contingency approaches;
- expectancy theory.

The development and implementation of reward systems available to managers as a means of motivating workers in different organisational settings is discussed. This discussion is followed by an analysis of the effect that empowering employees has on motivating workers in the modern business environment. The link between motivation and effective communications is made explicit and the chapter concludes with an analysis of information richness in communications and an overview of some of the barriers to effective communication.

Theoretical perspectives of motivation

Factors that motivate workers have been the concern of managers ever since the early days of industrial endeavour. It has already been noted that the likes of Frederick Taylor and Henry Ford had a rather simplistic view on motivation that extended no further than economic reward for prescribed sets of actions that constituted a day's work. More enlightened perspectives followed with the development of the human relations approach. In the modern era it is clear that a wide range of different motivators are evident in the workplace and that they span a broad array of different human needs and emotions. To better understand the contribution that theory has made to our understanding of motivation in the workplace, this section offers an explanation of the characteristics of different theoretical perspectives and provides analysis of their effectiveness in shedding light on this important aspect of management.

The instrumental approach

Early management theorists viewed the employee as a totally rational creature whose motivation was purely economic. As noted in Chapter 2 on Management Theory, the essence of Frederick Taylor's concept of 'Scientific Management' was that it was in an employee's own best (economic) interest to put in a fair day's work (Taylor, 2003). This gave rise to payments on the basis of 'piece-rates' that rewarded efficiency. Piece-rates is a wage determination system whereby the employee is paid for each unit of production at a fixed rate. Economic return was seen as the only incentive or motivator that was required in the factory system that characterised the industrial landscape of the nineteenth and early twentieth centuries. As economic incentives are under the control of the organisation, the worker is merely a passive agent who can be motivated, manipulated, and controlled by the provision or withdrawal of economic reward. Inefficiency, in terms of a worker's inability to meet targets and production quotas, could be met with dismissal. Thus managers traditionally 'motivated' their workforce by a combination of fear and reward. The characteristics of this traditional view of how management can direct and control the behaviour of its workers relies on a series of assumptions about human nature. These were labelled by Douglas McGregor (1960) in *The Human Side of Enterprise*, as 'Theory X' assumptions. (See details of McGregor's work later in this chapter.)

One should not assume that these traditional assumptions have totally disappeared from the managerial consciousness. Neither should we assume that aspects of Taylorism, albeit in a somewhat diluted form, are unacceptable to workers. Variations of his piece-rate systems are common in manufacturing industries, as are the time and motion studies to ascertain output and the setting of rates. His concept of measured day work, albeit in a tempered form, is a characteristic of much manual work. Both are frequently applied with the active encouragement and enthusiasm of trade unions. Similarly the modern concept of the productivity bonus, seen as a means of increasing output and hence enhancing a firm's competitive position, is widespread. The bonus culture in the financial services industry has attracted some criticism in the wake of the 'credit crunch'. As the nature of work, and indeed the wider society in which it takes place, changes, so the emphasis swings towards other types of motivators. As the weaknesses and limitations of the traditional view became increasingly obvious, the alternative 'human relations' approach gained in currency.

Maslow's Hierarchy of Needs

Maslow's 'Hierarchy of Needs' theory has influenced both the clinical school of psychology, which is based on the motivational concept of 'drive', and the very different experimental school, which has produced the 'choice' or 'contingency' theories. Maslow (1943) postulated that human beings possessed five categories of needs, arranged in a specific hierarchical order, so that, once one need had been satisfied it no longer acts as a motivator, and a higher level need emerges which requires satisfaction. He also made the controversial assumption of 'prepotency', that is, that the higher-level needs would not manifest themselves until the lower-level needs had first been satisfied. Figure 9.1 illustrates Maslow's hierarchy of needs.

Physiological: basic survival needs of a physical nature—air, water, food

Security: a feeling of well-being and safety

Belongingness: an emotional need to feel wanted and part of a society

Esteem: feelings of self-worth and value

Self-actualisation: fulfilment of ambition and desired life goals

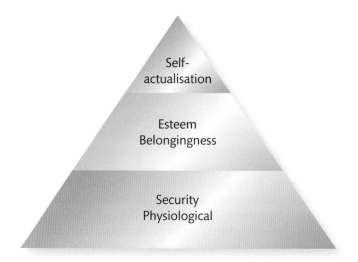

Figure 9.1 Maslow's Hierarchy of Needs

Critical reflection
Do pay increases lead to the increased motivation of workers?

There have been numerous studies into the link between pay and motivation in different organisational settings. Whereas the rational goal school discern a positive link, researchers from the human relations schools note that economic reward alone does not motivate, especially over a protracted period of time. Of course, it is necessary to view the investigations in their historical context as there was a time when workers' expectations regarding reward extended no further than receiving wages for their time and effort. Where consensus exists is in the finding that when pay is static, motivation tails off. Therefore, the debate surrounds the link between incentive payments and motivation. That is, paying additional wages to boost the productivity of the employee. This can take on different forms such as performance-related pay, merit pay, profit-sharing, variable pay plans, bonuses, or gain-sharing. Again, protagonists of the rational goal school believe that there is a direct link between incentive pay and motivation as it is, in their view, economic reward that brings people to work in the first place. Conversely, the human relations school believe that workers only derive short-term utility from pay rises and that its motivating powers are limited. In fact, the human relations school note a negative correlation between increased pay and psychological well-being. McClelland (1988), for example, classifies employee needs as being achievement, affiliation or power, with no mention of wealth accumulation.

Two influential studies illustrate how this subject can elicit different outcomes. Jenkins et al. (1998) analysed thirty-nine studies conducted over four decades and concluded that economic reward does motivate workers irrespective of the working conditions or environment. Their conclusions also noted that the lack of adequate economic rewards leads to worker resentment and dysfunctional teams. A further review of literature by Perry et al. (2006) found that financial incentives did improve performance but that the effectiveness of this was dependent on organisational conditions such as employees' preferences for specific incentives. An interesting finding of Perry's analysis was that small group incentives tend to sustain high levels of productivity and satisfaction for group members. These incentives may be financial (increased pay), non-financial (greater autonomy in decision making), or social (greater freedom to interact as a group). Despite some differences in findings and interpretations of studies, many modern employers retain faith in the motivational effects of pay and use it as a means of attracting, retaining, and motivating workers.

Maslow's concepts are not without problems. First, there is no evidence to suggest that a hierarchy of needs actually exists; it remains speculation, a hypothesis only. Secondly, the ideas that a rank order exists and that pre-potency is a necessary condition are valid only in a very limited and simple sense. There is evidence to suggest that overlapping occurs. There are instances where higher needs are given priority over lower ones. For instance, an individual worker may pursue a grievance for a long period, to his own disadvantage, rather than concede a principle. However, Maslow's work strongly influenced Douglas McGregor whose Theory X/Theory Y has informed management education for many years.

McGregor: Theory X/Theory Y

Douglas McGregor, as one of the protagonists of the human relations approach, was primarily interested in discovering what motivates workers and how managers can influence motivation in the workforce. His main legacy is the Theory X/Theory Y model. A number of key assumptions underpin the model.

Theory X assumptions:

(i) the average human being has an inherent dislike of work and will avoid it if he can;

(ii) humans have a characteristic dislike of work meaning that most people must be coerced, controlled, directed, and threatened with punishment to get them to put forth adequate effort toward the achievement of organisational objectives;

(iii) the average human being prefers to be directed, wishes to avoid responsibility, has relatively little ambition, wants security above all.

Theory Y assumptions:

(i) the expenditure of physical and mental effort in work is as natural as play or rest;

(ii) external control and the threat of punishment are not the only means of bringing about efforts towards organisational objectives—man will exercise self-direction and self-control in the service of objectives to which he is committed;

(iii) commitment to objectives is a function of the rewards associated with their achievement—the most significant of such rewards, e.g. the satisfaction of ego and self-actualisation, can be direct products of effort directed towards organisational objectives;

(iv) the average human being learns, under proper conditions, not only to accept but to seek responsibility;

(v) the capacity to exercise a relatively high degree of imagination, ingenuity, and creativity in the solution of organisational problems is widely, not narrowly, distributed in the population;

(vi) under conditions of modern industrial life, the intellectual potentialities of the average human being are only partially utilised.

McGregor believed that Theory Y would lead to higher motivation. He considered traditional assumptions (his Theory X) as both limiting and unrealistic because they relied on authority as the primary means of control, which he saw as likely to generate resistance, restriction of output, indifference to organisational objectives, and the refusal to accept personal responsibility. McGregor's theories have influenced many academics and practitioners of management. An understanding of Theory Y assumptions and their implications is central to understanding human resource management. However, the process of converting these theoretical assumptions into practical management strategies, such as schemes of job enlargement, job enrichment, and job redesign, owes less to the contribution of McGregor, rather it is the output of American psychologist Frederick Herzberg that carries more significance in this regard.

Herzberg: Hygiene factors and motivators

After collecting and reviewing literature on job satisfaction, Herzberg and his collaborators developed a new method of investigation known as 'factor analysis of critical incident'. The result of the initial application of this 'critical incidents' technique on 200 engineers and accountants were deemed by his peers to be of ground-breaking significance. The key discovery

Mini case 9.1
Motivating the workforce at the Polish Competence Centre

The Polish Competence Centre (PCC) was established in 2005 in Warsaw as an independent and not-for-profit organisation with the aim of supporting partners from the public sector in e-government and e-education development and implementation. The Centre comprises three main partners: the Foundation for Economic Education (Warsaw), Poznan Supercomputing and Networking Centre (Poznan), and the Fraunhofer Institute for Open Communications Systems (FOKUS) based in Berlin. The PCC is concerned with the design, planning, and implementation of projects and supports its partners and clients in acquiring funding for their chosen projects (FOKUS: Polish Competence Centre, 2013).

The majority of workers at the PCC are relatively young, most commonly recent graduates, or in the 21–28 age group. The typical profile of the workers is young, university educated, technology literate, problem solvers with good communications skills. Workers are generally self-motivated as there is a certain kudos attached to working in an organisation that has technology, design, and education at the core of activities. Many of the workers view their time at the PCC as a good investment for their future career trajectory, especially given the range and profile of partner organisations they work with including *Microsoft*, *Siemens*, and *Cisco Systems* (FOKUS: partners, 2013). Thus, it is not money or status that motivates the workforce but rather the opportunity to hone their skills in areas where they perceive a value in terms of future career prospects.

There is a mutual benefit from the recruitment policy as the PCC gain access to young, talented, motivated, and skilled workers and the workers gain access to opportunities for developing their skills and applying them in the real world. This combination has created a symbiotic relationship between managers and workers that has added real quality to the products and services provided. In particular, the public sector in Poland has benefited from the innovative new ways of applying e-government services as a means of improving transparency, accountability, and democratic processes at local and central government level. Citizens can now readily access the voting record of all public officials and monitor the alignment between promises made and political action. The openness of government processes in Poland has enhanced the country's reputation for implementing the type of democratic reforms that encourage inward investment. The pace of change would have been much slower but for the contribution made by the highly motivated workforce at the PCC.

Sources:

FOKUS (2013) Partners: Polish Competence Centre. http://www.fokus.fraunhofer.de/en/elan/projekte/international/pcc/index.html#PARTNERS

FOKUS (2013) Partners http://www.fokus.fraunhofer.de/en/elan/projekte/international/pcc/index.html#ACTIVITIES

Discussion point

Do most university graduates trade-off financial rewards for a first step on the career ladder?

Questions

What are the main rewards for workers at the Polish Competence Centre (PCC)?
Is the motivation model adopted at the PCC sustainable?
How can managers at the PCC measure the motivation of workers?

Online Resource Centre

Author commentary on this discussion point and questions can be found on the Online Resource Centre at: www.oxfordtextbooks.co.uk/orc/combe1e/

303

http://www.fokus.fraunhofer.de

http://www.fokus.fraunhofer.de

was that two separate scales were required, one to measure satisfaction, and one to measure dissatisfaction. For example, a worker may complain of dissatisfaction because he or she is underpaid. To give that worker a pay rise would not, according to Herzberg, make that worker satisfied or motivated to become more productive; it would merely stop him or her expressing dissatisfaction. As a result, Herzberg (1959) claimed that the opposite of being dissatisfied is not being satisfied, but rather being not dissatisfied. To make the worker in question satisfied would require more than raising the level of remuneration. In the study, the factors associated with being satisfied included:

- obtaining a sense of achievement from their work;
- having autonomy and responsibility;
- receiving recognition for their efforts or aptitudes;
- being asked to perform challenging, interesting, and worthwhile tasks.

The major dissatisfactions on the other hand were:

- company strategy;
- administration;
- supervision;
- salary;
- interpersonal relations;
- working conditions.

Herzberg called the factors associated with dissatisfaction the 'hygiene factors' because they were generally associated with environmental conditions that surrounded the job. The factors associated with satisfaction he termed 'motivators'.

The implications of Herzberg's theory are that, whilst it is important to get the hygiene factors right (i.e. good working conditions, salary, supervision, etc.) this does not guarantee good organisational health; it merely provides a necessary precondition for it. The factors which provide job satisfaction, i.e. the motivators, also have to be provided. However, Herzberg's work is not without its critics, and the methodology of both the original and later studies is far from rigorous in scientific terms (Hinrich and Mischkind, 1967). Nevertheless, the work of Herzberg did pave the way for the study of motivation at a practical level, being applied by industrial concerns in both the USA and the UK. Herzberg's theories suggest that it would be possible to design or redesign jobs in a way that makes them more satisfying for employees—what he termed 'job enrichment'. Forms of 'enrichment' may include:

- an increase in responsibility;
- a decrease in supervision;

Term
Definitions

Motivators: aspects of work that influence people to deliver superior performance.
Job enrichment: the design or redesign of jobs to make them more satisfying for employees.

Critical reflection
Is job enrichment a key motivator?

Job enrichment is a common feature in organisations as managers attempt to improve morale and the motivation of workers. This is especially the case in working environments that are characterised by repetition and low skills. However, job enrichment is not without its limitations when it comes to its actual implementation. For instance, the concept of job enrichment is built on the assumption that workers want it and perceive a benefit from it. This is not always the case and in some instances workers may resent the imposed change. Workers may fear that they do not possess the training or skills to undertake the new challenges that job enrichment presents. Also, in some factory settings, technology is used to undertake the majority of tasks and processes, leaving little scope for introducing job enrichment activities. The cost of applying job enrichment can also be prohibitive, especially if it exceeds any gains in productivity. Managers would have to assess the value of the intangible asset of improved morale alongside that of increased productivity to attain a real value of applying job enrichment innovations. Finally, workers may very quickly become familiar with the new job enrichment activities whereupon the motivating dimension to the innovation dissipates. So, although it is a useful technique that is widely adopted, job enrichment has to be thought through carefully to ensure that expected benefits are realised.

- freedom to schedule one's time and work activities;
- increased direct feedback on performance;
- opportunities for developing and expanding skills.

Contingency approaches

The human relations theorists (Follett, 1920; Mayo 1939) considered that in all cases all employees sought self-actualisation. This implies that what is 'good' or 'best' for one employee will be 'good' or 'best' for all. What is 'good' for one organisation will be equally 'good' for all organisations. If one employee becomes more highly motivated by job enrichment, so will others. This is a rather simplistic assumption as it is known that organisations are very different in practice, as are people. Within the same organisation and among people doing the same job there will be various different opinions about self-development or job enrichment. This necessarily undermines the robustness of the assumptions that there exists one right strategy for an organisation, and that employees are essentially undifferentiated in terms of what motivates them. This 'unitarist', and essentially prescriptive approach, ignores two important features:

- Individuals, even within the work context alone, will have different perceptions, attitudes, and motivations with regard to their tasks, even if the tasks performed are identical.
- Psychological explanations alone are insufficient to explain concepts like motivation. There is a sociological and cultural dimension which affects our attitudes, perceptions, and motivations, and which is not left behind when we enter our place of work.

There is no 'one best way' approach for organisations or individuals. What may be more appropriate is an approach to motivation which takes account of contingencies. One such approach is known as 'expectancy theory'. This theory emphasises that people make choices as to how they will behave, and that these choices will be affected by the extent to which the probable outcome of such behaviour is valued. Thus, in order to understand how employees behave and how they are motivated to perform their tasks, it is necessary to examine what 'outcomes' they value.

The pioneering work underlying this approach was first proposed by Victor H. Vroom in 1964. He was concerned with the individual in the workplace and how he or she behaves. He assumed that much behaviour was motivated as a result of individuals deciding between various possible outcomes, and was likely to be related to that which was valued most. Therefore expectations would motivate people to behave in a way that would enable them, potentially at any rate, to attain their preferred outcome. Vroom was interested in the value that outcomes had for individuals, and the theory which resulted from his work became generally known as 'valency theory'. Writers who followed, such as Hackman and Porter (1968), and Nadler and Lawler (1983), presented Vroom's concepts in a way that was more directly related to managers, and the theoretical approach they developed came to be known as 'expectancy theory'.

Nadler and Lawler: Expectancy theory

Nadler and Lawler (1983) criticised existing approaches to motivation as being based on the false assumption that all employees were alike, that all work situations were alike, and that consequently there was one best way to motivate employees. Instead, they postulated four assumptions about the causes of the behaviour of people in organisations:

(i) behaviour is determined by the combination of forces in the individual and in the environment;

(ii) each individual has a unique set of needs deriving from past experiences which will have coloured the way he or she perceives the world and the expectations he or she has of the organisation—these expectations and values will influence the individual's response to the workplace;

(iii) the work environment itself will influence the individual such as in terms of supervision or pay;

(iv) these factors lead to the conclusion that dissimilar people will behave differently in similar environments, and similar people will behave differently in dissimilar environments.

People make their own conscious decisions about their behaviour in the context of organisational life, even though they are also operating within environmental constraints. For example, they make decisions about membership behaviour (whether to accept a particular job, and with whom to be associated when engaged in it), and decisions about task performance (for example, how hard to work, how much output to produce, and how much to care about its quality). Teaching provides some good examples in this respect, since there are few supervisors checking on the extent or quality of either the input or the output. Different people have different needs and desires and, therefore, will value different outcomes or rewards differently. Finally, and most importantly, people will tend to adopt behaviour which will lead to the outcomes and rewards they value, and will avoid doing things that they have no desire for, that is, they will behave in ways that they believe will satisfy their needs. Nadler and Lawler emphasised that people are neither inherently motivated nor unmotivated. Whether or not one is motivated thus depends on the situation one is in and the extent to which a given behaviour is perceived as being likely or unlikely to satisfy one's needs. Thus expectancy theory is essentially a diagnostic tool—an attempt to map out the

Term
Definition

Expectancy theory: identified values and beliefs that motivate action.

values or beliefs which must normally be present before an individual is motivated to act. There are three such values/beliefs:

(i) Improvement in performance is possible (effort–performance expectancy)

For an individual to be motivated to improve, he or she must consider it worthwhile to increase effort. This implies a belief that performance can be improved, i.e. if the individual exerts effort, a higher performance will result. Individuals may not hold this belief because they think their performance cannot be improved, i.e. they assume that exerting greater effort will not result in a higher performance.

(ii) Available rewards are desirable (valence)

One member of staff may value being promoted because of a strong need for achievement or the acquisition of power, while another may place a stronger value on remaining a member of the group/department because he or she has a strong 'social affiliation' need. Consciously or unconsciously, many individuals base such decisions on a kind of personal cost–benefit analysis.

(iii) Improved performance will lead to attaining the desired reward (performance–outcome expectancy)

If at the age of forty-five you believe that, even if you achieve high performance, you have a less than 20 per cent chance of gaining further promotion, this may cause you to 'coast'. Or if you are convinced you will not gain promotion or may even be dismissed, then you might decide to 'retire' but omit to tell your employer.

Mini case 9.2
Smoke-free factory boosts worker motivation at Azucarlito

Work on understanding the effect of the physical working environment on the motivation of workers has a long history and much of the knowledge gained has been reflected in the way that working environments are designed. The discipline of ergonomics grew out of the growing body of knowledge created by industrials, academics, environmentalists, and other key contributors to this field of study (Bridger, 2008). However, it is only relatively recently that public policy and private sector initiatives have focused attention on the effects of smoking in the workplace. Many western governments have now implemented legislation to ban smoking

http://www.
azucarlito.com/

http://www.
azucarlito.com/

in public places, many of which are workplaces such as pubs, museums, and universities. Many private sector organisations are following suit as the benefits to health and staff morale are becoming clear. Some cultures are more difficult to change than others, with traditionalists resisting change. Nevertheless, even in the most challenging environments, there is evidence that a change in habit can lend a significant boost to staff morale.

Uruguay is a country renowned for its exports of beef. Less well-known is the production of sugar which forms an important commodity generating much needed revenue. The sugar factories of Uruguay are a challenging environment for workers with many tasks relying on physical labour in hot conditions. Added to this was the traditional macho culture of workers that invariably involved the heavy consumption of cigarettes. However, in the early 2000s a group of workers at the *Azucarlito* factory in Paysandu, Uruguay approached management with an interest in making the factory smoke-free. They cited the poor morale of the majority of non-smoking workers as the main reason for the request. On investigation the management discovered that only 10 per cent of workers smoked, but the effects had a disproportionately negative impact on the health and motivation of the non-smoking workers (University of Kansas, 2013).

The strategy to tackle the problem was, first, of education and support followed by sanctions for miscreants. The management put in place several initiatives such as educational programmes designed to help workers understand the health implications of smoking (including passive smoking), peer group support mechanisms, access to health promotion specialists and doctors, and the establishment of smoking cessation support groups. After a period of six months management implemented a policy declaring the *Azucarlito* factory a 'smoke-free' zone. It was at this stage that the management were confident enough in their efforts to gradually reduce incidences of smoking that they first introduced sanctions against those violating the new policy. The initiative not only changed the physical working environment for the better but also brought about a change in culture whereby the link between smoking and manliness was replaced by one where health promoting activities were dominant. Importantly, in the years following the implementation of the initiative, productivity increased, fewer sick days were taken by workers, and the quality of work improved. Anecdotal evidence from workers suggested a significant rise in motivation due to the cleaner environment in which they were expected to work. The initiative proved to be the catalyst for the government to introduce national Decree 268/05 that banned smoking from all enclosed spaces in Uruguay.

Sources:

Bridger, R. S. (2008) *Introduction to Ergonomics* (3rd edn), London, CRC Press.

University of Kansas (2013) 'The Community Toolbox: Documenting Health promotion initiatives Using the PAHO Guide, Example 13: Azucarlito: A Company Free of Tobacco Smoke Workplace Initiative in Uruguay', Kansas, KA, University of Kansas.

Discussion point

Do the non-smoking policies of organisations undermine the job prospects of smokers?

Questions and task

Choose an organisation and highlight its policy on smoking.

Does the implementation of sanctions against non-conforming smokers at *Azucarlito* violate their human rights?

What did management do to help smooth the transition to a smoke-free factory at *Azucarlito*?

Online Resource Centre

Author commentary on this discussion point and questions can be found on the Online Resource Centre at: www.oxfordtextbooks.co.uk/orc/combe1e/

Reward systems

Previously it has been noted that the reward system used throughout the Industrial Revolution from the eighteenth century was purely economic. That is, workers gave of their time, effort, and skills in exchange for wages. This system still operates in many working environments today, especially in low skilled jobs where workers get paid an hourly rate for carrying out prescribed duties. Thus, fast food restaurants, production lines, call centres, etc. tend to operate this simple wage/labour system. Nevertheless, even within this narrowly defined reward system there are differences in how the economic returns are derived. Payment may be based on a fixed salary, piece-rates, time rates, bonus systems, or a combination of these. Much depends on the nature of the work being carried out and the activities expected of workers to complete tasks. The more quantifiable the activities and outcomes, the closer match there is likely to be between output and reward.

The wage/labour system dominated well into the twentieth century but around the 1960s the working environment started to change such that the modern business environment is characterised by the deployment of a wide range of vastly different skills, experience, and expertise required in a much wider range of activities. Globalisation and the effect of mass consumerism have played a catalytic role in fostering change in the working environment. The demise of heavy industry (coal mining, shipbuilding, steel making) and the rise of the service sector along with a burgeoning public sector have also defined change. The types of products and services produced have not only expanded greatly, but also their method of production and the support activities designed to ensure quality and customer satisfaction. Value chains of organisations have become ever more complex with a host of different activities being undertaken to deliver products and services. The nature of work itself has changed with an upsurge in freelance workers negotiating their own rewards and managing their own time; the use of flexitime, teleworking, and other forms of working arrangements feature prominently across different industries. There are more women in work now than at any time in the past, placing a greater emphasis on devising family-friendly and work/life balance working arrangements.

Within this complex social and economic environment, managers have to devise suitable reward systems that not only reflect the quality and volume of output produced, but also act as a motivator for workers to improve the quality of what they do or contribute to the long-term prospects of the organisation (Perkins, 2008). Beyond simple economic rewards there are a host of other ways that managers can use rewards as a motivating factor. In fact, rewards have become an important strategic issue in many organisations (Thorpe and Homan, 2000). Figure 9.2 outlines some reward systems that include economic and non-economic criteria.

Performance-related pay

This form of reward system requires agreement between the employer and employee regarding what constitutes an acceptable output. Some activities are easily quantified and therefore designing a performance-related pay structure is simply a matter of negotiation. A bricklayer may get paid for completing a wall and perhaps a bonus if it is completed within an agreed timeframe. Factory workers can be paid by the hour but with an additional performance-related pay element linked to levels of output. There is also evidence that this form of motivation is increasingly being implemented in the public sector in Europe and the USA (Forest, 2008). Even at the executive level of industry this form of reward system is prevalent. Most controversially, executive bankers have come in for criticism for the performance-related pay

Figure 9.2 Motivation-oriented reward systems

structure they have negotiated with their ultimate employers, normally the remuneration committee who act on behalf of the shareholders. The controversy arises because of the tenuous link between performance and the bonuses awarded.

Often it is not possible to make a detailed quantitative link between the contribution of executives and their performance-related payments. Nevertheless, there are some compelling reasons why this type of reward system may be deemed suitable for both employers and employees. First, the nature of the work may be conducive to this system. Some work activities are measurable and form discrete and independent activities. Once the work is completed satisfactorily then the performance-related payment can be made. Secondly, some employees prefer to have their rewards linked to performance as they perceive themselves to be in a position to meet or exceed the expectations of employers. Thirdly, such a system can act as a key motivator or target for employees to aim for, thereby improving their own performance and that of the organisation. Mutual benefits, clearly defined performance targets, and trust are prerequisites for the successful implementation of performance-related pay schemes.

Peer recognition

Some professions attract people who seek more than monetary reward for their contributions. In many fields of activity the respect and recognition of peers acts as a barometer of performance and is a key motivator in the pursuit of excellence. One measure of esteem in the academic world is to have written papers peer reviewed and published. The approbation of peers is an important aspect of career progression and recognition of a standard of performance. Some organisations build peer recognition into their formal practices. For example, office equipment firm *Xerox* have different levels of engineer quality standards that align to a peer recognition system of the problem solving capabilities of their engineers. Engineers can disseminate information on how they solved an office equipment problem to peers using hand held electronic devices. If the solution is adopted by other colleagues the engineer may be awarded with a higher quality standard. This acts as a reward for attainment with the highest level providing an aspiration for engineers (this case is discussed in Mini case 11.1 in Chapter 11 on Organisational Structure).

Promotion and status

Most organisations operate a promotion system where superior performance is formally recognised by assigning more responsibility and status to employees. A personal performance and development plan is standard in many organisations and is used as a means of human resource management. This document outlines the goals that are linked to an employee's development within the agreed job specification, what targets can be agreed with line managers that aid development, and what support is required to achieve those targets. The document is one piece of evidence that can help inform managers as to whether or not an employee is deserving of promotion. Very often higher status is given alongside promotion as a means of recognising the higher level of responsibility conferred on the promoted employee. In some work settings this is a formal process underpinned by regalia or symbols (stripes signifying rank in the army), title (professor at universities), or business arrangement (partner in a law firm). In some industries the status is more subtle and nuanced, for example in the creative industries where formality is minimal but peer recognition of status is displayed in the form of loyalty and mentoring (top chefs are highly sought after as mentors by those who aspire to their level of expertise).

Greater freedom

An important form of reward that can act as a key motivator is to demonstrate an enhanced level of trust by offering greater freedom to employees. This is especially relevant to industries where creativity and innovation form the key to competitive advantage. A great deal of trust is placed on employees when given the freedom to explore new opportunities, build relationships, or seek inspiration by operating 'out of office'. Some working environments are more conducive to facilitating this than others. For example, the scope for freedom in a production line is very limited compared to that of the antiques or arts industries. Some firms are able to exploit the value of freedom to influence the organisational culture and attract a particular type of employee. New media firm *Google*, for example, offer a great deal of freedom to their employees at their headquarters in California to the extent that they can organise their working day around their life interests. The type of employee attracted to *Google* ensures that their contribution is high and they remain driven and motivated. Here, the unconventional approach to managing the working arrangements appeals to the type of employee they seek. Again, there are mutual benefits to be gained from this arrangement. Since the company has expanded into a global operator, the management team have introduced new software technology hosted on *Google* servers that helps workers fully engage with each other and heighten the creative tension that drives innovation (*The Economist*, 2009a). Other industries have high levels of freedom, such as in academia where the principle of 'academic freedom' is firmly engrained in the culture and proffers significant advantages for employees. The success of this type of reward system depends on the level of trust and the effect it has on achieving organisational aims and objectives. Managers need to think through the level to which this form of reward can and should be implemented based on their analysis of the type of work to be carried out, the type of employees they hire, the organisational culture, the monitoring and control of employees, and so on.

Decision making power

Decision making power is linked to promotion and status in organisations and can act as a key motivator. All organisations are political to a greater or lesser extent, and part of that process is access to power. Power and decision making ability are interlinked and this is something that individuals or groups often seek in order to leverage advantages to achieve their own aims which may be linked to ambition, influence, control, and so on. However, with this form of reward comes increased responsibility and it is incumbent on managers to ensure that greater decision making power is dispensed for the correct reasons. That is, they need to be sure that the recipients of increased decision making powers will use it to further the aims of the organisation rather than as a means of achieving their personal ambitions. In some organisations the decision making power is formally linked to roles and responsibilities (such as in the civil service), in others it may be part of a more consensual culture where others share the same level of decision making power (the formation of project-led teams is often characterised by an egalitarian approach to decision making).

Professional development

All organisations need to develop the skills of their staff and to put into effect plans for achieving this. Professional development helps workers to improve their skills and expertise and to contribute more to the aims of organisations. In some instances professional development is a necessary aspect of gaining promotion or access to more decision making powers or influence. It may be through formal courses leading to qualifications or simply an update on existing skills and competencies. Whatever the nature of the development it can be perceived as a reward for superior performance. Although many professional development opportunities are open to all staff, there will be some of a specialised nature that are limited to a select few. This may be due to budgeting constraints or the fit with the human resource requirements of the organisation. Where development opportunities exist that may lead to advancement, there is likely to be greater demand. It is therefore necessary for managers to select those staff members who they deem most deserving and capable to fill those slots. Thus, some professional development opportunities are a reward rather than a right.

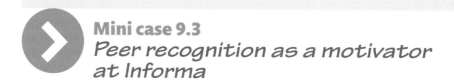

Mini case 9.3
Peer recognition as a motivator at Informa

http://www.
informa.com/
http://www.
informa.com/

Swiss-based global business information services provider *Informa* established a peer-recognition initiative in 2004 as a means of extending their reward system to align more with the company mission of providing world-class service. Managers at the company wanted to encourage and motivate staff not through the traditional means of managers rewarding subordinates, but rather peer-driven recognition. This, they believed, was a much more powerful tool for recognising excellence as very often it was the peer approbation that workers valued most (Coleman, 2010). Other benefits beyond motivation include increased loyalty, staff retention, and improved productivity and quality of service. There are nineteen different award categories under headings such as productivity, individual and team performance, and corporate social responsibility (CSR). By 2011 the awards were open to around 8,500 workers around the globe. Key to the success of the initiative is the ability of managers to communicate expectations to workers so that exceptional performance can be identified and recognised. Workers nominate peers for awards and management decide who is most deserving of the award based on analysis of performance against a range of set criteria. Also, there is no heavy cost burden on the organisation for running the scheme as the whole process (except the public award ceremony itself) is undertaken online. Peer recognition schemes are a popular and effective means of driving forward corporate core values and provide a means of empowering workers to recognise peer excellence in performance. The scheme won an award from employment specialists the Employee Benefit Group in 2009 (Informa, 2013). The management at *Informa* intend to extend the initiative further by adding new categories as the business grows and extend the range of skills and experience of workers in a multitude of different roles.

Sources:

Coleman, A. (1 February 2010) Peer recognition schemes pay off. http://www.employeebenefits. co.uk/resource-centre/analysis/peer-recognition-schemes-pay-off/9861.article

Informa (2013) Careers. http://www.informa.com/Careers/Why-work-for-us/Benefits/

Discussion point

Why is peer-recognition perceived as more valuable than that of management?

Questions

Can you detect any flaws in the *Informa* peer-recognition initiative?

What are the main advantages of the peer-recognition initiative at *Informa*?

How can the effectiveness of the peer-recognition awards initiative at *Informa* be measured and assessed?

 Online Resource Centre
Author commentary on this discussion point and questions can be found on the Online Resource Centre at: www.oxfordtextbooks.co.uk/orc/comb e1e/

Empowerment

The theoretical perspectives outlined in this chapter have revealed some of the motivations evident among workers. Economic reward, status, esteem, power, personal satisfaction, peer recognition, and so forth are all well-known motivators. One of the most common means of motivating the workforce in the modern era is for managers to offer greater levels of empowerment to their employees. In some industries the issue of empowerment has become an important aspect of human resource management whereby added value and competitive advantage can be gained from allowing workers greater autonomy in decision making (Chiles and Zorn, 1995). Project-led work is particularly conducive to this type of management where small groups of workers are given a task and specific aims, but how they undertake the task and achieve the aims is entirely up to them to manage. The rationale for this approach stems from the recognition that skilled and knowledgeable workers are best positioned to fully understand what is required to achieve the desired outcome.

Essentially, empowerment is about presenting employees with an opportunity to be more enterprising and delegating power and authority to them to facilitate added value outcomes. Inherently, there is a level of risk involved in empowerment as managers can never

Term
Definition

Empowerment: the delegation of a level of authority that extends the scope of workers to act autonomously from line management.

be certain how the delegated power and authority will be exercised by empowered workers. Nevertheless, the benefits of empowerment can make this risk worthwhile. For the most part, the risk is limited as the extent of empowerment is such that it cannot affect the strategic direction or values, mission, or vision of the organisation before intervention can take place. Empowerment can be bestowed at the individual worker level, on a small group, or company-wide. Participative management techniques refer to empowerment that is suffused throughout the organisation. This gives an egalitarian feel to the way power and authority is dispersed but it can be complex and difficult to manage unless clear lines of authority are well understood. It is useful to outline the advantages and disadvantages associated with empowerment.

Advantages of empowerment

One of the most commonly cited reasons for implementing an empowerment policy is the effect it has on worker morale and motivation. Very often workers will feel a greater affinity with what the organisation is trying to achieve if the management demonstrate trust in them by proffering greater responsibility. This can lead to greater job satisfaction, increased productivity, efficiency, and, ultimately, better performance. Employees have the scope to become creative and innovative within a regime characterised by empowerment. This results from the greater freedom afforded workers when it comes to exploring new ideas, experimenting with new processes, or building relationships. With empowerment comes the ability to act on intuitive instincts and take certain risks, which are often the source of competitive advantage. As more and more workers take 'ownership' of their own work schedule, decision making, and risk taking, this can lead to improved efficiency and better quality outputs. Much of this stems from the fact that empowered workers are acutely aware that the quality of their output is determined by themselves rather than being one stage removed from their responsibility by having a layer of management between them and their actions. This helps to concentrate their minds more closely on the need to deliver added value and to justify the faith placed in them by management. In an era defined by quality, empowering workers has the potential to enhance the value adding across the value chain of an organisation. Empowerment also means that managers can concentrate on business level or strategic level decision making as there is less need for direct supervision at the operational level. Again, this helps to increase efficiencies by deploying management capacity in areas where it is most effective.

Disadvantages of empowerment

The most concerning aspect of empowering workers is the risk that it entails. Delegating authority and power entails risk and managers have to be able to strike a balance between monitoring how the empowerment is put into action whilst maintaining a suitable distance to allow the workers to dispense power and authority as they see fit. There is also risk attached to allowing workers greater scope to explore new opportunities or create new products or services, as these can turn out to be failures as well as successes. Very often workers can generate good ideas but lack the wider entrepreneurial skills to commercialise them. It is at this point that managers may draw the line at empowerment. This requires some deft communications skills as this reining in of power may be received negatively by workers. Another risk is that of security of information. As empowerment spreads throughout an organisation, so does access to sensitive commercial information which may be of value to rivals in an industry. Organisations need to ensure the integrity of their information by putting in place robust security measures to prevent inappropriate dissemination of that information. Another risk linked to empowerment is the change in the nature of the relationships with representatives of the workforce, in particular the trades unions. By empowering workers, the organisation may be giving an insight into the *modus operandi* of managers that could perhaps be exploited by union leaders in future negotiations. Finally, there is always the issue of personalities to contend with. Empowering some workers may have a detrimental effect on organisational harmony as the newly acquired power and authority is dispensed in inappropriate ways or in ways that alienate co-workers. The ego-enhancing effect of empowerment can often be the downfall of a well-intentioned policy of dispersing power and authority more widely. Table 9.1 provides a summary of the main advantages and disadvantages associated with empowerment.

Table 9.1 Advantages and disadvantages of empowerment

Advantages	Disadvantages
Job satisfaction and better motivation and worker morale	Risk of compromise to information security
Enhanced creativity and innovation	Lack of commercial expertise to follow through on ideas
Increased efficiency and productivity	Risk of unions exploiting the type of relationship with workers
Less need for supervision	Difficult to balance control and monitoring with delegating power
Improved quality of outputs	Difficult to control ego-enhancing effect of empowerment
Greater entrepreneurial spirit and risk taking	Employees may receive feedback negatively

? Critical reflection
Should managers expand worker empowerment during periods of economic downturn?

Normally under conditions of economic downturn managers become more cautious, especially regarding the delegation of power and authority to employees. However, this could be a mistake and one that could result in an organisation finding it more difficult to emerge from recession stronger and more competitive. The credit crunch of 2008 led to a downturn in the economic fortunes of many countries including the United States. This resulted in a decrease in demand for goods and services and a squeeze on profit margins for firms. Unemployment in Europe and the United States reached worryingly high levels as firms shed workers as a means of reducing costs in the short term. Under such conditions it is difficult for managers to take risks when making investment decisions, especially since the availability of investment funding was low due to the banks and other financial institutions being more risk averse in their lending policies. It is hardly surprising that under such circumstances the empowerment of workers may come under pressure. However, there is a compelling argument for allowing workers ever greater freedom during hard times as the workers are the potential source of innovation and creativity. During periods of economic downturn, these factors play a key role in lending impetus to growth and recovery. Nevertheless, it takes brave management to extend worker empowerment during times of economic uncertainty and many are reluctant to do so.

Communications

Communications are key to effective management and feature in each of the chapters in this book in some form. The functions of management, such as planning, organising, leading, and controlling all require effective communications skills (either verbal or non-verbal) in transferring information from sender to receiver. In the modern business environment good communications skills have never been more important, even though the media through which the communications are channelled have been broadened significantly. Interpersonal and communications skills lie at the heart of what management is all about, which is 'getting people to do things'. Often good communications skills are linked to emotional intelligence. That is, an acute understanding of how one comes across to others, and how the behaviour and actions of others is perceived by us. A heightened sense of what motivates people to act in the way they do aids understanding and can help frame appropriate responses.

Communications can be structured in different ways according to what is appropriate and available. In an organisation communications can be configured:

One way:	information communicated to a target audience with no need or expectation of a response;
Two way:	information passes back and forth between different senders and receivers in the form of discussion, teamwork, consultation, etc.;

Upward:	information channels that give access to different layers of management including top executive level;
Downward:	information from management downwards towards groups of workers;
Laterally:	information that passes between different departments or functions within the organisation.

Formal communications structures are underpinned with policies, regulations, and procedures relating to who, how, and why certain types of information are communicated throughout the organisational structure. For instance, the prevailing command structure within an organisation informs the types of communications necessary and identifies the appropriate recipients. The formal approach is necessary to maintain certain standards of communication as workers deal with each other, the organisational management, suppliers, consumers, etc. Most organisations form formal committees to examine certain issues and to put forward plans for action.

Running in parallel with the formal approach to communications is the informal approach where individuals or groups of workers communicate in a more free-flowing and natural manner. Much depends on the organisational culture as to how the informal channels of communication work. In some instances, they can support the aims of the organisation (informal discussions between creative people may generate new ideas) or they may prove negative (rumour-mongering about management intentions). It is necessary for managers to recognise the influence that informal channels of communication have on the operations and functions within the organisation, and to make value judgements regarding when and how to try to influence it. Understanding the key characteristics of communications goes a long way to helping them make those judgements.

Communication is made up of numerous different factors including language, sound and tone, eye contact, body language, pitch, culture, norms, and so on. Here, the discussion focuses on issues of verbal and non-verbal communication, perception, and the use of electronic media in communications. One of the most important pointers to the effectiveness of communications in terms of influencing motivation among the workforce is that of information richness. This concept refers to the amount of information that a communication channel can carry, and the extent to which it enables sender and receiver to achieve a common understanding (Daft and Lengel, 1984). Figure 9.3 outlines several different types of communications and their attendant level of information richness.

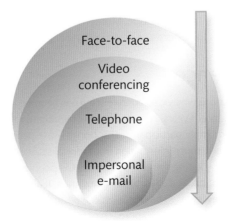

Figure 9.3 Types of communication and information richness

Impersonal e-mail

If information richness refers to the capability of channels of communication to facilitate and promote common understanding between sender and receiver then electronic forms of communication that are impersonal form the least effective. Here, it is evident that the scope for misunderstanding is heightened due to the lack of visibility. Body language and intonation are missing from the communication making it more difficult for the receiver to decipher the message and its true meaning. There have been many instances where e-mail has been the catalyst for conflict due to its impersonal (and very often curt) nature. Invariably e-mails are sent with the sole purpose of imparting information. Social manners are often dispensed with in this medium. This works as long as the sender and receiver expect the same thing. Problems arise when the receiver perceives the communication to be lacking in sensitivity. For managers, this can prove a barrier to the effective motivation of workers as the richness of the communication is low leading to potential for conflict, misunderstanding, ineffective interpersonal relationships, and lack of cohesion within the working group. However, in recent years attitudes to electronic forms of communication have changed as the advent of *Twitter* and Short-Message-Service (SMS) have become an increasingly prevalent part of everyday communications both in and out of the workplace. The ubiquity of such social networking media has resulted in a growing acceptance of the very short, sharp, and concise form of communications that characterise their use.

Telephone

Information richness is enhanced using the telephone as a medium relative to impersonal e-mail. The receiver benefits from the intonation of the caller and can use this to aid understanding. This means of communication benefits from the real-time and flowing nature of the two-way communication. It is quick, easy, and one of the most commonly used channels of communication in the workplace. Increasingly, mobile telephones are being used in the workplace to link workers engaged in different parts of the production or service delivery. Sales people often use mobile phones to contact prospective buyers, suppliers, and managers. Such is the ubiquity of the mobile phone that the etiquette surrounding its use is still being worked out. In some settings, such as lectures at a university or during a theatre production, it may not be deemed appropriate to have a mobile phone switched on, let alone field a call. In the workplace some people would resent having their time with a manager usurped by a mobile telephone caller. The other issue regarding the telephone as a medium for communication relates to the lack of visibility of the body language of the sender and receiver. Body language can inform a great deal on the true feelings of those engaged in the communication. Some managers prefer to see people face-to-face for this very reason. Modern technology, such as Skype, allows a visual image of the participants to be accessed when undertaking communications by telephone.

Video conference

There are a number of reasons why video conferencing has become a popular means of communication in business in recent years. First, it offers the combination of visual, audio, and oral contact, potentially with multiple participants. This brings more people into the conversation and helps managers to receive more information from specialists. Video conferencing facilitates rich information exchange by letting the participants see the people they are engaged with, the body language, voice intonation, and other important signals. It also offers access to a wider set of participants so that the key issues to be discussed can be addressed at one conference, rather than the more fragmented and disruptive approach of reporting the key issues back to relevant people and then waiting for feedback. There are also good economic reasons for the increased preference for video conferencing. Many businesses are cutting back on their managers' and executives' travel costs during times of economic downturn. A video conference can be a relatively cheap way of circumventing the cost in terms of both time and money.

Although this is a useful means of enriching information, there are some disadvantages to video conferencing. Invariably, there is a delay between sender communication and receiver. This can be problematic if participants are uninitiated in how to cope with what is an unnatural pause in the flow of conversation. Experienced video-conference participants will be able to adjust their communications style to deal with this, but others may find it difficult leading to voice cross-overs, potential for misunderstanding, and an unsatisfactory meeting. Advances in information and communications technologies (ICTs) have helped to reduce this delay but nevertheless it takes some understanding and knowledge of the technology to be able to adjust the communications to the appropriate timing and pace. The scope for this being a problem increases as more participants are included in the conference.

Face-to-face

By far the most information rich form of communication is the face-to-face format. Here, all the criteria for ensuring that the communication is transferred effectively are present. Participants benefit from real-time, interactive communications with high visibility and access to body language and voice intonation. Problems of explanation or understanding can be dealt with immediately as clarification can be instant. There is also the potential for the emotional aspects of the communication to be transferred more clearly. People can express human warmth, frustration, persuasiveness, anger, and so on more effectively during a face-to-face meeting. Managers are better able to motivate workers when they have a physical presence and adopt a range of communications techniques. It is ineffective to try to motivate workers from behind a 'screen' whether it be e-mail, telephone, or even a video conference. Van der Kliej et al. (2009) provide a valuable insight into how conversations change over time in face-to-face and video-mediated communications.

Sometimes it is necessary to adopt these forms of communication media are because of the nature of the business structure (subsidiaries remote from headquarters, virtual organisations, etc.) but there is no better way to communicate effectively than through face-to-face contact. Here, the interpersonal skills of managers are key. Unlike other media for communication, the face-to-face format requires managers to project their personality into the conversation much more explicitly. Issues of personality, charisma, charm, persuasiveness, inspiration, and other personal assets that facilitate effective communication will be much more important in face-to-face meetings compared to other forms.

Term
Definition

Information richness: the extent to which a communication achieves a common understanding between sender and receiver.

Barriers to effective communications

Very often management failure stems from a lack of effective communication. The scope for misunderstanding, confusion, cross-purposes, and other forms of ineffective transmission of information is significant and can multiply according to the size and complexity of an organisation. Managers can sometimes be responsible for poor communication as a result of their inability to articulate commands, ideas, concepts, and feedback in a meaningful and motivating manner. However, there are many barriers to effective communication that can lead to inefficiencies, poor quality products and services, low morale, an unmotivated workforce, and disgruntled customers and suppliers. Some of these barriers are of the organisation's own making, such as the structure or level of control; others will be the effect of factors in the external environment, such as communications infrastructure or language. Figure 9.4 outlines some of the main barriers to effective communications.

Internal barriers

Three areas of an organisation that can lead to potential barriers to communication are the organisational structure, organisational culture, and the control mechanisms put in place.

Organisational structure

The organisational structure has a direct influence on the communication channels evident within an organisation. Tall, hierarchical organisations have many layers through which communications have to travel. The scope for misunderstanding and ineffective transfer of information is heightened. A flat organisational structure makes communication easier but can also create problems. For example, when different departments all operate at the same level in terms of power and authority, then there is likely to be an increase in political activity as each tries to maximise the influence they wield. This can result in suppressing information rather than sharing it openly. Some organisations are structured in a way that means that many functions are carried out remotely from headquarters. Firms with subsidiaries around the globe have to contend with the barriers to communication (time differences, language, norms of doing business, culture, etc.) that this inevitably brings. Managers have to weigh the risks associated with barriers to communication with the benefits of expanding into other regions.

Organisational culture

The dominant culture within an organisation can create barriers to communication. Conversely, the culture may be the basis for effective communication. Much depends on the nature of the

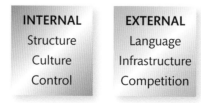

Figure 9.4 Barriers to communication

products or services being produced, how they are produced, the level of integration required throughout the organisation, and the need for knowledge sharing both internally and externally. There are some industries, such as publishing, gaming, hi-tech software, public relations, marketing, and other creative industries where knowledge sharing is an essential ingredient for success and the type of personnel recruited into those industries tends to exhibit free-flowing communications and good interpersonal skills. However, in other settings, the culture may be one of protecting information rather than sharing it. This is especially the case where departments are competing for their share of resources from the centre, often found in public sector organisations, educational institutions, or even in the armed forces, police, or the National Health Service (NHS) in the UK. The culture of protecting rather than sharing knowledge may be self-defeating in the long term but in an environment characterised by shrinking budgets and political interference, this type of culture can easily come to dominate. Although policies and procedures may be put in place to encourage more effective communication, it is really a change of culture that is required to break down the barriers.

Control

Linked into structure and culture is the element of control in organisations. The extent to which control is exercised within an organisation has a profound effect on the ability and willingness of workers to communicate effectively. In highly controlled environments there are likely to be set procedures and regulations underpinning what is communicated, to whom, and when. Even so, there is likely to be some form of informal communications systems that run parallel to the formal communications system. An emphasis on control may stem from the need to ensure minimum standards or where freedom of expression and communication may compromise the mission or values or strategic aims of the organisation. Certainly, in the military environment there are strict rules relating to communications for security reasons. However, in many industries it is evident that the free flow of information and knowledge lies at the heart of strategies for competitive advantage and, therefore, the control element is significantly lower. In media industries for example, comment, debate, and critique is the lifeblood of many organisations. Any barriers to communication in the newspaper, broadcasting, or multimedia industries would place firms at a competitive disadvantage.

External barriers

Language

Language is one of the most obvious barriers to communication. In business, it is generally accepted that English is the most used language, although Mandarin and Cantonese have the most speakers. Language is an important part of cultural identity and something that has to be protected and nurtured. Many businesses offer their staff opportunities to learn a language, especially those spoken in areas where they have a business presence or a relationship. It is not uncommon for mainland Europeans to speak several languages, whereas in the UK relatively few people are fluent in a second language. Various theories have been put forward to explain this: geography (an island nation set apart from Europe), culture (the attitude that 'everyone speaks English'), and education (languages are not always compulsory subjects in high schools). In future, it may be that being able to compete in global markets requires a better understanding of the culture of target countries, the methods of doing business, and at least a rudimentary understanding of language. Fast developing countries such as Russia and Brazil offer opportunities for investors, but in a highly competitive environment it is those firms who can offer added value skills, products, and services that are most likely to succeed. This added value is also likely to include the ability to communicate effectively in the language of the target country.

Infrastructure

A considerable amount of communication in modern business is undertaken via information and communication technologies (ICTs) and a host of digital and multimedia channels. This includes telephony, internet, mobile, video conferencing, teleconferencing, and so on. The effectiveness of communications using technology depends largely on the quality of infrastructure that supports it. This varies markedly around the world with developed nations such as the USA, South Korea, and Germany leading the way in terms of quality and access to a wide range of support technologies for communication. Other regions and countries fare less well and form a barrier to communication, leading to competitive disadvantage. For example, parts of Africa are almost devoid of reliable and effective ICT infrastructure, partly due to geographical and terrain difficulties but also because of a lack of investment and political instability. While the infrastructure to support communications is constantly being upgraded and expanded, it is clear that the major trading regions of the globe (North America, Europe, and Far East) have the most sophisticated and reliable systems in place. This creates a distinct trading advantage but also creates a barrier to communication on a global scale as the concentration of investment marginalises other regions.

Competition

Competitive pressures can also have a role to play in the way in which communications are disseminated throughout an industry. Much of the internal information of organisations will be sensitive and efforts will be made to ensure that it is not spread to competitors. This is a natural barrier to communication for competitive reasons. However, since the early 1990s there has been a distinct trend towards greater collaboration between firms either at the operational or strategic level. This has required a change in emphasis regarding how information is disseminated and protected. For example, a strategic alliance between partners can only work if a certain amount of knowledge sharing takes place to inform decisions and formulate a plan. Previously, it was noted that firms are sometimes characterised by a lack of knowledge sharing internally, perhaps for cultural, economic, or political reasons. This is likely to be more intense when dealing with external third parties and may require a significant shift in culture for it to be effective. Competitive pressures are driving organisations towards partnerships, alliances, and collaborative ventures, but one of the most significant hurdles to overcome is the barriers to communication that so often thwart the participants' best intensions.

Case study
Total worker empowerment at Semco

Semco is an industrial machine manufacturing company based in Brazil. The main output of the company is machine pumps for the Brazilian shipbuilding industry. The company was established by Antonio Semler in the early 1950s and had some success before hitting on hard times during the recession of the early 1980s. This era was characterised by organisations with typically hierarchical management structures with a patriarchal figure as leader. *Semco*, like many similar sized organisations, had set rules and regulations that controlled every aspect of the activities undertaken in the firm.

Faced with the disastrous effects of recession, Antonio's son Richard Semler assumed control of the business and immediately set about radically transforming the organisation as a means of dealing with consistently poor performance. He explains his rationale and *modus operandi* in an article for the *Harvard Business Review* (Semler, 1989). First, Semler immediately dismissed all top management (including many of his father's close friends) and dismantled the existing layers of management, reducing the hierarchy from seven to three. Job titles were eliminated with only the Chief Operating Officer (COO) retaining a title, a position that is rotated among workers every six months. There is complete transparency in salaries and workers are empowered to set their own working hours. Managers are chosen via a democratic process of voting by workers with the outcomes publicly communicated. The Semco Way is outlined on the company website (www.semco.com/br). Semler also implemented a change of strategy for the business, one that embraced diversification rather than heavy reliance on one industry.

The stress of implementing the radical overhaul of the business took its toll on Semler's health and it was during his rehabilitation from illness in 1985 that his radical plan for running the business started to emerge. One idea was to establish self-managed teams of no more than eight production workers who would be in full control of their production remit including controlling budgets and setting targets. The reward structure was designed to match the set targets and almost immediately costs started to diminish, productivity rose, and the company returned to profit. Profit sharing was another radical new way of motivating workers. Each division of the business received around 25 per cent of net profits. Those profits were then divided among workers according to the decision of a democratically elected committee. The next phase of change was the most risky. Semler did not know if his empowerment strategy would be successful throughout the entire business. Also, almost an entire layer of middle managers left the business in little over a year, most complaining that their authority had been undermined by newly empowered subordinates. Undaunted, Semler pressed on with his plans. The empowerment plan was extended throughout the plant and resulted in workers accepting more responsibility for managing multiple duties and using their knowledge to generate new and innovative ideas on how to reduce costs and improve quality. The workers decided how best to organise themselves for the challenges they faced. For example, some were divided into small groups while others were in divisions numbering over 150 and covering manufacturing, sales, and finance. Workers even had the power to hire and fire people according to a democratic vote. Decisions are made after discussion and debate rather than through set procedures. The manuals that defined factory life in the previous regime were disposed of. Siehl et al. (1999) provide a valuable case study of how Richard Semler restructured Semco.

Such was the success of the empowerment plan that by the early 1990s the company had given permission for a group of engineers to form what was termed the Nucleus of Technological Innovation. This group had full autonomy to act in ways that they deemed necessary to advance innovation in technology at the plant. Although their performance is reviewed every six months, the group operate independently of the main Semco structure. Payment is based on a percentage of sales. Eventually, this model became the blueprint for how the rest of the business would be structured. That is, a series of self-regulating, democratic, independent groups with their own aims, strategy, and performance indicators. Thus, the structure does not fit any of the traditional designs such as functional, geographical, or matrix, but rather resembles a series of concentric circles that operate independently but who report to a core of democratically elected counsellors and, of course, Richard Semler himself. Each elected leader of the independent groups takes it in turn to be CEO on a six month rotating schedule. Partners make up the second circle and are comprised of six leaders from each of *Semco's* divisions. The rest of the workforce is termed 'associates'. The associates set their own salaries which are posted on noticeboards for complete transparency. Associates can attend any meeting within the organisation. Maresco and York (2005) provide an appraisal of the empowered leadership at Semco. Figure 9.5 illustrates the Semco structure.

Figure 9.5 Semco organisational structure

The *Semco* structure is one of small, free-standing units who have autonomy to make decisions regarding how best to achieve their aims. One of the advantages of this type of structure is that it is agile and flexible enough to cope with change. Whether by accident or design the structure that evolved was perfectly suited to the changing global competitive environment of the 1990s where firms had to move quickly to seize opportunities as they arose. The previous structure at the company would have been too rigid and unwieldy to respond to change quickly enough to be competitive. To effect this transformation required a change in culture and the new arrangements put in place by Richard Semler initiated that cultural change. Much was based on trust. Semler took a huge risk by placing all responsibility for overseeing processes, managing output, and ensuring quality in the hands of the workers. That the concept was extended to managing salary levels, bonuses, decision making processes, and so on was radical and unique in a business of that size. In subsequent years, others firms have tried, with varying results, to copy the *Semco* transformation. *Google*, for example, have a liberal approach to work arrangements at their headquarters in California. The balance between work and play is not demarcated, to the extent that workers can manage their own schedules to whatever suits their lifestyle. In similar fashion to the culture at *Semco*, the management believe that self-motivated workers will always deliver more under conditions of freedom than command.

The success of the radical transformational strategy at *Semco* has encouraged other firms to mimic the formula, but to limited effect. The most obvious reason is that it is almost impossible to replicate a distinct culture that exists in any one organisation. The nature of work, interpersonal relationships, group dynamic, and management style, among other factors, will play out differently in different organisations even if they are engaged in the same industry and producing the same product. At *Semco* a unique set of circumstances and personnel came together at the right time to ensure the success of the plan. Within that plan a number of key motivators proved critical to its success. These involved economic factors (workers controlled the reward structure); social factors (small groups formed a social bond with common aims); democratic processes (transparency and accountability formed the basis of trust-forming relations through applying a democratic process); leadership (Richard Semler trusted his instincts by empowering workers and workers repaid the trust by responding positively to his leadership); and innovation (a highly motivated group of key workers formed an innovation-oriented team dedicated to developing new products and processes). Fundamentally, the workers at *Semco* believed in what the organisation was trying to achieve, felt that they had a stakeholding in the organisation, and embraced the values that underpinned Richard Semler's vision of how the organisation should be managed. These factors created a strong psychological contract between workers and the aims and objectives of the organisation. That is, the motivators ensured that the workers were prepared to put in more than they took out of the organisation without any formal direction to do so. This type of motivation is often considered the 'holy grail' of management as it invariably means that workers are self-motivated, self-managed, and focused on adding value without the time and cost associated with high levels of monitoring, control, direction, and reporting that characterises many mainstream organisational structures.

Sources:

Maresco, P. A. and York, C. A. (2005) Ricardo Semler: Creating Organizational Change through Employee Empowered Leadership. http://www.newunionism.net/library/case%20studies/SEMCO%20-%20Employee-Powered%20Leadership%20-%20Brazil%20-%202005.pdf

Semler, R. (1989) 'Managing Without Managers', *Harvard Business Review*, Sept/Oct, pp. 1–10.

Siehl, R., Killian, D., and Perez, F. (1999) 'Richard Semler and Semco S.A.', *Harvard Business Review* (28 January 1999).

Discussion point

Is the transformational plan implemented at *Semco* universally applicable?

Questions and tasks

Outline the main changes at *Semco* that improved the motivation of workers.

Identify possible sources of tension within the existing structure at *Semco*.

What were the biggest risks taken by Richard Semler in implementing the new regime at Semco?

Online Resource Centre

Author commentary on this discussion point and questions can be found on the Online Resource Centre at: www.oxfordtextbooks.co.uk/orc/combe1e/

Summary

● **Understand the components of the job characteristics model and the role of job design in worker satisfaction and motivation**

Job characteristics and the job design have important roles to play in motivating workers depending on the expectations and attitudes of workers and managers. Job characteristics have changed over time according to the types of work carried out, the expected outcomes, and the relationships within organisations. Job design has also been transformed from one that was based on the wage/labour dichotomy to ones that reflect a wider range of the physical, social, and emotional needs of workers that stimulate and motivate them.

● **Critically assess the theoretical perspectives on motivation**

The use of theory has helped to provide a framework for analysis and discussion and has been used as a basis for identifying and examining the key factors that affect motivation. The chapter critically evaluated a number of theoretical perspectives relating to motivation including the instrumental approach, Maslow's Hierarchy of Needs; McGregor's Theory X/Theory Y; Herzberg's hygiene factors and motivators; contingency approaches; and expectancy theory. The analysis highlighted some of the limitations of these theories (such as the simplicity of Maslow's hierarchy, or the polemic of McGregor's Theory X and Y) but noted the enduring relevance of others such as contingency approaches.

● **Evaluate the effect of worker empowerment as a key motivator**

Very often motivation is linked to reward and this chapter has outlined how the reward system within organisations has evolved from a very simple wage/labour relationship to ones that feature a broad range of motivation-enhancing rewards. In particular, the incentives of empowerment and access to decision making suggest that some workers are more motivated by what they can deliver for the organisation rather than the more narrowly defined economic rewards.

● **Understand and assess the different reward systems in terms of motivation**

The chapter highlighted and discussed a number of different reward systems, mostly non-economic in nature. For example, peer recognition and esteem of colleagues have emerged as goals through which managers can develop a reward system. The nature of the modern, multicultural, multi-skilled working environment means that managers have to be more innovative when designing reward systems as well as the methods adopted for enhancing motivation in the workforce.

● **Assess the information richness of communications media and understand the barriers to effective communication**

Information richness is a measure of how effective communications systems are in providing the basis for information and knowledge sharing. The analysis of this highlighted some of the persisting barriers to effective communication, some of which require the support of government to resolve (such as infrastructure) while others are essentially a management issue (such as organisational structure and control).

Conclusion

Motivating workers is one of the key skills of management but how it actually works is often a result of a combination of factors, some of which are not immediately apparent. For example, the need for effective interpersonal skills is paramount as workers can quickly feel distant and alienated from management without constant dialogue. This dialogue is part of a wider conversation that constantly takes place both internally and externally to the organisation. Communications is a vital component of modern businesses and requires investment, nurturing, and renewal. There is an economic imperative to effective communication as competitive advantage can be gained from information and knowledge sharing. Some organisations produce nothing but knowledge, and therefore their entire business strategy is built around effective communication. One of the key issues discussed in this chapter was that of empowerment as a method of motivating workers. A key trend in recent years has been to empower groups or teams of workers to take charge of their work and to find innovative ways to problem solve, make decisions, and achieve their aims. Such is the importance of this trend in defining the modern workplace that it is worthy of more detailed investigation. As such, the formation and use of teams is the focus of attention in the next chapter.

Chapter questions and tasks

Think about what the main motivators for you would be on entering a new job. Highlight what they would be and place them in a priority list.

Highlight five ways managers can influence the motivation of workers.

Identify five key factors that can undermine worker motivation.

Do modern information and communication technologies (ICTs) help or hinder effective communications?

Online Resource Centre

Author commentary on these questions can be found on the Online Resource Centre at: www.oxfordtextbooks.co.uk/orc/combe1e/.

Further reading

- Blundel, R. and Ippolito, K. (2008) *Effective Organisational Communications: Perspectives, Principles and Practices*, Harlow, Financial Times/Prentice Hall.

  A comprehensive introduction to principles of communication within and between organisations. The authors use robust theoretical perspectives and illuminating real–world examples to explain and evaluate communications skills evident within a wide range of organisations.

- Idr Awan, A. B. (2011) *Motivational Management: Managing Factors affecting Work Motivation*, Saarbrucken, Germany, LAP Lambert Academic Publishing.

  A short account of employees' experiences in terms of motivation. The book offers a valuable insight into how employees perceive motivation, how it affects their actions, and why it is important.

- Pritchard, R. and Ashwood, E. (2008) *Managing Motivation: A Manager's Guide to Diagnosing and Improving Motivation*, Abingdon, Routledge Academic.

  A concise and usable book that bridges the gap between academic research on motivation and the practical application of motivational techniques. The author uses well-chosen theories as a basis for developing mental models to support management actions to diagnose and improve the motivation of workers.

- Wargborn, C. (2009) *Managing Motivation in Work Organizations: Why Employee Relationship Management Matters*, Saarbrucken, Germany, VDM Verlag Dr Muller.

  Motivation as a concept is explored through the lens of the science of organisational behaviour. The author investigates the costs associated with low morale and postulates that few managers understand the reasons for motivation beyond salary as a reward. The book is differentiated from many others in the field as it focuses mostly on individual human differences, and in particular the relationships that emerge in organisations that influence levels of motivation.

Online Resource Centre

For more information, updates, and multiple-choice questions, please visit the Online Resource Centre at: www.oxfordtextbooks.co.uk/orc/combe1e/

327

Skillset 9
Presentation skills

9(a) Introduction

One of the most important skills in life is the ability to communicate with others whether in a face-to-face conversation, as part of a small group, or to a large audience. Communication skills are a vital part of successfully meeting the challenges presented by study, work, and life in general. Good communication skills are a prerequisite for so many job roles in the modern business environment and it is a key differentiator in the jobs market if prospective employees can demonstrate the ability to communicate effectively to a wide range of different people. There are many different forms of communication, but one that is likely to feature at some point in study and professional life is the presentation.

A presentation is a communication to a group of people. At university or college it is likely that students will be required to give a presentation as part of an assessment exercise. Often the presentation is delivered as part of a team with each participant allocated a topic or theme and a time slot for delivering their part of the presentation. However, sometimes it may be an individual effort whereby the student is required to present to a small group of people or even an individual. This can happen as part of a viva (an oral examination between a student and members of staff). A viva for a PhD usually includes a presentation by the student to a panel of experts. Presentations will be a feature of life after formal study too. It is often the case that employers will ask a prospective candidate for a job to deliver a short presentation to the interview panel or to staff members. Once in employment, presentations are a common feature of communicating ideas and concepts, news and plans to a wide range of stakeholders. This may involve explaining the company strategy to staff members; pitching a new product to potential buyers; delivering a training programme; addressing shareholders; inducting new recruits; and so on. As presentation skills are such an integral part of modern life it is important to understand the techniques that underpin their effective execution. This skillset focuses on the skills and techniques required to deliver an effective presentation.

Activity 1:
Complete the table for presentations you have given in the past

Presentation Where and when	Purpose and audience	Key presentation learning outcomes

9(b) Preparing for a presentation

The first thing to recognise is that a presentation takes people out of their comfort zone and presents a personal challenge. Apart from seasoned professionals, most people have an element of fear associated with the prospect of delivering a presentation to an audience. The fear is a natural human emotion as it stems from being sensitive about oneself and how we appear to others. A presentation puts the individual in the spotlight and they receive the full attention of the audience. This is a very unusual state of affairs and so it is important to prepare for the feeling of being exposed and isolated in this way. Nerves are a normal physical reaction to the fear that is associated with giving a presentation. The adrenalin produced by the onset of nervous tension can be harnessed in a positive way (it makes us more alert and energised). However, nerves can also suppress the ability to think in a logical and systematic way, undermining the quality of the presentation. Some of the most common problems leading to ineffective presentation delivery include:

- reading directly from a prepared sheet;
- not making eye contact with the audience;
- too fast in delivery;
- over-compensating by appearing to be overly relaxed and uninterested;
- adopting the wrong tone for the type of audience;
- not fully grasping the ideas and concepts around the presentation topic.

Good preparation can help to alleviate some of the tensions surrounding a presentation. Some key points are worth bearing in mind when preparing a presentation. These include:

(i) What is the purpose of the presentation?

This ensures that you fully understand the reasons for the presentation, the remit, and the key issues that should be covered.

(ii) Who is the audience and what do they expect?

The type of audience will determine a number of important things such as the correct tone to use (serious, humorous, formal, informal, fact-based, free-flowing, etc.); the extent of technical knowledge required; the length of the presentation; what they expect to learn from the presentation.

(iii) How do you intend to deliver the presentation?

There are many different ways to deliver a presentation ranging from a monologue to full audience participation. Here, understanding the type of audience and the purpose of the presentation is a guide to what is appropriate in terms of type of delivery. Some presentations will require interaction with the audience, others will be supported by multimedia technology or hand-outs; in some cases it may be appropriate to ask questions of the audience or to bring in a second presenter to deliver part of the presentation. The judgement on this will depend on knowing the answers to parts (i) and (ii).

9(c) Use of technology

If multimedia technology such as PowerPoint®, video streaming, whiteboard applications, etc. are to be used then you must ensure that these are in full working order ahead of the presentation. Seek technical assistance to ensure that this is the case and practise with the technology. Nothing undermines confidence and audience attention than a hiatus of silence that technological failure brings. You must also ensure that the link between the use of technology, such as a video or podcast, and the resumption of the presentation is as seamless as possible.

329

Audiences will be tolerant of a slight delay but if this is elongated you risk losing their attention. Do not add layers of complexity by using several different types of multimedia unless it is absolutely necessary. This will only add to the risk of disruption without adding much value to the quality of the presentation. Keep things simple. Ensure that the media you use are appropriate and effective. For example, a PowerPoint® slide should feature at least a 23-point font using a style such as Arial, Calibri, or Verdana for best effect. Lower case letters are easier to read than ALL CAPITALS. Video screenings or podcasts should only last a few minutes and not dominate attention. They should be used to illustrate specific points or issues rather than be deployed as a substitute for your own presentation.

9(d) Structure of the presentation

The structure of the presentation is also important. There should be a logical progression of ideas, knowledge, and learning. Normally, there is an informal preamble as you introduce yourself to the audience, remind them of the purpose of the presentation and what you intend to deliver. You may also explain how you intend to deliver the presentation (for example, you may want to talk for twenty minutes then take questions; or you may be happy for the audience to interrupt with queries or questions as the presentation progresses). The presentation should have a discernible beginning, middle, and end. The end should always summarise the key issues or points you want the audience to remember.

9(e) Practice

Finally, you should practise and rehearse the presentation so that you get the timings correct, ensure you cover the key issues you want the audience to know; and better understand the sequence of topics to be discussed. If possible, familiarise yourself with the room in which the presentation is to take place. This will help prevent any last-minute surprises regarding layout, lighting, sound, etc. Good preparation and practice will help to lessen the negative influence of nerves when it comes to delivering the presentation.

9(f) Presentation techniques

The requirements for a good presentation are to know your subject, understand the audience and their expectations, and apply some good techniques. The following can be used as a guide to good presentation technique.

Time

Always be aware of the time. Take a clock (do not glance at your watch as it gives the impression you just want the presentation to end) and place it within easy sight. Your practice should give you an indication of how the time allocated to each topic will play out. Remember it may not match that of the rehearsal because the different environments may influence the pace of delivery. To help the time management you may consider using cards with small notes as an *aide memoire* covering the sequence and topics to be covered in the presentation.

Introduction

The introduction is important because it sets the scene for the relationship between yourself and the audience. You may want to make this relatively informal to get the audience to relax and enjoy the experience. Striking the correct tone is important at this stage and much will depend on the nature and characteristics of the audience and what they expect. Here, emotional intelligence comes into play as you make the correct judgement regarding the approach and tone adopted. The introduction should set out the purposes of the presentation and the key issues to be addressed. This part of the presentation can be used to control the pitch and pace of delivery so that you can communicate in a clear and understandable manner. Good control of the pace of delivery at this stage will set an appropriate level for the rest of the presentation and boost your confidence.

Style of presentation

The style of presentation should be calibrated to the type of audience, the subject matter, and the understanding of the most appropriate means of communicating what you want to put across. For example, a presentation as part of a job interview will focus on your ability to deliver in an effective manner, whereas a presentation to a research conference has to demonstrate a deep understanding of the subject matter. A presentation at a wedding or other social gathering will probably be infused with humour and amusing anecdotes; whereas a presentation to potential investors for a new business venture needs to be persuasive and compelling. Each will entail a different style of presentation according to the circumstances and purpose of the presentation.

No matter what the presentation is for or the type of audience, there are a number of techniques that should always be applied. First, your body language should be open and engaging. Where you have an opportunity to walk about you should use the space to engage with the audience, not by standing in the same spot throughout but by using the space to make the audience feel included. Do not become part of the audience, keep a distance, but where possible use the space available to good effect. Sometimes you will be limited in terms of the space provided. You may, for example, be delivering from behind a barrier or a podium. In this case you rely on eye contact, gestures, and tone of voice to engage with the audience. Eye contact is an essential technique for maintaining audience interest and ensuring that they feel included in proceedings. You should share out the eye contact, not just focusing on a few audience members at the front but in all parts of the room. Do not focus on just one or two audience members as this will quickly make them feel uncomfortable.

The tone of your voice is also important. You need to maintain clarity of expression but you also need to inject some interest, even passion into what you are saying. If you do not sound interested then the audience will not be either. Again, the tone will depend on your understanding of the circumstances. A eulogy at a funeral will be set in a very different tone from a valedictory speech after an achievement. Similarly, a presentation to your peers as part of an assessed piece of work will be delivered in a different tone to that of a viva in front of two academics.

Content

Fundamentally, the audience has turned up to hear you talk about a specific subject and to learn something from it. The content of the presentation has to cover the key issues, raise some new insights or learning, and be relevant to the audience and their interests. PowerPoint® slides and other multimedia technologies can be used to support the presentation of ideas and concepts but they should not dominate. Too much information on slides requires too much investment in effort from the audience and detracts from the main points you want to make. There should be just a few key points highlighted on screen, or a graphic that visually represents the key issues under discussion. The use of visual aids is important not just for conveying messages to the audience but also helps to strike a balance between the attention focused on you the presenter and other points of interest. Applied properly, this can also help to ease nerves and focus attention on effective delivery. It is important that you allocate sufficient time to cover the most salient parts of the presentation. A number of key issues should be identified and discussed as the main body of the presentation. If these are missing the audience will depart feeling 'short changed' or dissatisfied.

Activity 2:
Identify TEN key techniques for effective presentations and briefly outline the
value they bring

Presentation technique	Value of technique

9(h) Evaluation

It is important to use each presentation as a valuable learning experience, something you can
reflect on and use to hone your skills and techniques. Some key questions to ask are:

- Did I prepare properly?
- Was the content relevant and insightful?
- Was my time management accurate?
- Did I explain the key issues clearly?
- Was the style of delivery appropriate?
- Did I use appropriate body language and eye contact?
- How effective were my visual aids?
- Was I able to maintain the attention of the audience?
- Did the presentation achieve its aims and objectives?
- What can I do better next time?

Activity 3:
Use these questions as a template for reflection after your next presentation.

10 Managing Groups and Teams

Learning outcomes

- Understand the reasons for the formation of groups and teams

- Apply models for the development and implementation of forms of teams

- Identify and evaluate teambuilding and empowerment strategies

- Critically evaluate the advantages and limitations of teams

- Assess the relative merits of the development and use of virtual teams

The Great Britain athletics team returned from the Beijing Olympics in 2008 with a disappointing four medals. The sport's governing body was rightly concerned that a similar performance when London hosted the games in 2012 would be a national embarrassment. There was a desire among officials to appoint a team manager with a working philosophy that the athletes could relate to and be inspired by. The appointment of Dutch coach Charles van Commenee in 2009 was a decisive factor in delivering a successful team performance culminating in some outstanding individual performances from Jessica Ennis and Mo Farah. The performance of Team GB in athletics was largely down to the dedication and talent of the athletes, but the team philosophy and coaching expertise of van Commenee also played a pivotal role. On arriving in the post he immediately sacked many of the existing coaching staff, reorganised the structure of UK athletics, and brought in his own trusted assistants. However, it was the team philosophy and the culture of a zero tolerance of failure that he communicated that made the difference. In particular, van Commenee saw the value of a team ethic that could spread positive energy to individual athletes. This was a method of tackling what he perceived as a 'soft excuse' culture for failure (Hart, 2012). Thus, by giving each athlete a real feeling of being responsible for their part in a team, rather than perceiving their role as an individual, van Commenee was able to harness the advantages of team spirit in what is essentially a series of individual events. As a means of communicating the need for each athlete to push themselves beyond their existing personal best performances, van Commenee set himself highly challenging medal targets. Although the six medals eventually won (the haul of four gold medals was the best performance since the Tokyo Olymipcs in 1964) fell below his target, the purpose of the exercise was achieved. Team GB athletes met the expectations of the British Olympic Association and, more importantly, those of the watching UK public.

334

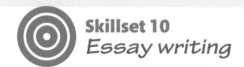

Skillset 10
Essay writing

At some point in their academic career students will be required to compile an essay. This is a common assessment instrument. Essay writing requires a combination of key skills that have previously been covered in the Skillsets on reading skills, sourcing materials, time management, and literature review. Skillset 10 outlines a number of effective techniques for structuring and writing an essay.

Student study skills

Skillset 10 outlines how to structure an essay, disciplinary skills such as referencing, the role of paragraphs, headings, how to build in arguments and analysis, presentation, etc.

Workplace skills

Writing in a coherent and formally structured manner is a key skill in many organisations, especially in business-orientated professions such as consultancy. This Skillset contributes to students' abilities to deliver high quality written outputs as part of a portfolio of communications skills.

Definitions

A group can be defined as two or more individuals who are connected to one another by social relationships. A team is a group who work intensively with each other to achieve a specific common goal. Teamwork is the collaborative and coordinated effort of that group to achieve a common goal.

Introduction

Human beings are social and possess a natural instinct to become part of a group. When two or more people have something in common, it is normal for those people to interact, share knowledge, offer support, and recognise the formation of a group. When members of a group have complementary capabilities that can be combined to achieve a stated aim, they may be brought together to form a team. This has been a key trend that has emerged in the last two decades. Rather than viewing the workforce as individuals who congregate in the same location and undertake a series of tasks, managers see the value of bringing together a group of workers with combined skills, experience, and expertise to form a team that is capable of achieving more than a group of individuals. In this instance the saying that 'the whole is greater than the sum of the parts' holds true as, in collaboration, a team can deliver a number of advantages that a dispersed group of individuals cannot. For example, team members can bring a number of different but complementary attributes or skills to form a more complete understanding of a problem. A marketing person and an engineering person will both add value, but together they may combine to determine the feasibility of developing new products from both a technical and commercial perspective.

335

Teams and organisational structures

Teams have become an integral part of organisational structures to the extent that some are afforded semi- or full autonomy to make decisions and act in ways that not only achieve their aims and objectives but add further value by experimenting with new ideas, reforming processes, creating networks and partnerships, and so on. Escriba-Moreno and Canet-Giner (2006) provide research evidence to link team performance to organisational structures of small and medium sized enterprises. It is the role of senior management to determine the extent to which teams can exercise autonomy in decision making and the type of leadership and structure that characterises them. Some teams may be task specific or project oriented, others may have strategic responsibilities. They may be temporary or permanent. Teams have a great deal of flexibility linked to them in terms of the scope of their activities, membership, and structure. This presents managers with opportunities to exploit them to gain maximum returns but also to change and adapt them according to need.

Teams and workers

Workers similarly benefit from being part of team as they gain a broader understanding of key factors affecting the processes and outputs of the organisation, acquire valuable knowledge-sharing insights, attain a greater stakeholder investment and engagement in the organisation and its aims, and build morale and motivation. Nevertheless, there are some challenges associated with teams, for example, finding the correct dynamic between team members, integrating workers from different disciplines and skillsets, finding a positive culture that is sustainable, and ensuring that there is no abuse of power (Levi, 2013). The success or otherwise of a team depends on the level of trust placed in the members and how they respond to acquiring higher levels of responsibility. Teams have been a feature of organisations and management for a long time and have attracted the interest of academic writers. One of the aims of this chapter is to present some of the theoretical models devised by academics for the formation, development, and implementation of teams and the means by which managers can derive added value from teamwork.

The chapter begins with definitions of groups and teams before going on to highlight the key differences between them. These formations are often confused so this part of the discussion provides clarity in differentiating groups and teams. Theoretical models of the development of groups and roles within them are also used to set the scene for an analysis of teams and teamwork, including explanations of different types of teams with insights into the reasons for their formation. The discussion of the advantages of teams is counterbalanced by setting out some of the limitations associated with this approach. Managing effective teams and teamwork includes discussion on teambuilding and the activities that support it, and implementing empowerment strategies. The chapter also considers the development of virtual teams in the context of the global economy and discusses the relative merits of this model for achieving organisational aims.

Groups and teams

It is important to note that teams can be a form of work group, but that not all work groups are teams. In fact, work groups are more prevalent than teams even though the latter has seen an increase in organisations in the last decade or so. To distinguish work groups from teams it is useful to look at them from three different functional levels: dependent, independent, and interdependent.

Dependent work groups

Dependent work groups are the most familiar form. They are groups of workers in a demarcated unit or department with a line manager. Typically each employee in a work group has an assigned task or job and is supervised by the line manager. The line manager has a direction-oriented role, issuing commands and monitoring performance. For example, line maintenance workers for *Network Rail* are tasked with jobs by foremen who take their direction from engineers and line managers. Although they work as a group there is no expectation that the workers will be asked to form a team. Dependent work groups are effective in the short term for the purposes of completing a particular task, but they do not evolve into anything more complex or sophisticated and, therefore, have limited strategic significance. The emphasis in dependent work groups is on maintaining the status quo and ensuring that tasks are completed. There is limited scope for improvement, innovation, problem solving, or other developmental activities in this type of work group.

Independent work groups

Independent work groups are the most prevalent in organisations. In a similar fashion to dependent work groups, each worker is assigned a task or job, but the main difference lies in the fact that line managers are more distant and less controlling in their management of workers. Line managers may offer general guidance and support but direct supervision is kept to a minimum. This form of work group is evident in professions such accountancy, research, law, teaching, and design. *GE Healthcare* sales staff spend most of their time travelling to prospective clients and are well used to working independently. There are a great number of freelance workers who operate in a similar fashion. Although it is likely that a work group will be allocated a department or working unit, they tend to work independently.

Interdependent work groups

There is a high level of co-dependence between workers as part of an interdependent work group. Here, collaboration is essential to complete the tasks or jobs. In some instances workers will have their own tasks and jobs and can work independently, but in other aspects of their work they are required to collaborate with others and the responsibility for producing the desired outcome is shared. Interdependent workers at this functional level form a team.

Independent work groups can be mobilised more quickly than interdependent ones as forming a team invariably takes time and some initial coordination (Benson, 2000). However, once the team is established, an interdependent work group can produce much better quality output such as commercially viable ideas and innovations, creativity, and problem solving. High-performing teams can deliver the added value that creates a competitive advantage and enhance the reputation of the organisation. The Formula 1 racing teams such as *McLaren*, *Ferrari*, and *Lotus* all comprise interdependent work groups as they constantly strive for the incremental innovations that give them a competitive advantage. Consequently, teams have a strategic dimension as they contribute to the long-term aims and objectives of organisations. In essence, work groups tend to exhibit strong individual characteristics, whereas collaboration is the hallmark of teams. Table 10.1 outlines the main differences between work groups and teams.

Table 10.1	Key differences between work groups and teams	
	Work groups	**Teams**
	Individual accountability	Individual and collaborative accountability
	Minimal and formal knowledge sharing	Knowledge-sharing culture underpinned by formal and informal communications systems
	Individual goals	Team goals
	Discrete individual outputs	Collective output
	Clearly defined tasks	Fluid dimension to roles and tasks depending on team needs
	Emphasis on individual rewards	Emphasis on team rewards
	Purpose, goals, and scope of work shaped by the line manager	Purpose, goals, and scope of work shaped by team leader in consultation with team members

One of the key differences between work groups and teams is the level of communication that exists. Managers may periodically convene meetings with work groups to share information and to impart knowledge on issues such as performance or strategy. Teams meet much more regularly and there are distinct outcomes and plans decided at those meetings. Team meetings can involve issues of problem solving, planning, work scheduling, performance, and so on. The team leader plays the role of organising, coordinating, and overseeing the management of the work, but this is done in close collaboration with team members. Some teams require very little management as the members are adept at self-managing and are motivated by the independence this brings.

Informal groups

It is worth noting that not all teams are formally constructed. Some are the result of informal interactions between workers with a common goal. That goal may be wide and varied and include everything from simple friendships through to political manoeuvring for some work-based advantage. Informal groups are a feature of internal organisational relationships in many different contexts and cultures. For example, Farivar and Esmaeelinezhad (2012) analyse this phenomenon in the context of businesses in Iran. Most informal teams are formed to satisfy the need for human interaction and social support. For the most part, managers should encourage these as they provide an important means for workers to share experiences without the pressures of formality that characterises most work-based relationships. Some teams will form as an interest group (such as a football team or other leisure activity). Managers should observe interest groups to better understand what employees see as being important.

The development of groups

Groups are subject to change and adaptation over time with members arriving and leaving on a continuous basis (Surowiecki, 2004). Sometimes group members leave of their own volition, at other times they are required to leave due to under-performance, their skills and experience no longer fitting the objectives of the group, conflicting views, and so on. Group development is important to ensure that the aims and objectives of bringing people together can be met. However, groups do not form and gel immediately, but instead go through phases of increasing integration and maturity, a process highlighted by Kurt Lewin (1948) who was one of the early pioneers of studying group dynamics in the working environment. One of the most cited models of group development is that of Tuckman (1965). The simplicity and continuing relevance of the model accounts for its longevity of use by practitioners and academics alike. Figure 10.1 illustrates Tuckman's model.

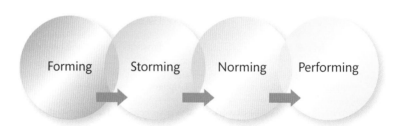

Figure 10.1 Tuckman's model of group development

Forming

The forming phase of group development refers to the initial point when people come together to form a group. Each member will have their own expectations of the group and their place in it. At this stage the members are sizing each other up to determine whether or not they want to continue to be part of the group. Caution is exercised before going on to the next stage.

Storming

The storming phase refers to the point when group members start to share more information about themselves and their expectations, and absorb those of others. The storming phase entails expressing feelings about areas of concern, tension, or potential conflict and can lead to a certain level of antagonism between group members.

Norming

The process of moving beyond storming to norming is the vital one if the group is to function effectively. Norming refers to the point when the group reaches some form of consensus about acceptable forms of behaviour and attitude that allows the group as a whole to move forward and function as a unit. At this point group members are proactive in aligning their skills, experiences, and capabilities to the needs of the group.

Performing

The final phase is putting into action the tasks for which the group was established. Here, roles of the members are defined and shared according to need. As group members increasingly collaborate on defined tasks, so the work group becomes a team.

There is no set timeframe for how long it takes a work group to become a team or how long it takes for them to work through each of the phases. Much depends on the types of personalities involved, the work tasks assigned, the resources available, management and leadership styles, time pressure, and so on (Shaw, 1981). In some instances the linear process illustrated in Figure 10.1 is not followed. For example, a work group may be formed with people who already know each other and have experience of working together, thereby making the 'norming' phase redundant. In other cases the storming phase may create a residual ill-feeling that makes the journey to the norming phase difficult and then, ultimately, proves a constraint to performance.

Development of group roles

The attitude and behaviour of group members goes a long way to determining the type of roles they will enact in the team that emerges. Here, a myriad of different social and

Term
Definition

Group role: set of behaviours a group member is expected to perform because of their position in the group.

psychological factors can potentially come into play including life experience, education, class, religion, beliefs and values, ethics, peer group influence, intellectual agility, culture, temperament, and personality among others. For example, if a group member exhibits high levels of anxiety but is creative then the challenge is to fit those traits into a suitable role whereby the effects of the anxiety can be tolerated or helped in order to benefit from the creative outputs that person will bring to the team. Alternatively, a team member may possess a strong personality and uses that to control and influence the actions of others. Again, there is a role for that type of personality whereby benefits are accrued but only if the negative aspects are tolerated. Teams are usually comprised of people with different personality traits and it is very difficult to pinpoint what mix of traits is most likely to lead to success. Several management writers and psychologists have attempted this task with varying levels of success. Perhaps the most famous is that of Meredith Belbin (1981) who devised a list of roles, key characteristics and positive and negative attributes of team members. This list is outlined in Table 10.2.

Table 10.2

Belbin's team roles and characteristics

Role	Characteristics	Positive attributes	Negative aspects
Implementor	Conservative, cautious, dutiful, methodical	Organising, common sense, hard work, self-discipline	Inflexible, deaf to untested ideas
Co-ordinator	Calm, self-confident, controlled	Treating all contributions fairly, sense of objectives	No more than average intellect or creativity
Shaper	Excitable, outgoing, dynamic	Drive, opposes inertia, complacency or self-deception	Provocative, impatient
Plant	Individualistic, serious, unorthodox	Genius, imagination, intellect, knowledge	Impractical, dreamy, ignores protocols
Resource investigator	Extroverted, enthusiastic, curious, communicative	Makes contacts, checks out new ideas, responds to challenges	Loses interest after initial obsession
Monitor-evaluator	Sober, unemotional, prudent	Judgement, discretion, hard-headedness	Lacks inspiration, cannot motivate
Team worker	Social, mild, sensitive	Responsive to people and settings, promotes team spirit	Indecisive in a crisis
Completer-finisher	Painstaking, orderly, conscientious, anxious	Follows through, perfectionist	Worries about small matters, reluctant to let go

Source: © Belbin, 2011. www.belbin.com

Factors that determine group effectiveness

There are numerous factors that affect how successful a group is likely to be, including the personality traits of group members, changes in the environment, perceptions of rewards, and so on. There are some criteria that determine the effectiveness of groups that are seen as pre-requisites for the group to function properly (Doel, 2005). These include:

- group composition;
- group norms;
- cohesiveness.

Group composition

The effectiveness of a group is largely dependent on the composition of its members. The composition is a difficult task as there is no template for deciding what mix of personalities, skills, and experience is required for success in different contexts. One composition may create a group dynamic that is positive whereas another with almost the same attributes and characteristics may fail. It is not an exact science and the process involves an element of trial and error to see how the group integrates and achieves the stated aims. Groups will exhibit their own 'personality' and this will influence how roles, tasks, and conflicts are dealt with (Anderson, 2009). Groups formed to achieve specific task-oriented outcomes may be comprised of members with identified key skills. However, this is no guarantee of success as it may be that the group requires a non-specialist leader who possesses good communication, organisational, and motivational skills. Some groups may be comprised of members from diverse backgrounds who bring forward new ideas and different perspectives. However, it is not a given that all members embrace diversity. Group composition is a dynamic, uncertain, and risky function for managers and much will depend on an intuitive understanding of how the various personalities that comprise the group will work together to achieve stated aims.

Group norms

For groups to function effectively there has to be acceptance by members of the norms of behaviour and attitude that binds them in pursuit of a common cause. Group norms are either explicit or implicit rules that members have to understand and adhere to (Tuckman, 1964). Rewards for adherence include continued membership of the group, the respect and friendship of other group members, and a feeling of belonging. These are important human psychological needs and may be the motivation for joining a group in the first place. New recruits often have to undergo an 'initiation ceremony' as an informal means of establishing the process of communicating group norms. Conformity brings such rewards whereas deviance or challenges to the group norms are likely to be met with sanctions ranging from mild rebuke through to expulsion. However, this can be a disadvantage in some groups where there is a need for innovation and creative thinking. Very often new ideas are generated by those who step out of the norm and challenge the status quo. In high performing groups and teams it is necessary to accommodate this type of personality to nurture some of these attributes.

Critical reflection
What makes a good team?

There are so many different factors that influence the effectiveness of teams that it is almost impossible to create a formula for success. Any one, or a mix, of these factors can undermine the best laid plans for creating a team to achieve stated aims and objectives. Some factors are easier to deal with than others. For example, good managers should be able to identify and communicate the goals, purpose, and mission of the team. This informs potential members of the purpose of the team formation and they can then decide if they want to be a part of that team. Allocating roles and responsibilities for the tasks to be carried out should also be within the scope of managers. However, things can become complex when emotive factors play a role. For example, teams are formed by bringing together different personalities. How relationships are formed and maintained throughout the time the team is expected to operate is a largely unknown factor until such times as the team comes together. Leadership roles will form as the team begins to operate, but here again there is no guarantee that an effective leader will emerge from the chosen personalities that comprise the team. Other factors such as power and influence are similarly difficult to contrive. Determining who has power and influence and how they exercise it may be a fruitless endeavour as the reaction of others in the team will be largely unknown. Finally, the mix of skills allied to personality types is another key challenge facing those who have the duty of forming a team. Experience can help managers make informed choices but the way a team gels and operates is not easily given to scientific approaches.

Group cohesiveness

The cohesiveness of a group is determined by the loyalty that members exhibit. This can be gauged by the level of participation in the activities of the group in all its manifestations, including social gatherings. High levels of performance and achievement can enhance group cohesiveness and some managers are especially aware that celebrating success is an important aspect of building a cohesive working unit (Johnson and Johnson, 2003). Care needs to be taken to ensure that the group does not focus entirely on their own performance at the expense of the wider strategic aims and objectives of the organisation. Several factors combine to determine the level of cohesiveness of a group including group size (the bigger the group the more difficult it is to maintain universal acceptance of group norms and consensus on key aims); levels of diversity (much depends on the extent to which members embrace diversity); group identity (a common understanding of why the group formed, its aims, and dominant culture); and level of success (groups tend to have longevity when they consistently achieve outcomes as a group that they could not as individuals).

Types of teams

Formal teams can be created by managers to meet the organisation's aims and objectives. Team composition is a key element of building effective teams and much depends on the type of team required (Mello and Ruckes, 2006). Figure 10.2 highlights some of the most common types of teams in organisations.

Figure 10.2 Types of teams in organisations

Some teams are formed on the basis of self-management whereby the majority of decisions affecting their processes and activities are taken by team members or a designated leader of the team. For example, at Hewlett Packard self-managed work teams make decisions on work schedules and production-related issues. This form of empowerment has a number of advantages, the most obvious being that the team members acquire a heightened sense of responsibility which can improve motivation. Giving teams responsibility can improve innovation, problem solving, creativity, speed, or productivity as employees react to the greater sense of stakeholder engagement that self-management brings. Thus, their own success is inextricably linked to that of the organisation.

To create effective self-managed teams it is necessary to provide the necessary support mechanisms. These can be broad ranging but the most critical involve ensuring the team is afforded enough responsibility and autonomy to become truly self-managing. Senior managers need to devise terms of reference that clearly state the level to which the team can make decisions. This may simply be operational or functional, or may extend to strategic issues depending on the scope of autonomy that senior managers deem appropriate. The composition of the team is also a critical success factor and should encapsulate diversity, skills, and value adding personal traits such as dedication, motivation, and enthusiasm. The culture of the team needs to support the aims and objectives. Management style needs to be supportive and guiding rather than directive and supervisory. Also, to merit autonomy, the self-managed team needs to be able to identify a distinctive and complex set of tasks that benefit from the advantages of self-management.

Cross-functional teams

Members of different departments can be brought together to form cross-functional teams. This has the benefit of aiding knowledge sharing between members but also, crucially, it gives members an insight into the working processes, pressures, and technical aspects of work in different departments. The main motivation for forming cross-functional teams is to encourage members to use and share their knowledge and expertise in a cooperative and integrated way (Ghobadi and D'Amba, 2012) and to become more innovative and creative around processes, ideas on developing new products or services, packaging, distribution, marketing, customer service, or other functions that add value. Cross-functional teams have been a feature of organisations for many decades. In the 1950s American insurance company *Northwestern Mutual Life* pioneered a cross-functional team comprising departmental staff from finance, insurance brokerage, actuarial, investment analysis, and other areas to assess the effect of computers on the work processes at the company. The company were first-movers in developing a bespoke information system in their industry that leveraged a competitive advantage.

The challenge facing managers of cross-functional teams is to create a dynamic that is positive and integrated. Team members come from an array of different backgrounds featuring different views on how things should be done and they will invariably have acquired different forms of language associated with the activities and culture in their respective departments. Consequently, strong leadership needs to communicate clear and well-understood aims and objectives. Members need to know why the team has been formed, what its structure is, what the expected outcomes are, and what the benefits of participation will be. Some managers in organisations draw up a formal team charter that states exactly what these are as a means of establishing the basic protocols and standards that working as a team entails. Another challenge is to ensure that departmental goals align to those of the cross-functional team. If the activities of a cross-functional team are unrelated to the usual duties of a team member there may be competing responsibilities that lead to confusion and lack of engagement. Aligning cross-functional goals and departmental goals helps members understand the rationale for the team's formation and boosts cooperation and positive participation.

Cross-cultural teams

As discussed in Chapter 8, Human resource management, the issue of diversity has become key to gaining a competitive advantage for many organisations operating in global markets with global customers. This has led to an increased awareness among managers of the need to integrate workers from different backgrounds. Cross-cultural team formation is an effective way of bringing together people from a range of different backgrounds reflecting their ethnicity, culture, religion, values, beliefs, customs, etc.

The benefits of creating cross-cultural teams can be significant as knowledge sharing between members encapsulates a broad range of different cultural values and norms (Thomas and Inkson, 2003). For example, customer service can be improved by team members explaining the appropriate way of communicating with particular ethnic groups who exhibit distinct customs and beliefs. The etiquette of doing business is a subtle but influential means of gaining brand loyalty. Appreciating how to deal with people from different backgrounds can lead to valuable partnerships. Cross-cultural teams can swap ideas; generate insights from the integration of cultural values and ways of doing things; find ways of working through issues that affect the cohesiveness of a multi-ethnic workforce; and better understand the perceptions and behaviour of customers, co-workers, and others along the supply chain. Importantly, cross-cultural teams can deliver real added value in bringing forward new ideas for products and services that customers will find novel and compelling. There are some ventures that require cross-cultural awareness and understanding to become successful. This is often the case with large-scale international collaborations such as the development of the *Eurofighter* fast-attack military jet aircraft that involved cooperation between four different countries, or the completion of the *Eurotunnel*, which was an Anglo-French collaboration.

It should be noted that forming a cross-cultural team is also fraught with danger. There is no guarantee that the mix of diverse cultures will gel in the way imagined. There may be tensions between team members as they try to work through their differences and the implications those differences have for work processes, relationships, leadership, communication, norms of doing business, and so on. It is important that managers are able to identify the correct people to form the team and to ensure that they possess the necessary emotional awareness and cultural sensitivity and embrace diversity so that the members are committed to achieving the stated aims and objectives of the team.

Research and development teams

Research and development teams are brought together to create new products and services. Innovation, creativity, knowledge sharing, and ideas are the core characteristics of R&D teams and define the types of personnel who are chosen to participate. It is important that managers populate the R&D team with the most able workers who possess the skills and attributes to contribute to the generation of innovation and new ideas that deliver new products and services. Invariably, R&D teams have both cross-functional and cross-cultural characteristics as the team members are drawn from any and all departments of the organisation.

R&D teams have become a locus of skills and experience, creativity, and innovation for carefully chosen staff within modern organisations seeking competitive advantage in global industries. The modern business environment is knowledge-driven, and it is within this environment that R&D teams need to discover and develop new concepts, products, or processes. Of all the teams formed within organisations, the R&D team is under the most intense pressure to perform, as their outputs ultimately determine what products or services the organisation provides. Very often the timeframe for delivering a new innovation is exacting and this requires a highly motivated and able workforce to collaborate effectively. Mini case 10.1 featuring the *Nordstrom Innovation Lab* is a prime example of the benefits that can be derived for customers and the organisation when this form of teamwork succeeds. In other cases the innovation team may fail to deliver. For example, the innovation team at photographic equipment specialist *Kodak* led the way in digital photography but failed to transform the lead into a sustained competitive advantage by neglecting the commercialisation aspect of their strategic aims (Kain, 2012).

Managers have to resource and support R&D teams by carefully thinking through the choice of key personnel to participate, the type of work to be undertaken (a mix of research and product development), and the expected outcomes. Crucially, though, research has revealed that the key to the success of an R&D team is the form of leadership employed (Mann, 2005). A transformational style of leadership is closely linked to success of R&D teams as it is seen to motivate and inspire members by establishing trust and setting clear goals. Transformational leaders are skilled communicators who can liaise with a wide range of stakeholders to gain support. These are often the building blocks for creating an effective innovative team.

Project-based teams

Project-based teams are most closely associated with research and development but can be formed for other specific purposes such as identifying potential new markets, undertaking an employee feedback survey, redesigning internal governance procedures, and so on. The project may be multidisciplinary and/or multicultural. For example, the Swiss-based nuclear research organisation *CERN* brings together scientists and business people from all over the world to work on the delivery of particle accelerators for physics research.

The most important aspect of project-based teams is choosing the members (Brown and Hyer, 2010). One of the dangers in the management of teams is the temptation to continually go back to the personnel who have comprised previous successful teams. This may be a mistake as each team needs to be refreshed with new people with new ideas and vigour. Also, the tendency to choose people with similar views and attitudes may undermine the type of creative tension that drives innovation and the generation of ideas. Just as with other types of teams, project-based teams rely on effective leadership. This may involve breaking up a cohesive and successful team and replacing it with another. Leaders have to look to the bigger picture by reinvigorating teams at the expense of 'tried-and-tested' ones that are at risk of stagnating. This might be indicated by outcomes that have been successful but sub-optimal. Maintaining the status quo risks losing competitive advantage as the organisation slips into a 'comfort zone' of acceptability rather than pushing forward towards innovative excellence. Very often, using the same people in teams lead to the same type of results rather than the exponential leaps in returns associated with new and highly motivated teams.

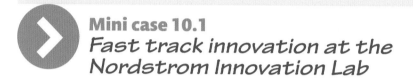

Mini case 10.1
Fast track innovation at the Nordstrom Innovation Lab

John H. Nordstrom was a Swedish immigrant to the United States with a flair for commercial retailing. In 1887 he opened his first shoe shop in Seattle (Nordstrom company history, 2013). Today the company has expanded across the USA and specialises in developing as well as selling a range of fashion products. As a means of maximising returns on innovation, the company established the Nordstrom Innovation Lab, a lean start-up that operates within the Nordstrom organisational structure. Through the design-led innovation process, the company attracts people with the mindset of design thinking, agile development, and lean manufacturing. These provide the basis for moving ideas along quickly to test which creative outputs are feasible and viable. Lab staff are multicultural, multidisciplinary, and team-driven and work in a collaborative open space to maximise communication efficiencies and knowledge sharing. New ideas go through several iterations (including customer feedback) before prototyping and development. What sets Nordstrom apart from rivals is the ability of the team to fast-track the innovation process with the benchmark of one week for the creation of a new product from conception to completion. One example is the iPad app that was developed within one week which was designed to help customers choose a pair of sunglasses. For this initiative the team based themselves in the flagship Seattle store where they could access the customers for feedback on how effective the app was for their shopping experience. This concept was borrowed from the Toyota production system called 'genchi gembutsu' which broadly translated means 'go and see for yourself'. By accessing the key people in the process (customers, sales staff, managers, etc.) the innovation team can gain valuable information that helps them to test, validate, and complete the development of new products or services within very tight timeframes (Fossell, 2011). The key to success is the team ethic that permeates throughout the Lab, a mindset of innovation and ideas generation, and an open, collaborative, and integrated approach to achieving value added outcomes.

http://
nordstrominnovationlab.
com/
http://
nordstrominnovationlab.
com/

Sources:

Fossell, B. (20 December 2011) Nordstrom Innovation Lab: Sunglass iPad Case Study, Crowdsourcing.org. http://www.crowdsourcing.org/index.php/video/nordstrom-innovation-lab-sunglass-ipad-app-case-study-/9484/related

Nordstrom company history (2013). http://shop.nordstrom.com/c/company-history

Discussion point

Are Japanese working methods, such as *genchi gembutsu*, easily transferred to organisations in the west?

Questions and task

What are the key characteristics of the Nordstrom Innovation Lab?

What is the *modus operandi* of the Nordstrom Innovation Lab team?

Access YouTube and identify the main activities in the development of the iPad app for sunglasses. www.youtube.com/watch?v=szr0ezLyQHY

or Google: Nordstrom Innovation Lab: Sunglasses iPad App Case Study–YouTube

 Online Resource Centre
Author commentary on this discussion point and questions can be found on the Online Resource Centre at: www.oxfordtextbooks.co.uk/orc/combe1e/

Advantages of teams

Managers will be motivated to create teams for a number of different reasons. The advantages associated with teams and teamwork are numerous and account for the prevalence of them in recent years in organisations across the spectrum including public, private, and voluntary sectors. The main advantages of teams and teamwork are:

- improved performance;
- responsiveness to customers;
- innovation and creativity;
- knowledge sharing;
- integrated organisational culture;
- diversity economies;
- organisational reengineering;
- motivation and morale;
- pushing boundaries;
- speed and efficiency.

Improved performance

The main reason for forming teams is to enhance performance (Franz, 2012). There may be direct and tangible results such as the increased revenue derived from the formation of a sales team, or intangible effects such as the enhanced reputation of the organisation as a result of the successful development of a new product through the activities of the research and development team. The synergy created by bringing people together from different parts of the organisation may result in improved processes, productivity, and output (tangible returns) or increased innovation, ideas generation, and creativity (intangible returns).

Responsiveness to customers

Teams can be established with the aim of undertaking activities that improve the organisation's responsiveness to customers. For example, a project-based team may be established to examine customer responses to the organisation's health and safety record for affected stakeholders. Part of the remit for an R&D team may be to discover customers' reactions to new products or services. Alternatively, a team may be formed to find new means of engaging and communicating with customers, perhaps through social media or digital technology.

Innovation and creativity

One of the main reasons for creating a team is to enhance innovation and creative thinking that leads to ideas for new products and services or improved processes. Teams can comprise diverse members with a range of different skills and experiences that can be used as a basis for viewing the environment from different perspectives, challenging the status quo, and pushing the boundaries of knowledge, all of which help the process of innovation and creativity.

Knowledge sharing

Team members are in an environment where knowledge sharing is easy and accessible and is a feature of the culture. Innovation and creativity are linked to knowledge sharing and a team formation is designed to encourage this important value adding activity. Some knowledge sharing between team members will occur through formal means such as weekly meetings, project management meetings, appraisals, reviews, etc, but a great deal will be through the informal interpersonal relationships that a close-knit team is designed to nurture. Some of the best ideas are generated in informal settings such as break-times or even during social gatherings.

Integrated organisational culture

Teams create their own unique and distinctive culture replete with its own terminology and use of language, informal relationships, hierarchies, conflicts, tensions, success recognition customs, and so on. The formation of a distinct culture is an important cohesive element that binds the team and underpins the special nature of the relationships therein. Managers have to be proactive in helping to create a positive culture within the team but for the most part the dominant culture that emerges is a result of the myriad of different interactions between the team members. This aspect of the team is the most difficult to control and the dynamic that emerges is one that is self-determined rather than one of design.

Diversity economies

Managers can form a team comprised of members from diverse backgrounds, skills, and experiences. This not only helps in the drive to improve diversity awareness, but also allows participants to understand different perspectives, views, and interpretations of the world around them. Exposure to these different perspectives is often the catalyst for the generation of new ideas and innovations. In many industries it can be a source of competitive advantage and something that can be managed closely through the formation of a carefully chosen team. Investment in the team can yield economies that only diversity can bring, that is, novelty, insight, different perspectives, and inspiration.

Organisational reengineering

Project teams can be established to focus on ways in which the organisation can be radically transformed to improve processes and communications. This may involve detailed investigations into each functioning part of the organisation to determine where improvements can be made or if the existing processes need to be altered, adapted, or totally replaced. In some instances external teams, such as consultants, are brought in to carry out the investigation as a means of ensuring that a critical and unbiased assessment is carried out. Organisational reengineering is transformational in scale and scope and requires the deployment of specially trained team members to identify, assess, and recommend changes that will help the organisation achieve its long-term aims and objectives, or to become more competitive.

Motivation and morale

Teams can bolster morale and improve motivation among the members. There is a psychological effect associated with being chosen for membership of a team. It suggests that an individual possesses skills or attributes that are especially valued by the organisation and are recognised by inclusion into a team set up for a specific purpose. Members may also derive greater satisfaction from the added responsibility that a greater level of autonomy in decision making brings. Members may have been chosen because they react positively to being given increased responsibilities or because of their capacity to take control of the management of their work tasks. The increase in trust and responsibility can be key motivators for team members and can encourage members to work in an integrated and cohesive manner to achieve stated aims and objectives. Scannell and Scannell (2009) outline a number of practical examples of team motivation games that can be applied in different contexts.

Pushing boundaries

Some teams are established with the remit of challenging the status quo, to push the boundaries of knowledge, and to recommend radical changes to the existing means of doing business. Team members may be chosen for their abilities to think differently, to step out of the norms of everyday business processes, or to exhibit innovative and creative abilities that can deliver new and better products and services. In some ways the mavericks within the organisation may be best placed to form a team as they habitually exhibit modes of behaviour that challenge the norm. Care needs to be taken not to populate the entire team with such personality types, as even in the most radical team formation there needs to be some discipline and focus. Nevertheless, it often the most challenging of personalities that prove to be the most effective in terms of pushing boundaries.

Speed and efficiency

Chapter 11 on Organisational Structure highlights the reasons for the trend towards flatter and less hierarchical organisational structures. One reason is to accommodate teams of workers with specific aims and objectives and with a certain level of autonomy in decision making.

?

Critical reflection

What factors should be considered when forming a team?

Much has been said about the way in which teams can improve innovation by sharing ideas and bringing forward new perspectives. However, simply bringing together a number of people to form a team does not in itself improve the chances of increasing innovation. The team needs to possess a number of important characteristics and motivations for innovation to flourish. Although, as has been noted, there is no scientific approach that can guarantee the success of any given team formation, there are a number of key management principles that can improve the chances. First, it is important to establish the reasons for the team formation, set out the goals, and then set about recruiting the people who have the identified attributes and skills to comprise the team. To operationalise the team it is essential that the team plan and future direction is articulated. Both task and relationship functions should be clearly set out. Leadership roles should either be assigned or allowed to emerge. Group norms needs time to become established but the outcomes need to be monitored to ensure that they inform positive team behaviours. When these management principles have been put in place, there is a greater chance that team members will understand the reason for their team's existence, the structure and their roles within it, and the expected outcomes. This is the basis around which an effective team can unleash its innovative and creative ideas that then transfer into real added value for the organisation.

A hierarchical organisational structure is not conducive to speed and efficiency as initiatives have to be authorised higher up the hierarchy before being implemented. Giving autonomy in decision making to teams facilitates a quicker response to change initiatives and makes the organisation more agile, flexible, and, ultimately, more competitive. The need for this has never been greater as in the modern business environment it is speed to market and first-mover advantages that are key sources of competitive advantage.

Limitations of teams and teamwork

The myriad advantages of teams and teamwork account for their prevalence in organisations, but it is important to recognise some of the limitations associated with this form of delegating authority and power. Managers have to be able to assess how team dynamics are working (or not) and act quickly to make changes or adaptations where necessary. There are numerous stresses that can undermine the structure and cohesiveness of a team and it is the role of management to recognise and deal with them. The main limitations associated with teams and teamwork include:

- team dynamics;
- abuse of power;
- cross-functional tensions and conflict;
- elitism.

Team dynamics

The success of teams depends on how well the team members integrate, collaborate, and share common aims and objectives. It is difficult for managers to predict how the different personalities that comprise the team will gel when it finally comes to them working together. Humans are complex and subject to changes in mood, motivation, and commitment. In some instances teams can be successful even if the individuals that comprise them do not share similar interests or perceptions. In others, teams may fail even though they comprise personalities that are similar. Flaherty and Moss (2007) provide some insight into the impact that personalities have in a team context and that can introduce counterproductive work behaviour. Different factors will create different dynamics such as the size of the team, leadership positions, how decisions are to be arrived at, reward systems, and so on. It is not possible to predict how a team will fare until they actually start working together. Team dynamics can be changed or adapted as things progress but newcomers still have to be initiated and accepted by the group which can prove destabilising and undermine the existing and more mature relationships that have been established (Levi, 2013). Team dynamics has been of interest to academics and practitioners as they search for the 'holy grail' of a combination that works every time. In the meantime, it is the role of management to bring together teams that they think will best achieve their remit.

Abuse of power

For teams to work effectively requires management to bestow a level of autonomy in decision making and self-management. Necessarily, this entails delegating power to the team to act in ways they see appropriate for the achievement of their stated aims and objectives. This opens the possibility of an abuse of power whereby the team (or individuals within it) act in a manner that is beyond the limits of their powers, whether those are stated explicitly or implicitly. Managers have the dilemma of allowing teams to manage their remit in a manner they see fit, whilst ensuring that their self-management does not undermine the wider aims and objectives of the organisation, or alienate other workers. Abuse of power can manifest itself in many different ways including issuing commands to subordinates not directly in their line of management; making decisions that have strategic implications; making decisions that have significant resource implications for the whole organisation; changing the composition of the team; or taking decisions that set the team adrift from the strategic aims of the organisation. Managers can circumvent many of these by setting out, in writing, the terms and conditions under which the team operates.

Cross-functional tensions and conflict

As has been noted, the formation of cross-functional teams has a number of potential advantages. However, tensions and conflict may also be a feature as bringing together people from different parts of the organisation may result in a power struggle. Each functional area will be used to a certain way of operating, and have their own distinct culture and use of terminology. Tension arises when one faction wants to dominate and continue to operate in the manner to which they have become accustomed. An example of cross-functional team failure was the *Taurus* project initiated in the early 1980s by the *London Stock Exchange*. The aim was to deliver a paperless share settlement system that would greatly add to the efficiency and speed with which trade could be concluded. However, the project comprised many different people from a broad range of backgrounds including IT, business, policy, human resources, logistics, and others. The lack of coordination and demarcated roles and authority combined with on-going

IT problems meant that by 1993 the project was abandoned as the original budget of £6 million had ballooned to almost £100 million (Morris and Pinto, 2007).

It is for management to recognise whether or not individuals or groups are team players and form judgements about their suitability for participation in a team. However, it is not always possible to determine how people will react once confronted with the pressures of teamwork. Very often it is a risk-based endeavour built on known but limited information of the types of personalities involved. For the most part it is up to the team members to resolve tensions and conflicts as they arise as this is part of the remit of forming a team. If higher level management have to intervene to resolve conflicts, it is a sign that the team is not working and may have to be abandoned or reshaped.

Elitism

The reason for forming a team is to derive some output that other forms of organising staff cannot deliver. This may be through integrating specific skillsets, bringing together creative minds, facilitating collaboration to complete a project, and so on. Teams are formed because of the distinct added value they can bring to an organisation. By implication, a team is regarded as having specialist skills or knowledge that sets it apart from other workers or groups of workers in an organisation. This is likely to have an effect on other workers who are excluded from the team. The elitist nature of the team (or the perception of elitism) may cause resentment among other workers and lead to conflict, tension, lowering of morale, and a downturn in productivity. Managers need to explain the reasons for the formation of the team, make access available to those who possess the correct attributes and characteristics for participation, and ensure that the work of those not included is fully recognised and valued.

Managing effective teams and teamwork

Teambuilding

The underlying assumption behind teambuilding is that group activity is basic to organisational functioning. The aim is to induce high levels of group loyalty and develop interactive skills which will lead to the achievement of high performance goals. Teambuilding is an attempt to structure activities so that learning occurs which will benefit the organisation in the long term—this is often referred to as T-group training (the 'T' refers to being under the guidance of a 'trainer'). T-group training is an agenda-less training experience in which the data for discussion arise out of the interaction of the group members as they strive to create a viable mini-society for themselves. The group dynamics are such that participants are informed by other members exactly how they are perceived, both positively and negatively. Advocates of this technique claim that it creates in the participant an increased self-awareness, making that individual more sensitive to emotional reactions in him- or herself and in others, which it is claimed leads to an 'understanding' that will make the participant a better manager of people. However, in unskilled hands, the emotional stress it can induce in individuals is such that it can prove to be a destructive experience, with long-term consequences for the individual. For this reason, T-group training has largely been superseded by teambuilding techniques which have a degree of structure to the activities and are less threatening to the participants.

Teambuilding activities

There are a number of ways of classifying teambuilding activities, but three of the most commonly employed are worth highlighting. First, techniques can be used both within and between groups. Secondly, they may be focused on either process issues, that is, concentrating on the dynamics of how people in a group interact, or task issues, that is, constructed on the basis of some actual work-based task common to all the participants or group members. An 'activity' is structured in such a way that it generates greater group cohesiveness around a common problem or issue. A good example of this is the quality circle, where a group of both workers and managers get together to review production procedures and suggest improvements and how to implement them, the emphasis being on improving the quality of the output. This has had mixed success, but where it has worked, management has tended to see it as a means of fostering employee involvement rather than just as a potential source of cost savings. Thirdly, although most teambuilding techniques can be classified as predominantly process- or task-oriented, many task techniques indirectly entail process matters, that is, group members learn about interaction and group dynamics (process issues) by involvement in a work-related task. Also, teambuilding techniques concentrating on process issues often use various kinds of task to highlight the process aspects of group behaviours. Car manufacturer *BMW* has developed a compelling teambuilding training programme that takes account of these factors.

Mini case 10.2
Team building the BMW way

Excellence in engineering, manufacturing, and design has been key to the success of German car manufacturer *BMW* for decades and has been well documented by Robson (2008). However, managers at BMW have also long held the belief that the most effective means of achieving high quality performance is through the trust-forming relationships that their employees have in each other. Sustainable leadership practices and teambuilding are important aspects of the company strategy for supporting this fundamental principle (Avery and Bergsteiner, 2011). In fact, such has been the success of the BMW teambuilding training programmes that they have diversified by delivering training programmes for employees of other companies. The BMW Performance Center in Greer, South Carolina is one of a number of training facilities where employees from other companies learn to trust each other, and to cooperate and communicate more effectively. One exercise in trust building involves two employees from different departments working as a team. One is the driver of a BMW who is blindfolded, the other is the navigator (Davis, 2010). There may have been tensions at work between the two participants as they operate in different departments, undertake different functions, and have a diffident organisational work group culture. However, in the exercise the driver has to listen intently and obey every command of the navigator if he is to negotiate the track successfully. The exercise is then extended to involve a blindfolded driver and front seat passenger with instructions coming from a third occupant in the back seat. These are two of a number of techniques designed to break down barriers and engender a higher level of trust between employees. Such has been the demand for the BMW training programme that the company now runs them throughout the year. Training managers at BMW believe the value of the programme lies in the new level of respect and trust between participants who can then relate the experience to their workplace and the relationships they have therein. Effective relationships are often key to performance in many industry sectors and the popularity of the BMW training programme in teambuilding is testament to the growing awareness of managers of the potential added value associated with this aspect of their human resources.

Sources:

Avery, G. C. and Bergsteiner, H. (2011) 'How BMW successfully practices sustainable leadership principles', *Strategy & Leadership*, Vol. 39, No. 3, pp. 5–15.

Davis, A. (6 March 2010) BMW program offers businesses team-building help, GreenvilleOnline.com. http://www.greenvilleonline.com/article/20100307/BUSINESS/303070014/BMW-program-offers-businesses-team-building-help?nclick_check=1

Robson, G. (2008) *Inside the BMW factories: The Ultimate Driving Machine*, Osceola, WI, Motorbooks International.

Discussion point

Do employees take company training days seriously?

Questions and task

Identify one of the training activities in the BMW teambuilding training programme.

What is the most common feature of the BMW training programme activities?

How do the training activities at BMW transfer to the workplace experience?

Online Resource Centre
Author commentary on this discussion point and questions can be found on the Online Resource Centre at: www.oxfordtextbooks.co.uk/orc/combe1e/

Empowerment

Empowerment in organisations has, and continues to be, created in many ways. Training, self-managed work groups, eliminating whole levels of management in organisations, and the use of automation are some of the techniques introduced by managers. At the heart of the effort is the need to ensure that decision making is consistent with the mission, strategy, and tactics of the business while at the same time allowing considerable latitude to operating personnel. One way operating managers do this is through the use of policies that facilitate the formation of teams with a clearly stated level of autonomy in decision making and control. Empowerment through self-managed teams is the key theme of the training programme run by human resource specialists *Bowes Consulting*.

Virtual teams

Modern technology has allowed groups and teams to work together even though they are physically dislocated. This gives rise to the concept of the virtual team where the main form of interaction is conducted electronically through various forms of digital media (internet, e-mail,

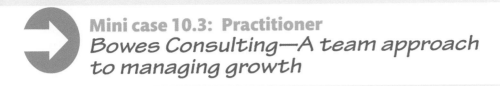

Mini case 10.3: Practitioner
Bowes Consulting—A team approach to managing growth

Established in 1994 by project manager James Bowes, Glasgow-based Bowes Consulting specialises in helping small and medium sized enterprises (SMEs) realise their growth potential through the strategic development of people and processes. In many cases this involves managing the transition from a start-up company to a larger entity with increasing functions such as production, marketing, packaging and distribution, and customer service. As distinct functional areas are created, so too does the drift from a small, integrated organisation to one that comprises a number of self-contained silos of activities. Managing Director James Bowes reflects on this by stating that 'In this scenario it is common for staff to concentrate on their own activities, meet their own performance targets and communicate only with those who immediately affect their everyday work experience. Very often this leads to a fragmented organisation where workers are neither integrated or working to a common vision. I see our role as designers and facilitators of solutions to this problem'. To achieve this, the consultants create teams of people who are tasked with working on a project that encapsulates activities across the organisation from procurement to distribution and customer service.

Key to team formation is the 'buy-in' of employees. Here, the key communications skills of James Bowes and his team are deployed to good effect. These skills are demonstrated in different ways including oral, visual, and experiential types of communication. In some instances the challenge of getting 'buy-in' is relatively easy as the participants display little resistance to what is proposed. Oral explanations often suffice in this instance. However, more commonly there has to be an element of persuasion. Here, a combination of practical demonstrations and visual aids, such as short videos or podcasts of previous participants discussing their experience, can prove decisive. These skills underpin the principal aim of ensuring that staff members understand the benefits of teamwork, the potential that it creates for greater job satisfaction, and the rewards that are associated with it. To this end the consultants concentrate the training on collaboration skills and teambuilding sessions. These include group tasks, problem solving, and role playing. By assessing the responses of participants (focus group sessions are also included in the assessment phase) it is possible to establish teams, some of which are self-managed and others not depending on the outcome of the assessment. James Bowes outlines the rationale for the approach—'the ultimate aim is to identify the means by which the client can build in self-managed teams from their recruitment strategy. The feedback from the self-managed teams relating to their experiences on the assigned project gives managers a better handle on the link between effective self-managed teams and the type of new recruits they are looking for'.

There are a number of advantages to this form of teamwork in firms undergoing a transition from small to larger scale. These include the wider communications that emerge between groups of workers; the increased feeling of being part of a wider organisation with common goals; greater and better knowledge sharing opportunities; better understanding of how the organisation as a whole operates and works; increased motivation and morale; a greater feeling of being valued; increased willingness to accept responsibility; and greater contributions to innovation, creativity, and problem solving.

Source: Based on author interview (2013)

355

http://www.
bowesconsulting.
co.uk/

http://www.
bowesconsulting.
co.uk/

What can consultants deliver on teambuilding that organisations cannot manage themselves?

Questions and task

Give an example of role playing in a teambuilding exercise.

Are there any dangers associated with self-managed teams?

What are the main reasons for establishing self-managed teams?

Online Resource Centre

Author commentary on this discussion point and questions can be found on the Online Resource Centre at: www.oxfordtextbooks.co.uk/orc/combe1e/

video-conferencing, teleconferencing, etc.). Ebrahim et al. (2009) provide a useful review of literature on virtual teams in the context of small and medium sized firms. Large corporations also feature virtual teams as they seek to integrate workers on a global scale. The BP Virtual Network allows workers to access video and teleconferencing facilities anytime, anywhere through their own home page on the company intranet.

Lipnack and Stamps (2000) define virtual teams as 'Groups of people who work together without boundaries of time or space using technology'. Although there is scope for team members to meet face-to-face the majority of the interactions are undertaken remotely. Buhlmann (2006) explains the key issues relating to the management of virtual teams using theory and practical examples. Managers can hire workers from anywhere around the globe to be part of the team thereby greatly increasing access to key skills. For example, a web design company can build a team that comprises a designer from India, quality assurance engineer from Germany, a project manager from Hong Kong, and an advertising specialist from the USA. Figure 10.3 illustrates this virtual team. As the final product can be produced and delivered via the internet there is no requirement for any of the service providers to physically meet. The team can each contribute their skills, collaborate on the project, and deliver their aims all through electronic media.

Virtual teams have become increasingly prevalent among industry structures due to the flexibility they offer. Key advantages include:

- Team members can be located anywhere in the world where access to electronic means of communication exist.
- Team members can be recruited for their specific skills or expertise.
- The team can be operational quickly and disbanded on completion of the aims.
- No overhead costs associated with physical buildings.
- Low transport or commuting costs.
- Team members can work around the clock in different time zones.
- Team members can organise times when they 'meet' via video-conferencing or other electronic media.
- The entire organisation can be virtual or some task teams set up to complete a specific task.
- Teams can be established to focus on a specified product or market.

Managers have to take into account some limitations associated with virtual teams. Although the advantages do outweigh the disadvantages there are some factors that can undermine the effectiveness of this form of working. First, the lack of face-to-face human interaction can suppress

Figure 10.3 Virtual team for a web design company

357

the team ethic or the spirit that teamwork is based on. Some team members may possess the necessary skills and competencies but prefer to work in physical proximity to co-workers. Virtual team members require a great deal of self-discipline as their work commitments are largely self-managed. If this attribute is missing it may undermine the whole team effort. Finally, working via electronic means requires a different set of communication skills compared to face-to-face relationships. Some team members may not be adept at using electronic media or understand the distinct communication skills that it requires. In fact, the business etiquette associated with new media technologies is not well developed and can vary markedly between different workers in different cultures. Managers have to help team members work through these issues to ensure that the full benefits of virtual teams are realised. Bergiel et al. (2008) provide a clear explanation of the various advantages and disadvantages associated with virtual teams and Daft and Lengel (1984) consider the effects of dislocated teams in the context of information richness.

Term
Definition

Virtual team: a team who are brought together to achieve specified aims and objectives but who are located remotely from each other and communicate via electronic media.

Case study
Les Folies Bergère Theatre

Introduction

Les Folies Bergère is a world famous, old style music hall that has been in existence since the late nineteenth century. Located in the 9th Arondissement in Paris it was originally designed and built as an opera house but also featured popular music, comedy, dance, and even gymnastics. Derived from the Latin word for leaves—'foliae', the music hall management wanted to emphasise an out-doors feel to the venue based around the Rue de Bergère. Hence, the name *Les Folies Bergère*. The venue was immortalised in art when Edouard Manet completed his famous painting *A Bar at the Folies Bergère* in 1882. The *Les Folies Bergère* caters to popular taste with shows featuring elaborate costumes and often containing a great deal of nudity. Shows also play up the 'exoticness' of persons and things from other cultures. Librizzi (2008) provides a well-researched and insightful history of the company.

Other than the performers and artists, a large, highly skilled team is needed to produce and present the shows. Most are never seen by the audience but they each play a vital role in delivering high quality productions. Although each role has distinct functions and skills, it is the ability of the back stage people to work together as a team that allows the performers to deliver an entertaining spectacle. The key is for the audience to be focused on the show and unaware of the back stage activity that supports it. Hawkins and Menear (1988) explain the roles of the back stage team:

Producer

The main responsibility of the producer is to source finance to fund the show and to manage the financial risks. Sourcing performers is another important duty of the producer. Some theatres have their own in-house producers, but most outsource this role to specialist production companies.

Artistic director

The artistic director is the creative force behind the show and delivers the programme to be presented to audiences. As the name suggests, the artistic director has to direct the production. Typically, once the production opens, the director instructs the stage managers who then 'opens the book'—the script, prompts, and cues for the performers. Lighting, sound, and scenery also come under the direction of the artistic director.

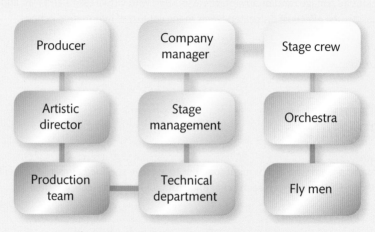

Figure 10.4 Production team at Les Folies Bergère

Production team

The role of the production manager revolves around ensuring that all technical and staging requirements are met. *Les Folies Bergère* maintains its own production and technical managers who work closely with the artistic director, the musical director, choreographer, and the engineering team. The combination of these roles helps deliver the creative team's vision for the show.

Company manager

Staff welfare is the responsibility of the company manager and can cover a multitude of activities including negotiating payments, liaising with producers on performers' welfare, accommodation, and so on.

Stage management team

The role of stage managers is to direct the performances for the show. The team of stage managers includes the stage manager (SM), the deputy stage manager (DSM), and one or more assistant stage managers (ASM). The DSM is usually positioned to the left of the stage so that he/she can issue prompts to performers. The DSM coordinates the show using a book of prompts that will include stage lighting, sound, and all scene changes. The DSM must also ensure that the performers appear on stage at the correct time and will relay 'calls' to them using a tannoy system. The calls are made at intervals of thirty, fifteen, and five minutes prior to curtain up on the show. Another important duty of the DSM is to inform the audience that it is time to move from the 'front of house' to the auditorium at the beginning of the show and at the interval. Again, a tannoy system is used for this purpose. The main task of the ASMs is to set up the props and undertake scene changes (Hawkins and Menear, 1988).

Technical department

Technicians are responsible for ensuring that the show runs smoothly and safely and that all equipment is performing properly. Technicians are responsible for sound, lighting, and any special effects. Technicians have to work closely with the artistic director to advise on what is possible and demonstrate how the application of equipment can match the creative vision.

Stage crew

The stage crew are responsible for moving props and free-standing scenery during the show. As noted above, they may be helped by ASMs in these tasks. The stage crew take charge of all the machinery that operate lifts, revolving platforms, trapdoors, bridges, etc. Very often stage crew are freelance workers hired on a casual basis.

The orchestra

The orchestra provides the music for the shows. Most orchestras are hired for the purpose, but *Les Folies Bergère* retains a resident orchestra.

Fly men

Fly men are responsible for operating scenery from walkways above the stage called 'fly floors'. Before power-flying systems became the norm, the scenery was operated manually by teams of men using ropes made from hemp. Theatres using this method were known as 'hemp houses'. Some older theatres still are 'hemp-houses' but *Les Folies Bergère* uses counterweights and power-flying.

Cross-functional team at *Les Folies Bergère*

The back stage staff at *Les Folies Bergère* form a cross-functional team taken from different departments or areas of specific skills and competencies. The team comprises a mix of artistic, technical, and managerial competencies that come together to produce the shows. A crucial element of the effectiveness of the team is the knowledge and understanding that each member has of the roles and skills of others in the team. This helps members appreciate the distinct skills, pressures, and requirements associated with the myriad roles that comprise the back stage team. This aids team cohesion and bolsters the intangible quality of team spirit that is so valuable to maintaining morale and motivation among members. The team work in an integrated and collaborative way because they understand what needs to be done and share a similar desire to achieve a specific output—namely a high quality show that audiences appreciate.

The culture of the team also helps to forge an integrated unit (Librizzi, 2008). Although there is a form of hierarchy, the knowledge that each member possesses regarding the distinct roles that each member plays dissipates any notion of a command culture whereby orders are issued and are obeyed without question. Rather the culture at *Les Folies Bergère* is one of collaboration, united by a common language and heightened understanding of why direction is issued by managers. The positive culture underpins team bonding and *esprit de corps*. In essence, the team members understand why the team has been formed, what the expectations and objectives are, and the rewards for achieving outcomes. In the case of *Les Folies Bergère* the rewards extend beyond simple monetary remuneration but include the satisfaction of contributing to an artistic output of high quality in a world famous setting. Thus, many of the motivational factors that bind the team are intangibles such as job satisfaction, being part of a team, audience reaction, and so on. Many of these intangible rewards are experienced as a team thereby further bonding the members together in a shared and common goal.

It is not uncommon for teams to work effectively in the creative industries as they pursue the type of satisfaction that more process-driven jobs cannot deliver. Hawkins and Menear (1988) provide a useful glimpse into the world of stage management and theatre administration. That is not to say that tensions do not arise. In fact, the theatre is awash with anecdotes about 'creative tensions' behind the scenes that can either spur the team on to greater accomplishments, or fatally undermine the production. One advantage for *Les Folies Bergère* is that many of the personnel are long-standing employees and have worked together for some time. In other settings the team has to collaborate and bond very quickly even though they know that they will disband after the production run ends. The context within which teams form goes a long way to determining how well they will collaborate and integrate to gain the benefits of teamwork.

Sources:

Hawkins, T. and Menear, P. (1988) *Stage Management and Theatre Administration*, London, Phaidon Books.

Librizzi, A. (2008) *Folie raconte-moi: La Fabuleuse histoire des Folies Bergère*, Paris, L'Harmattan.

Discussion point

Is teambuilding more problematic in the creative industries?

Question and tasks

Make a list comprising functions that are 'artistic' and others that are 'production' oriented at *Les Folies Bergère*.

Choose any two functions from Figure 10.4 and explain why they need to know and understand what each other is doing.

Identify five potential sources of tension and conflict in the production team at *Les Folies Bergère*.

Online Resource Centre

Author commentary on this discussion point and questions can be found on the Online Resource Centre at: www.oxfordtextbooks.co.uk/orc/combe1e/

Summary

● **Understand the reasons for the formation of groups and teams**

Managers should be able to see the value of forming a group or team of workers with combined skills, experience, and expertise that can be used to achieve more than a group of individuals. The chapter highlighted a number of examples where, in collaboration, a team can deliver more than an individual such as the output of bringing together complementary attributes or skills to form a more complete understanding of a problem.

● **Apply models for the development and implementation of forms of teams**

A number of models of team formation and development were presented as a basis for discussion. These included Belbin's model of team roles and characteristics and different types of teams such as cross-cultural, cross-functional, research and development, and project-based teams.

● **Identify and evaluate teambuilding and empowerment strategies**

The T-group model was used for evaluating teambuilding where participants reveal the positive and negative aspects of how others are perceived with the aim of increasing self-awareness and bolstering team cohesion. Empowerment of workers can be distributed using a number of different techniques including training, self-managed work groups, eliminating whole levels of management in organisations, and the use of automation.

● **Critically evaluate the advantages and limitations of teams**

The chapter included a critical evaluation of the advantages of teams and teamwork including the effect they have on improving performance, responsiveness to customers; and boosting innovation, creativity, and knowledge sharing, among others. A number of limiting factors were also presented such as the problems associated with creating positive team dynamics; the impression of elitism that they create (thereby alienating other groups of workers); cross-functional tension and conflict; and so on. Managers have to make judgements regarding the relative benefits that teams bring against the evident disadvantages that may occur.

● **Assess the relative merits of the development and use of virtual teams**

The discussion was extended to include the influence of modern technology on teams and teamwork, in particular, the formation of virtual teams who are physically dislocated but who can use digital media to communicate. This and other new forms of organisational structure indicate new ways in which people can come together to achieve aims and objectives for the benefit of the organisation. However, managers need to be aware of the problems that dislocation may have on team spirit and morale, or the need for deploying specific types of communications skills to ensure the workforce are integrated and effective.

Conclusion

Developing teams is an important but difficult management task. Difficult in the sense that there exists no formula that guarantees success; it is not a scientific endeavour. However, there are some guiding principles that improve the chances of success including giving a clear understanding of team goals, undertaking a rational analysis of the attributes and personalities of team members, creating a structure to the team, allowing strong leadership to emerge, and empowering the team by delegating responsibility and decision making powers. Groups and teams will continue to form an important part of working relationships; the type and structure of them may change, as may the means by which they communicate but the basic reasons for their existence remains the same, namely to add value to the organisation and, ultimately, its customers and other stakeholders. Modern communications technologies such as internet or video conferencing means that teams may be formed but the members remain dislocated from each other. This has given rise to the concept of the virtual organisation. A virtual organisation is a form of organisational structure and is one of a number of examples used in the next chapter to illustrate how this feature of organisations is designed and implemented to achieve specified aims and objectives.

Chapter question and tasks

Summarise the main advantages associated with virtual teams.

Why have cross-cultural teams become more prevalent in organisations in the last two decades?

Explain the difference between groups and teams.

Using Belbin's role model, identify what role(s) best suit your personal characteristics.

Online Resource Centre
Author commentary on these questions can be found on the Online Resource Centre at: www. oxfordtextbooks.co.uk/orc/combe1e/

Further reading

● Belbin, M. R. (2010) *Management Teams: Why They Succeed or Fail* (3rd edn), Oxford, Butterworth-Heinemann.
  Meredith Belbin's work on teams has become part of everyday language in organisations. The book provides a comprehensive account of teams and team behaviours. Of practical use is the self-perception inventory that readers can apply to match their own personalities to particular team roles.

● Belbin, M. R. (2010) *Team Roles at Work* (2nd edn), Oxford, Butterworth-Heinemann.
  Another important work by Belbin relates to team roles in the workplace. Students can match their personality to particular types of team roles. This work is a useful starting point for students and practitioners wishing to understand the complexities of team role formation in the workplace.

● Harvard Business Review (2011) *Harvard Business Review on Building Better Teams*, Boston, MA, Harvard Business Review Press.
  The *Harvard Business Review* series provides a practical and useful insight into a range of management issues including leadership, teambuilding, and strategy. This book focuses on teambuilding and offers the reader a clear and insightful account of the key issues relating to effective teambuilding. The work provides a step-by-step account of the ways in which managers can build a team that is fit for purpose and can be applied in real-life settings.

- Lepsinger, R. and DeRosa, D. (2011) *Virtual Team Success: A Practical Guide for Working and Leading from a Distance*, New York, NY, John Wiley & Sons.

  This is a highly practical and easy to read guide to the effective management of virtual teams. The book leverages the authors' robust global research study and hands-on experience to provide a useful resource for virtual team members and team leaders. The author provides a practical toolkit backed up with examples and insights to enhance the virtual team experience for all interested parties.

Online Resource Centre

For more information, updates, and multiple-choice questions, please visit the Online Resource Centre at: www.oxfordtextbooks.co.uk/orc/combe1e/

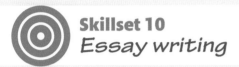

Skillset 10
Essay writing

10(a) Introduction

Many of the assessments undertaken as part of formal study involve essay writing. It is one of the most common forms of assessment and calls on a number of key skills such as research, sourcing materials, writing, and critical analysis among others. Essays provide a means through which students can demonstrate an ability to apply those skills to produce good quality academic output.

10(b) Essay writing skills

An essay should bring together both knowledge of the subject matter and the technical skills needed to compile the work. These skills include understanding when to describe things and when to offer critical analysis, use of source material, referencing, use of examples, evidence to underpin assertions, making judgements, and presentation. Other key skills include being able to:

- comprehend and interpret the question;
- articulate your understanding of the subject and the key issues;
- demonstrate analytical and evaluation skills by presenting different views and perspectives and developing logical arguments;
- source and provide evidence to support the assertions made;
- express, ideas, concepts, and judgements in an appropriate academic writing style.

> **Activity 1:**
> Find and familiarise yourself with your academic department's guidance on the compilation of essays.

10(c) Analysing and understanding the question

In the first instance, you need to comprehend and understand what the essay question is asking of you. What are the key theme, topics, and issues that are to be investigated and discussed in the essay. To help in this process you need to concentrate on three things—the content, the focus, and the task set.

- The content: the subject or topic you have been tasked to write about.
- The focus: the perspective or key issue to be considered.
- The task(s): what you need to address. Note that there can be more than one task.

10(d) Example of an essay question

Critically assess the practical application of scientific management in the modern business environment.

By identifying the key words in the task it is possible to deconstruct the question for a better understanding of what the task is asking of you. In this example the key words (in bold) focus on a number of key areas:

Critically assess:	Key academic skill that tells you that a description is not sufficient, you have to go further and offer some level of evaluation of the topic under discussion. This can be based on evidence and judgement.
practical application:	This requires the use of knowledge of how the issue under discussion can be applied in a practical way. This usually requires the use of examples.
scientific management:	The concept or perspective chosen as the main focus of the discussion.
modern business:	The context in which the discussion should take place.

Activity 2:

Find an essay question that has been presented to students in the past by your departmental staff and deconstruct it to discover exactly what is being asked for and expected.

10(e) Planning the essay

Once the essay question has been effectively analysed, and a full understanding gained of what is being asked for and expected, it is then appropriate to start the planning part of the work. In particular, the planning phase should focus attention on:

- the main content of the essay;
- the types of source information required to compile the work;
- identifying those areas that rely on current knowledge;
- identifying those areas that rely on the acquisition of new knowledge;
- identification of key theoretical perspectives as a focus of the work;
- compiling a list of key issues relevant to the discussion.

These planning elements should work in conjunction with your reading to form the draft outline of the essay.

10(f) Reading

Before embarking on the reading you should satisfy yourself that the necessary planning actions have been completed. Part of this is to confirm the main topic to be investigated and discussed. This will help you to focus your search for relevant literature on the topic. Background reading is an essential part of essay writing. Do not be tempted to start writing before you have read and fully understood the key issues surrounding the essay topic. When undertaking the reading it is useful to:

- Use a range of materials, which present different views, perspectives, and arguments.
- Have a clear focus on the essay topic.
- Read purposefully. Do not read whole books or articles (look at abstracts/summaries/ introductions/conclusions to see if they are relevant). Focus on what you need to extract from the books and journals.

The reading should be complemented by note taking. Remember to think critically about what it is you are reading, rather than simply take the word of the author as being correct. The author may be discussing the topic from a certain perspective or to further a specific point of view. Some useful questions to consider in support of the reading include:

- What are the main findings in the literature?
- Are the main findings supported with evidence?
- What are the limitations of the chosen theory?
- What do other studies have to say about the subject?
- Are the arguments presented convincing?
- Are the findings too narrowly defined to significantly add to knowledge?
- Does the author support a specific viewpoint or school of thought?

10(g) Note taking

Both in the planning and execution of the essay you should get into the discipline of note taking of relevant issues or key points. For example, you need to note the details of books, articles, and other literature for the purposes of a reference or bibliography section. It is much more difficult to revisit the source of material after the work has been compiled compared to doing so as you go along. Thus, the book title, author, year of publication, publisher, and location of publisher should all be noted. If you use internet sources you should note the full URL and the last date accessed. Ensure you know how to source information and use the library effectively. If you need help you should contact your allocated departmental librarian for guidance and advice.

Activity 3:
Find out who your academic librarian is.

10(h) Structuring the essay

Once the planning and reading phase of the work is complete, it is time to turn your attention to the actual writing of the essay. This involves structuring the work so that it has a beginning, middle, and end. This is normally set out as:

1 An introduction
2 A main body
3 A conclusion

Ensure that the essay is continuous narrative and keep bullet points or sub-headings to a minimum. Remember that bullet points are only statements of fact or opinion and do not add anything to the depth of understanding of the topic under discussion. If they are used then they should be the starting point of a discussion or analysis rather than an end in themselves. Ensure that you fully understand the guidance given by your tutor as this may vary.

General guidance relating to the structure of the work includes:

Introduction

The work often begins with a general overview statement. This part is where it may be appropriate to be descriptive in style. It may involve highlighting key issues or definitions of concepts. Invariably this includes quotations from leading writers in the field or the provision of key facts or data. The introduction can be used to map the key stages that comprise the essay and the key issues to be discussed. The introduction is usually no more than 10 per cent of the overall word count. Do not waste word count by repeating the question or task.

Main body

The main body is where the key arguments are developed and discussed from different perspectives. It is by taking different perspectives that a critical element of the work can be introduced. This is an important essay writing skill and underpins the academic aspect of the work. The judgements made must be on the balance of arguments provided and underpinned by supporting evidence. The evidence has to be robust, relevant, and achieved through the application of effective research methods. You must reference all sources in the appropriate manner (see Skillset 2, Referencing).

Use paragraphs to express ideas. Each paragraph should have an opening statement which informs the reader about the topic under discussion. Clearly identify when you are moving on to a different stage of your argument or a new area of discussion by providing an appropriate 'signpost', for example, 'However, Smith (2004) explains . . .' or 'Another perspective is provided by Jones (2007) . . .'.

The work should follow a logical progression, be coherent, and lead to the presentation of key findings.

Conclusion

The conclusion draws together the main strands of arguments presented and highlights the key points. It should be a summary of the key findings and should demonstrate that you have understood the question and answered it by retaining a focus on the main topic. The conclusions should not feature new information or new arguments. It is standard practice for a full reference section to be provided and sometimes a bibliography. A reference section consists of all those works that have been cited in the essay. A bibliography is a list of all literature that you have accessed and used, but that are not cited in the essay. When you have finished your essay always proofread carefully, checking for any errors or omissions plus grammar and spelling mistakes.

Activity 4:
Using the task set out in 10(d) the passage below has numerous mistakes and examples of bad practice when writing an essay. Try to identify what they are. Compare and contrast it with HOW TO write an essay below.

Sample essay question

Critically assess the practical application of scientific management in the modern business environment.

HOW NOT TO write an essay

For this assignment I went to the library and found some books on management. I have chosen scientific management as an example of how my company XX Ltd treats its staff. Scientific management is a subfield of the classical management perspective that emphasises scientifically determined changes in management practices as the solution to improving labour productivity. This is true in XX Ltd because we always get monitored by the line managers and the boss is really horrible. The work is boring and everything we do gets measured. We are even timed when we want to go to the toilet. Scientific management is the way our company operates because they can make more profits by making the workers work long hours for little pay with no prospect for promotion.

HOW TO write an academic essay

This essay links the operating methods of XX Ltd with the theoretical management perspective of scientific management first developed by Frederick Taylor in the late nineteenth century. Kinicki and Williams (2003) describe scientific management as 'the scientific study of work methods to improve the productivity of individual workers' (p39).

By researching the working practices at XX Ltd it is possible to discern elements of scientific management in operation at the organisation. For example, the activities of the front line workforce are subject to constant monitoring by line managers and productivity is measured. The aim of this is to ensure that no workers are underachieving or as Taylor termed it 'soldiering'.

Although there is some evidence to suggest that scientific management has helped increase performance of XX Ltd (appendix 1) there are a number of disadvantages associated with this management style. Anecdotal evidence from co-workers at XX Ltd suggests that staff morale is low. The symptoms of this are absenteeism, large-scale staff turnover, and widespread sick leave. However, the cause of the low staff morale lies in the restrictive working practices and poor working conditions that characterises the working environment at XX Ltd.

Reference

Kinicki, A. and Williams, B. A. (2003) *Management: a practical introduction*, London, McGraw Hill.

Appendix

Appendix 1: Operating profits of XX Ltd 2000–2003

367

Part

Management and Organisations

3

11 Organisational Structure

Learning outcomes

- Recognise the design of different types of organisational structure

- Understand the reasons for implementing the chosen organisational structures in different contexts

- Identify and assess the key factors that influence the choice of organisational structure

- Critically evaluate the effectiveness of organisational structures in different contexts

Organisational restructuring is a common means of effecting change and reallocating resources to achieve strategic aims. When organisations have a new management team, restructuring is often high on the agenda of the new regime leading to a period of uncertainty and change. Sometimes the restructuring is part of a planned strategy, whereupon a measure of deliberation and control is exercised. In other situations, restructuring is forced upon an organisation as the environment changes and this reactive approach is not conducive to boosting confidence among investors. Such a scenario has played out at *International Airline Group* (IAG) formed by a merger between *British Airways* and the Spanish carrier *Iberia*. In December 2012 chief executive officer Rafael Sanchez-Lozano reported that the company was losing €1.7 million per day and that the only way for the airline to survive was to initiate a radical restructuring of the business that would entail some 4,500 job losses and a very much slimmed down version of the organisation. Sanchez-Lozano declared that the company was in a 'fight for survival' and that only radical action could prevent its demise (BBC News, 2012). In such a situation organisational restructuring plays a critical role in cutting costs and capacity, changing working practices, increasing competitiveness, and realigning the activities of the organisation with prevailing market conditions.

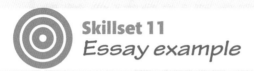

Skillset 11
Essay example

Following on from Skillset 10, this Skillset provides an example of a well-composed essay.

Definition

A structure is the grouping of organisational activities to promote the attainment of the organisation's goals and objectives. Each sub-division of the organisation makes a contribution to organisational effectiveness and within each sub-division there is a further breaking down of tasks into more focused areas of activity, which eventually translates into individual roles and responsibilities that are formalised in job descriptions.

Introduction

Organisational restructuring has become a common feature of management to the extent that many stakeholders perceive it to be an on-going, continuous process. The scenario that feeds this perception is a familiar one, that is, a new management team arrive and want to stamp their mark on the organisation and a reorganisation of human resource deployment is usually the most visible and widely felt manifestation of this. In an era marked by a turnover of managers across a wide range of industry sectors, it is not surprising that organisational restructuring is seen as a prevalent phenomenon. Nevertheless, there are some compelling reasons why organisational restructuring can deliver results as it has implications for a wide range of issues including organisational culture,

Organisational structure: the formal division of human resources and tasks as a means of managing and coordinating activities in an organisation.

staff motivation, communications, power, authority, innovation, growth, and so on. Although not a panacea for the myriad problems facing managers in the modern business environment, organisational structure can significantly contribute to achieving strategic and operational aims.

Other factors have also contributed to the prevalence of organisational restructuring. The opportunities for growth presented by the globalised economy have made restructuring a necessity as managers seek to organise resources to maximum effect in an increasingly complex and fast-moving business environment. Very often the speed with which firms can grasp opportunities in global markets determines whether or not they able to gain a competitive advantage. This invariably requires a structure that is conducive to speed, flexibility, and agility to meet the demands of customers as they emerge. In other instances, firms reorganise in order to influence the actions and behaviours of key stakeholders such as customers, suppliers, and strategic partners. However, in other settings it is not speed of change or flexibility that informs the type of organisational structure implemented. Rather, stability and security of output may be the overriding criteria that characterises the activities of an organisation. For example, the civil service in many countries depends on the quality of a process that underpins the smooth administration of a vast array of different service demands such as pensions, welfare benefits, support for public services, and so on. The organisational structure is likely to reflect the need for process control, order, and stability with clearly defined roles and lines of authority.

Technology has greatly contributed to the development of newer forms of organisational structure. For example, the possibilities for remote working have lessened the need for large physical buildings where workers traditionally congregate for a set period of time to carry out a range of tasks. Flexible working, outsourcing, and freelance work are just some of the characteristics of the modern working environment that have ensured that managers have to devise appropriate organisational structures very different from the traditional ones based on the congruence of resource deployment in one location. Indeed, it can be argued that formal organisational structures may be irrelevant in some settings where remote, temporary, and specialised resources and skills are hired for a specific purpose only.

This chapter aims to outline the evolution of the formation of different forms of organisational structure from the bureaucratic formats that characterised factories during the Industrial Revolution through to virtual organisations in the twenty-first century. The chapter begins by offering a rationale for the importance of organisational structure in modern management and discusses the key determinants of organisational structure. There follows a description, analysis, and examples of different types of structure including functional, multidivisional and strategic business units, geographical, matrix, project-team based, and virtual organisations. The discussion extends to cover the emergence of strategic alliances as a form of collaborative arrangements for achieving the stated strategic aims. Key issues for discussion also include communication, authority, span of control, centralisation/decentralisation, and the role of restructuring as part of corporate strategy. The chapter offers discussion and analysis of the effectiveness of implementing organisational structural change as a means of achieving organisational goals.

Determinants of structure

There are numerous factors that influence and determine the choice of organisational structure. They are not mutually exclusive but, rather, all play a contributory role in informing decisions about the appropriate structure to choose in order to fulfil the strategic and operational aims and objectives of organisations. Although not an exhaustive list, Figure 11.1 outlines some of the key determinants of organisational structure.

Environment

Organisations are open systems and are therefore subject to a range of internal and external influences on structure. The pace of change in the environment influences the choice of organisational structure with more flexibility and speed required in organisations that operate in rapidly changing environments such as in the financial or hi-tech sectors. Burns and Stalker (1961) emphasised the importance of environment by asserting that it is the key determinant of organisation structure. Organisations operating in turbulent environments need to have a capacity to respond to environmental constraints. Burns and Stalker (1961) termed the flexible, responsive structure as being 'organic' as opposed to the 'mechanistic' structure that is more

Figure 11.1 Determinants of organisational structure

suited to stability in the organisation's environment. Lawrence and Lorsch (1967) identified that this responsiveness to environmental influences can take place at sub-divisional levels within organisations. Some sub-divisions operate in more turbulent conditions than others and therefore require greater flexibility in their structure. Structure as contingency is the key to understanding the ways in which organisations sub-divide their activities. Structure depends on the influences exerted on organisations by a range of factors, each of which may change in intensity over time. Effective organisations are able to respond appropriately to dynamic variables such as changes in the performance of the economy; levels of employment and skills; industry regulation; availability of raw materials; the cost of production and so on.

Technology

Patterns of organisation, such as span of control and scalar chain (a system whereby authority passes downwards from the top executive level of an organisation to the lowest level), were found to be related more to similarity of objectives and production techniques than to size, type of industry, or the business success of the firm. Firms with unit and small batch production engaged in traditional activities tended to have classical pyramid organisation structures. Firms engaged in mass production tended to have flattened hierarchies but with large numbers of operatives at basic organisational levels such as in car manufacturing. In process production such as petro-chemicals, the organisation was diamond shaped with middle management being the numerically largest group responsible for a range of direct and indirect services. There were relatively few operatives as the organisation's technology required limited supervision and servicing.

Studies by Woodward (1965) have stood the test of time with the focus being on how the dominant technology impacts on the structure of an organisation. The 100 firms studied by Woodward were divided into three main groups according to the type of production system. These consisted of:

1 Unit and small batch production: firms with this structure do what the names suggest, they produce small quantities of one-of-a-kind products. The quality of the output determines that workers require a flexible structure to facilitate specialisation and innovative new designs of high quality products.

2 Large-batch or mass production: this requires a more formal structure in settings where workers perform repetitive tasks or where automated machines make high volumes of standard products. This is often to be found in settings where standardised products are produced in large quantities such as electronics or food production.

3 Automation: this third element of Woodward's studies is where a flexible structure is required in fully automated processes but where workers need to be able to react quickly to solve problems in the process production line. This is evident in some car manufacturing organisations such as Fiat or Toyota.

Technology has provided the means for expanding the types of organisational structures available. In particular, information and communications technologies facilitate relations between partners who are remote from each other. Technologies such as the internet, intranet, social media, teleconferencing, and cloud computing offer opportunities for much greater flexibility in the types of relationships and business arrangements that underpin activities of organisations. For example, the scope for outsourcing work to freelance workers has gained in currency in recent years as managers take advantage of the global labour market to acquire the skills and expertise needed to fulfil parts of their production process or service delivery. Workers or groups of workers may form effective and temporary alliances to deliver a bespoke service to an organisation via information and communications technologies. Real-time interaction speeds the productive process and allows workers and managers to communicate from remote locations. This type of structure is explored in more detail later in the chapter. Clearly, technology has had an influential role to play in all aspects of business and has been the catalyst for change in the way that managers view organisational structure in many modern business settings.

Human resources

Workers will have an influence on the chosen structure as it is they who have to operate within its construction. Enlightened management should consult workers regarding the most suitable choice of structure. However, they cannot be dictated to in this regard as other factors have to be taken into consideration too, such as the fit with strategy or the reorganisation of working practices. The nature of the organisation and the activities that are undertaken in large measure determine the type of organisational structure that is appropriate. For example, a learning organisation has to adopt a particular type of structure that facilitates knowledge sharing and has a communications system that is flexible and network oriented. Ashton (2004) analysed the impact of organisational structure on learning in the workplace.

The quality of human resources plays an integral part in this process. For example, highly skilled and creative workers who work in teams usually need a more flexible structure, neither tall nor flat, but one that allows communications to flow freely in a network of inter- and intra-organisational relationships. Felstead and Ashton (2000) trace the link between structure and the formation of skills in different settings. Workers who are specialists in a particular skill or activity within a process-oriented organisation may achieve their aims in a more controlled environment characterised by departments and hierarchical structures. These two examples are almost polar opposites and most implemented organisational structures fall somewhere in between. The key is to ensure that the organisational structure has the design attributes that facilitate human resources achieving the aims and objectives of their job. An effective organisational structure should facilitate good internal communications that can improve staff motivation and job satisfaction. Mini case 11.1 is an example of this in action.

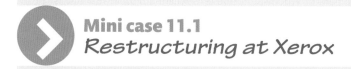

Mini case 11.1
Restructuring at Xerox

Xerox is one of the most famous names in office equipment manufacturing but it also specialises in troubleshooting repairs and problem solving when office equipment breaks down. The company has hundreds of engineers working in many different locations around the globe. The engineers have a wealth of experience and can be creative in problem solving technical problems on a wide range of different Xerox office equipment. Traditionally, the knowledge acquired by the engineers was not shared to any effective extent. Prior to the mid-1990s the knowledge that was stored and made available to others entailed a paper trail through a maze of departments in an organisational structure that was hierarchical with vertical communications systems. By the early 2000s *Xerox* was in the throes of a turnaround strategy under new Chief Operating Officer (COO) Anne Mulcahy. A strategic review resulted in a flatter and more networked organisation with information and communications technologies playing a central role in coordinating activities and improving internal efficiency. This was complemented by a restructuring of sales compensation to ensure better customer satisfaction (Cholewka, 2001).

The review also led to investment in technology that was designed to facilitate knowledge sharing among all employees in the company. The company termed the initiative 'communal expertise sharing' (PARC, 2002). Each engineer was issued with an electronic pad that could be used to log problems presented and the means by which it was solved. The information was freely available to any other employee. This way, other workers could suggest quicker, more efficient methods of problem solving, or tap into the information repository and access the range of solutions that had been logged. The savings in time and the improved efficiencies that the company could offer clients created a means of achieving competitive advantage. However, making the technology available to workers was only part of the strategy. The other part entailed changing the organisational structure as a means of influencing the formation of a dominant culture where knowledge sharing became the norm. Workers were given a range of incentives to participate in the new knowledge sharing culture including training programmes and a certain level of empowerment in decision making. Importantly, *Xerox* created a staff grading structure that included a tier of elite problem solvers among the engineers. This peer recognition of excellence provided the standard that a significant number of engineers in the organisation aimed to achieve. The organisational structure was designed to facilitate the new working arrangements and the network communications system that underpinned them. Former COO Anne Mulcahy reflects on the changes in an article for the journal *Research Technology Management* (2009).

377

Sources:

Cholewka, K. (2001) 'Xerox's Saviour', *Sales and Marketing Management*, April, 147, pp. 36–42.

Mulcahy, A. (2009) 'XEROX', *Research Technology Management*, Vol. 52, No. 6, p. 3.

PARC (2002) Xerox Corporation: Harnessing communal expertise sharing to enhance services, Ethnography in Action, Palo Alto, Xerox/PARC. http://www.parc.com/content/attachments/xerox_cs_parc.pdf

Discussion points

Can organisational structure influence culture?

Technology has been the main catalyst for structural change in the last ten years. Discuss.

Questions and tasks

What organisational type is most suited to what Xerox is trying to achieve?

What were the main challenges facing Xerox when implementing the new structure?

Do sophisticated information and communications technologies (ICTs) make traditional organisational structures less relevant in the modern business environment?

Online Resource Centre

Author commentary on these discussion points and questions can be found on the Online Resource Centre at: www.oxfordtextbooks.co.uk/orc/combe1e/

Size and control

As organisations grow in size there is less opportunity for direct supervision by senior management of the organisation's activities. In order to maintain coordination and control, structural changes are required that introduce delegation and specialisation. In large, complex organisations multidivisional or matrix structures may be the only viable means of exercising control. Size and control are interrelated. The bigger and more complex the organisation becomes, the greater is the need for formal control mechanisms. In small-scale organisations it is possible to maintain control informally as managers can see what is happening on a daily basis. This becomes increasingly problematic as the size of the organisation increases. The structure of the organisation may be designed specifically for control purposes. In settings where the emphasis is on process and output, the control function is likely to be formalised within a very distinct and hierarchical structure. As organisations expand in size or scope (perhaps to other regions of the world) it may be necessary to delegate control away from the centre. This may be in the form of subsidiary companies, strategic business units, or strategic alliances with partner firms. The extent to which control is delegated or shared will also inform the type of structure required to achieve stated aims and objectives. These are all issues that managers have to address and make decisions on. How managers arrive at decisions regarding organisational structure is well explained in Legerer et al. (2009).

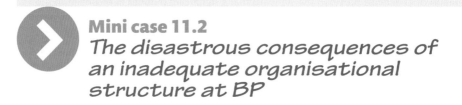

Mini case 11.2
The disastrous consequences of an inadequate organisational structure at BP

British Petroluem (BP) is one of the largest and most complex organisations in the world, primarily concerned with oil exploration and the commercial retailing of petrol products. In 2010 one of BP's oil rigs in the Gulf of Mexico suffered a blowout. The Deepwater Horizon disaster killed three workers and caused widespread environmental damage across a large swathe of the southern US coastline that seriously affected the livelihoods of many communities in the region. Various investigations were ordered into the cause and effects of the disaster and led to a raft of reports from a wide range of agencies including the Congressional Research Service in Washington DC that focused attention on the on-going efforts to address key economic and environmental issues (Ramseur and Hagerty, 2013). BP also undertook an internal investigation to pinpoint the reasons for an incident that caused considerable damage to their reputation. The final report from the company highlighted eight technical faults as the main cause of the blowout. No mention was made of how the company managed safety or how failings in their system had contributed to the disaster. In particular, BP ignored the failure of their organisational structure as a contributory factor. There is a direct link between the structure put in place for ensuring maximum attention to safety and the prevailing organisational culture (National Commission on the BP Deepwater Horizon Oil Spill and Offshore Drilling, 2011). History should have taught BP a lesson in this regard. In 1988 the Piper Alpha platform exploded in the North Sea killing 167 men. The subsequent investigation blamed an ineffective organisational structure at owners *Occidental Petroleum* (The Cullen Report, 1990). Lack of communications between one shift of workers and another led to a safety valve failing and a subsequent explosion. The disaster was compounded by the neighbouring rigs that continued to pump gas to Piper Alpha even after the initial explosion. It transpired that no operative on the rigs had the authority to turn off the gas supply. Although engineers could point to key operational failings for these incidents, the role of an ineffective organisational structure cannot be underestimated in understanding the real causes of the disasters.

Sources:

National Commission on the BP Deepwater Horizon Oil Spill and Offshore Drilling (January 2011) *Deepwater: The Gulf Oil Disaster and the Future of Offshore Drilling: Report to the President*, Washinton DC, United States Government Printing Office.

Ramseur, J. L. and Hagerty, C. L. (2013) *Deepwater Horizon Oil Spill: Recent Activities and On-Going Developments*, Washington DC, Congressional Research Service.

Cullen Report (November 1990) *The Cullen Report on Piper Alpha*, London, HMSO.

Discussion points

Do major oil companies such as *BP*, *Shell*, and *Exxon* put profit before safety?

Has *BP* become so large and complex that it is almost impossible to manage effectively?

Questions and task

Apart from the Deepwater Hozizon incident, identify and describe two major disasters in the oil industry in the last thirty years.

What type of organisational structure is in place at *BP*?

What organisational structural factors contributed to the Deepwater Horizon disaster?

379

Online Resource Centre
Author commentary on these discussion points and questions can be found on the Online Resource Centre at: www.oxfordtextbooks.co.uk/orc/combe1e/

Strategy

Different strategies require the use of different structures. A differentiation strategy needs a flexible structure, a low cost strategy may need a more formal structure. Increased vertical integration or diversification also requires a more flexible structure. (see Chapter 14 for a more detailed treatment of these concepts). Another key factor is the extent to which managers are prepared to delegate responsibility and decentralise control. In some organisations managers are reluctant to decentralise control, principally because they fear the effects of strategic drift. That is, local managers may take decisions that are in direct conflict with the desired and stated aims of the organisation. It may mean that the reputation and image of the organisation is compromised because of the increased power being exercised at the local level. The lack of strategic control from the centre may lead to the diminution of competitive advantage as the coherence of strategy is compromised. Many managers prefer to maintain a close control of operations to ensure accountability and control spending. This may explain the longevity of the functional or divisional types of structure in many industrial settings.

One of the enduring debates in management surrounds the issue of whether strategy follows structure, or if structure follows strategy. Different writers take different views on this conundrum. Chandler (1962) believes inefficiencies result unless structure follows strategy. Structure in this regard is seen as being subordinate to strategy. Others believe this underestimates the true role of structure and that strategy should follow on from the formation of structure. Hall and Saias (1980) recognise the importance of strategy but emphasise that an organisation's structure determines the strategy that management should adopt. Research by Amburgey and Dacin (1994) into 200 US companies revealed that moves towards decentralised structures were often followed by diversified strategies, thus structure determined strategy (but not all the time). With no firm conclusion forthcoming it is a debate that is likely to continue into the future.

Culture

The dominant organisational culture can influence the choice of structure. Culture can be considered as a feature of a society and also an intra-organisational phenomenon. Hierarchy can be a reflection of an organisational culture that seeks to distance operatives from decision making processes. Different countries have different structural forms in their organisations and these are a reflection of features of societal norms and expectations. Hierarchy is the norm in Indian and Japanese society and is reflected in the types of organisational structures evident in the companies and public offices in those countries. Hofstede (1989) contrasted India and Japan with countries such as the Netherlands and Denmark where there is a much greater desire for equality in society which consequently impacts on the design of organisational structure, that is, there are fewer hierarchical structures.

Culture at the organisational level also influences structure. For example, groups who acquire power and influence in an organisation can position themselves further up a hierarchy or at least be considered 'first among equals' in a flat structure. This is often the case with finance departments where the power to influence resource allocation underpins a lofty position within the structure. In some cases, it is the specialised nature of activities that determines a powerful position in the organisational structure, such as in the case of a legal department in a public agency or research and development in a pharmaceutical company. As organisational culture is dynamic and subject to change, so organisational structures are subject to change to reflect the evolving power and authority within organisations.

Stakeholders

Stakeholders can influence structural forms in situations where they can exert influence on the organisation's executive to meet their demands for greater transparency, accountability, and control. This often applies to public sector organisations responding to pressure from government, funders, and audit agencies. However, with the rise of due diligence as a control mechanism, private sector organisations in the modern business environment have to cope with ever-increasing scrutiny and monitoring of activities from key stakeholders, primarily shareholders. For example, the excessive risk taking by bankers that led to the credit crunch of 2008 has resulted in tighter regulation and closer inspection of activities and decisions by shareholders. To facilitate this, organisations need to configure a structure that allows greater communication between the management team and stakeholders. In some instances, stakeholders may form part of an internal committee overseeing activities such as corporate ethics, investment plans, or mergers and acquisitions. The ethical dimension to management activities on behalf of shareholders and other stakeholders is another important aspect that has an influence on organisational design.

Ellman and Pezanis-Christou (2010) undertook some enlightening research into the linkage between structure, communications, and group ethics in a study of US companies.

The key issues summarised offer some insight into the factors that help managers decide what sort of structure to impose. Although a minority of organisations operate with minimal formal arrangements or unconventional structures (decision making at *Semco* in Brazil is the preserve of workers rather than management, see the Case study in Chapter 9), for the vast majority of organisations there is a formal structure that underpins their activities and how they are carried out. That is why a great deal of time and effort is spent on determining the most optimally efficient structure. Child (1984) highlighted the consequences of structural deficiencies such as poor decision making, low motivation and morale, the potential for conflict through ineffective coordination of activities, poor response to new opportunities, and ineffective control of costs. For these reasons it is necessary to understand the attributes and limitation of the types of organisational structures available to managers.

? Critical reflection
Which organisational structure supports innovation and creativity?

The key determinants of organisational structure have been outlined above. However, in the modern business environment it is possible to discern another key factor—the importance of creativity and innovation as drivers of competitive advantage. To leverage advantage from creativity and innovation, managers need to be able to foster a culture that supports these activities. An appropriate organisational structure must also be carefully chosen as it is known that overly bureaucratic arrangements restrict and undermine creativity and innovation whereas fluid, dynamic, and free-flowing structures are known to be more supportive. Thus, structure can either inhibit or foster creativity and innovation.

The challenge facing management is to adopt or design a structure that supports creativity and innovation. This is potentially complex given the myriad different factors that influence structure such as history, size, growth, product diversity, skills and so on. Teece (1996) attempted to match organisational structures to types of technological innovations albeit without any firm conclusion on what type is most suited. King and Anderson (1995) and Morris (2005) point to some consensus that organic structures are more appropriate than mechanistic structures for the purposes of fostering creativity and innovation. This then provides a starting point for the type of design that is appropriate. The parameters can be defined by the attributes that a chosen structure must display. These include an emphasis on decentralisation, tasks being loosely defined, horizontal communications, greater individual authority, and flexibility. Further to these it is necessary to ensure that there is a direct line of communication to decision makers and that there is a tangible progression of ideas from problem to solution and onwards to product development and commercialisation. The structure should be flexible enough to accommodate workers operating externally but with links to the organisation. As many workers perceive some form of hierarchy within their organisations it can be argued that there is a great deal of restructuring to be done before these criteria can be met across many industry sectors.

Types of organisational structures

As organisations respond to changing circumstances, they adopt a structural form that best meets their requirements at that point in time. Traditionally structures have been divided into either tall or flat organisations. Tall structures have many levels of authority relative to the organisation's size. As levels in the hierarchy increase, communication gets difficult. The extra levels result in more time being taken to implement decisions. Communications can also become distorted as this is repeated through the firm. Flat structures have few levels but wide spans of control which can result in quick communications but can increase the workload of managers, some of whom should be concentrating their efforts on strategic issues rather than operational ones.

The issue of whether to centralise or decentralise control also determines the type of structure. The merits and demerits associated with this were discussed in Chapter 4 on Organising. However, it is worth revisiting this issue in the context of organisational structure. Decentralised operations put more authority at the lower levels and leads to flat organisations. Here, workers must be able to reach decisions. Divisions and functions can begin to lose sight of organisational goals and focus only on their small area. In many modern businesses the concept of the empowerment of workers has been given impetus by the decentralisation of power from headquarters. This allows for teams of specialist workers to take charge of projects, make decisions, and complete the work more efficiently. Decentralisation makes communications within organisations smoother and limits bureaucratic practices that stifle innovation and creativity. Here, the problems of one-way and distorted communications are minimised as decision making is carried out lower down the organisation and closer to customers. This also allows top managers to concentrate on strategic rather than operational issues. Furthermore it allows local managers the scope to negotiate contracts with suppliers that offer best value. Local managers are also better informed about their competitive environment and can make better judgements about the types of plans and decisions that bring about the achievement of specified aims. Additionally, the empowerment given to local managers can act as an important motivator and instil loyalty.

It is worth noting that during times of economic downturn, managers often become more risk averse. A consequence of this is a reining in of power and authority within organisations. A drift to centralisation of control is a rational strategic choice during times of economic downturn, although it may not always be the optimal decision (Polak et al., 2011). Even during times of economic prosperity, managers need to ensure that divisions or departments are not given too much authority such that they pursue their own goals and objectives rather than those of the organisation as a whole. There is also the danger that different divisions or departments see themselves as isolated and independent units rather than part of an integrated organisation. In some cases different divisions may view each other as rivals for resources or top management support. This can lead to a lack of communication, coordination, and knowledge sharing between divisions or departments.

Now that the key issues that contribute to determining organisational structure have been set out, it is necessary to turn our attention to the different types of structure that have been implemented by organisations. These range from traditional and long-standing types (bureaucratic, functional, multidivisional), structures that are designed to deal with increasing complexity and growth (multidivisional and matrix), and more modern forms that use technology to integrate relationships and coordinate activities (virtual and network organisations). Choosing an appropriate structure is vital for achieving stated organisational aims and objectives and requires a systematic and analytical approach (Anand and Daft, 2007).

Mini case 11.3
Restructuring at Gazprom

Russian company *Gazprom* is the world's largest gas business with core activities covering oil and gas prospecting, production, transmission, processing, and marketing. With over half a million shareholders the company operates as an open joint stock company. However, the Russian government is the largest and majority shareholder in the company with 51 per cent ownership. *Gazprom* possesses around 17 per cent of the world's gas reserves and employs over 430,000 people in Russia and its neighbouring countries. The company is a vertically integrated organisation meaning that the structure is designed around activities spanning exploration and production (close to the raw materials) through to marketing and service (close to the customers). In 2006 the company began a process of restructuring designed to improve operating efficiency by creating wholly owned subsidiaries that would be the locus of the core activities. The restructuring was designed to align with the key strategic goals of the company which included expansion and diversification of operations, improving corporate governance and transparency, enhancing the leadership's personal responsibility for decision making, and enhancing efficiency throughout the entire value chain of the organisation. The previous structure was deemed too bureaucratic and too slow to exploit opportunities in areas where oil and gas exploration showed potential but had yet to be realised. The subsidiary companies were more agile and proactive in pursuing opportunities in regions such as neighbouring Kazakhstan and Turkmenistan as well as further afield in Venezuela. *Gazprom* has also used its growing share of European markets to wield political and economic power by controlling gas supplies and influencing wholesale prices (Schaffer, 2008).

The governance of the Russian gas sector has been one that central government has been determined to reform. The previous structure exhibited all the characteristics of a large-scale bureaucratic organisation where transparency and accountability were often compromised within the complex administration-oriented environment. The wholly owned subsidiaries are independent legal entities owned by shareholders to whom the management must report and on whose behalf they manage the business. Thus the structural reform 'unbundles' the accounts relating to the core activities of production, transmission, processing, storage, and marketing and with it enhances the transparency of the costs related to these activities (Gazprom Annual Report, 2011). The restructuring has also created a mechanism for monitoring the activities of the key decision makers in the wholly owned subsidiaries by formalising shareholders' rights. *Gazprom* was the first Russian company to adopt the Corporate Governance (Behavior) Code that is used as a basis for shareholders to exercise their rights and allow the Board of Directors to exercise control over the company's executive bodies. Although the restructuring has created an organisational design similar to that of many commercial enterprises seen in free market western economies, it is worth noting that the Russian government remains the majority shareholder in this strategically important company.

Sources:

Gazprom (2011) Annual Report. http://www.gazprom-neft.com/company/organization.php

Schaffer, M. B. (2008) 'The great gas pipeline game: monopolistic expansion of Russia's Gazprom into European markets', *Foresight*, Vol. 10, No. 5, pp. 11–23.

Discussion point

Can a company be considered privatised if the government owns over 50 per cent of the shares?

http://www.
gazprom.com/
http://www.
gazprom.com/

383

Questions and tasks

Define a wholly owned subsidiary.

Is there a direct link between organisational structure and good corporate governance at Gazprom?

Explain the rationale for the implementation of the new structure at Gazprom in relation to the strategic aim of expansion of activities.

Online Resource Centre

Author commentary on this discussion point and questions can be found on the Online Resource Centre at: www.oxfordtextbooks.co.uk/orc/combe1e/

Bureaucratic structure

As noted in Chapter 6 covering Control, bureaucracies are concerned with the implementation of rules, regulations, and procedures underpinned by formal authority as a guide to how employees should behave. The design of the organisational structure reflects the characteristics of centralised power, clear lines of authority, discipline, clearly defined roles, and an ordered set of activities that transform inputs into outputs. This type of structure was typical during the halcyon days of the Industrial Revolution when the factory system dominated the industrial landscape. However, bureaucracies still exist today in settings defined by stability and control, such as in large-scale public sector organisations. Figure 11.2 illustrates a hierarchical structure typical of a bureaucracy as described by its leading protagonist and designer, the German industrialist Max Weber (1864–1920).

According to Weber, the main advantage of a hierarchical and bureaucratic structure was the clear chain of command (scalar chain) that ensured maximum efficiency in the coordination of activities. Each worker knew where they fitted within the structure and what they had to do. The span of control was small to ensure that work was supervised and carried out according

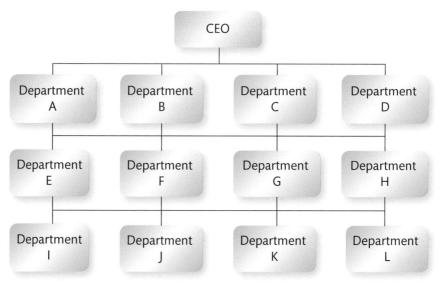

Figure 11.2 Hierarchical structure

Term
Definition

Bureaucratic structure: a tall, hierarchical arrangement of human resources and tasks based on clearly defined roles, rules, span of control, and authority.

to set procedures and targets. The structure offered certainty, order, discipline, and stability that underpinned efficiency of output. In a more modern context, it can also be argued that this type of structure offers workers a clear career progression pathway through the hierarchy.

Hierarchical structures have not been without their critics. The main disadvantages include the slow decision making process as communications have to work their way down through the hierarchy. This is because decisions tend to be top-down, emanating from top management and then being communicated downwards. This can lead to distortion of the communication that leads to inefficiencies and potential conflict. Those at the lowest end of the hierarchy may feel so distanced from the top that they feel alienated and this can lead to poor morale. Also, top level managers are far removed from other stakeholders such as suppliers and customers. This can lead to poor decision making and a lack of focus on what customers want.

Perhaps the most cited limitation of this type of structure is its slow reaction to changes in the environment. Bureaucracies tend to evolve slowly and incrementally and are not designed for speed, agility, and flexibility—many of the key characteristics of modern competitive organisations. The strict demarcation of roles and responsibilities is not conducive to the knowledge sharing that is the basis of innovation and creativity that can lead to a competitive advantage. Again, for these reasons, bureaucratic organisations tend to be found in large-scale, public sector settings rather than commercial ones. Table 11.1 summarises the advantages and disadvantages of hierarchical structures.

385

Table **11.1**	Advantages and disadvantages of hierarchical structures	
	Advantages	**Disadvantages**
	Clear chain of command	Communication and decision making tends to be slow
	High level of coordination	Communication tends to be from the top down
	Small span of control	Communication may become distorted
	Certainty and order	Poor morale at the bottom of the structure
	Discipline and stability	Slow to react to changes in the environment
	Clear career pathway	Tend to restrict innovation and knowledge
	Maximum efficiency potential	Top far removed from operations and/or customers

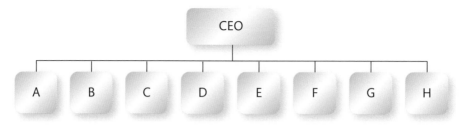

Figure 11.3 Flat structure

Flat structures

In response to some of the criticism associated with hierarchical structures, managers sought to flatten the design. The entails stripping out layers of management or setting all departments and attendant management teams on an equal footing. Figure 11.3 illustrates a flat organisational structure.

One of the main reasons for introducing a flat structure is to overcome the limitations that hierarchies place on communications and knowledge sharing. These factors have become increasingly important to modern businesses leading to a trend towards flatter structures. There is less scope for information distortion in this type of structure as communications are lateral rather than top-down. However, the main disadvantage is that managers have a great deal more employees to supervise. Also, with all departments set on an equal footing the political manoeuvring to gain the support of the top manager becomes more intense, taking attention away from core activities. The decision making process may not be any faster than under hierarchical structures as the egalitarian design means that many more views and opinions need to be heard before a decision is reached. Also, unlike the hierarchical design, workers may not be able to discern a clear career pathway in a flat structure leading to the potential erosion of morale and motivation. Table 11.2 summarises the advantages and disadvantages of flat structures.

Functional structure

Functional structures involve specialisation according to organisational activity or function. This sub-division by function remains commonplace where each key activity is carried out by a semi-autonomous group, for example finance, production, marketing, human resources. Functional structures are most commonly implemented in organisations with a relatively

Table 11.2	**Advantages and disadvantages of flat structures**	
	Advantages	**Disadvantages**
	Fewer levels encourage communication and knowledge sharing	Larger span of control means that managers' supervisory roles increase
	Less risk of information distortion	Decision making can be slowed by increased number of views and opinions
	More egalitarian and democratic	Employees have a less clear career pathway that could compromise morale and motivation

Term
Definition

Functional structure: an arrangement of similar human resources and/or tasks grouped together into departments.

narrowly defined range of products or even a single product where there is an emphasis on deploying key skills or specialisations as a means of gaining a competitive advantage. The division of labour into a series of specialised tasks allows workers to concentrate their effort on only one aspect of the necessary work, thereby potentially increasing efficiency.

Figure 11.4 illustrates a functional structure.

Perhaps the most important advantage associated with the functional structure is that it allows personnel to build specialisms in terms of skills and expertise. Once deployed in a particular function, workers can hone their skills to become highly efficient and add value to the organisation by delivering quality outputs. For example, people in the legal department become highly specialised in all aspects of the law as it affects the organisation; marketing specialists design and implement campaigns that deliver customers and boost sales; production staff ensure that the manufacturing process is running smoothly and efficiently; and so on. This makes monitoring and evaluation of performance easier for managers as it is easier to pinpoint which functions are being carried out and by whom. More broadly, the functional structure allows managers the scope to scan and assess the environment in a more detailed and systematic manner based on functional activities.

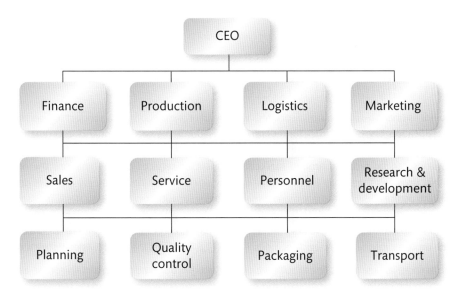

Figure 11.4 Functional structure

Table 11.3   **Advantages and disadvantages of functional structures**

Advantages	Disadvantages
Specialisation	May lack cooperation between functional departments
Better monitoring and evaluation of performance	Focus on functional goals at the expense of organisation-wide goals
More efficient environmental scanning	

Functional structures are the most commonly deployed structure, especially among small and medium sized enterprises (SMEs). However, there are some limitations to their effectiveness. For example, in a similar fashion to flat structures, the effectiveness of functional structures depends on the quality of relationships between the different functional areas that comprise the organisation. Sometimes tensions can exist between functional departments that form barriers to knowledge sharing. There may be a concentration on functional goals rather than the wider organisational aims and objectives. Table 11.3 summarises the advantages and disadvantages of the functional structure.

Geographical and product-based structures

In geographical and product-based organisational structures firms often grow by expanding the sale of their products or services to new geographic markets or they expand their product portfolio. In the case of geographical growth, organisations frequently encounter differences that necessitate different approaches in producing, providing, or selling their products or services. Structuring by geographic areas is usually required to accommodate these differences. In product-based growth the organisation specialises in activities that support the specific products or services being produced. Figure 11.5 illustrates the geographical and product-based structures.

When firms experience growth in markets and products then a multidivisional structure may be necessary to control the expansion.

Multidivisional structure

Multidivisional structures are associated with market expansion and product or service diversification. The driving force for multidivisionalisation is the need to enhance coordination and control. Each main division operates as a profit-centre with a high degree of autonomy. Divisions can be grouped around markets, products, or services or combinations thereof. Within divisions there may be functional sub-divisions. A divisional/strategic business unit (SBU) structure allows corporate management to delegate authority for the strategic management of distinct business entities—the divisions or SBUs. This expedites decision making in response to varied competitive environments and enables corporate management to concentrate on corporate-level strategic decisions. Figure 11.6 illustrates the multidivisional structure.

The main advantage of creating a multidivisional structure is that it helps to maintain control and direction whilst experiencing growth and expansion of products and/or markets. Workers can

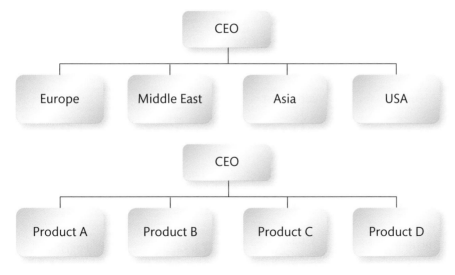

Figure 11.5 Geographical and product-based structures

maintain specialisms that focus on customer needs, something that is enhanced by the distinctive characteristics of the functional departments within the structure that are set up to meet those customer needs more quickly. This customer focus can be an integrating mechanism that binds the culture of the different divisions that comprise the organisation. The main danger of this type of structure is the escalating costs associated with creating ever-increasing numbers of divisions. There may be a duplication of effort and resources across divisions. In fact, there is just as likely to be a conflict over resource allocation as in more modest functional types of structures. Table 11.4 summarises the advantages and disadvantages associated with multidivisional structures.

Strategic business units

A strategic business unit (SBU) is a business entity within an overall corporate enterprise which is set apart from other areas of the business. This is because it exists to serve a specifically defined external market where the management team can undertake strategic planning relating to the product and market portfolio. An SBU can comprise an entire enterprise or can be a smaller

Term *Definitions*

Multidivisional structure: an arrangement of human resources and/or tasks grouped into products, customers, or regions.

Strategic business unit (SBU): an autonomous business entity within a corporate enterprise established to serve an identified external market.

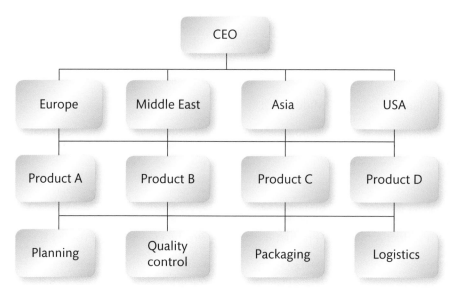

Figure 11.6 Multidivisional structure

entity set up to achieve specific aims and objectives. Crucially, managers of an SBU are given scope to develop and implement their own strategy to achieve aims and objectives that may differ from those of the parent company. Some organisations allow many different SBUs to operate independently from the centre. For example, computing firm *Hewlett Packard* is comprised of many dozens of SBUs located around the world. Figure 11.7 illustrates the SBU structure.

Breaking an organisation down into smaller SBUs gives the flexibility to adjust the structure as required and enables the organisation to change quickly in a dynamic environment. This may be as a result of changes in technology, the competitive environment, the effects of globalisation and so on. The main advantage of SBUs is the strategic use of the knowledge and expertise of managers who understand the environment in which the organisation competes much more deeply than anyone from corporate headquarters. Tapping into this bank of knowledge can leverage advantage in highly competitive industries.

Matrix structure

As organisations experience ever-increasing growth and complexity, the effectiveness of functional and multidivisional structures comes under strain. Managing organisations characterised

Term
Definition

Matrix structure: an arrangement where personnel undertaking tasks report to both functional and divisional line managers.

Table 11.4	Advantages and disadvantages of multidivisional structures	
Advantages	**Disadvantages**	
Maintains control	Escalating costs	
Maintains direction	Increasing complexity	
Helps manage growth	Risk of duplication of effort	
Retains specialisms of workers	Risk of duplication of resources	
Focus on customer needs	Inter-divisional rivalry	
Customer focus integrates culture	Risk of 'strategic drift'	

by multiple products and services across different functions in different locations is a major challenge that traditional forms of structure cannot support. The development of the matrix structure was as a response to managing high levels of complexity brought about by increasing growth and scale of operations. Matrix management is characterised by the dual-reporting relationships that underpin the communications system, rather than the linear arrangement most commonly associated with traditional structures. The matrix structure combines functional and product departments and operates a system of dual authority. Work teams operate across different functional areas. These teams are comprised of individuals who may report to different parts of the organisational line management, but who collaborate to complete projects or tasks. Figure 11.8 illustrates a matrix structure.

Matrix structures are mostly implemented in highly complex projects where collaboration is a necessary working practice. One of the first organisations to implement a formal matrix structure was the National Aeronautical and Space Agency (*NASA*) in the 1960s as a means of managing the challenge of the space programme, culminating with putting a man on the moon. One of the biggest challenges facing *NASA* management was how to coordinate the activities of the many

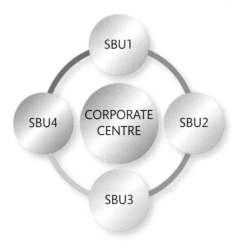

Figure 11.7 Strategic business units

391

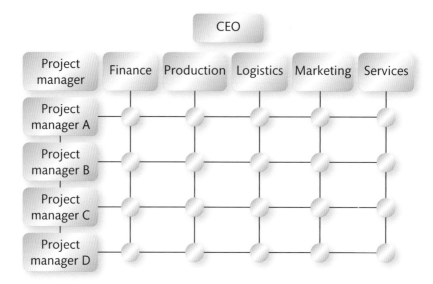

Figure 11.8 Matrix structure

hundreds of organisations that comprised the programme. Many different functions and projects had to be simultaneously coordinated and integrated in a seamless and synergistic manner. That is, no one function or project could be considered as more important than another. Traditional forms of organisational structure, such as functional or multidivisional, were deemed to be too slow and cumbersome to cope with demands of the programme and, therefore, the matrix structure was adopted as the most efficient means of meeting the challenges presented.

The successful implementation of the matrix structure in the early *NASA* space programme gave this type of organisational structure sufficient credibility for it to become a favoured choice of many large-scale corporate bodies such as *Shell*, *Matsushita*, *Nike*, and *General Motors* throughout the 1970s and 1980s. The rise of globalisation as an economic phenomenon in the 1980s gave an impetus to firms seeking to expand beyond domestic markets. As this expansion involved increasing complexity, the matrix structure was commonly used as the model to cope with the challenges that rapid expansion presented. Matrix structures were viewed as being more flexible and capable of dealing with complexity. There was the added advantage of tapping into human resource skills and experience from a wider pool of talent to ensure quality. Teams could be formed and then disbanded as required. Thus, advantages could be derived from the specialisation of work in a functional unit combined to that of working in a product team. This type of structure helps the coordination of activities and has the potential for enhancing communications and knowledge sharing. Table 11.5 summarises the advantages and disadvantages of the matrix structure.

Project-team based structure

The project-team based structures are to be found in most organisations. They can be permanent or temporary and involve the coming together of a team from different organisational functions and from different organisational levels for the purpose of responding to organisational requirements for multidisciplinary inputs to decision making. Such approaches can create problems in the relationships between the temporary matrix arrangements and the permanent functional relationships. In large companies, increased diversity leads to numerous

Table 11.5	Advantages and disadvantages of the matrix structure	
	Advantages	**Disadvantages**
	Flexible to support growth	Lack of clarity in command
	Teams form and disband as required	Complex reporting network
	Maintains specialisation of workers located in functional units and working in a product team	Politically motivated factions may emerge that undermine integration
	Helps communications and knowledge sharing	Ill-defined command can result in conflict
	Integrates functions and product areas	Increased pressure of workload on management

393

Critical reflection

Why has the matrix structure become less popular among managers in the twenty-first century?

By the mid-1990s the popularity of the matrix structure had reached its zenith. More and more companies started to struggle with the huge demands it placed on managers to coordinate the complexity and growth that the structure was designed to help manage. Part of the problem was the emergence of politically motivated factions within functional or product areas that distorted the need for coordination and integration throughout the organisation. However, perhaps the most telling disadvantage associated with the matrix structure is that each individual could potentially have to report to more than one superior. Referring back to one of Fayol's principles of management (Chapter 2, Management Theory), the unity of command remains an important axiom of management. Any confusion among workers as to who to report to inevitably leads to inefficiencies and has an eroding effect on the level of coordination and integration throughout the organisation. In some instances, this imprecise reporting structure can lead to conflict and tensions that undermine the cohesiveness that a matrix structure is designed to encourage. Finally, the sheer number of managers involved in supporting the structure can be costly, lead to indecision, and create conflict regarding the span of control that each manager has.

product and project efforts of major strategic significance. The result is a need for an organisational form that provides skills and resources where and when they are most vital.

Virtual organisational structure

Information and communications technologies (ICTs) have played a key role in the development of more fluid and dynamic forms of organisational structure. The ability of people to communicate from anywhere around the globe in real time has offered opportunities to expand the range of skills acquired, increase collaboration (permanently or temporarily), organise new forms of working arrangements, and deliver customised or personalised products and services that fit customer needs to exact specifications. One such structure is that of virtual organisations that consist of a group of companies, acting as one company to fulfil a need in the marketplace.

The participant companies in a virtual organisation collaborate on the production of the product or service by sharing knowledge, expertise, skills, and experience to produce a high quality outcome that adds value to customers. Although the companies work independently of each other, they also collaborate to meet common goals. The flexibility of the arrangement gives scope for companies to participate in more than one virtual organisation simultaneously. In fact, to emphasise the flexible characteristic of this type of structure, virtual organisations may consist of any form and number of people including individuals, teams, or whole companies. Some will be virtual workers, others will take on virtual leadership or management roles designed to aid coordination and liaise with clients. Invariably, there is a central or hub organisation that coordinates the link between the needs of the client and the formation of the virtual organisation. The scope of activities has great flexibility too. Some activities may have strategic goals, others may be short-term and task-based. The virtual organisation supports activities along the spectrum from individuals or ad hoc groups performing tasks to deliver a product or service to a client, all the way through to the coordination of large groups of people or companies to deliver a range of products and services in support of a strategic aim of a client company. Figure 11.9 illustrates a simple virtual organisation structure.

The virtual structure is created to meet a range of client objectives and aims and to respond to changes in market dynamics. Satellite organisations may come and go depending on the needs of clients and of the hub organisation. The organisation at the hub directs change and the partner organisations react to that change. The organisation at the hub does not manage the partners but rather manages the relationship between itself and the partners, and between the partners as required. Crucial to the success of a virtual organisation is a reliable and sophisticated IT system that facilitates the free flow of information in real time between all interested parties.

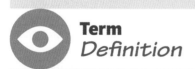

Term
Definition

Virtual organisation: an organisation that uses information and communications technologies (ICTs) to coordinate activities without physical boundaries between different functions.

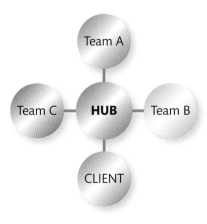

Figure 11.9 Virtual organisation

There are a number of key principles that underpin the success of virtual organisations. These revolve around:

- goals;
- processes;
- systems;
- metrics.

First, it is essential that partners agree on common goals based on the needs of identified clients and customers. There is also a need to clearly map out the process underpinning customer satisfaction from first enquiry through to completion and then on-going customer relationships if required. Virtual organisations also need to identify, install, and work with a suitably robust IT system that supports a wide range of applications including real-time communications between multiple partners and clients or customers. There is also a need for a performance measuring system to ensure that service levels and profitability are maintained. The role of the hub organisation is to organise people and match skills, expertise, and experience to the specifications of the client or customer.

One of the main drivers of the emergence of virtual organisations is the technological advances that have made communications easier and more flexible on a global scale. This has coincided with the rise of globalisation as an economic phenomenon that is characterised by increasingly dynamic and growing markets (the credit crunch of 2008 put the brakes on this as economic downturn constrained global demand for products and services). The changing nature of demand also played a role in the emergence of virtual organisations. Customers are more knowledgeable and demanding than in the past. Access to market information that was once the preserve of the supplier is readily available to customers now via the internet. This has raised expectations and ensured that companies need to provide added value in products and service in order to compete effectively.

Customisation and personalisation are key features of demand that are more readily serviced by the collaboration of partners with a range of skills and expertise that can deliver quality to specification, on time and at cost. There is also added value for clients or customers to deal with a one-stop-shop and to have end-to-end service. Virtual organisations deliver on this through the coordination expertise of the hub organisation. On the supply side, there is a distinct cost advantage of participating in a virtual organisational structure as the cost of

Table 11.6	**Advantages and disadvantages of virtual organisations**	
	Advantages	**Disadvantages**
	Flexible, dynamic, and quick to respond to market opportunities	Relies on mutual understanding of goals across potentially multiple partners
	Cost effective due to lower overheads	Relies on high level of understanding and integration across different cultures, regions, time zones, etc.
	Access to a wide range of skills, experience, and expertise	May not fit the preferred lifestyle of some workers
	Customisation and personalisation according to customer needs	Provision of training across different partners dislocated from each other is difficult to achieve
	Choice of participation entails less risk	High expectations from clients and customers

merger or acquisition is prohibitive and risk bearing. The risk factor prevents companies from acquiring other companies to fulfil customer needs. Finally, in an era marked by shrinking profit margins, many firms view participation in virtual organisations as a means of protecting against economic pressures brought about by a downturn in global demand for products and services. Table 11.6 summarises the advantages and disadvantages of virtual organisations.

Strategic alliances

A strategic alliance is a formal agreement committing two or more firms to exchange resources to produce products or services. Normally strategic alliances involve two or more organisations entering into long-term, formal relationships which are mutually beneficial, albeit all parties remain independent organisations. There are a number of advantages that have seen a rise in strategic alliances since the late 1990s. Foremost among these is that each participant organisation can concentrate on their core business whilst taking advantage of the expertise, skills, and assets of the other participants. In terms of innovation, organisations may access increased capital for research and development, but without the high level of risk associated with individual organisational effort. Participating firms may also benefit from technology transfer through the acquisition of knowledge and expertise beyond organisational boundaries. Importantly, as part of a strategic alliance, an organisation may achieve economies of scale and/or critical mass that allows them to compete more vigorously in industry sectors characterised by large-scale powerful entities. There is also scope for enhancing credibility among consumers and raising brand awareness.

There are also some pitfalls associated with strategic alliances that managers need to be aware of before committing to them. The most obvious one relates to the risk associated with entering into a long-term agreement with a partner or partners. Effective research has to be undertaken into the motives of partners for the alliance as well as their commitment to it and their ability to resource it. Partnerships are only as strong as the weakest link and it is necessary to ensure that all partners are equally capable of delivering on their commitments. Much

Term Definition

Strategic alliance: formal agreement committing two or more firms to exchange resources to produce products or services.

of the success of strategic alliances is based on trust as it inevitably requires organisations to reveal some strategic information. Trust is a dynamic concept that has to be monitored and evaluated based on experience. It is, therefore, important that each participant demonstrates trustworthiness in a meaningful way so that the agreement can prosper. Trust is closely related to expectations. Again, it is important to ensure that each partner understands what is expected of them and what they can expect from the alliance. Unrealistic expectations can damage strategic alliances and diminish trust. It may be the case that one or more parties begin to drift from the strategic aims that brought the organisations together in the first place. This could be the precursor to ending the relationship. However, as long as each partner is benefitting from the alliance, it makes economic sense to maintain the relationship.

Sometimes alliances are formed along the supply chain to include suppliers, producers, distributors, and so on. This is termed a network structure and involves a whole series of strategic alliances. Network structures allow organisations to bring resources together in an organisation without boundaries. The main advantage lies in the possibilities for sharing resources and risk. The competencies of each partner in the network may be complementary, thereby creating synergies that derive benefits to all in the network. The greater economic power created by the network allows the firms to compete more effectively and achieve greater market reach. Table 11.7 summarises the advantages and disadvantages associated with strategic alliances.

Table 11.7 Advantages and disadvantages of strategic alliances

Advantages	Disadvantages
Access to wider skills and expertise	Success based on trust
Technology transfer economies	Only as robust as weakest partner
Shared risk	Shared benefits
Increased brand awareness	Risk of sharing strategic information
Increased competitiveness	Exit strategy could be costly
Increased credibility	Difficult to manage expectations

Critical reflection
What are the dangers in forming a strategic alliance?

Strategic alliances are common feature in many industry sectors, especially ones characterised by powerful competitors in global markets. Such arrangements allow companies to combine in order to compete more vigorously and to build market share. However, many well-intentioned alliances have failed to live up to expectations. The most frequently cited reasons for failure tend to focus on management failure, culture clashes, intense competition, or lack of trust. Perhaps the most obvious reason is the lack of clear goals at the outset. History shows that the structure of the alliance has often taken precedence over the formulation and implementation of clearly stated strategic aims. For example, in the late 1980s, *Mitsubishi* and *Daimler-Benz* formed a strategic alliance for the purposes of marketing a range of cars in Japan. Although the intensity of global competition brought the companies together, it was the perceived synergies in competencies that proved the catalyst for formalising the relationship. The structure of the alliance was formulated and agreed but the strategic aims were never clearly stated. No major projects emerged from the alliance and it eventually petered out amid managerial acrimony and escalating costs (*New York Times*, 1990). The case of *Apple* and *IBM* is even more telling. These companies formed a strategic alliance in 1990 to challenge the dominance of *Microsoft* and *Intel*. Again, the structure of the alliance was established but the strategic intent was never fully formulated leading to the break-up of the alliance in 1998 (Robinson, 2002). The clear lesson is that formulating an alliance is the easy part; actually determining a strategic direction and set of aims is the more difficult but necessary part.

Case study
Organisational structure at the Ministry of Health in Oman

Introduction

Oman is situated at the head of the Persian Gulf in the Arabian peninsula. A strategically important country, it forms the gateway to the shipping lanes from the oil rich countries of the Gulf. The interior of the country is mostly desert with the majority of the population residing in coastal areas or around the capital Muscat. The rugged nature of the terrain and the remoteness of many villages make healthcare provision a major challenge for providers. Nevertheless, a well-organised and sophisticated healthcare system has emerged since a major restructuring of the Ministry of Health took place in the mid-2000s. Oman has traditionally featured as a World Health Organization (WHO) top ten ranked effective healthcare provider (MiddleEastHealthMag.com, 2005). This case study uses the Seventh Five Year Plan

http://www.moh.
gov.om/
http://www.moh.
gov.om/

(2006–2010) to outline the mission of the Ministry of Health in Oman and presents the organisational structure of the Ministry, the rationale for its design, and comments on the effectiveness of its implementation.

Mission of the Ministry of Health in Oman

The mission of the Ministry of Health (MOH) is to enhance the health and well-being of all the people of Oman by ensuring the availability of comprehensive health services throughout the Sultanate. In order to attain and sustain the highest possible level of health, MOH will co-operate and collaborate with other social and economic sectors, to protect and promote the health of the people in their bid to achieve a better quality of life. The Ministry of Health will share with the people the responsibility for achieving a state of health, which will permit them to lead a socially and economically productive life.

The Ministry of Health of Oman

The healthcare provision in Oman is mostly through the public sector with about 90 per cent of all hospitals coming under the aegis of the Ministry of Health. The public sector accounts for around 80 per cent of doctors and over 90 per cent of all nurses in the country. The remainder is in the fledgling private sector healthcare sector in the country that caters for those able to afford private health insurance. The Ministry of Health is responsible for the provision, governance, and management of the healthcare system in the country. It also performs a strategic role by overseeing the development of the sector. As part of this responsibility the Ministry is required to design a healthcare system that integrates the various specialist providers (social welfare, surgeries, disease, pharmaceuticals, consultants, and so on). As well as setting and implementing health-related policies, the Ministry has to design an organisational structure that is capable of supporting the integration of activities across the whole spectrum of healthcare provision. Ministry of Health officials are also responsible for resource allocation from government, including finance, for all health-related areas under their governance (Health Systems Profile—Oman, 2013).

Other government healthcare service providers work closely with the Ministry. These include the medical services for the armed forces and police, the petroleum industry medical corp, and the Sultan Qaboos University Hospital. There are also a number of health centres which work closely with Community Support Groups across the country and who are involved in the process of planning, monitoring, and implementing healthcare provision in their particular regions. The organisational structure of the Ministry of Health is designed to coordinate the numerous different functions that comprise the healthcare system. Figure 11.10 illustrates the organisational structure of the Ministry of Health in Oman.

The structure can be described as a functional hierarchy with the Ministry of Health at the apex and three supporting Undersecretaries covering planning, health, and administration and finance. Subordinate to the Undersecretaries are a series of director generals and directors who oversee a wide range of functions ranging from patient care to the rational use of drugs. Non-clinical bodies act as consultants and advisors to the Minister for Health and include departments covering legal affairs, public relations, international relations, and audits. The country's flagship hospital is the Royal Hospital which reports directly to the Ministry of Health thereby reflecting its status. The office of the Undersecretary for Health Affairs is pivotal to the mission of delivering universal healthcare to the citizens of Oman. Although this office is ostensibly on the same level as administrative affairs and planning, its importance is recognised by the fact that there is a more direct reporting line to the Ministry of Health. This is because the core activities of the office align more closely to the reason why the Ministry exists, namely, to provide healthcare services.

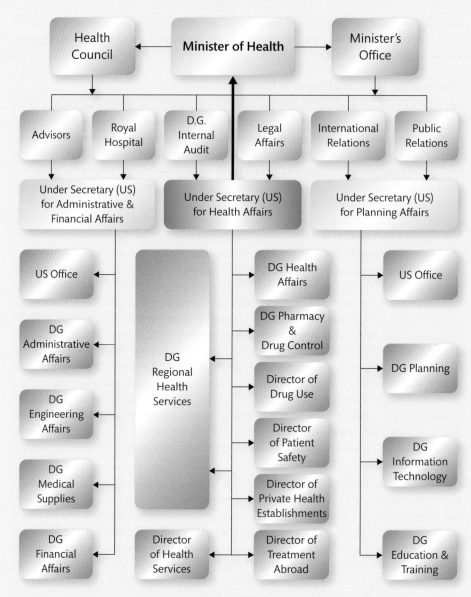

Figure 11.10 Organisational structure of the Ministry of Health in Oman
Source: Based on Regional Health Systems Observatory.

The Director General for Health Affairs (who reports to the Undersecretary for Health Affairs) oversees a wide range of functional areas including Family and Community Health, Disease Control, Environmental Health, Public Health, and Health Education, among others. The office of the Director General for Health Affairs collaborates with the directorates to develop and implement strategies for delivering healthcare to the citizens of Oman. The other two Undersecretary offices cover planning and administrative and financial affairs. Planning involves collaboration with other directorates to fulfil health planning needs and coordinates activities with providers of statistics, information, and research. Monitoring and evaluation functions feed into this process too. The offices of administrative and financial affairs cover contracts, purchasing, revenue, expenditure, and accounting and financial procedures. It also oversees employment and recruitment policies.

Rationale for the organisational structure

At first glance the organisational structure of the Ministry of Health resembles a typical tall, hierarchical structure mostly associated with large bureaucratic organisations. There are numerous functional departments that comprise the structure and there is a distinct hierarchy. Compared to the preceding organisational structure, the one illustrated is designed to decentralise control of health provision to regions rather than concentrate power and authority at ministerial level. This has to be undertaken against a backdrop of the need for delivering a wide range of different services across a diverse geographical region. The structure has to accommodate types of activities that are not necessarily process driven and therefore require some flexibility. In others, process, rules, and regulations predominate. For example, the delivery of healthcare services has a number of different dimensions to it. Some healthcare is preventative and requires innovation and experimentation to see what works best. Alternatively, the control of drugs has to be prescriptive and highly regulated to ensure patient safety. Thus, it is not possible to design a standard organisational structure that incorporates both flexibility and rigid hierarchical features.

The structure implemented at the Ministry of Health is one that demarcates key functional activities (clinical and non-clinical) so that resources can be managed in each according to need. The structure also helps the reporting system that is an important feature of healthcare and helps to inform future policy making. Here, the structure is conducive to letting personnel know exactly who they have to report to and their place within the hierarchy of management in the organisation. In a healthcare setting it is of vital importance that the decision making process is clearly understood by personnel. In a hospital, for example, this can mean the difference between life and death as some decisions have to be made and implemented quickly. The structure and underpinning command system ensures that issues of authority, span of control, and decision making power are well understood. The functional aspect of the structure also allows for specialisation. This is important in a healthcare context as the quality of provision relies on the distinctive skills and expertise of health professionals, both clinical and non-clinical staff, although the primacy of the expertise of clinicians in the profession is well understood. The functional structure also makes monitoring and evaluation of activities easier as it is possible to pinpoint the location where activities are undertaken and to put in place appropriate standards and procedures that can be measured for outcomes and then evaluated against set targets.

The effectiveness of the organisational structure

There is an evolutionary aspect to the way in which the Ministry is gradually devolving responsibilities to the regions. The structure devised and described above is the first stage of a policy to decentralise control and delegate more responsibility to the regions. In the structure, health services are delivered through ten regional health directorates. The structure is effective in the sense that it provides the mechanism for these regional directorates to plan, implement, monitor, and evaluate their own health service provision programmes within a framework set by the Ministry of Health. Importantly, the national headquarters retains responsibility for policy making, strategic decision making, national health planning, and programme design. The structure ensures that the key decisions regarding strategic issues are retained at the executive level of the organisation. Where the policy of decentralisation is most evident and most effective is in the migration of responsibility from the Director General for Health Affairs to the regional directorates. Although it will be some time before a definitive assessment of how effectively this has been carried out, nevertheless, the organisational structure as designed constitutes an important step in the direction of decentralisation.

Sources:

Health Systems Profile—Oman (2013) Regional Health Systems Observatory—EMRO. http://gis.emro.who.int/HealthSystemObservatory/PDF/Oman/Health%20system%20organization.pdf

MiddleEasthealthMag.com (2005) Regional profile-Oman: rapid progress. http://www.middleeasthealthmag.com/cgi-bin/index., cgi?http://www.middleeasthealthmag.com/sep2005/feature4.htm

Ministry of Health, Seventh Five Year Plan for Health Development 2006–2010 , Muscat, Sultanate of Oman, Ministry of Health. http://www.moh.gov.om/en/nv_menu.php?o=fiveyearplan/fiveyearPlan.htm&SP=1

Discussion points

In large-scale, complex organisations such as a healthcare provider, is a hierarchical structure inevitable?

Is healthcare service provision easier to manage in the public sector or the private sector?

Questions and tasks

Identify the type of organisational structure at the Ministry of Health in Oman.

What is the purpose of the new structure? What is it designed to achieve?

Identify and discuss some of the main challenges when implementing the new structure at the Ministry of Health in Oman.

Online Resource Centre

Author commentary on this discussion point and questions can be found on the Online Resource Centre at: www.oxfordtextbooks.co.uk/orc/combe1e/

Summary

● **Recognise the design of different types of organisational structure**

The main types of organisational structures presented in this chapter included flat and hierarchical structures, functional, geographical, and matrix structures. The discussion also included other types of structures such as virtual organisations and strategic alliances. Each were graphically represented and explained.

● **Understand the reasons for implementing the chosen organisational structures in different contexts**

The structure has an influence on so many different aspects of an organisation that it is of vital importance to get the choice correct. Not only that, but it is also important to implement a structure effectively. Issues of resourcing, organisational culture, morale of staff, communications systems, decision making, power, authority, control, and many others are affected by the type of structure implemented.

● Identify and assess the key factors that influence the choice of organisational structure

Key factors that influence the choice of organisational structure were identified as technology, culture, size and control, stakeholders, strategy, and human resources. Each will have its own level of influence in determining the correct structure for the organisation depending on what goals and objectives need to be achieved. For example, if management seeks to achieve a more integrated workforce, the organisational structure may change from hierarchical to flat to allow quicker and easier communications between workers.

● Critically evaluate the effectiveness of organisational structures in different contexts

This chapter has highlighted examples of both effective and ineffective structures and explained the reasons why the outcomes were derived. The organisational structures presented were critically evaluated for their strengths and limitations. The discussion has placed different types of structure in their correct context and outlined the aims and rationale for their implementation. Even with the correct choice, it can be seen that getting the implementation part of the process right can be fraught with difficulty. Much depends on how well management communicate the rationale for the structure to workers and how well they receive the communication. Workers need to see and feel the benefits of working within the new organisational arrangement.

Conclusion

The discussion and explanation of organisational structure in this chapter has provided some clarity on why this aspect of management is so prevalent and so important. The prevalence of organisational restructuring has reached such a level that it has become part of the stories often recited by workers as part of the narrative underpinning organisational culture. A pattern has emerged whereby a new management team arrive and prioritise stamping their mark on the organisation. The most tangible way of doing this is often seen as restructuring activities and resources. The turnover of management in modern business settings has been a key influencing factor on the prevalence of restructuring as the drive for competitive advantage. Even the public sector has not been immune from the trend with such diverse organisations as the National Health Service in the UK and the civil service in India both undertaking significant restructuring processes. The benefits that accrue to organisations that get it right are enough to ensure that this type of activity is likely to remain a common feature of management into the future. One of the key benefits is the effect it has on generating a positive organisational culture. It is, therefore, appropriate that attention is turned to this feature in the next chapter.

Chapter questions and tasks

What are the disadvantages of tall, hierarchical organisational structures?

Define a virtual organisation. What are the advantages associated with a virtual organisation?

Highlight four key factors that managers should consider when choosing the type of organisational structure.

Find an example of a company that has implemented a matrix structure. Explain why the company has chosen this type of structure.

Discuss the risks and benefits associated with strategic alliances.

Online Resource Centre

Author commentary on this discussion point and questions can be found on the Online Resource Centre at: www.oxfordtextbooks.co.uk/orc/combe1e/

Further reading

● Cuneen, P. (2008) *Organisational Structure: An Essential Lever in Managing Change*, Dublin, Blackhall Publishing.

A concise text that offers a market-led perspective to designing an organisational structure that is capable of flexibility and adaptability in a changing environment. The concept of change has been discussed in many textbooks but few have focused on the implications for organisational structure. The book is of use to both students and practitioners.

● Galbraith, J. R. (2008) *Designing Matrix Organizations That Actually Work: How IBM, Procter & Gamble and Others Design for Success*, New York, NY, Jossey-Bass Business and Management.

Galbraith starts from the premise that organisational structures that fail are down to the failure of management to implement them effectively. Galbraith focuses attention on how to operate a matrix structure effectively using case studies. The author uses examples to explain how matrix structures help companies manage multiple products, in multiple countries, and to many different types of customers. There is a systematic outline of the identified critical success factors for the implementation of the matrix structure.

● Stanford, N. (2007) *Guide to Organizational Design: Creating High Performance and Adaptable Enterprises*, London, Economist Books.

The key strength of this book is the treatment of models, approaches, and designs for organisational structures and the links to culture and group processes. The book emphasises project management as a means of problem solving in the context of structure. There is a practical exercise using a list of questions as a basis for choosing a model or design. This helps users to identify the benefits or limitations of different structural types in a practical and meaningful way.

● Thurrow, K. (2011) *Virtual Organisations—The Creation of Value Networks*, GRIN Publishing, San Francisco, CA (Kindle edition—eBook).

Thurrow discusses how the emergence of virtual organisations has had a strong impact on how companies organise in the modern business environment. This eBook offers a definition of virtual organisations and highlights some of the defining characteristics in different settings. The case study of Dell Corporation is used to good effect with a clear and lucid account of the development of the virtual organisation as the dominant organisational structure. The author then goes on to explain the key differences between virtual organisations and vertical organisations.

Online Resource Centre

For more information, updates, and multiple-choice questions, please visit the Online Resource Centre at: www.oxfordtextbooks.co.uk/orc/combe1e/

Skillset 11
Essay example

Identify the strategic aims and undertake an internal and external analysis of a chosen company. Evaluate the rationale of the chosen strategy.

2500 words

Amazon.com

Introduction

In the early 1990s Jeff Bezos left his job as a Wall Street trader to embark on an entrepreneurial venture that would lead to the creation of one of the world's most successful online businesses. The era coincided with the development and commercialisation of the internet as a means of channel communication between firms and their suppliers, customers and partners. Bezos resolved to formulate a strategy for retailing online that would harness the wide-ranging attributes of the new technology. Arriving in his home town of Seattle in 1993 he decided that his first venture into the embryonic online retailing industry would feature bookselling, with his new venture being called *Amazon.com*. The rationale being that if the transaction did not meet customer expectations their loss would be minimal in financial terms (Combe, 2006). The risk lay mostly in the reputation of the business as customers could easily switch allegiance in the e-commerce environment.

This work focuses on the formulation of strategy at *Amazon.com* in the initial phase of the firm's development between 1993 and 2000. In the first instance, the key strategic aims of the firm are identified. This is followed by an internal and external analysis using the theoretical perspectives of generic strategy, value chain, and five forces models developed by Porter (1980, 1985). The theoretical perspectives provide the basis for a critical analysis of the coherence of the firm's stated strategic aims and the choice of strategies to achieve those aims adds the necessary academic rigour to the work.

The formulation of strategy: strategic aims

All organisations need to identify their strategic aims within the constraints of current resources and capabilities. It is possible for firms to extend their current portfolio of resources and capabilities through organisational learning, redeployment of existing resources in new and more effective ways, knowledge generation and sharing and so on (Barney, 1991). As first movers in the online bookselling industry, *Amazon.com* could not take advantage of these resource and capability extending sources as the industry was in its infancy. The resources the company possessed extended to little beyond the drive and determination of Bezos to explore the opportunities that the internet offered. However, the key strategic aims of the firm were built around the capabilities that the new technology offered for creating added value to customers. Amit and Zott (2001) focus attention on value creation in e-business. Related benefits of using the internet for book buying are extensive and include convenience, greater selection, ease of use, information search and retrieval, ease of access, competitive pricing, price comparisons, and even the potential for the personalisation and customisation of service.

The strategic aims of the firm in the period 1993 to 2000 were to become the world's leading online retailer not just of books but a wide range of products and services. Another strategic aim was to extend the business model to include other multimedia offerings such as e-mail, SMS, search engines, auction sites, business hosting, and so on. The long-term strategic aim of *Amazon. com* from the mid-1990s was to become a global player in the highly competitive multimedia industry (Stockport and Street, 1999). To achieve these aims *Amazon.com* would have to become technological leaders in their industry, acquire the best skills, develop partnerships across multiple supply chains, and leverage advantage from the host of first-mover advantages such as brand recognition, customer loyalty, influence on the developing shape of the industry, and creating barriers to entry.

Internal analysis: generic strategy

Determining the generic strategy of a business is a vital decision that strategic managers have to make. In the case of *Amazon.com* the choice was relatively simple. Although the firm sought to lower costs where possible, the key to competitive advantage lay in the quality of the service they could provide to customers. The business model for the online bookselling venture entailed receiving information from customers on what book they wished to buy, relaying that information to the warehouses where the books were held, and then transporting the books to the customer. In effect, *Amazon.com* is a logistics and distribution company. The quicker and more efficiently they could achieve this process the more customers would be attracted to their website. The key to achieving this was to differentiate their service against both online rivals and traditional bookshops.

The key differentiators were the huge array of titles available to customers, 24 hour service, greater convenience, and quick delivery. Another compelling differentiator was the lower prices *Amazon.com* could offer. In the traditional economy prices are determined by the cost of adding value in the process of the supply chain. The manufacturer, wholesaler, distributor, and retailer all provide services that add value and cost. The margins added by the retailer provide the final cost to the customer. In the online environment, firms such as *Amazon.com* by-pass some of the players in the supply chain, thereby reducing the cost burden and allowing the product to be offered to customers at a lower price.

As the business model became increasingly successful in the late 1990s, so more customers were attracted to the website. The more customers that the website attracted the greater the *Amazon. com* brand became known. The global recognition of the brand acted as a barrier to entry in the online bookselling industry and, later, general retailing. Although the internet economy is well populated with potential rivals, few could match the market share acquired by *Amazon.com*. Each time a web user clicked on the *Amazon.com* website, the brand was being marketed and promoted. This so-called 'virtuous cycle' was another important differentiator that underpinned the firm's strategy for competitive advantage. Finally, the software developed by the company helps to differentiate the service from rivals. The acquisition of key skills led to the development of software that facilitates quicker and more efficient services to customers; makes navigation of the website easier; smoothes the process of ordering, transactions, and distribution; and helps build knowledge about customers through database management and customer relationship management (CRM). The relationship that *Amazon.com* has with customers accounts for the ability of the firm to sustain its competitive advantage despite many potential rivals imitating their business model.

Internal analysis: value chain analysis

The value chain analysis focuses on how much value an organisation's activities add to its products or services compared to the costs incurred in utilising resources in the productive process. Every product that is produced is the result of organising and using resources in a particular way. Value chain analysis helps managers to focus attention on configuring and coordinating resources on those activities that produce the product in the most efficient and effective way. The main questions managers have to address when conducting a value chain analysis are: what activities should the firm perform, and how? What is the configuration of the firm's activities that best enables added value to the product and allows the firm to compete in the industry? The internet adds the further dimension of a virtual environment to the working of the value chain (Rayport and Sviokla, 1995, Bhatt and Emdad, 2001). Indeed, Porter (2001) had to revisit his concept of the value chain in light of the emergence of the internet onto the business landscape.

As noted previously, *Amazon.com* can be viewed as a logistics and distribution company. The key value adding activities that can be identified using Porter's (1985) Value Chain model are inbound and outbound logistics. Service can be added to these as, ultimately, the success of the business model is determined by the superior service provided to customers. The software developed and implemented by the firm allows information from suppliers, customers, and partners to be received, synthesised, disseminated, and used as a means of setting in train a process that ends with the customer receiving the product or service more quickly and efficiently than any rival can offer. Thus, the support activity underpinning the added value is in technology development. An example of this is in the *'One Click'* technology the company developed and patented that allows the communications interactions between the firm and customers to be logged and used for marketing and other functions that improve customer service. Combined, these attributes create a distinctive capability that rivals find difficult to match and lead to a competitive advantage. Since the late 1990s the firm has substantially extended their value adding activities to include community building (customised services for customers/partners); sales interface (direct customer order intake); core information management (data management); and core handling and processing (full electronic distribution and transaction fulfilment).

External analysis: Five Forces model

The Five Forces model developed by Porter (1980) is designed to help strategic managers understand an industry's attractiveness and the influence that each of the five forces has on the firm's ability to compete. Combined, the five forces determine the potential for achieving profit within an industry sector. Each force will exert a different level of influence depending on the type of industry under scrutiny. With this in mind, it is relevant only to discuss the forces that determine the online retailing industry. Of significance here are the bargaining power of buyers and the threat of substitutes. There is intense rivalry in the online retailing industry but *Amazon.com* has been able to acquire a large enough market share to elevate the firm above the vast majority of rivals that compete for a relatively small market share. There is always a high threat of entry into the industry because capital costs of doing so are small. However, few firms could enter the industry and pose a direct threat to *Amazon.com* because of their market share and economic power. Although they have some power as suppliers, the firm is aware that customer allegiance can be easily switched with one click of a mouse. Hence, they do not exploit their supplier power to the fullest extent.

The two most important forces affecting the attractiveness of the online retailing industry are the power of buyers and the threat of substitutes. The internet empowers buyers (consumers) because they have access to the type of market information previously closely guarded by suppliers. Hence, issues related to price, quality, quantity available, delivery times, comparisons with substitutes, and so on are now readily available to consumers. Firms have to compete more vigorously for the attention of online buyers with compelling offers and high quality service. The industry is only attractive to those firms who can match or exceed customers' high expectations. The second important feature is that of the threat of substitutes. In this regard, other forms of accessing products become relevant such as traditional shopping, mobile commerce, catalogues, and so on. *Amazon.com*, like all online retailers, has been affected by these forces and has had to continue to add value to customers in order to sustain their competitive advantage. Innovations include one-to-one services, network communities, secure transactions, interactivity, reviews, book recommendations, and so on. These innovations, as key differentiators that underpin strategy formulation, are designed not only to add value to customers but also to undermine the attractiveness of substitute forms of shopping.

Strategic rationale

The internal and external analyses provide the basis for assessing the coherence of the firm's strategy given their resources and capabilities. The combination of deployed resources and resultant capabilities in adding value that leads to superior service stems from the first-mover advantages of brand loyalty, brand recognition, high market share, and economies of scale by accessing global markets. Capabilities within the organisation are manifest in the generic strategy of differentiation which is bolstered in many different ways including the promotion of the brand every time a customer logs on to the website; patented software capability that enhances logistics and distribution; continuous innovation; effective partnerships; and so on. All these either directly or indirectly lead to added value service for the customer. The value chain highlights where *Amazon.com* has channelled their resources to underpin differentiation and create a competitive advantage. Innovation in inbound and outbound logistics leads to greater customer service (such as order tracking, customised delivery schedules, etc). The support activity of technology management underpins this strategy by enhancing the efficiency and speed with which orders are taken and products delivered to customers.

Conclusion

There is a high level of coherence between the strategic aims of *Amazon.com* and the strategic choices, resources, and capabilities that have been used to achieve this. The strategic choice of differentiation has enabled the firm to focus on developing capabilities that improve performance and add value to customers. This, in turn, has led to the exponential growth of the business throughout the period 1993 to 2000 evidenced by increasing market share, turnover, expansion of products and services for sale, increasing strategic alliances and partnerships, and access to global markets (Saunders, 1999). The five forces analysis revealed that the industry remains attractive for firms such as *Amazon.com* which have been able to create a sustained competitive advantage by exploiting first-mover advantages, continuing to innovate, extend market reach, and acquire the capabilities that rivals find difficult to match.

References

Amit, R. and Zott, C. (2001) Value Creation in eBusiness, *Strategic Management Journal*, 22, pp 493–520.

Barney, J. (1991) Firm Resources and Sustained Competitive Advantage, *Journal of Management*, 17, pp 99–120.

Bhatt, G. D. and Emdad, A. F. (2001) An analysis of the virtual value chain in electronic commerce, *Logistics Information Management*, Vol. 14, Issue 1/2, pp 78–84.

Combe, C. A. (2006) *Introduction to e-Business: Management and Strategy*, Oxford, Butterworth-Heinemann.

Porter, M. E. (1980) *Competitive Strategy*, New York, The Free Press.

Porter, M. E. (1985) *Competitive Advantage: Gaining and Sustaining Superior Performance*, New York, The Free Press.

Porter, M. E. (2001) Strategy and the Internet, *Harvard Business Review*, March, pp 63–78.

Rayport, J. and Sviokla, J. (1995) Exploiting the virtual value chain, *Harvard Business Review*, Vol. 73, No. 6, pp 75–85.

Saunders, R. (1999) *Business the Amazon.com way: secrets of the world's most astonishing Web business*, Washington DC, Capstone.

Stockport, G. J. and Street, D. (1999) Amazon.com: from start-up to the new millennium, European Case Clearing House, No. 300- 014-1.

12 Organisational Culture

Learning outcomes

- Understand the definition of organisational culture

- Comprehend the key elements of the formation of organisational culture

- Appreciate and apply models of organisational culture

- Compare and contrast the different approaches to influencing culture

- Critically assess the means of creating a positive organisational culture around concepts of knowledge sharing and the agile organisation

Understanding and influencing organisational culture is one of the most difficult tasks facing managers. This is due to the intangible and dynamic nature of culture as a phenomenon that is present in all organisations. In fact, a culture can inform modes of behaviour across whole industries, regions, and countries. Many of these environments will host multiple sub-cultures thereby adding to the complexity. One industry that has had a problem managing a negative culture is that of financial services and banking. Barclays Bank has been one of a number of institutions that have been guilty of mismanagement, malpractice, and in some instances there have been allegations of criminality with the subsequent negative effect on its reputation and standing in the wider community (Chapman et al., 2012). Barclays Chairman Sir David Walker recognised the magnitude of the problem when he warned that banks in general had to prioritise reputation over profits if they are to overcome cultural problems across the industry. In particular, he criticised banks for the culture of paying staff sales-based commissions and excessive bonuses. Barclays, he claims, is at the forefront of actively contributing to changing the culture across the industry (Quinn and Ahmed, 2012). Clearly the new executive management at the company has a lot of work to do. Previously the bank management presided over a culture that allowed the illegal fixing of inter-bank lending rates (LIBOR) and the mis-selling of insurance policies. Other banking institutions have similarly been battered by the effects of a culture that put market share and profit before the interests of its customers and the wider economy.

Skillset 12
Critical analysis

Students from diverse backgrounds and cultures have different learning experiences. Some countries such as India and Korea place the emphasis on learning by rote where comprehension is the key aim. Others, such as in western European countries, have a more critical element to the learning process. This chapter helps to address the gap by focusing on what critical analysis is, how it is incorporated into academic discourse, and its value in delivering judgements on various business phenomena. The link to organisational culture is to recognise that diversity needs to be addressed and managed.

Student study skills

Critical analysis is a vital skill that students need to become competent at to produce good quality outputs. Critical skills help to shape cognate reasoning and form the basis for making rational judgements based on evidence. This Skillset explains the importance of critical analysis and offers examples to illustrate the difference between descriptive accounts of a business topic and a critical analysis of it.

Workplace skills

Critical skills are highly valued by organisations as they transcend merely process-driven activities to incorporate business and strategic thinking. This Skillset is designed to provide an introduction to the concept of critical analysis using examples to highlight the application of the technique. This is a starting point for those who are relatively new to the concept of critical analysis and will initiate a life-long learning approach to honing this crucial skill.

Definition

Organisational culture refers to the collective behaviour of people who are part of an organisation and the meanings that the people attach to their actions. Organisational culture includes values, norms, working language, systems, symbols, and beliefs.

Introduction

Organisational culture is often cited as a key factor in determining an organisation's performance such as the output of human resources, the achievement of strategic aims, or the effectiveness of change. However, it may be overly simplistic to view culture as a panacea for all of an organisation's ills or the catalyst for achieving superior performance and competitive advantage. Organisational culture is dynamic, ephemeral, and sometimes difficult to identify (Baker and Newport, 2005). As business guru Warren Buffett noted, 'Trust is like the air we breathe. When it's present nobody really notices, but when it's absent, everybody notices' (Sandlund, 2002). These characteristics present problems for managers when they seek to influence the formation of a positive organisational culture. As a phenomenon that is intangible and subject to change, managers require some help in finding the means by which they can identify, influence, and manage the formation of a positive organisational culture that is conducive to achieving their stated aims.

One of the problems relating to the management of organisational culture is the different perspectives of the phenomenon offered by different disciplines and schools of thought. For example, in management and business organisational culture is viewed predominantly as a variable factor that can be identified and managed accordingly. Alternatively, a sociological perspective of culture is interpretive and intangible thereby requiring some subjective analysis of the concept. This latter perspective makes the management of culture more problematic as it cannot be readily identified and characterised.

The output of key writers in the field over the last three decades gives an insight into the different perspectives that can be adopted when analysing organisational culture. In an important work, Deal and Kennedy (1982) asserted that 'strong cultures' had a positive effect on organisational performance. Their research noted that strong cultures emerge as a result of a close correlation between the organisation and the environment in which it exists, underpinned by shared values and well-defined behavioural rituals. Peters and Waterman (1982) took a similar view of culture and used it as a basis for prescribing means by which managers (predominantly in American firms) could motivate workers and develop a positive organisational culture. It is important to note that organisational culture does not operate in isolation from other culture-forming influences. For example, organisational culture is influenced by the social culture in which it exists. It may have an influence on the culture within other business units but it will not wholly determine it. Figure 12.1 illustrates the different layers of cultural influence.

A conceptual model of corporate culture was developed by Schein (1985) whose basic premise was that organisational culture emerged from the learning process that is a direct consequence of group interaction. His three-level hierarchy as illustrated in Figure 12.2 began with the simple notion of underlying assumptions held by workers about their working environment and the relationships that are formed within it. Many of these assumptions

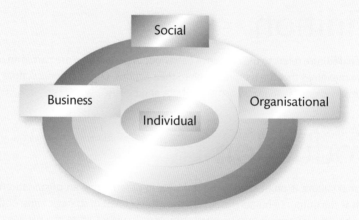

Figure 12.1 Layers of cultural influence
Source: Based on Schein (1985).

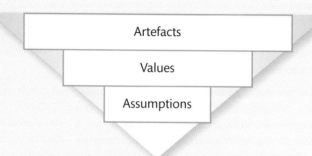

Figure 12.2 Layers of corporate culture
Source: Based on Schein (2004).

refer to experiences that are 'taken-for-granted' but that also help form beliefs and cultural values which occupy the intermediate section of Schein's model. The top section shows culture as a set of artefacts such as visible behaviour patterns, technology, and the physical environment.

This chapter presents a discussion of organisational culture. Theoretical models of organisational culture provide the basis of understanding that formation in different contexts. This is followed by analysis of how managers can manage and influence a positive organisational culture with examples of how this is formed and managed. The discussion then focuses on managing culture in the context of the modern business environment with an emphasis on knowledge sharing and the agile organisation. First, though, it is useful to provide an expanded definition of organisational culture.

Organisational culture: a system of shared beliefs and values held by workers that form a dominant culture that is unique to the organisation.

Organisations and organisational culture

Organisations exist as ordered and purposeful collections of people drawn together to produce an outcome, that is, to achieve the organisation's goals (Keyton, 2005). Sanchez (2004) asserts that the culture of an organisation dictates how that organisation is going to achieve success. There are many different definitions of organisational culture and this tends to reflect the intangible and elusive nature of the topic. However, there is consensus around the importance of key factors of shared values, shared beliefs, norms of behaviour, individual and group behaviour, and reinforcing outcomes that combine to form organisational culture as illustrated in Figure 12.3.

Formation of organisational culture

Shared values and beliefs coalesce to deliver what is understood to be the dominant culture within organisations. Values and beliefs refer to consensual, enduring, and implicit assumptions held by groups within an organisation that influence behaviour and ways of doing

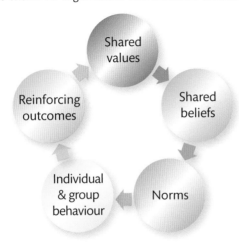

Figure 12.3 Formation of organisational culture

things within the environment. These determine how people perceive and react to changes within various environments. These values and beliefs manifest themselves in many different ways but will merge around the formation of norms of behaviour and conduct. Many organisations seek to influence the formation of a dominant culture that reflects their mission and vision. For example, South Korean car manufacturer *Hyundai* emphasise the 'spirit of creative challenge' as one of their core beliefs that they incorporate into all induction programmes for employees. Lunenburg (2011) notes that newcomers to an organisation will be exposed to these values, beliefs, and norms of behaviour in both explicit and subtle ways as part of their initiation into the fold. Acceptance within the organisation will be largely dependent on how quickly and how well newcomers adapt their behaviour to fit into the dominant culture. This form of socialisation underpins the dominance of the culture and helps it to endure.

As it is not possible to replicate cultures across different organisations, each organisation has its own unique culture that sets it apart from others. The norms of behaviour inform and link into both individual and group behaviour. Various reinforcing outcomes ensure that the dominant culture is maintained. These may range from formal codes of conduct (as drawn up in some professional organisations such as solicitors and accountants) to more informal reminders of expectations regarding behaviour.

The process of forming an organisational culture invariably begins with the core beliefs, values, vision, and philosophy of the founders of the organisation. Sometimes these dissipate over time and are replaced by new ones, at other times they endure the test of time and dominate for many decades. What is clear is that they have a strong influence on the formation of culture by guiding the behaviour of managers at all levels of the organisation, informing recruitment criteria and the types of staff they employ, and determining the socialisation process that matches new recruits' values and beliefs to those of the organisation.

Cultural norms may be communicated to workers in both explicit and implicit ways, sometime formal and at other times informal. Figure 12.4 illustrates a paradigm for communicating cultural signals in an organisation.

The cultural web is a paradigm that highlights the key points of reference from the internal environment that combine to influence the formation of an organisational culture. These inform

Term
Definitions

Socialisation: the process of persuading individuals to behave in ways that are acceptable to a group or society.

Dominant culture: a culture that reflects the core values and beliefs that are shared by the majority of an organisation's workers.

Rhetoric: artificial or exaggerated use of language.

Paradigm: example serving as a model.

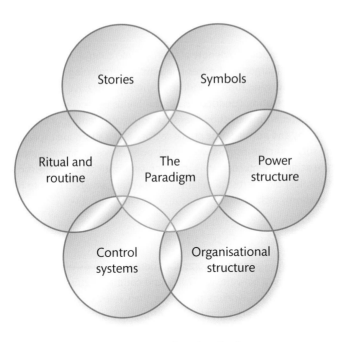

Figure 12.4 The cultural web

the beliefs, values, and assumptions that underpin the dominant culture. The key points of reference include:

- stories;
- symbols;
- organisational structure;
- power structure;
- control systems;
- ritual and routine.

Stories

The recounting and telling of stories as anecdotes about previous attitudes, beliefs, values, routines, activities, individual characters, and performance acts as an important means of communication that links historical events to the formation of a dominant culture. Stories, myths, and legends proliferate in most organisations to varying degrees. In the armed forces stories of past exploits not only serve to motivate new and existing recruits but also have an effect on the enemy. For example, the stories of operations carried out by the British Special Air Service (SAS) have helped to create an aura and mystique around their exploits that serves to underpin their status as one of the world's elite fighting forces. The stories reinforce the soldiers' dominant culture of seeking achievement in dangerous situations as they seek to live up to the regiment's motto of 'Who Dares Wins'.

Symbols

Symbols act as a reference point to denote authority, rank, control, activities and duties, company and product logos, jargon and other linguistic or terminology characteristics that are commonly used in the organisation or industry. Symbols can have the effect of guiding or influencing behaviour; creating connotations in the minds of receivers of the visual symbol; signposting socialisation norms; creating a sense of corporate identity; or communicating various forms of hierarchy and power. Some public sector organisations are explicit in linking symbols to authority, such as in the insignia worn in the police force. Academics are assigned status titles to reflect the achievements such as 'Doctor' for gaining a PhD or 'Professor' as recognition of standing in their field of expertise. Similarly, managers are assigned titles to reflect their status within organisations, such as deputy, executive, or chief executive.

Organisational structure

Formal organisations have formal structures that demarcate lines of authority, span of control, levels of power, types of activities and roles, and communication channels. Each of these sets parameters around which workers undertake their roles and fit into the specified formal structure. This constraint is designed as a control mechanism to ensure activities, power and authority, lines of communication, etc. are recognised and adhered to. In organisations where prescribed processes and outcomes are the dominant characteristics of the workplace, it would be expected that the structure would be hierarchical, rigid, and well understood to reflect these principal aims. In the UK the civil service is an example of an organisation where process and stability are the dominant features rather than innovation and change that is more evident in many small and medium sized hi-tech companies. The organisational structures are designed to align with the type of activities that are carried out and the outcomes expected.

Power structure

Formal organisations invariably distribute power to chosen individuals or groups and this is another key factor in determining the formation of the dominant culture. Here, the ability of chosen individuals or groups who are empowered to exert greater influence on work activities, routines, schedules, commands, performance targets, and other organisational issues is likely to elicit a response from the individuals or groups to whom these communications are directed. The response may be positive, negative, or relatively neutral, but each will contribute to the formation of the dominant culture by characterising the types of relationships that exist within the organisation. In some cases the power structures are formal and rigidly enforced, such as in the armed forces where rank and authority is clearly symbolised and explicit. Others are more informal and require more nuanced forms of enforcement featuring motivation techniques, communication, empathy, roles, leadership styles, and so on.

Control systems

Power distribution is one means of control system within an organisation. Others exist too including the rewards for performance, means of measuring performance, work schedules, duty rosters, quality assurance methods, reporting systems, and accounting and financial control. In process-driven industries such as manufacturing, these types of control systems are prevalent and characterise the working environment. *Vee Technologies* based in Bangalore, India specialise in business process outsourcing by carrying out back office services for companies in the insurance, banking, and healthcare sectors. The company has a highly specialised control system that records all calls and transactions in and out of the call centre; closely monitors and records the activities of workers; and structures rewards around performance as well as constantly updating quality assurance procedures. The working environment is characterised by close control and the dominant culture is performance-driven within a well-defined process (Vee Technologies, 2013). In other sectors, such as the creative industries, the control systems are more subtle and do not dominate the work activities carried out. These types of control mechanisms influence relationships, attitudes, values, and perceptions about the working environment on the part of workers. These transfer into the formation of a dominant culture.

Ritual and routine

Control systems are inextricably linked to rituals and routines evident within an organisation. Some rituals and routines are formal in character and are carried out by workers as a matter of course during their normal working duties. Air stewardesses, for example, habitually demonstrate safety procedures prior to take off as part of their routine duties. Some Japanese workers undertake group exercises before starting work, a ritual that was adopted by British workers at *Nissan's* Sunderland car plant. Others emerge informally as part of the socialisation process or may be the preserve of particular groups of workers as a sub-culture. For example, fishermen around the world display a diverse range of rituals prior to embarking on an expedition. These may involve religious prayer, drinking a toast, singing a song, or saluting an icon such as the patron saint of fishermen. Individuals may display their own routines and rituals that are personal to them. Combined, these rituals and routines contribute to the formation of the dominant culture.

417

? **Critical reflection**
What skills and attributes do managers need to understand organisational culture?

The cultural web is a useful model for focusing attention on how organisational culture is formed. Another important question that needs to be addressed, but which is often ignored, is why is organisational culture important? First, organisational culture features the human side of organisations. Understanding human characteristics and group and individual dynamics is a vital skill of management as it informs performance-related issues such as motivation, morale, and work ethics. Also, formal approaches to understanding the formation of organisational culture helps managers develop systems of shared meaning that encourage effective relationships in the workplace. This is vital in many modern businesses where issues of collaboration, knowledge sharing, and project-led teamwork are common themes. Most importantly it focuses attention on the self-reflection and self-awareness of workers themselves. In particular, understanding organisational culture helps workers to understand what impact their behaviour has on other workers and, by extension, on the organisation as a whole. This understanding is a key asset in many modern businesses where behaviour needs to be modified to align with changes in the working environment.

Cultural change

When workers refuse to absorb and react to these messages, the dominant culture starts to lose its strength and is replaced by a new culture that becomes dominant. Many factors may initiate this change. For example, the nature of activities within the organisation may change radically over time and make comparisons with the past irrelevant. Similarly the relationship between workers and technology may have a key influence on the formation of culture. Invariably technology has a role in determining work activities, schedules and design, organisational structure, skills and capabilities, rewards, and so on. Attitudes of workers to change brought about by the introduction of new technology has the potential to change the dominant culture depending on the level of acceptance or resistance to change. The 1986 dispute between members of the UK printing unions and newspaper publishers *News International* was partly over the introduction of new printing technology that was designed to change working practices and skills. The formerly powerful printing unions resisted the change but eventually capitulated after a bitter and sometimes violent dispute ended in favour of the company. The changes ushered in not only new working practices but an entirely new culture in the printing and publishing industry.

Stakeholder relations

Relationships with stakeholders may also determine the formation of a dominant organisational culture. Here, the relative depth of relations between workers and other workers, customers, suppliers, citizens, partner agencies, contractors, etc. will have an influence on culture. Some organisations require close-knit groups of workers to collaborate effectively to achieve their aims. This may create a sub-culture within an overarching dominant culture (McShane and Travaglione, 2005; Vecchio et al., 2005). By creating divisions or departments, managers create a structure that is designed to compartmentalise groups of workers and set them apart from each other. This may encourage the emergence of several sub-cultures rather than one dominant organisational culture. The reason for doing so may stem from managers' perception that the dominant culture is not conducive to achieving their aims and so they deliberately fragment it by creating barriers to the development of one dominant culture. Alternatively, managers may require greater innovation within the organisation and seek to facilitate this with the creation of small groups of workers engaged on specific projects with their own set aims and empowered to make decisions (Robbins et al., 2004).

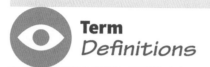

Term
Definitions

Sub-cultures: separate and distinct mini-cultures that form among groups of workers who are separated from other workers through geographical location, function, or structure.

Stakeholders: individuals or groups who affect, or who are affected by, the activities of an organisation.

Management style

The management style is another relationship-orientated factor that influences culture. Workers will react differently to different types of management style such as unitary, pluralist, cooperative, autocratic, or coercive (see also Chapter 1). The management style has a direct impact on the relationships that exist within an organisation. Workers and managers will have expectations of each other in terms of how their mutual working relationship should be. The potential for conflict is heightened where gaps exist between those expectations. Formal methods of aligning the expectations have to be implemented alongside informal methods and this is where the management style becomes important. Issues of communication, motivation, leading, interpersonal skills, empathy, inspiration, and others may all feature to varying degrees in the management style evident within an organisation and from which organisational culture is influenced.

Organisation size and location

The size of the organisation will have an influence on the chosen structure, power relations, and working practices and, by consequence, the emergence of the organisational culture. Culture-influencing factors such as rules and regulations, reporting procedures, communications systems, coordination, and control will be created according to the overall size and complexity of the organisation. Even the geographical location of the organisation will influence culture as workers will react differently to being situated in urban areas as compared to industrial parks on the edge of towns; or in areas physically distant from customers or suppliers; or where the business is close to competitors. This is particularly relevant to many modern businesses where even their own staff may be physically remote from the corporate headquarters or business units. Outsourcing services is a common feature of modern businesses where workers rarely, if ever, meet physically and their tenure of work may be temporary. This type of business will have a distinctly different type of culture compared to one where all staff are physically located in the same building.

Critical reflection
Can individuals influence the formation of a dominant organisational culture?

Much of the discussion on organisational culture assumes that it is a group dynamic that is co-ordinated and self-contained. This ignores the fact that some individuals within organisations may have the ability to influence the way in which a dominant culture emerges. Individuals can acquire status by displaying attitudes, values, and beliefs that are in conflict with the prevailing dominant culture, but which may reflect the aspirations of others. This may initiate a following that translates into a new sub-culture or even a dominant organisational culture. Individuals can use personal characteristics such as charisma, personality, communications skills, and empathy to influence culture. For example, Lech Walesa of the Polish shipyard workers' trade union achieved iconic status in the early 1980s through his personality and his pursuit of greater workers' rights changed the organisational culture from one of passive resistance to active disobedience and was the catalyst for change in the working environment.

Term
Definition

Outsourcing: arranging for a function or activity to be undertaken by an external agency rather than by those within the organisation.

Models of organisational culture

Models of organisational culture help to focus attention on the key characteristics of culture, the means by which it develops and the influence it has on determining the dominant culture in an organisation. Handy (1976) outlined four main types of organisational culture including power culture, people culture, task culture, and role culture as illustrated in Table 12.1.

Power culture

A power culture is one characterised by the relationship between workers and the individual upon whom power is bestowed. Consequently, a power culture has at its core the individual who wields power. The way in which this power is used is crucial in understanding the effectiveness of a power culture. Workers will react in different ways according to the means by which a power culture is expressed by the individual at the core. In many ways the efficiency and performance of the organisation depends on how this dynamic plays out. A power culture is sustained when workers believe in and follow the leadership of the individual with power. Without followers there can be no leadership, and without leadership there can be no legitimate power (Drucker, 1997). Alternatively, those with power may lose trust in the ability of workers to achieve stated aims. Here, the power culture is likely to be eroded unless replacement workers can be found who are deemed capable of sharing the confidence of the individual with power.

Other factors that undermine the sustainability of a power culture are the increasing size of an organisation and the departure of the individual with power from the organisation. In the former, control of power becomes more problematic as its influence is spread more thinly. In

Table 12.1 Types of organisational culture

POWER CULTURE	PEOPLE CULTURE
TASK CULTURE	ROLE CULTURE

the latter, it may not be possible to replicate the same power culture when a dominant individual leaves the organisation. That individual may have displayed attributes or characteristics that are unique to the individual such as management style and flair, respect among peers and workers, influence in political circles, distinct interpersonal skills, or a persona that is inextricably linked to the brand.

People culture

A people culture results from the coordinated efforts of a group of people to create an organisation with the purpose of mutual benefits to the members of that group. The organisation may exist within a bigger organisation such as a special interest group or research group, or it may be a separate entity formed for a specific purpose such as a sports club or protest group. There has to be a common interest and shared aims that provides the cohesion for the maintenance of the group and the sustainability of the people culture. Charities and voluntary organisations typically exhibit characteristics of a people culture where the overriding aim of the organisation is the key factor in bringing people together. One of many such organisations is Dutch charity *Vialisa* that specialises in bringing together volunteers to support the improvement of future prospects for working youngsters in Bangladesh. The culture of the organisation is people centred whereby ideas can be transformed into practical measures to contribute to the organisation's aims.

Task culture

Task cultures are linked to particular activities that take place within organisations such as sales, marketing, production, customer service, logistics, and so on. Groups of workers will be assigned to carry out specific tasks and are very often formed into groups to effect this. The groups can specialise in achieving specified aims by adopting a flexible and dynamic culture that is capable of accommodating workers from across the organisation depending on need and experience and the skills that they can offer. Project management is often based on a task culture where the combination of various staff skills and expertise are brought to bear in the quest to complete set tasks. In many modern businesses this is necessary for innovation in product and service development, testing, and commercialisation that adds value to customers and helps gain a competitive advantage. The task defines the culture and informs the attitudes and behaviours of people operating within the groups assigned to complete the tasks.

Role culture

The activities undertaken in an organisation determine the types of roles that need to be carried out by individuals or groups therein. These roles are likely to be well-established in the organisation and are created to lend a certain level of stability and efficiency to the activities, processes, and outcomes of the organisation. Role cultures are often associated with hierarchical structures where authority and span of control are well-defined and specific roles are universally recognised. Although close to power cultures, role cultures emphasise the nature of the activities undertaken rather than any power or authority that aligns to those roles.

The models presented are useful for setting the scene and identifying possible determinants for the formation of an organisational culture. However, it is necessary to bear in mind the limiting effect that building in assumptions has to theoretical models. Sometimes the assumptions merely reflect the ideology or rhetoric of management rather than help to support a greater insight of organisational culture as a phenomenon. The idea that managers can undertake forms of 'social engineering' to deliver a strong and positive culture for the achievement of corporate aims and objectives is dubious at best. Some influence may be exerted but the link to the formation of a distinct organisational culture that fits in with management desires is unlikely. The complexity of organisational culture and the myriad of sub-cultures that comprise it makes effective intervention problematic and unwieldy. The sub-cultures are often the source of tension and conflict and are often found to be working against each other. That is, organisational culture rarely, if ever, comprises a single and unified entity. Nevertheless, managers do seek to exert some influence on the formation of a positive organisational culture and it is worth exploring this in more detail.

Managing and influencing a positive organisational culture

Since organisational culture contributes to effective relationships, efficiency of tasks, acceptance of change, performance and other key organisational issues, managers have a vested interest in how best to exert an influence that helps to create a positive culture. Some organisations exhibit strong cultures where the organisation's values and beliefs are firmly held and widely shared among the workforce. In others the link is tenuous or weak. The relative strength or weakness of an organisational culture will have a bearing on the level of behavioural control. For example, in organisations with a strong culture shared beliefs manifest themselves in the form of loyalty, workforce cohesion, commitment, and unity of purpose. In organisations where the culture is weak there is more likely to be fragmentation of workers' attitudes as there is no evident sense of purpose that bonds workers. This may be reflected in relatively high staff turnover as loyalty and commitment are less evident in weak cultures.

An aim of management is to influence the creation of a strong and positive organisational culture. Some critical success factors underpin this, including devising and communicating a clear vision of what the organisation stands for and what its strategic aims are. Workers need to be able to 'buy into' the vision of the organisation in order to make sense of their role in attaining the ideals that underpin the vision. Here, managers need to be able to communicate their vision for the future that is both understandable and attractive to workers. The development of a strategic direction for the organisation that workers perceive as coherent and achievable

Term Definitions

Strong culture: a culture in which the organisation's core values and beliefs are widely and intensely shared by the majority of workers.

Vision: desired future state; the aspiration of the organisation.

also acts as a means of building a strong and positive organisational culture. A strategy is a set of plans designed to achieve the long-term aims of an organisation. It requires change, a significant reallocation of resources, reconfiguration of the organisational structure, and different approaches to undertaking activities internally. This presents a challenge to the workforce who may prefer the status quo. In strong and positive cultures the workforce may be open to change and accept it as a necessary part of their working environment. In weak cultures the response may be negative and lead to resistance. Readiness to change will vary across national cultures, industries, and organisations (Susanto, 2008).

Managers can influence a positive organisational culture by delegating more responsibility and power to workers. This may lead to higher levels of commitment as the stakeholder value is increased by offering a greater vested interest in the welfare and performance of the organisation. Research by Dennison et al. (2004) pointed to the empowering of employees and how restructuring around the creation of project teams acts as a stimulus to the development of a strong and positive culture and the enhanced performance that stems from it. It is worth noting that these influencing factors generate different responses in different parts of the world. For example, in countries with well-defined and rigid social norms such as Japan and South Korea, ideals of empowerment elicit a weaker response than societies that are more individualistic, liberal, and diverse such as the United States. Thus, making generalisations about the effectiveness of particular influential factors is inappropriate. This is particularly the case when trying to transfer management techniques developed in one country to that of another when the two exhibit vastly different cultures, traditions, social structures, and levels of development. National cultures have an influential role in determining the effectiveness of organisational cultures. Hofstede (1980) derived distinctions between national cultures using four key dimensions including:

- *Power distance*: the level of acceptance among less powerful members of organisations or institutions that power is distributed unequally. The physical and psychological distance that exists between people and the sources of power (e.g. high power distance–Malaysia, low power distance–Sweden).
- *Individualism versus collectivism*: the extent to which individuals expect to take care of themselves or expect to collect into groups to achieve a common good (e.g. individualist–USA, collectivist–Indonesia).
- *Masculinity versus femininity*: assertiveness and competitiveness versus modesty and caring. Masculinity exhibits values of money, power, material wealth, and success; feminine values are concerned with sensitivity, caring, welfare, the needs of others, and the quality of life (e.g. masculine–Argentina, feminine–Denmark).
- *Uncertainty avoidance*: level of tolerance towards uncertainty and ambiguity (e.g. high uncertainty avoidance–Greece, low uncertainty avoidance–Singapore).

Some countries have social and cultural dimensions that more easily adapt to change than others. Western nations such as the Netherlands and the UK absorb new cultural influences far more easily than traditional countries where deeply embedded belief systems are evident. Mini case 12.1 discusses the problems facing Saudi Arabia as the country seeks to become more competitive in global markets within a very traditional, tribal, and strict religious-centred society. The case illustrates the difficulties of integrating western methods of business in a strong and deeply entrenched culture.

Managers may try to influence the creation of a positive culture by introducing incentives and opportunities for workers to bond more closely as a unit. Incentives may include economic rewards for enhanced performance that is reliant on group or team cohesion. This may encourage the development of *esprit de corps* and create a positive and collaborative work ethic.

Critical reflection
How robust is Hofstede's national trait model in a global economy characterised by diversity?

Although Hofstede undertook extensive research covering many organisations across some forty different countries, it is necessary to exercise some caution when interpreting the outcomes. First, cultures are dynamic and evolving, making the assignment of traits or characteristics to them problematic. Any national trait is likely to be short-lived as new influences change the nature of the culture. For example, the Americanisation of many cultures around the globe through media communication, advertising, and consumerism has eroded the strength of indigenous cultures in some parts of the globe. Also, globalisation, political change, and social mobility have created a more multicultural and diverse national characteristic in many countries such as the UK. Demographic, social, and political change has been the catalyst for many different cultures to co-exist in the same country. These changes have been evident within organisations too, as their human resources are inevitably a reflection of the society in which they operate. These factors make it difficult to fully subscribe to the findings presented by Hofstede and point to the need to update and revise the research framework in light of the considerable changes to national cultures that have evolved since his seminal work was first published in the early 1980s.

Mini case 12.1
Organisational culture in Saudi Arabia

The work by Hofstede initiated a period of further research into the role of national and organisational cultures on the performance of companies or industry sectors. American, Japanese, and Chinese cases have been well-represented in the literature, but less so in the Middle East. The Kingdom of Saudi Arabia, for example, has a significant role in driving the global economy due to its vast oil reserves. The Saudi government has been instrumental in diversifying the portfolio of businesses that defines the industrial landscape in the country. As this process continues, a better understanding of the distinct national and organisational cultures begins to emerge.

Most businesses are family-owned enterprises and the leadership and management style in the Kingdom is mostly determined by precedents set through family customs that are passed down through the generations. The national culture is collectivist (centred around the Islamic religion), whilst the dominant organisational culture displays attitudes and beliefs that underpin respect for the forebears who devised the business practices and a prohibition on questioning or challenging the dictat set by historical precedent (Deresky, 2005). The dominant culture is informed by the history of the business, the respect for the legacy of the patriarchal founders (power culture), and the deferential attitude of the workers to authority. Walker et al.

(2003) found that this is a common feature of the dominant organisational culture across the Islamic world where tribal custom holds sway.

Managers in Saudi organisations act as a father-figure to the employees. The style of management is command and control and studies by Alanzi and Rodriguez (2003) discovered that this approach finds favour with the workforce who prefer to be directed and closely managed. Ideals of empowerment, change, and innovation are largely alien concepts to many Saudi companies and this tends to set them adrift from the trends evident among many other firms operating in the global economy. Some studies have found that the work practices and organisational cultures of Saudi firms have been responsible for a lack of innovation and growth leading to poor performance (Yavas, 1997; Bhuian et al., 2001). Organisational culture is inextricably linked to national customs and traits and as such is likely to take some time to change. Resistance to change in this context is likely to be strong as centuries of custom and practice have become firmly embedded in the national psyche. More fundamentally, many people from Islamic countries would treat with suspicion the imitation of what would be perceived as a western, non-Islamic set of values, beliefs, and behaviours that defined organisational culture.

Sources:

Alanzi, F. and Rodrigues, A. (2003) 'Power bases and attribution in three cultures', *The Journal of Social Psychology*, Vol. 143, No. 3, pp. 375–95.

Bhuian, S., Abdulmuhmin, A. and Kim, D. (2001) 'Business education and its influence on attitudes to business, consumerism and government in Saudi Arabia', *Journal of Education for Business*, March/April, Vol. 76, No. 4, pp 226–30.

Deresky, H. (2005) *International Management: Management Across Borders and Cultures*, Harlow, Pearson/Prentice-Hall.

Walker, D., Walker, T., and Schmitz, J. (2003) *Doing Business Internationally*, New York, McGraw-Hill.

Yavas, U. (1997) 'Management know-how transfer to Saudi Arabia: A survey of Saudi managers', *Industrial Management and Data Systems*, July, pp 280–6.

Discussion points

Are Islamic countries competitive in global markets?

Is there a management role for women in organisations in Saudi Arabia?

Questions

What are the key national characteristics associated with Saudi Arabia?

Is the organisational culture evident in Saudi Arabia helpful to firms seeking to compete in global markets?

What is the dominant organisational culture in most Saudi Arabian enterprises?

 Online Resource Centre
Author commentary on these discussion points and questions can be found on the Online Resource Centre at: www.oxfordtextbooks.co.uk/orc/combe1e/

Even so, economic rewards may have a limited effect as the reward for performance becomes the norm. Other, more subtle and 'care' orientated forms of influencing culture may be appropriate such as improving the physical working environment; allowing workers more freedom and opportunities to make decisions that affect their role within the organisation; introducing

Term
Definition

Esprit de corps: team spirit.

job rotation or changes to the job design that encourages multi-skilling and multi-tasking; organising social events where workers can share experiences outside the working environment; or introducing peer reward schemes where the attainment of qualifications, skills standards, or other attributes are formally recognised by workers.

When workers feel they have a real stake in the welfare of the organisation then a more positive culture is likely to emerge. Riordan et al. (2005) refer to this as the 'climate of employee involvement in the organisation'. A culture where workers can challenge and question the strategy, goals, decisions, and common practices with a view to improvement can be viewed as an asset rather than a threat by managers. Mini case 12.2 highlights the strategy developed by managers at animation studios *Pixar* as the company tries to influence an organisational culture that emphasises collaboration, teamwork, and *esprit de corps*. Formal or informal mechanisms can be established to facilitate this type of dialogue between workers and management. *Microsoft*, for example, have created focus groups of employees to elicit feedback on a range of organisational issues and use the MSPoll® as an online survey that allows staff to communicate ideas, feedback, concerns, and complaints that inform managers and can initiate real change. These approaches link into another key factor in influencing the formation of a positive organisational culture—the level of trust that exists between all members of staff and at all levels in the organisation.

Mini case 12.2
Generating a culture of creativity at Pixar University

Pixar Animation Studios is a subsidiary of The Walt Disney Company specialising in computer animation production. The company is best known for producing some of the most successful animated films of all time including *Finding Nemo* and *Toy Story*. Key to the success of the company (by 2010 they had notched up over twenty Academy Awards, four Golden Globes, and three Grammy's) is innovation derived from the unique environment that facilitates effective working relations between their creative people. The environment is characterised by a team ethos with the emphasis on collective strength rather than individual performance. The core activity of film production is necessarily a team effort and, therefore, the dominant culture is people orientated rather than based around the technology or processes (Catmull, 2008). Equal status is afforded workers in the creative as well as the technological aspects of the work. Managers at *Pixar* work hard to ensure that one activity-based group does not dominate another.

One method of supporting this egalitarian philosophy is through the education and training programmes the company delivers to workers through the establishment of the Pixar University.

In similar vein to traditional universities, Pixar University delivers lectures, seminars, courses, and practical workshops where formal training combines with the forum for allowing workers to generate and share ideas. All aspects of the production process are included in the curriculum, as are specialist activities such as dancing, voice, and movement. All workers are entitled to sign up to four hours of paid education per week and all workers are encouraged to exhibit their work or express ideas and to take risks. Risk is the driver of much innovation and creativity and it is the deliberate exposure to risk that managers seek to benefit from in the creation of new ideas from their workers whether they be animators, sculptors, storywriters, or software developers.

According to Purkayastha (2009) two main benefits derive from the Pixar University initiative. First, it is a forum for generating new ideas that is the raw material the company uses to transform into creative output. Secondly, it provides a forum for interpersonal relationships to flourish and enrich the company with the collaborative flair that underpins the innovative and creative culture. These attributes also make Pixar a magnet for some of the world's most creative talents who seek a working environment where their skills and expertise can be nurtured and enhanced through close collaboration with other creative people.

Sources:

Catmull, E. (2008) 'How Pixar Fosters Collective Creativity', *Harvard Business Review*, September, pp 1–11.

Purkayastha, D. (2009) Pixar University: A Distinctive Aspect of Pixar's Organizational Culture and Innovation, Hyderabad, ICMR Center for Management Research.

Discussion points

What is meant by innovation?

Do formal educational courses help or hinder everyday activities in organisations?

Questions

What do managers at Pixar do to encourage the team ethic among workers?

Explain how the organisational culture at Pixar helps the company achieve its aims.

What organisational benefits derive from the educational programmes run by Pixar for workers?

Online Resource Centre
Author commentary on these discussion points and questions can be found on the Online Resource Centre at: www.oxfordtextbooks.co.uk/orc/combe1e/

427

Trust

Trust can be viewed as a psychological 'contract' that is consciously or sub-consciously reviewed based on experience. The economic recession sparked by the financial crisis of 2008 has eroded the level of trust in institutions such as banks and public services. Trust is vital to reinvigorate enterprises by improving the quality of relationships that underpin so many activities that organisations are engaged in. The correlation between levels of trust between emploees and employers and business performance is widely recognised, making it all the more important for organisations to manage the re-emergence of trust as a catalyst for renewal and growth across economies. This can be initiated by re-establishing trust as a principal aim in the organisation. Managers need to be proactive in trust-forming relationships by using effective communications techniques for engagement, openness, and transparency with workers, suppliers, customers, clients, and other stakeholders to ensure that the people who contribute to the organisation's aims feel valued (Adonis, 2006). This acts as a vital motivating factor that drives performance.

As noted previously, in some regions of the world the empowerment of workers can bolster the development of a positive culture. In times of recession there is a tendency among managers to become more risk-averse and to increase the monitoring and control of workers. This often has the effect of eroding trust and is counter-productive in encouraging the employee commitment that underpins a positive organisational culture that is needed to boost performance. Clarke et al. (2010) suggest that a distinction be drawn between motives-based trust (Do I trust you as a person?) and competence-based trust (Do I trust you to do the job?). The former is characterised by low levels of trust but the latter, perhaps by necessity, is significantly higher. Managers have to place a higher level of trust in employees to do a job in order to influence a positive organisational culture and to demonstrate faith in the organisation's recruitment decision making. A distinction has to be drawn between levels of trust in the context of relationships in the wider society compared to that employed in the working environment.

Managing culture in the modern business environment

If it is accepted that trust is a vital component of creating a positive organisational culture, then the development of the knowledge economy has placed greater pressures on the trust-forming relationships between managers and workers. The knowledge economy is characterised by the use of digital technologies, fast, agile organisations that respond quickly to opportunities in the global marketplace, flexible working arrangements and practices, and high levels of trust. This has led to the dismantling of traditional, hierarchical structures of organisations to be replaced by flatter, more democratic forms of structure that facilitate better knowledge sharing. Autocratic and controlling forms of management have been replaced by styles that reflect the egalitarian and trust-based relationships that characterise many modern businesses. In many instances workers are located away from the physical building of their employers, requiring a higher level of trust in their self-discipline to work anywhere at any time and still achieve their goals. Knowledge sharing and an agile organisation are two important attributes underpinning strategies for gaining a competitive advantage. Key to the success of these strategies is how effective managers are at influencing the creation of a positive organisational culture around these key concepts.

Knowledge sharing culture

The aim of creating a knowledge sharing culture has become almost a 'holy grail' for managers since the advent of the digital revolution in the late twentieth century. The reasoning goes that knowledge sharing is the means by which innovation and creativity can deliver added

Innovation: the introduction of new ideas or methods.

value products and services, more efficient internal processes, and smoother relationships with stakeholders that combine to create a competitive advantage. This type of culture is facilitated by new communications technologies such as the internet and mobile phones.

Managers may establish formal and informal mechanisms for workers to share knowledge internally, such as the creation of special interest groups comprised of staff from different departments, conferences, dedicated web pages, workshops, publications, and so on. However, simply providing the means through which knowledge sharing is possible is not sufficient to create a culture of knowledge sharing. For example, the dominant culture may be one of knowledge protection in a highly politicised working environment where different groups of workers have to compete for resources. This would require a significant cultural change to gain benefits from knowledge sharing. Nevertheless, organisational culture plays a pivotal role in determining how well knowledge is shared. An assertion supported by DeLong and Fahey (2000) who argue that culture:

- shapes people's assumptions about what knowledge is important;
- determines the relationship between levels of knowledge, such as what knowledge belongs to the organisation and what belongs to the individual;
- creates a context for social interaction about knowledge—for example, what is deemed sensitive information, how much interaction or collaboration is desirable, and which actions or behaviours are rewarded or punished;
- shapes the creation and adoption of new knowledge.

Care needs to be taken in how the process of cultural change is managed. It may be that some of the benefits associated with the previous dominant culture become diluted or lost. For example, the tensions created by increased internal competition may instigate greater performance. Power cultures may be less amenable to knowledge sharing but may still be the preferred culture in some organisations that are performance-driven such as stockbrokers in the financial sector of the City of London or in recently privatised organisations in Russia such as energy giant *Gazprom*. In others, such as in the creative industries, task or people cultures are more prevalent as these are more conducive to facilitating knowledge sharing.

It can be seen that managers need to be able to exert some influence on the creation of a dominant culture that is appropriate to their activities and stated goals. That is, managing knowledge sharing will require different approaches depending on the level of cooperation or competition that characterises the dominant culture in an organisation. Jashapara (2003) noted that successful organisations tend to operate in a 'zone of knowledge creation' that resides between the internal forces of cooperation and competition as illustrated in Figure 12.5. The tension between competition and cooperation acts as a spur to the development of creativity and the knowledge that flows from it. For example, firms specialising in the production

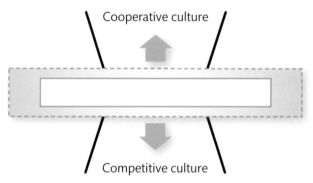

Figure 12.5 Zone of knowledge creation
Source: Based on Jashapara (2003).

of luxury brands such as Louis Vuitton, Dior, and Hermes rely on the effective collaboration of creative staff. However, they also exhibit management styles designed to heighten the creative tensions between designers, production staff, merchandisers, marketers, and others involved in the supply chain to stimulate innovation and maintain the pursuit of excellence that underpins their world-class reputation.

Note that an over-emphasis on either cooperation or competition is likely to undermine the creation and sharing of knowledge that they are designed to encourage. Organisations that exhibit knowledge sharing cultures are characterised by on-going battles between groups of workers who seek to impose their values and beliefs on others and ensure control over the dominant culture. Here, the dominant culture may emerge regardless of managers' attempts to engineer an outcome they deem preferable. In other instances the workforce may be passive or open to management influence resulting in a compliant culture. In countries characterised by a strong tradition of patriarchal dominance such as Saudi Arabia, Iran, and South Korea, organisations are invariably comprised of cultures that are reactive and compliant with the commands from the hierarchy of management.

Some writers have offered some insights into the means by which managers can attempt to influence a knowledge sharing culture. Newall et al. (2002) advise that managers should:

- link knowledge sharing to business goals and objectives;
- link the organisational management style to the types of intervention, such as the use of language, social events, or websites;
- promote appropriate reward and recognition interventions;
- provide the resources to support human networks that facilitate knowledge sharing;
- link knowledge sharing with core values and beliefs;
- encourage individuals who can communicate and transfer knowledge across different groups (such as in Mini case 11.1, Restructuring at Xerox).

Knowledge sharing is an important aspect of creating a positive organisational culture in the modern business environment. Strategies for developing mechanisms for facilitating knowledge sharing are now prevalent in public, private, and voluntary sector organisations. Mini case 12.3 outlines the means of, and reasons for, the introduction of knowledge sharing initiatives at the World Bank. The organisation generates a huge array of information and knowledge that is of value to its many stakeholders and the case highlights not only how that knowledge can be shared but also the rationale underpinning the development of a knowledge sharing culture among employees at the organisation. However, it can be argued that to fully reap competitive

Mini case 12.3
Knowledge sharing at the World Bank

The World Bank is a not-for-profit organisation funded by loans provided by its 184 member states. It was formally established in December 1945 with the remit of organising financial aid to help the reconstruction of Europe and Japan after the Second World War. As those regions recovered and enjoyed economic growth, the focus of the bank shifted towards developing under-developed regions of Africa, South and Central America. The mission of the World Bank is to help eliminate global poverty. In the mid-1990s the president of the bank, John Wolfensohn, announced the strategic aim of transforming the World Bank into a 'knowledge bank' (Inside Knowledge, 2004). By the early 2000s the bank was one of the most high-profile institutions investing heavily in knowledge management. The World Bank gathers, stores, and disseminates a huge array of financial, economic, social, political, technological, legal, and regulatory information and makes it available to the community of stakeholders including clients and employees.

The primary aim of the bank's strategy is to make the work that goes into achieving the mission of the elimination of global poverty faster and more efficient. Knowledge sharing is a key element of this strategy and by the year 2000 several programmes had been implemented to support this. These included:

- the establishment of communities of practice (thematic groups);
- the roll-out of the Development Gateway website as a knowledge sharing platform (http://www.developmentgateway.org/);
- investment in web-based resources to enable knowledge sharing;
- training and educational programmes for employees to understand how the knowledge sharing systems worked and to embed the concept into the culture of the organisation.

The transformation to a knowledge sharing organisation was not just a technological and logistical challenge but also represented a test for managers to effect cultural change among the workforce. The thematic groups were to prove critical in this process. The thematic groups are informal groups of people brought together through shared or related work activities covering issues of environment, education, poverty, child development, etc. The importance of the thematic groups is reflected in the 90 per cent of the knowledge sharing annual budget allocated to this initiative.

Key to the success of the knowledge sharing initiative among the thematic groups is the synergies derived from keeping people connected. The previous culture was characterised by caution among the workforce when expressing their opinions or thoughts (Regani, 2004). The thematic groups provided a forum of like-minded people where frank and open discussion could take place. Workers felt they could speak more freely among their thematic group colleagues and this lent impetus to the process of embedding knowledge sharing in the organisation. New media technology such as the intranet and video conferencing allowed people from different parts of the globe to communicate and share ideas on a single platform.

Importantly, as the concept of knowledge sharing became the norm, managers noted the increasing trend towards people seeking information from other people rather than from the impersonal databases available. To coordinate activities each thematic group had a leader but participation was voluntary among the workforce. Workers could move between groups according to their shifting work priorities. These empowering characteristics helped develop the culture of knowledge sharing as participation rates increased year on year throughout

http://www.worldbank.org/

http://www.worldbank.org/

431

the 2000s (Gwin, 2005). The informality of the initiative proved more effective than imposing procedures through a formal organisational structure. Knowledge moved faster and more efficiently between groups of workers. Shared knowledge on best practice, problem solving, news, story telling among others quickly became part of the organisational culture that has helped to make the World Bank one of the world's most effective knowledge sharing organisations. Importantly, the quest for new and better means of knowledge sharing goes on in the bank with new challenges being identified and solutions sought (Gwin, 2005).

Sources:

Gwin, C. (2005) *Sharing Knowledge: Innovations and Remaining Challenges,* Washington DC, The World Bank.

Inside Knowledge (29 February 2004) The Evolution of the Knowledge Bank, Vol. 7, No.6. http://www.ikmagazine.com/xq/asp/sid.0/articleid.65628363-55E1-494E-B3E1-284EBF2B5944/qx/display.htm

Regani, S. (2004) Knowledge Sharing Initiatives at the World Bank: Creating a Knowledge Bank, Hyderabad, ICMR Center for Management Research.

Discussion points

Is voluntary participation in organisational change initiatives an effective means of achieving a positive organisational culture?

Is effective knowledge sharing always likely to be limited by internal politics in organisations such as the World Bank?

Questions

What are communities of practice?

What initiatives did the World Bank introduce to facilitate knowledge sharing? Separate out the technology-based ones from the human-based ones.

How does the mission of the World Bank influence the creation of a strong and positive organisational culture?

Online Resource Centre

Author commentary on these discussion points and questions can be found on the Online Resource Centre at: www.oxfordtextbooks.co.uk/orc/combe1e/

benefits from culture, managers have to go much further by integrating knowledge sharing with a raft of other attributes to create an agile organisation that is better able to respond to changes in the environment.

Culture and the agile organisation

An agile organisation is one that adapts to changes in the environment by quickly responding to shifts in supply and demand conditions. The means of achieving this is by creating a culture of collaboration, knowledge sharing, innovation, and flexibility and supporting it by designing an appropriate organisational structure, creating a learning organisation, and introducing leadership styles that proactively encourage the development of agile workers through the delegation of responsibility, building trust-forming relationships, and acting as facilitators of change. Trompenaars and Hampden-Turner (2006) note that the effectiveness of a business is dependent on how closely culture and change are intertwined.

Agile working is a concept devised by the Japanese car manufacturer *Toyota* with the aim of improving efficiency and speed of production lines. This chapter's Case study featuring *Toyota* discusses the effectiveness of introducing the concept of the agile organisation into one of the world's largest car manufacturers. In Brazil, manufacturer *Semco* has adopted agile organisation principles to underpin their philosophy of worker empowerment, in Canada generic pharmaceutical company *Strategic Pharmaceutical Procurement* has embraced agile principles in outsourcing to ensure rapid product development and market access to a range of quality medicines. In the UK companies such as *BT* and *Sky* have similarly adopted agile organisation principles and the topic has attracted the attention of academics and industry consultants. The founding principles are detailed on the website www.agilemanefesto.org whilst www.agile.org.uk is a dedicated website of business consultants The Agile Organisation.

The concept of the agile organisation requires a distinct shift in cultural norms among the workforce as it involves breaking down traditional structures, working practices, and relationships. Agile working in an organisation focuses on performance rather than what can be termed 'presenteeism'. That is, workers need to be able to go beyond simply attending the workplace for a set period of time and undertaking a set number of tasks. Agile working environments are characterised by high levels of trust underpinning relationships across the organisation. Traditional hierarchical structures are replaced with flatter and less bureaucratic structures that encourage interactive knowledge sharing and innovation. Organisational components underpinning the concept of agility include market focus and position, organisational structure, human resources, flexibility, and change. However, the key to success lies in the organisational culture as illustrated in Figure 12.6.

Market focus and position

This is the capability the organisation has to understand and respond to changing market conditions. Leveraging analytics and diagnostic tools for generating market intelligence is a means of informing the market focus and position when the outcomes create knowledge about how the organisation's resources and capabilities can be deployed to take advantage of market opportunities.

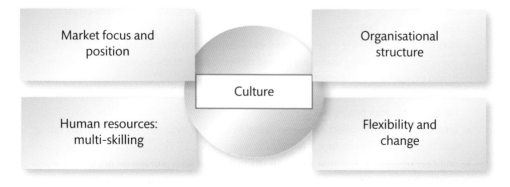

Figure 12.6 Components of the agile organisation

Organisational structure

The agile organisation dispenses with hierarchical and bureaucratic structures in favour of a design that resides somewhere between centralised and decentralised structures. This balanced design encourages innovation without slowing productive processes.

Human resources

The agile organisation plans the strategic use of human resources by developing people with the correct portfolio of skills and competencies and who can adapt quickly in response to changes in the market. Multi-skilling and re-skilling within a learning organisation underpins this organisational component for developing agility.

Flexibility and change

The ability to adapt quickly and respond with speed to changes in the market environment informs the dominant culture where the concept of change is a constant in the workers' everyday experience. In agile organisations workers do not just accept the need for change but actively pursue change and the opportunities it presents.

Organisational culture

Workers who have a collaborative culture, underpinned by an acceptance of change, display behaviours that are conducive to developing an agile organisation. The culture is defined by a mindset that involves:

- perceiving market change as an opportunity rather than a threat;
- focusing on new and better ways of doing things as opposed to relying on the 'comfort zone' of traditional practices;
- proactively sharing knowledge and collaborating across the organisation rather than operating within 'silos' where activities and knowledge are constrained by the organisational structure.

Managers can lend support to the development of such a collaborative culture by:

- creating an organisational structure with fewer layers of management;
- promoting continuous learning among the workforce through educational programmes, review workshops, and feedback mechanisms for knowledge sharing;
- devolving authority and responsibility to individuals and groups of workers across the organisation;
- configuring the working environment that allows workers easy access to each other;
- moving top performing managers around different parts of the organisation to ensure broad exposure to good practice and effective leadership;
- deconstructing projects into smaller, more manageable components that can be checked for quality as work progresses;
- creating an ethos of collective responsibility to increase innovation, creativity, risk taking, and enterprise and to reduce the fear of failure;
- engineering a people-orientated organisation rather than a process-driven one;
- leading the cultural change by explicitly adapting their own behaviours to embrace learning, change, knowledge sharing, and all the other attributes associated with the agile organisation.

Many organisations aspire to become agile organisations without putting into effect the support mechanisms that influence the development of a positive organisational culture that is the basis for adopting the characteristics of agile working. Here, it is necessary for managers to communicate the ideas and concepts behind agile working to the workforce, the benefits to be derived from it, and the rationale for introducing the support mechanisms that underpin its implementation.

Case study
The Toyota Way

Introduction

Toyota is one of the world's biggest and most successful car manufacturers with some 80,000 employees in many countries around the globe. In 1959 the Japanese city of Koroma was renamed Toyota City in recognition of the influence the company had on the economic and social welfare of its citizens. The operating philosophy, manufacturing techniques, sales, and design functions of *Toyota* have formed the standard for many manufacturing companies to emulate and are the foundations of the company's success over many decades. By 2005, business report experts Forbes 2000 placed *Toyota* eighth in the list of the world's leading companies. However, by the late 2000s a series of malfunctions in their cars resulted in the biggest crisis the company has faced in modern times. Although the focus of the crisis was the highly publicised accelerator pedals failures that resulted in the recall of millions of cars worldwide, the underlying problem was a failure of management. In particular, the organisational culture that had served the company so well in the past had become a liability that no one noticed until it was too late. This case study explains how organisational culture contributed to the success of *Toyota* for many years, but also discusses its role in the crisis that engulfed the company in 2009.

History

The Toyota car manufacturing company was formally established in Japan in 1937 by Kiichiro Toyoda as an automobile spin-off from his father's Toyota Industries company. The first Toyota passenger car was produced two years previously with full production starting in 1936. The end of the Second World War ushered in a period of severe austerity in Japan and Toyota teetered on the brink of bankruptcy before being saved by a consortium of financial institutions. After a damaging workers' strike in 1950 company president Kiichiro Toyoda resigned to be replaced by Taizo Ishida. Contracts to supply vehicles to the US military for their intervention in the Korean War (1950–53) revived the fortunes of the business and marked the start of a significant infrastructure investment programme. By the mid-1950s Toyota was exporting cars to the lucrative American market followed by global expansion throughout the 1960s as plants were set up in Brazil, Australia, and Europe. By the end of the decade Toyota had sold over one million cars worldwide.

The oil crisis of the early 1970s, when prices quadrupled, proved a challenging time for car manufacturers as demand for their products dipped due to the global recession. This led to a change in demand characteristics with consumers placing greater emphasis on efficiency and economy in their choice of car. Toyota quickly reconfigured their design and production techniques to deliver the smaller, gas-efficient models that matched consumer demand. The

435

company was a powerful global operator in the car industry and by the beginning of the 1980s was manufacturing in the USA and forming a partnership with the giant General Motors to broaden the brand range, including the luxury model the Lexus. Innovation continued into the 1990s with the roll-out of their first hybrid car, the Prius, as well as a range of SUVs (sports utility vehicles) and models designed for the young, affluent clientele. Meanwhile the company's European ventures were expanded, including operations in the UK. This growth was the catalyst for the company's listing on the New York Stock Exchange in 1999.

The new millennium saw further expansion by Toyota including diversification into banking and a presence in Formula One racing. Although the company was posting good financial returns, the first signs of weakness can be traced to the mid-2000s when major shareholder United Financial of Japan became embroiled in a corruption scandal that rocked the Japanese political establishment. There followed a financial meltdown in the Japanese economy upon which so much of Toyota's success had been built. The new era demanded a new outlook but the executives at Toyota failed to respond to, or even recognise, the need for cultural change in the organisation (*The Economist*, 2009). Before discussing the implications of this, it is worthwhile outlining the components of the Toyota organisational culture that had formed the cornerstone of the company's success since its formation.

Organisational philosophy

The genesis of the Toyota philosophy stemmed from the post-war austerity suffered by Japan when scarcity led to maximising returns from very little. This social mindset was transferred to the manufacturing environment as managers sought to eradicate waste and maximise efficiency. This philosophy informed the dominant culture and resulted in the development of the Toyota Production Schedule (TPS) which introduced the concept of 'lean manufacturing'. Lean manufacturing dispenses with stocks and inventory by employing 'just-in-time' delivery techniques whereby suppliers bring components to the production line only when needed. The organisational philosophy underpinning TPS is termed '*kaizen*'—Japanese for 'continuous improvement'. Also, many of the characteristics of the agile organisation formed the basis of the company's efforts to adapt quickly to changes in the global environment that affected demand conditions for the types of cars in different market segments. Dominici (2010) provides a detailed account of the roots of lean production techniques in Japanese business culture.

The distinct organisational philosophies of Japanese firms have been the subject of much academic attention, especially when compared to approaches adopted by western firms. As global trade has gathered pace, and with it the 'export' of Japanese organisational methods, the differences between western and Japanese approaches has become increasingly evident. Takamiya and Thurley (1985) provide a valuable insight into what these differences are and how they can be reconciled. That Toyota failed to reconcile these differences lies at the root of the problems the company experienced in the late 2000's.

Organisational culture: The Toyota Way

The Toyota Way is a set of principles that underpin the Toyota Production Schedule. Key overarching philosophies revolve around issues of challenge, *kaizen* (improvement), *genchi genbutsu* (go and see), respect, and teamwork. Liker (2004) outlines the fourteen principles of the Toyota Way:

1 base management decisions on long-term philosophy, even at the expense of short-term goals;
2 create continuous process flow to bring problems to the surface;
3 use 'pull' systems to avoid overproduction;
4 level out the workload;

5 build a culture of stopping to fix problems, to get quality right the first time;
6 standardised tasks are the foundation for continuous improvement (*kaizen*) and employee empowerment;
7 use visual control so no problems are hidden;
8 use only reliable thoroughly tested technology that serves your people and processes;
9 grow leaders who thoroughly understand the work, live the philosophy, and teach it to others;
10 develop exceptional people and teams who follow the company's philosophy;
11 respect your extended network of partners and suppliers by challenging them and helping them to improve;
12 go and see for yourself to thoroughly understand the situation (*genchi genbutsu*);
13 make decisions slowly by consensus, thoroughly considering all options, implement decisions quickly;
14 become a learning organisation through relentless reflection and continuous improvement.

Before going on to identify what parts of the Toyota Way failed and why, it is useful to outline the theoretical underpinnings of the approach. Managers at Toyota believe that the key to the successful implementation of the Toyota Way, and by extension the formation of a positive and strong organisational culture, is the empowerment of all those workers who are involved in the work process. This allows them to actively participate in the improvement of the work process alongside their routine activities. Empowerment in this context goes well beyond suggestion boxes or informal dialogue with decision makers, but involves procedures whereby ideas and innovation can be analysed, evaluated, and acted upon if consensus is reached with other workers and managers (Liker, 2004).

The concept of *kaizen* or continuous improvement applies to people as well as processes and empowerment is seen as one means of creating a culture that leverages optimal performance from human resources. This element of the Toyota Way was arguably the most difficult for managers to implement as it necessarily ran counter to many of the national traits associated with Japanese culture. The desire to avoid 'losing face' is deeply embedded in Japanese culture and acts as a barrier to questioning authority or the perceived superiority of others. Putting in place a mechanism for empowering workers to challenge the decisions of superiors was not translated into actions by those whose dominant national culture was informed by ideals of compliance, respect, and deference.

Another Japanese approach designed to underpin empowerment is the concept of *'jidoka'* which loosely translated means automation but with a human touch. The idea behind *jidoka* is to allow workers the scope to highlight defects, bad practice, or process inefficiencies without fear of accusations of insubordination. Toyota attempted to introduce this concept whereby any individual worker could stop production if a fault or problem was detected. However, the fact that so many faults went undetected in the run up to the 'accelerator pedal' crisis points to a failure of this system to be implemented.

Crisis and culture

In November 2009 Toyota had to announce the recall of over nine million cars worldwide after faulty accelerator pedals made the cars unsafe. In a particularly harrowing case a driver and his three passengers were killed when the pedal of his Lexus ES 350 became stuck. The final mobile phone communications from the driver to an emergency worker were broadcast to a global audience via newswires and the internet. Poor crisis management and public relations (they initially blamed consumers for improperly installing the floor mats) compounded the already disastrous situation for Toyota. The key question being posed at the time of the recall was: is this a one-off or part of a more long-term systemic failure? In time, the answer was found to be the latter. Consumer group Safety Research & Strategies reported an increase in the number of reported acceleration-related problems with Toyota cars as far back as 2002. In the USA the National Highway Traffic Safety Administration (NHTSA) initiated several investigations the following year and there were two small recalls announced by Toyota in 2003 and 2007. Once the company finally accepted their responsibility a large-scale recall was announced. However, it was too late to save the reputation of a company once renowned for quality, safety, and efficiency (*The Economist*, 2009).

The causes of the 2009/10 crisis that overwhelmed Toyota have been investigated at length by the company, health and safety regulators, government agencies, academics, and industry commentators. Each has put their own slant on the events leading up to the crisis and drawn their own conclusions. However, there is general consensus around the theory that the organisational culture at Toyota transformed from being an asset to a serious liability. This was particularly evident in the high growth phase between the late 1990s and the time of the crisis towards the end of the 2000s. In that decade Toyota doubled its output to ten million cars per annum and increased its manufacturing plants from fifty-eight to seventy-five as part of their strategic aim to become the world's leading car manufacturer.

Although the capacity for producing cars was put into place through infrastructure investment, the know-how and technological capabilities proved much more difficult to diffuse across an increasing number of plants located in many different countries with vastly different languages and cultures. Essentially, the growth strategy of the organisation had failed to account for the cultural challenges that global expansion entailed (Harden, 2010). Re-locating Japanese managers and workforce specialists to overseas plants to transfer their knowledge took a long time and was less effective than anticipated. This was a clear signal to Toyota management that the revered organisational culture that had served them so well in the past had been diluted by the pursuit of growth. Unfortunately, the warning was not heeded by Toyota management (Takeuchi et al., 2008).

Three key factors lay behind the management failure. First, the ability of the company to adapt to changing internal and external conditions had been compromised but managers failed to perceive this shift. Secondly, the pace of expansion led to ever-increasing levels of complexity that the company found difficult to manage. Toyota had posted losses in the financial year leading up to the crisis and the industry was characterised by over-capacity and falling demand. The economic pressures and increasing complexity of their manufacturing processes did nothing to ease the burden of managers.

Thirdly, and perhaps the most telling factor, was that the management culture was informed by continuous success for the best part of half a century, making acceptance of failure more difficult to detect and act upon. Also, as noted previously, the approach of *jidoka* had not transferred to other cultures where Toyota had expanded their business, leading to a higher risk that faults would go undetected. Far from reporting weakness or failure, company investigations found that many workers baulked at the prospect of delivering unwelcome news to their superiors who were already under pressure to deliver on set targets.

The Japanese style of management plays a central role in defining the formation of the dominant organisational culture in the Japanese working environment. This style is defined by a focus on consensus rather than strong leadership where the managers lead from the front, motivate through communicating a clear vision, and reward or punish where appropriate. In Japan, top managers rise through the ranks and promotion is often based on seniority rather than ability. The dominant culture at Toyota is one of compliance and conflict-avoidance rather than questioning and reaching a consensus around future action (*The Economist*, 2009). Also, the emphasis on consensus and conflict-avoidance undermines creative tension and the drive to-wards radical reform as a means of exploiting opportunities in the modern global marketplace. Furthermore, the board at Toyota (and most other Japanese firms) comprises only Japanese nationals making for a very insular and parochial cultural view from the executive (Hiten Amin Reports, 2012). This again is not conducive to operating successfully in the modern global economy. This style of management is not easily transferred across national and organisational cultures thereby increasing the physical, social, and psychological distance between management and workers that undermined so many of the principles of the Toyota Way.

Sources:

Dominici, G. (2010) *From Business Systems to Supply Chain and Production in Japan: lean production and its roots in Japanese Business Culture*, Frankfurt,VDM Verlag Dr Muller Aktiengesellschaft & Co KG.

Harden, B. (13 February 2010) 'Toyota Way' lost on the road to growth, *The Washington Post.* http://articles.washingtonpost.com/2010-02-13/business/36849595_1_toyota-way-toyota-way-shinichi-sasaki

Hiten Amin Reports (2012) *Traditional Employment Practices in Japan*, Tokyo, Japan, DISCO Inc.

Liker, J. (2004) *The Toyota Way: 14 Management principles from the World's Greatest Manufacturer*, Maidenhead, McGraw-Hill Professional.

Takamiya, S. and Thurley, K. E. (1985) *Japan's Emerging Multinationals: An International Comparison of Politics and Practices*, Tokyo, University of Tokyo Press.

Takeuchi, H., Osono, E. and Shimizu, N. (2008) The Contradictions That Drive Toyota Success, *Harvard Business Review*, June.

The Economist (10 December 2009) Toyota: losing its shine. http://www.economist.com/node/15064411

439

? Critical reflection
What are the limitations of the 'Toyota Way'?

The Toyota case illustrates the difficulty managers face in translating a theoretical framework into practical application in the workplace. The Toyota Way served as a template for the philosophy and working ethos of the organisation for many years and formed the guiding principles around which many of the activities in the company were organised. The effectiveness of the Toyota Way lay in its simple construction and articulation. The main problem was its reliance on a different set of cultural characteristics to those evident in the wider society from which the workers were selected. This disconnect between theory and practice was largely disguised by many years of high performance in the global car manufacturing industry. As the company rapidly expanded throughout the globe in the late 1990s and 2000s the inability of managers to transfer the Toyota Way into other cultures mirrored the problems facing managers in their Japanese plants. So, although many commentators point to mechanical failures of some of their cars as the cause of the company's woes, the reality is that a failure of management to identify and address weaknesses in the organisational culture was an underlying reason for the crisis that engulfed the company in the late 2000s.

Questions and tasks

Research Hofstede's findings on national cultures and list the key characteristics of the Japanese national culture.

Using the cultural web model, compile a summary of the key factors that determine the formation of the organisational culture at Toyota.

What type of organisational culture is in evidence at Toyota? Explain your answer.

Highlight the key weaknesses in the organisational culture at Toyota that have contributed to the company's problems since 2000.

What can managers at Toyota do to influence the formation of a strong and positive organisational culture that can be transferred to workers in different countries?

Online Resource Centre

Author commentary on these questions can be found on the Online Resource Centre at: www.oxfordtextbooks.co.uk/orc/combe1e/

Summary

● **Understand the definition of organisational culture**

Many definitions of organisational culture have been postulated by writers but there is a general consensus that it refers to the collective behaviour of people who are part of an organisation. The level of understanding of organisational culture depends on the ability of observers to understand the meaning behind people's actions.

● **Comprehend the key elements of the formation of organisational culture**

Key elements in forming an organisational culture include shared values and beliefs, norms, individual and group behaviour, and reinforcing outcomes. These elements help to guide behaviour and inform the type of dominant organisational culture. Formation is also influenced by factors such as company history, rewards, rules and regulations, rituals, symbols, management style, organisational structure, and power, among others.

● **Appreciate and apply models of organisational culture**

Different models were presented to help understand the formation and effects of a dominant organisational culture. These included the cultural web that highlighted key points of reference for the formation of a dominant organisational culture, Hofstede's national cultures model, and the zone of knowledge creation. Examples were used to illustrate the application of these models. The limitations or weaknesses of the models were also recognised and discussed.

● **Compare and contrast the different approaches to influencing culture**

This chapter identified and discussed some of the ways in which managers can influence the development of a strong and positive culture that is conducive to leveraging advantage from these concepts. In particular, restructuring the organisation to permit more collaboration between workers, empowerment of workers, peer recognition as a reward mechanism, multi-skilling and multi-tasking are just some of the myriad ways that managers can influence the environment within which such positive cultures may emerge. Trust is another important factor in this process. Managers need to be proactive in developing trust-forming relationships with workers that are both meaningful and enduring.

● **Critically assess the means of creating a positive organisational culture around concepts of knowledge sharing and the agile organisation**

The chapter focused some attention on the emergence of dominant cultures within modern business settings where concepts of innovation, creativity, change, knowledge sharing, speed, and agility are the key drivers of value and competitive advantage. It was noted that such influence is likely to be ineffectual unless the overarching philosophy of the organisation—its mission, vision, and goals—represent ideals that workers can 'buy into' and can inform the types of values, beliefs, and norms of behaviour that underpin the formation of a positive and strong organisational culture.

Conclusion

This chapter has highlighted the importance of organisational culture in determining the ability of organisations to achieve their aims and objectives. It also plays a key role in determining many of the goals and aspirations of employees in the workplace as it is seen to affect motivation, morale, team spirit, and performance. Also, it is clear that constant up-dating and monitoring of the key characteristics of culture is necessary to maintain the relevance of its identification in any particular setting. The dynamic and elusive nature of organisational culture makes it difficult and inappropriate to assign any level of certainty to what is perceived to be a dominant culture.

The emergence of a dominant and distinct organisational culture will also be influenced by the ethical and moral stance that individuals and groups display within the organisation. Ethics provide the basis for developing the moral codes that help shape and govern modes of behaviour that are deemed acceptable to stakeholders. The concept of ethics can be extended into the business environment in the form of corporate social responsibility. That is, there is an increasing recognition that organisations' activities have an impact on the wider community and that it is incumbent on managers to proactively seek to incorporate an ethical code of conduct around their activities. The next chapter explores the concepts of ethics and corporate social responsibility in more detail.

Chapter questions and tasks

Define organisational culture. Highlight the key characteristics of organisational culture.

What are the main factors that determine the formation of an organisational culture?

How can managers influence the formation of a strong and positive organisational culture?

Research what Hofstede's model of national culture has to say about the country you are from. Does it ring true or is the outcome dubious? Explain your answer.

What factors constrain the ability of managers to transfer the characteristics of a positive organisational culture from one company to another?

Online Resource Centre
Author commentary on these questions can be found on the Online Resource Centre at:
www.oxfordtextbooks.co.uk/orc/combe1e/

Further reading

- Alvesson, M. and Sveningsson, S. (2007) *Changing Organizational Culture: Cultural Change Work in Progress*, London, Routledge.

  This book discusses how people react to significant organisational change and poses some searching questions about how we see ourselves in the change process. It features analysis of a range of reactions such as adaptability, resistance, and support. The work uses an extended case study to focus on change from the perspectives of planning, inception, project management, and engagement of workers to change. It calls on real-life change processes to reveal how various stakeholders react to change. The value of the book lies in the illuminating discussion around how managers can promote change without alienating the people needed to implement it.

- Driskill, G. W. and Laird Brenton, A. (2005) *Organizational Culture in Action: A Cultural Analysis Workbook*, Thousand Oaks, CA, Sage.

  The book begins with an overview of organisational culture theories and then progresses to discuss methods of improving organisational performance. The book helps students to apply cultural insights to aid a range of key management issues including organisational change, leadership, fostering diversity, and understanding the link between ethics and culture.

- Gobillot, E. (2008) *The Connected Leader: Creating Agile Organizations for People, Performance and Profits*, London, Kogan Page.

  This book offers an invaluable insight into the development and application of the agile organisation. Key features of the discussion are how an agile organisational environment can extend the skills of workers; enhance performance; and boost the bottom line in terms of increased profitability. The book helps students understand how corporate leaders can implement the concept of agility in an organisational context.

- Handy, C. (1996) *Understanding Organizations*, New York, Penguin.

  This celebrated work by management guru Charles Handy provides an illuminating discussion on issues of culture, motivation, power, role-playing, and teamwork. The work includes a practical guide on how to transform the six key concepts into valuable tools for effective management. Issues of reward, structure, and conflict among others are featured as determinants of the organisational culture.

- Herzberg, F. (1967) *Work and the Nature of Man*, Boston, MA, Harvard University Press.

  One in a series of books by Herzberg specialising in the working environment. The book considers the aspects of work within the organisational setting including issues of culture, motivation, and the need for people to work.

- Ihlenfeld, J. (2007) *The Impact of Knowledge Sharing on Corporate Culture—An Outlook on Small and Medium Sized Enterprises*, Saarbrucken, Germany, VDM Verlag and Dr. Mueller.

  This book provides a valuable insight into the process of knowledge sharing in the context of small and medium sized enterprises. The discussion and analysis focuses on the ways in which knowledge can be disseminated across an organisation and the performance and learning enhancements that can derive from it. The book also highlights some barriers to knowledge sharing in organisations, with an emphasis on the SME sector.

- Liker, J. and Hoseus, M. (2008) *Toyota Culture: The Heart and Soul of the Toyota Way*, Maidenhead, McGraw-Hill.

  For students seeking a more in-depth examination of the case study of Toyota, this book provides an excellent insight into the Toyota Way. The book explains the introduction of the 4P model for organisational excellence (philosophy, people, process, and problem solving). The discussion goes on to reveal how Toyota selects, develops, and motivates its people to become committed to building high quality products. Further analysis focuses on the human element of the organisation by examining how Toyota implements its founding principles of trust, mutual prosperity, and excellence.

- Morrison, E. W. (2002) 'Newcomers' relationships: the role of social network ties during socialization', *Academy of Management Journal*, 45, pp 1149-60.

  This journal article focuses on the importance of developing social networks as part of the socialisation process for new recruits into an organisation. The work focuses attention on the form of relationship building by new entrants into an organisation and the subtle processes of developing interpersonal relationships that smooth the transition of new recruits into a working environment.

- Robbins, S. P., Judge, T. A. and Campbell, T. T. (2010) *Organizational Behaviour*, Harlow, Pearson Education, (ch. 17).

  This textbook is a valuable source of knowledge on organisational behaviour. The content covers issues of decision making, motivation, mood and emotions, perceptions, etc. in a work setting. For the purposes of organisational culture, chapter 17 provides an insight into what culture can do in organisations, methods of creating and sustaining culture, how employees learn culture, and creating a positive organisational culture.

- White, E. (2006) 'Culture Shock: learning customs of a new office', *Wall Street Journal*, 28 November, p B6. http://online.wsj.com/article/SB116466660952733780.html

  This short article provides an anecdote to the learning process that underpins the initiation of a new recruit into a working environment and the customs and rituals that have to be quickly absorbed in order to gain acceptance.

Online Resource Centre

For more information, updates, and multiple-choice questions, please visit the Online Resource Centre at: www.oxfordtextbooks.co.uk/orc/combe1e/

443

Skillset 12
Critical analysis

12(a) Introduction

If a friend asked you to analyse a film you had seen recently—how would you answer them?

Would telling your friend what happened in the film minute-by-minute be an analysis of the film? If not, why not?

If your line manager asked you to evaluate the products offered by one of your rivals— how would you answer them?

Would giving your line manager a list of the products offered by your rival be an evaluation of the products? If not, why not?

Although we might not realise it, analysis and evaluation are activities which we undertake in many parts of our working, academic, and personal life. Having the skills to analyse and evaluate effectively helps to shape your ability to reason, and forms the basis for being able to make rational judgements based on evidence. What we call 'critical analysis' is a vital skill that students need to become competent in to produce good quality outputs. In the workplace, critical skills are highly valued by organisations as they transcend merely process-driven activities to incorporate business and strategic thinking.

This Skillset explains the importance of critical analysis and offers examples to illustrate the difference between descriptive accounts of a business topic and a critical analysis of it. It provides a starting point for those who are relatively new to the concept of critical analysis and will initiate a life-long learning approach to honing this crucial skill. The Skillset provides a worked example linking a theoretical framework concerning organisational culture (Chapter 12) to the analysis of the internal organisational culture of the Brazilian organisation *Semco*.

12(b) What is 'analysis'?

Analysis is a systematic process which looks at all sides of an issue, breaks a topic down into parts, and explains how these components fit together (adapted from McMillan and Weyers, 2009: 550). For our purposes this definition has four elements which are discussed in greater detail below.

Firstly, as it is a *systematic process* this implies that analysis should done in an ordered, step-by-step way. There are inputs, a process of transformation, and clear output(s) or goal(s) in mind.

Practical tips:
- Clearly identify what is the purpose/goal of your analysis. Why is the analysis being carried out? What will the key output be? Who is your audience?
- Map out a step-by-step process for what you will do at the start—rather than just 'leaping in'.

Secondly, analysis *looks at all sides of an issue*. This helps ensure there are no gaps or omissions in your analysis. In a management context there may be many different stakeholders (senior management, employees, government, customers, suppliers, trade unions, and so on) all with different views which should be considered. Regarding academic work, different authors may have different and contrasting views on a topic. More generally, analysis may involve examining a topic from the perspective of both advantages and disadvantages; barriers and drivers; strengths and weaknesses; and so on.

Thirdly, analysis *breaks a topic down into parts*. Many management issues and challenges are highly complex and it can be very difficult to look at the big picture all at once. This is where, for management and academic work, the use of theories, frameworks, models, and so on ('theory' or 'tools' for short) can be helpful. These tools can be used to identify discrete issues, concepts, or topics around which you can assemble your thoughts and analysis. For example, in relation to organisational culture, you could analyse organisational culture within an organisation in terms of its assumptions, values, and artefacts.

Practical tips:
- One general way to break a topic down into parts is to use the standard journalist's questions of: What? Where? When? How? Why? and Who?

Finally, analysis explains how the *various components fit together*. Having disaggregated an issue or topic into many parts—another role for analysis (and theory) is to identify how the various components of a topic can, or might, fit together. This is an important stage which sometimes gets overlooked.

Breaking down a topic, issue, or challenge into parts and investigating how the various components fit together is a key role for management theory and can provide added value and understanding to many management situations. This understanding, in turn, informs management's decision making and actions. Far from theory being dry and dusty, social psychologist Kurt Lewin noted that 'there is nothing as practical as a good theory' (Lewin, 1951: 169).

12(c) Critical thinking

In everyday use 'being critical' of something or someone has a negative connotation with criticism stereotypically relating to what are perceived as negative or unhelpful comments. However, the judges in television shows such as *America's Next Top Model* or *The X Factor* (to give two popular examples from around the time this Skillset was written) offer 'critique' (critical thinking on their performance) to the participants (and indeed ask participants to critique themselves)—in this case both 'positives' and 'areas for enhancement' are (should be) identified!

Critical thinking entails neither a 'positive' nor a 'negative' mindset but requires you to undertake the 'examination of facts, concepts and ideas in an objective manner [and demonstrate the] ability to evaluate opinion and information systematically, clearly and with purpose' (adapted from McMillan and Weyers, 2009: 552). In both your studies and in management, this ability to examine and evaluate evidence (facts, figures, opinions, body language, and so on) in an objective and dispassionate way is crucial. It requires the ability, and willingness, to put your own personal feelings and biases to one side in order to understand the topic or issue. It is rare that there is only 'one best way' and adopting a critical mindset requires you to be open to alternative points of view. For example, Hofstede's work on national culture (see Chapter 12) is widely cited and has a certain reputation. However as noted in Chapter 12: 'it is necessary to exercise some caution when interpreting the outcomes [of Hofstede's work]' due to, for example, the dynamic, changing nature of some national cultures.

Practical tips:
- Techniques such as having a two-column list of advantages/disadvantages or benefits/challenges or strengths/weaknesses can be a simple but effective way of developing material where you consider different sides of a topic around which to build a critical analysis or evaluation (see below).
- However, note that although such lists help you structure your thoughts, they are not enough by themselves. Rather than just having a list of points, think about: What are the most important points being made here? (It is unlikely that all the points made will be of equal value.) Do points in the different list(s) fit well together like different sides of the argument? (So these could be written up joined by a word/phrase such as 'however' or 'on the other hand' or 'in contrast'.)
- More generally, appropriate use of a graphical/diagrammatic/tabular presentation of your analysis can help you/the reader structure and understand your thoughts. Although in your final documentation this should normally complement, not replace, a prose-based discussion and analysis.

12(d) Critical evaluation

Evaluation relates to identifying or measuring the value of something. The concept of value has a number of different meanings but, for our purposes, we can regard it as the extent to which we perceive something meets our needs in order to efficiently and effectively achieve a particular task or goal. Note that the perceived value depends on our needs and that weighing up the value requires us to have some measure/criteria against which to judge what we are evaluating. These needs and criteria may vary depending on the context: on a cold morning, the value of a mug of hot coffee may be as much in the warmth provided as its taste and caffeine!

Depending on the task you have to undertake (in your studies or your workplace), evaluation may take many forms:

Evaluation of a concept, theory, or model: is it the right tool for what you are trying to do?

This is something which is often overlooked—why have you chosen that particular tool and how will you use it to address the task at hand. There may be a tendency to choose a tool because it is available (e.g. it was covered in class) rather than on the basis of the tool being the most appropriate based on a proactive and thoughtful choice.

Many students find it hard to evaluate the theory they have used. It is not enough just to say that, for example, 'the cultural web is . . .'; that is description and not evaluation. Similarly, quoting a general point that, for example, 'the cultural web is used to analyse the internal culture of an organisation' is not sufficient. It is more powerful to say what you think about the theory at the generic level, *and then* say how did (or not) the theory actually help you to unlock the topic you are addressing. An imperfect and simplistic example/analogy could be:

> 'A saw is a good tool for cutting wood. I used a saw to make my tabletop.' **[Generic statement about a tool then describes what was done.]**

Versus:

> 'I'm making a tabletop from a piece of wood I bought. **[Overall aim.]** I have to cut the piece of wood to the correct shape of the tabletop. **[Need for some form of tool.]** A saw is a good tool for cutting wood. **[Generic justification for using a saw, i.e.** *why* **use a saw.]** I used a saw to cut my original piece of wood into shape for the tabletop I was making. **[***How* **I used the saw to help achieve my goal.]** The finished edge made by the saw was rather ragged, so I will also need to sandpaper the edge and the rest of the tabletop to prepare it for varnishing. **[***Limitations* **of using the saw in helping me achieve my goal. Link to next part of the process.]**'

This second example is more focused on why the tool was chosen, how the tool was used, and the tool's limitations in achieving the purpose/overall goal it was used for—in other words it is more evaluative overall.

Evaluation of the argument(s) that are presented: the work of Stephen Toulmin has been influential in thinking about how to make, or evaluate, an argument. Detailed discussion of Toulmin's ideas is beyond the scope of this Skillset but in general terms a 'good argument' has six elements:

- Claims—what you are asking the reader to accept. With a 'critical analysis' mindset the reader should not accept a claim unquestioningly at face value.
- Grounds—what is the basis (e.g. evidence) for making the claim?
- Warrants (justifications)—this is an argument (explicit or implicit) which links the grounds to the claim.
- Backing—which gives additional support to the warrant. For example by considering the general principle(s) which underpin the warrant(s).
- Modal qualifiers—not all arguments are 'certain'. The argument may (or should) be qualified by words such as usually, possibly, normally; and so on. This is something to look for (and adopt) in academic or business writing. For example there is a large difference between a sentence in a report which states 'launching this new product will double our turnover' and 'launching this new product will *possibly* double our turnover'.
- Possible rebuttals—a good argument will also consider the conditions, circumstances or arguments which may counter the argument being made. In academic work it is good practice to acknowledge limitations in your work as, at the very least, it demonstrates that you have been self-critical and are not seeking to make more of your argument than can be supported by the evidence (and so on).

This brief overview of Toulmin's work illustrates that creating a strong argument is complex and requires thought and effort. Simply expressing your own opinion cannot stand up to this critical analysis; and so it becomes discredited.

Evaluation of the evidence presented: is the evidence you present accurate and free of bias? If not then this will undermine the arguments that you are building. For academic writing it is usually also important to provide a trail for your evidence in the form of references. See the Skillset in Chapter 2 for discussion of why referencing is important, and good practice regarding referencing.

Practical tips:

- Be cautious in your use of bullet points as part of your work (particularly academic work). In general terms, a list of bullet points is unlikely to have the depth of critical analysis/ evaluation which is expected. Imagine you have a limited number of 'bullets' and choose carefully when and where to use ('fire them'!) them in your text.
- Read your own work, or other peoples', and look for words or phrases that indicate an argument/analysis/evaluation is being made. These might include, but are not limited to: however, but, therefore, on the other hand, etc.

12(e) Activity: analysing Semco's organisational culture using the Cultural Web

Perhaps the best way to understand what 'critical analysis' is and how to do it—is to try it for yourself!

Semco is a Brazilian-based company which started manufacturing centrifuges for the vegetable oils industry. By 2009 it had expanded into a range of other areas such as environmental consultancy, facilities management, and industrial equipment.

Imagine you are set the following assessment question:

> Critically analyse the internal organisational culture of the Brazilian company Semco in order to determine the extent to which they have a strong and positive organisational culture.

How would you approach answering this question? The following activity leads you through one process for answering this question. Please note that the process/activity below is intended to illustrate the principles and discussion in the first part of this Skillset; it is not intended to be definitive and the only way to approach answering the question.

1 Understanding key concept(s)

What are the key concept(s) which you must understand as prerequisites for answering the question? In this case the key concepts relate to the nature of (internal) organisational culture and what a 'strong and positive' organisational culture might be. At this stage you may wish to review the chapter.

2 Clarify what you are being asked to do

How will you know when you have fully answered the question? Many students think that their job is complete when they have used some theory to analyse Semco's organisational culture. However that is not enough to fully answer the question—you must also determine *the extent* [so there is an evaluation here] to which Semco has a positive and strong organisational culture.

3 What theoretical frameworks/models will you use?

As noted above, analysis requires a systematic approach—so just finding information about Semco is useful, but not enough by itself. How will you make sense of all the various materials you could find about Semco? Typically we would use one of the theoretical frameworks to help us analyse Semco by giving us some labels/concepts upon which to 'hang' the material we have found. Looking at the content of Chapter 12, you could (for example) use the cultural web, Handy's cultural types, or perhaps Hofstede's work on national cultures. For some assessments, particularly at higher levels of study such as Masters programmes, you may be expected to critically evaluate why you have chosen particular aspect(s) of theory to inform your analysis/evaluation.

For our purposes we will assume that you have chosen to use the cultural web, which highlights the key points of reference from the internal environment that combine to influence the formation of an organisational culture.

4 Understand the theoretical frameworks/models you will use

Read or reread Chapter 12 if appropriate. In particular, review material on the cultural web and what constitutes a strong and positive organisational culture.

5 How will you use the theory?

Your use of the theory will be in two phases:

First, we will use the various categories of the cultural web to investigate Semco's organisational culture: stories, symbols, power structures, organisational structures, control systems, and rituals and routines. This should give us a clear insight into the nature of the organisational culture within Semco.

Secondly, based on our cultural web analysis we will evaluate the extent to which Semco has a strong and positive organisational culture.

6 The Semco video

For the purposes of this exercise, rather than reviewing published materials from corporate websites, journal articles, books, and so on, we will use a YouTube video (see link below) as the basis for our evidence of Semco's organisational culture:

The Caring Capitalist—Brazil [Semco]

http://www.youtube.com/watch?v=gG3HPX0D2mU

The video lasts for around 15 minutes and you may wish to view the video more than once. Remember that, typically, you can use the software to pause or rewind the video when appropriate.

7 A table for analysis

Rather than just watch the video and see what you find out, create a table (see below; to give yourself space to add comments you may wish to create it in a 'landscape' format) within which you can record and structure your thoughts regarding Semco and the various dimensions of the cultural web.

Dimensions of the cultural web	Evidence	Strong/weak culture?	Positive culture?	Reasons for your view(s)
Stories				
Symbols				
Power structure				
Organisational structure				
Control systems				
Ritual and routine				

8 Analysis: Phase 1

Column 1 of the table lists the various dimensions of the cultural web. Based on your viewing of the Semco video, is there any evidence of (for example) Stories or Symbols which might indicate the nature of organisational culture within Semco? Enter the 'evidence' in Column 2.

9 Analysis: Phase 2

After you have looked at the video at least once and have gathered some evidence for the various elements of the cultural web, the analysis starts in earnest. Examining the evidence you have gathered (e.g. for the Stories dimension), does this suggest to you that there is strong or weak organisational culture in Semco (Column 3)? Similarly, does the evidence suggest a positive organisational culture within Semco (Column 4)? You may need to remind yourself of what might constitute a strong/positive organisational culture, for example factors such as evidence of workers 'buying in' to the vision of the company.

Be careful to document the reasons for your views (Column 5). Also, in the spirit of thinking critically, you should be sensitive to alternative explanations for the evidence you have gathered. For example, does a particular point made in the video relate to a symbol or a ritual? Does it illustrate a positive culture (or a less positive one, or both depending on the interpretation)? Try and avoid coming to quick judgements—think about your answers.

10 Conclusion

Column 2 provides the evidence for your views regarding the culture at Semco based around the cultural web framework. Columns 3, 4, and 5 are important as they will document evidence of your reasoning when you argue your case on the extent to which Semco has a strong and positive organisational culture. The final stage would be to weigh up and present your evidence/analysis and come to a conclusion (i.e. evaluation) regarding the extent to which Semco has a strong and positive organisational culture.

12(f) Summary of the Skillset

This Skillset unpacked the nature of critical analysis and evaluation. An activity examining the organisational culture of the Brazilian company Semco was used to illustrate the process of analysis/evaluation. The ability to critically analyse and evaluate are key higher order skills for both studying and in management; they take time to develop and merit a life-long learning approach to honing these crucial skills.

References

McMillan, K. and Weyers, J. (2009) *The Smarter Study Skills Companion* (2nd edn), Harlow, UK, Pearson Education.

Web links for Skillset

American Evaluation Association http://www.eval.org/

Research Methods knowledge base—introduction to evaluation http://www.socialresearch-methods.net/kb/intreval.htm

Overview of Toulmin's argument model http://changingminds.org/disciplines/argument/making_argument/toulmin.htm

Writing Guides at Colorado State University http://writing.colostate.edu/guides/

13

Ethics and Corporate Social Responsibility

Learning outcomes

- Understand the concepts of management ethics and corporate social responsibility (CSR) and the link to stakeholders

- Critically evaluate the ethical dimensions of management

- Apply models of management ethics

- Understand the importance and different perspectives of CSR

- Reflect upon the role of ethics and CSR in formulating the mission and goals of organisations

Anita Roddick created *The Body Shop* in 1976 by opening a small shop to sell herbal products. An activist at heart, Roddick was determined to pursue her business aims within a strict ethical code that meant fair treatment for her suppliers and employees. *The Body Shop* was to become a global brand partly on the back of the customer goodwill that the company built up through demonstrating ethical business practices. This included travelling extensively to source ingredients for the range of natural cosmetics that formed the core products, meeting and building relationships with suppliers, and offering fair prices that allowed the suppliers to make a living and support the development of their communities. Other ethical practices have come to define the company's business philosophy such as never buying products that are tested on animals or made from animal products and supporting the fight against labour exploitation in developing nations. Although Anita Roddick died in 2007 her legacy lives on and in 2011 the company produced a report called 'Striving to be a Force for Good' that sets out how companies can work towards eradicating child labour, discrimination, poor working conditions, and low wages. Even though *The Body Shop* has been innovative in the way it manages corporate ethics the company has not been without its critics. In particular, Entine (2002) has consistently questioned the claims of Anita Roddick to be both caring and capitalist in the way *The Body Shop* is run.

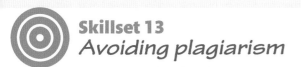

Skillset 13
Avoiding plagiarism

This chapter focuses attention on ethics and corporate social responsibility and highlights the reasons why an ethical dimension to business is an important aspect of the practice of modern management. Similarly, students also have a responsibility to act in an ethical manner when it comes to academic practice. One particular area of concern is that of plagiarism or copying of other people's work. Plagiarism is a growing problem in higher education partly due to the ease with which new technologies facilitate copying of text from one document to another. Skillset 13 is designed to help students avoid an accusation of cheating but also emphasises the moral and ethical responsibilities they have to ensure compliance. Likewise, organisations have a moral duty to act responsibly in their activities and to recognise and act upon ethical imperatives.

Student study skills

Students will be able to understand the reasons why plagiarism is a problem that needs to be addressed and the means available to them to ensure compliance. Different cultures have different attitudes to plagiarism, some actively encourage it (India) whilst others display an ambivalence towards it (Nigeria). This Skillset is presented from the perspective of European and American stances on plagiarism that recognise copyright law and ethical stances on the copying of work without proper referencing.

Workplace skills

Organisations need to protect themselves from potential litigation for infringement of copyright. Plagiarism is an offence that can have economic and reputational costs and workers need to be aware of their responsibilities in complying with standard practices. This Skillset gives students an understanding of what those responsibilities are and what measures they can take to avoid plagiarism.

Definitions

Ethics refers to moral principles that underpin modes of behaviour. Corporate social responsibility (CSR) refers to the commitment shown by business to behave in an ethical manner. The ethical dimension to corporate business activity is the extent to which enterprises improve the quality of life for stakeholders in the course of their economic development activities.

Introduction

Since the credit crunch of 2008 the issues of ethics in business and corporate social responsibility (CSR) have become increasingly prevalent in the discourse between the business community, government, academics, regulators, and the wider public. Part of the reason for closer scrutiny of these issues has been the perception among consumers and the public at large that corporate bodies have failed to strike a balance between the need to achieve economic growth and profits, and their duty of care towards their stakeholders. In particular, the highly publicised and disastrous risk taking ventures of some of the leading financial institutions around the world has focused attention on the diminished confidence that the general public has in the ability of organisations to undertake ethical and socially responsible actions that account for the welfare of the wider community that they serve as well as their own economic aspirations.

Of course, examples of poor ethical behaviour in organisations have been around since the inception of trade and there is nothing new about the types of mismanagement and lack of social responsibility witnessed in the run up to the credit crunch. Prior to that, the *Enron* scandal rocked corporate America to its foundations in the 1990s. In that case not only was the company engaged in corrupt and fraudulent behaviour (overstating the share price for the benefit of executive staff) but the auditors sent in to oversee accountability were also embroiled in the scheme to defraud. This almost unprecedented scenario led to a radical overhaul of corporate governance procedures in the USA. In 1984 the American-owned *Union Carbide* chemical plant in Bhopal, India, leaked toxic gas killing many thousands in the surrounding area. The company had set up in India as a deliberate act to circumvent tight safety regulations in the USA and Europe (Cassels, 1993). The lax regime led to disaster but the culpability for the incident is still being fought over decades after the event. In the wake of the disaster *Union Carbide* was bought by the American company *Dow Chemical* who have subsequently refused to accept any responsibility for the events at Bhopal (*The Economic Times*, 2013).

In some instances organisations build their mission and reputation on corporate social responsibility. In the UK, the *Cooperative Bank* has set out to ensure that it only engages in ethical investments. What is and is not considered ethical is a debate that surrounds the business practices of the organisation, but nevertheless there is a concerted effort on behalf of the bank to build its mission around the ethical dimensions of business. Prior to its takeover by cosmetics giant *l'Oréal*, *The Body Shop* placed a great deal of emphasis on corporate social responsibility and a high ethical stance. The firm traded on the idea that none of its products was tested on animals or used animal products. This struck a chord with the buying public and many consumers bought into the trading ideals of the company. Examples of good and bad ethical business practices abound and the reasons for them can be a combination of:

- business pressures;
- culture;
- consumer attitudes;
- regulation;

- political climate;
- opportunity;
- greed;
- social conscience, etc.

This chapter will begin with an overview of some of the main philosophical approaches to ethics that have been evident through the ages. This section brings understanding up to date by highlighting the key characteristics of the human rights approach that informs much of current thinking on ethics in business and the wider society. The advantages of adopting ethical business practices and CSR are outlined before the work focuses attention on the relationship between ethics, CSR, and stakeholders. The discussion features the means by which ethics are recognised and codified and identifies and analyses some of the competing responsibilities that help shape a CSR stance by managers in organisations. The implementation of CSR actions has implications for performance in organisations, and forms the basis for discussion on how this may affect profitability. The means by which ethics and CSR can be included in mission statements and form organisational goals is also discussed. The chapter concludes with the presentation and analysis of a framework for CSR and an outline of how organisations can achieve different levels of CSR.

Philosophical approaches to ethics

There is no one dominant ethical or moral code that is universally accepted as different peoples, creeds, and cultures view the world differently. Over the centuries different philosophical approaches to ethics have emerged. The main ones are outlined in Figure 13.1.

Figure 13.1 Philosophical approaches to ethics

Term
Definition

Moral principles: fundamental principles that underpin understanding and knowledge of what is right and wrong.

Moral principles

This approach is adopted when people are confronted with an ethical dilemma. In essence, decisions are made on the basis of a recognised moral code or accepted mode of behaviour. These are generally accepted by members of society and act as a guide to what is considered right and wrong. In some instances the understanding of moral principles is almost universally accepted (such as the understanding that it is wrong to kill someone) but each has to be set in context (it is not considered wrong to kill during war). Moral principles also feature in the business environment as managers and workers need to follow parameters of behaviour that are deemed to be generally acceptable in the workplace. For example, the relationships managers have with subordinates need to be built on mutual respect and an understanding that the manager has the right to issue orders and instruction. The manner in which this plays out in reality depends on the style of management and the extent to which an understanding of the unwritten moral principles are understood and acted on by personnel.

Utilitarianism

This approach to ethics relies on the pursuit of maximising utility (or a favourable outcome) for the greatest number of people. English philosopher John Stuart Mill (1861) coined the term 'consequentialism' as a means of defining the essence of utilitarianism. That is, the moral value of any course of action is determined by the result of the outcome. Thus, it is only possible to know the morality of an action once all the relevant consequences are known. Utilitarianism necessarily means that a certain number of losers will be tolerated if the majority of people are winners. This is one of the weaknesses of the approach and one that has been used as a basis for adopting a human rights approach where issues of equality inform the philosophical underpinning. That said, in a business context there are many examples of managers making decisions based on the notion that the outcome will benefit the majority but not all.

Human rights

This approach is based on widely held beliefs and consensus on how actions affect the human rights of individuals or groups. The human rights approach has been dominant since the end of the Second World War when the United Nations delivered the Universal Declaration of Human Rights in December 1948, which the majority of countries are signatories to. Part of the motivation for taking a human rights approach was to enshrine in law the basic principle that every citizen of the world should be afforded a minimum right to life, and freedom of speech and movement. Today, human rights underpin much of the employment laws that govern the way organisations deal with workers. However, the application of human rights varies markedly not just between different organisations but between different regions and cultures around the globe. This has led to the establishment of various monitoring organisations such as *Human Rights Watch* who seek to identify, record, and rectify cases of human rights abuses.

Individualism

This approach is taken by individuals who view and evaluate the environment in terms of the effect it has on them as individuals. Actions are deemed to be right if they serve an individual's self-interest. This philosophy was the basis behind the seminal work of economist and philosopher Adam Smith (1776) who argued that if each individual concentrated on their own self-interest then society as a whole would benefit. In a business context the philosophy has it that risk takers and entrepreneurs should only act in their own self-interest and that by doing so they would benefit others. Chicago school economist Milton Friedman (1962) was one of the proponents of this approach. Indeed, he viewed the role of business as being separate from that of the wider society by emphasising that the reason commercial organisations exist is to maximise returns for shareholders. If they can do this without causing harm to others, then Friedman viewed that position as fulfilling their *raison d'être*. This approach found some support in the 1980s when the credo of 'greed is good' informed much of the business philosophy of the era, especially in the financial and stockbroking sectors. Although the emphasis on individualism has waned in the intervening years, there remain a significant number of people in the business community who adopt this approach. Whether or not they look beyond self-interest as a motivator is open to debate.

455

Critical reflection
How can the moral integrity of managers be determined and evaluated?

Although this chapter focuses on ethics and corporate responsibility at the organisational level, it is as well to remember that these stem from decisions made by individuals or groups within organisations. Ultimately, managers and workers have to make their own judgements and decisions regarding the manner in which they carry out their duties in accordance with accepted modes of behaviour. Clearly, it is vital that managers lead by example and this requires the demonstration of integrity. Managers who lack integrity are more likely to commit or tolerate unethical acts. No matter what short-term gains may be derived from this, the ultimate effects are a loss of reputation and goodwill amongst stakeholders, mistrustful employees, and poor motivation and morale. Integrity lies at the heart of knowing what is right and wrong and then transforming that understanding into actions. Fundamentally it underpins ideals of honesty, fairness, character, and conduct.

The best way to assess a manager's integrity is to ask his or her peers. Key pointers are the level of trust that workers have in the manager; the extent to which they display high standards of conduct; the reputation the manager has for telling the truth; and the extent to which the manager's concern for the organisation is greater than that of his- or herself. The consistency of integrity bearing behaviour is another key criterion. Besides peer assessment, the integrity rating of managers can be assessed by their line manager (top-down) or from subordinates (bottom-up). An assessment that comprises all three levels is termed a 360° appraisal. This comprehensive approach has value because it reveals a manager's behaviour in many different settings and situations; it irons out personal grudges or close relationships; and is more likely to deliver greater insights. The key to ensuring high levels of integrity in an organisation is to transform those insights into actions that influence a culture of high integrity. This may require top managers to take the lead and formulate means of communicating how integrity should be demonstrated throughout the organisation. There may be formal assessment exercises carried out periodically. Such actions help to demonstrate a zero tolerance attitude to unethical behaviour or lack of integrity by staff.

Advantages of ethical business practice and CSR

There are a number of advantages associated with ethical business practice and corporate social responsibility. These include economic advantages, competitive advantage, enhanced image and reputation, improved stakeholder relationships, increased lobbying power, accreditation, safer products and processes, and environmental benefits and sustainable business.

Apart from the moral imperative of acting in a correct manner, there are a number of advantages to ethical business practice and a corporate social responsibility stance. In the first instance it can have a direct impact on performance. Consumers are increasingly aware of the effects of modern lifestyles on the environment and have concerns for future generations. The issue of sustainability has become an increasingly important aspect of how consumers perceive organisations and the means by which they produce products and services. Organisations that damage the environment or deplete the planet's resources faster than they can be replenished are more likely to be shunned by consumers, thereby affecting profitability and growth (Harrison et al., 2005). Some debate exists as to the extent to which this happens. For example, Devinney et al. (2010) argue that although consumers are more aware of the environmental issues, very little of their knowledge is expressed in the form of transformations in buying behaviour.

In some cases it is the treatment of workers that undermines the image of the organisation. For example, *Nike* had to recalibrate the entire human resource strategy in their overseas manufacturing plants after human rights groups exposed poor and illegal working conditions in their factories in developing countries (Shah, 2006). There is an on-going online petition aimed at encouraging oil giant *Shell* to make reparations for the environmental damage caused by exploration in the Nigerian delta region. *BP* has paid out billions of dollars in compensation and fines after the Deepwater Horizon blowout in the Gulf of Mexico (Lustgarten, 2012). Sometimes it is the manner in which organisations exploit customers that forms the basis of a backlash. Many UK financial institutions have been forced to pay compensation to customers for the mis-selling of pension protection packages. These are just some of the many examples that exist to illustrate how unethical behaviour or a lack of corporate social responsibility can affect the ability of organisations to achieve their performance targets, which may include gaining and sustaining a competitive advantage. As such CSR has become a strategic issue for many organisations as they seek competitive advantage over rivals. Porter and Kramer (2006) explore the link between CSR and competitive advantage in some detail. A proactive approach to drawing up plans to implement effective CSR policies and actions can lead to brand loyalty, enhanced image and reputation, and provide a means of gaining and sustaining competitive advantage. For a more in-depth understanding of this process, McWilliams and Siegel (2011) outline the conditions under which CSR can contribute to sustainable competitive advantage.

Image and reputation

The image of an organisation is a valuable asset that can be used to build customer loyalty and create a competitive advantage. Many organisations are sensitive to the way they are perceived by stakeholders, particularly customers. Understanding the stakeholders' needs, wants, and expectations can inform the way the organisation should behave and what is expected of them. Research has shown that an endorsement of social responsibility can have a positive response from the market (Doh et al., 2010). In the last two decades the 'green' credentials of organisations has become a litmus test of how they impact the environment and acts as a check on how they manage their operations in line with heightened expectations regarding respect for the environment. The mission statements of many modern organisations feature some reference to their ecological awareness and commitment to sustainability even though, as Moore (2008) reveals, markedly different approaches to this are evident in different regions of the globe. Also, when they do feature in mission statements they are often characterised by a high level of rhetoric and not followed through. Nevertheless, it is revealing that the greater focus of attention on these issues demonstrates the importance of them to organisations. In some instances, organisations can lobby government or regulators with added credibility if their practices are demonstrably ethical and/or they have complied with officially recognised standards.

Accreditation and standards

Another compelling reason for pursuing ethical business practices or demonstrating corporate social responsibility is to maintain the right to compete in an industry. Increasingly these issues are featuring as part of accreditation or standards criteria that permit organisations to carry out operations and activities. For example, car manufacturing companies operating within the European Union have to meet stringent standards for carbon emissions before being given a licence to produce. In the USA, the Sarbanes–Oxley Act (2002) was introduced in the aftermath of the *Enron* scandal to ensure minimum standards of corporate governance are adhered to by companies. In contrast to other countries (in the UK codes of conduct are on a 'comply or explain' basis) the Act is mandatory for all registered companies in the USA. There are serious sanctions brought against directors who fail to ensure that their organisations comply with the provisions laid down in the Act. The accreditation of industry standards has become an industry in itself with a wide range of organisations involved in setting standards and monitoring compliance in many different industry sectors ranging from agriculture to zoology. Some industries draw up a code of conduct themselves to ensure a closer system of monitoring of employees' behaviour. In the legal and accountancy professions, for example, the relationship with clients is often the key to success and has to be underpinned with high standards of integrity. In the UK legislation has been introduced as a means of deterring corruption through the UK Bribery Act (2010). Also, industry standards and accreditations such as ISO (International Organization for Standardization) are used to ensure that products and services meet agreed health and safety standards.

Stakeholder communication

As has been noted previously, the influence that stakeholders wield on organisations can affect performance, strategy, and consumer and public opinion. It is important for organisations to understand the relative power and influence that each stakeholder group has and to engage in dialogue with them to prevent negative publicity. Very often this may require organisations to communicate with groups who are fundamentally opposed to their activities. Nevertheless, there is value in forming some communication channel with stakeholders so that the business perspective is heard. For example, there is a close dialogue between representatives of the farming community and the pressure group *Compassion in World Farming*. Whilst the latter opposes many of the practices seen in modern agricultural business, the channel of communication is a positive and constructive means of airing different views and seeking solutions to difficult problems. The farming industry benefits from being seen to be actively engaged in problem solving some of the ethical issues related to their practices, and the pressure group gets access to the key decision makers in the industry. Constructive engagement is a focus of academic attention as well as activists and business practitioners. For example, Argenti (2004) outlines the strategy of *Starbucks* in entering constructive collaboration with activists.

Pressure from stakeholders can force organisations to act ethically or adopt a corporate social responsibility stance. This can manifest itself in changes to the way products are produced (exposing the exploitation of cheap labour in least developed and developing world countries by leading Western brands such as *GAP*, *Next*, and *Nike*) (Birch, 2012), packaged (imported goods to the USA are rigorously checked for safety), advertised (products aimed at children are banned from advertising on television in Sweden), and consumed (smoking in public places has been banned in many EU member states). Some stakeholders form formal organisations to pursue their agenda. For example, *Fairtrade* is an organisation set up to champion the cause of poor and marginalised producers of crops around the world. The group has had some success in influencing organisations to adopt fairer and more equitable buying policies to help the economic and social development of subsistence farmers and labourers. An example of this is given in the chapter case study featuring coffee retailer *Starbucks*. The extent to which stakeholder groups have organised and created strategies to lobby corporate bodies over a wide range of issues has been a feature of globalisation and the rapid development of information and communications technologies. The role of stakeholders in encouraging ethical business practices and CSR is worthy of deeper analysis.

Term
Definition

Corporate governance: a system of control over the actions and practices of managers in organisations through an agreed set of relationships between a company's management, board, shareholders, and other stakeholders.

> ## Mini case 13.1
> ## *Managing the ethics of stem cell research at Pfizer*

In 1848 Charles Pfizer and Charles Erhart created what was to become the world's largest research pharmaceuticals company. Heading a company at the cutting edge of technology, the management of *Pfizer* have always had to deal with ethical dilemmas, particularly in the area of medical research. No more so than in the highly controversial development of stem cell research. Researchers at Pfizer laboratories use embryonic stem cells from animals or humans to help screen new compounds and identify safer and more effective medicines. Human embryonic stem cell (HESC) research offers hope for millions of people who suffer debilitating and often life-threatening diseases and conditions (Mullin, 2008). HESCs have the capacity for self-renewal and have the capability to differentiate into all types of cells of the body. The research that Pfizer scientists carry out with their partner organisations has the aim of identifying the mechanisms that govern cell differentiation and to turn HESCs into specific cell types that can treat disease and debilitating conditions. As a sign of the commitment of Pfizer to this type of research, the company announced a £41 million investment in research facilities in Cambridge, UK in 2008 (Cookson and Jack, 2008). The facility will work jointly with a sister facility in Cambridge, Massachusetts in the USA.

There has been heated debate over the ethical issues that this research involves as the harvesting of the HESCs can involve the destruction of a human embryo. Opponents of stem cell research argue that it is immoral to carry out this procedure as it necessarily requires the ending of human life, albeit consisting of only a few cells. Advocates of the technique argue that the therapeutic benefits of the research outcomes far outweigh the costs. Essentially, those against stem cell research adopt the human rights philosophy to the ethical question (equal rights for all) and those in favour argue from a utilitarian perspective (the greatest good for the greatest number). So far Pfizer have decided to press ahead with their stem cell research programme and have drawn up a Pfizer Stem Cell Policy Guide to help formulate standards and guidelines for employees to follow. Whilst the policy outlines the company's continued investment in this type of research, it also addresses the ethical issues by stating that:

* *Pfizer* acknowledges the sensitive issues raised by this research, and we support proper ethical safeguards that take into account both the moral issues and public sensitivities.
* *Pfizer* will only engage in stem cell research projects that meet the highest ethical standards set by leading scientific authorities around the world, including the Guidelines developed by the National Academy of Sciences in the USA.
* *Pfizer* strongly opposes any efforts to clone human beings.

It is doubtful that these policy guidelines will appease the individuals and groups who are opposed to stem cell research, some of whom have powerful voices in the corridors of power both in the USA and elsewhere around the world. This case highlights the increasingly complex ethical issues faced by commercial companies as research and technology advances at a rapid pace. Companies, such as *Pfizer*, have ethical, moral, as well as commercial decisions to make. This latter point cannot be ignored as it is known that if one company in one region opts not to pursue research on ethical grounds, rivals elsewhere will. For example, public funding for stem cell research in the USA was banned until a court ruling overturned it in 2011. Since the mid-1990s companies in India and

http://www.pfizer.
co.uk/

http://www.pfizer.
co.uk/

the Far East where no such restrictions exist have been forging ahead with research in the field and creating a competitive advantage. Renwick-Monroe et al. (2007) provide some valuable insights into the debates surrounding stem cell research from a range of different perspectives.

Sources:

Cookson, C. and Jack, A. (13 November 2008) Pfizer to build £41 million UK stem cell centre, ft.com.

Renwick-Monroe, K., Miller, R. B., and Tobis, J. (2007) *Fundamentals of the Stem Cell Debate: The Scientific, Religious, Ethical and Political Issues*, Berkeley, University of California Press.

Discussion point

Is stem cell research ethically and morally acceptable?

Questions and task

Research and highlight the main points of the Pfizer Stem Cell Policy Guide.

What are the key issues that managers have to address at Pfizer when deciding on whether or not to pursue stem cell research?

If Pfizer do not invest in stem cell research then rivals in other countries will. Is this a suitably compelling argument for deciding to undertake stem cell research?

Online Resource Centre

Author commentary on this discussion point and questions can be found on the Online Resource Centre at: www.oxfordtextbooks.co.uk/orc/combe1e/

Ethics, CSR, and stakeholders

In defining or redefining the company mission, managers need to recognise the legitimate rights of the stakeholders. Stakeholders are all those who affect, or are affected by, the activities of the organisation. These include not only stakeholders and employees but also outsiders affected by the firm's activities. These typically include customers, suppliers, governments, unions, competitors, local communities, and the general public. Effective CSR requires organisations to incorporate the interests of these groups into their mission statement. Key steps in this process include:

- Identification:
  in defining the organisation, managers must identify all of the stakeholder groups and weigh their relative rights and their relative influence in affecting the organisation's activities.
- Understanding:
  decision makers need to understand the specific demands of each group.
- Reconciliation and priorities:
  claims must be reconciled in a mission statement that resolves the competing, conflicting, and contradictory claims of stakeholders.
- Coordination with other elements:
  the demands of stakeholder groups, the managerial operating philosophy and the determinants of the product-market offering constitute a reality test that the accepted claims

must pass. The key question is: How can the firm satisfy the claims of stakeholders and at the same time achieve its stated strategic and economic aims?

Ethics and stakeholders

Ethics can be thought of as a set of beliefs about right and wrong (Weiss, 2008). At a societal level, ethics constitute acceptable standards of behaviour that people adopt when dealing with each other and are based on values founded in society's legal rules, norm, and mores. Norms dictate how people should behave and can vary according to different cultures and forms of society. Ethics also feature in professional life and play out in the form of values and standards used by individuals and groups in the workplace. Another ethical dimension is at the individual level. Here, the individual as a free thinking entity has choices to make in terms of actions and modes of behaviour. Again, core values and beliefs and an understanding of society's norms help inform acceptable and ethical modes of behaviour in any given environment. In some instances it is extremely difficult to codify ethics and, therefore, individual choice becomes more important in ensuring that behaviour keeps within expected levels of acceptability (even though consensus may be difficult to ascertain). An example is the freedom of the press to go about their business in upholding the values of a free and democratic society where free speech and opinion are cornerstones of a civil society. In the UK this has been seriously undermined by the malpractice and unethical behaviour of certain sections of the press (see Mini case 13.3: Moral meltdown at News International), for example, phone hacking and serious breaches of personal privacy. The Leveson Inquiry was set up to establish the extent to which the press contravened ethical standards and to investigate ways and means of ensuring that the principles of the freedom of speech are upheld within a recognised moral and ethical code. However, one of the recommendations set out in the Leveson Report (2012) that there should be a formal committee established to oversee self-regulation of the press was not accepted by the UK government. The main difficultly is in establishing exactly what constitutes an ethical code of practice.

A multitude of factors help to form an understanding of ethical modes of behaviour at the individual level including parental guidance, schooling, peer group, formal agents of social control, and so on. At the managerial level in organisations, ethics act as a guide when dealing with stakeholders and others, as they help determine appropriate actions. Often, managers have to make choices when dealing with the conflicting interests of stakeholders. A key ethical issue is how to disperse harm and benefits among stakeholders as these are inevitable consequences of business activity. It is generally accepted that managers should behave ethically to avoid harming others and should act responsibly to protect and nurture resources in their charge. These are termed 'normative' statements whereby an understanding of what should happen is understood by a majority view. Ethical stances are often built on normative perspectives of the world around us. However, it is known that sometimes managers stray from

Term
Definition

Normative: relating to an ideal standard or model. The way things should be.

Figure 13.2 Competing responsibilities that influence CSR

adhering to a normative perspective when acting on behalf of stakeholders. To fully under-stand ethics and corporate social responsibility it is necessary to understand the pressures on management from competing stakeholders that influence their actions and behaviour (Kotler and Lee, 2005). These place in context the decisions and actions of managers as they seek to achieve the stated aims of the organisations they represent. Figure 13.2 outlines a range of competing responsibilities that help to shape attitudes and determine actions by managers in the context of corporate social responsibility.

Corporate social responsibility and stakeholders

Corporate social responsibility refers to the duty of management to nurture, protect, and enhance the welfare of stakeholders (Blowfield and Murray, 2008). There are many ways managers respond to this duty including:

Obstructionist response: managers choose not to be socially responsible.

Defensive response: managers stay within the law but make no attempt to exercise additional social responsibility.

Accommodative response: managers realise the need for social responsibility.

Proactive response: managers actively embrace social responsibility. Managers accrue ben-efits by being responsible.

Whistleblower: a person reporting illegal or unethical acts. In many countries, whistleblow-ers are now protected by law.

The various stakeholders of an organisation can be divided into internal and external stakeholders. Internal stakeholders are the individuals or groups that are stockholders, directors, management, or employees of the organisation. External stakeholders are all the other individuals or groups that affect the organisation or are affected by the organisation's actions. Different approaches adopted by different organisations reflect differences in factors such as the competitive position, industry, country, environmental and ecological pressures,

Mini case 13.2
Whistleblowing on GlaxoSmithKline in Puerto Rico

In 2010 Cheryl Eckard was awarded $96 million as her share of a $750 million criminal and civil settlement between US regulators and the UK pharmaceutical company *GlaxoSmithKline* (*GSK*). Eckard's reward for exposing contamination problems at a drug manufacturing plant in Puerto Rico, and a subsequent cover-up by management, was one of the largest ever pay-outs to an individual for whistleblowing on corporate malpractice and criminal behaviour (Wearden, 2010).

As Quality Control manager, Eckard was sent by *GSK* to investigate production problems at the company's huge *Cidra* plant in Puerto Rico in 2002. She quickly identified a number of violations and reported them to *GSK* executives. After repeated attempts to highlight the failings and the cover-up to executives, including a direct approach to chief executive J. P. Garnier, Eckard was sacked in 2003. It was then that she decided to report the case to the powerful *Food and Drug Administration* (FDA). The FDA investigation revealed a catalogue of malpractice and criminal activity including contamination of drugs. The plant produced anti-depressant *Paxil* and diabetes medication *Avandia*, both on the list of the top 50 bestselling drugs at the time. Drugs of varying types and strengths were discovered in the same bottle, some were distributed with the wrong strength whilst others were found to be contaminated with micro-organisms linked to various ailments and diseases. The investigation also revealed connections between a senior Cidra manager and companies who were alleged to be selling and distributing *GSK* drugs on the black market across South America. The investigation also highlighted that *GSK* employees had lied to FDA inspectors and that senior executives were implicated in a cover-up. Eckard's lawsuit was filed under the False Claims Act, a legal instrument in the USA that offers private citizens with knowledge of fraud, corruption, or unethical behaviour by organisations to share in any recovered proceeds from a successful prosecution (Connor, 2010). Whistleblowers can receive legal protection but it takes some bravery to expose malpractice in powerful organisations. Eckard's intervention could possibly have saved many lives as production at the Cidra plant was quickly stopped and the plant finally closed down in 2009. Whistleblowing is an important means of exposing unethical behaviour in organisations and many governments around the world have been active in formulating procedures that encourage reporting of malpractice as well as offering more robust protection for those who bring cases into the public domain.

Sources:

Connor, M. (26 October 2010) GSK to pay $750 million fine, Whistleblower to get $96 million, *Guardian*, Business Ethics. http://www.guardian.co.uk/business/2010/oct/27/glaxosmithkline-whistleblower-awarded-96m-payout http://www.ft.com/cms/s/0/9f12390e-b1b7-11dd-b97a-0000779fd18c.html#axzz2R5sSrI4C

Wearden, G. (27 October 2010) GlaxoSmithKline Whistleblower awarded $96 m payout, *Guardian*. http://www.guardian.co.uk/business/2010/oct/27/glaxosmithkline-whistleblower-awarded-96m-payout

Discussion point

Should 'whistleblowers' be financially rewarded for exposing wrong-doing?

463

http://www.gsk.com/

http://www.gsk.com/

Identify four examples of management failure in the GSK case.

Who is to blame for the unethical practices at the Cidra plant?

What can GSK do to ensure that malpractice of the type outlined in the case cannot happen again?

Online Resource Centre
Author commentary on this discussion point and questions can be found on the Online Resource Centre at: www.oxfordtextbooks.co.uk/orc/combe1e/

and so on. A CSR approach can manifest itself in many different ways within an organisation or through the way the organisation interacts with external stakeholders. For example, marketers have attempted to incorporate a CSR element into their activities by developing the so-called '4 Es' principles into their activities. These include guiding principles that:

(i) make it **easy** for the consumer to be green;

(ii) **empower** consumers with solutions;

(iii) **enlist** the support of the consumer;

(iv) **establish** credibility with the wider public.

Some critics have questioned the motivation of managers who seek to gain value from adopting a CSR stance or overtly extol the virtues of their organisation's ethical credentials. Asongu (2007) offers some insight into this phenomenon.

Social audits

Organisations can be seen to be taking a proactive approach by linking CSR into their performance targets. One technique is to undertake a social audit whereby key ethical and business metrics are incorporated into the decisions on performance targets. For example, reductions in carbon emissions may form part of a performance target over a stated period of time. Social audits measure actual social performance against pre-set targets. Although many social audits are carried out by organisations internally, more credibility can be gained

Term
Definition

Social audit: a process that enables an organisation to assess and demonstrate its social, economic, and environmental benefits and limitations. A measure of the extent to which an organisation matches its actions with actual commitment to agreed shared values and objectives.

by hiring independent external consultants to undertake the work. The reputational benefits of a positive audit carried out by external consultants will be greater than that which could be derived by the same outcome carried out by internal employees. Once completed, the audit results can be disseminated both internally and externally to maximise transparency of performance. Some annual reports have a special section dedicated to the CSR efforts and performance of the organisation. In other instances, organisations may publish periodic reports covering their CSR performance. The value of social audits can extend beyond monitoring and evaluating social performance. The information they provide can help managers to scan the external environment, identify internal weaknesses, and/or embed CSR within the organisational culture.

There may be strategic advantages associated with CSR such as increased relational or reputational capital. A proactive approach may entail establishing an ethical control system that formalises types of actions and behaviours that encourage CSR. In some instances, organisations may appoint a specialist in business ethics or CSR to monitor practices and communicate standards to all employees.

Corporate social responsibility and profitability

Corporate social responsibility is a highly contentious issue that has attracted vigorous debate among a wide range of stakeholders including the business community, pressure groups, government agencies, academics, citizens, and employee representatives such as trade unions. Managers have come to realise the benefits of embracing CSR and incorporating it into their strategic decision making. There are numerous reasons why CSR has a raised profile in managerial decision making in the last two decades. Foremost among these include the support it gives to the mission of organisations and their right to exist; the threat of externally imposed regulation if they fail to attain minimum standards of corporate behaviour; and the effect it has on economic performance through brand loyalty and accessing new customers in new and emerging markets.

A distinctive characteristic of CSR is that the costs and benefits are both economic and social in dimension. Whilst economic costs and benefits are mostly quantifiable, social cost and benefits are not. This increases the risk of managers accounting for economic variables at the expense of social ones when making decisions. The dynamic between CSR and economic performance is complex. Whilst one concept is not mutually exclusive of the other, neither is one a prerequisite for the other. Rather than view these two factors as competing, the challenge for managers is to determine a viable and compelling means of integrating them into their strategies so that both economic and social targets can be achieved.

Whilst there is wide consensus that incorporating CSR into strategy is a laudable and effective approach to corporate governance and performance, the issue is not without its critics, most notably Friedman (1962, 1970). Numerous research studies have been undertaken to shed light on the relationship between CSR and organisational performance (McWilliams and Siegel, 2000; Orlitzky et al., 2003; Wang, 2010). However, to date, the true nature of the relationship remains elusive. Consequently, much of the contemporary thinking concerning performance and CSR focuses attention on creating value rather than the pursuit of profit (Kearns, 2007).

? Critical reflection
Are reputational benefits the main reason for organisations engaging in CSR activities?

As has been noted some critics regard the efforts of organisations in the areas of business ethics or CSR as being piecemeal, self-serving and, ultimately, short-term in effect. Examples abound of organisations sponsoring events designed to improve social cohesion, welfare, the environment, and so on. To counter these arguments some organisations have become involved in social enterprises that are designed to help fill a gap in provision not served by either the market or the public sector. For example, in 2012 *British Gas* formed a partnership with the charity *Social Business Trust* to help start up social enterprises (Bentley, 2012). Partnerships between the private sector and social enterprises have a much more strategic aspect to their goals and objectives, part of which may be to proactively deliver socially responsible business practices for the welfare and benefit of the community. These arrangements tend to be long-term and require a commitment in resources that goes beyond some of the one-off initiatives that have traditionally formed the basis of private sector involvement in community projects. For example, *Deutsche Bank* in Germany was one of the first private banks to join the *European Investment Bank Group* set up to mobilise funds to support the Social Impact Accelerator (SIA)—the first pan European public–private partnership for social impact investment (European Investment Fund, 2013). Although it is not the primary reason for participation, the reputational benefits to the organisation can be significant as the company name becomes synonymous with the civil society benefits delivered by social enterprises. For example, *Unilever* (through the brand detergent Persil) has joined forces with a social enterprise to deliver active playing areas for children in inner city areas blighted by dilapidation and neglect.

More and more private sector companies are looking beyond short-term CSR initiatives or contrived marketing techniques to bolster their ethical credentials by forming partnerships with social enterprises. The financial arrangements underpinning such partnerships can also encourage participation. For example, under a social enterprise partnership, the participants are not liable for tax on profits (once costs are accounted for, all profits are poured back into the social enterprise). So, although not a registered charity, the organisation has a charitable mission. Private sector organisations can bring their skills, experience, and expertise to bear on the social enterprise to create social value and clearly demonstrate their ethical business credentials. In an economic climate characterised by austerity and shrinking public sector budgets, this form of partnership strikes a more coherent and substantial resonance with communities than traditional attempts at delivering CSR.

◉ Term
Definition

Social enterprise: a business that trades for a social or environmental purpose.

The role of CSR in mission and goals

Mission statement

Whether an organisation is developing a new business or reformulating the direction for an on-going business, it must determine the basic goals and philosophies that will shape its strategic posture. This company mission is defined as the fundamental purpose that sets an organisation apart from others of its type and identifies the scope of operations in product and market terms. Essentially, a mission statement embodies the overriding philosophy of the firm's strategic decision makers, implies the image the organisation seeks to project, reflects its self-concept, and indicates the principal product or service areas and the primary customer or stakeholder needs the organisation will attempt to satisfy. No external body requires that the company mission be defined, but rather it is a statement of attitude, outlook, and orientation. The objectives of mission statements are multifarious but may include:

- To ensure unanimity of purpose within the organisation.
- To provide a basis for motivating the use of the organisation's resources.
- To develop a basis, or standard, for allocating organisational resources.
- To establish a general tone or organisation climate, for example.
- To serve as a focal point for those who can identify with the organisation's purpose and direction.
- To facilitate the translation of objectives and goals into a working structure involving the assignment of tasks to responsible elements within the organisation.
- To specify organisational purposes and the translation of these purposes into goals in such a way that cost, time, and performance parameters can be assessed and controlled.

The role of CSR in mission formulation

Three indispensable components of the mission statement are specification of the basic product or service, specification of the primary market, and specification of the principal technology for production or delivery. Often the most referenced public statement of an organisation's selected products and markets appears prominently in the mission statement. These economic goals guide the strategic direction of almost every business organisation. Whether the mission statement explicitly states these goals, it reflects the organisation's intention to secure survival through growth and profitability. In the public sector, organisational goals are different and tend to reflect issues related to accountability, transparency, and best value.

An organisation's philosophy usually appears in a mission statement. Mission statements reflect the fundamental beliefs, values, and aspirations of the strategic decision makers in the organisation. Mission statements should also communicate the organisation's philosophy to external stakeholders and should reflect the public's expectations of the organisation and what it stands for. This is necessary to maintain and develop a positive public image and reputation as these play a role in building effective relationships and brand loyalty. Mission statements vary in the type of message they seek to convey. The mission statement of *Starbucks* is 'To inspire and nurture the human spirit, one person, one cup and one neighbourhood at a time' (Starbucks, 2013). The message emphasises the notion that Starbucks customers are considered part of a community. Others emphasise performance criteria. Part of the mission statement of insurance and fund management company *Aviva* reads 'to grow our long term savings business aggressively and profitably. . .' (Aviva, 2012). In the wake of the Deepwater Horizon disaster (see Mini case study 11.2), oil giant *BP* emphasise their commitment to preserving the environment and the communities they affect. In part of a document entitled 'What we stand for', the company states that 'We are committed to the safety and development of our people and the communities and societies in which we operate. We aim for no accidents, no harm to people and no damage to the environment' (BP, 2012).

CSR as organisational goals

A goal, according to Etzioni (1964), is 'a future state of affairs that an organisation attempts to realise'. This definition can be applied to all organisations. Stated goals exist to provide a focus for the activities of internal stakeholders. In most organisations, goals incorporate a general statement of organisational purpose or 'mission' and a set of more detailed aims and objectives that guide strategic and operational decision making. Perrow (1970) identified five categories of goals including:

Societal goals: goals as perceived by the wider society such as the standard of health and safety of products, carbon emission levels, welfare rights of workers, etc.

Output goals: production targets over a set period of time.

System goals: goals relating to the process stage of organisational activity such as production rates, system failure rates, etc.

Product goals: relate to the characteristics of the output and may be expressed in terms of quantity, quality, or availability.

Derived goals: goals that may not be formally stated in the organisation's mission statement but are pursued by organisational activity. Examples include lobbying activity to exert political influence, active involvement in charitable concerns, or forms of community engagement.

In the context of ethics and corporate social responsibility it can be seen that each of the types of goals set out above can be the focus of attention. Clearly, the societal and derived goals feature most commonly in the action of organisations in support of CSR or wider ethical goals. Nevertheless, it is possible to discern examples of these in the productive processes of firms, procurement activities regarding access to raw materials, advertising campaigns, workers' welfare, and in a host of other activities undertaken by organisations. In fact, the emphasis on CSR and ethics has been subject to change over time as attitudes, beliefs, and values in the wider society change. Consequently, it is inevitable that the goals of organisations change over time for reasons not just to do with economic returns, but also to reflect the expectations of customers and other stakeholders. In modern businesses the goal of profit maximisation has often been subject to goal displacement as new goals are developed which entirely change or go counter to previous goals. This has been evident in the trend towards incorporating a more socially responsible aspect to the activities of organisations, improving internal corporate governance, and better engagement with the wider society. In some circumstances CSR is a focus of goal succession where new or modified goals are incorporated into existing ones in such a way that the broad organisational focus remains the same.

Mini case 13.3
Moral meltdown at News International

What happens when influential and powerful managers of large-scale global corporate bodies fail to create a moral and ethical code of conduct for their staff to follow? What happens when the top executives of any business fail in their duty of care to wider stakeholders? What happens when unethical behaviour becomes the dominant culture in an organisation? All of these questions have been answered in the investigation and exposure of Rupert Murdoch's global media firm *News International*. In May 2012 a *Culture, Media and Sport* select committee of the UK government delivered a damning verdict on the conduct of top managers at the company, concluding that Rupert Murdoch himself was 'not a fit person' to exercise stewardship of a major international company (House of Commons, Culture, Media and Sport Committee, 2012).

What brought the committee to that conclusion was evidence of a corporate culture based on illegal and unethical practices, and the inadequacy of management to deal with it appropriately. There is no doubt that many critics believe that a major cover-up operation at the company was put into action to limit the damage caused by revelations into practices such as illegal hacking of private individuals' mobile phones. Under a significant weight of evidence, *News International* was forced to accept the verdict and conclude that its response to phone hacking allegations was 'slow and too defensive' (Mooney, 2012). These related to the activities of journalists and other employees of *News International*—an organisation that dominated media ownership in the UK including the newspapers *The Sun, The Times*, and the *News of the World*. In the wake of the scandal, James Murdoch (son of Rupert Murdoch) resigned his position as chairman.

The scandal revealed the extent to which the Murdochs and their close associates were prepared to go to dominate the industry in which they compete. It also revealed the dangers of having too much power vested in a few dominant players in the global media industry. Pluralism and independence are two vital characteristics of an industry that has a powerful voice in a free and democratic society. When those are compromised then the scene is set for widespread abuse of power. In the case of the Murdochs, it emerged at the official Leveson Inquiry (2012) that they had excessive patronage and influence on key decision makers in the areas of politics, media, the police, and others. The extent to which the unethical practices were diffused throughout the Murdoch empire may never be known but it is significant that the tone set by Rupert Murdoch himself could not have failed to encourage a culture of disregard for basic ethical principles. Significantly, the commons select committee concluded that he had been guilty of 'wilful blindness' to the unethical behaviour of his staff. *News International* executive Les Hinton was branded as complicit in the cover-up, whilst the company lawyer Tom Crone and former *News of the World* editor Colin Myler were condemned for misleading parliament.

The *News International* case shone a light on the darker recesses of British corporate and public life. Collateral damage was felt by the Metropolitan Police (some senior officers were in the pay of the company for revealing case information), successive government ministers, celebrities, rival media companies, regulators (the Press Complaints Commission was revealed to have been wholly ineffective), among others. Following on from the loss of public confidence in the integrity of financial institutions after the credit crunch, it is evident that public and corporate bodies have to radically alter the culture within organisations to create a climate of trust between themselves and their wider stakeholders.

Sources:

House of Commons, Culture, Media and Sport Committee (2012) *News International and Phone Hacking, Eleventh Report of Session 2010-12*, Vol. 1, London, The Stationery Office.

The Leveson Inquiry (2012) *Culture, Practices and the Ethics of the Press*, London, The Stationery Office.

Mooney, A. 2012 (1 May 2012) Rupert Murdoch 'Not Fit' to Lead a Major International Company, campdenFB. http://www.campdenfb.com/article/rupert-murdoch-not-fit-lead-major-international-company

Discussion point

Are governments in free market democracies powerless to prevent the power being vested in just a few firms in the global media industry?

Questions and task

Identify the world's five most powerful media organisations.

Can regulation work in controlling the excesses of the media and in particular the activities of newspapers?

Where did the culture of unethical behaviour by managers and staff at the *News of the World* and *The Sun* newspapers stem from? Consider the role of individual staff members, line managers, top executives, rivals, government, consumers, police, the wider society, etc.

Online Resource Centre

Author commentary on this discussion point and questions can be found on the Online Resource Centre at: www.oxfordtextbooks.co.uk/orc/combe1e/

A framework for CSR

Since 2004 the UK Government has supported the first CSR Academy and has offered a basic CSR competency framework for managers. For the Department of Trade and Industry, CSR will improve business efficiency and competency, and business education and training is an important means to achieve this. The framework, as illustrated in Figure 13.3, consists of six core characteristics and is designed for application across the full spectrum of business functions including operations, planning, supply chain logistics and procurement, finance, human resources, customer service, marketing, and sales.

Perhaps the most important characteristic of CSR is an understanding of the society in which organisations operate and in particular how government, business, educational institutions, security and control organisations, and civil society support organisations operate. An appreciation of how economic and social structures are created and organised underpins knowledge on how to operate within those structures. It is from this knowledge and understanding that a sense of an organisation's role and responsibilities within them starts to emerge. Very often organisations do not create and implement strategies in support of CSR in isolation but, rather, they seek suitable partnerships to help them achieve their objectives. Building capacity for delivering on strategic plans that incorporate CSR is an important aspect of management whereby networking skills are the catalyst for creating external partnerships, strategic alliances,

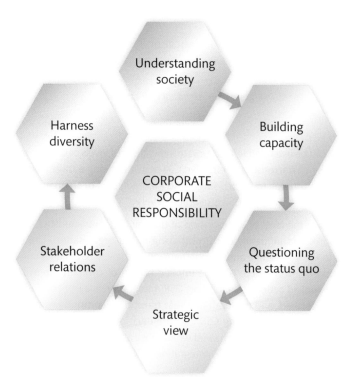

Figure 13.3 Key characteristics of a CSR framework

or at least channels of communication. For example, where once power generation companies were in direct opposition with ecology protection groups such as *Greenpeace*, there is now effective dialogue and consultation between the two camps. For example, a *Greenpeace* delegation attended the European Nuclear Energy Forum in Bratislava, Slovakia in 2008, which demonstrated a willingness to engage in direct communication and discussion even though agreement on key issues has remained elusive.

Another characteristic underpinning effective CSR includes questioning the status quo or 'business-as-usual' approach to addressing some of the most pressing global issues such as climate change, structures of economies, social welfare, political reform, and so on. Testing times require sometimes radical new ideas and innovative methods of problem solving. In terms of CSR it can be seen that more and more organisations are adopting a proactive approach to dealing with their responsibilities to the wider society by adopting new forms of doing business (such as public service partnerships, or partnerships with social enterprises). Part of this process is to have better and more effective relationships with stakeholders that may include giving them a platform or channel of communication that informs change within organisations. All of these characteristics need to be part of a strategy that includes CSR. This requires organisations not only to take a strategic view of the business environment, but to build in a strategic view of how their activities can be undertaken without harming the wider environment or the people that inhabit it. Finally, in a globalised economy, effective CSR can only be achieved through embracing diversity and adjusting the lens through which managers view the world around them. Understanding and harnessing diversity is a prerequisite for dispensing CSR in the modern global economy.

Figure 13.4 Levels of CSR attainment

The framework can be extended to incorporate indications of levels of CSR attainment. The aim is to transform the characteristics of effective CSR activities along a trajectory from awareness of the need for CSR through to embedding it into the leadership of an organisation. Figure 13.4 illustrates the components of the CSR attainment levels.

Awareness refers to the level of appreciation of the key CSR characteristics and the extent to which they inform and influence decision making in the organisation. The level of understanding links to the knowledge and comprehension of the key issues affecting the formation of CSR as a concept. Here, there is some implied notion of competence in transferring the knowledge into applied actions that support CSR. Integration is a level of understanding that is more focused, detailed, and in-depth and that transforms comprehension and knowledge into specific expertise in embedding CSR into the decision making process in the organisation. Finally, effective leadership is achieved when those at the executive and strategic decision making level support managers for fully integrating CSR activities across the organisation.

? Critical reflection
Does active CSR by organisations help tackle issues such as crime, child labour exploitation, poverty, and disease?

Although there is a general consensus that CSR is a force for good within organisations and for the welfare of the wider society, it is not without its critics. Some, such as Doane (2005), point to the fact that very often CSR initiatives become obscured by wider corporate interests. For example, some CSR initiatives have been designed to ensure a greater community engagement from organisations. This may benefit a minority of the population but the main advantage resides with the organisation in the form of enhanced reputation and goodwill among stakeholders. So, for a minimal investment, organisations can derive significant marketing economies at low risk. In some cases the public can only benefit if they actually purchase products. Organisations that deliver benefits such as sportswear to youth clubs or computers to schools can link the 'benevolence' to sales. This can be done through setting targets for returns of product wrappers, for instance. Critics argue that this type of approach is a cynical exploitation of a market demographic that has little understanding of sophisticated marketing techniques. Also, the nature and scope of such initiatives have only a marginal effect on societal change. Again, critics point to the fact that the majority of CSR-related initiatives fail to really address the major issues of the day such as climate change, social transformation, universal healthcare, economic reform, and so on.

Case study
The Fairtrade credentials of Starbucks in Guatemala

The *Fairtrade Foundation* is a UK-based charity that aims to help economically disadvantaged producers in developing countries by addressing inequalities in conventional trade. They do this by encouraging consumers to support the concept of fair trade through their purchasing power. The key asset of the *Fairtrade Foundation* is the ability it has to bestow enhanced reputational capital on organisations through the promotion and licensing of the *Fairtrade* Mark. The *Fairtrade* Mark is awarded to organisations that can provide evidence that the production of retail products sold in the UK have been produced in accordance with internationally agreed *Fairtrade* standards. The *Fairtrade* logo, which signifies that producers have met these rigorous standards, has become a sought-after form of accreditation for organisations which want their ethical trading activities recognised.

Starbucks is one the world's best-known brands with coffee shops located in many countries around the globe. A traditional feature of the marketing strategy of the company has been to project an ethical trading image. A large percentage of their target customers are relatively young, university-educated professionals who have an appreciation of sustainable, ecological, and ethical trading (Moon and Quelch, 2003). It is important for Starbucks that the target core market perceives the organisation to be demonstrably supportive of ethical standards. By the late 2000s the company had embraced the reputational potential of *Fairtrade* and built it into their multi-million dollar advertising campaigns. The campaigns are designed to complement the policy of paying local producers higher than market prices; however, that is only one part of the company's strategy. Other elements of the Starbucks growth strategy have included buying out independent producers and competitors' land leases. The company has also successfully lobbied national governments of producer nations to create an economically advantageous market presence that has driven out competition. The marginal increase in prices offered to local producers is a fraction of the returns the company enjoys in almost unfettered expansion across the coffee producing regions of the world. In some coffee growing regions, such as Central America, the Starbucks presence may be viewed as a contributory factor in perpetuating wider social and economic inequalities (Thompson, 2006). In 2011 *Fairtrade* accounted for around $1.75 billion sales—a small fraction of the overall $70 billion market. Of that, small-scale producers retain only around 7 per cent of the retail price (Fairtrade, 2012).

The situation in Guatemala (the biggest producer of coffee in the region) provides an example of how this inequality plays out in the coffee growing industry. The country has the most unequal land tenure in all of Latin America with 2 per cent of landowners owning around 65 per cent of the land. The remainder is comprised of smallholders. Thousands of workers toil on the large-scale coffee plantations (known as *fincas*). These indentured labourers are charged for accommodation and food leaving no surplus for education, healthcare, or any other basic human needs. Starbucks buys around 25 per cent of all the coffee grown in Guatemala, but up to 2009 only a small percentage of it was through *Fairtrade* arrangements. There have been occasions when Starbucks have deliberately held back from buying coffee until a cheaper price from growers can be attained (Seager, 2007). Here, the economic power of the biggest buyer is being wielded to best advantage. As the incomes of the growers and landowners is squeezed, so the plight of the workers worsens as the meagre incomes they already earn are further reduced.

The negative publicity generated by these practices forced the company to reassess their buying policies such that by 2012 Starbucks had doubled their *Fairtrade* commitment in Guatemala.

Even so, the economics of the industry for small farmers and labourers means that even with *Fairtrade* their incomes have been in decline. In 2012 the average small-scale coffee grower in Guatemala earned $1.55 per pound for their produce through *Fairtrade*—almost 10 per cent higher than the market price. However, after growers have paid the *Fairtrade* cooperative fees, government taxes, and farming expenses that figure is reduced to 50 cents per pound. For most that means earning around $1000 per annum or the equivalent of $2.75 per day—the cost of a Starbucks café latte (Fairtrade, 2012). Even though small-scale farmers would probably cease growing coffee if it were not for *Fairtrade*, the economics of the industry makes the future of this level of production unsustainable. Some may argue that the large-scale growers are simply waiting in the wings to acquire land sold by impoverished small-scale farmers. Put simply, *Fairtrade* prices have failed to keep pace with market prices to an extent that it offers small-scale producers a sustainable future.

Research by Bacon et al. (2008) revealed that a minimum price that farmers would need to raise their incomes above subsistence level is $2 per pound. The dilemma faced by *Fairtrade* advocates is that such a price would deter buyers such as *Starbucks* from participating in the scheme. It would mean that fewer farmers would receive the economic support that *Fairtrade* can bring. Instead, the main strategy of *Fairtrade* bodies has been to concentrate on recruiting more buyers such as *Starbucks*. This, it is argued, is the only viable means to increase the market for small-scale farmers.

The increased commitment to *Fairtrade* has been a feature of the *Starbucks* strategy from the late 2000s. The company has made a concerted effort to display their *Fairtrade* credentials to the wider public, especially in the UK and Ireland where all their espresso-based coffee products have been sourced through *Fairtrade* producers. The company now claims that around 12 per cent of their coffee purchases derive from *Fairtrade*, thereby securing the futures of many thousands of small-scale and independent coffee producers around the world. These efforts have formed a major part of the advertising and marketing campaigns of the company with a view to extracting maximum reputational capital from the investment in *Fairtrade*. However, critics have argued that the company has overstated its *Fairtrade* credentials and that much of the advertising was based on emphasising the fact that 100 per cent of their espresso-based coffee is *Fairtrade* certified. Although correct, the reality is that only around 12 per cent of all their coffee products sold came from this source (*Guardian*, 2011). *Fairtrade* has been a force for good in a world defined by economic inequality, but it can also be a target for global corporate bodies seeking to exploit the label to enhance the perception of their ethical trading credentials. Valiente-Riedl (2012) provides a critical investigation into the 'fairness' of Fairtrade as an ethical trading mechanism.

Sources:

Bacon, C. M., Mendez, V. E., and Fox, J. A. (2008) 'Persistent Paradoxes in Efforts to Cultivate Sustainable Coffee' in C.M. Bacon, V. E. Mendez, S. Gliessman, D. Goodman, and J. A. Fox (eds), *Confronting the Coffee Crisis: Fair Trade, Sustainable Livelihoods and Ecosystems in Mexico and Central America* (Food, Energy and Environment Series), Cambridge, MA, MIT Press.

Fairtrade Commodity Briefing (May, 2012) London, Fairtrade. http://www.fairtrade.org.uk/includes/documents/cm_docs/2012/F/FT_Coffee_Report_May2012.pdf

Guardian (28 February 2011) 'Fairtrade beans do not mean a cup of coffee is entirely ethical', London, *Guardian*. http://www.theguardian.com/environment/green-livingblog/2011/feb/28/coffee-chains-ethical

Moon, Y. and Quelch, J. (2003) 'Starbucks: Delivering Customer Service', Boston, Harvard Business School, Harvard College, pp 1–20.

Seager, A. (9 January 2007) Starbucks stirred by fair trade film, *Guardian*. http://www.theguardian.com/business/2007/jan/29/development.filmnews

Thompson, T. (February 4, 2006) The dark story of poverty in your coffee cup, Seattlepi. http://www.seattlepi.com/local/opinion/article/The-L dark-story-of-poverty-in-your-coffee-cup-1194935.php

Valiente-Riedl, E. (2012) *Is Fairtrade Fair?* Basingstoke, Palgrave Macmillan.

Does *Fairtrade* help or hinder the economic prosperity of small-scale coffee farmers?

Questions and task

Research and list the countries that Starbucks buys coffee from.

Explain how the concept of Fairtrade works.

Do Starbucks act ethically in their dealings with coffee growing stakeholders in Guatemala?

How do Starbucks demonstrate their CSR credentials in Guatemala?

Online Resource Centre

Author commentary on this discussion point and questions can be found on the Online Resource Centre at: www.oxfordtextbooks.co.uk/orc/combe1e/

Summary

- **Understand the concepts of management ethics and corporate social responsibility (CSR) and the link to stakeholders**

The concepts of ethics and corporate social responsibility (CSR) are closely linked. Where ethics refers to moral principles that underpin modes of behaviour, CSR focuses on the commitment shown by business to behave in an ethical manner. The link to stakeholders of ethics and CSR stems from the principle that corporate bodies and enterprises should strive to improve the quality of life for consumers, suppliers, and the wider citizenship and communities.

- **Critically evaluate the ethical dimensions of management**

This chapter has described how the ethical dimensions of management differ from those of economic performance and profit. Increasingly, ethics and CSR have a focus on the role of business in the wider society and a commitment to social welfare. Here, it was noted that some organisations are actively involved in partnering with social enterprises to demonstrate a strategic and long-term commitment to CSR, rather than the traditional marketing-oriented approaches that were deemed opportunistic and short-term. Good corporate citizenship requires management to look at a wide range of issues including the safety of products and services, the effect on the environment of their production, workers' rights and welfare, the economics of doing business, and so on.

- **Apply models of management ethics**

Theoretical perspectives were used as a basis for understanding management ethics. These included moral principles, utilitarianism, individual, and human rights approaches to ethics. Management has operated within these moral dimensions in different eras and different cultural and political environments. For example, the dominant moral philosophy in the

United States tends towards the individual which is a reflection of the national culture and identity. This contrasts with the human rights approach that dominates in Europe and where equality and fairness are the key guiding principles.

● **Understand the importance and different perspectives of CSR**

A CSR framework was used to identify and discuss different perspectives including harnessing diversity, stakeholder relations, understanding society, building capacity, questioning the status quo, and the strategic view of CSR. Each plays an important role in influencing the management of CSR and the approach that organisations take in incorporating it into their activities and goals.

● **Reflect upon the role of ethics and CSR in formulating the mission and goals of organisations**

The role of ethics and CSR usually features as a statement of an organisation's philosophy or core beliefs and values as part of the mission statement. It reflects the priorities to which strategic decision makers are committed in managing the company. Some may incorporate specific ethical or CSR-related issues such as commitment to reducing carbon emissions or the health and safety of new products. Managers need to devise mission statements that accurately reflect the organisation's commitment to ethics and CSR as a means of maintaining credibility and reputation in the minds of the wider public. Thus, mission statements should reflect the public's expectations, as well as organisational goals and beliefs.

Conclusion

This chapter has outlined the key advantages associated with adopting ethical business practices and corporate social responsibility (CSR). It was noted that these issues have a raised profile in the modern business environment as the trust between the business community and the wider public has been eroded by successive cases of unethical behaviour and a lack of CSR. The discussion and cases highlighted have revealed some pressing ethical dilemmas that face managers. In particular, the advance of technology into areas with fundamental human rights issues, such as stem cell research. Managers have to weigh the commercial benefits against the deeper moral questions relating to their activities. In some cases organisations take a moral stance, in others it is left to the individual to determine what course of action is appropriate given each set of circumstances. Thus, it can be seen that establishing a generic code of conduct covering all circumstances is impossible and not something that could be underpinned by consensus given the diverse nature of cultures, interpretations of morality and ethics, and the prevailing attitudes at any given time.

Attitudes to business ethics and CSR evolve and change over time. This change is sometimes brought about by changes in society itself (attitudes, values, and beliefs are constantly changing and evolving); sometimes organisations initiate change; and in some cases pressure groups or other stakeholders prove the catalysts for change. Consumers have become more aware of the effects that the business community has on their economic, social, and environmental welfare. The combination of these factors has ensured that the issues of business ethics and CSR have found a more prominent place in the strategic plans of organisations. To explore the extent of this and other important factors that derive organisations' aims and objectives, the next chapter focuses attention on the management task of formulating and implementing strategy.

Chapter questions and task

Identify a moral dilemma you have experienced in your life. How did you resolve it?

Explain the term 'Corporate Social Responsibility (CSR)'.

Explain the difference between utilitarian and human rights approaches to ethics.

What is a 'social audit'?

Online Resource Centre

Author commentary on this discussion point and questions can be found on the Online Resource Centre at: www.oxfordtextbooks.co.uk/orc/combe1e/

Further reading

- Burrough, B. and Helyar, J. (2010) *Barbarians at the Gate: The Fall of RJR Nabisco*, London, Arrow.

  A classic book detailing the story of the battle for control during one of corporate America's largest ever takeovers. This book gives a real insight into the motivations and ambitions of ruthless businessmen in an era characterised by greed and egotism. The difference between the academic treatment of business ethics and the stark reality of unbridled ambition is simultaneously fascinating and disturbing.

- Griseri, P. and Seppala, N. (2010) *Business Ethics and Corporate Social Responsibility*, Basingstoke, Cengage.

  This book focuses firmly on the management challenges and realities of introducing business ethics and CSR into operational and strategic practices in organisations. The book has an international perspective and delivers a reflective account of some of the pitfalls evident in applying CSR principles in the modern business environment. The book has effective additional online materials and well-chosen cases studies for students to supplement their learning.

- Horrigan, B. (2010) *Corporate Social Responsibility in the 21st Century: Debates, Models and Practices*, Cheltenham, Edward Elgar Publishing.

  This inter-disciplinary and cross-jurisdictional analysis includes debates on governance, practical guidelines for responsible businesses, and government roles in supporting CSR. The book has an international flavour and introduces some compelling controversies in different regions of the globe. The discussion provides a useful insight into dealing with ethical issues in business from different cultural and legal perspectives.

- Lange, H., Lohr, A., and Steinmann, H. (2010) *Working Across Cultures: Ethical Perspectives for Intercultural Management*, New York, Springer.

  Based on academic discussions, the book addresses potential ethical solutions to managing dilemmas in a world characterised by cultural diversity. The narrative discourse is aimed at higher level academics but the subject matter is of interest to anyone with a learning or research focus on business ethics and CSR. The book also gives a useful insight to students into how academic professionals frame arguments and deal with argument.

- Mullerat, R. (2010) *International Corporate Social Responsibility*, London, Kluwer Law International.

  The author starts the discussion and analysis by offering a definition of the sometimes vague concept of corporate social responsibility. The analysis then goes on to focus on the role of corporate bodies in formulating and shaping an understanding of what CSR is and how it can be applied in the modern business environment. The discussion is well-crafted and accessible to a wide readership including undergraduate and postgraduate students.

● Trevino, L. K. and Nelson, K. A. (2010) *Managing Business Ethics* (5th edn), Chichester, John Wiley & Sons.

Trevino and Nelson focus on the whole business ethic rather than the more narrowly defined decision making at the individual level. The discussion moves seamlessly from the individual to the managerial level and then on to the organisational contexts to help and guide readers in the process of understanding the complexities of human behaviour that underpins the development of business ethics. One of a number of textbooks aimed at bringing clarity to a complex set of issues, this book is well written, easy to follow, and provides a solid foundation for students new to the study of business ethics.

Online Resource Centre

For more information, updates, and multiple-choice questions, please visit the Online Resource Centre at: www.oxfordtextbooks.co.uk/orc/combe1e/

Skillset 13
Avoiding plagiarism

13(a) Introduction

Plagiarism is a growing problem in Higher Education partly due to the ease with which new technologies facilitate the copying of text from one document to another. This Skillset is designed to help you avoid being accused of plagiarism but also emphasises the moral and ethical responsibilities you have to ensure compliance. Likewise, organisations have a moral duty to act responsibly in their activities and to recognise and act upon ethical imperatives.

This Skillset will help you to understand the reasons why plagiarism is a problem that needs to be addressed, and offer strategies to ensure you comply with good practice. Different cultures have different attitudes to plagiarism; some actively encourage it (India) whilst others display ambivalence towards it (Nigeria). This Skillset is presented from the perspective of European and North American stances on plagiarism that recognise copyright law and ethical stances on the copying of work without proper citation/referencing.

13(b) What is 'plagiarism'?

Precise definitions of plagiarism may vary but at its heart, plagiarism is: the unacknowledged passing off of other peoples' words, works, or ideas as your own (adapted from Glasgow Caledonian University, 2012, Section 7.5.1).

The following 'dialogue' illustrates examples of plagiarism by posing typical questions students ask about the nature of plagiarism, along with typical responses from a tutor. [The list of 'questions' is adapted and extended from examples of plagiarism given by Glasgow Caledonian University (2012, Section 7.5.1). The 'tutor advice' is original.]

Student Question 1

Can I use another person's work or ideas without an appropriate citation or reference?

Advice from Tutor

No you cannot. As discussed in Skillset 2 (Referencing), good practice in citing and referencing the words, work, and ideas of others is core to the whole process of academic writing. It demonstrates 'honesty' and 'integrity' by acknowledging the work of others.

Student Question 2

Can I summarise someone else's work and present it as my own? For example: by rewriting it with some of my own words.

Advice from Tutor

No you cannot. Even if the specific words are different from the original you should still acknowledge the original source(s) as the ideas are not your own.

Student Question 3

Can I using someone else's ideas without appropriate acknowledgement via citation/referencing?

Advice from Tutor

No you cannot. Again, you must be diligent in acknowledging the works and ideas of others.

Student Question 4

Can I copy another student's work?

Advice from Tutor

No you cannot. This may be regarded as a more serious breach of the regulations as there cannot be any mitigation that there was merely 'poor academic practice' in terms of citation/referencing. If you undertook an examination then you would (I assume) know that copying someone else's work is not allowed. The same applies to written assessments (e.g. reports).

Be aware that if copying another student's work was discovered then there may be serious consequences not only for you—but also for the person you copied from (if they agreed you could copy them). At the very least you may subject your colleague to a very stressful investigation where they have to (for example) prove that you had copied their work without their permission. If they left their work unattended and you reviewed it/copied it—would they have been negligent in leaving the work unattended/not password protected? Or could there be a suspicion that they left the work unattended 'knowing' you might look at it (so tacit approval of your actions)? You should not wish to put your colleagues into this difficult situation.

Finally, it may be that you copy the work from a previous student (whether for payment or not) who has now graduated. This is not acceptable and as well as consequences for yourself, it could be that your actions may lead to severe consequences for the graduate.

Student Question 5

Can I purchase an 'answer' to my assignment online (or pay someone to write it) and then submit it as my own work?

Advice from Tutor

No you cannot. This may be regarded as a particularly serious case as it undermines the psychological contract between tutor and student that they are working together to engage in a learning process. Instead you would have, in effect, purchased your degree (via a third party who acted as your 'ghost writer') rather than have undertaken the learning process yourself. From an ethical point of view 'your work' must be your own work. In submitting your assessments you may be required to make and sign a declaration that it is your own work; so passing off another person's work as your own is fraud.

If you were to purchase materials from online 'paper mills' note that they are often careful to present the material you purchase only as 'examples'—it is up to you to make sure that you do not plagiarise and pass them off as your own work, no matter how tempting that might be.

Student Question 6

Can I work with my fellow students to produce an assessment together?

Advice from Tutor

Just to clarify your question: is the assessment you are working on a 'group assessment'? If so then, providing your group does not plagiarise (see the answers to your other questions), that would be acceptable.

If your assessment is an 'individual assignment', in other words you are expected to be producing the submission on your own, then **this is not acceptable**. Working together when you should be working as individuals is called 'collusion'. This is a form of cheating and, as a by-product, you would effectively be plagiarising each other's work by (I assume) not acknowledging that words and ideas came from the colleagues with which you were colluding. In any case, if individual submissions are required, working as a group in this way may be comparatively easy to detect as there may be several very similar responses to the task set!

This is not to say that you cannot have discussions with your colleagues about an assessment, but there is a difference between these general discussions and co-creating documents when the task set requires your own individual (non-collaborative) work.

Student Question 7

If I have written material for one assessment, can I use it again (all of it or significant parts exactly the same) for a different assessment?

Advice from Tutor

No you cannot. Taking your own work from one assessment then reusing it for another is what is called 'self-plagiarism'. It may be expressly forbidden by your institution's regulations; when submitting your work you may have to sign a statement to the effect that what you submit has not already been submitted for another piece of work. Taken to its (admittedly extreme) conclusion—imagine writing one assessment then resubmitting that same piece for all your other assessments and being awarded a degree! Of course, in practice the assessment tasks you are set are different. To obtain a good mark, significantly reworking any material you may have already written is both expected (so you do not self-plagiarise) but also in your own interests so that the material is appropriate and fit for purpose.

Student Question 8

Why do I have to provide a citation/evidence when we all know whose ideas these are? We were told in the lectures! Can I not assume that my tutor must know where the material came from?

Advice from Tutor

Your questions here relate to what is regarded (or not) as 'common knowledge'. A starting point is that for an assessment it is important that *you* demonstrate that you know where the ideas came from. As you develop higher level skills in analysis and evaluation then part of this is being aware that different authors may hold different points of view or have a different way of justifying the same point—it is important that the reader knows what the evidence base is and where the evidence came from.

More generally, common knowledge can be contested territory which may vary with academic discipline, industry sector, an individual's own experiences, and so on. As a general rule, it is better not to assume that it is common knowledge who wrote particular words or had a particular idea—better practice is to provide the relevant citation/reference.

Student Question 9

What if I am just poor at citation/referencing and have not wilfully set out to plagiarise/cheat? In other words I did not 'deliberately' miss out acknowledgement of the words, work, and ideas of others.

Advice from Tutor

As can be seen from the answers to your earlier questions, some forms of plagiarism may (as you suggest) relate to poor practice—but they are still plagiarism. Others, such as buying your answer online, are clearly plagiarism and ethically questionable.

In practice, it may be difficult to argue that your plagiarism is not deliberate given the time and attention which is usually given in your programme to highlighting good practice in terms of academic writing, avoiding plagiarism and (in contrast) the challenges and penalties which may occur if you do not adopt good practice and plagiarise. I suggest you read the advice in this Skillset and other Skillsets in this textbook.

Student Question 10

This all sounds very complicated! On the one hand, I am expected to use the work of others to provide theoretical underpinning for my work and to provide evidence for the points I make. On the other hand there seems to be lots of ways I can plagiarise and break the regulations. What can I do?

Advice from Tutor

I understand your dilemma! The best advice I can give is to reflect on what plagiarism is and how to avoid it—this Skillset and others will help with this. At its core, avoiding plagiarising relates to the key academic skills of citation and referencing. Work on developing these skills and seek advice from your tutors.

13(c) Why is avoiding plagiarism important?

From an ethical perspective, plagiarism is regarded within European and North American educational cultures as 'wrong'. Plagiarism is seen as a form of 'cheating' or 'academic dishonesty' and there may be severe penalties for breaking the rules. These may range from: a reduction in the mark given to your submission; a mark of zero being awarded; and, for particularly serious cases, expulsion from your programme of study.

Perhaps it is no surprise that an academic institution such as a university treats using other people's words, work, and ideas without acknowledgement as very poor ethical behaviour. After all, in common with academics and others, your tutors may have spent considerable time and effort carrying out research, writing articles, reports, and books all to extend knowledge within their discipline and also their own (and their institution's) reputation. 'Stealing' this work by copying it or using it (without due acknowledgement) undermines the value of all their efforts.

There is another aspect to this, which is that when you have graduated and are working for an organisation, your employers will expect that you behave in an ethical and appropriate way. Since plagiarism can be regarded as cheating, dishonest, or unethical, there may be professional repercussions later in your career if you are found to have plagiarised. For example the German Education Minister Annette Schavan resigned from her post after the University which awarded her doctorate revoked the award of the degree following an investigation into alleged plagiarism (BBC, 2013). In addition, employers will expect you to have the skill and understanding which your degree signifies—not that, in fact, it was others (whom you copied from) who actually have that expertise and knowledge!

13(d) Plagiarism detection software

The rise of the World Wide Web as a repository of materials, including the ability to access academic journals online, has been of great benefit to students in conducting research for their studies. No longer are the few copies of books, journals, or reports held in the library 'like gold dust'. Similarly word processing software enables us to construct well-presented documents. However, there is a danger that a 'copy and paste' mentality may occur, as it is a matter of a few key strokes to bring text from a document found on the Web to our own word processing software. This may then, without further attention, lead to others' work being plagiarised—deliberately or inadvertently. Consequently, 'plagiarism detection software' has been introduced which can allow both students and tutors to review and monitor work. This section briefly outlines how plagiarism detection software works.

In essence, plagiarism detection software (such as Turnitin) matches your work against the database which they hold of: material published on the Web (websites, reports, journal articles, and so on) as well as student work which has already been submitted to their database. Before such software existed, tutors might type a phrase into a search engine to see if there were any 'matches'—plagiarism detection software can perform this task efficiently and effectively on a much larger scale. For example, Turnitin can be customised by your tutor to include (or not) references or vary the extent of the size of the 'match' which is shown between your work and the material found on the database (matches of five words might show more comparison than matches of twenty words). The tutor can also vary whether you can resubmit work (perhaps to receive feedback from the software and an opportunity to enhance your work) or make the first submission the only one which is possible.

A typical process might be:

1 Student drafts assessment.
2 Student submits an electronic version of the draft to the plagiarism detection software.
3 Student can access a report indicating the similarity between the submitted document and material held by the software's database.
4 Student amends draft in light of the feedback from the software.
5 Steps 2–4 may be repeated.
6 Student submits the final version of their work to the software. In this case no further submission is possible.

The software may generate a number which indicates the similarity between what is submitted and materials 'matched' from the software's database; and may also indicate where in your document there is a 'match'. Key indicators that there may be a plagiarism issue are:

- A particularly high score for 'matches' against the software's database.
- Large parts of particular parts of your work matching other sources (e.g. Conclusion) Some tutors may have a percentage figure in mind (for example 20 per cent), above which they may examine your work in more detail. However there is no hard and fast rule regarding this as (depending on what is submitted) it may be that much of a particular score relates to citation/references which, not surprisingly, are commonly used in work written about management. So the raw score would typically require further interpretation. When in doubt about what the software's report is showing you, please ask your tutor for further clarification.

13(e) Plagiarism detection software as an enhancement tool

If you can submit a draft of your work and then review it before final submission, there is an opportunity to use what the software is 'telling you' to enhance your work. Key aspects to consider (based on a Turnitin Originality Report being generated; other software may work slightly differently) include:

- Where blocks of text are highlighted as 'matching' material from the database then check good citation practice (see Skillset 2). For example, do quotation marks indicate the start *and* end of a quotation correctly; are name, date, *and* page number given? Plus any other good practices which are applicable such as the quotation is indented from both sides. Correct any citations not following good practice. You may have to decide how small a block of text is worth your while investigating—start with the larger blocks.
- If there are 'matches' but no quotation marks and so on (and there was no intention that this text should be a quotation) then this may suggest that you have further work to do to paraphrase that part of your work and put it in your own words rather than drawing heavily on the words of others.
- Look at the location of the copied/highlighted text. Even if quotations are correctly cited, too many grouped together in one area may suggest that your writing adopted a strategy of 'he said', 'she said', and 'they said'. In other words there is a series of direct quotes (such as definitions of terms) which offers little in the way of analysis and evaluation. So consider amending this to reflect where the definitions agree or disagree, with a more limited number of quotations to provide key examples where appropriate. See Skillset 12 on critical analysis.
- A second tip regarding the location of matching text is that there may be certain areas of your work where it is unlikely or unexpected that your work would match the work of other people. For example, in the conclusion section where you are drawing together *your* own thoughts on *your* own work for the reader, it should be very unlikely that your words would 'match' those of someone else. In this case revising your work is strongly advised.
- Where certain key terms or phrases are matched by the software and they are in common use within your discipline you could read the sentence just to make sure that there is a citation to acknowledge that these concepts/ideas are not your own.

13(f) Activity

Consider the following questions in relation to regulations and practice regarding plagiarism detection/avoidance *at your own academic institution*:

- How is plagiarism defined?
- What counts as plagiarism?
- What are the penalties for plagiarising?
- Is plagiarism detection software available? How is it used and can you use it to receive feedback on drafts of your work?
- What support is available to help you develop your skills in avoiding plagiarism? Online? Academic tutors? Support staff specialising in academic skills? And so on.
- Consider whether you would benefit from contacting staff at your institution to help you enhance your academic writing skills (including citation/referencing; using/interpreting plagiarism detection software).

13(g) A checklist to help you avoid plagiarism

In conjunction with the material above, the following brief checklist can help you avoid plagiarism (there is some overlap with Section 13(f)). Ask yourself the following questions, reflect on your answers, and take action as required to fill any gaps in your knowledge.

1 Do I understand what plagiarism is and why it is such an important issue that I should make sure I avoid any charges of having plagiarised?

2 Have I identified what good citation/referencing practice looks like for my discipline and institution? Am I confident that I can consistently meet this good practice when I write assessments? [Where is the evidence for my 'confidence'?]

3 What processes and help do I have access to that will provide me with an opportunity to 'self-detect' and: (a) avoid any allegations of plagiarism; (b) develop my ability to write without plagiarising? This might include: access to plagiarism detection software to submit drafts; being reflective when reading others' work to identify good and not such good practice; support from tutors and others; and so on.

4 Am I making use of the processes and so on I identified from Point 3? If not, why not? Remember that prevention is better than having to deal with allegations of plagiarism.

5 How would I react if I was accused of plagiarism? If it was found that I had plagiarised—what would I do? The most important thought here is to decide that you would actively learn any lessons and strive to ensure that there were no further allegations of plagiarism.

13(h) Summary of the Skillset

Within European and North American academic cultures, to be held to account for plagiarism is a serious matter with potentially serious consequences for your academic (and future) career. Similarly, in the workplace, copying or passing off others' work as your own may have legal repercussions. This Skillset outlined what plagiarism is and why it is important to avoid it. Through a student–tutor dialogue and a number of self-reflective questions, you are encouraged to develop the skills to make your work 'plagiarism proof'. This Skillset should be read in conjunction with Skillset 2 on citation/referencing.

References

BBC (2013) *German minister Annette Schavan quits over 'plagiarism'*, 9 February. [Online resource] Available from: http://www.bbc.co.uk/news/world-europe-21395102

Glasgow Caledonian University (2012) *University Assessment Regulations: October 2012.* [Online resource] Available from: http://www.gcu.ac.uk/media/gcalwebv2/theuniversity/gaq/gaqfiles/University%20Assessment%20Regulations%202012_13.pdf

Further Resources

Plagiarism, org [Online Resource] Available from: http://plagiarism.org/ [A website devoted to plagiarism and avoiding it.]

PLATO (Plagiarism Teaching Online) [This is a very useful online interactive tool which explains what plagiarism is and how to avoid it. The software was developed by the University of Derby. See: http://www.preventplagiarism.co.uk/index.asp?pageId=167. It may be that PLATO is available within your institution or you could search for it online. As there is a cost for institutions to use the software (see http://www.preventplagiarism.co.uk/index.asp?pageId=171) a direct link has not been given here.]

TurnitinUK [Plagiarism detection software (and more)] Available from: http://www.submit.ac.uk/ [Note this is the home page for the site, your institution may already have its own links to Turnitin via, for example, your virtual learning environment.]

Write Check [Plagiarism detection (and more) site] Available from: https://www.writecheck.com/static/home.html

Writing Center (The), 2012, *Plagiarism*. [Online Resource] Available from: http://writingcenter.unc.edu/handouts/plagiarism/

See also the references/sources for Skillset 2 on citation/referencing.

Managing Strategy, Change, and Innovation

14 Strategic Management

Learning outcomes

- Understand the development of strategic management thinking

- Apply internal and external environmental analysis models

- Evaluate the options and choices available to strategic managers in a global environment

- Comprehend the dynamics of strategy in a global context

Michael Porter is one of most cited authors in strategy and his work on understanding why some firms are more competitive and profitable than others has been used by academics, students, and practitioners for many decades. Porter is one of the leading lights of the Harvard School of strategic thinkers who view strategy from the perspective of competitive positioning to gain a competitive advantage. Importantly, Porter emphasises that even where a firm has demonstrably achieved a competitive advantage, it is not a simple matter of rivals trying to replicate their effort that will achieve results. It is important that firms follow their own pathway to achieve a competitive advantage based on their unique bundle of resources, skills, competencies, and capabilities. To do so requires an understanding of both the supply and demand sides of the consumer/producer dynamic. Thus, strategic managers need to understand what customers want, but also they need to understand what value adding activities can be undertaken internal to the organisation that derives a distinctive capability and a competitive advantage as it delivers something different and better for consumers. Porter views strategy as being the link between the choices made on the demand side with unique choices on the supply side—or what he terms the value chain (Porter, 1985). Achieving competitive advantage requires both of these working together. Although other writers on strategy take a different perspective to Porter, the longevity of his theories and models is testimony to the clarity of exposition, his ability to adapt and update them in line with environmental changes, and his knowledge around strategy processes.

Skillset 14
Personal Development Planning

Personal Development Planning has a strategic dimension to it as students need to focus on where they aim to be at some point in the future. This may involve aspirations, continuous professional development, accreditation, and so on. Strategic management is about positioning an organisation to achieve its stated aims over a particular timeframe beyond the short or medium term.

Student study skills

Personal development planning is an integral part of students' abilities to effectively plan for their future and is key to organising their skills and capabilities around their professional aspirations. Students will be presented with a template they can use as a personal development plan which can be completed as their studies progress. Key elements of the plan will be described and an example of how to compile the plan will be a key feature.

Workplace skills

Personal development plans are a component of human resource requirements in most organisations and are used to reflect on past performance, monitor current performance, and set a plan for future targets and outcomes. This Skillset provides an opportunity for students to engage with the concept of personal development planning in a practical way and to initiate strategic thinking about their career goals.

Definitions

Strategy refers to a plan that helps to achieve particular stated aims, typically over a long period of time. There are many different definitions of strategy because it is a term used in many different contexts (business, military, sport, etc.). A strategy necessarily involves undertaking a series of actions to achieve stated aims (Bayliss et al., 2012). The management of the resources required to make this happen is what is referred to as strategic management. Strategic management involves determining the vision and mission of the organisation; setting aims and objectives; choosing the means and actions required for achieving those aims and objectives; and ensuring that the performance of the organisation is of a standard to achieve the stated aims and objectives over a set time period. Strategy is a process that can be either a deliberate set of actions that are prescribed, planned, and monitored or an emergent phenomenon that follows a pattern of behaviour that is consistent but without any pre-determined route to achieving a stated aim or aims. Strategic management is therefore characterised by feedback, knowledge, learning, and analysis, each of which contributes to the experience that managers call on for making future decisions.

Introduction

Chapter 14 begins with an overview of the strategic process and the different levels of strategy, followed by a discussion of the development of strategic management thinking since the 1950s when it first emerged as a distinct area of study. This is followed by a formal approach to understanding the means by which strategic managers can analyse the external and internal environments by the application of theoretical models, leading on to a discussion of how managers can make effective strategic choices given the resources and capabilities of the organisation. The chapter concludes with a discussion of the importance of globalisation by focusing attention on the methods by which strategic managers can exploit opportunities in the international environment. Opportunities and challenges within the global context are discussed and examples given for illustrative purposes.

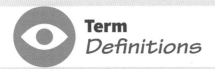

Term
Definitions

Strategy: the determination of long-term aims and objectives of an organisation and the plan of action to achieve them.

Strategic management: the use of theories, frameworks, models, and techniques to inform strategic thinking about the plans and actions designed to achieve long-term aims and objectives.

Figure 14.1 The strategy process

The strategy process

Key elements of the strategy process include formulating a mission statement (see Chapter 13) and overall purpose of the organisation; undertaking internal and external analysis; analysing the range of options available; choosing a strategic option; and implementing measures to achieve the aims and objectives and evaluating the performance of the chosen strategy (Lampel et al., 2013). Key stages are formulation, implementation, and evaluation and control. The value of undertaking a strategy process is that it allows managers to follow a systematic pathway to achieving stated objectives. Following a strategy process allows managers to evaluate each stage towards goal attainment. The process helps to clarify what is feasible and desirable for their organisation and focuses attention on the key elements for analysis by the company. Figure 14.1 illustrates the strategy process.

Levels of strategy in organisations

The key differences in business level and functional level strategies is reflected in the different levels of decision making power delegated to managers at these levels (Campbell et al., 2011). The business level is comprised of both corporate managers and business managers and it is their task to translate the statements of direction and intent generated at corporate level into objectives and strategies to be implemented at the functional level. Business level strategies set out how the company intends to compete in the selected product/market area. They must secure the best available market segment and control it to ensure they maintain a competitive advantage. Functional strategies are sometimes referred to as tactics because of their distance from corporate level strategy. Business strategists are the link between corporate and functional managers. Functional managers are responsible for product, geographical, and productive areas of operations. Functional managers develop short-term objectives based on annual targets for production, accounting, marketing, human relations, etc. This is the way firms can measure and control short-term performance. The data provided forms the basis for the evaluation of performance and corrective action.

The development of strategic management

As noted in the definition above, strategy is a long-term plan featuring a series of actions that combine to help achieve a stated aim (or aims) of an organisation, mostly some form of competitive advantage. Although it is not widely considered a discipline in itself, strategic management is a key element in the study of organisations. One striking characteristic of strategic management is the emphasis on 'top-down' decision making structure in organisations. That is, the role of strategy development and implementation invariably resides at the executive level of organisations. Ultimately, the strategy of an organisation determines its success or otherwise and, therefore, responsibility lies with those charged with the duty of overseeing the direction and performance of the organisation. Whilst business level managers may be involved in an advisory capacity in the strategy process, the key decisions are usually taken by those at corporate and executive level.

Strategic management as a recognised area of study emerged from the compilation of a series of business case studies in the 1950s by prominent management writers Peter Drucker (1954) and Philip Selznick (1957). Drucker pioneered the concept of management by objectives (MBO) that included the need to recognise the value of intellectual capital assets within an organisation—an insight that retains great relevance to strategy in the modern era. Indeed, Drucker coined the term 'knowledge workers' that is still in common usage by academics and practitioners today. Selznick's work has also endured with analysis of internal and external factors remaining an integral part of the strategy process. The determination of the strengths and weaknesses of an organisation is similarly a standard approach that matches internal and external factors affecting the organisation under study. The era in which Drucker and Selznick operated was characterised by planning, forecasting, and control mechanisms in organisations.

The origins of strategic management can be detected in work emanating from the discipline of industrial organisation or industrial economics with the structure-conduct-performance (S-C-P) model informing the dominant paradigm. Although the S-C-P approach was initially developed by Mason in the 1930s it was not until the 1950s that its expression found widespread favour after further elaboration by Bain (1959). Conceptually the model is linear in design with performance being dependent upon the conduct of buyers and sellers in any given market. Conduct is variously determined by factors such as prices, investment, marketing, technology,

Term
Definition

Competitive advantage: a competitive advantage is gained through the implementation of a value creating strategy by a firm that is not simultaneously being implemented by rivals (or potential rivals).

partnerships, and so on. It is also deemed to be dependent on the structure of each given market defined by the number and size distribution of sellers and buyers, the degree of product differentiation, entry barriers, cost structures, integration, and diversification.

The S-C-P model failed to stand the test of time as critics challenged the limiting effects of the linear relationship between the three elements. By the the 1970s the S-C-P model as the dominant paradigm gave way to the Positioning approach as championed by the Harvard School, even though key elements of S-C-P such as entry barriers and industry concentration remained salient to the discourse. This gave rise to the intellectual rivalry between the Harvard School and the Chicago School of thinking on strategic management. The Harvard School perceive these key elements (entry barriers and industry concentration) as a means of achieving above average industry profits; in contrast the Chicago School (as described by Demsetz, 1973, 1982; Barney, 1986) perceive entry barriers as informational and concentration as a result of efficiency. Fundamentally, Chicago School thinking focuses on the better use of underlying assets deployed by the firm (such as knowledge or innovation) as the means of achieving superior performance rather than the exercise of economic power. This thinking informed the development of the Resource-Based View (RBV) of the firm that has been prominent since the early 1990s and which is discussed in more detail later in this chapter.

The 1970s was a time of economic malaise and market turbulence leading to great uncertainty. In 1973 OPEC (Organisation of the Petroleum Exporting Countries) tripled the price of crude oil sending economic shockwaves around the world. Many economies slid into recession, including the UK. The seismic shift in economic performance proved a catalyst for the emphasis of strategic management to move away from rigid planning processes to a focus on methods to improve performance and profitability. Thus criteria relating to the size of firms, growth, and asset management became more prominent. Models such as the Profit Impact of Marketing Strategies (PIMS) were developed and applied with the purpose of creating a link between strategy and profitability. Much of the output relied on the robustness of the assumption that large firms with high market share were most likely to be the most profitable, a position later challenged by Harvard School writers such as Porter (1980) who pointed to the success of small and medium sized firms in securing high profits. Porter argued that profitability stemmed from the firm's ability to position itself in the market—hence the creation of the Positioning approach. The Positioning approach dominated the 1980s with many of the frameworks and models developed to aid analysis still widely used today.

Influential Harvard School writers on strategic management include Learned et al. (1965), Andrews (1971), Porter (1979, 1980, 1985, 1996, 2001), Ghemawat (1991), and the consultants from McKinsey and the Boston Consultancy Group. Seminal works have included the strengths, weaknesses, opportunities, and threats (SWOT) framework as a basis for analysing internal and external environments. Porter (1979) combined the SWOT framework with identified key concepts from industrial economics to create the five-forces (external) and value chain (internal) models, which will both be discussed later in the chapter. Applying these theoretical models can offer insights into why some industry sectors are more attractive than others (Five Forces) and why some firms' strategies perform better than others (value chain). Importantly, the value chain model underpinned the realisation by the Harvard School that internal activities of organisations are strategically significant and may be a source of competitive advantage—key tenets of the increasingly significant Resource-Based View during the 1990s.

In light of the insights offered by the RBV approach, the Harvard School revisited their interpretation of what strategy is. In particular, Porter (1996) adopted some RBV ideas when revising the definition of strategy including the acceptance that firms have to make trade-offs between value adding activities and the need to create a *'hard-to-replicate'* fit among parts of the chosen value adding activities carried out. Still, the 1990s marked a swing away from the Positioning approach to those with RBV ideas. The RBV takes account of the broader range of resources available to firms when setting strategies for competitive advantage. This includes those intangible resources such as experience, goodwill, and reputation alongside tangible ones of skills, finance, capital, etc. Of particular relevance are the assets that workers can bring to the firm in the form of skills, knowledge, competencies, and ideas. Combined, these form the organisation's resources and capabilities. Resources are the portfolio of available assets that are owned by the firm, and organisational capabilities are the attributes that transform those resources into added value. The coherence of the RBV approach in emphasising the importance of internal analysis encouraged Porter (1996) to re-evaluate his concept of strategy.

Beyond the RBV there have been other developments in strategic thinking throughout the 2000s and beyond. For example, the dynamic capabilities approach stemmed from the long-held belief that so many of the models and frameworks developed by academics and consultants were static in their construct. There is a consensus that the environment is dynamic and changeable but most of the models fail to reflect this key characteristic. Teece et al. (1997) initiated the quest to address this shortcoming by developing the concept of dynamic capabilities where the key to competitive advantage lies in the ability to integrate, build, and reconfigure internal and external competencies with competitive environments characterised by rapid change. There is a more fluid dimension to dynamic capabilities theory that is palpably missing in the RBV. It provides a focus for managers when deciding how to deploy resources that can be further developed internally and then released as a means of creating a competitive advantage. This ability is resonant with the challenge of formulating and implementing strategies in a rapidly changing environment. Strategic management has undergone significant transformations since the 1950s with further adaptations likely to emerge in future. Table 14.1 summarises the development of strategic management since the 1950s.

Table 14.1 Development of strategic management thinking since the 1950s

	1950s	1960–1976	1977–1987	1988–1999	2000s
Dominant paradigm	Case studies of chosen organisations	Corporate-level strategies and planning	Positioning approach	Resource-based view	Dynamic capabilities
Focus of attention	Planning and control	Growth	Industry and market choice	Competitive advantage	Innovation, creativity, knowledge, and change
Techniques	Structure-Conduct-Performance	Forecasting	Five Forces, generic strategy, value chain	Knowledge management, organisational learning, change	Collaboration, alliance, knowledge

Environmental analysis

Environmental analysis involves scanning the macroenvironment to detect signs of any change that is likely to impact the organisation. These changes may be political (change in the regulatory regime of an industry), economic (changes to inflation or interest rates or levels of employment), social (changes in tastes and fashions, attitudes, values, cultures), or technological (rate of innovation, infrastructure investment, new products). Brought together these factors form what is termed the PEST analysis—political, economic, social, and technological (various adaptations of it have been mooted such as SPENT or PESTLE, the former includes the natural environment (N) such as the earthquake and tsunami that struck Japan in 2011; the latter includes the legal (L) and environmental (E) factors). PEST is a useful starting point for trying to make sense of the wider environmental factors that affect businesses and the industries in which they compete. Managers need analytical skills to determine the level of influence that each factor change may have on their strategic aims, their rivals, partners, customers, and other stakeholders. Strategic managers need to monitor the macroenvironment to help them understand the factors most likely to affect their decision making, which in turn will affect the ability to achieve the stated aims of the organisation. Table 14.2 outlines possible PEST factors.

Table 14.2   **PEST factors**

Political	Social	Economic	Technological
Regulation	Tastes	Employment	Innovation
Law	Fashions	Interest rates	Technology development
Economic policy	Attitudes	Inflation	Technology investment
Public sector	Beliefs	Incomes	New products
Foreign policy	Values	Spending/debt	Patents awarded
Welfare	Culture	Consumer spending	Intellectual property rights
Health	Control	Investment	Communications
Education	Demography	Tax rates	Transport
Pensions	Ethics	Government spending	Research and development
Political system	Social structures	Exchange rates	Production

The competitive environment

Strategic managers need to understand the competitive environment in which their organisation competes. The greater the knowledge and understanding of the myriad factors that combine to form an industry sector, the better informed will be the decisions that managers make that determine the level of success for the organisation. Theoretical models can form the basis for helping managers in the process of generating knowledge about the competitive environment. Porter (1980) designed a model specifically for private sector organisations where the aim was profit maximisation. The Five Forces framework is a tool for analysing the key theme of relating average profits of industry competitors to the competitive forces affecting the industry. The identified key forces are the:

- threats posed by existing or new potential rivals;
- entry barriers to the industry;
- bargaining power of suppliers;
- bargaining power of buyers;
- threat or availability of new substitute products or services.

The Five Forces each have an influence on the level of competitiveness of a firm in the industry. Together the Five Forces determine the profit potential in the industry, and in turn the attractiveness of the industry. This is important because it helps managers of firms currently competing in the industry decide whether or not to stay in the industry. Also, it helps managers of firms currently competing in other or related industries decide whether or not they should seek to enter the industry. In both situations the Five Forces analysis helps managers formulate strategy by informing decisions regarding where and how to deploy their resources; and how they can improve their current competitive position and achieve a competitive advantage. The model provides a useful set of parameters around which investigation can reveal the conditions that determine the attractiveness of an industry. It should be noted that the Five Forces model focuses on the key factors that determine the competitive environment at industry level. It is not suitable for understanding the strategies of individual firms.

The value of the model lies in its simplicity and conceptual relevance to a range of industry sectors. The chosen Five Forces are typical external factors that determine the competitive environment in many sectors. The longevity of the model as a means of analysing the competitive environment owes much to its ease of application. Strategic managers can apply the model as a tool for better understanding the environment in which their organisation competes. First, though, it is useful to add definition to each of the Five Forces.

The threat of new entrants to the industry

The ease or difficulty with which firms can enter the industry determines the threat level of potential new competitors for established firms in the industry. There are some factors that deter entry, called entry barriers. These include economies of scale (McDonald's volume sales), high initial investment costs (the nuclear power companies), access to distribution channels (electronics and 'white goods' such as washing machines and refrigerators), legislative and regulatory measures (defence industry), cost advantages of existing firms (Amazon and eBay—first movers in the internet economy with high brand loyalty), and high levels of differentiation and brand loyalty enjoyed by existing firms (Mercedes Benz and BMW cars).

Threat of substitute products

The threat of substitute products that perform the same function and are produced in other industries can be a threat to established firms in an industry. The closeness of the substitute to replicating the function determines the level of the threat posed. If a firm produces a drink in a glass bottle it will face the threat of a substitute by a firm producing a similar drink in a plastic bottle. Substitutes constrain the ability of firms to raise prices because by doing so they will lose some customers to cheaper alternatives. This results in a reduction of industry attractiveness. The media industry is characterised by a high threat of substitutes. News can be accessed through many different media channels—newspapers, television, radio, internet, and each presents a viable substitute for customers.

Bargaining power of buyers

Buyers usually seek either low prices or higher quality at constant prices. Both of these force prices down below what businesses prefer and affect industry profitability. Suppliers will attempt to force prices upwards. The success they have in this depends on the power that buyers have in the market. In this context, buyers are assumed to be consumers of commercial products and businesses who buy products from other businesses. Buyer power is high when the buyer buys in bulk from the supplier; when there are available substitutes; the product represents a large portion of the buyer's total costs (this would induce buyers to seek lower prices); and where buyers have the potential to produce their own supply such as supermarkets producing their 'own brand' products.

Bargaining power of suppliers

Not surprisingly, the conditions that increase the bargaining power of suppliers are the converse of those that increase the bargaining power of buyers. The power of suppliers is high when there are few of them competing for the target customers; when their product is easily distinguishable from rivals (maintains customer loyalty); the costs of switching to another supplier is high for customers; when the supplier can extend their business to compete with the customer; or when the customer has little importance or influence.

Intensity of rivalry

Intense competitive rivalry pushes prices downwards and results in low profitability in an industry. Strong competition occurs when there are many competitors; there is slow market growth; fixed costs are high; there are high exit costs (initial investment may be high, so exiting the industry is the least attractive option); and where products are similar so that customers can easily switch between suppliers.

The Five Forces model is useful for gaining an understanding of the competitive environment facing firms. However, there are some limitations attached to it. First, it can only be a snapshot of the competitive situation at any one time. The model is not dynamic and, therefore, does not reflect the fast-changing environment that is a characteristic of the modern industrial landscape. Secondly, the model assumes that all firms are in competition with each other. However, this is far from the case. Collaboration, alliances, and partnerships between firms are a common feature of modern business. That such arrangements occur across the supply chain of industries makes the Five Forces model weak in terms of truly reflecting the nature of competition in the modern era. Nevertheless, its longevity can be put down to its relative simplicity and the ease of use to which it can be put in a number of different industry settings.

Mini case 14.1
The structure of the petrol retailing industry

A Five Forces analysis can be undertaken to give an insight into the competitive environment in a particular industry sector (Porter, 2008). The petrol retailing industry provides a good example. This industry is dominated by just a few big players (*Shell, BP, ESSO*) making the industry structure an oligopoly. The companies that comprise an oligopoly have a mutual vested interest in ensuring that prices remain high and stable. Therefore, competition tends to be on differentiating the products through advertising and free gifts rather than through price. This arrangement ensures that all members receive economic benefits. This structure characterised the industry for many years.

In the 1990s the supermarkets started to take an interest in petrol retailing because they saw it as an ideal opportunity to take advantage of the fact that 85 per cent of people who shop in their supermarket arrive by car. Supermarkets such as Tesco and Sainsbury entered the industry by cross-subsiding investment in petrol retailing from the profits made from food sales. This competitive force undermined the oligopolistic structure of petrol retailing and ushered in a period of price competition that has continued ever since (Macalister, 2013). Nevertheless, entry barriers remain steep for any prospective new rival since investment costs in petrol stations are expensive and links to distributors of petrol are difficult to achieve.

A Five Forces analysis of this industry could be summarised as:

Threat of entry: relatively low because of high initial investment costs and the need to break down established relationships between existing firms and their distributors.

Availability of substitutes: there are some substitute products available such as gas or electric cars, but to date no substitute has been close to matching petrol as a type of fuel for cars.

Power of buyers: buyers are unorganised, fragmented, and individualistic. Although there have been some attempts in the past to organise drivers to boycott petrol stations in protest at escalating prices, the effects have been short lived and ineffective.

Power of suppliers: suppliers of petrol have huge power because, at present, there is no viable substitute for the product. As long as this situation persists demand will always be high even if prices continue to rise.

Extent of rivalry: although the supermarkets have increased the level of competition in the industry, there remain relatively few firms that dominate in this sector. As long as this is the case, prices will remain high and relatively stable excepting for external factors such as war in the Middle East or increasing demands from developing nations such as China and India.

Sources:

Macalister, T. (19 April 2013) Supermarkets cut petrol prices again, *Guardian*. http://www.guardian.co.uk/business/2013/apr/19/supermarkets-cut-petrol-prices-again

Porter, M. E. (2008) 'The five competitive forces that shape strategy', *Harvard Business Review*, January, pp. 86–104.

Discussion points

Are oligopolistic industry structures good for the consumer?

Should government intervene to ensure minimum levels of competition exist within industry?

Questions and tasks

Describe what strategy is.

Choose an industry and undertake a Five Forces analysis.

Explain how to apply the value chain model for a company in a chosen industry.

Outline the limitations of the Five Forces model.

Online Resource Centre

Author commentary on these discussion points and questions can be found on the Online Resource Centre at: www.oxfordtextbooks.co.uk/orc/combe1e/

By determining the relative 'power' of each of these forces, an organisation can identify how to position itself to take advantage of opportunities and circumvent threats. The strategy of an organisation can be designed to exploit the competitive forces at work within the industry. When applying the model, it is important that strategic managers identify which of the Five Forces are the key forces at work in their industry sector at any given time. As the competitive environment changes rapidly, it is necessary to undertake a Five Forces analysis on a regular basis in order to adjust or align strategy to the key forces at work within the industry sector.

Critical reflection
Are there inherent weaknesses in Porter's Five Forces model?

There are a number of important limitations to the model that constrict its effectiveness. One of the key assertions made by Porter (1980) was that the Five Forces model enabled the assessment of the potential profitability of a particular industry. Although some evidence exists to support this claim, equally, there is evidence to suggest that company-specific factors (such as individual competences) are more important to profitability than industry factors (Rumelt, 1991). Also, the model implies that the Five Forces will apply equally to all competitors whereas, in reality, the strength of the forces differs markedly from business to business. For example, the model suggests that if supplier power is strong, then this will apply equally to all businesses across the industry. This is far from the truth, as large businesses face less of a threat from powerful suppliers compared to small businesses. The application of the Five Forces model is only relevant when the macroenvironment is stable, a scenario that is most rarely observed. The dynamic nature of the macroenvironment determines that the model needs to be constantly updated to preserve any relevance, a weakness acknowledged by Porter. Finally, the model assumes that all firms are in competition with each other. In light of changes in the nature of industry competition in the last decade or so, Porter revisited the model to take cognisance of the fact that partnerships, alliances, and joint ventures are a common feature of the environment. That the model is still widely used as a means of analysing the competitive environment by managers in the modern business environment is testimony to Porter's rigour in updating and revising the model as the macroenvironment evolved.

Internal analysis: the Positioning approach

The Positioning approach can be used as a basis for discussion. Porter's models of generic strategy, Five Forces, and value chain provide the theoretical underpinnings of the analysis. The generic strategies model is, as the name suggests, applicable to many firms and provides strategic choices for managers to follow. The Five Forces model is similarly generic and focuses on competitiveness and external factors. The value chain model, on the other hand, has an internal focus and can be applied to individual firms.

The value chain

Porter (1985) proposed the value chain model as a means of identifying those activities that form the basis of a firm's strategy for achieving competitive advantage by driving down costs or differentiating the product or service. Figure 14.2 illustrates the value chain model.

Primary activities directly add value to the end product or service. The support activities indirectly add value by providing the support necessary for the effective execution of the primary activities. A typical value chain analysis is likely to include:

- a breakdown of all the activities that are undertaken by the organisation;
- identification of the core activities of the organisation and their relationship with the current organisational strategy;
- evaluation of the effectiveness and efficiency of individual activities;
- identification of linkages between activities for additional added value;
- identification of blockages that prevent the organisation achieving competitive advantage.

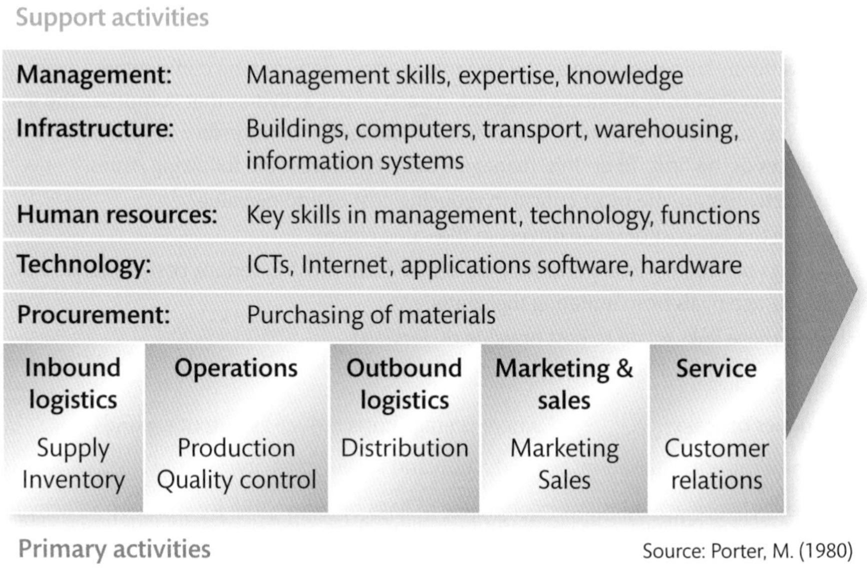
Support activities
Management: Management skills, expertise, knowledge
Infrastructure: Buildings, computers, transport, warehousing, information systems
Human resources: Key skills in management, technology, functions
Technology: ICTs, Internet, applications software, hardware
Procurement: Purchasing of materials
Inbound logistics
Supply Inventory
Operations
Production Quality control
Outbound logistics
Distribution
Marketing & sales
Marketing Sales
Service
Customer relations
Primary activities
Source: Porter, M. (1980)

Figure 14.2 The value chain model

Source: Adapted with the permission of Free Press, an imprint of Simon & Schuster Inc., from COMPETITIVE ADVANTAGE: Creating and Sustaining Superior Perfomance by Michael E. Porter. Copyright © 1985, 1998 by Michael E. Porter. All rights reserved.

Term
Definitions

Consumer value added: the organisation's ability to position a product or service better than rivals so that consumers are persuaded to recognise, buy, and value it accordingly.

Firm value added: the organisation's ability to create and sustain competences that underpin competitive advantage.

Porter's definition of value is determined by the amount buyers are willing to pay for a product or service. Added value is measured by the total revenue after the cost of production has been met. Differentiation of products or services can add value in all the value chain activities. Key sources of added value derive from the choices of activities that are to be undertaken; the links between primary and support activities; integration of supply chain partners; the timing of activities; or location advantages. The value chain model is most appropriately applied to manufacturing firms (although Porter and Millar, 1995, recognised the value adding potential of information technology) characterised by physical flows of materials. Thus, adaptations were needed for firms with core activities involving information flows (such as insurance, banking, stock trading, etc.).

Applying the value chain

The value chain recognises that each individual activity in the production process plays a part in determining cost, quality, and image of the end-product. According to Porter (1985) each activity contributes to the firms' overall cost position and creates a basis for differentiation. Cost and differentiation are seen as the two main factors determining competitive advantage. A minimum level of competence is required in each of the activities that comprises the value chain, but to succeed in gaining a competitive advantage it is necessary to identify the core competences of the firm. To do this, managers need to address the following issues:

- Which activities are the most critical in reducing cost or adding value?
- What are the key cost or value drivers in the value chain?
- What links between primary and support activities do most to reduce cost, enhance value, or discourage rivals from imitating the strategy?
- How do these links relate to cost or value drivers?

Cost drivers include:

Economies of scale:	where average costs reduce as output expands
Pattern of capacity utilisation:	production and labour capacity
Linkages between activities:	coherence of links between primary and support activities
Interrelationships:	alliances, collaboration with supply chain partners
Geographical location:	key advantages of proximity to resources or customers
Policy choices:	product range, suppliers, wage structures, human resource
Institutional factors:	political, legal, regulatory issues

Critical reflection
*How has the internet changed
the value chain?*

The emergence of the internet, and with it e-business and e-commerce, made the need for a new value chain model acute as firms sought to contextualise their strategies around the new medium of communication. Rayport and Sviokla (1995) developed the virtual value chain model that more closely matched the activities of firms engaged in gathering, organising, selecting, synthesising, and distributing information via electronic means. There is a strategic dimension to the role of information in the virtual value chain when it is integrated with physical activities to create value added products or services. For example, activities may include the gathering of information necessary to organise and coordinate the logistics of matching demand with supply criteria. The physical value chain activities may include the actual distribution of the product to customers. This is evident in the virtual value chain of postal distribution companies such as *FedEx* and *DHL*.

Value drivers

Value drivers refer to those features of added value perceived by customers other than low price. Such value drivers derive from closely understanding the needs and characteristics of customers. Value drivers include policy choices on product features, design, applications, and the skills and expertise of staff. Value is also added where there are clear benefits derived from the linkages between primary and support activities.

It is the role of strategic managers to choose the most appropriate elements of the value chain to focus resources on, build capabilities and core competences, and leverage the added value into a competitive advantage. Much depends on the links between the primary and support activities and how they come together in coherence with the firm's strategy. Although firms may not be responsible for all the activities that come together to deliver their product to customers, they need to take an active interest in the performance of those who fulfil the activities along the supply chain. For example, many firms outsource the customer service activity of their business but they need to ensure that good standards of service are observed (McIvor, 2005). Likewise, a firm may depend on a road haulage firm to deliver products to retailers. Here, they need to ensure that the products are delivered on time and in good condition. To sustain a competitive advantage over time requires a core competence. Core competence refers to the ability of a firm to sustain a competitive advantage over the long term by adding value to consumers that other rivals find difficult to match (Barney, 2010). An organisation can achieve a core competence by focusing on excellence in one or more parts of the value chain. There is usually a coherent link between the primary and support activities that underpin the value adding for customers. Examples include linking inbound and outbound logistics with technology (*FedEx*), linking human resource management with service (professions), linking operations with management (car industry), or linking the marketing function with procurement (Marks & Spencer). These firms all excel at their core activities such that their reputation is enhanced, customers recognise the added value, and brand loyalty results.

Mini case 14.2
Adding value at AES Cargo, Hungary

One way Hungarian freight logistics and distribution company, AES Cargo, succeeds in achieving a competitive advantage is to take advantage of their central European location and to offer customers added value service by developing and implementing software that automates every aspect of internal processes. Customers can track the progress of their items from sender to destination. In many organisations this is a vital added value as important functions and decisions may rely on the delivery times of packages. For example, the transport of drugs in the medical sector may mean the difference between life and death for a patient. Perishable goods such as flowers and fruit rely on quick delivery to maintain their value. If customers can closely estimate arrival times of packages they can organise their business model around it. This added value increases their brand loyalty to their distributors.

The key linkages in the value chain for AES Cargo are between the primary activities of inbound and outbound logistics and the support activity of technology. Although this type of software is diffused throughout the industry now, the Hungarian logistics industry were pioneers of this added value service and this built upon their existing competitive position in the global distribution services industry. Figure 14.3 highlights the value adding activities of AES Cargo.

Discussion points

How important is the role of distribution to determining competitive advantage?

Is it possible to sustain a competitive advantage by successfully linking key activities in a value chain?

Questions and tasks

Explain how to apply the value chain model.

Choose two rival companies at the same level of supply in the same industry and compare and contrast their value adding activities.

Support activities

Infrastructure:	Buildings, computers, transport, warehousing, information systems			
Human resources:	Key skills in management, technology, functions			
Technology:	ICTs, Internet, applications software, hardware			
Procurement:	Online purchasing of materials			
Inbound logistics	**Operations**	**Outbound logistics**	**Marketing & sales**	**Service**
Real-time supply inventory	Automated distribution Quality control	Distribution tracking systems	Online marketing	Personalise customer relations

Primary activities

Figure 14.3 The value chain for AES Cargo

Explain the rationale behind the chosen linkages in the value chain for AES Cargo, Hungary.

What distinct advantage does Hungary have as a centre for distribution in Europe?

Online Resource Centre
Author commentary on these discussion points and questions can be found on the Online Resource Centre at: www.oxfordtextbooks.co.uk/orc/combe1e/

Strategy options and choice

Strategic analysis highlights the range of options available to decision makers and provides the basis for making choices about strategy. The options available can be widespread or limited depending on the resources available and the organisation and the extent of its ambitions. Strategic choices will decide the future prospects of the organisation so the importance of getting it right cannot be overstated. Options available may cover a number of areas of activity including customer base, product portfolio, technology investment, human resources, market development, etc. There are also choices to be made regarding the alternative ways of delivering the chosen strategy.

Strategic options

A useful model for highlighting the strategic options available to firms is Ansoff's (1987) product/market matrix. Apart from market withdrawal, each element of the matrix assumes growth. Of course, growth is not usually an aim of public sector organisations more likely is alterations to the mix service provision. The construct of the matrix consists of existing and new markets and existing and new products/services. Figure 14.4 illustrates Ansoff's product/market matrix model.

Existing market/same product or service

The stage of maturity in the market plays a key role in determining choice in this segment. Markets follow a common trajectory of growth, maturity, and decline. Each segment of the matrix contains strategic options.

Term *Definition*

Strategic options: potential solutions to questions of how to position the organisation in relation to product and resource markets, competitors, and macroenvironmental forces.

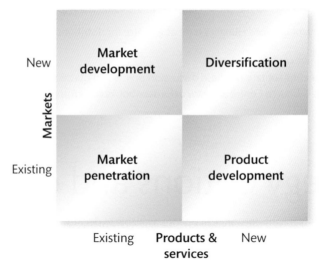

Figure 14.4 Ansoff's product/market matrix

Source: Based on Ansoff (1957).

Market penetration

This stage is designed to increase market share. It is easier to manage growth in market share in a growing market compared to one that has reached maturity. Firms may choose to lower price, increase promotional and advertising spend, or improve distribution.

Consolidation

Consolidation refers to protecting and maintaining market share in existing markets. In growth markets this requires an increase in the volume of business. Mature markets would possibly entail improving cost efficiency and customer service in order to retain custom. Acquisition of other rivals may be the preferred option in declining markets; this would help the organisation consolidate their position.

Withdrawal

Withdrawal is an option where there is intense competition in a market with no prospect of increasing market share. Changing circumstances may determine that resources are better deployed elsewhere.

Existing market/new product

A strategy of product development allows a firm to retain a relatively secure hold of its present markets while altering products or developing new ones. Many industries are characterised by rapidly changing product offerings, especially in the hi-tech and creative industries, where consumer demand is variable and subject to changes in trends and fashions. The car industry is also an example of change where manufacturers continually update and upgrade features or extend their model range. New product development incurs a risk because there is no guarantee that customers will buy the new products.

Term
Definition

Growth strategy: long-term action plan for expansion of new or existing markets and products.

New market/present product/service

Market development requires seeking new markets for existing products or services. Three main ways of doing this are by entering new geographical markets (perhaps by becoming more international in scope); targeting new market segments (by age, gender, income, lifestyle, etc.); and developing new uses for a product.

Diversification

There are two main forms of diversification: related and unrelated.

Related diversification

Related diversification entails developing competing or complementary activities to the existing business. With related diversification there is some link between existing and new activities. This type of diversification has the advantages of allowing the firm some control over inputs and the opportunity to expand by using existing skills.

Managers of a manufacturing business may decide to diversify into making their own components rather than buying them from a supplier. This is diversification in new products for existing markets. Alternatively a manufacturer may produce existing products but sell them in new markets.

Unrelated diversification

Unrelated diversification refers to developing new products for new markets outside the existing business. This is a high risk strategy because the firm will need to develop its capabilities and competences from scratch in an industry where they have no real experience. However, some organisations, such as multinationals or conglomerates, have the resources to manage this transformation and very often have vast and widely different products and services in their portfolio. This is why unrelated diversification is sometimes termed 'conglomerate diversification'. Examples include supermarkets, such as *Tesco*, moving into financial services or sportwear manufacturers, such as *Adidas*, moving into personal hygiene products.

Alternative methods for delivering strategy

It is worth considering other ways in which firms can deliver a strategy including internal development, acquisition or joint ventures.

505

Internal development

Internal development relies on the expansion or redeployment of relevant resources at the firm's disposal. The advantage to the firm is that it retains full control over all aspects of developing new products and services. This is especially important for firms which are innovative and creative and seek to protect their new products from imitation by rivals. Firms engaged in developing new fighter aircraft have a vested interest in keeping all aspects of their activities secret. By keeping all activities in-house, they lessen the risk of imitation and copying. Other industries, such as pharmaceuticals, biochemistry, life sciences, and computing, develop new products in-house for this reason. Traditionally, the public sector sought this strategy to ensure control over important services such as repair and maintenance of buildings. More recently, government policy has been to encourage local authorities to contract out such services to the private sector, thereby lessening the scale of this approach in the public sector.

Acquisitions and mergers

Acquisitions occur when one firm takes over ownership of another firm. Mergers are when two firms agree to merge their activities to become one larger organisation (Johnson et al., 2011). There are numerous reasons why firms seek acquisition as a strategy. First, and most commonly, it is to gain the market share of a rival, thereby simultaneously increasing their industry power by reducing the competition. Other reasons include accessing key skills owned by rival firms; acquiring valuable brands (an example is *Nestlé's* takeover of *Rowntree* with their portfolio of world renowned confectionery products such as Kitkat); acquire technological advantage; gain marketing and sales expertise; or to break up and sell for a profit.

Mergers have become more common in recent years as the price of acquisitions has escalated (Caruso, 2013). Mergers have the advantage of being agreed upon by the two sets of owners. This harmony does much to ease the amalgamation of the two firms. Mergers are especially advantageous where there is synergy of activities between the firms. That is, their activities complement each other in the process of creating and selling the output. For example, one firm may possess production capacity and expertise in manufacturing process, another may operate in the same industry but have expertise in marketing and sales. If these two firms merge it is possible to extend the value adding activities along the value chain and create a competitive advantage that rivals find difficult to match.

Acquisitions and mergers have been a key feature of the global industrial landscape in the last decade with many important industries subject to structural change as a result of increasing economic power being vested in ever fewer firms (Faulkner et al., 2011). This trend has been evident in financial services (the merger of *Halifax* and *Bank of Scotland* to form *HBOS*, now owned by *Lloyds Banking Group*); media industry (consolidation of the UK independent television (ITV) industry from sixteen firms to one that has no franchise); *Time-Warner* and *AOL* (one of the biggest mergers in history); telecommunications (Vodafone's acquisition of *Mannesmann* of Germany); car manufacturing (*Rover* taken over by a Chinese conglomerate), and so on.

Even though acquisitions and mergers have been commonplace in recent years their record of success is not inspiring. Around 70 per cent of acquisitions end in failure. The main reason for this is the lack of time firms have to undertake proper research into the true financial and trading position of firms they seek to acquire. Shareholders very often put pressure on managers to achieve quick returns on their investments leading to injudicious takeover decisions. Very often the post-acquisition period is marked by disharmony within the new organisation. Workers sometimes do not perform to the same level when they are owned by a distant and invisible

Acquisition: the joining of unequal partners by the process of one organisation buying another.

Merger: the joining together of two organisations to become one by the mutual consent of the majority of shareholders.

corporate entity. Also, there is likely to be a period of flux as new systems and styles of management bed in, new structures are devised and implemented, and new methods of dealing with customers, partners, and suppliers are introduced. All these factors can combine to lead to escalating costs which add to the financial burden already accrued by the price of buying a rival firm.

Joint developments and alliances

Sometimes it is more prudent for firms to engage in joint developments or alliances with other partner firms to achieve a particular strategic aim. Acquisitions and mergers, by their nature, are permanent arrangements and once finalised become part of an organisation's business. Joint developments or alliances have the advantage of being temporary coalitions between firms with mutual benefits to gain from such arrangements. Arrangements can vary between highly formal contractual obligations that clearly set out the scope and extent of the arrangement to loose, informal understandings based on trust.

The main attraction associated with joint developments or alliances is the limits it places on risk. Acquisitions and mergers incur high risks of failure whereas less formal or temporary arrangements permit both partners to review the arrangement and make changes at any time. Such arrangements can bring together the most unlikely of partners for specific purposes. An example of a joint venture is the one arranged between *Kentucky Fried Chicken* (*KFC*) and the Japanese electronics firm *Mitsubishi*. *KFC* wanted to enter the Japanese fast food retailing industry but had no experience of marketing, sales, and supply chain issues in the country. *Mitsubishi* have long established contacts in many different sectors of Japanese industry and wield much influence in the Japanese market. For a percentage of the profits generated, *Mitsubishi* agreed to a joint venture with *KFC* to introduce the brand into the Japanese market.

Strategic choices

Porter (1980, 1985) identified two basic types of competitive advantage—cost leadership or differentiation. From this basic premise, he devised the generic strategy model for competitive advantage which comprises:

- cost leadership;
- differentiation;
- focus.

Cost leadership

A cost leadership strategy is one where the firm seeks to be the least-cost producer of the product or service in the industry. Cost leadership can be gained in many different ways but the cost leader must be able to produce and distribute the product or service to customers at prices lower than any of its rivals. This strategy requires economies of scale in production and close attention to reducing costs at every opportunity throughout the productive process. Means of lower costs includes imitating and copying existing products, minimising marketing and promotional spend, minimal training of staff, producing mass market standardised products, setting up close to customers, and offering minimal customer service. Customers will then be faced with a simple trade-off between low price and quality. If price is the dominant trigger for buying, then the least-cost producer would be able to satisfy that market demand. Customers seeking quality would look elsewhere. The cost leadership generic strategy is most evident in industries that produce mass market products, where switching costs are low for consumers and where competition is based predominantly on price. Some food retailers and supermarkets such as *Lidl*, *Kwiksave*, and *Iceland* operate cost leadership strategies.

Mini case 14.3
The rise and rise of Air Asia

One of the best examples of a cost leadership strategy is that of Malaysian budget airline *Air Asia*. The company is a low cost airline that operates both domestic and international flights based on a low fare, no frills business model. Under the energetic leadership of founder Tony Fernandes, the company has sought to reduce operating costs in every aspect of their business activities to be able to offer the lowest prices to customers (Paulsen, 2013). Cost leadership has stemmed from having low levels of service, automating the sales and distribution function, minimising advertising, using low cost, out-of-city airports, minimising the amount of luggage per passenger, employing fewer staff at their Kuala Lumpur headquarters, and having quick turnarounds of their aircraft (aircraft incur most costs when on the ground). The airline was the first in the region to introduce ticketless travel and unassigned seats (Harvard Business Case Study, 2011). Many aspects of the business model mirror that of the pioneer of low cost flights—SouthWestern Airlines in the USA. However, the roll-out of the strategy coincided with a huge rise in demand for air travel in South East Asia that ensured high levels of maximisation of capacity on scheduled flights. The business model and the generic strategy have proved to be highly successful for the airline in terms of profit, turnover, and sales. The airline is expanding their routes to include many destinations across the highly lucrative Chinese market. Consolidating their position as the least cost supplier of budget flights in the region has delivered a competitive advantage to the airline.

Sources:

Harvard Business case Study (2011) Air Asia, Cambridge, MA, Harvard Business School. http://mygreenztech.blogspot.co.uk/p/harvard-business-case-study-air-asia.html

Paulsen, J. H. (2013) *De- and Restructuring Leadership: The Leadership of Tony Fernandes—Air Asia*, Santa Cruz, Grin Verlag.

Differentiation

Differentiation refers to a strategy where a firm offers a product or service that is distinctive from the offerings of rivals and is valued by customers. Porter (1985) argued that differentiation has to be something beyond low price, something unique that adds value to customers, and for which they can charge a premium price. Differentiation has the potential to be more profitable than cost leadership if customers are prepared to pay premium prices for a higher quality product or service.

Differentiation can be achieved in many different ways, including advertising, promotion, marketing, design and applications of products, packaging, image, reputation, etc. Many industries are characterised by high levels of differentiation such as the mobile phone industry. Mobile phone companies try to differentiate their offerings by advertising and promotion of their products but there have also been significant advances in technology that underpin the strategy too. The basic mobile phone product offered only communications between one person and another. However, with each successive generation of mobile telephony there has been the roll out of differentiating features such as photographic capability, internet access, MP3 players, and so on. The design of mobile phones has also been used as a differentiator with different designs aimed at different market segments. In other industries the differentiating aspect may revolve around quality of service (hospitality), distribution (postal services), or branding (fashion items).

The sportswear company *Nike* is a good example of a firm engaged in differentiation as a generic strategy. *Nike* is in intense competition with rival *Adidas* for domination of this very lucrative and global market. One of the main competitive forces is advertising and marketing of the brands. *Nike* and *Adidas* have been busy buying up the rights to use the world's leading sportsmen and sportswomen as a promotional front for their goods. The rivalry is intense and this is reflected in the amount of money these companies are prepared to pay the leading sports people to be part of their marketing strategy. In the case of *Nike* one of the most important sports contracts was signed with basketball icon Michael Jordan. Of course marketing strategies based on sports stars is a precarious business as *Nike* discovered when golfer Tiger Woods' reputation was irreparably damaged by lurid stories concerning his private life. Sometimes a new star bursts on to the scene before firms can exploit their newfound fame. Jamaican sprinter Usain Bolt had already signed up to *Nike's* rival *Puma* prior to his stunning

Term
Definition

Generic strategy: strategy for competitive advantage based on value adding activities that aligns most closely to the organisation's competitive environment.

performance at the Beijing Olympics. Differentiation in this case covers design of the products, advertising campaigns, promotional tours, marketing material, logos, reputation, and image.

Focus

A focus strategy involves competing in a particular market segment, such as targeting a specific customer group by age, gender, income, location, etc. There are two variants to the focus strategy—cost focus and differentiation focus. There are numerous examples of firms pursuing a focus strategy. Some travel companies target a specific market segment (*Club Med 18–30* or *Saga* for the over 60s), others target the whole market (*Thomson*). *Rolls Royce* target a wealthy market segment for their cars, whereas *Ford* take a broader view with different types of cars for many different market segments. A generic strategy can offer firms protection against the pressures created in the Five Forces model. For example, cost leadership through economies of scale is a powerful entry barrier and one that some mass market producers use to maintain their competitive advantage. Differentiation can also create entry barriers by creating a powerful brand or image that prospective newcomers to the market would find difficult to emulate.

Interestingly, it was Porter's contention that firms ought to choose between a cost leadership strategy (narrow or broad focus) or a differentiation strategy (narrow or broad focus) or else risk being 'stuck in the middle'. Porter believed that firms need to have clarity and coherence in their choice of generic strategy and stick with it. However, in the years since the generic strategy model was devised, it can be seen that some companies can successfully operate both a cost leadership and differentiation strategy simultaneously. For example, *Honda*, the car manufacturer, is able to produce a range of cars for many different market segments at low cost because of their long-standing expertise in design, engineering, manufacturing, and operations. However, the company also differentiates the range of cars they make in terms of design, advertising, and marketing.

Global perspectives on strategy

So far the discussion of strategy has been focused on formulation. Once the internal and external analysis has been undertaken and options and choices made, attention turns to implementation. The implementation of strategy may involve a number of different activities all of which are designed to put into action the plans for achieving stated aims. Some examples of implementation include key issues that are discussed elsewhere in this book, such as human resource management (Chapter 8), changes to the organisational structure (Chapter 11), influencing changes to the organisational culture (Chapter 12), or means of improving innovation through organisational learning (Chapter 16). In this section the focus turns to strategies for internationalising the organisation's activities.

Whilst some companies are only concerned with operating in domestic markets, a great many more have expanded operations in the last two decades to the international arena as a result of political (collapse of communism in Eastern Europe, opening up of markets in China), economic (increasing affluence and consumerism in key areas of the globe such as the Far East), social (increased mobility and multiculturalism), and technological (digital economy, logistics, distribution, telecommunications) factors. Firms have exploited these changes by adopting international or global strategies (Ghemawat, 2007). Firms who are said to be 'international' are those who carry out some of their activities in a foreign country or countries. Firms become 'global' when they compete in industries that span the globe (media, software development, cars, pharmaceuticals, etc.), set up, manage, and integrate wholly owned subsidiaries in foreign countries, and take advantage of the global consumer culture for products such as fashion, music, transport, telecoms, food, and entertainment. Levitt (1983) first coined the phrase the 'global village' to mean the homogenisation of consumer culture around the globe. Thus, *Levi's*® jeans, *Sony*'s Walkman®, and *McDonald's* burgers are as culturally relevant in Tokyo or Madrid as they are in Los Angeles or Rio.

To understand the concept of globalisation it is necessary to know the extent to which it exists in any particular industry and the types of activities within the industry that can be considered either global or not global in characteristic. For this a useful theory is that of the global drivers framework developed by George Yip (1992). The four drivers are:

- market;
- government;
- cost;
- competition.

Yip's framework helps to determine which parts of an industry can be considered global and which are not. Importantly, this offers a more insightful basis for analysis compared to the rather limiting approach of determining whether an industry as a whole is global or not. The framework also helps managers to develop a coherent global strategy by focusing attention on the key drivers. Yip also emphasises that firms may have a global strategy but also operate a local strategy simultaneously. Managers seek to exploit the benefits of globalisation such as access to new markets, greater market share, potential for increased profits, and so on but to do so they need to understand the characteristics of global markets. Figure 14.5 highlights some of the possible drivers of globalisation.

Term
Definition

Globalisation: the extent to which competition in one country is influenced by competition in other countries.

Market drivers	Cost drivers
• Convergence of consumer demand • Global customers • Global distribution channels • Global marketing campaigns • Presence in lead countries	• Global economies of scale and scope • Sourcing efficiencies • Logistics advantages • Comparative advantages in costs • High product development costs
Government drivers	Competitive drivers
• Advantageous trade policies • Global technical standards • Common marketing regulations • Government-owned competitors or customers • Host government concerns	• High exports and imports • Competitors from across the globe • Country interdependence • Globalised competitors

Figure 14.5 Global drivers

Market drivers

Market drivers are perhaps the most important catalyst for the emergence of globalisation in the last two or three decades. As noted previously the extent to which common customer needs converge around certain types of products provides opportunities for a firm if they can understand and exploit the distinct cultural, legal, economic, and social characteristics of the market. Many leading firms such as *Apple*, *Nike*, *Volkswagen*, and *Vodafone* have accessed global markets by adapting to customer demands. Global customers buy products and services from the global suppliers. A distinction can be made between national global customers (those who buy from global suppliers for use in one country, such as Chinese firms sourcing copper from global markets to service their growing telecommunications infrastructure industry) and multinational global customers (those who buy from global suppliers for use in several countries, such as computer manufacturers who source software globally and who sell their end product in different countries).

An added advantage is the access to global distribution channels (Sreenivas and Srinivas, 2008). Industries such as consumer white goods (refrigerators, washing machines, etc.), cars, and sports apparel have well-established distribution channels that can act as a barrier to entry against prospective rivals of leading firms. Global marketing campaigns also help firms access global customers, especially in lead countries such as the USA, the UK, China, and Japan. In line with the homogenisation of consumer cultures, the advertising and promotional campaigns that underpin the marketing of products and services can be designed in a way that appeals to a global target market. The more transferable the marketing, the more economies of scale can be achieved in the marketing spend. However, it should be noted that a trend has emerged in many regions where consumers are turning towards products and services that more closely align to their domestic culture. Consequently, companies such as *McDonald's* and *Coca Cola* have increasingly adapted their advertising to match local characteristics. Banking giant *HSBC* incorporate this idea into their advertising with the slogan 'The world's local bank'.

Cost drivers

There are opportunities for reducing the costs by engaging in globalisation. Global markets are of such significant size that economies of scale can be derived. This is where the average cost of production declines as more products are sold. Similarly, there are economies of scope to be gained as activity in one product or market area leads to benefits in another. For example, pharmaceutical companies benefit from the research and development and technology innovation not only in the delivery of new drugs but also in the methods by which those drugs are produced. Companies can also gain cost advantages by outsourcing activities to global markets or by accessing cheaper raw materials or labour. This has been a contentious issue as some firms have been accused of exploiting low cost economies in least developed or developing countries for the purposes of economic gain. Other cost drivers of globalisation are those associated with logistics or the sourcing of raw materials. Thus, low distribution and transport costs and levels of local pricing of raw materials will generate activity in the globalisation process.

Government drivers

Governments (both individually and collectively) have sought to enable the free trade of goods and services around the globe since the end of the Second World War. Free trade encourages wealth creation, makes goods and services available to customers, broadens the range of products and services available, and encourages entrepreneurship. Where barriers to trade exist, wealth creation is stifled and this can lead to a contagion around the world. For example, in the run up to the Second World War many countries were suffering from economic downturn. In response some countries erected trade barriers to protect their own producers against competition. However, other countries simply retaliated and similarly erected trade barriers. Soon the free flow of goods and services started to dry up and the whole international community suffered. Global recession ensued raising further the political tensions between nations which contributed to the outbreak of war. Since 1945 various bodies have been set up to ensure that the same scenario is avoided. These include the World Trade Organization (WTO) and the General Agreement on Tariffs and Trade (GATT).

Beyond the setting up of bodies geared towards encouraging the free flow of trade, other 'governmental' factors drive globalisation. Common technical standards mean that products produced in one country can be sold in many others. Therefore, there are common standards for everything from packaging sizes to telecommunications, machine components to air traffic control, and so on. Government drivers also include state-owned organisations such as parts of the aerospace industry in France or *Petrobras*, the state-owned oil company in Brazil. These industries are deemed so strategically important to the economy that state intervention has ensued. Critics point to this being a barrier to globalisation rather than a driver as it interferes with the free market mechanism. Very often state-owned organisations are subsidised to protect them from the competitive forces of the free market. However, the trend in the last thirty years has been for governments around the world to sell off previously state-owned organisations (such as *BT* in the UK) to the private sector. Governments around the world have different perspectives in relation to globalisation. Some countries, such as the UK, Poland, and Mexico, are closely aligned to the concept of the free market and have relatively liberal regimes for attracting inward investment. Others, such as Japan, have a history of protecting key industries such as car manufacturing and the electrical goods sector. Thus, host government concerns can either hinder or help the extent of globalisation.

Competitive drivers

There are a number of factors that determine the strength of competitive drivers, and in turn, an industry's level of globalisation (Yip, 1992). High levels of global competition are correlated to high levels of imports and exports between trading nations, especially where those nations are geographically spread out across the globe. It is also determined by the level of economic interdependence between trading nations. The global economy is very much interdependent in the modern era as the performance of one region affects the prospects of others. For example, the USA is the biggest economy in the world and sucks in huge amounts of imported goods from other countries. As the US economy slowed in the wake of the credit crunch of 2008, so less consumer demand meant that less imports were demanded leading to an economic downturn in those countries exporting to the USA. This is a scenario that is played out across the globe as countries readjust to economic structural transformation.

The combination of the global drivers determines the extent of globalisation. This phenomenon grew throughout the 1990s and into the 2000s before the financial meltdown of 2008 slowed its progress. However, it was not just economic factors that slowed the march of globalisation. Managers had to think clearly about their marketing strategies and the types of products they were offering in global markets in more detail as the nature of consumer demand started to change. Even prior to the credit crunch there was evidence of the market demand characteristics changing. The established model of selling mass produced, homogenised products supported by global marketing campaigns was giving way to a more sophisticated demand by consumers around the globe. The challenge was to operate globally, but deliver goods and services that closely matched the demand characteristics of local consumers.

514

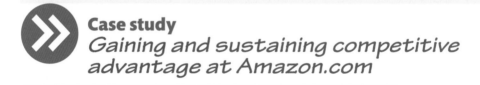

Case study
Gaining and sustaining competitive advantage at Amazon.com

www.amazon.com
www.amazon.com

Introduction

In the early 1990s Jeff Bezos left his job as a Wall Street trader to embark on an entrepreneurial venture that would lead to the creation of one of the world's most successful online businesses. The era coincided with the development and commercialisation of the internet as a means of channel communication between firms and their suppliers, customers, and partners. Bezos resolved to formulate a strategy for retailing online that would harness the wide-ranging attributes of the new technology. Arriving in his home town of Seattle in 1993 he decided that his first venture into the embryonic online retailing industry would feature bookselling, with his new venture being called *Amazon.com*. The rationale being that if the transaction did not meet customer expectations their loss would be minimal in financial terms (Combe, 2006). The risk lay mostly in the reputation of the business as customers could easily switch allegiance in the e-commerce environment.

This case focuses on the formulation of strategy at *Amazon.com* in the initial phase of the firm's development between 1993 and 2000. In the first instance, the key strategic aims of the firm are identified. This is followed by an internal and external analysis using the theoretical perspectives of generic strategy, value chain, and Five Forces models developed by Porter (1980, 1985). The theoretical perspectives provide the basis for a critical analysis of the coherence of the firm's stated strategic aims and the choice of strategies to achieve those aims adds the necessary academic rigour to the work.

The formulation of strategy: strategic aims

All organisations need to identify their strategic aims within the constraints of current resources and capabilities. It is possible for firms to extend their current portfolio of resources and capabilities through organisational learning, redeployment of existing resources in new and more effective ways, knowledge generation and sharing and so on (Barney, 1991). As first movers in the online bookselling industry, *Amazon.com* could not take advantage of these resource and capability extending sources as the industry was in its infancy. The resources the company possessed extended to little beyond the drive and determination of Bezos to explore the opportunities that the internet offered. However, the key strategic aims of the firm were built around the capabilities that the new technology offered for creating added value to customers. Amit and Zott (2001) focus attention on value creation in e-business. Related benefits of using the internet for book buying are extensive and include convenience, greater selection, ease of use, information search and retrieval, ease of access, competitive pricing, price comparisons and even the potential for the personalisation and customisation of service.

The strategic aims of the firm in the period 1993 to 2000 were to become the world's leading online retailer not just of books but a wide range of products and services. Another strategic aim was to extend the business model to include other multimedia offerings such as e-mail, SMS, search engines, auction sites, business hosting, and so on. The long-term strategic aim of *Amazon.com* from the mid-1990s was to become a global player in the highly competitive multimedia industry (Stockport and Street, 1999). To achieve these aims *Amazon.com* would have to become technological leaders in their industry, acquire the best skills, develop partnerships across multiple supply chains, and leverage advantage from the host of first-mover advantages such as brand recognition, customer loyalty, influence on the developing shape of the industry, and creating barriers to entry.

Internal analysis: generic strategy

Determining the generic strategy of a business is a vital decision that strategic managers have to make. In the case of *Amazon.com* the choice was relatively simple. Although the firm sought to lower costs where possible, the key to competitive advantage lay in the quality of the service they could provide to customers. The business model for the online bookselling venture entailed receiving information from customers on what book they wished to buy, relaying that information to the warehouses where the books were held, and then transporting the books to the customer. In effect, *Amazon.com* is a logistics and distribution company. The quicker and more efficiently they could achieve this process, the more customers would be attracted to their website. The key to achieving this was to differentiate their service against both online rivals and traditional bookshops.

The key differentiators were the huge array of titles available to customers, 24 hour service, greater convenience, and quick delivery. Another compelling differentiator was the lower prices *Amazon.com* could offer. In the traditional economy prices are determined by the cost of adding value in the process of the supply chain. The manufacturer, wholesaler, distributor, and retailer all provide services that add value and cost. The margins added by the retailer provide the final cost to the customer. In the online environment firms, such as *Amazon.com*, by-pass some of the players in the supply chain, thereby reducing the cost burden and allowing the product to be offered to customers at a lower price.

As the business model became increasingly successful in the late 1990s, so more customers were attracted to the website. The more customers that the website attracted the greater the *Amazon.com* brand became known. The global recognition of the brand acted as a barrier to entry in the online bookselling industry and, later, general retailing. Although the internet economy is well populated with potential rivals, few could match the market share acquired by *Amazon.com*. Each time a web user clicked on the *Amazon.com* website, the brand was being marketed and promoted. This so-called 'virtuous cycle' was another important differentiator that underpinned the firm's strategy for competitive advantage. Finally, the software developed by the company helps to differentiate the service from rivals. The acquisition of key skills led to the development of software that facilitates quicker and more efficient services to customers; makes navigation of the website easier; smoothes the process of ordering, transactions, and distribution; and helps build knowledge on customers through database management and customer relationship management (CRM). The relationship that *Amazon.com* has with customers accounts for the ability of the firm to sustain its competitive advantage despite many potential rivals imitating their business model.

Internal analysis: value chain analysis

The value chain analysis focuses on how much value an organisation's activities add to its products or services compared to the costs incurred in utilising resources in the productive process. Every product that is produced is the result of organising and using resources in a particular way. Value chain analysis helps managers to focus attention on configuring and coordinating resources on those activities that produce the product in the most efficient and effective way. The main questions managers have to address from conducting a value chain analysis are: what activities should the firm perform, and how? What is the configuration of the firm's activities that best enables added value to the product and allows the firm to compete in the industry? The internet adds the further dimension of a virtual environment to the working of the value chain (Rayport and Sviokla, 1995; Bhatt and Emdad, 2001). Indeed, Porter (2001) had to revisit his concept of the value chain in light of the emergence of the internet onto the business landscape.

As noted previously, *Amazon.com* can be viewed as a logistics and distribution company. The key value adding activities that can be identified using Porter's (1985) Value Chain model are inbound and outbound logistics. Service can be added to these as ultimately, the success of the business model is determined by the superior service provided to customers. The software developed and implemented by the firm allows information from suppliers, customers, and partners to be received, synthesised, disseminated, and used as a means of setting in train a process that ends with the customer receiving the product or service more quickly and efficiently than any rival can offer. Thus, the support activity underpinning the added value is in technology development. An example of this is in the '*One Click*' technology the company developed and patented that allows the communications interactions between the firm and customers to be logged and used for marketing and other functions that improve customer service. Combined, these attributes create a distinctive capability that rivals find difficult to match and lead to a competitive advantage. Since the late 1990s the firm has substantially extended their value adding activities to include community building (customised services for customers/partners); sales interface (direct customer order intake); core information management (data management); and core handling and processing (full electronic distribution and transaction fulfilment).

External analysis: Five Forces model

The Five Forces model developed by Porter (1980 is designed to help strategic managers understand an industry's attractiveness and the influence that each of the Five Forces has on the firm's ability to compete. Combined, the Five Forces determine the potential for achieving profit within an industry sector. Each force will exert a different level of influence depending on the type of industry under scrutiny. With this in mind, it is relevant only to discuss the forces that determine the online retailing industry. Of significance here are the bargaining power of buyers and the threat of substitutes. There is intense rivalry in the online retailing industry but *Amazon.com* has been able to acquire a large enough market share to elevate the firm above the vast majority of rivals that compete for a relatively small market share. There is always a high threat of entry into the industry because the capital costs of doing so are small. However, few firms could enter the industry and pose a direct threat to *Amazon.com* because of their market share and economic power. Although they have some power as suppliers, the firm is aware that customer allegiance can be easily switched with one click of a mouse. Hence, they do not exploit their supplier power to the fullest extent.

The two most important forces affecting the attractiveness of the online retailing industry are the power of buyers and the threat of substitutes. The internet empowers buyers (consumers) because they have access to the type of market information previously closely guarded by suppliers. Hence, issues related to price, quality, quantity available, delivery times, comparisons with substitutes, and so on are now readily available to consumers. Firms have to compete more vigorously for the attention of online buyers with compelling offers and high quality service. The industry is only attractive to those firms who can match or exceed customers' high expectations. The second important feature is that of the threat of substitutes. In this regard, other forms of accessing products become relevant such as traditional shopping, mobile commerce, catalogues, and so on. *Amazon.com*, like all online retailers, has been affected by these forces and has had to continue to add value to customers in order to sustain their competitive advantage. Innovations include one-to-one services, network communities, secure transactions, interactivity, reviews, book recommendations, and so on. These innovations, as key differentiators that underpin strategy formulation, are designed not only to add value to customers but also to undermine the attractiveness of substitute forms of shopping.

Strategic rationale

The internal and external analyses provide the basis for assessing the coherence of the firm's strategy given their resources and capabilities. The combination of deployed resources and resultant capabilities in adding value that leads to superior service stems from the first-mover advantages of brand loyalty, brand recognition, high market share, and economies of scale by accessing global markets. Capabilities within the organisation are manifest in the generic strategy of differentiation which is bolstered in many different ways including the promotion of the brand every time a customers logs on to the website; patented software capability that enhances logistics and distribution; continuous innovation; effective partnerships; and so on. All these either directly or indirectly lead to added value service for the customer. The value chain highlights where *Amazon.com* has channelled their resources to underpin differentiation and create a competitive advantage. Innovation in inbound and outbound logistics leads to greater customer service (such as order tracking, customised delivery schedules, etc.). The support activity of technology management underpins this strategy by enhancing the efficiency and speed with which orders are taken and products delivered to customers.

Conclusion

There is a high level of coherence between the strategic aims of *Amazon.com* and the strategic choices, resources, and capabilities that have been used to achieve this. The strategic choice of differentiation has enabled the firm to focus on developing capabilities that improve performance and add value to customers. This, in turn, has led to the exponential growth of the business throughout the period 1993–2000 evidenced by increasing market share, turnover, expansion of products and services for sale, increasing strategic alliances and partnerships, and access to global markets (Saunders, 1999). The Five Forces analysis revealed that the industry remains attractive for firms such as *Amazon.com* which have been able to create a sustained competitive advantage by exploiting first-mover advantages, continuing to innovate, extend market reach, and acquire the capabilities that rivals find difficult to match.

Sources:

Amit, R. and Zott, C. (2001) 'Value creation in eBusiness', *Strategic Management Journal*, Vol. 22, pp. 493–520.

Barney, J. (1991) *Firm Resources and Sustained Competitive Advantage* (4th edn), Harlow, Pearson.

Bhatt, G. D. and Emdad, A. F. (2001) 'An analysis of the virtual value chain in electronic commerce', *Logistics Information Management*, Vol.14, Nos. 1–2, pp. 78–84.

Combe, C. A. (2006) *Introduction to e-Business: Management and Strategy*, Oxford, Butterworth-Heinemann.

Porter, M. E. (1980) *Competitive Strategy*, New York, The Free Press.

Porter, M. E. (1985) *Competitive Advantage: Gaining and Sustaining Superior Performance*, New York, The Free Press.

Porter, M. E. (2001) 'Strategy and the Internet', *Harvard Business Review*, March, pp. 63–78.

Rayport, J. and Sviokla, J. (1995) 'Exploiting the virtual value chain', *Harvard Business Review*, Vol.73, No.6, pp. 75–85.

Saunders, R. (1999) *Business the Amazon.com way: Secrets of the world's most astonishing Web business*, Washington DC, Capstone.

Stockport, G. J. and Street, D. (1999) Amazon.com: from start-up to the new millennium, European Clearing House, No 300-014-1.

Discussion points

Amazon.com only exists today because of the goodwill it maintained with key shareholders throughout its early unprofitable years. Discuss.

Is online book buying destroying traditional bookshops?

Questions and tasks

Identify the key value adding activities of Amazon.com that underpins the company's competitive advantage.

What key innovations have Amazon.com implemented that underpins their sustained competitive advantage?

Undertake a SWOT analysis for Amazon.com.

What, if any, core competence does Amazon.com possess?

Online Resource Centre

Author commentary on these discussion points and questions can be found on the Online Resource Centre at: www.oxfordtextbooks.co.uk/orc/combe1e/

Summary

● **Understand the development of strategic management thinking**

The subject of strategy is relatively new in terms of formal academic study and discourse. However, this chapter identified and discussed several schools of thought that have emerged to forward different arguments and perspectives on what strategy is, what it does, and how it should be implemented.

● **Apply internal and external environmental analysis models**

A number of different models were used as a basis for analysing the internal (generic strategy, value chain) and external (Five Forces) environments. The analysis of the information and data relating to these models forms the basis of understanding the internal strengths and weaknesses of the organisation as well as the opportunities and threats from the external environment. These help strategic managers make choices regarding what strategies to implement to achieve stated aims.

● **Evaluate the options and choices available to strategic managers in a global environment**

Ansoff's growth model was used as a model to describe and illustrate how strategic managers can evaluate the options available to them as a consequence of the outcomes of the internal and external analysis. The discussion and analysis focused on strategies in the global environment characterised by hyper-competition and change.

● **Comprehend the dynamics of strategy in a global context**

To understand globalisation and the dynamics of strategy in a global context it is important to determine the extent to which it exists in any particular industry and the types of activities within the industry that can be considered either global or not global in characteristic. For this the global drivers framework developed by George Yip was used as a basis for explanation and discussion. The four drivers of market, government, cost, and competition help determine the extent of globalisation in an industry. The framework helps to determine which parts of an industry can be considered global and which are not and helps managers to develop a coherent global strategy by focusing attention on the key drivers.

Conclusion

This chapter has given an insight into the process of strategy and outlined how to apply various models and frameworks to aid strategic management in organisations. The key issue emanating from this chapter is to view strategy as a process rather than an end in itself. It has been noted that the environment in which managers operate is necessarily changeable and this takes on an added dimension when one considers the long timeframe that strategic management deals with.

The chapter has highlighted some of the more modern trends in strategic thinking including the dynamic capabilities approach that is a further development from the Resource-Based View. This can be seen as an attempt to address one of the main criticisms of academic contributions to strategy, namely that the models and frameworks are invariably static in design and fail to reflect the dynamic nature of the modern international business environment. This dynamic permeates throughout all activities in organisations including the value adding activity of marketing and the need for constant innovation. Analysis and discussion of these two important aspects of modern organisations form the next two chapters and provide a coherent thread following on from the treatment of strategic management.

Chapter questions and tasks

Discuss the advantages to managers of undertaking analysis based on Porter's Five Forces model.

Outline the key elements of the strategic process and discuss the value of it to managers.

Identify and discuss the roles of business level and functional level managers in an organisation.

Highlight some examples relating to each of Yip's global drivers.

Describe the concept of core competence and evaluate how it can help an organisation sustain a competitive advantage.

Online Resource Centre

Author commentary on these questions can be found on the Online Resource Centre at: www.oxfordtextbooks.co.uk/orc/combe1e/

Further reading

- Campbell, D., Edgar, D., and Stonehouse, G. (2011) *Business Strategy: An Introduction* (3rd edn), Basingstoke, Palgrave Macmillan.

  A well-conceived textbook that is suited to those approaching strategy for the first time. The book has a distinct international flavour with cases and examples from around the globe featuring contemporary issues. The narrative is well-crafted and written in a style that is accessible to a broad range of readers. The text comes with an impressive array of additional materials including review questions, PowerPoint® slides, weblinks, and audiovisual links.

- Coulter, M. K. (2009) *Strategic Management in Action* (5th edn), Harlow, Pearson.

  Coulter presents contemporary theoretical perspectives in an engaging manner that will capture the interest of students and practitioners of strategy. As a supplement to the theoretical approach, Coulter also provides practical examples of strategy in action by the effective use of ideologies, ethical dilemmas, and identified strategies of contemporary managers. The book includes case studies of global firms; key issue boxes featuring strategic management in an e-business context; and a global perspective for mini cases featuring international strategies. There is also an opportunity for students to examine and analyse ethical dilemmas in strategic decision making.

- Dess, G. G. and Lumpkin, G. T. (2003) *Strategic Management: creating competitive advantages*, New York, McGraw-Hill.

  As the title suggests, this textbook focuses on the means of achieving competitive advantage. Strategic management is explained in a coherent manner and there is a common theme throughout the book featuring the role of strategy in the digital economy, most notably the realm of e-commerce. Methods of creating a competitive advantage are underpinned by clear explanations, effective articulation of frameworks for analysis, and relevant case studies and examples.

- Johnson, G., Scholes, K., and Whittington, R. (2009) *Fundamentals of Strategy*, Harlow, Prentice Hall.

  For students who feel daunted by the full text on the 'Essentials of Strategy' this abridged version by Johnson and colleagues has much to commend it. A succinct and articulate text with clear explanations of key strategic issues. Students will gain in confidence from accessing this source as it helps the preparation process for more in-depth and complex issues of strategy.

- McGee, J., Thomas, H., and Wilson, D. (2010) *Strategy: Analysis and Practice* (2nd edn), Maidenhead, McGraw-Hill.

  There is a contemporary feel to the text with many up-to-date cases featuring key issues of strategy such as risk, decision making, and corporate governance. Cases are of globally recognised firms that students will be familiar with and the style of discussion is analytical and precise.

Online Resource Centre

For more information, updates, and multiple-choice questions, please visit the Online Resource Centre at: www.oxfordtextbooks.co.uk/orc/combe1e/

Skillset 14
Personal Development Planning

521

14(a) Introduction

Personal Development Planning (PDP) has become an integral part of the management of the learning process for students, ensuring that the skills around the technical aspects of learning as well as interpersonal competencies are planned and thought through carefully.

14(b) The importance of Personal Development Planning

Personal Development Planning provides a means through which you can improve your capacity to learn by focusing attention on the reflective aspect of the learning process. That is, the questions of why and how you are learning and the effectiveness of the approaches used. PDP is designed to enable you to reflect, review, assess, and take responsibility for learning. This process should be fully supported by academic staff designated in support roles such as personal academic tutors or advisors. The key purpose of undertaking a PDP is to help you to:

- become a more effective, independent, and self-confident learner;
- better understand how you are learning;
- improve your general study skills;
- improve your employability and career management skills;
- realise your aspirations and personal goals and self-evaluate your learning progress and performance;
- develop a positive attitude to learning, life, and work.

14(c) Advantages of Personal Development Planning

There are a number of distinct advantages associated with effective PDP. These include:

- the enhancement of interpersonal and social skills that facilitate better communications and boosts personal confidence;

- improving emotional intelligence such as self-awareness, sensitivity to the needs and expectations of others, character forming qualities, and positive attitudes;
- understanding and managing aspirations and career-oriented decision making;
- improving time management and self-discipline;
- developing independence in life and learning environments.

14(d) The Personal Development Planning pathway

It is important that PDP follows a pre-determined pathway, one that helps students to better understand and manage the myriad challenges they face in a learning environment. Four key stages can be identified as a framework for mapping this pathway. These include:

Stage 1: Foundations of the learning process

The foundation refers to the understanding and knowledge required for the chosen area of study including the key aspects of the discipline, basic theoretical perspectives, ideas, and concepts. This requires some discipline around core skills of sourcing relevant materials and undertaking the necessary background reading into the subject matter. This paves the way for undertaking more targeted reading as part of the formal and structured learning around the chosen subject.

Stage 2: Acquiring core discipline skills

Once the foundations of learning have been established, you can go on to further hone your understanding and knowledge of the subject area and start to engage with reading and insights from related areas of study. The core disciplinary skills require a deeper understanding of theory, concepts, and ideas around the subject matter and require you to undertake effective independent learning supported by tutor guidance and recommended reading lists and other source materials.

Stage 3: Consolidation of core discipline skills

Stage 3 requires you to consolidate your learning and begin the process of adding quality to your academic output by focusing attention on developing critical, analytical and evaluation skills that follow on from comprehension and knowledge of your chosen subject. This helps to hone the skills required to make sense of what the information means and to understand the consequences or effects of the application of theory or the implementation of ideas and concepts in different contexts.

Stage 4: Specialisation and managing the future

The final stage of this process requires you to develop a specialist knowledge and understanding of the subject, to be able to apply models and frameworks effectively, undertake analytical and evaluation work, critically assess outcomes and the findings of study or research, and manage your learning independently through self-discipline and effective time management. This stage also includes planning and preparing for the future including managing the final stages of study and proactively pursuing career opportunities (such as networking) and improving employability prospects.

14(e) Personal Development Planning: managing and monitoring progress

Personal Development Planning is designed to help you develop as an independent and confident learner, and to help you utilise the skills that incorporate PDP in your future career. Importantly, a PDP record helps you update and monitor progress relating to the development of key skills throughout your academic career. This helps you to identify areas where you may require extra guidance or support, or where you have made particular progress and seek ways in which you can consolidate or use those skills more effectively. PDP also helps you to firmly embed the concept of Continuous Professional Development and Lifelong Learning. PDP prepares you for the discipline of undertaking effective self-evaluations regarding your performance and needs, honing your self-awareness so that you able to make well-balanced judgements and decisions in the workplace.

14(f) The implementation of a Personal Development Plan

Personal Development Planning should be a continuous process throughout your academic career. It should be designed to align with each level of study and be constantly updated, monitored, and reviewed. The first exposure to the PDP process may be during the first induction programme where an academic advisor or tutor should be allocated to each student. The academic advisor or tutor can play a key role in monitoring and advising on PDP issues and should be proactive in helping you to use the PDP to identify and access further support and guidance where appropriate.

Each university or college will have their own arrangements for student support but it is now recognised standard practice to implement a PDP process. Academic staff play a vital role in the effectiveness of any PDP and it would be expected that students meet with their allocated advisor or tutor to discuss progress, reflect on performance, and map a way forward according to the identified needs of each student. It is important that students ensure they prepare for and attend scheduled meetings, undertake agreed actions, and regularly report on progress to their allocated advisor or tutor. It is also important that the relationship between the advisor/tutor and student is based on trust and that the dialogue is underpinned by honesty, integrity, and respect. Students will gain by the efforts they make to strike a good rapport and working relationship with their academic advisor or tutor.

Once the PDP has been initiated by the distribution of relevant documents and files, and the allocation of student advisors or tutors, then it becomes a continuous process designed to encourage student reflection on academic learning, personal development, and the basis for documenting evidence to support the evaluation of progress. Often, certain milestones or targets linked to achievement may be set, either as part of university or departmental policy or by individual advisors/tutors. It is normal practice for students to meet face-to-face with their advisor or tutor at least once or twice per semester. The dialogue should feature a range of issues including assessing progress across a number of identified skills (such as sourcing materials, interpersonal skills, time management, etc.), monitoring the record of progress, and guidance on the content and direction of the student learning experience. Much of the discussion is based on evidence provided and, therefore, it is essential that students maintain an updated and accurate record of their learning and study experience. Students are solely responsible for the input of information into their PDP file.

Personal statement

The starting point of a PDP often includes a personal statement compiled by the student. The personal statement sets out the current situation relating to the student including past achievements, reasons for choosing the course of study, aspirations, and targets for both current academic and future work careers. The personal statement can be part of the PDP at each level of study so that changes can be documented as appropriate. For example, a student may start off their studies with a clear idea of what qualifications they need to pursue a certain career (law or accountancy, for example) but they may change their mind at some point during their academic career and want to focus attention on some other area of study to support a different aspiration (for example, a student may decide they may want to become an entrepreneur running his/her own business or to work for a voluntary organisation). It is important that these changes in attitudes and aspirations are documented and notes made regarding why this decision came about and what the student is doing to support it.

Learning plan

In conjunction with the personal statement, you should initiate the PDP with a learning plan that outlines what subjects you intend to study, how and why you made the choice, the mode of study, support and development needs for the learning process, and the key skills and competencies needed to undertake effective learning in the chosen subject. Most departments or schools within universities and colleges have a formal learning support team who can help with the compilation of the learning plan. Invariably they will deliver a template that you can use to input information relating to progress in each of the elements that comprise the learning plan. This is often linked to the personal statement. A typical template for the personal statement and learning plan is set out below.

PERSONAL STATEMENT

Name	
Matriculation number	
Programme	
Level of study	
Semester	
Academic Tutor	
Personal statement	Summarise academic achievements; reasons for undertaking the programme of study, career aspirations, and any previous work experience.

LEARNING PLAN

Key skills	Status	Action needed
Comprehension and understanding		
Writing skills		
Sourcing materials and reading		
Analytical and critical skills		
Referencing		
Presentation skills		
Seminar preparation and contribution		
Exam revision and techniques		
Working in groups		

Additional comments

The learning plan should also have a space where students can document their successes or where they have made significant progress in developing key skills. This is important as it provides students with a record of confidence-boosting achievements that can be used as a source of encouragement for meeting future challenges. Examples of what to include under 'Additional Comments' include:

- successful completion of academic tasks;
- evidence of personal development (such as giving a presentation);
- list of transferable skills attained over the period (such as report writing or sourcing information);
- details of effective time management and work scheduling;
- non-academic activities such as work experience, participation in extra-curricular activities such as volunteering, sports, etc., or networking activities.

It is important that all the academic and extra-curricular activities that contribute to the development of key skills are documented and supported by evidence. Here, it is useful to keep a portfolio of achievements so that each is documented and can be used as evidence later for assessing performance or as part of a job application. Evidence can take the form of coursework and feedback, exam results, assessments from tutors, references, certificates or accreditations, attendance at events or conferences, audio or visual evidence of presentations, teamwork, independent study, etc. Students should also keep evidence of having met with advisors or tutors, the outcome of the meetings and challenges set, and how those challenges were met.

525

Task:
Use the templates above to input data and information relating to your personal statement and learning plan to develop key skills.

14(g) Assessing progress using the Personal Development Plan

The Personal Development Plan should be used as a helpful document to monitor and assess the progress made towards developing key skills. This helps to identify areas where progress has been made, recognise success, but also to identify areas where further work or guidance is needed. The learning plan and other supporting evidence such as the record of achievement will help the advisor or tutor to understand what progress has been made and to devise ways of addressing gaps or areas where further development work is needed. This will usually result in an action plan that details what the student needs to focus on in future. A typical progress assessment and action plan template is outlined below.

PROGRESS ASSESSMENT:

STUDENT NAME:

MATRIC NO:

PROGRAMME:

ACADEMIC ADVISOR:

DATE OF PROGRESS MEETING:

Key issues discussed:

Development of personal skills:

Attitude to learning

Time management

Interpersonal skills

Writing skills

Working in a group

Other

Evidence of progress:

Areas for improvement:

Agreed objectives for action:

ACTION PLAN

SKILLS DEVELOPMENT OBJECTIVE	METHOD OF ACHIEVEMENT	TIMESCALE FOR ACHIEVEMENT

Task:
Compile your Curriculum Vitae using the template below.

CURRICULUM VITAE

  PERSONAL DETAILS

  NAME:

  DATE OF BIRTH:

  CURRENT POSITION:

  TELEPHONE:

  E-MAIL:

QUALIFICATIONS

Year   Institution   Qualification

EMPLOYMENT

Year(s)   Organisation   Position & Core activities

ACADEMIC ACHIEVEMENTS

Key skills   Evidence

EXTRA-CURRICULAR ACTIVITIES

Further reading

Cottrell, S. (2010) *Skills for Success: Personal Development and Employability*, Basingstoke, Palgrave.

Smith, J. (2011) *Personal Development Planning—What You Need to Know: Definitions, Best practice, Benefits and Practical Solutions*, Ruislip, Tebbo.

15 Marketing

Learning outcomes

- Understand the characteristics and types of marketing strategies

- Develop and apply a marketing plan

- Identify and evaluate appropriate marketing strategies for different market segments

- Recognise the components of the marketing mix

- Assess the use of new media applications for marketing purposes

- Understand the concept and application of Customer Relationship Management

Marketing is a highly competitive global industry and requires sound business acumen, creative flair, and a superior understanding of consumers and their wants and needs. One of the most successful companies in this field is UK-based *Bartle, Bogle and Hegarty*, founded in 1982 by John Bartle, Nigel Bogle, and the now Sir John Hegarty. The company rose to prominence by being able to design advertising campaigns that fitted the mood and fashion of each era in which they were launched. For example, the *Levi's®* jeans advert featuring Nick Kamen in a launderette became an iconic image in the 1980s. Slogans such as 'Vorsprung durch Technik' (lead through technology) for *Audi* and the 'Lynx effect' for *Unilever's* branded body spray have all found their way into the consciousness of consumers over the last three decades. The company has consistently won awards for achievement in the marketing and advertising industries based on their competitive advantage in planning, creating, and crafting branding campaigns across different media and geographical regions. In particular, the creative capital of the designers ensures that the messages communicated have an endurance that rival campaigns find difficult to match.

Skillset 15
Reflective practice

Skillset 15 outlines techniques that help students to reflect on their learning experience. Reflection is an important part of the learning process as it helps students to focus on areas they recognise as being challenging; to think through how they set about overcoming the challenges; to identify areas where they displayed good practice and competence; and to think through ways in which they can improve. Skillset 15 asks students to look back and choose three topics from the book and think about interactions between them. This is a short activity-based Skillset that helps students integrate different aspects of the subject.

Student study skills

Reflection is a key part of the learning process for any student. This technique allows students to make honest and balanced judgements regarding their own performance and their ability to put into action learning techniques that help them to comprehend, understand, apply, and critically evaluate and analyse key concepts, theories, and ideas. The reflective learning is a means by which future performance can be improved or identified areas of good practice consolidated.

Work study skills

Being able to reflect honestly about performance is an aspect of emotional intelligence that is a valuable asset when honing skills and building competencies within a working environment. Reflecting on aspects of performance with a balanced and accurate analysis helps the learning process that is the catalyst for better and improved performance in future.

Definition

Marketing is a function carried out within organisations that is concerned with identifying, anticipating, and satisfying customer and other stakeholder requirements in an effective and profitable manner. Marketing involves communicating the value of the brand, products, services, and other organisational assets to the wider community.

Introduction

This chapter focuses on key elements of managing the marketing function in organisations. It begins with a definition of marketing and then highlights and discusses the different types of marketing strategies available to managers to achieve stated aims. This is followed by an outline of the development of the marketing plan as a key component of the marketing process. The chapter uses models of marketing to analyse the challenges and opportunities that present themselves through the identification and exploitation of different market segments and links into the marketing mix using the four P's model featuring product, place, price, and promotion. New approaches to marketing are highlighted and discussed. Also included is analysis of the use of new media applications as a means of spreading the marketing message to consumers and other stakeholders. Finally, the chapter concludes by highlighting the advantages and problems associated with the application of customer relationship management systems for marketing purposes.

Types and aims of marketing

Marketing has become a vital component of business strategy and commands a great deal of time and resources in organisations. Its importance can be gauged in the huge sums of money spent on advertising budgets by companies as they seek to maximise the exposure of their products and services to consumers. Traditional forms of marketing focused on advertising in broadcast media such as newspapers, television, and radio. Billboards were another popular means of spreading the message. However, in the last two decades there has been an increase in the types of media through which the marketing effort can be channelled. New media technologies, such as the internet, have opened up possibilities to extend the types of marketing of products and services. The scope for accessing new customers on a global basis is another major change in the marketing function. In line with the new opportunities for spreading the message has been an increase in the types of marketing techniques applied. Some of the most prominent ones are outlined in Table 15.1.

Marketing aims

There can be a number of aims associated with the marketing function but the four main ones include:

- increasing brand awareness;
- increasing the product or service penetration into targeted markets;

Table 15.1	Types of marketing	
Type of marketing	**Examples**	
Traditional	Newspapers, television, radio adverts	
Online	Video and banner adverts, search engines, e-mail	
Outbound	Cold calling, billboards, newsletters	
Inbound	Search engines for customers to find companies or products	
Article	Free written articles produced by the company about the company for distribution to customers, clients, suppliers, etc.	
Trade shows	Participation in public trade shows to display or demonstrate products and services	
Direct	Send messages directly to customers, direct mail, direct selling, telemarketing	
Niche	Companies focus on filling an identified gap in the market	
Drip	Send scheduled targeted e-mails that are coordinated to the specific goal of client conversion	
Social media	Use of YouTube, Twitter, Facebook, and other social media to support marketing efforts	
Referral	Customers refer new customers to a company, includes viral marketing (word of mouth)	
Promotional	Contests, prizes, coupons, free samples	

- increasing customer acquisition;
- increasing customer retention.

Marketing plan

The marketing plan is part of a broader business strategy designed to help organisations achieve their aims and objectives (McDonald and Wilson, 2011). Marketing plays a key role in the business strategy and can involve a number of different but linked activities such as research for consumer and market intelligence, communications with customers or other stakeholders using a range of media, managing the brand and the intellectual property that underpins it, and designing advertising campaigns. The scope of the marketing plan depends on the amount of resources channelled into supporting the marketing function. Normally, a marketing budget is allocated according to the calculated benefits that are expected to be derived from the investment. Although not an exact science, managers need estimates of the return on investment in marketing in order to make valid judgements regarding the amount of

Figure 15.1 Marketing plan

resources spent on it and its contribution to achieving stated aims and objectives. The added value benefits of a marketing plan and the marketing objectives therein must be clearly stated to ensure that it is in alignment with the business strategy. A key element of a marketing plan is the consumer, competitor, and market intelligence which provide the data and information that allows organisations to develop and implement strategies aimed at identified targets. In this instance, the marketing mix is the model used for this purpose and forms the basis of discussion later in this chapter. Also, there is a requirement for performance measurement and assessment of the marketing plan to provide managers with an insight into how closely matched the outcomes of the plan are to set targets. The marketing plan process is illustrated in Figure 15.1.

Objective setting

The marketing plan is based on clearly defined objectives which will vary between organisations. These objectives may include increasing sales, establishing new products in the marketplace (Higgins, 2001), broadening the customer base, enhancing customer service, diversifying the product range, reducing costs, or any of the other benefits associated with undertaking the marketing function. Whatever objective or objectives are chosen, it is important to ensure that they are achievable. Many firms have failed in their marketing strategy

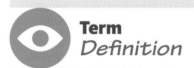

Term
Definition

Marketing plan: an outline of the specific actions to be carried out to encourage potential customers to buy the products and services for sale.

because they do not link their plan to the capabilities and resources of the organisation when setting objectives. The objectives must be measurable in order to form part of the marketing audit. Some objectives, such as improving the company reputation, may take some time to be achieved and even then may be difficult to measure. Nevertheless, it is necessary for managers to determine how much of a contribution the marketing effort makes to organisational improvement and performance (Gok and Hicioglu, 2010).

Demand and competitor intelligence

The basis of acquiring effective intelligence on the market and industry is through demand analysis and competitor analysis.

Demand analysis

The effectiveness of a marketing plan is largely dependent on how well workers and managers understand the nature and dynamics of the market. Typically, this involves analysis of current levels of demand, historical levels of demand, and then using the information to project forward and predict future demand. Various research and statistical techniques can be applied for this purpose including longitudinal studies and regression analysis. The scope of this activity ranges from analysis of the whole market, to that of a specified and targeted market segment. There are many factors involved in demand analysis; some of the most common are:

- the number of customers who purchase products or services currently and in the past;
- the method through which the purchase was made;
- the age, gender, location, income group, and other personal profile data;
- the type of products bought, by whom, and when;
- income and spending habits of individuals and targeted profile groupings;
- satisfaction ratings for the products or services consumed.

Identifying customer segments is important when marketing specific types of products. While some products and services are sold to the whole market, such as fast food or budget airline tickets, others are designed for specific customers or customer groups. For example, *Saga Holidays* is a UK-based travel agency that specialises in holidays for the over 50s age

Term
Definition

Market segment: that part of a market that is defined by specified characteristics.

533

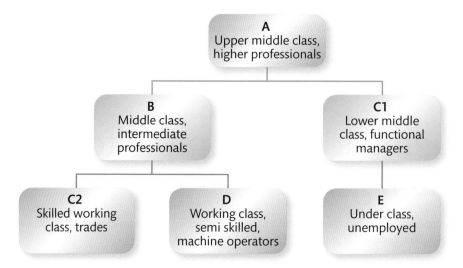

Figure 15.2 Consumer categories

group. Skin care specialists *Olay* target women, and *Mercedes Benz* design their marketing campaigns around certain income and lifestyle groups of customers. Market segments include:

- socioeconomic groups;
- geographic positioning;
- gender;
- age and demographics;
- tastes and fashions;
- business sectors.

Socioeconomic groups

Consumers can be divided into six broad groupings based on socioeconomic criteria as outlined in Figure 15.2.

Geographic positioning

The geographical location of customers is important information for organisations as it can help reveal information of interest to those involved in marketing. For example, some areas are marked by high or low incomes, different ethnographic and demographic characteristics, different population densities, urban or rural environments, industrial or residential, access to services and infrastructure, and so on. These all have an influence on the demand characteristics of the local population.

Gender

Products and services can be targeted to particular customers based on gender. Often there is a correlation between gender and identified types of consumer behaviour such as the extent to which consumers use products and services, their level of brand loyalty, buying habits, and the key benefits they seek from products and services. Psychographic variables are also of interest such as lifestyle, attitudes, personality traits, interests, and leisure activities.

Age and demographics

As noted previously the age profile of customers or customer groups is another key element of customer segmentation. It is possible to catagorise people into age groups such as infants, children, teenagers, young adults, middle aged, retired and elderly. Demographic change relating to the age distribution in different regions has a fundamental impact on the demand function for products and services. Some countries such as India and China have experienced population explosions in the last thirty years leading to high demand for a wide range of products and services, but bringing with it significant social and economic stresses on the population. In other regions change in the age distribution has been marked. In Scotland, for example, the population over the last thirty years has been around the five million mark. However, in the last two decades it has been evident that an increasing proportion of this population is over the age of 60. This is likely to increase in future as people live longer due to factors such as access to better healthcare. This has implications for government (fewer people of working age contributing to the tax revenues), social services (increased demand for healthcare), and businesses (specific types of products and services designed for an older demographic). Private healthcare provider *Bupa* tailor their insurance policies according to the age profile of customers.

Tastes and fashions

One of the most difficult aspects of marketing is to predict how tastes and fashions change over time. However, this is a crucial element of the marketing plan as it allows firms to plan and resource the production of products and services that may be in demand in future. Sometimes they are adaptations of existing products or services, but often they are new and innovative products and services that have been developed and designed based on the outcome of market research and analysis. This allows a much more specific marketing effort to be implemented knowing that the target market has already expressed an interest in the types of products and services being offered. Some industries are proactive in shaping and influencing tastes and fashions. For example, fashion houses collaborate with retailers in pushing products towards the customer, rather than the customer taking the lead in determining the next season's offerings.

Business sectors

It is not just retail consumers who provide demand for products and services. Businesses are also important customers as they have on-going demand for everything from stationery to supplies of raw materials. Thus businesses sell to and buy products from other businesses. This can also be divided into segments or sectors such as financial services, retail, transport, healthcare, public sector, leisure and entertainment, and so on. The level of demand for so-called business-to-business (B2B) products and services depends on the added value that businesses as customers receive from other businesses.

Competitor analysis

Generating and analysing knowledge of competitors is an integral part of developing a marketing plan. Competitor intelligence and analysis involves a number of integrated activities including the sourcing and gathering of relevant information on a wide range of criteria such as identifying who the competitors are, the products and services they produce, their market performance, the types of communication channels used, and their marketing strategies. Competitor analysis has both operational and strategic value as it helps firms respond to current campaigns run by rivals and helps to inform long-term investment decisions on the types of products and services to produce in future. This latter strategic dimension is informed by the number and size distribution of firms entering or leaving the industry depending on the profit potential it exhibits. Monitoring the actions of rivals gives managers important insights into the growth potential of an industry and the marketing effort plays a role in this process.

A great deal of the information required for competitor analysis can be accessed from stakeholders such as suppliers, employees, and customers. Information provided by rivals is another important source and may include different types of promotional material, advertisements, and company reports. These can be a source of information on new products, prices, availability, quality, discounts, promotions, and target customers. Extra-industry sources are also valuable in this regard and may include industry reports, government reports, press releases, and academic case studies.

Marketing audit

The marketing audit is designed to review the performance of the marketing plan. In particular, the marketing audit assesses the performance of the integrated factors in the objective setting model.

The effectiveness of the marketing plan forms a key part of the marketing audit. The analysis of performance focuses on three key areas:

- contribution to business performance;
- marketing effectiveness;
- consumer reaction.

Contribution to business performance

The implemented plan has to make a contribution to the economic performance of the company in the form of additional revenue and profitability.

Marketing effectiveness

The plan has to deliver greater sales and will be subject to monitoring for measures of effectiveness in attracting, retaining, and repeating customers. Feedback from customers on quality of service and satisfaction rates also feature in the measures of marketing effectiveness.

Consumer reaction

Consumers will have a reaction to marketing material that they are exposed to, whether it is a banner advertisement on a website, a television advertisement, or a flyer posted through general mail. One of the functions of the marketing department is to assess consumer reaction to their campaigns. Clearly, a positive reaction is the ideal, but this has to be transformed into improved performance for the marketing to be considered effective. Consumer reaction can be part of market research using techniques such as a vox pop (stopping people in the street and asking their opinion of a marketing format), focus groups (getting the reaction of a selected group of people), surveys (getting reactions from a wider number of people perhaps using a questionnaire), or telephone interviews (soliciting opinions via telephone). The metrics generated form the basis of analysis and informs as to the effectiveness of the marketing techniques in terms of customer reactions.

The marketing mix

Once the target market has been identified the next stage in the development of the marketing strategy is to focus attention on the marketing mix. The marketing mix is a combination of product, price, place, and promotion that helps increase sales to the target market (McCarthy, 1960). Firms can improve their competitive position by applying a unique mix of the elements that comprise the marketing mix.

Product

A number of factors come together to determine the effectiveness of products and services in the marketplace including quality, availability, application, construction, packaging, image, customer service, and ease of use. Critical to the success is the capability of the product or service to match or exceed the expectations of customers. It is important that the marketing information sets out clearly what the product or service is, what it does, and what buyers can expect from it. One of the challenges facing marketing managers is the trend towards ever-increasing customer expectations that has been evident since the emergence of the internet as a medium of communication in the mid-1990s. Consumers now have access to market information that was once the preserve of suppliers. Information on price, product quality, consumer reviews, and so on are a feature of the modern consumer environment.

Usually, to meet the demands of consumers it is necessary for firms to vary the product offerings and/or provide additional features that add value to the customer. This is the difference between a core product that meets basic consumer expectations, and an extended product that has additional features that takes the product beyond basic consumer expectations. For example, education is now available in a myriad of different formats. Although this can significantly reduce the cost of delivery, it also has the effect of raising consumers' expectations regarding the quality of the product or service. Firms or educational institutions now have to compete more vigorously by delivering added value products or services such as real-time interactive facilities, easy search facilities, moving images for illustration, access to a greater amount of information, and customer support. Another feature of the internet in this context is the potential it offers for delivering mass customisation of products. Mass customisation is a means of personalising a product or service on a large scale. Mass customisation relies on technology to create economies of scale where the low average cost of production makes it cost effective to provide tailored products to individual customers or groups of customers. The increasing demand for online learning products and services has given rise to many educational establishments offering mass customised learning products to individuals and groups of learners around the globe (Combe, 2006). Chaffey and Smith (2001) suggest some typical added value marketing techniques to support the promotion of products or services. These include:

- endorsements;
- awards;
- testimonies;

Term
Definitions

Mass customisation: the development and design of added value products and/or services to meet the demand characteristics of a large number of consumers.

Personalisation: the development and design of value adding products and/or services to meet the demand characteristics of individual customers.

- customer lists;
- customer comments;
- warranties;
- guarantees;
- money-back offers;
- personalised customer service;
- incorporation of tools for using the product.

Another method of varying the product is by bundling, where the benefits of the whole product package are emphasized. The main advantage to producers is that consumers cannot compare prices of individual items that when combined form the whole package. This is a well-used tactic in broadcasting where companies such as Sky bundle packages of programmes (for example, the premium sports channels may have to be bought alongside a news or game show channel) and sell them through subscription as a package. It may be that the consumer only really wants one channel but is forced into buying others in the package. Some critics point to this as a potential source of consumer exploitation (Crawford and Cullen, 2007). After all, it would be unacceptable for consumers to go into a supermarket to buy milk only to be told that they have to buy biscuits and bread too. Bundling only works for certain types of products, and in certain industries. The main advantage from the company's perspective is that it allows premium prices to be charged for the product bundle.

Price

A number of factors come together to form the price at which any product is sold including the cost of raw materials, production and distribution costs, the level of return on investment, and the producer's target profit margin. Part of the marketing department's remit is to monitor the reaction of customers to the initial price charged for any product or service. In economics, the price elasticity of products and services refers to the extent of changes in demand in response to changes in price. From the consumers' perspective the power dynamic regarding price has changed in recent years due to the plethora of price comparison websites that have appeared on the internet. This gives important market information to consumers that was previously unknown and helps them to form their judgements regarding which products and services to buy (Sinha, 2000). This has added to the pressure on companies to be ever more price competitive in the industries in which they operate. The reaction of customers to the initial price may influence price changes.

In response to the challenges presented by power shifts in supply and demand that have characterised markets in the last decade or so, companies have been forced to adopt a much more dynamic approach to their pricing policies. Dynamic pricing is a key characteristic of markets that are subject to rapid changes. Prices can be updated almost instantly as market conditions change. There may be many factors that act as a catalyst for this change ranging from changes in tastes and fashions, weather conditions, trade regulations, currency exchange rates, access to distribution channels, or raw materials, and so on. Most industries have access to instant, real-time information on trading conditions that influences their pricing policies. Managers need to be able to analyse the information and make quick decisions on the appropriate response and the marketing department plays a key role in this process. For example, potential new customers can be targeted with discounts, free gifts, or other incentives to buy depending on the ability of the company to manipulate price to make access to the products and services more inclusive. The more information firms have on customers the more able they are to align prices towards individual customers or groups of customers.

One further market phenomenon that has become increasingly prevalent since the late 1990s is the increased interactivity between buyers and sellers. Again, the internet has played a key role in facilitating greater price negotiation between buyers and sellers. This again changes the traditional way in which products and services are marketed and the type of relationship between commercial bodies and the consumer.

Place

The place element of the marketing mix refers to the channel through which companies bring products or services to the customer. These can include a communications channel (e.g. e-mail), a distribution channel to intermediaries (e.g. to customers via wholesalers), or direct selling to customers (disintermediate middlemen in the supply chain). It is important that companies establish effective communications systems that allows information to flow along the supply chain, and between seller and buyer and vice versa. These ensure that orders can be taken from customers and the information passed on to intermediaries such as wholesalers and distributors to deliver the products or services to customers. The choice of place depends on a number of factors including the nature and characteristics of the products or services for sale, the power of intermediaries in the supply chain, the effectiveness of traditional supply chain mechanisms, the scope of channel conflict, and the closeness and depth of relationship that firms seek with customers.

Promotion

Promotion is the element of the marketing mix that involves communication with customers regarding products and services for sale. There are a number of different methods of promoting products and services including branding, advertising, public relations, sales promotions, in-store displays, web promotion, sales promotions, and personal selling. These are all designed to inform customers of products and services for sale, the types of communications media available for completing the transaction, the quality and/or application of the products or services, the availability of discounts or special offers, and so on. Promotion is usually a combination of market push and market pull. Market push refers to activities undertaken to communicate the value of products or services to customers. The company is in control of the format of the communication, how it is seen, when, and where. Market pull refers to marketing strategies that involve advertising and promotional activities designed to entice potential customers to buy the products or services. Half-price discounts or BOGOF (Buy One Get One Free) are two typical examples. Mostly, it is the element of market pull that informs the promotion strategy. There are a number of ways firms can reach out to potential customers. These include:

- use of traditional media such as newspapers, magazines, radio, and television to promote the website;
- direct mail or e-mail to promote as a means of attracting customers with information on product and services or details of special offers;
- website information designed to enhance the customer experience or make the transaction smoother for the customer.

The success of promotion is highly dependent on the effectiveness of the two-way communications between buyer and seller. Customer loyalty is one of the keys to creating a competitive advantage in the modern business environment and part of this is dependent on effective customer relationships.

Mini case 15.1
The marketing mix at Nokia

Nokia is a Finnish-based multinational electronic communications manufacturer employing over 120,000 people in 120 countries around the world. With sales worth €13.4 billion in 2012 (Nokia Annual Report, 2012) it is one of the world's leading manufacturers of mobile phones. Part of the reason for the company's success is the effectiveness of the marketing effort that has brought the brand of *Nokia* to the attention of consumers on a global scale despite some fierce competition. The returns from marketing within this competitive environment are the subject of investigation by Choi et al. (2007). The marketing mix of the company gives an insight into how the key areas of price, place, promotion, and product have combined to leverage a competitive advantage.

Price

Nokia have been able to build the value of the brand through innovation and quality such that premium prices can be charged. Customers equate the *Nokia* brand with a level of quality that meets or exceeds their expectations and transfers into their buying behaviour.

Place

Nokia phones are distributed globally and in the UK usually sold in established retail outlets and electrical suppliers. *Nokia* prefer to deal with established retailers to ensure that customers receive a level of service that aligns to the quality of the product.

Promotions

The promotional strategy for new technologies and mobile devices at *Nokia* is consistent and focuses on a single, highly resourced advertising campaign for a single technology launch rather than for each individual mobile device. This creates economies of scale in advertising as it appeals to a large number of different markets simultaneously through an individualised campaign effort.

Product

Innovation lies at the heart of the added value *Nokia* seek to build into their product range. This may include new apps, differentiated designs for market segments, customised services, additional functionality, accessories, and so on. The company has been at the forefront of taking the basic mobile phone device and extending the product offering through adaptation and innovation. The emphasis on innovation has been an important element of the company's strategy in a saturated market.

The marketing mix at *Nokia* has been managed effectively and has contributed to the global brand recognition and loyalty of customers. Evidence of this is provided by Ali (2008) who links the brand reputation to the management of the marketing mix to explain *Nokia's* expansion in the Pakistani market. However, the challenge facing the company is to continue to innovate and provide continuous improvement and quality. The mobile phone has become a ubiquitous device on a global scale and has evolved into a device supporting a wide range of applications. How these value adding applications can be further extended and promoted to key target markets is the challenge facing the company in future and forms a central part of *Nokia's* strategy for growth, especially in fast-developing regions such as India and Brazil.

Sources:

Ali, S. E. (2008) 'Marketing Mix and the Brand Reputation of Nokia', *Market Forces*, Vol. 4, No. 1, pp. 23–32.

Choi, C. J., Millar, C. C. J. M., Chu, R. T. J., and Berger, R. (2007) 'Increasing returns and marketing strategy in the twenty-first century', *Journal of Business and Industrial Marketing*, Vol. 22, No. 5, pp. 295–301.

Nokia Annual Report (2012) http://i.nokia.com/blob/view/-/2268488/data/3/-/NSN-form-2013.pdf

Discussion point

Has innovation in mobile phones reached its peak?

Questions and tasks

Access a Nokia mobile phone product on the internet and describe its key features.

What differentiates Nokia products from those of rival firms?

Is Nokia's success all down to the way in which the products are marketed?

Name five characteristics that you think are key to the mobile phone as a product.

Online Resource Centre

Author commentary on this discussion point and questions can be found on the Online Resource Centre at: www.oxfordtextbooks.co.uk/orc/combe1e/

Managing the brand

The name, term, or symbol given to a product to set it apart from others produced by rivals is called a brand. Brand management is the process of creating and developing brands that are designed to add value to consumers (or are perceived by consumers to have added value). One of the sources of competitive advantage is that of differentiation, and branding comes into that category (Gaski, 2011). Thus, for example, the choice of name for the business is an important branding exercise. The name values of *Coca Cola* or *Microsoft* are almost incalculable. The brand name chosen should have some key attributes including the capability of identifying the unique aspects of the company and its products; communicating the company aims and objectives to a wide audience; and helping to protect the intellectual property of the company. Three main types of brand names can be identified including free-standing (designed to be unique and memorable such as *Yahoo!*); associative (linked to quality or an abbreviation of the

Term
Definition

Branding: name, term, or symbol given to a company, product, or service to differentiate it from others.

Table 15.2	Consumer and brand values		
		Consumer values	**Brand values**
	Core values	Lifestyle, aspirations, attitudes, beliefs	Shared values of the consumer and brand
	Expressive values	Personality type	How the brand symbolises personality traits
	Functional values	Demand for types of products and services	How the brand fulfils consumer expectations

Source: Adapted from Hart and Murphy (1998).

company name such as *BP* or *HSBC*); or descriptive (where the name links to the products or service such as *General Electric* or *Legal & General*).

To exploit the value of brands it is necessary to match consumer values with brand values. Hart and Murphy (1998) highlighted three main values that underpin the matching of consumer values and brand values. This is illustrated in Table 15.2.

In the modern business environment, effective brand management can create a competitive advantage but it requires very different marketing and promotional strategies from traditional marketing. A key difference is the extent to which companies now engage in meaningful dialogue with consumers about products or services. This is called one-to-one marketing and facilitates the building of relationships with customers to derive valuable information about the nature of demand. This feeds into the factors that drive innovation in companies in the form of new processes or the development of new products or adaptations to existing ones.

Other sources of competitive advantage are customisation and personalisation as distinct value adding services for customers. The benefits of personalised promotions are at their greatest when customers are interested in detailed product information (Allan and Fjermestad, 2000) that can form the basis of brand loyalty in customers. There is evidence to suggest that as consumers become more sophisticated in their demand characteristics, they will only buy products or services that precisely match their needs (Sealy, 1999). To meet these expectations firms need to adopt brand management strategies that go beyond product characteristics but also include criteria such as values, beliefs, emotions, memories, and attitudes.

http://www.adidas.com/

http://www.adidas.com/

Mini case 15.2
Global branding at Adidas

The German sports apparel company *Adidas* is one of the most globally recognised brands, thanks mainly to the exposure the company achieves from the huge interest in sport both in terms of spectators and participants. The company has successfully exploited the phenomenal interest in sport, and football in particular, to position their brand to support the strategic aim of being the world's leading sportswear company. To help achieve this aim the company established the *Global Brands* arm of the business which oversees all marketing activities linked to the long-term development of the *Adidas* brand as well as its sister brand *Reebok*.

Key to the success of *Global Brands* is the ability of managers to identify and exploit market opportunities on a global scale. This requires a clearly defined marketing strategy linked to the distinctive characteristics of the target market. These can be varied and complex depending on the myriad factors that define the nature of demand including incomes, culture, type of sport, distribution, and so on. The link between corporate branding and high-profile sports individuals or teams is key to this strategy too. Motion et al. (2003) provide details on the co-branding efforts of *Adidas* and the New Zealand All Blacks rugby team. Furthermore, there is a high emphasis on innovation in the design and materials used for the range of sportswear and these too vary according to the environment in which the target market is located. For example, climate plays a key role in determining the different types of materials used and the design of the apparel. Each brand has to be supported by effective communications strategies that express the brand values to customers in many different formats including web-based, television, billboards, advertising hoardings at sports events, workshops, coaching sessions, and so on.

Global Brands plays a key role in the long-term and sustainable growth of *Adidas* by ensuring that consumers have a positive perception of the brand values (Joseph, 2013). To this end, in 2010, *Global Brands* contributed to the development of *Route 2015*, the group's five-year strategic plan. The plan details the role of branding in the ambitious aims. The *Adidas* and *Reebok* brands have been set targets of delivering 90 per cent of the growth projections for the company by the end of the strategic cycle (Adidas Global Brands, 2012). Key to this is a number of identified areas that drive performance. These include the *Sports Performance* brand linked to tapping into the growing global interest in running and basketball; expanding the fashion brand *Adidas Sports Style*; and building the *Reebok* brand by focusing on fitness and training. Underpinning many of these is the customisation and innovation that builds brand loyalty. The company has put together a coherent and ambitious strategic plan that has branding at the core of activities.

There are significant challenges ahead for the company if they are to realise their targets. The changing nature of sport as a cultural activity is one that needs to be constantly monitored. An economic downturn on a global scale affects the amount of disposable income spent on what may be considered luxury, or at least non-essential, products such as sportswear. And, of course, there is the on-going head-to-head competition with main rival *Nike* to contend with. However, it is evident that *Adidas* have been proactive in formulating and implementing a coherent strategy to meet those challanges.

Sources:

Adidas Global Brands (2012) http://www.adidas-group.com/en/investorrelations/strategy/global_brands/default.aspx

Joseph, S. (2013) Adidas unveils new global brand strategy, London, *Marketing Week*. http://www.marketingweek.co.uk/news/adidas-unveils-new-global-brand-strategy/4005658.article

Motion, J., Leitch, S., and Brodie, R. J. (2003) 'Equity in corporate co-branding: The case of Adidas and the All Blacks', *European Journal of Marketing*, Vol. 37, No. 7/8, pp. 1080–94.

Discussion point

Is the dominance of *Adidas* and *Nike* in the sports apparel industry good for the consumer?

Questions and tasks

Link five high-profile sportsmen to the brand of Adidas.

What key characteristic defines the Adidas brand?

Identify three types of marketing employed by Adidas.

List the top five sporting events where Adidas would focus their marketing efforts.

Online Resource Centre
Author commentary on this discussion point and questions can be found on the Online Resource Centre at: www.oxfordtextbooks.co.uk/orc/combe1e/

New approaches to marketing

Marketing involves targeting customers or customer segments with information about the company, its activities, and its products and services. As noted previously, there is a disruptive characteristic to traditional forms of marketing that often intrude on the lives of consumers. Mail shots promoting products and services are often ill-received by consumers and discarded quickly. The residual resentment at being targeted with offers of no interest to them has a negative effect on customer relationships and undermines brand loyalty. In the internet economy, research has shown that consumers do not react positively to banner advertisements as they are perceived as an unwanted distraction to the content the user logged on to view (Adobe, 2013). Perhaps the most disruptive form of marketing is the unsolicited recorded telephone messages from telemarketers that have become a blight on modern living. In response, companies have explored means of using less disruptive techniques such as permission marketing, request marketing, and opt-in marketing.

Permission marketing

Consumers are increasingly playing an active role in determining the type and content of advertising they receive (Greenberg, 2000). The advent of permission marketing is one manifestation

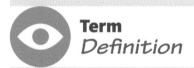

Term
Definition

Permission marketing: the process of sending marketing and promotional information to consumers with their express agreement to receive it.

of this whereby a potential buyer agrees to receiving marketing information in advance. The internet is an ideal medium for this with consumers having the option of receiving 'opt-in' e-mails about products and services or future promotions. This form of permission marketing is more effective than a 'scatter gun' approach to saturating the market with largely unwanted promotional material. Permission marketing means that consumers who choose to agree to being targeted with promotional material are likely to be more receptive to messages received. There are also cost advantages to the company because their marketing effort is more targeted and well-defined. Permission marketing is effective as long as mutual benefits exist for buyer and seller. One of the advantages is the prospects for building long-lasting relationships between the parties. Firms get to know the customers' profiles in some detail, and customers feel as if they are receiving a personalised service. Thus, the longevity of permission marketing techniques is based on the rational calculations and perceptions of all parties. As computer guru Seth Godin (1999) noted, there is an initial cost of establishing permission marketing but the benefits quickly accrue as attention turns into permission, permission into learning, and learning into trust.

Economic theory can help give an insight into how the process of permission marketing works. In the first instance, consumers have disposable income they wish to spend on products and services. However, they want to minimise the transaction costs in the process of turning their wants into a completed purchase by minimising the time spent evaluating products and evaluating the competence of, and trust in, the sellers. As self-interest lies at the heart of permission marketing, consumers will only allow companies to forward information to them if they are fully aware of the benefits that will be derived from it. In effect, companies have to offer some inducement or reward for consumers' permission to forward marketing material to them. On the other hand, from a company's perspective, once a consumer has given permission, the cost of sending additional information via electronic means is almost zero. In particular, as e-mail incurs low marginal costs this encourages companies to continue communicating with customers who have given permission. This helps educate consumers about the benefits of products and services they can provide, and continue to turn them into paying customers.

? Critical reflection
Is permission marketing ideal for the internet age?

It could be argued that permission marketing does not go far enough as it is based on the transmission of messages from companies to the consumer. In the language of the internet economy this is business-to-consumer or B2C. The acronym suggests a one-directional communication process. Companies that employ permission marketing techniques will only send consumers information if they have explicitly agreed to receive it. However, this is one-directional. The internet and permission marketing work in opposite directions. Whereas permission marketing is business to consumer, the nature of the internet economy as expressed in website applications and usage also features consumer-to-business communications. Thus, it needs to be viewed as a customer-driven medium where the company only sends messages that the customers or users have specifically requested. This is termed request marketing.

Request marketing and opt-in

Request marketing, or opt-in marketing, is ideally suited to the fixed internet or to the mobile wireless internet where intrusive messages are especially received with dismay by consumers. Unlike permission marketing where companies proactively seek the permission of consumers to send information, consumers engaged in request marketing are proactive in seeking information on products or services from companies even if there has been no history of communication between the two parties. There is a close link between request marketing and opt-in marketing. Customers who 'opt-in' agree to receive further marketing material after they have already received some information. For example, they may have received a direct e-mail promoting a product, became intrigued by it, and agreed to opt-in to the process of receiving further information.

Marketing using new media applications

The development and application of a host of new media technologies, most prominently the internet, has created opportunities for consumers, suppliers, and others along the supply chain to communicate with each other on a global scale. Traditional boundaries that constrain activities, such as time, geography, and access to information, have been largely dismantled by the advent of the internet. One of these activities is the marketing function. The internet offers a number of advantages that can be exploited by companies to improve their marketing strategy. Timmers (1999) identified key attributes of the internet as ubiquity, information richness and density, global reach, interactivity, customisation, and personalisation. Buyers and sellers can interact in a more cost-effective manner than under traditional forms of marketing (Kiang and Chi, 2001). This accounts for the exponential growth in e-commerce and e-business since the commercialisation of the internet in the mid-1990s.

The marketing function consists of identifying, anticipating, and satisfying customer needs profitably. As noted previously, the key market variables to be taken into account when implementing a marketing strategy are price, promotion, place, and products. Understanding the profile of targeted customers is a critical success factor in the implementation of a marketing strategy. In this regard the internet provides a valuable additional means of support for the marketing strategy. For example, the high level of connectivity of customers to internet websites provides a considerable and on-going source of customer information. The marketing strategy can be designed around the applications of the internet. This process is termed e-marketing and involves the use of electronic communications technology in all its formats and platforms as a means of achieving marketing aims and objectives. As we have seen, internet generated information also empowers customers and can help them achieve their own aims and objectives. Such is the importance of the internet in altering the way marketing is managed in the modern business environment that it is worth exploring this in more detail.

The e-marketing environment

Understanding the differences between traditional and e-marketing is an important step in the development and implementation of an e-marketing plan. An effective e-marketing plan is developed from an understanding of new perspectives relating to customer relationships, different types of interactions with customers, and different approaches to marketing products and services (Harris and Dennis, 2008). As the internet economy has evolved, and consumers become more sophisticated in their usage, so their expectations and demand characteristics have changed. Promotion and marketing of products and services has similarly been subject to change within this new environment. Thus, prior to devising an e-marketing plan, some key questions need to be addressed.

What are the critical success factors for e-marketing?

The most critical factor in an effective e-marketing campaign is the same as in traditional forms of marketing. That is, consumers must perceive added value. This added value may be real in the sense that buying the product derives a certain level of satisfaction, or it can be imagined. Advertising is about influencing perceptions as much as anything else and as long as consumers believe that they are experiencing added value from the product or service then that constitutes effective marketing. For example, some marketing campaigns are aspirational in character where the message communicated is designed to tap into this particular emotion. Perfume, designer dresses, shoes, cars, sportswear, and jewellery are marketed as aspirational products linked to a glamorous and desirable lifestyle. Sports apparel marketing makes buyers feel as if they can mimic their sporting idols. In the e-marketing arena the images can be adapted to different formats such as banner advertising, video, pictures, logos, endorsements, etc.

Another critical success factor is the ability to create partnerships along the supply chain. It is unlikely that one producer would be able to deliver expertise in all aspects of bringing the product to the consumer. The most successful e-commerce firms, such as *ebay* and *Amazon*, have built effective partnerships with suppliers, distributors, software developers, and, of course, marketing specialists. In e-marketing the key to success is an understanding of the appropriate way of harnessing the power of the internet and other new media technologies to spread the message. This understanding extends to knowing the best platform to use for different customer segments, how the targeted audience accesses and reacts to the messages, and how interest can be transformed into sales. The marketing function adds value to the productive process by enticing consumers, facilitating sales, and building a relationship with consumers to create brand loyalty. This latter point is achieved by having on-going communications and interactivity with consumers such that they perceive a personalised service.

What is the position of the marketing function in organisations?

Marketing and information systems help to drive product development in organisations. Therefore, there has to be an integrated marketing function with other functions such as IT and business development.

How are customers perceived in the online environment?

The biggest difference between the online trading environment and traditional ones is the access that consumers have to market information. The internet allows customers to compare prices, check quality and availability, and access a wide range of different suppliers. Consumers can also build a greater understanding of organisations and how they operate, their performance, and reliability using websites such as Tripadvisor.com or comparethemarket.com. The behavior of consumers is also different in the online environment with much more browsing and impulse buying taking place. The behaviour of consumers can be monitored and the data used to inform e-marketing strategies. These characteristics have ensured that the pressure to deliver added value in quality of products, delivery, and customer service is of a high order. The expectations of consumers have been ratcheted upwards in the online environment and the e-marketing campaigns have to reflect this new reality. Consumers perceive themselves to be

> ## Mini case 15.3
> ## *Marketing at IKEA using social media*

Headquartered in Delft in the Netherlands, *IKEA* is an iconic brand designing and manufacturing self-assembly furniture. The company has always tried to project an image of being young, energetic, quirky, and cool. This is played out in the advertising and promotion of their products where the emphasis is on attractive colour schemes, functional but stylish design, and innovative layouts. A key aim of the company is to make the brand relevant across different cultures and market segments (Tarnovskaya and de Chernatony, 2011). One of the most important market segments for *IKEA* is the youth market, young people who perhaps are living independently for the first time. The promotional campaigns aimed at this market segment are designed to positively project the role of *IKEA* products in the lifestyle of young people. As a means of communicating that message it was natural for *IKEA* to explore opportunities presented by social media. Social networking is a phenomenon on a global scale, but most prominently by an under-30 age group—the Generation Y age group who grew up in the age of the internet. Rydne (2013) reveals some seven of the best ideas generated by IKEA in the social media space.

IKEA use a number of social media sites such as *Twitter* and *YouTube* for posting information about their products and the values they can bring to consumers. However, the use of *Facebook* has proved one of the most effective means of engaging with a young target market. *IKEA* wanted to use *Facebook* as a vehicle for creating a buzz about a new store opening in Malmo. Rather than using the logo *IKEA* they decided to personalize it by creating a Facebook profile of the store manager Gordon Gustavson. The campaign then used the default tagging tool on *Facebook* to create interest in an online competition. Users were drawn to the profile of Gustavson who had uploaded pictures of his showrooms. The competition was based on the first person to tag their name on any item would win it. This created a viral effect as the instant that something is tagged by a user the information is passed on to that user's network of contacts who quickly become aware of the opportunity of winning some free furniture from *IKEA* and so log on to the site. Very quickly thousands of users were converging on the *IKEA* site to try to win something.

The success of the *IKEA* campaign was based on some simple but effective rules for using social media for marketing and promotional purposes. First, it used existing applications on the *Facebook* site. There was no complex third party involvement; the campaign was personalised by using the store manager's profile; the campaign lasted only a short, fixed time and created a sense of immediacy in users who all had an opportunity to win. Finally, the method of communication ensured that news of the opportunity went viral very quickly. The use of social media by *IKEA* was a success because it was simple, innovative, and smart.

Sources:

Rydne, A. (27 March 2013) Ideas to Steal from IKEA's Content Strategy, socialmediatoday.com. http://socialmediatoday.com/coskills/1326216/social-media-7-actions-copy-ikea-s-content-strategy

Tarnovskaya, V. V. and Chernatony, L. (2011) 'Internalising a brand across cultures: the case of IKEA', *International Journal of Retail and Distribution Management*, Vol. 39, No. 8, pp. 598–618.

Discussion point

Is *IKEA* perceived as a company catering for all types of customers or as one that focuses on particular market segments?

http://www.
ikea.com/
http://www.
ikea.com/

individuals rather than part of a mass consumer body when operating in the online environment and through social media (Semple, 2012). Thus, personalisation of the message in e-marketing has become both a challenge and an opportunity for firms engaged in e-commerce.

Customer relationship management

Most business models are designed with market, price, or cost criteria as the main focus for generating profits. However, the issue of customer loyalty has become a key criterion in recent years leading to managers giving more attention to how this can be achieved. As a general rule, it costs as much as twenty times more to acquire a new customer as it does to retain an existing one (Lykins, 2002). The increasing importance attached to the process of building long-term customer relationships gave rise to the development of a formal approach called customer relationship management (CRM). Combe (2006) explains the concept of CRM in some detail. The three component parts to a CRM model are customer acquisition, customer retention, and customer extension.

Customer acquisition

Customer acquisition involves any technique used to form relationships with new customers including advertising, marketing, and promotion; the offering of discounts, loss leaders, or

Term
Definition

Customer relationship management: the process of managing customer service and long-term relationships with customers.

other incentives to attract new customers; value adding services offered to new customers; and targeting groups of customers through direct mailshots or e-mail.

Customer retention

Customer retention refers to any technique used to retain existing customers including using information on customers to offer a personalised service, access to a community of buyers, discounts for loyalty, or access to specialist promotional material.

Customer extension

Customer extension includes any techniques used to encourage and facilitate customer inter-activity or involvement in the activities of an organisation. This may include sending additional information via direct mail or e-mail relating to the types of products and services the organisation has for sale or information on the organisation itself.

There are a number of marketing applications of CRM. Chaffey (2004) highlights the main ones: sales force automation (SFA), customer service management, and campaign management.

Sales force automation (SFA)

This is where sales representatives are supported in their accounts management through tools to arrange and record customer visits.

Customer service management

This refers to sales representatives in contact centres responding to customer requests for information by using an intranet to access databases containing information on the customer, products, and previous enquiries.

Campaign management

This is achieved through managing advertising and promotion material, direct mail or e-mail, or other marketing techniques.

Customer analysis

Data warehousing and data mining provide the storage and retrieval mechanisms that form the basis for analysis of buyers' characteristics, habits, and behavioural responses.

Since the late 1990s the adage that 'the customer is king' has become firmly embedded in the consciousness of business managers. Business models have been developed that are termed 'customer-centric' thereby lending emphasis to this philosophy. CRM is a method of firmly placing the needs of customers at the forefront of the business model (Buttle, 2008). Information technology plays a key role in this process as it helps to gather, store, and disseminate information about consumers' behaviour and buying habits to all personnel with an interest in the marketing and sales of products and services. It also forms the basis of personalising a service as a means of building longer-lasting relationships with customers. Information gathered from multiple sources, such as direct contact, online, mobile, or any other medium all passes into a common repository for later use (Dutta and Segev, 1999). Analysis of the information from these multiple channels helps managers make decisions on the marketing of new or existing products and services. Although this process has been a key feature of marketing for many decades, the development of sophisticated information and communications technologies

(ICTs) has taken this process to a new level in terms of tracking, monitoring, and analysing customer data for strategic marketing purposes. For example, *Tesco* has created a system that tracks purchases of individual products over a period of time. The knowledge generated allows them to better control warehousing and supply dynamics as they can closely predict how many items of a product will be bought at any given time period in different stores.

A central respository for storing customer information is a standard facility for many organisations in the modern business environment where information and knowledge make significant contributions to seeking competitive advantage. It helps in the aim of creating stronger and longer-lasting relationships with customers by providing added value in service based on all previous interactions between the customer and seller. When customers make enquiries about any aspect of the supply of products and services, the interaction is logged and stored in the central repository. All future contact with customers benefits from the knowledge gained from the previous interactions (O'Brien et al., 2002).

Managers need to ensure that the CRM system is integrated throughout the organisation (Chen and Popovich, 2003). This requires harmonisation and interoperability of systems across the organisation no matter where the locus of activity is (different departments, different regions, or countries). Having customer data spread across multiple platforms diminishes effectiveness. For example, premium paying customers may be lost in the time it takes to track down important information from different sites. It is the duty of managers to provide direction on how best to use the data that supports their business aims and objectives including that of the marketing function. This can be a complex management challenge if different groups within the organisation have different CRM needs. Much depends on the capability of managers in applying the CRM system to leverage a competitive advantage. To evaluate a CRM strategy, managers need to focus attention on five key criteria as outlined in Figure 15.3.

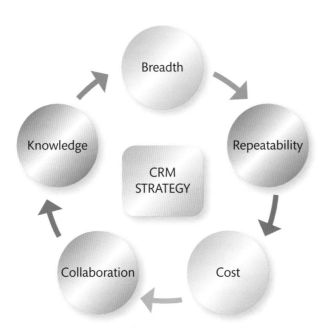

Figure 15.3 Five key criteria for evaluating CRM strategy

- *Breadth*
  Expectations and return on investment of a CRM system. This is often closely related to the number of people or groups involved in using the system.
- *Repeatability*
  The potential returns of the CRM system depending on the frequency of the activity or transaction that the application supports.
- *Cost*
  The cost of the solution must be lower than the cost of the system it replaces.
- *Collaboration*
  CRM applications that support collaboration across organisations can increase efficiency, lower costs, and help leverage a competitive advantage.
- *Knowledge*
  CRM applications that support knowledge sharing can create a competitive advantage.

Critical reflection
Why is CRM considered by many to be a disappointment?

It is important that managers understand the objectives that CRM systems are designed to help achieve. Conflicting objectives lead to confusion, duplication of effort, inefficiency, and, ultimately, a waste of resources as the lack of focus and coherence in the rollout of the CRM strategy fails to bring returns on investment. Davis (2002) and Ebner et al. (2002) report only a 3 per cent success rate of firms adopting CRM systems. There may be a number of reasons for this. There may be hidden problems in usability where staff members require additional training to glean maximum potential from CRM or there may be conflicting ideas about how best to use the data that leads to inefficiency. Disappointment relating to the performance of CRM systems stems from five main areas: knowledge management capability; measuring of CRM performance; customer expectations; managing cost reductions; and industry saturation (Combe, 2006).

Most CRM systems are ideal for collecting and managing customer data. However, they lack features for problem solving or handling complex questions. CRM systems lack knowledge management capability and, therefore, additional software (Primus being one example) is required to plug the gap. This allows employees to access the knowledge database, ask questions, and get quick replies. They can also add information to the knowledge bank for others to use (Combe, 2006).

Combe (2006) notes that the poor success rates associated with implementing CRM systems may stem from the economic limitations of their use. The ubiquity of CRM across significant numbers of industry sectors has eroded the potential for competitive advantage by its utilisation. Also, there is no clear causal link between CRM and returns on investment. Measuring the performance of CRM systems is fraught with difficulty. Even firms who report increases in revenues post-CRM implementation cannot be sure how much, if any, of the increase has been garnered through CRM utilisation. Similarly, decreases in revenues of firms utilising CRM may not be wholly, or even in part, the responsibility of CRM systems. Other inflexibilities and inefficiencies in those firms or changes in the external environment may account for the downturn in performance.

Customer satisfaction has been another measure used to determine the success, or otherwise, of CRM. However, this poses problems too. The advent of the internet has radically altered consumers' CRM applications and their expectations (Combe, 2006). Expectations of reduced delivery times are now fully embedded in the psychology of consumers and firms have had to meet those expectations. There has been some evidence to suggest the internet has increased satisfaction rates among consumers, especially in the USA where internet firms frequently top the American Customer Satisfaction Index (ACSI) compiled by the University of Michigan.

The extent of cost reductions has been used as a performance measure of CRM systems. The most commonly cited example is the efficiencies gained from increasing the availability of information to customers. Again, there are difficulties associated with this measure because efficiencies can be eroded by the empowerment of consumers by allowing free access to information. Consumers can match prices, determine availability, reduce search costs, and build communities to increase their market power based on information garnered from websites. Efficiency gains from CRM utilisation need to be weighed against the potential for diminishing competitive advantage in the face of increasing consumer power.

A source of potential savings using CRM is in the acquisition of customers. It costs less to increase sales to existing customers than it does to acquire new ones (Birkin and Harris, 2003). However, there is still the process of industry saturation to contend with. Continued acquisition of new customers alongside increasing revenues from existing customers means that the total market is being reduced. Firms may decide to focus on acquiring new customers or on existing customers, but to do both quickly erodes the market. Without tacit collusion which is (illegal) industry revenues would start to decline. This economic reality determines that firms need to pursue a strategy that brings industry leadership in order to gain and sustain competitive advantage. Consequently, it is unlikely that industries with CRM at the heart of their operations will have a high success rate and this accounts for the disappointments associated with CRM. The case of CRM is a good illustration of how assumptions around a new application of technology can prove to be erroneous and how managers need to be cautious when assessing their likely benefits.

553

Case study
New media marketing strategies for wine—from Chile to China

Introduction

The global wine industry is highly competitive and generates significant revenue for countries in wine growing regions of the world. In 2010, some three billion 9-litre cases of wine were sold and total wine consumption amounted to an average of 4 litres per person worldwide. The global wine trade registered 1.3 per cent growth between 2005 and 2010 but this is projected to increase to 3 per cent by 2015 (Euromonitor International, 2012). The United States is the biggest consumer market for wine with around 12 per cent of volume, followed by China with 7 per cent. China and Brazil are two of the fastest-growing wine consuming countries in the world.

Euromonitor International have estimated that China will overtake the USA in wine consumption by 2015 and that the Asia/Pacific region will be the most significant for driving growth in future.

China is clearly becoming a key market for wine exporters and this has presented challenges as well as opportunities. Wine producers need to understand the profile and dynamics of the Chinese market for wine and tailor their products and services to meet the demand characteristics of consumers in that country. In 2012 France was the leading exporter of wine to China with just over 73 million litres sold in the previous year (Euromonitor International, 2012). France has a competitive advantage due to the reputation of quality wines, strong brands, and established distribution channels. Australia sold around 56 million litres of wine to China in 2011 (Euromonitor International, 2012) and benefits from proximity, closer cultural links (there is a significant Chinese population in Australia), and strong marketing and promotional campaigns. Almost on a par with Australia is Chile with around 55 million litres sold in the same period. Compared to the early 2000s Chilean wine has emerged as one of the fastest growing brands in the world, partly due to a more coherent strategy for building relationships, but crucially for a more effective long-term promotional campaign that not only educates consumers about the wine but also of the country and its culture (Thomson, 2012). This case focuses attention on the strategic aim of increasing exports of Chilean wine to China through effective marketing. First, though, it is useful to highlight the key drivers of that global trade.

Key drivers of the global wine trade

Different countries have different demand characteristics for wine depending on tastes, culture, geography, demographics, etc. However, there are a number of key trends and drivers of the global wine trade that are generic to all regions. The ability of wine producers to meet the challenges plays a key role in determining their performance in export markets and requires a significant investment based on a clearly defined strategy in which marketing is a vital element. Figure 15.4 highlights the key drivers of the global wine trade.

Figure 15.4 Key drivers of the global wine trade

Value for money is an important driver because of the customer profile and characteristics of consumers that buy the products. Market research has helped to inform understanding of the profiles of consumers and their perceptions of wine as a product. Consumers tend to be professionals, over 30 years of age, technology savvy, and discerning in their tastes. Producers need to demonstrate value for money to an audience that is well-educated and sophisticated in their understanding of quality and price and who are living through times of austerity.

The ability to exploit opportunities in emerging and growing markets is another key driver and will determine where the competitive advantage is gained in the intensely competitive wine producing industry. Key markets are China and Brazil but there are also opportunities in Russia and South East Asia. Understanding the distinct demand characteristics in these regions is key as well as building relationships along the supply chain with host partners. The marketing of wine products has to be distinctive and culturally relevant to the target audience. Again, partnerships in the marketing effort are an important part of this process and may be based on the effectiveness of building long-term relationships.

As well as price, consumers of wine are interested in quality. Wine as a product is perceived by a great many consumers as a high quality item, and in some instances a luxury item. Although the industry has explored opportunities for innovation in packaging that can add value and is another key driver, producers need to recognise the enduring quality of glass and cork as part of the bottling, packaging, and presentation of the product.

Innovation has played a significant part in transforming consumers' perceptions of wine in recent years. New types of packaging offer opportunities for differentiating the product in new and exciting ways. The trend towards more innovative approaches started with cases for wine, and has now developed to include metal cans, small individual plastic bottles, cartons, wine glasses filled with the product and topped with a peel back label, and so on. These provide opportunities for extending the market to include a younger audience who seek portability, convenience, and value. A further characteristic of a younger target audience is an awareness of the importance of sustainability issues and the environment. Innovation has extended towards delivering materials that meet eco-friendly credentials. New, robust, and flexible types of materials for packaging help to reduce distribution and breakage costs.

Wine producers can use new media technologies such as the internet and mobile devices to help improve their business processes, market their products, and communicate with customers. To reach out to a younger audience, producers need to access the media that the target demographic uses. Social networking sites such as *Twitter* and *Facebook* have become almost standard communication channels in modern businesses and can be invaluable for building a relationship with customers, receiving reviews, and disseminating information. The ease with which new media users can disseminate information can be exploited with tailored marketing techniques. With internet retailing accounting for around 13 per cent of global wine sales compared to 2.5 per cent from supermarkets and around 2 per cent from discounters (Euromonitor International, 2012), it is clear that new media technologies will continue to play a crucial role in the marketing and promotion of the products and driving sales in the industry in future. Those producers that can meet the challenges presented by the key drivers in the industry will be the ones most likely to achieve a competitive advantage. Since the early 2000s the wine producers of Chile have been proactive in that process.

Marketing Chilean wines to China

In the early 2000s the Chilean wine industry was losing ground in world markets to rivals in South Africa, New Zealand, and Australia. This was largely due to a lack of any integrated strategy for the industry as it consisted of many disparate and individual producers. The marketing of Chilean wines was primitive and had no real global outlook. This perilous situation was finally addressed by the industry in the mid-2000s with the first attempts to create a marketing strategy that would reach out to consumers in growing markets and showcase the quality and diversity of Chilean wines. The marketing campaign utilised new media as a communications channel, comprised three phases, and was specifically targeted at the Chinese market, one of the fastest growing in the world (www.chileanwines.org).

The Chinese market for alcoholic drinks is defined by a distinct target audience of the 25–35-year-old age group. This age group is predominantly resident in urban areas, especially the metropolises of Beijing and Shanghai. They are urban professionals, well-educated, relatively affluent, and culturally sophisticated. This generation has grown up in an era of increasing freedom and have emerged as a middle class with discerning tastes and wide choice. The profile also reveals that this section of Chinese society are technology savvy with social networking and online buying an everyday experience. This is the environment in which they derive their information on products and services that fit their lifestyles much more than traditional forms of mass advertising.

Although Scotch whisky is a leading product in China, the target audience is an older generation than that for wine. Red wine is the fastest growing of all alcoholic products in terms of sales in China (Woke, 2012). One reason for this is the effective marketing of the product which has helped to educate the Chinese consumer about the quality and different flavour characteristics of wine. However, they sought this information not by word of mouth, but via the internet, and in particular through the social networking sites that proliferate in Chinese cyberspace. Consequently, this form of communication played a key role in the three-phase strategy of the Chilean wine producers' marketing strategy (Chinatraveltrends.com, 2010).

The three-phase strategy

The internet and social media that it facilitates were the key communication channel for the campaign. The aim was to use the technology to send information that both educated and empowered Chinese consumers to form judgements about Chilean wine products. Images of the products, the vineyards, and wider Chilean landscapes were posted on the sites to lend context to the campaign. These formed a consistent backdrop to the imagery that supported the message. The three-phase strategy consisted of:

Phase 1: 'I love wine'. This phase was designed to educate the target audience about wine growing and appreciation and was aimed at current and potential wine drinkers.
Phase 2: 'I love Chilean wine'. This phase focused attention on the specific qualities of Chilean wine emphasising issues of affordability, taste, aroma, growing practices, sustainability, and the distinctiveness that sets Chilean wines apart from wines from other regions.
Phase 3: 'I love Chile'. This phase set the context in which Chilean wine is grown by highlighting the social, economic, cultural, and environmental aspects of Chile as a country.

The use of social media was identified for making the marketing message go viral. In particular, the Chilean marketeers identified four influential Chinese bloggers and requested that they set up competitions online in exchange for bottles of Chilean wine and facts about the country. This was a tactic to get the bloggers to discuss the products and the country online and spread the message. The aggregated bloggers' postings were recorded and analysed for effect. Over the course of the campaign over 70,000 bloggers participated in the competition, many of whom won bottles of Chilean wine. The campaign was extended by continually updating content via social media to help create a community of social media users discussing wine. For example, *Kaixin* is a Chinese social media site where wine lovers can communicate and share experiences and tips. *Youku* is a Chinese version of *YouTube* where video sharing of content relating to Chilean wine can be uploaded and downloaded. So-called 'webisodes' provide short introductions to wine tasting and related topics.

The Chilean producers collaborated with the *ProChile in China* group, set up to encourage export trade, and between them they created an interactive e-book featuring a range of wine related content. Other initiatives followed including increasing their presence on the main Chinese websites *Sina* and *Sohu*. The campaign proved to be the catalyst for a much greater awareness of Chilean wine in China leading to the country's elevation from fifth largest exporter of wine to the fourth in two short years. Clearly, the superior understanding of the target market and knowledge of means to reach them played a key role in ensuring that Chilean wines have a strong market presence in China.

Sources:

Chinatraveltrends.com (January 5, 2010) using social media to promote China via Chilean wines. http://chinatraveltrends.com/case-study-promoting-chilean-wine-in-china

Euromonitor International (2012) Wine. http://www.euromonitor.com/wine

Thomson, A. (1 October 2012) Chilean winemakers set sights on China, ft.com. http://www.ft.com/cms/s/0/5d6afed2-0889-11e2-b37e-00144feabdc0.html#axzz2R5sSrI4C

Woke, L. (7 September 2012) Alcoholic drinks sales hit a high, Chinadaily.com.

Questions and tasks

What are the key drivers in the global wine trade?

Identify five main challenges facing firms seeking to increase exports to China.

What are the main consumer characteristics of the target market for Chilean wines in China?

Highlight a key attribute that differentiates Chilean wines from rivals.

Outline five key advantages of using social media for communicating a marketing message.

Online Resource Centre

Author commentary on this discussion point and questions can be found on the Online Resource Centre at: www.oxfordtextbooks.co.uk/orc/combe1e/

Summary

● **Understand the characteristics and types of marketing strategies**

This chapter has highlighted a number of different types of marketing strategies including traditional forms such as direct messages, trade shows, and promotions to more contemporary ones based on social media and permission marketing. The characteristics and purpose of these have been discussed and the effectiveness of them reviewed.

● **Develop and apply a marketing plan**

The marketing plan has become a vital element in the business strategy of many firms who seek competitive advantage. The chapter explained that the success of a marketing plan is dependent on the ability of firms to use information relating to customers and competitors in ways that contribute to the overall strategy. Managers need to determine clearly defined and measurable objectives for the marketing plan such that performance of the marketing effort can be evaluated.

● Identify and evaluate appropriate marketing strategies for different market segments

The characteristics of different market segments vary considerably according to criteria such as age, gender, income, etc. Consequently, it is necessary to apply different marketing strategies that fit the profiles of those segments.

● Recognise the components of the marketing mix

The marketing mix is another key element of the marketing plan and comprises product, place, price, and promotion criteria. In the modern era the use of internet applications now plays a significant role in determining the marketing mix adopted by firms when positioning their products or services in the marketplace. The chapter gave an explanation of the components of the marketing mix and gave examples to place these in context.

● Assess the use of new media applications for marketing purposes

Firms need to understand the differences between traditional forms of marketing and e-marketing, focus on the critical success factors in the e-marketing environment, and alter their perceptions of, and relationships with, customers in the new trading environment. The discussion of new media for marketing purposes highlighted internet technologies, mobile communications, interactive television, and social media and gave examples of how these can be applied to good effect in the marketing function of organisations. For example, the internet provides valuable information about customers and this can be used to inform the strategies for branding the products or services and determining the method and form of targeting of customers. Firms are able to collect and use a huge amount of information on customers and their online behaviour to inform future marketing efforts.

● Understand the concept and application of Customer Relationship Management

Customer relationship management is the process of managing customer service and long-term relationships with customers. The chapter highlighted three key components including customer acquisition, customer retention, and customer extension. The discussion focused on some of the advantages that can be gained through CRM such as matching customer data with promotional efforts, better informed campaign management, and improved customer service. However, the analysis also noted the fact that CRM has not delivered the competitive advantage many managers had hoped for as its limitations have become clearer.

Conclusion

Marketing is a key function within organisations and invariably forms part of business strategy for competitive advantage. The value of marketing is not always easy to measure but the huge sums of money spent on advertising and promotion of brands and products is an indication of its worth to organisations. Traditional forms of marketing remain important even in the internet age with television, radio, and the print media remaining important communication channels. However, the breadth of marketing activity has increased significantly due to the advent of new media such as social media channels. The number and type of platforms through which marketing and promotional messages can be channelled has increased hugely, giving rise to new forms of marketing strategies. Information and communications technologies (ICTs) have also played a key role in opening up global markets and giving organisations access to a much wider audience. This has presented challenges too, as the cultural diversity and distinct demand characteristics of global customers have had to be catered for. As new opportunities for spreading the message emerge, so too does the need for understanding the application of marketing techniques in the modern age. This chapter has identified and explained some of the innovative techniques applied to the marketing function. Of course, innovation is a concept that permeates throughout modern organisations and is often the source of competitive advantage. The final chapter focuses attention on change management and innovation as these have become key themes concerning management in the modern global environment.

Chapter questions and task

What are the main benefits of using the internet for marketing purposes?

Highlight the differences between traditional marketing and e-marketing.

Choose an internet-based firm and:

(i) undertake a profile of their customer base using demand analysis;

(ii) undertake a profile of their marketing mix;

(iii) identify the values that underpin the brand.

Explain how the marketing function of an organisation can benefit from using a customer relationship management (CRM) system.

Further reading

- Baines, P., Fill, C., and Page, K. (2010) *Marketing*, Oxford, Oxford University Press.
  A comprehensive and multifaceted text with many cases and illustrations to help guide readers through the key issues relating to modern marketing theory and practice. The clarity with which the key concepts are explained offers readers an understanding of how marketing strategies can be developed and successfully implemented in many different settings. A useful text for students, academics, and practitioners.

- Brown, E. (2010) *Working the Crowd: Social Media Marketing for Business*, Swindon, British Computer Society.
  This book helps to demystify social media as a means of marketing and promoting products and services. Brown has brought logic and clarity to a complex set of issues to provide a useful guide for applying social media applications to the marketing effort of organisations.

- Doyle, P. and Stern, P. (2006) *Marketing Management and Strategy* (4th edn), Harlow, Financial Times/Prentice-Hall.
  A concise text, but one that delivers a useful insight into advanced marketing techniques as part of an organisation's strategy. The link to strategic development is the key advantage of the text as its well-crafted narrative clearly explains the role of marketing in the strategy of organisations.

- Kotler, P., Keller, K., Brady, M., Goodman, M., and Hansen, T. (2009) *Marketing Management* (European edn), Harlow, Prentice-Hall.
  The European edition of this text is a useful addition to the American version and one that will appeal to students in the UK and other parts of Europe. The text reveals contemporary thinking in marketing theory and practice. Case studies proliferate throughout and there are exercises to help students engage their learning as the ideas and concepts develop. The book successfully articulates the scope, range, and fast pace of change in modern marketing and presents the challenges faced by managers in this environment.

Online Resource Centre

For more information, updates, and multiple-choice questions, please visit the Online Resource Centre at: www.oxfordtextbooks.co.uk/orc/combe1e/

Skillset 15
Reflective practice

15(a) Introduction

This Skillset outlines techniques that can help you reflect on your learning experience. Reflection is an important part of the learning process as it helps you focus on areas you recognise as being challenging; thinking through how you went about overcoming these challenges; identifying areas where you displayed good practice and competence; and thinking through ways in which you can improve. In the workplace, being able to reflect honestly about performance is an aspect of emotional intelligence that is a valuable asset when honing skills and building competencies. Reflecting on aspects of performance with a balanced and accurate analysis helps the learning process that is the catalyst for better and improved performance in future. The Skillset includes a short activity to help you relate the different contents of the textbook—encouraging you to be reflective.

15(b) Reflective practice

Reflective practice is what soccer teams do at half-time before coming out for the second half of the match; it is what search and rescue services do after they attend serious incidents. Reflective practice is about reviewing your performance, thinking about what you have learned, and considering what you might do differently in the future to enhance your performance.

There are a number of different models of reflective practice, but a critical distinction is made between what Schon (1991) calls 'reflection-in-action' (thinking and reflecting while engaged in a particular activity) and 'reflection-on-action' (thinking and reflecting after the particular activity has finished). Given the multi-dimensional and complex nature of being a manager then, clearly, the ability to think and reflect while engaged in undertaking a particular management task or activity is important. For example, implementing a marketing strategy you have formulated without reflecting that a significant change in the organisation's external environment has made the strategy out-dated may lead to difficulties for your organisation. Reflection-on-action is about taking stock and looking back to see what lessons can be learnt from past performance for the future. This section is largely concerned with reflection-on-action.

Imagine you have completed a module on management, using this textbook as core reading, and have undertaken the assessments related to the module. As part of reflecting back on the module you may wish to ask yourself the questions (adapted from Gibbs, 1988) in Table 15.3.

These questions are indicative and are simply designed to prompt your thinking. As a general model for reflective practice consider the following seven interrelated themes:

1 What did I expect from the activity?
2 How did I expect to perform during the activity?
3 What happened during the activity?

<table>
<tr><td colspan="2">

Table 15.3

Gibbs Learning Cycle
</td></tr>
</table>

Gibbs Learning Cycle	Ask yourself ...
Description	What happened during the module? What did I do? How and when did I study?
Feelings	What was I thinking and feeling? What were my expectations for the module?
Evaluation	What were the good and bad things about the experience? Were there parts of the module syllabus I liked? What parts did I like less? What parts was I good at? What parts required more time and effort?
Analysis	Taking some of my earlier answers: why did I feel that way? For example, why were some parts of the syllabus more challenging for me than others?
Conclusion	What could I have done to gain more from the module?
Action plan	If I was doing this module again (or something similar) what would I keep doing? What would I do differently? What did I learn from this module that will help me with other modules in the future? What lessons did I learn that others might benefit from?

4   What were the strengths and weaknesses of my performance during the activity?
5   What would I keep doing if I did a similar activity in the future?
6   What would I change if I did a similar activity in the future?
7   More widely—what are the lessons learnt for my future practice?

There should, naturally, be some evidence base for your answers to the questions. For example: Why did I expect to perform well during this module (Theme 2)? Perhaps because I have studied management before; or I have work experience where I have acted in a management role. Although I enjoyed the module, my performance was weak in the assessments (Theme 4). Why was this? Although my work experience as a manager helped, it also reduced the time I was able to spend revising for the examination. In the future I would try and reduce the hours I work in the weeks leading up to the exam (Theme 6). Why? It would give me more time and less pressure when revising for the exam.

How do you engage in reflective practice? There are two general approaches. One is to keep a diary or journal or, making use of technology, possibly a blog. There is a power in writing things down, in whatever form, as it encourages you to engage in thinking and formalising your thoughts. You may wish to set some time aside every day or week to reflect on the past (in writing or not). With this approach reflection is a regular activity, comparatively embedded into the fabric of your other everyday activities.

A second approach to reflective practice is to conduct what organisations call an 'after action review'. Again, you might gather your thoughts in writing or otherwise. The difference from the first approach is that this reflection tends to occur after particular activities or incidents, rather than being a more continuous process. For example, Table 15.3 helps you with an 'after action review' having completed a module.

Whichever approach to reflective practice you undertake (or both), you could consider sharing these thoughts (written or not) with a colleague (fellow student or worker) for their input and own reflections. Indeed in some situations such as search and rescue or military operations, an after action review is standard operating procedure so that lessons can be learnt and processes enhanced where necessary.

15(c) Management as an integrative activity

You are now nearing the end of this textbook. In reading this book and having worked through the various tasks and questions, you explored the nature and practice of management across a diverse range of topics, contexts, and countries. In doing so you have adopted what is termed a 'reductionist' approach—you have reduced and separated the theory and practice of management to its constituent parts. For example: planning, organising, or control. Alternatively: managing strategy, marketing, or decision making. This reductionist approach is a powerful tool which enables you to specialise and focus on understanding particular aspects of the theory and practice of management, rather than facing the challenge of trying to look at the whole spectrum of management activity all at once. However, as noted in Chapter 1, management is a complex and multifaceted concept and managers typically undertake in parallel, or in series, a range of (after Mintzberg) interpersonal, informational, or decisional roles. At some point, it is important to rebuild and reintegrate the dimensions of management to reflect, in part at least, the complexities and realities of management.

15(d) Activity

The following activity will help you start to (re)think about management more holistically. In other words, the activity will encourage you to link together the various concepts, theories, and models which bind together to describe 'management' as a whole.

1 Choose an organisation that you know well and/or you have access to a substantial amount of information about.
2 Choose three chapters of this book.
3 From each of the three chapters choose one particular theme. So, for example, you might choose the following chapters and themes.

Chapter number	Title of chapter	Theme from chapter
6	Controlling	Types of control systems
9	Motivation and Communications	Reward systems
12	Organisational Culture	Managing and influencing a positive organisational culture

Or, another example:

Chapter number	Title of chapter	Theme from chapter
3	Planning	Contingency planning
10	Managing Groups and Teams	Types of teams
16	Change Management and Innovation	Managing resistance and barriers to change

These are just examples—please choose your own chapters/themes.

4   Critically assess the organisation you have chosen in relation to the three themes you
    have chosen in point 3 above. This assessment should have three dimensions:

    (i)   *First*, assess the extent to which each theme contributes to the organisation's
          performance (successful or otherwise). So, for example, contingency planning
          may be particularly important for the management of a nuclear power station.

    (ii) *Secondly*, explicitly consider the extent to which the three themes *interact* to facilitate
          the effective management and performance of the organisation. For example, a
          nuclear power station may depend on contingency planning which is facilitated by
          the effective management of teams and their resistance to change (to ensure a culture
          of safety first and safety enhancement).

    (iii) *Finally*, reflect on what the challenges are for managers in your chosen organisation in
          relation to your three themes.

The activity is deliberately open ended. It is intended to encourage you to reflect on the content
of the book in a holistic manner and apply the concepts, theories, models, and so on from different chapters to your chosen organisation. You may spend time reflecting and carefully choosing
themes which seem to 'go together' in relation to your organisation. For instance, in the first example given, reward systems and organisational culture may have a natural link. Alternatively you
may choose themes you are interested in and then see if you can 'fit them to your organisation'.
There are no 'right or wrong' choices or answers—it is the process of thinking more holistically
which is important. If you choose a theme which does not seem to fit your organisation (based on
the information you have available) then that, in itself, may be an interesting insight into the practice of management there. In addition, carrying out this exercise should encourage you to draw
upon several of the Skillsets such as time management, sourcing materials, and critical analysis.

15(e) Integrating the Skillsets

The activity above encourages you to look at several chapters of this book in order to build up a holistic view of the theory and practice of management. Within this textbook each chapter has been
accompanied by a Skillset which imparted concepts, practices, and activities to help you develop
and enhance your abilities in relation to a number of key practical skills of value to both your studies and the workplace. As with the main chapters of this book, each Skillset is reductionist in that it
focuses on a particular skill such as time management or avoiding plagiarism. However, once again,
in the real world of study or work the Skillsets intertwine and as an experienced student or manager
you will draw on a range of the Skillsets which are appropriate to the nature of the task facing you.

Table 15.4 presents some ideas of how several Skillsets might intertwine to help you with particular tasks you may face in your studies. For example, writing an essay may draw upon Skillsets
relating to reading skills and time management along with more obvious ones such as essay
writing/examples. As this will be an academic piece of work, referencing and avoiding plagiarism will be required. Finally, skills in critical analysis will be important, particularly if you wish
to obtain a good mark for the work you submit. The lists are indicative and depending on your
needs and current skill levels you may vary these as you see fit to meet your own requirements.

13(f) Summary of the Skillset

Reflective practice is a critical skill for both your studies and in the workplace. It is at the heart of
developing yourself as a student or manager—learning from the past and enhancing performance
for the future. This Skillset outlined the nature of reflective practice and provided some key questions which enable you to be reflective. The second part of the Skillset noted that both the main
chapters and Skillsets adopted, for good reasons, a reductionist approach so that particular aspects of management/skills could be the focus. However, management and the application of

Table 15.4	How Skillsets combine to aid particular tasks and activities		
I would like to ...	**Review the following Skillsets ...**		
... write an essay.	Skillset 1	Reading skills	
	Skillset 3	Time management	
	Skillset 10	Essay writing	
	Skillset 11	Essay example	
	Skillset 4	Sourcing materials	
	Skillset 7	Literature review	
	Skillset 2	Referencing	
	Skillset 13	Avoiding plagiarism	
	Skillset 12	Critical analysis	
... avoid plagiarism.	Skillset 13	Avoiding plagiarism	
	Skillset 2	Referencing	
	Skillset 4	Sourcing materials	
... revise for an exam.	Skillset 8	Exam techniques	
	Skillset 6	Exam questions	
	Skillset 7	Literature review	
	Skillset 12	Critical analysis	
	Skillset 3	Time management	
... prepare for a presentation.	Skillset 9	Presentation skills	
	Skillset 12	Critical analysis	
	Skillset 3	Time management	

skills are rarely one-dimensional so this Skillset provides an activity to encourage you to think and reflect more holistically about the nature and practice of management. Finally, some possible ways of navigating through the Skillsets was given to show how particular tasks, such as writing an essay, depend on a range of interlocking skills to provide a high quality output.

References

Gibbs, G. (1988) *Learning by Doing: A guide to teaching and learning methods*, Oxford, Further Education Unit, Oxford Polytechnic

Schon, D. A. (1991) *The Reflective Practitioner: How professionals think in action*, Farnham, Ashgate Publishing

Further resource

Finlay, L. (2008) *Reflections on 'Reflective practice'*, PBPL paper 52. [Online resource] Available from: http://www.open.ac.uk/cetl-workspace/cetlcontent/documents/4bf2b48887459.pdf [A review of a number of models relating to reflective practice.]

16

Change Management and Innovation

Learning outcomes

- Understand the application of models of organisational change

- Comprehend and assess the change process from introduction to implementation

- Critically assess the role of change in the processes of innovation and be able to synthesise and evaluate the impact of innovative activities

- Use theory to understand the management of information systems

- Identify resistance and barriers to change and the management techniques for overcoming them

Change and innovation have become two key words in the lexicon of management in recent times. This is because the global market environment is one defined by fluctuating tastes and fashions, and the demand for new and novel products and services has become seemingly insatiable. The most successful companies are the ones that can change quickly and innovate to deliver new and better products to customers anywhere around the globe. Household appliance specialists *Dyson* are a good example of these attributes in action. James Dyson is an innovator with a host of highly valued product developments already selling on a global scale. Perhaps his most famous invention is the vacuum cleaner that bears his name and that works using cyclonic separation to ensure that no loss of suction occurs as the vacuum picks up dirt. The 2012 version combines the cyclone vacuum technology with the ball design for added manoeuvrability and suction power. The results mean that a *Dyson* vacuum is highly efficient and easy to handle in tight spaces. Crucially, the appliance was unique for that type of product as it did not require a bag to collect the dust. This found favour among the buying public and ensured the success of the innovation. Companies such as *Dyson* thrive on innovation and creativity and seek to acquire the best talent to follow the lead given by the now knighted Sir James Dyson.

Skillset 16
Overview

Skillset 16 draws all the themes together and shows the holistic nature of these skills.

Definitions

Change in an organisational context refers to methods and/or techniques for initiating and implementing alterations to how the organisation operates in relation to processes, systems, organisational structure or job roles and responsibilities. Change management is the process, tools, and techniques to manage the people-side of change to achieve a required business outcome. In a business context, innovation refers to the successful exploitation of new ideas around the technical, design, manufacturing, management, and commercial activities involved in developing new products or services, processes or equipment.

Introduction

Combe (2006) describes change management as major alterations to an organisation's processes, structure, technology, staff, or culture. Change management is necessary when firms seek to improve their current performance through changing their infrastructure and internal processes and activities. Usually, change management is necessary when a performance gap emerges. That is, when there is a disparity between existing and desired performance levels. To effect change management it is necessary for managers to understand what forces drive change and what forces restrain change.

There are numerous factors that have to be taken into consideration when undertaking change management. These may include the:

- scope of change required;
- timeframe for undertaking each successive stage of change;
- financing of change;
- identification of resources required for implementing a strategy of change;
- resources to be retained and the procurement of new resources;
- design of the most appropriate organisational structure;
- human resource management implications of introducing large-scale change;
- level of technology required for effective change;
- level of risk and the likely benefits involved in implementing change management.

At the organisational level, change can be viewed as a deliberate attempt to improve organisational performance by changing one or more aspects of the organisation. The main elements where change can be focused within organisations may include objectives, such as developing new products or markets; altering the overall mission of the organisation; or undertaking a review of human resource needs. Technology also features whereby change may take the form of investment in new information systems; building new infrastructure; or integrating communications systems with suppliers. Another is the business processes where there may be a need for a radical rethink of how business services are delivered to customers; or the introduction of new systems for handling cash flow. In some organisations the focus of change may be on the people employed or the organisational structure within which their skills and competencies are deployed. Thus, changes to human resource policies are a common feature of organisations and can include new training programmes, diversity awareness workshops, new roles and responsibilities.

Change may also involve implementing strategies designed to create a more cohesive and positive culture involving renewed reward systems, changes to the physical working environment, incentive schemes, or peer recognition. Structural reorganisation is one of the most common forms of change in organisations and may be implemented to improve communications, encourage teamwork, or to help the sharing of skills and experiences. Finally, one of the most politically charged issues in organisations is the distribution of power. Change may involve reorganising that distribution to empower more workers in the decision making process. Alternatively, some organisations may initiate policies to centralise power. Often this is closely linked to the distribution of financial resources which may involve changes such as rationalising the workforce, closing offices, or restructuring salaries in order to reduce costs. These, and related issues, feature as part of the explanation and discussion on change management and innovation.

The chapter begins with a rationale for the reasons why change is necessary in modern organisations. Detailed accounts of types of organisational change are outlined, such as incremental, step change, and business reengineering. Management issues relating to the change process are discussed such as identifying areas of change, design, implementation of change, and managing resistance to change. The discussion is linked to innovation with an emphasis on managing and influencing the development of innovation. A deeper discussion calling on influential contributions from academic writers on information systems as a catalyst for change will be included. The chapter concludes by identifying barriers to change and a discussion on managing resistance to change.

Models of organisational change

Managers need to understand what forces drive change and what forces restrain change. These form the basis of a force-field analysis. In a seminal piece of work, Lewin (1952) suggests a three-step approach to understanding these forces:

(i) *Unfreezing*: finding ways of making the need for change so clear that most people will understand and support it;

(ii) *Changing behaviour*: bring to bear new attitudes, values, and behaviour that become the dominant culture within the organisation;

(iii) *Refreezing*: introduce supporting mechanisms that consolidate and maintain the new behaviour patterns.

Managers can use force-field analysis to complement market information that illustrates the competitive position to employees in an effort to reinforce the need for change. Refreezing can be achieved by creating a culture of continuous change whereby innovation and creativity flourish. For example, computer and electronics giant *Hewlett Packard* initiated a restructuring of their entire global business in the 1990s that involved setting up strategic business units as a means of better managing change for improved innovation and speed of response to market opportunities. This can be achieved through developing teamwork, emphasising peer group acceptance as part of the reward structure, empowering workers to take responsibility, and authorising workers to make decisions. The aim is to ensure that workers become proactive in the change management process. The force-field analysis model is illustrated in Figure 16.1.

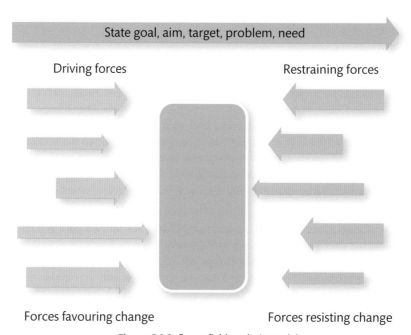

Figure 16.1 Force-field analysis model

Each arrow is labelled and the arrow size reflects the strength of the force, either a driving force or a restraining force. The number of arrows reflects the breadth of the force. The length of the arrow represents the length of time taken to put into operation a driving force or overcome a restraining force. This can be the catalyst for changing behaviours that form the basis for improved performance.

Other key aspects of change that need to be addressed include the business model adopted for achieving competitive advantage, and the organisational structure and culture that exists within the organisation. Change management is used to alter the culture and behaviour of workers and this can be facilitated by structural change. As noted previously, structural change can influence culture by altering control functions, decision-making processes, lines of authority, and span of control (Combe, 2006). These measures can be implemented to varying degrees depending on what managers seek to achieve. For example, the case studies of *Semco* in Chapter 9, the Ministry of Health in Oman in Chapter 11, and the *BBC* later in this chapter illustrate radical change management programmes in action. In other cases, change may be more incremental in scope, such as the case of *Azucarlito* in Chapter 9 where the aim was to influence changes in attitudes and behaviour.

Critical reflection
Has the usefulness of the force-field analysis model been overstated?

The force-field analysis model has been used by academics and practitioners for many decades with mixed results. Its longevity suggests that some value can still be derived from its use. However, there are some significant limitations to the model. For example, it is unlikely that full participation of employees is possible, thereby limiting the objectivity of the analysis. In fact, there may be a requirement to run multiple sessions thereby placing even greater demands on the time of staff. If group sessions become fragmented the effectiveness of force-field analysis as a change tool may be constrained. The personalities of participants also play a role in determining the effectiveness of the model's application. For example, some members of a group may come to dominate the discussion thereby skewing the outcome towards their views at the expense of others. Alternatively, participants may all be confident about contributing their views but the outcome may be confused or unclear.

The role of the facilitator also has an impact. Where group participation is needed, the role of the facilitator takes on added importance. Not only does the facilitator need to keep the group focused and on task, but he or she is instrumental in setting the pace and determines the environment in which the conversations take place. Any type of analysis will fail if 'group think' and other types of subjective thinking form the basis of analysis. Facilitators need to ensure an open environment, where all participants can air their views, but the task of identifying a suitable person for the role is not always straightforward. Two other limitations can also be in evidence. First, participants may disagree with opposing views thereby running the risk of conflict and tension—a possible source of a further restraining force. Finally, the outcome of a force-field analysis requires management to act in response to the findings for it to have proved a useful exercise. This is very often not the case thereby raising questions as to the purpose of the exercise.

Scale of change

Managers have to determine the appropriate scale of change that is necessary for firms to undertake in order to achieve their aims. Change can differ in scale and intensity ranging from a paradigm shift to radical change through business process reengineering (BPR) then to the lower scales of incremental change through business process improvement (BPI) and automation. Each level of change brings with it its own level of risk and reward.

Paradigm shift

A paradigm shift refers to a radical rethinking of the nature of the business and the nature of the organisation. This scale of change usually occurs when the organisation finds it difficult to compete effectively in the industry sector. Their inability to compete will be reflected in poor performance, loss-making, and low market share. Firms need to reassess their entire *raison d'être* (reason for existing), processes, and structures under circumstances where their current capabilities are inadequate to make returns on investment. For example, the e-commerce environment (Combe, 2006) attracted many suppliers in the early years of internet trading in the mid-1990s. However, few firms achieved their objectives. In the wake of the dot.com crash of 2000 many firms ceased to exist. Others, however, were able to undertake a paradigm shift by reinventing the organisation based on an entirely new business model. In some instances the e-commerce environment proved too complex and costly to operate their business model in. For example, *Levi Strauss* adopted an e-business aspect to augment its existing bricks-and-mortar activities, subsequently reverting back to its original model. Many such firms were to return to the online environment later once key lessons had been learned and so-called 'second mover' advantages became apparent. These are advantages associated with the learning experience gained by firms who are not part of the first wave of entrants into an emerging industry.

Business Process Reengineering

Business Process Reengineering (BPR) is a relatively new concept developed by Michael Hammer in 1990. Hammer argued that computerising existing processes wasted the opportunity to use modern IT systems as a means of remodelling business processes from scratch. He believed that waste and duplication of effort between departments could be avoided by entirely rethinking processes. Hammer advocated a plunge approach to conversion whereby the change over to a new system should occur in one radical swoop. Oil giant *Royal Dutch Shell* undertook just such a radical reengineering of its worldwide business starting in 2009. This involved a restructuring that led to the company shedding over 10,000 jobs (10 per cent of its workforce) (Webb, 2009); closer and integrated relationships with key stakeholders; cost reductions through increased efficiency in internal communications, command structure, and decision-making; greater emphasis on Total Quality Management techniques; and a transformational restructuring of its research and innovation capabilities by building in greater flexibility and integration of departments. The process was the biggest and most ambitious of its type in the company's history.

Davenport (1992) suggests a five-step model of Business Process Reengineering. This includes:
- developing the business vision and process objectives;
- identifying the business processes to be redesigned;

Term
Definition

Business Process Reengineering (BPR): radical reorganisation of internal business processes.
Business Process Improvement (BPI): incremental change to processes using information technology.

- understanding and measuring the existing processes;
- identifying IT levers or key IT capabilities;
- designing and building a prototype of new processes.

Davenport's model has been used as a guiding principle in many different industry settings. BPR has become an important method of implementing strategies in e-business. BPR involves radical alterations to the design of business processes to improve the firms' product quality, efficiency of production, and service to customers. It has an emphasis on linking innovation to improvements in business processes to improve the performance of the firm and helps achieve a competitive advantage. Mini case 16.1 on the *State Bank of India* reveals some of these characteristics in action. In e-business, BPR has most commonly focused on technology as a means of implementing change management. For example, the types of applications software used for e-business, such as Enterprise Resource Planning (ERP), are used to reengineer, automate, and integrate functions in the organisation such as production, inventory, distribution, and human resources management. This has enabled firms to create new ways of working. However, installing new technology may not, in itself, bring improved performance.

The redesign of organisational structure is an enabler of BPR. This has become an integral part of change management in e-businesses alongside that of introducing new technology. As noted previously, the trend in the e-business industry is for firms to organise projects around teams of workers who are empowered to make decisions affecting their project management. These teams are invariably cross-functional or multidisciplinary groups who can communicate electronically within the organisation (using the intranet) or with external partner organisations (using the extranet). The technology and the structure combine to make the organisation more flexible, responsive to change, innovative, and efficient.

Business Process Improvement

Business Process Improvement (BPI) is a less radical approach to change than BPR. It is incremental in scale and involves introducing change to optimise existing processes using information technology. BPI offers an alternative to the more radical scale of change represented by BPR. Small, incremental changes are easier to manage and control since they focus attention on identified activities within an organisation. For example, new applications software may be introduced to increase efficiency and service in distribution. This improves a current business process by investing in a particular information technology that is designed for that chosen process. Over a period of time other business processes can be improved by introducing

When is it necessary to implement Business Process Reengineering in an organisation?

Many organisations have benefited from radical internal change in the form of BPR. In most cases the risks have been carefully analysed and weighed against the long-term strategic benefits of change. It is not a course of action to be undertaken lightly and requires an acceptance that existing norms of behaviour and process are inevitably going to be extensively altered or even abandoned. Invariably this form of reorganisation entails change across functional boundaries that may result in those functions no longer being part of the activities of the organisation. The risk analysis of BPR necessarily has to be extensive and in-depth to ensure that the long-term benefits outweigh the short-term costs. Perhaps the most common risk factor is the implementation of the wrong processes.

Business process reengineering requires radical change and should, therefore, focus on core activities. If non-core activities are the focus then the desired effect will be diluted and the costs of implementation will outweigh the benefits. This error often stems from inadequate planning and analysis leading to substandard process design. Ultimately, if there is no process improvement or added value to customers from the upheaval then the exercise has been ill-judged. Sometimes the timescale for implementation becomes stretched leading to increasing costs which can undermine the value of the process. However, the most common reason for failure of BPR is lack of leadership or failure to accept responsibility by key staff engaged in the change process. Leadership should be inclusive meaning that workers across all parts of the organisation need to understand and engage with the rationale for change. In fact, very often it is deemed good practice to involve people from lower levels of the organisation in the design phase of the process. This can lessen resistance to change and help ensure a smoother transition. These risks need to be factored into the analysis prior to a decision being taken on adopting a BPR approach to change.

appropriate information technology. The risks and rewards associated with BPI are less than those associated with BPR. BPI may be an option for firms who lack the resources, either financial or human, to undertake radical change. Alternatively, incremental change may be the most appropriate approach for the organisation. They may be risk averse but need to take measures to improve performance over time (Combe, 2006). BPI has become an important tool for many organisations seeking to improve processes to such an extent that internationally agreed standards have been developed around a range of implementation models. Compliance with global standards such as ISO 9001, ITIL, and Six Sigma certifications are valuable sources of recognised quality in BPI within organisations.

Automation

As noted previously, automating business processes can bring cost savings and increase efficiency for organisations. Most modern organisations have some element of automation of processes even if it only entails simple answerphone software. The attraction of automation to many firms is the scope it offers for using technology to improve their operations and to undertake a large number of tasks that previously required human resources. Although automation can bring distinct benefits to organisations, its implementation requires careful planning and analysis. Automation can improve business processes, but those business processes have to be the right ones. A poor choice of business model or business process means automation serves only to improve the process of doing the wrong thing. This will undermine the organisation's costs, product quality, and ability to achieve its strategic aims. The French cement manufacturer *Lafarge* undertook some radical alterations to its portfolio of factories in North America through automation of processes in the 1980s. This not only stripped away many of the monitoring roles that were previously undertaken by workers, but also included the calibration of machinery that determined inputs of materials throughout the manufacturing process. The results showed in increased efficiency and lower costs (Hoovers. com, 2013). In general, organisations need to address the issue of what business processes need to be improved before investing in the information technology that can facilitate the improvement.

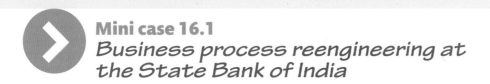

Mini case 16.1
Business process reengineering at the State Bank of India

573

The State Bank of India undertook radical restructuring in the early 2000s to align itself more to the market realities of modern global banking (Goyal et al., 2004). Traditionally the *State Bank of India* initiated change through organisational restructuring. Although this approach was instrumental in ensuring that working relationships and processes kept pace with changes to the external environment, strategic managers sought a more robust solution to the deployment of human resources, especially those of management. To effect this, the company streamlined its management structures through the implementation of BPR. In conjunction with consultants McKinsey the bank identified a nine-stage roll-out of the process (Dasgupta, 2003). This included:

- migration to automatic telling machines (ATMs);
- designing a flowchart of all the bank's activities;
- centralisation of retail assets processing;
- creation of small enterprises credit (SECC);
- drop boxes;
- outbound sales forces;
- currency administration;
- micro-market;
- relationship management.

The aim of the roll-outs was to shift the emphasis away from back-office duties of managers to one where their input more directly supported the marketing of the range of products and

http://www.sbi.co.in/

http://www.sbi.co.in/

services delivered by the bank to different customer groups. Where once branch managers were in control of cash transactions, the introduction of automation means their skills could be deployed elsewhere. Similarly, all loan processing work is now handled by a specific group of employees (small enterprise credit control) freeing up time for branch staff to concentrate more on marketing the bank's products and services.

Further to the BPR the bank has undertaken extensive internal surveys to determine the attitude to change by employees. Although there are always questions of validity, nevertheless, this is an important indicator of how well the process has been received and implemented by workers throughout the organisation. The outcome of the BPR was to make the bank more competitive in the burgeoning small and medium sized enterprise market which was experiencing high growth in India through the 1990s and into the 2000s. It also allowed more specialisation among bank staff that resulted in more customised service delivery to their core customer groups. Thus, BPR was a radical but necessary transformation in the way the bank operated and utilised its human resources.

Sources:

Dasgupta, S. (13 August 2003) State Bank of India Hires McKinsey for BPR, *The Economic Times*. http://articles.economictimes.indiatimes.com/2003-08-13/news/27527010_1 _purwar-sbi-chairman-mckinsey

Goyal, P., Sharma, K., and Jauhari, V. (2004) 'The State Bank of India: A Progressive Study of Transformation of a Socialistic Welfare Organisation into a Market Entity', *Journal of Services Research*, Vol. 4, No. 2.

Discussion point

Does the transformational scope of business process reengineering deter most managers from pursuing this approach?

Questions and task

What are the advantages of business process reengineering?

What were the key motivating factors behind the implementation of business process reengineering at the State Bank of India?

What are the main risks associated with business process reengineering?

Online Resource Centre
Author commentary on this discussion point and questions can be found on the Online Resource Centre at: www.oxfordtextbooks.co.uk/orc/combe1e/

Managing change for developing innovation

Much of the focus of internal activity in modern organisations revolves around innovation whether it is for developing new products and services, improving internal processes, or increasing organisational learning. To effectively manage innovation requires change, and change

<table>
<tr><td colspan="3">Table 16.1   Internal and external factors for learning and knowledge</td></tr>
</table>

Internal	External
Decision making processes	Industry competitiveness
Power structures	Technological development
Operational issues	Demographic change
Organisational life-cycle position	Changing customers' demands
Leadership and authority	Macroeconomic performance
Relationships with partners	Social change
Organisational structure	Political influences
Mission, aims, objectives, and goals	Changing regulation and legislation
Empowerment of employees	Natural environmental change

requires creating, diffusing, and embedding learning and knowledge throughout the workforce. Most commonly, the workforce and the organisation as a whole tend to absorb learning as a reaction to internal or external developments in the environment. That is, management have traditionally relied on incentives to motivate workers to use existing knowledge to best effect. Current thinking on innovation takes this a stage further by focusing attention on the key factors that encourage greater investment in the types of new learning that are a catalyst for innovation. Maintaining a focus on people as generators of innovation is important. For example, global design consultants *IDEO* deliberately recruit from a wide range of disciplines and areas of expertise such as psychologists, anthropologists, sociologists, philosophers, and others as a means of embedding the human element into their service delivery innovations (Bloomberg Business Week, 2001). These factors are broad ranging and sometimes complex. Table 16.1 outlines the internal and external factors that each contributes to organisational learning and knowledge.

Innovation emerges as a response to some of the factors outlined in Table 16.1. Specific types of innovation emerge as a response to specific changes in the environment. For example, climate change has presented some pressing challenges for organisations but also initiated innovative solutions to some of the problems it presents, especially in areas such as agriculture, natural sciences, environmental management, and others. The operating environment in those and other industries is characterised by uncertainty and risk, but is also one of opportunity. Managing change and innovation in dynamic and unpredictable environments requires investment in learning and knowledge creation in areas of change that can deliver sustainable growth. While managers have some measure of control over internal factors, the external environment is beyond the scope of their influence and is characterised by a risk/opportunity dichotomy. Industry competitiveness, for example, can be intense because certain rivals may embed learning from a strategy of copying ideas and innovations and adapt them slightly to bear their own brand and design. This raises the risk of innovation and careful analysis of trading conditions needs to be undertaken before committing to investment. Consequently,

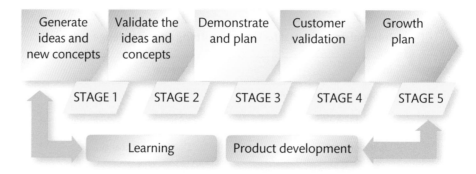

Figure 16.2 Stage gate process

Source: Stage-Gate ® is a registered trademark of Product Development Institute Inc.

managing change and innovation in such an environment requires a focus on some key issues including:

● identifying and measuring the cost (direct and indirect) of innovation;
● estimating the returns on investment in innovation;
● estimating the sunk costs and consequences of failure;
● deciding if the current business model is sustainable for what is required, if it is not then . . .;
● creating a new business model built around innovation.

Stage gates

The concept of 'stage gates', first designed by Dr Robert Cooper, can help managers make decisions throughout the learning investment process (Cooper, 2008). Figure 16.2 illustrates the components of a stage gate process.

In uncertain environments, the learning investment decision entails high risk and is difficult to determine. The type of change management required needs to focus on learning that reveals information that underscores the potential for returns on investment. Stage gates are learning milestones that are designed to help manage the learning investment by providing a framework for managing change and innovation. Two key elements underpin the framework. First, the stage gates must be fully understood by those in decision making roles within the organisation. Secondly, the innovations must be catalysts for accelerated learning that helps to reduce uncertainty. Thus, the decisions made at each stage gate should be supportive of the change process that, in turn, facilitates organisational support for the successful implementation of innovations. There are five main components of the framework that lead to stage gate decisions. These include:

Generation of ideas and concepts

Ideas and concepts need to be evaluated to determine their viability, especially when assessed within the existing business model. If a new business model has to be developed to accommodate the idea or concept then the risk factor increases as the cost of implementation will inevitably rise. Managers need to make decisions regarding what ideas and concepts to run with and those to drop. This is necessary to ensure that resources are only allocated to those that offer a realistic prospect of a return on investment.

Validation of ideas and concepts

At this stage the concept or idea is developed to a level whereby some insight can be derived as to its viability in terms of value proposition, scope for achieving a competitive advantage, return on investment, or some other business criterion.

Creation of a demonstration development plan

This stage involves the development of a plan or a proof of concept demonstration to potential buyers or end users. The key here is to demonstrate the value proposition of the innovation without incurring excessive costs.

Validation of customer value

Feedback from external end users or customers will form the basis of establishing the value of the innovation. In particular, the customer validation should be measurable so that managers can get an insight into the extent to which the investment in learning reduces uncertainty.

Create a growth plan based on commercialisation

If the innovation can be commercialised within an existing business model then a growth plan will be relatively easy to compile. Where it has to be incorporated into a new business model then the growth plan needs to take into account the higher risk and cost associated with developing and implementing a new business model.

Uncertainty and risk are diminished the further along the process the innovation goes. Each gate along the process signifies a milestone towards full implementation and commercialisation. This framework provides a systematic and logical progression that helps to guide managers through the decision making process around change and innovation. Fundamentally, it is a framework that helps managers deal with uncertainty and risk in a dynamic and unpredictable environment. And it is not only commercial enterprises that have to deal with uncertainty. Social enterprises thrive on innovation but are similarly confronted with a dynamic and changeable environment. For innovation to flourish in such a setting requires the implementation of some effective change management techniques. The case of the social innovation support organisation *The Melting Pot* is an example of this in action.

Mini case 16.2: Practitioner
Managing social innovation at The Melting Pot

Social innovation refers to new ideas (products, services, and models) that simultaneously meet social needs (more effectively than alternatives) and creates new social relationships or collaborations. Social innovation is the generation of new ideas that resolve existing social, cultural, economic, and environmental challenges for the benefit of people and the environment. It is systems-changing—it permanently alters the perceptions, behaviours, and structures that previously gave rise to these challenges. A social innovation must work for the public good.

The Melting Pot is an Edinburgh-based, not-for-profit social enterprise that aims to stimulate and support social innovation by providing help and support for social innovators. In particular, the organisation provides spaces and services that enable individuals and other organisations to work, connect, learn, meet, and hold events. The vision of the enterprise was created by founding director, Claire Carpenter, and implemented by a wide range of people over many years. *The Melting Pot* began trading in October 2007, and after a period of development work Claire and her colleagues set about creating solutions to some pressing social needs. Claire identifies the key aspects of this by highlighting:

> Our need to respond personally, professionally and collectively to the many ecological-social-economic problems that we face and are constantly creating. Change relies on the creative, industrious and imaginative efforts of many talented, dedicated people working on great initiatives to improve our collective wellbeing. (Interview with Claire Carpenter, *The Melting Pot*, 7 February 2013)

Claire decided to create an independent, low-carbon, financially self-sufficient resource base—a melting pot—to bring together talented people to contribute to the achievement of the vision. Key skills and attributes required to bring this vision to reality included effective networking skills, the ability to communicate the essence of social innovation to diverse stakeholders, and to implement change actions in a meaningful and added value manner. By deploying her networking skills, Claire was able to recruit a team of volunteers to turn the idea into a reality, and together they set off on a journey where the principle of 'the only constant is change' could be put into effect. Effective communications and marketing skills ensured that awareness of the venture rose quickly throughout the social innovation community. Also, the pace of change picked up after securing the top floor of 'Thorn House'—the Ethical Property Company's first centre in Scotland, which was fitted out largely through volunteer input. In the first few years *The Melting Pot* has supported hundreds of members (both individuals and whole organisations) and hosted well over a thousand events and meetings, involving tens of thousands of people. *The Melting Pot* currently has more than 150 members using the workspace and network. It forms a dynamic, diverse, and supportive community for the purposes of social change.

Source: www.themeltingpotedinburgh.org.uk

Discussion point

Are social problems best tackled by public sector agencies?

Questions and task

Define social innovation.

Give an example of a social innovation.

What added value does The Melting Pot deliver to their clients?

 Online Resource Centre
Author commentary on this discussion point and questions can be found on the Online Resource Centre at: www.oxfordtextbooks.co.uk/orc/combe1e/

www.themeltingpotedinburgh.org.uk

www.themeltingpotedinburgh.org.uk

Managing information systems

Innovation can be applied to the development of technologies that can be a product in themselves or a means of improving process efficiency. For example, the development of information systems (IS) and information technology (IT) have been used to deliver a wide range of benefits to organisations when managed effectively. Indeed, such has been the impact of IS on organisational performance that it has become a focus of much academic attention. For example, IS as a resource features in the study by Kettinger et al. (1994) into the sustainability of competitive advantage and firm performance; Bharadwaj (2000) undertook an empirical investigation into IT capability and firm performance; Duncan (1995) examined measurements of IT infrastructure; while research by Ray et al. (2005) linked IT and the performance of the customer service process.

There is a need for firms to implement strategies to acquire their information systems infrastructure. This can be achieved in two main ways, internally, through the development of their IS function, or, externally, through outsourcing all or part of the delivery of the development, maintenance, and operation of their systems. Throughout the 1980s IT was increasingly being used as a means of implementing strategies and as a result the attention of academics turned to creating theoretical frameworks capable of supporting analysis. For example, Porter's (1985) competitive strategy model was often used as a means of linking the use of IS to the development and implementation of strategies capable of achieving sustained competitive advantage. Henderson and Venkatraman (1993) emphasised the need for coherent links between IS strategies and organisational change strategies as a prerequisite for improved firm performance. Success relied on the alignment of the IS functions to stated business goals, rather than the traditional emphasis on user needs. Key writers in the field recognised the broader IS functions that incorporated competence in organisational skills alongside the development of value adding applications. Sustained competitive advantage in this context could be derived through synergies derived from the integration of these attributes.

The issue of competitive advantage has been the focus of much of the development of theory relating to IS and IT. In particular, the identification of the types of resources and capabilities linked to gaining competitive advantage formed the basis of many studies. For example, Feeny and Wilcocks (1998) take a broad view of IS capabilities by identifying business and the IT vision, architecture and design, and delivery as being key to gaining a competitive advantage. Core IS capabilities may feature leadership, business systems thinking, relationship building, architecture buying, contract facilitation and monitoring, and vendor development.

Alternatively, Mata et al. (1995) identify key issues as being switching costs enabled by technology, access to capital, proprietary technology, and technical and managerial IT skills. They note that this latter capability is critical to developing and implementing IS strategies, and in particular, the acquisition of information systems architecture (either through internal development or outsourcing). Outsourcing is often viewed by managers as a means of reducing costs or freeing up resources to concentrate on core activities. Also, the organisation may not possess the required skills to develop the IS system internally. Although there is evidence to suggest that savings can be made through outsourcing, the long-term benefits to firms is less clear (Elmuti, 2003). If IT is viewed simply as a factor of production, then it would be a relatively simple task to meet requirements from the vast array of software and hardware on the market. This, though, is unlikely to yield a competitive advantage in itself. Rather, it is the organisational skills that transform resources and capabilities into competitive advantage.

Figure 16.3 Information systems implementation activities

Change management requires managers to address a number of key issues, and technology infrastructure is one of them. Often, organisations undertake an audit of technology performance to ascertain information that informs the need for change. It is important that the implementation of technology follows a process. Figure 16.3 illustrates implementation activities for the conversion of information systems as described by Mallach (2009).

The implementation process can only begin once a thorough evaluation of appropriate activities has taken place. This includes a number of key activities such as ensuring that:

- the correct hardware and software have been selected;
- the systems have been rigorously tested;
- an efficient user documentation system has been developed;
- all staff have received suitable training.

> ## Mini case 16.3
> ## *IT project failure at the NHS*

One of the problems associated with IT infrastructure projects is that managers often believe that their roll-out is sufficient to deliver transformational change in organisations. One such example was the ambitious plan by the UK government to create the world's largest single civilian computer system designed to link all parts of the National Health Service (NHS). In August 2011 the government announced it was to abandon the project which to that date had racked up a cost of some £11.4 billion to the taxpayer, over £6 billion more than had been originally forecast (Martin, 2011). The fall-back position is to allow local healthcare trusts to either develop or buy-in computer systems to serve their own needs. In a damning report by the House of Commons Public Accounts Committee (PAC) the project was deemed to be beyond the capability of the Department of Health to deliver. The main reasons for the failure of the project were identified as being changing specifications, technical challenges, and problems with suppliers. For example, management consultants *Accenture* walked away from the project in 2006 costing the company many millions of pounds and plunging the project into disarray. Several other suppliers, such as *BT*, failed to fully deliver on their contract agreement (Wray,

2006). Significantly, the PAC reported that the transformational change that the IT system was designed to deliver was never a realistic prospect owing to the lack of effective leadership surrounding the implementation of the project.

The debacle surrounding the centralisation of the NHS computing system illustrates the risks associated with implementing transformational change in organisations, especially ones that are characterised by complexity. The lesson to be learned in the case of the NHS is that large-scale IT projects need effective leadership, clear and integrated planning, cost control, relationship management along the supply chain, and a commitment to deliver by all stakeholders (Dinwoodie, 2013). The main motivation for implementing the ambitious centralised system was to improve efficiency and to act as a catalyst for transformational change throughout the organisation with patient-centred care at the core of activities. The computer system was designed to facilitate integrated care delivery by allowing patient care teams to access all relevant information on their patients in a secure environment. The case illustrates the problems associated with having IT at the core of transformational change rather than viewing it as a facilitator for change alongside effective management, processes, and cultures.

Sources:

Dinwoodie, R. (12 April 2013) Controversial NHS patient system axed, *heraldscotland*. http://www.heraldscotland.com/politics/political-news/controversial-nhs-patient-records-system-axed.20640741

Martin, D. (22 September 2011) £12bn NHS computer system is scrapped . . . and it's all YOUR money labour poured down the drain, London, *MailOnline*. http://www.dailymail.co.uk/news/article-2040259/NHS-IT-project-failure-Labours-12bn-scheme-scrapped.html

Wray, R. (28 September 2006) Accenture confirms quitting NHS work, *Guardian*. http://www.theguardian.com/technology/2006/sep/28/news.business1

Discussion point

Are publicly funded projects always more expensive than ones financed by the private sector?

Questions and task

What were the main causes of the failure of the proposed NHS computer project?

Highlight the critical success factors in the successful implementation of change management featuring IT.

Where does the main responsibility for failure of the NHS computer project lie?

Online Resource Centre

Author commentary on this discussion point and questions can be found on the Online Resource Centre at: www.oxfordtextbooks.co.uk/orc/combe1e/

The implementation process also involves the conversion from a previous system to the new system. Combe (2006) outlines conversion methods that smooth the transition from old to new systems. These include:

- *Parallel conversion*: old and new systems run in tandem until the development team and management agree to switch permanently to the new system.
- *Phased conversion*: only parts of a new system or only a few departments, offices, or business units are converted at a time.

- *Pilot conversion*: one department or business unit acts as a test site for conversion.
- *Plunge conversion*: the whole organisation converts to the new system at the same time.

No matter which method is adopted there are risks associated with the implementation of computer systems. The case of the planned centralised computer system project at the NHS in the UK is an example of how a major IT investment can go very wrong.

Managing resistance and barriers to change

If organisations are to survive into the future they must be aware of the need to adapt to changing circumstances. If they cannot, then the consequences are very serious. Change management is concerned with the way successful change can be implemented in an organisation. Not all change is instantly acceptable to the organisation's members and on many occasions there is strong resistance. Managers must carefully consider the nature of the resistance and do their best to overcome it. There will be various reactions to change ranging from extremely favourable (*Tesco, Sainsbury's*, and other supermarkets hire people who wish to prolong their working lives) to the downright hostile (*British Airways* have had a long-running dispute with cabin staff over new working practices). Some individuals will be pleased, some annoyed, and some upset, and this kind of mixed reaction is likely to occur whenever change is suggested. Generic types of responses to change include acceptance, indifference, and resistance. Figure 16.4 highlights typical responses to change.

Acceptance

People who accept change can be found in all walks of life. They are a great asset in any organisation that needs to make changes, because their enthusiasm for the new ideas can carry along the more reluctant members of the group.

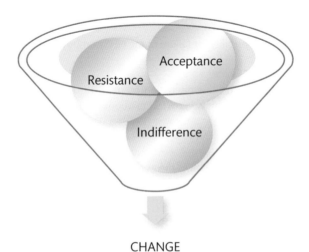

Figure 16.4 Potential individual responses to change

Indifference

Many changes are met with indifference, even apathy, especially if the people concerned perceive that their overall state will be unchanged.

Resistance

People who resist change may do so passively or actively. Passive resistance will include those who will not learn about new ideas or who will do everything to avoid being faced with something different. At the extreme end of the spectrum there are actively hostile resisters. These individuals will express their resistance in such activities as go-slows, strikes, sabotage, sit-ins, etc.

Influences on responses to change

Many factors have been proposed which might account for a particular individual's attitude toward a change, and any manager wishing to make a change should be aware of these underlying influences.

Personality

Some people are sensitive to any form of change and will react accordingly. This may be positive or negative but the reaction is very much linked into a distinct personality type that stimulates a response which takes the form of either a general resistance to, or acceptance of, changes. A feeling of insecurity often leads to strong resistance. It is important in these instances for managers not to be influenced by the response of certain individuals within the organisation. Some may have vested interests in resisting change (trade union representatives may view change as a threat to their members' welfare) or embracing it (some workers may view change as a career opportunity). Whatever the response, managers must maintain a focus on implementing and managing change effectively so that the aims of change are realised.

Values and beliefs

Individuals, organisations, and groups build up their own value systems, codes of conduct, or behaviour. Change that runs counter to these is likely to be met with strong resistance. However, invariably, part of a change agenda is to alter values and beliefs so that they more closely align to the new reality within the organisation. Again, managers have to concentrate on the bigger picture by ignoring the short-term responses to change and focusing on the long-term cultural changes that are more conducive to helping achieve stated aims.

Past experience

Individuals often evaluate changes that affect them by looking for similar occurrences in the past and reacting in similar ways. This presents an obvious problem for managers as the reason for change is most likely to be built around a departure from past practices. It is essential that managers can communicate the reasons for the change and why past practices are no longer effective in achieving stated aims. The most effective form of management is one that communicates the reasons for change, gets workers to 'buy-into' the vision presented, and is implemented with the goodwill and support of staff. This is never an easy task as most organisations are comprised of people with very different views and expectations, ambitions and interests. To achieve full consensus for change is rare but the most effective managers are the ones who are able to implement change without major disruption or dissent.

Reasons for resistance

It can be said that people do not resist change itself. What they are resisting are the implications behind the change which may be detrimental to them. Some possible reasons for resistance to change include the perceived effects of economic implications. If a change is perceived as going to affect levels of income, or in the amount of work required to generate the same income, then resistance is likely to be high. Also, resistance may be greater if the change is going to make life more difficult. This often occurs when workers, offices, or factories are being relocated. Psychological feelings of security and well-being may also feature. For example, if an individual feels that his or her freedom is going to be diminished, then there will be resistance. Greater control is desirable in certain circumstances, but that may not be how it is perceived by the individuals who are going to be controlled. One of the most prevalent reasons for resistance to change is the impact on job security. If a proposed change suggests that there may be a threat to the security of jobs, then it is likely that there will be some resistance to it. Again, much will depend on how those affected perceive the future, even if there is no explicitly stated intention of implementing job losses.

? Critical reflection
Do traditions, customs, and rituals restrain necessary change in organisations?

In classical economics much of the output of writers such as Adam Smith and Alfred Marshall has been concerned with rational decision making and notions of 'equilibrium' and 'rational choice'. In contrast, the evolutionary school of economics challenges these concepts by arguing that they are incapable of offering insights into the actual operation of the economy. Protagonists of this school, such as Thorstein Veblen (1919) and Clarence Ayres (1961), argue that all cultures since the dawn of civilisation have been confronted by two opposing forces. Those are technology and institutions rooted in what they term 'ceremonialism'. The former is seen as dynamic, forward looking, accepting of change, and cumulative (one discovery builds on another). This, they argue, is the building block of human progress. Conversely, the latter is static and consists of restraining factors such as customs, beliefs, taboos, rituals, and ceremonies that act as a barrier to change. According to Veblen, human progress is inextricably linked to the ability of individuals and groups to not only accept change but to embrace it.

Managing successful change

Effective implementation of change invariably features a number of key attributes of management. These include keeping people informed of progress throughout the change phase. Withholding information and not consulting encourages rumour and speculation. If people are kept informed, they are less likely to be suspicious of change. Group involvement is also important as group decision making can increase the commitment of the members. Although group involvement is not a panacea for all the challenges presented by change, it is important to obtain the group's reaction to the change proposal. Dialogue with workers is essential to elicit information on the reaction and needs. For example, there may be a requirement to introduce more training and development to facilitate acceptance of change. Staff may require new skills to carry out their changed duties and responsibilities. Comprehensive training programmes should equip staff with those competences essential for the successful implementation of change. Finally, there should be continued support after the change. Support should not be regarded as a one-off isolated activity but part of a strategy for developing new competencies in staff members.

Tactics for overcoming resistance to change

According to Kotter and Schlesinger (1979), managers must have at their disposal a range of tactics for addressing resistance to change. These include:

Education and communication

Resistance can be reduced through communicating with employees to help them see the rationale for change. This tactic assumes that the source of resistance lies in misinformation or poor communication, that is, if employees receive the full story then potential resistance will subside. Communication can be achieved through one-to-one discussions, memos, group presentations, or reports. Communication is effective provided that the source of resistance stems from inadequate communication and that management–employee relations are characterised by mutual trust and credibility. If these conditions do not exist, the change is unlikely to succeed.

Participation

It is difficult for individuals to resist a change decision in which they have participated. Prior to making a change, those opposed can be brought into the decision process. Assuming that the participants have the expertise to make a meaningful contribution, their involvement can reduce resistance, obtain commitment, and increase the quality of the change decision.

Facilitation and support

Change agents can offer a range of supportive efforts to reduce resistance. When employees' fears and levels of anxiety are high, employee counselling, new-skills training, or a short period of absence may facilitate adjustment. The drawback of this tactic is that, as with the others, it is time consuming and potentially costly with no guarantee of positive outcomes.

Negotiation

A change agent can reduce the level of resistance to change by engaging in negotiation. This invariably involves compromise by way of offering something of value in exchange for a reduction in resistance. Negotiation may be with a powerful individual, small groups or representatives of a larger group such as trade union shop stewards. Although negotiation can succeed in the primary aim of reducing resistance, it will involve a cost. That cost is likely to manifest itself in many different ways. For example, those resistant to change may view compromise as a weakness to be exploited; they may find more subtle means of resistance whilst continuing to benefit from the reward; if one group perceives that another group has benefited through the tactic of resistance it may encourage them to do likewise; or it may spread discord among workers if there is a perception of inequality from the outcome of the negotiations. Managers need to balance these risks against the benefit of reducing resistance to change.

Manipulation and co-optation

Manipulation is a means of influencing outcomes through distortion of facts, misinformation, withholding of information, or devious modes of behaviour designed to achieve a desired outcome. Co-optation refers to the means by which resistance can be reduced by bestowing key roles in the change decision to leading figures in the resisting group. Both these approaches are fraught with risk. There is a cost to the corporate ethic by behaving in such a manner. If stakeholders such as suppliers or shareholders become aware of this type of management then they may consider switching allegiance to a rival. Also, should the manipulation or co-optation become known amongst the majority of workers, it could seriously undermine labour relations and diminish the credibility of management.

Coercion

Last on the list of tactics is coercion, that is, the application of direct threats or force upon the resisters. Coercion differs from manipulation or co-optation as it involves a threat or sanction if those exhibiting resistance do not comply. For example, if the corporate management were determined to close a manufacturing plant if employees don't acquiesce to a pay cut, then coercion would be the label attached to the change tactic. Other examples of coercion are threats of transfer, loss of promotions, negative performance evaluations, and poor letters of recommendation. The advantages and drawbacks of coercion are similar to those highlighted under 'manipulation and co-optation'.

Organisational development

Organisational development (OD) is another important aspect of change. OD covers a wide range of different activities designed to improve the effectiveness of the organisation and the well-being of employees within it. OD aims to support human and organisational growth through the integration and collaboration of workers. Robbins et al. (2010) identify the key underlying values in OD as being:

- *Respect for people*: Individuals are perceived as being responsible, conscientious, and caring. They should be treated with dignity and respect.
- *Trust and support*: The effective and healthy organisation is characterised by trust, authenticity, openness, and a supportive climate.

- *Power equalisation*: Effective organisations de-emphasise hierarchical authority and control.
- *Confrontation*: Problems should not be ignored, rather they should be openly confronted.
- *Participation*: The more that the people who will be affected by a change are involved in the decisions surrounding that change, the more they will be committed to implementing those decisions.

Case study
Change management at the BBC

Introduction

The *BBC* has been at the fulcrum of public service broadcasting in the UK for over 80 years. During that time it has built an enviable reputation for producing quality programmes for diverse audiences and set standards for production values in broadcasting. As a public service broadcaster the *BBC* has a duty to provide services for a broad constituency of cultures, tastes, and social groups. It must reach out to society as a whole. Consequently, it delivers programme genres unwanted by commercial channels alongside the more populist ones; generates new ideas and experiments with new formats; fulfils a role as a vehicle for social cohesion at significant moments in the nation's history and provides an impartial window on the world through its news output. The public service remit of the *BBC* differentiates it from most commercial broadcasters. Although *ITV* have a public duty to provide a minimum range of quality programmes, the commercial aspect of their business determines that they can focus more on popular programmes that attract the biggest audience share as well as advertising revenue. Until the advent of *Channel 4* in 1982 the *BBC* and *ITV* had no other competition for audiences. The *BBC* monopolised licence fee income and *ITV* monopolised advertising revenue.

Concern over the future of the *BBC* has its roots in a host of economic, technological, political, and legislative changes that have been brought about by the introduction of the Broadcasting Act (1990). The availability of other delivery systems such as cable, satellite and digital has altered the structure of the industry. The *BBC* is no longer viewed as the dominant provider of entertainment, information, and education in broadcasting and now has to justify its role as a publicly funded body in the largely privatised broadcasting arena. Public service broadcasting in the UK is still in the early stages of adapting to the increased competition from new commercial services and of redefining their role in the multi-channel environment.

This case study charts the process of managerial and strategic change at the *BBC* in response to the challenges facing the organisation in the 1990s. In particular, the case focuses on the highly controversial changes brought in during the 1990s as the regime of director general John Birt (1992–2000) implemented radical change in order to make the *BBC* a more accountable and efficient organisation.

Producer choice

In early 1990 the *BBC* set out a five-year plan for restructuring and reorganising the corporation. The objectives of the changes were to cut costs; to re-introduce in-house production capacity; to seek to maximise income from sources other than the licence fee; to investigate opportunities for commercial partnerships; and to compete in global markets (Harris and Wegg-Prosser, 1998). To oversee the implementation of many of these changes the *BBC* announced the appointment of John Birt as director general in 1992. Birt set about attempting the major task of restructuring large parts of the *BBC*, particularly the areas concerned with programme production. Over the next few years, in conjunction with a myriad of consultants, Birt and a team of senior managers began to spearhead moves to increase efficiency under a wide-ranging set of new initiatives that were branded under the label *Producer Choice*.

Felix (2000) maps the change process at the *BBC* in the period 1993–99. The main thrust of *Producer Choice* was to create an internal market in programme making resources by separating the purchasing and supply of these resources within the *BBC*. This meant that the internal purchasing of in-house facilities used to make programmes such as studios, lighting, editing suites, and so on, as well as personnel, would now be financially distinct from the cost of providing them from within the organisation. A price would be put on these facilities so that in-house users and purchasers, in this case the *BBC* producers, would have greater flexibility and a more accurate and accountable way of budgeting and monitoring the production costs of their programmes. This system offered the *BBC* an opportunity to compare production costs in-house with those of outside suppliers such that producers could make a choice as to which offered the better value.

The greater accountability offered by *Producer Choice* also enabled a 'slim down' of production and administrative areas where there was deemed to be over-capacity. By 1996 the number of permanent jobs in BBC Resources (the division set up to oversee the working of *Producer Choice*) was reduced from 11,000 to around 6,800. By the end of 1996/7 BBC Resources announced a trading surplus of some £15 million while supplying 78 per cent of the BBC's facilities requirements. Other saving were made by merging skills. Thus, journalists who had previously only worked on television now had to service the needs of radio as well. Likewise, production staff were required to become more flexible in the tasks they performed across different media.

Resistance to change

Unsurprisingly, the wide-ranging changes and restructuring brought about by *Producer Choice* attracted criticism and reaction from *BBC* employees, as well as the in-house union. However, although there were some skirmishes with management there was no large-scale industrial action. There was a general move within BBC Resources towards employing production staff more on fixed-term contracts or on a freelance basis, as needed by programme making schedules, and away from full-time, permanent, salaried employment. Some full-time staff were offered, and chose to take, redundancy payments that were calculated on the basis of the number of years' service they had accrued. Many of these people were then re-employed by the *BBC* in similar roles on flexible, short-term contracts.

The effect of *Producer Choice* on programme makers at the *BBC* was felt almost immediately and involved increasing bureaucracy, an over-emphasis on accountability at the expense of creativity, and resistance to the required change from a public service to a 'marketisation' culture (Koenig, 1993). In this new, more commercial climate, producers also claimed to be increasingly unsure about what their goals were in making programmes. Were they supposed to be going all out to chase audiences and ratings, or were they to make shows that aimed for something higher, more in the public service *BBC* tradition? Harris and Wegg-Prosser (1998) provide valuable research findings from an investigation into the effects of *Producer Choice* on the creative output at the *BBC*.

The decision to merge the news and current affairs departments and combine radio and television news was also generally unpopular with many of the journalists employed at the *BBC*.

There was widespread dissatisfaction and claims that these moves would undermine the quality of news output, which was one of the *BBC*'s main strengths. Several journalists, some of them household names, took the opportunity to express their views by publishing articles in newspapers criticising the changes. Included in these tirades were criticisms of John Birt's management style. To most *BBC* staff, the director general was traditionally a remote figure. Birt, however, reportedly exacerbated this by communicating to employees through circulars and reports in a style loaded with management jargon that was derisively dubbed 'Birtspeak'. Respected *BBC* foreign correspondent Kate Adie joined the criticism by noting that John Birt bore responsibility for the collapse of internal confidence (Adie, 2003).

There were also problems with the implementation of *Producer Choice*. Apart from the employees' reluctance to change working practices and the difficulties in designing and putting into practice new processes and procedures, it was found that anomalies sometimes occurred in trying to make the internal market actually work. Transactions and trading between various *BBC* departments, for example, could become inordinately time-consuming, complex, and bureaucratic, causing frustration and increased costs. There was also the issue of whether it was really appropriate to compare and benchmark efficiency and performance measures derived from an examination of private sector industry firms with the internal departments of a large organisation like the *BBC*.

Producer Choice represented one of the most radical and divisive attempts to introduce change in a large, multifaceted, and complex organisation. The effectiveness of the strategy has been hotly debated by a wide range of commentators, but what is clear is that the increased accountability of the organisation was used by managers as leverage when lobbying government for the maintenance of the licence fee system that guarantees income for the corporation. In an era when the licence fee system was under unprecedented threat, the change management regime under the aegis of John Birt proved pivotal in ensuring support for the continuance of the funding system.

Sources:

Adie, K. (2003) *The Kindness of Strangers: The Autobiography*, London, Headline.

Felix, E. (2000) 'Creating radical change: Producer choice at the BBC', *Journal of Change Management*, Vol. 1, No. 1, pp. 5–21.

Harris, M. and Wegg-Prosser, V. (1998) 'The BBC and Producer Choice: A Study of Public Service Broadcasting and Managerial Change', *Wide Angle*, Vol. 20, No. 2, pp. 150–63.

Koenig, P. (27 June 1993) 'No choice at all: BBC programme makers are drowning in a sea of paper. The reason is Producer Choice—the drive by John Birt to set up an internal market', *The Independent*.

Discussion point

Is an internal market approach to resource allocation appropriate in a public sector organisation?

Questions and tasks

Explain the concept of *Producer Choice*.

Identify the key elements of change management under the Birt regime.

What were the reasons for resistance to change by some BBC staff members?

 Online Resource Centre
Author commentary on this discussion point and questions can be found on the Online Resource Centre at: www.oxfordtextbooks.co.uk/orc/combe1e/

Summary

● **Understand the application of models of organisational change**

Academics have tried to help managers seeking change by developing theoretical models and frameworks such as the force-field analysis model of Kurt Lewin, Business Process Reengineering, Business Process Improvement, or the process of automation. These provide the guidance around which change-oriented decisions can be taken. This chapter has presented and explained just a few of the many theories that are designed for this purpose. It may not always be possible for managers to comprehend and apply theoretical models in a business setting but they can at least understand the parameters of what it is they are dealing with. Those parameters are likely to include economic, social, political, technological, emotional, and strategic dimensions that make change potentially complex and difficult to manage. The chapter has used theory as a means of helping managers work through that complexity to achieve a measure of clarity in building an analytical insight into the areas where change can and should happen within their organisations.

● **Comprehend and assess the change process from introduction to implementation**

This chapter has explained that change takes on many different forms and varies markedly in both scope and scale. Managers need to make decisions regarding the extent to which their organisation seeks change, allocate appropriate resources to support it, build the capabilities to deliver it, and seek strategic advantages from its implementation. These have inevitably placed greater pressure on managers as they seek to identify, manage, and sustain change from introduction to implementation in a dynamic and unpredictable environment.

● **Critically assess the role of change in the processes of innovation and be able to synthesise and evaluate the impact of innovative activities**

This chapter has highlighted the types of change necessary to support the development of innovation within organisations. This was linked to the learning organisation and the generation and sharing of knowledge—key concepts that have gained in currency in the last decade or so. Many modern organisations undertake change (most commonly restructuring as a means of initiating a new culture of knowledge sharing) as a means of deriving increased capabilities and competencies of their existing staff or to facilitate the sharing of knowledge that acts as a stimulus to innovation.

● **Use theory to understand the management of information systems**

A framework for the implementation of information systems was used to explain the different options available to managers for introducing new systems to their organisations. These included the parallel, pilot, phased, and plunged approaches. Some key issues that help inform decisions were presented and discussed including the implementation activities of acquiring hardware and software services, software development, user training and development, and system documentation.

● **Identify resistance and barriers to change and the management techniques for overcoming them**

Responses to change can range from acceptance, to outright resistance, or just indifference. Managers may face different levels of resistance to change such as insubordination or lack of enthusiasm or even sabotage. Whatever the level of resistance, managers have to understand the reasons for the resistance and act accordingly. In some instances this requires superior communications skills in order to 'sell' the idea of change to workers. The chapter highlighted a number of techniques managers can apply to help overcome resistance to change including greater input to decision making or the change process, rewards for compliance, increasing access to training or education, and so on. It was recognised that acts of coercion are a sign of management failure to deal with resistance to change.

Conclusion

The concept of change has become an increasingly important issue in many organisational settings over the last two decades or so. Part of the reason for this has been the increased opportunities that present themselves in a globalised economy. Technological developments, increased mobility of people, better communications, and changing demand for products and services have contributed to change being put at the top of the strategic development agenda in many organisations. Whatever the aim of change is, it is clear that it has become firmly embedded in the culture of many organisations that require their workers to be catalysts for new and improved products and services. Workers react to change in different ways depending on the prevailing dominant culture of the organisation. In some instances change can be perceived as a threat by stakeholders whose lives or careers are affected by it. Resistance to change is an inevitable consequence of removing higher levels of certainty and stability within organisations. However, change may be necessary to remain competitive or to reinforce behaviours more suited to the modern business environment. This chapter has highlighted a number of practical measures that managers can take to try to overcome resistance to change. In many organisations, change has become firmly established in the culture of the organisation as successive generations of workers have been recruited with attitudes and values that include an appreciation of and engagement with change as a natural part of the modern working environment.

Chapter questions and tasks

Give a definition of change in an organisational context.

Your organisation is setting up a call centre facility 30 kilometres from the present location. It will be staffed by employees who are currently surplus to requirements in their own departments. What reasons for resistance to this change might you encounter and what could you do to address these concerns?

Give practical examples of the ways in which strategic change can be managed making use of the Kotter and Schlesinger framework of: education and communication; participation and involvement; facilitation and support; negotiation and agreement; manipulation and cooptation; and explicit and implicit coercion.

Research and describe a major IT-enabled project that has resulted in failure due to poor change management.

Online Resource Centre
Author commentary on this discussion point and questions can be found on the Online Resource Centre at: www.oxfordtextbooks.co.uk/orc/combe1e/

Further reading

- Brown, K. and Osborne, S. P. (2005) *Managing Change and Innovation in Public Service Organizations* (Routledge Masters in Public Management), London, Routledge.
  This book offers a useful insight into change in the increasingly complex environment of the public sector. The issue of innovation in the process of service delivery has become a key issue for public service managers and the authors have been able to articulate effectively the processes involved in understanding, managing, and sustaining change and innovation in a modern public sector environment.

- Cameron, E. and Green, M. (2009) *Making Sense of Change Management: A Complete Guide to the Models, Tools and Techniques of Organizational Change* (2nd edn), London, Kogan Page.
  Although it is stretching credibility to claim that this provides 'a complete guide', many of the relevant techniques and tools for managing organisational change are featured in this book. The authors have designed a logical and insightful account to help students and practitioners understand the key issues pertinent to making change happen. Techniques for managing and leading change in a range of organisational settings are explained and discussed in a clear and systematic fashion. The authors also utilise theory to underpin much of the discussion and use scenarios such as organisational restructuring, mergers and acquisitions, cultural change, and IT-based process change as examples of change in action.

- Hayes, J. (2010) *The Theory and Practice of Change Management* (3rd edn), Basingstoke, Palgrave Macmillan.
  A textbook designed for modules that feature change management. The author examines and applies key theoretical perspectives and models to change in a number of organisational settings. The book features the use of diagnostic tools and employs immersive learning techniques to help students identify change based on real examples, thereby lending a good balance between the theoretical and practical aspects of change.

- Manwani, S. (2008) *IT-Enabled Business Change: Successful Management*, London, British Computer Society.
  This book is compiled using the premise that many of the high-profile IT project failures have occurred because of poor or ineffective change management techniques. The author focuses on the types of business change processes that involve the use of IT. This includes the way that organisations use IT and how the change is identified, managed, and implemented. The structure of the book follows a new IT-enabled business change life-cycle which focuses on strategic alignment and delivering benefits rather than implementing a technology solution. The author aids comprehension by highlighting critical successful factors throughout.

- Paton, R. A. and McCalman, J. (2008) *Change Management: A Guide to Effective Implementation*, London, Sage Publications.
  A useful introductory textbook on change management that provides detailed explanations of key issues relating to the implementation of change. The discussion follows a logical and clear pathway to help guide students through the process of change, using effective examples by way of illustration. In particular, the treatment of the types of skills and competencies required for effective implementation is well explained and provides a basis for understanding the core attributes required of management when implementing change.

 Online Resource Centre
For more information, updates, and multiple-choice questions, please visit the Online Resource Centre at: www.oxfordtextbooks.co.uk/orc/combe1e/

Skillset 16
Overview

Skillset 16 is an overview of the Skillsets and provides a summary of what each Skillset can contribute to add to the effectiveness and quality of study techniques and disciplines of students. Figg et al. (2006) stress the importance of integrating skills as part of a developmental model for effective learning. Many of the Skillsets are interlinked and it should be clear that a holistic approach to building the skills and techniques is the best way to develop as a learner. So, for example, reading skills underpin the knowledge that is required to make sense of the world, be analytical, and deliver some critique. A number of techniques are highlighted that ensure students can approach the challenges of formal study equipped with the tools to deal with a range of assessments such as essays and exams. Progress towards building these skills can be recorded, monitored, and acted upon as part of a Personal Development Plan. Combined, these Skillsets provide the basis for meeting the expectations, standards, and challenges of study in modern universities or colleges.

Skillset 1: Reading skills
Key to gaining knowledge and understanding is the discipline of undertaking appropriate reading. This Skillset outlines the means by which students can become effective readers and highlights techniques for choosing appropriate reading and speed reading for maximum effect.

Skillset 2: Referencing
Students need to be able to reference works properly to reach the standard of academic quality required in assessments and other tasks. Referencing is a key skill that students need to master in order to submit comprehensive and academically robust written works. Referencing helps to underpin academic discipline and helps students to access key writers in areas of interest. It is also an important way of recognising the work of others and avoiding plagiarism.

Skillset 3: Time management
Students need to be able to manage their time effectively in order to keep pace with the learning process, assessment deadlines, and the work/life balance. This Skillset provides a practical insight into how to manage time by providing a template and example of a typical semester and the various activities that have to be managed within that timeframe.

Skillset 4: Sourcing materials
Closely linked to the Skillset of reading, students will benefit from taking a formal approach to sourcing materials by adopting the simple techniques outlined in this Skillset. Search techniques for sourcing appropriate materials saves time, aids the quality of output, and underpins the type of discipline that students require to navigate their way through the various academic challenges they are presented with.

Skillset 5: Analysing a case study
Case studies are frequently used to illustrate key issues and concepts in a practical and applied setting. Understanding the context and implications of business and management issues as part of a case study is a key skill that helps link academic theory to its application in the real world. This helps students to appreciate the issues, problems, and challenges facing managers in a range of industry and business environments. This Skillset outlines techniques for making the most of case studies by linking the structure and content to key learning outcomes.

Skillset 6: Exam techniques

At this stage of the Skillsets, attention turns to assessment in general and exams in particular. Students seek guidance on exam techniques and the areas for revision. This Skillset provides students with examples of typical exam questions related to the topics in the book, accompanied by model answers. Students will be able to discern exam writing techniques that are conducive to passing this type of assessment instrument. These will include writing concise responses that provide sufficient depth of knowledge and analysis, use of cases for illustration purposes, structuring a response, and focusing on the question asked.

Skillset 7: Literature review

A review of literature is a key element of students' project work, essays, dissertations, and other academic outputs. This Skillset provides students with clear guidance on how to compile a review that includes choices of which literature to include, how to make judgements about the value of literature to the understanding of a particular topic, and the importance of critique in the review.

Skillset 8: Typical exam questions and answer guidance

This Skillset links to Skillset 6—Exam technique, by providing a series of typical exam questions in management and follow up model answer guidance.

Skillset 9: Presentation skills

One of the most important skills in life is the ability to communicate with others whether in a face-to-face conversation, as part of a small group or to a large audience. Communications skills are a vital part of successfully meeting the challenges presented by study, work, and life in general. This Skillset focuses attention on the techniques for delivering effective presentations to a wide range of different audiences.

Skillset 10: Essay writing

Essay writing is a key skill that is a common feature throughout the academic career of students. This Skillset outlines how to structure an essay, disciplinary skills such as referencing, the role of paragraphs, headings, how to build in arguments and analysis, and how to deliver a high quality presentation of the work.

Skillset 11: Essay example

Linking in to Skillset 10—Essay writing, this Skillset provides an example of a well-written and structured essay. Further examples can be found on the Online Resource Centre (ORC).

Skillset 12: Critical analysis

Critical analysis is a vital skill that students need to become competent in producing good quality outputs. Critical skills help to shape cognate reasoning, and provide the basis for being able to make rational judgements based on evidence. This Skillset explains the importance of critical analysis and offers examples to illustrate the difference between descriptive accounts of a business topic and a critical analysis of it.

Skillset 13: Avoiding plagiarism

Using this Skillset students are better able to understand the reasons why plagiarism is a problem that needs to be addressed and the means available to them to ensure compliance. Different cultures have different attitudes to plagiarism, some actively encourage it (India) whilst others display an ambivalence towards it (Nigeria). This Skillset is presented from the perspective of European and American stances on plagiarism that recognises copyright law and ethical stances on the copying of work without proper referencing.

Skillset 14: Personal Development Planning

Personal Development Planning is an integral part of students' abilities to effectively plan for their future and is key to organising their skills and capabilities around their professional aspirations. In this Skillset students can access and use a template for a Personal Development Plan which can be completed as their studies progress. Key elements of the plan are described.

Skillset 15: Reflective practice

The Skillset provides students with an opportunity to look back, choose three topics from the book, and think about interactions between them. This Skillset provides a short activity that helps students integrate different aspects of the subject.

Skillset 16: Overview

This current Skillset provides an overview of the main added value elements of each Skillset in the book.

Glossary

Acquisition: the joining of unequal partners by the process of one organisation buying another.

Administrative management: ordered principles that guide activities throughout an organisation.

Administrative model of decision making: a model that recognises the limitations of decision making in ambiguous and unclear situations when information is incomplete.

Alienation: negative feeling of separation of workers from the core values or purpose of an organisation.

Analytical skills: ability to separate a whole into its component parts for study and interpretation.

Attraction: making the organisation the employer of choice for potential recruits.

Authority: power to command or control others.

Autonomy: the extent of decision making authority.

Behavioural theory: theoretical perspectives that support the view that particular behaviours separate leaders from followers.

Branding: name, term, or symbol given to a company, product, or service to differentiate it from others.

Bureaucracy: an organisational system tightly controlled through the application of strict rules, regulations, and procedures.

Bureaucratic structure: a tall, hierarchical arrangement of human resources and tasks based on clearly defined roles, rules, span of control, and authority.

Business Process Improvement (BPI): incremental change to processes using information technology.

Business Process Reengineering (BPR): radical reorganisation of internal business processes.

Centralisation: level to which decision making powers are concentrated among a few people at the top level of an organisation.

Chain of command: line of authority that extends from top to bottom in an organisation.

Communications skills: ability to connect with people through various media to achieve aims and objectives, to motivate and lead.

Competitive advantage: A competitive advantage is gained through the implementation of a value creating strategy by a firm, that is not simultaneously being implemented by rivals (or potential rivals).

Conceptual skills: problem solving by understanding complex environments.

Consideration: the extent to which a leader builds trust and respect of subordinates by considering their feelings.

Consumer added value: the organisation's ability to position a product or service better than rivals so that consumers are persuaded to recognise, buy, and value it accordingly.

Contingencies: key factors that reflect the situation of an organisation.

Contingency: something that might happen.

Contingency theory: that the effectiveness of groups depends on the fit between the leader's style of interactions with subordinates and the degree to which the situation bestows control on the leader.

Control: monitoring of activities and functions to ensure that outcomes are in line with set targets or align with plans and then acting to rectify any deviations.

Control process: the activity of setting performance targets, measuring and recording outcomes, and matching them against set targets or standards.

Control system: the chosen design and combination of elements in a control process.

Coordination: process of ensuring that activities occur in the correct sequence and at the right time.

Corporate governance: a system of control over the actions and practices of managers in organisations through an agreed set of relationships between a company's management, board, shareholders, and other stakeholders.

Cultural awareness: understanding of, and sensitivity to, cultural differences.

Culture: values, belief, and ideas that characterise individuals or groups.

Customer relationship management: the process of managing customer service and long-term relationships with customers.

Decentralisation: level to which decision making powers are delegated to lower levels within an organisation.

Diversity: range of varied personal characteristics including age, race, gender, nationalities, religions, cultures, beliefs, values.

Dominant culture: a culture that reflects the core values and beliefs that are shared by the majority of an organisation's workers.

Employee relations: the process of maintaining effective dialogue and communications with employees (or their representatives) to maintain a harmonious working relationship between staff and managers.

Empowerment: the delegation of a level of authority that extends the scope of workers to act autonomously from line management.

Entrepreneur: business person who seeks to make a profit by risk and initiative.

Equality and fairness: the formal and informal means of ensuring that each individual worker or potential recruit is treated with respect and dignity and that they are judged on merit and not on race, gender, age, or any other personal characteristic.

Esprit de corps: team spirit.

Expectancy theory: identified values and beliefs that motivate action.

Firm value added: the organisation's ability to create and sustain competences that underpin competitive advantage.

Flexible work schedules: the ability to design work schedules that operate across a broader time dimension.

Forecasting: process of assessing and predicting the future.

Formalisation: the level to which an organisation sets formal rules, procedures, and regulations for work tasks and activities.

Functional structure: an arrangement of similar human resources and/or tasks grouped together into departments.

Garbage can model: a model of decision making based on the assumption that the environment is characterised by extreme uncertainty and that responses to that environment are neither rational nor predictable.

Generic strategy: strategy for competitive advantage based on value adding activities that aligns most closely to the organisation's competitive environment.

Globalisation: the extent to which competition in one country is influenced by competition in other countries.

Goal: specified position the organisation seeks to attain.

Group role: set of behaviours a group member is expected to perform because of their position in the group.

Growth strategy: long-term action plan for expansion of new or existing markets and products.

HRM strategies: ways in which the skills, experience, and expertise of employees can be matched to the long-term aims and objectives of the organisation.

Human relations: system of management that places emphasis on social processes in the workplace.

Information richness: the extent to which a communication achieves a common understanding between sender and receiver.

Initiating structure: extent to which the leader defines his/her role and those of subordinates to achieve goals and objectives.

Innovation: the introduction of new ideas or methods.

Intuition: instinctive knowledge or insight without conscious reasoning.

Job enrichment: the design or redesign of jobs to make them more satisfying for employees.

Job specialisation: type of job that requires a specific skill or skills, experience or attributes to complete them effectively.

Kaizen: Japanese working technique for continuous improvement of processes.

Leadership: the ability to influence a group in the attainment of goals or objectives.

Leadership traits: personal qualities or attributes that differentiate leaders from non-leaders.

Learning organisation: the ability of an organisation to absorb experience, learn from it, and utilise that learning for greater effect.

Long term: one year and more.

Management: the organisation and coordination of activities to achieve stated aims and objectives.

Marketing plan: an outline of the specific actions to be carried out to encourage potential customers to buy the products and services for sale.

Market segment: that part of a market that is defined by specified characteristics.

Mass customisation: the development and design of added value products and/or services to meet the demand characteristics of a large number of consumers.

Matrix structure: an arrangement where personnel undertaking tasks report to both functional and divisional line managers.

Medium term: from six months to one year.

Merger: the joining together of two organisations to become one by the mutual consent of the majority of shareholders.

Moral principles: fundamental principles that underpin understanding and knowledge of what is right and wrong.

Motivation: the factors that encourage workers to act in ways that help achieve aims and objectives of the organisation.

Motivators: aspects of work that influence people to deliver superior performance.

Multidivisional structure: an arrangement of human resources and/or tasks grouped into products, customers, or regions.

New Public Management: market-oriented focus on public sector management.

Non-programmed decision: a decision that is unique to the situation and that requires a unique solution.

Normative: relating to an ideal standard or model. The way things should be.

Objective: clearly defined and measurable outcome to be achieved within a specified timeframe.

Open system: a system that interacts with the environment in which it exists.

Operational controls: control systems designed and implemented to support the organisation's short- to medium-term goals and objectives.

Organisational culture: A system of shared beliefs and values held by workers that form a dominant culture that is unique to the organisation.

Organisational skills: ability to coordinate resources and activities.

Organisational structure: the formal division of human resources and tasks as a means of managing and coordinating activities in an organisation.

Organising: arranging resources to achieve a stated outcome.

Outsourcing: arranging for a function or activity to be undertaken by an external agency rather than by those within the organisation.

Paradigm: example serving as a model.

Permission marketing: the process of sending marketing and promotional information to consumers with their express agreement to receive it.

Personalisation: the development and design of value adding products and/or services to meet the demand characteristics of individual consumers.

Political model: a decision making model that recognises the influence of groups with different interests, aims, and beliefs within an organisation.

Programmed decision: a decision that is routine and repetitive.

Quality: output that conforms to a pre-determined set standard.

Quality management: the act of overseeing activities and tasks required to achieve and maintain a pre-determined level of quality. This includes creating and implementing quality planning and assurance, and quality control and improvement.

Rational decision making: decisions based on consistent choices designed to maximise economic returns.

Recruitment: the process of assessing candidates' suitability for employment.

Resources: assets available to organisations for use in the productive process such as land, labour, machinery, intellectual and creative abilities, finance.

Retention: implementation of activities to ensure that employees remain loyal and that their terms and conditions of employment are met.

Rhetoric: artificial or exaggerated use of language.

Scenario: imagined sequence of future events.

Scientific management: science-based approach to optimising output in a production process.

Short term: from one day to six months.

Social audit: a process that enables an organisation to assess and demonstrate its social, economic, and environmental benefits

599

and limitations. A measure of the extent to which an organisation matches its actions with actual commitment to agreed shared values and objectives.

Social enterprise: a business that trades for a social or environmental purpose.

Socialisation: the process of persuading individuals to behave in ways that are acceptable to a group or society.

Span of control: the number of employees that a manager is responsible for.

Stakeholders: individuals or groups who affect, or are affected by, the activities of an organisation.

Strategic alliances: formal agreement committing two or more firms to exchange resources to produce products or services.

Strategic Business Unit (SBU): an autonomous business entity within a corporate enterprise established to serve an identified external market.

Strategic controls: control systems designed and implemented to support the long-term aims and objectives of an organisation.

Strategic management: the use of theories, frameworks, models, and techniques to inform strategic thinking about the plans and actions designed to achieve long-term aims and objectives.

Strategic options: potential solutions to questions of how to position the organisation in relation to product and resource markets, competitors, and macroenvironmental forces.

Strategy: the determination of long-term aims and objectives of an organisation and the plan of action to achieve them.

Strong culture: a culture in which the organisation's core values and beliefs are widely and intensely shared by the majority of workers.

Styles theories: theoretical perspectives that support the view that it is the style of management that separates leaders from followers.

Sub-culture: separate and distinct mini-cultures that form among groups of workers who are separated from other workers through geographical location, function, or structure.

Technical skills: knowledge or practical skills in specialised activities.

Theory: a set of principles designed to help explain a group of facts or phenomena.

Time and motion studies: the science of timing each action that contributes to the completion of a work task over a set period of time.

Total Quality Management: a method of ensuring quality that focuses on customer needs and expectations by emphasising continuous improvement.

Transactional leadership: leaders who guide, mentor, and motivate followers by clearly establishing roles and tasks for the achievement of the stated aims or goals.

Transformational leadership: leaders who inspire followers to act in ways that benefit the organisation or a wider cause other than their own self-interest.

Virtual organisation: an organisation that uses information and communication technologies (ICTs) to coordinate activities without physical boundaries between different functions.

Virtual team: a team who are brought together to achieve specified aims and objectives but who are located remotely from each other and communicate via electronic media.

Vision: desired future state; the aspiration of the organisation.

Work design: the method by which the work to be carried out is organised and scheduled.

Work schedules: detailed account of which work tasks need to be undertaken, the order in which they are to be completed, who is to undertake the tasks, and the timeframe for completion.

Work specialisation: the extent to which tasks and activities within an organisation are broken down into separate jobs.

References

Abernethy, M. and Stoelwinder, J. U. (1994) 'The role of professional control in the management of complex organizations', *Accounting, Organizations and Society*, Vol. 20, No. 1, pp. 1–17.

Acton, J. M. and Hibbs, M. (2012) Why Fukushima was preventable, Washington DC, Carnegie Paper.

Adair, J. (2006) *How To Grow Leaders: The Seven Key Principles of Effective Leadership Development*, London, Kogan Page.

Adair, J. (2009) *Effective Communication: The Most Important Management Skill of All*, London, Pan Macmillan.

Adler, P. S. (1992) Introduction, In P. S. Adler, (ed.), *Technology and the Future of Work*, New York, Oxford University Press.

Adobe (12 June 2013) 'Click here: The State of Online Advertising. New insights into the beliefs of consumers and professional marketers', Global Report, Regional Comparisons. <http://www.adobe.com/aboutadobe/pressroom/pdfs/Click_Here_Regional_Comparisons.pdf>.

Adonis, J. (2006) *The 4 Key Elements of Employee Engagement*, Sydney, Adonis.

Agor, W. H. (1986) 'The logic of intuition: How top executives make important decisions', *Organizational Dynamics*, Vol. 14, Winter, pp. 5–18.

Agor, W. H. (1990) *Intuition in Organizations: Leading and Managing Effectively*, Newbury Park, CA, Sage Publications.

Alberts, D. S. and Nissen, M. E. (2009) 'Towards harmonizing command and control with organization and management theory', *The International C2 Journal*, Vol. 3, No. 2, pp. 2–61.

Allan, E. and Fjermestad, J. (2000) E-Commerce Strategies: The Manufacturer Retailer Consumer Relationship, Proceedings of the 5th Americas Conference on Information Systems.

Allen, D. G., Mahto, R. V., and Otondo, R. F. (2007) 'Web-based recruitment: Effects of information, organizational brand, and attitudes to a web site on applicant attraction', *Journal of Psychology*, Vol. 92, No. 6, pp. 1696–708.

Allison, C. W., Chell, E., and Hayes, J. (2000) 'Intuition and entrepreneurial behaviour', *European Journal of Work and Organisational Psychology*, Vol. 9, pp. 31–43.

Amagoh, F. (2008) 'Perspectives on organizational change: Systems and complexity theory', *The Innovation Journal: The Public Sector Innovation Journal*, Vol. 13, No. 3, pp. 1–14.

Amburgey, T. L. and Dacin, T. (1994) 'As the left foot follows the right? The dynamics of strategic and structural change', *Academy of Management Journal*, Vol. 37, pp. 1427–52.

Anand, N. and Daft, R. L. (2007) 'What is the right organizational design?' *Organizational Dynamics*, Vol. 36, No. 4, pp. 329–244.

Anderson, M. H. (2009) 'The role of group personality composition in the emergence of task and relationship conflict within groups', *Journal of Management and Organization*, Vol. 15, No. 1, p. 82.

Andrews, K. R. (1971) *The Concept of Corporate Strategy*, Homewood, IL, Dow-Jones-Irwin.

Ansoff, I. (1957) 'Strategies for Diversification', *Harvard Business Review*, Vol. 35, No. 5, pp. 113–24.

Ansoff, I. (1968) *Corporate Strategy: An Analytical Approach to Business Policy for Growth and Expansion*, Harmondsworth, Penguin.

Ansoff, I. (1987) *Corporate Strategy*, London, Penguin.

Arango, T. (10 January 2010) How The AOL-Time-Warner Merger Went So Wrong, *New York Times*. <http://www.nytimes.com/2010/01/11/business/media/11merger.html?pagewanted=all&_r=0>.

Argenti, P. A. (2004) 'Collaborating with activists: how Starbucks works with NGO's', *California Management Review*, Vol. 47, No. 1, pp. 91–116.

Argyriades, D. (2002) *Governance and Public Administration in the 21st Century*, London, International Congress of Administrative Science.

Argyris, C. (1992) *On Organisational Learning*, London, Blackwell.

Ashour, A. S. (1973) 'The contingency model of leadership effectiveness: an evaluation', *Organizational Behavior and Human Performance*, Vol. 9, pp. 339–55.

Ashton, D. N. (2004) 'The impact of organizational structure and practices on learning in the workplace', *International Journal of Training and Development*, Vol. 8, No. 1, pp. 43–53.

Asongu, J. J. (2007) 'The legitimacy of strategic corporate social responsibility as a marketing tool', *Journal of Business and Public Policy*, Vol. 1, No. 1, pp. 1–12.

Aston, C. and Morton, L. (2005) 'Managing talent for competitive advantage', *Strategic HR Review*, Vol. 4, No. 5, pp. 28–31.

Ayres, C. (1961) *Towards a Reasonable Society: The Values of Industrial Civilisation*, Austin, TX, Texas University Press.

Bain, J. S. (1959) *Industrial Organisation*, New York, John Wiley.

Bain, P. and Taylor, P. (2002) 'Entrapped by the "electronic panopticon"? Worker resistance in the call centre', *New Technology, Work and Employment*, Vol. 15, No. 1, pp. 2–18.

Bak, R. (2003) *Henry and Edsel: The Creation of the Ford Empire*, New York, John Wiley & Sons.

Baker, R. and Newport, S. (2005) 'Dysfunctional managerial behaviour in the workplace: Implications for employees, supervisors, and organisations', *Problems and Perspectives in Management*, Vol. 1, pp. 108–13.

Banai, M. and Tulimieri, P. (2013) 'Knowledge, skills and personality of the effective business consultant', *Journal of Management Development*, Vol. 32, No. 8.

Bank of Japan (March, 2013) Reports & Research Papers: Questionnaire Survey on Business Continuity Management (September, 2012), Financial System and Bank Examination Department, Tokyo, Bank of Japan. <http://www.boj.or.jp/en/research/brp/ron_2013/data/ron130315a.pdf>.

Barnard, C. L. (1938) *The Functions of the Executive*, Cambridge, MA, Harvard University Press.

Barney, J. B. (1986) 'Organisational culture: Can it be a source of competitive advantage? ' *Academy of Management Review*, Vol. 11, pp. 656–65.

Barney, J. (2010) *Gaining and Sustaining Competitive Advantage* (4th edn), Harlow, Pearson.

Bass, B. M. (1985) *Leadership and Performance Beyond Expectations*, New York, The Free Press.

Bass, B. M. and Avolio, B. J. (1990) 'The implications of transactional and transformational leadership for individual, team, and organizational development', *Research in Organizational Change and Development*, Vol. 4, pp. 231–72.

Bass, B. M. and Avolio, B. J. (1991) *Transformational Leadership Development: Manual for the Multi-Factor Leadership Questionnaire*, Palo Alto, CA, Consulting Psychological Press.

Bass, B. M. and Avolio, B. J. (1993) *Improving Organizational Effectiveness through Transformational Leadership*, Thousand Oaks, CA, Sage.

Batty, D. and Mitchell, A. (2012) 'George Entwistle resigns as director general of the BBC', *The Guardian*, 11 November.

Bayliss, J., Wirtz, J. J. and Gray, C. S. (2012) *Strategy in the Contemporary World* (4th edn), Oxford, Oxford University Press.

BBC News (9 November 2012) Iberia to cut 4500 jobs under IAG restructuring plan. <http://www.bbc.co.uk/news/business-20264407>.

Belbin, M. (1981) *Management Teams*, London, Heinemann.

Bennett, J., Owers, M., Pitt, M., and Tucker, M. (2010) Workplace impact on social networking, *Property Management*, Vol. 28, No. 3, pp. 138–48.

Benson, J. (2000) *Working More Creatively with Groups*, London, Routledge.

Bentley, P. (6 December 2012) Social enterprises can benefit from private sector help, *The Guardian*. <http://www.theguardian.com/social-enterprise-network/2012/dec/06/social-enterprise-private-sector-help-skills>.

Bergiel, B. J., Bergiel, E. B. and Balsmeier, P. W. (2008) 'Nature of virtual teams: A summary of their advantages and disadvantages', *Management Research News*, Vol. 31, No. 2, pp. 99–110.

Bharadwaj, A. S. (2000) 'A Resource-based perspective on information technology capability and firm performance: An empirical investigation', *MIS Quarterly*, Vol. 24, No. 1, pp. 169–96.

Birch, S. (6 July 2012) How activism forced Nike to change its ethical game, GreenLivingBlog, *The Guardian*. <http://www.theguardian.com/environment/green-living-blog/2012/jul/06/activism-nike>.

Bird, C. (1940) *Social Psychology*, New York, Appleton-Century Company.

Birkin, S. J. and Harris, M. L. (2003) 'E-Business and CRM: Directions for the Future', in *Proceedings of the International Association for the Development of Information Systems (IADIS) Conference*, Carvoeiro, Portugal, 5–8 November.

Bloom, N. and Van Reenen, J. (2011) *Human Resource Management and Productivity*, Cambridge, MA, National Bureau of Economic Research.

Bloomberg Business Week (10 January 2001) Recruiting Q&A: IDEO. <http://www.businessweek.com/stories/2001-01-10/recruiting-q-and-a-ideo>.

Blowfield, M. and Murray, A. (2008) *Corporate Responsibility: a critical introduction*, Oxford, Oxford University Press.

Bolden, R., Gosling, J., Marturano, A., and Dennison, P. (2003) *A Review of Leadership Theory and Competency Frameworks*, University of Exeter, Exeter, Centre for Leadership Studies.

Bond, S. (2004) 'Organisational culture and work-life conflict in the UK', *International Journal of Sociology and Social Policy*, Vol. 24, No. 12, pp. 1–24.

Bono, J. E. and Judge, T. A. (2003) 'Self-concordance at work: Toward understanding the motivational effects of transformational leaders', *Academy of Management Journal*, October, pp. 554–71.

Bowman, R. H. (2008) *Business Continuity Planning for Data Centers and Systems: A Strategic Implementation Guide*, Chichester, Wiley.

Boyatzis, R. E. (1982) *The Competent Manager: A Model for Effective Performance*, New York, Wiley.

BP (2012) What we stand for <http://www.bp.com/liveassets/bp_internet/globalbp/STAGING/global_assets/downloads/W/what_we_stand_for.pdf>.

Bridger, R. S. (2008) *Introduction to Ergonomics* (3rd edn), London, CRC Press.

Bridges, W. (1994) 'The End of the Job', *Fortune* (19 September), pp. 62–74.

Brown, K. and Hyer, N. L. (2010) *Managing Projects: A Team-Based Approach*, New York, McGraw-Hill.

Bryan, S. (2010) *The Gold Standard at the Turn of the Twentieth Century: Rising Powers, Global Money, and the Age of Empire*, New York, Columbia University Press.

Buhlmann, B. (2006) *Need to Manage a Virtual team? Theory and Practice in a Nutshell*, Gottingen, Cuvillier Verlag.

Burns, J. M. (1978) *Leadership*, New York, Harper & Row.

Burns, T. and Stalker, C. M. (1961) *The Management of Innovation*, London, Tavistock.

Buttle, F. (2008) *Customer Relationship Management*, Oxford, Butterworth-Heinemann.

Campbell, A. (2007) *The Blair Years: Extracts from Alistair Campbell's Diaries*, New York, Knopf Publishing Group.

Campbell, D., Stonehouse, G., and Houston, W. (1999) *Business Strategy: An Introduction*, Oxford, Butterworth-Heinemann.

Campbell, D., Edgar, D., and Stonehouse, G. (2011) *Business Strategy: An introduction*, (3rd edn), Basingstoke, Palgrave Macmillan.

Carlyle, T. (1888) *Our Heroes, Hero-Worship and the Heroic in History*, New York, Frederick A Stokes & Brother.

Caruso, G.R. (5 June 2013) PitchBook reports that mergers and acquisition prices rise in first quarter 2013, Harvest Business Advisors. <http://harvestbusiness.com/pitchbook-reports-that-merger-and-acquisition-prices-rise-in-first-quarter-2013/>.

Cascio, W. F., (1995) *Managing Human Resources* (International edn), New York, McGraw Hill.

Case Study (2012) Scottish semiconductor firm chips in with the skills that matter:

Award-winning training promotes world-class performance, *Human Resource Management International Journal*, Vol. 20, No. 5, pp. 10–12. Available at <http://www.emeraldinsight.com/journals.htm?issn=0967-0734&volume=20&issue=5&articleid=17042769&show=abstract>.

Cassels, J. (1993) *The Uncertain Promise of Law: Lessons from Bhopal*, Toronto, University of Toronto Press Inc.

Chaffey, D. (2004) *E-Business and E-Commerce Management* (2nd edn), Prentice Hall, Harlow.

Chaffey, D. and Smith, P. R. (2001) *E-Marketing Excellence: At the Heart of E-business*, Oxford, Butterworth-Heinemann.

Chandler, A. D. (1962) *Strategy and Structure*, Cambridge, MA, MIT Press.

Chandler, C. and Ingrassia, P. (1991) 'Just as US Firms Try Japanese Management, Honda is Centralizing', New York, *The Wall Street Journal*, 11 April.

Chapman, J., Barrow, B., Sunderland, R. and Davies, R. (28 June 2012) 20 more banks were rigging interest rates: British bankers now facing criminal inquiry over scandal that was kept secret for years, MailOnline. <http://www.dailymail.co.uk/news/article-2166242/Barclays-20-banks-including-HSBC-facing-criminal-inquiry-rate-fix-scandal.html>.

Chen, I. I. and Popovich, K. (2003) 'Understanding customer relationship management (CRM): People, process and technology', *Business Process Management Journal*, Vol. 9, No. 5, pp. 657–88.

Chen, Y. C., Wang, W. C., and Chu, Y. C. (2011) 'Infiltration of the multicultural awareness: Multinational enterprise strategy management', *International Journal of Business Management*, Vol. 6, No. 2, pp. 72–6.

Chiarini, A. (2012) *Lean Organization: from the Tools of the Toyota Production System to Lean Office*, Rotterdam, Springer.

Child, J. (1984) *Organisation: A guide to problems and practice* (2nd edn), London, Harper & Row.

Childs, D. R. (2009) *Prepare for the Worst, Plan for the Best: Disaster Preparedness and Recovery for Small Businesses*, Chichester, Wiley.

Chiles, M. and Zorn, E. (1995) 'Empowerment and organizations', *Journal of Organizational Behavior*, Vol. 43, No. 1, pp. 207–42.

Clarke, M., Williams, A. and Smith-Gillespie, C. (2010) The Role of Trust in Employee Engagement, CIPD Conference, 26 January, London.

Coch, L. and French, J. (1948) 'Overcoming resistance to change', *Human Relations*, Vol. 1, pp. 512–32.

Cohen, S. (2002) *Negotiation Skills for Managers*, New York, McGraw-Hill Professional.

Collard, R. (1993) *Total Quality: Success Through People* (2nd edn), London, IPM.

Collings, D. G. and Mellahi, K. (2009) 'Strategic talent management: A review and research agenda', *Human Resource Management Review*, Vol. 19, No. 4, pp. 304–13.

Combe, C. A. (2006) *Introduction to e-Business: Management and Strategy*, Oxford, Butterworth-Heinemann.

Combe, C. A. (2009) 'Privacy guaranteed—to be violated. How the internet erodes rights to personal privacy', *Conference of the International Journal of Arts and Sciences*, Vol. 1 No. 6, pp. 88–101.

Conway, C. (2008) 'Business planning training for social enterprise', *Social Enterprise Journal*, Vol. 4, No. 1, pp. 57–73.

Cooper, R. G. (2008) 'The stage-gate idea-to-launch process, Update, what's new and Nex-Gen Systems', *Journal of Product Innovation Management*, Vol. 25, No. 3, pp. 213–32.

Covey, S. (1994) *7 Habits of Highly Effective People*, New York, NY, Simon & Schuster.

Covey, S. and Merrill, A. R. (1994) *First Things First*, London, Simon & Schuster.

Cox, T. H. and Blake, S. (1991) 'Managing cultural diversity: Implications for organisational competitiveness', *Academy of Management Executive*, Vol. 5, No. 3.

Crawford, G. S. and Cullen, J. (2007) 'Bundling, product choice and efficiency: Should cable television networks be offered a la carte?' *Information Economics and Policy*, Vol. 19, pp. 379–404.

Crisp, N. (2011) *24 Hours to Save the NHS: The Chief Executive's Account of Reform 2000–2006*, Oxford, Oxford University Press.

Crosby, P. B. (1979) *Quality is Free: The Art of Making Quality Certain*, New York, New American Library.

Crosby, P. B. (1996) *Quality is Still Free: Making Quality Certain in Uncertain Times*, New York, McGraw-Hill.

Crump, T. (2010) *A Brief History of How the Industrial Revolution Changed the World*, London, Robinson Publishing.

Cummings, T. G. (1995) 'Centralisation and decentralisation: the never-ending story of separation and betrayal', *Scandinavian Journal of Management*, Vol. 11, pp. 103–17.

Cummings, T. G. and Worley, C. G. (2001) *Organizational Development and Change* (8th edn), Cincinnati, OH, South-Western College Publishing.

Cunningham-Wood, J. and Wood, M. C. (2001) *Henri Fayol: Critical Evaluations in Business and Management: Pioneers of Business and Management Studies*, London, Routledge.

Cyert, R. M. and March, J. G. (1992) *A Behavioral Theory of the Firm* (2nd edn), New Jersey, Wiley-Blackwell.

Daft, R. L. (2003) *Management* (6th edn), Mason, OH, Thomson South-Western.

Daft, R. L. (2008) *New Era of Management* (2nd edn), Mason, OH, Thomson South-Western.

Daft, R. L. and Lengel, R. H. (1984) 'Information richness: a new approach to managerial behavior and organizational design', in Cummings, L. L. and Staw, B. M (eds), *Research in Organizational Behavior*, Homewood, IL, JAI Press, pp. 191–233.

Daft, R. L., Murphy, J., and Willmott, H. (2010) *Organizational Theory and Design*, Boston, MA, Cengage Learning Business Press.

Dahlgaard, J. J. and Dahlgaard, S. M. P. (2002) 'From defect reduction to reduction of waste and customer/stakeholder satisfaction (understanding the new TQM metrology)', *Total Quality Management*, Vol. 13, No. 8, pp. 1069–85.

Davenport, T. H. (1992) *Process Innovation: Reengineering Work Through IT*, Cambridge, MA, Harvard Business School Press.

Davies, R. (2002) 'The Wizard of Oz in CRMLand: CRM's Need for Business Process Management', *Information Systems Management*, Vol. 19, No. 4, pp. 43–8.

Davila, A. (2005) 'An exploratory study on the emergence of management control systems design in new product development', *Accounting, Organizations and Society*, Vol. 25 Nos. 4&5, pp. 383–409.

Davila, A., Foster, G., and Li, M. (2009) 'Reasons for management control systems adoption: insights from product development systems choice by early stage entrepreneurs', *Accounting, Organizations and Society*, Vol. 34, Nos. 3&4, April-May, pp. 322–47.

Davis, P. K., Bankes, S. C., and Egner, M. (2007) *Enhancing Strategic Planning with Massive Scenario Generation: Theory and Experiments*, Santa Monica, CA, Rand Corporation.

De Neve, J., Mikhaylov, S., Dawes, C. T., Christakis, N. A., Fowler, J. H. (2013) 'Born to Lead? A twin design and genetic association study of leadership role occupancy', *The Leadership Quarterly*, Vol. 24, No. 1, pp. 45–60.

Deal, T. and Kennedy, A. (1982) *Corporate Cultures: The Rites and Rituals of Corporate Life*, Reading, MA. Addison-Wesley.

DeLong, D. and Fahey, L. (2000) 'Diagnosing cultural barriers to knowledge management', *The Academy Management Executive*, Vol. 14, No. 4, pp. 113–27.

Deming, E. (1982) *Out of the Crisis*, Cambridge, MA, MIT Press.

Demsetz, H. (1973) 'Industry structure, market rivalry, and public policy', *Journal of Law and Economics*, Vol. 16, No. 1, pp. 1–9 April.

Demsetz, H. (1982) 'Barriers to Entry', *American Economic Review*, Vol. 72, No. 1, pp. 47–57.

Dennison, D. R., Haaland, S., and Goelzer, P. (2004) 'Corporate culture and organizational effectiveness: Is Asia different from the rest of the world?', *Organizational Dynamics*, February, pp. 98–109.

Department of Trade and Industry (DTI) (2004) *The CSR Competency Framework*, London, CSR Academy.

Desai, R. (2010) 'Understanding management control systems in call centers', *International Journal of Productivity and Performance Management*, Vol. 59, No. 8, pp. 792–810.

Devinney, T. M., Auger, P., and Eckhardt, G. M. (2010) *The Myth of the Ethical Consumer*, Cambridge, Cambridge University Press.

Dickens, L. (2012) 'Equality and Work/Life Balance: What's happening in the workplace', *Industrial Law Journal*, Vol. 35, pp. 445–9.

Dickens, L. and Hall, M. (2009) 'Legal Regulation and the Changing Workplace', in Brown, W., Bryson, A., Forth, J., and Whitfield, K. (eds), *Evolution of the Modern Workplace*, Cambridge, Cambridge University Press.

Digman, J. M. (1990) 'Personality structure: emergence of the Five-Factor Model', in M. R. Rosenzweig and L. W. Porter (eds), *Annual Review of Psychology*, Vol. 41, Palo Alto, CA, pp 417–40.

Doane, D. (2005) 'Beyond Corporate Social Responsibility: minnows, mammoths and markets'. *Futures* Vol. 37, pp. 215–29.

Dockel, A., Basson, J. S. and Coetzee, M. (2006) 'The effect of retention factors on organisational commitment: An investigation of high tech employees', *South African Journal of Human Resource Management*, Vol. 4, No. 2, pp. 20–8.

Doel, M. (2005) *Using Groupwork*, London, Routledge.

Doh, J. P., Howton, S. D., Howton, S. W. and Siegel, D. S. (2010) 'Does the market respond to an endorsement of social responsibility? The role of institutions, information, and legitimacy', *Journal of Management*, Vol. 36, No. 6, pp. 1461–85.

Doran, G. T. (1981) 'There's a SMART way to write management's goals and objectives', *Management Review*, Vol. 70, No. 1, pp. 35–6.

Drucker, P. (1954) *The Practice of Management*, New York, NY, Harper and Row.

Drucker, P. (1997) 'Introduction', in Hesselbein, F., Goldsmith, M., and Beckhard, R. (eds), *The Leader of the Future: New Visions, Strategies and Practices for the Next Era*, San Francisco, CA, Jossey-Bass.

Drucker, P. F. (2001) *The Essential Drucker*, New York, Harper Business.

Dubrin, A. (2008) *Essentials of Management* (International edn), Chula Vista, CA, South Western College.

Duncan, N. B. (1995) 'Capturing flexibility of information technology infrastructure: A study of resource characteristics and their measure', *Journal of Management Information Systems*, Vol. 12, No. 2, pp. 37–57.

Dutta, S. and Segev, A. (1999) 'Business transformation on the Internet', *European Management Journal*, Vol. 17, No. 5, pp. 466–76.

Dwyer, R. J. (2005) 'Formal organizations in contemporary society: the relevance of historical perspectives', *Management Decision*, Vol. 43, No. 9, pp. 1232–48.

Ebner, M., Hu, A., Levitt, D., and McCory, J. (2002) 'How to rescue CRM', *McKinsey Quarterly*, Special Edition, pp. 49–57.

Ebrahim, N., Ahmed, S., and Taha, Z. (2009) 'Virtual R&D teams in small and medium enterprises: a literature review', *Scientific Research and Essay*, Vol. 4, No. 13, pp. 1575–90.

The Economist (2008) 'Employment in Japan: Sayonara, Salaryman', 3 January. <http://www.economist.com/node/10424391>.

The Economist (2011) 'Middle Managers: Saving David Brent', 15 August. <http://www.economist.com/blogs/schumpeter/2011/08/middle-managers>.

The Economic Times (2013) 'Bhopal tragedy: Decision to summon Dow Chemical a big step, says Amnesty', 24 July.

Egremont (2007) HR Director Interview Series. <http://www.egremontgroup.com/thought_leadership/hr_director_interview_series/catherine_glickman_tesco.html>.

Eisenfuhr, F. (2011) *Decision Making*, New York, Springer.

Elbanna, S. (2009) 'Determinants of strategic planning effectiveness: an extension of earlier work', *Journal of Strategy and Management*, Vol. 2, No. 2, pp. 175–87.

Ellman, M. and Pezanis-Christou, P. (2010) 'Organizational structure, communications and group ethics', *American Economic Review*, Vol. 100, No. 5, pp. 2478–91.

Elmuti, D. (2003) 'The perceived impact of outsourcing on organizational performance', *American Journal of Business*, Vol. 18, No. 2, pp. 146–54.

Emery, F. E. and Trist, E. L. (1969) 'Sociotechnical systems', In F. E. Emery, *Systems Thinking*, London, Penguin, pp. 281–96.

Entine, J. (2002) Body Flops: Anita Roddick proclaimed that business could be caring and capitalist. Today The Body Shop is struggling on both counts, *Toronto Globe and Mail*, Business Magazine, 31 May.

Escriba-Moreno, M. A. and Canet-Giner, M. T. (2006) 'The combined use of quality management programs and work teams: A comparative analysis of its impact in the organizational structure', *Team Performance Management*, Vol. 12, Nos. 5/6, pp. 162–81.

Etzioni, A. (1964) *Modern Organizations*, Englewood Cliffs, CA, Prentice-Hall.

Euromonitor International: Wine (2012) <http://www.euromonitor.com/wine>.

European Investment Fund (EIF) (14 May 2013) EIF launches a social impact investment fund of funds. <http://www.eif.org/what_we_do/equity/news/2013/social_impact_accelerator.htm>.

European Nuclear Energy Forum (7 October 2008) Bratislava, Slovakia. <http://ec.europa.eu/energy/nuclear/forum/opportunities/doc/opportunities/2008_10_07/2008_10_07_minutes.pdf>.

European Patent Office, (2000) Patent Applications, Munich. <http://www.epo.org/applying.html>.

Ezigbo, C. A. (2012) 'Achieve organizational effectiveness by decentralisation', *European Journal of Business and Management*, Vol. 4, No. 20, pp. 125–34.

Facer, R. L. and Wadsworth, L. L. (2008) 'Alternative work schedules and work-family balance: a research note', *Review of Public Personnel Administration*, 28, pp. 166–77.

Falshaw, J. R., Glaister, K. W., and Tatoglu, E. (2006) 'Evidence on formal strategic planning and company performance', *Management Decision*, Vol. 44, No. 1, pp. 9–30.

Farazmand, A. (2002) *Administrative Reform in Developing Nations*, Westport, CT, Praeger Publishers.

Farivar, F. and Esmaeelinezhad, O. (2012) 'The effects of informal groups on organizational performance: A case study of Iran', *Interdisciplinary Journal of Contemporary Research in Business*, Vol. 3, No. 12, pp. 364–74.

Farmer, B. (15 November 2011) Afghan Loya Jirga national assembly to discuss peace, *Telegraph*. <http://www.telegraph.co.uk/news/worldnews/asia/afghanistan/8891152/Afghan-Loya-Jirga-national-assembly-to-discuss-peace.html>.

Faulkner, D., Teerikangas, S. and Joseph, R.J. (2011) *The Handbook of Mergers and Acquisitions*, Oxford, Oxford University Press.

Fayol, H. (1946) *General and Industrial Management*, London, Pitman.

Fayol, H. (1949) *General and Industrial Management* (trans C. Storrs), London, Sir Isaac Pitman & Sons.

Fearn-Banks, K. (2010) *Crisis Communication: A Case Book Approach* (4th edn), London, Routledge.

Feeny, D. F. and Wilcocks, L. P. (1998) 'Core IS capabilities for exploiting information technology', *Sloan Management Review*, Vol. 30, No. 3, pp. 9–22.

Feigenbaum, A. V. (1956) 'Total quality control', *Harvard Business Review*, Vol. 34, No. 6, pp. 93–101.

Feldman, M. S., Khademian, A. M. and Quick, K. S. (2002) 'Ways of knowing, inclusive management, and promoting democratic engagement', *International Public Management Journal*, Vol. 12, No. 2, pp. 123–36.

Felstead, A. and Ashton, D. N. (2000) 'Tracing the link: Organisational structure and skill formation', *Human Resource Management Journal*, Vol. 10, No. 3, pp. 5–21.

Fiedler, F. E. (1967) *A Theory of Leadership Effectiveness*, New York, McGraw-Hill.

Figg, K., McAllister, C., and Shapiro, A. (2006) 'Effective learning services: a developmental model in practice', *Journal of Access Policy and Practice*, Vol. 4, No. 1, pp. 39–52.

Finler, J. W. (1988) *The Hollywood Story*, New York, Crown.

Flaherty, S. and Moss, S. A. (2007) 'The impact of personality and team context on the

607

relationship between workplace injustice and counterproductive work behaviour', *Journal of Applied Social Psychology*, Vol. 37, No. 1, pp. 2549–75.

Flamholz, E. (1979) 'Organizational control systems managerial tool', *California Management Review*, Winter, p. 55.

Fleishman, E. A. (1953) 'The description of supervisory behavior', *Journal of Applied Psychology*, Vol. 37, No. 1, pp. 1–6.

Fleishman, E. A., Mumford, M. D., Zaccaro, S. J., Levin, K. Y., Korotkin, A. L., and Hein, M. B. (1991) 'Taxonomic efforts in the description of leader behavior: A synthesis and functional interpretation', *Leadership Quarterly*, Vol. 2, No. 4, pp. 245–87.

Follett, M. P. (1920) *The State: Group Organization the Solution to Popular Government*, New York, Logmans Green & Co.

Forbes Insights (2012) *Diversity and Inclusion: Unlocking Global Potential. Global Diversity Rankings by Country, Sector and Occupation*, Oxford, Oxford Economics.

Forest, V. (2008) 'Performance-related pay and work motivation: theoretical and empirical perspectives for the French civil service', *International Review of Administrative Sciences*, Vol. 74, No. 2, pp. 325–39.

Foss, N. (2001) 'Bounded rationality in the economics of organizations: Present use and (some) future possibilities', *Journal of Management and Governance*, Vol. 5, pp. 401–25.

Foss, N. (2003) 'Bounded rationality in the economics of organizations: "Much cited and little used"', *Journal of Economic Psychology*, Vol. 24, pp. 245–64.

Fox, C. R. and Tversky, A. (1995) 'Ambiguity aversion and comparative ignorance', *Quarterly Journal of Economics*, Vol. 110, No. 3, pp. 585–603.

Franz, T. M. (2012) *Group Dynamics and Team Interventions: Understanding and Improving Team Performance*, Chichester, Wiley-Blackwell.

French, E. and Tracey, N. (2010) 'Critical thinking and organisation theory: Embedding a process to encourage graduate capabilities', *eJournal of Business Education & Scholarship of Teaching*, Vol. 4, No. 1, pp. 1–10.

Friedman, M. (1962) *Capitalism and Freedom*, Chicago, IL, University of Chicago Press.

Friedman, M. (1970) 'The social responsibility of business is to increase its profits', *New York Times* Vol. 32, No. 13, pp. 122–6.

Friedman, S. D., Christensen, P., and DeGroot, J. (1998) 'Work and life: the end of the zero sum game', *Harvard Business Review*, November–December, pp. 119–29.

Friend, G. and Zehle, S. (2009) *Guide to Business Planning*, London, Bloomberg Press.

Gantt, H. (1919) *Organizing for Work*, New York, Harcourt, Brace, and Howe.

Garvin, D. A. (1988) *Managing Quality*, New York, New York Free Press.

Gaski, J. F. (2011) *Branding in Commerce and Marketing* (Management Science—Theory and Application), Hauppauge, NY, Nova Science Publishers.

Ghemawat, P. (1991) *The Dynamic of Strategy*, New York, NY, The Free Press.

Ghemawat, P. (2002) 'Competition and business strategy in historical perspective', *Business History Review*, Vol. 76,) Spring, pp. 37–74.

Ghemawat, P. (2007) *Redefining Global Strategy: Crossing Borders in a World Where Differences Still Matter*, Mason, OH, Cengage Learning EMEA

Ghobadi, S. and D'Amba, J. (2012) 'Knowledge sharing in cross functional teams: a coopetitive model', *Journal of Knowledge Management*, Vol. 16, No. 2, pp. 285–301.

Gilbreth, F. B. and Gilbreth, L. M. (1917), *Applied Motion Study*, New York, Sturgis & Walton.

Gilbreth, L. M. (1914) *The Psychology of Management*, New York, Sturgis & Walton.

Gillard, S. (2009) 'Soft skills and technical expertise of effective project managers', *Issues in Informing Science and Information Technology*, Vol. 6, pp. 724–9.

Gillespie, R. (1993) *Manufacturing Knowledge: A History of the Hawthorne Experiments* (Studies in Economic History and Policy: the USA in the Twentieth Century), Cambridge, Cambridge University Press.

Godfrey, G., Dale, B. G., Marchington, M., and Wilkinson, A. (1997) 'Control—A contested concept in TQM research', *International Journal* of Operations and Production Management, Vol. 17, No. 6, pp. 558–73.

Godin, S. (1999) Permission Marketing, New York, Simon & Schuster.

Goetsche, D. L. and Davis, S. (2011) Quality Management for Organizational Excellence: Introduction to Total Quality (7th edn), Harlow, Pearson.

Gok, D. and Hicioglu, G. (2010) 'The organizational roles of marketing and marketing managers', Marketing Intelligence and Planning, Vol. 28, No. 3, pp. 231–309.

Gomez-Majia, R., Luis, R., Balkin, D. B. and Cardy, R. L. (2008) Management: People, Performance, Change, New York, McGraw-Hill.

Gouldner, A. (1954), Patterns of Industrial Bureaucracy, New York, Free Press.

Graham, P. (1995) Mary Parker Follett: Prophet of Management, Beard Books, <www.beardbooks.com>.

Graicumas, V. A. (1933) 'Relationship in organization', The Bulletin of International Management Institute, Vol. 7, March, pp. 39–42.

Gray, P. A. (1991) Open Systems: A Business Strategy for the 90's, Maidenhead, McGraw-Hill.

Greenberg, K. (2000) 'Golden Age of Wireless (Marketing via wireless devices)', Mediaweek, May, p. 102.

Greenleaf, R. K. (1977) Servant leadership: A Journey into the Nature of Legitimate Power and Greatness, Princeton, NJ, Paulist Press.

Grieves, J. (2008) 'Why we should abandon the idea of the learning organization', The Learning Organization, Vol. 15, No. 6, pp. 463–73.

Griffin, E. (2010) A Brief History of the Industrial Revolution, Basingstoke, Palgrave Macmillan.

Guttman, H. M. (2008) Overcome Resistance 'Give change a chance to succeed' (11th edn), New York, Prentice-Hall.

Hackman, J. R. and Porter, L. W. (1968) 'Expectancy theory predictions of work effectiveness', Organizational Behavior and Human Performance, Vol. 3, pp. 417–26.

Hackman, J. R. and Wageman, R. (1995) 'Total quality management: Empirical, conceptual and practical issues', Administrative Science Quarterly, Vol. 20, No. 2, pp. 309–42.

Hackman, J. R. and Wageman, R. (2005) 'When and how team leaders matter', Research in Organizational Behavior, Vol. 26, pp. 37–74.

Hackman, J. R. and Walton, R. E. (1986) 'Leading groups in organizations', in P. S. Goodman, (ed.), Designing Effective Work Groups, San Francisco, CA, Jossey Bass.

Hales, C. P. (1986) 'What do managers do? A critical review of the evidence', Journal of Management Studies, Vol. 23, No. 1, pp. 88–115.

Hall, D. J. and Saias, M. A. (1980) 'Strategy follows structure!', Strategic Management Journal, Vol. 1, No. 2, pp. 149–63.

Hammer, M. (1990) 'Re-engineering work—Don't automate, obliterate!', Harvard Business Review, July/August, pp. 104–12.

Handy, C. (1976) Understanding Organizations, London, Penguin Books.

Hanke, J. E. and Wichearn, D. (2008) Business Forecasting (9th edn), Upper Saddle River, NJ, Pearson.

Hannagan, T. (2008) Management: Concepts & Practices, Harlow, FT/Prentice Hall.

Harris, L. and Dennis, C. (2008) Marketing the e-Business (2nd edn), London, Routledge.

Harrison, R., Newholm, T., and Shaw, D. (2005) The Ethical Consumer, London, Sage Publications.

Hart, S. (10 September 2012) Charles van Commenee leaves British athletics in rude health after golden London Olympics for Team GB. <http://www.telegraph.co.uk/sport/olympics/athletics/9534354/Charles-van-Commenee-leaves-British-athletics-in-rude-health-after-golden-London-Olympics-for-Team-GB.html>.

Hart, S. and Murphy, J. M. (1998) Brands: The New Wealth Creators, New York, New York University Press.

Hartvigsen, H. (2007) Successful Spokespersons Are Made, Not Born, Milton Keynes, Authorhouse.

Harvard Business School (2007) Creating a Business Plan: Expert Solutions to Everyday Challenges, Boston, MA, Harvard Business School Press.

Henderson, J. C. and Venkatraman, N. (1993) 'Strategic alignment: Leveraging information technology for transforming organizations', *IBM Systems Journal*, Vol. 32, No. 1, pp. 4–16.

Hersey, P. and Blanchard, K. H. (1969) *Management of Organizational Behaviour: Utilizing Human Resources*, Englewood Cliffs, NJ, Prentice-Hall.

Herzberg, F., Mausner, B., and Snyderman, B. B. (1959) *The Motivation to Work*, New York, NY, Wiley & Sons.

Higgins, A. (2001) 'Designing with the new Internet', *Machine Design*, Vol. 73, No. 14, pp. 90–4.

Hinrich, J. R. and Mischkind, L. A. (1967) 'Empirical and theoretical limitations of the Two-Factor hypothesis of job satisfaction', *Journal of Applied Psychology*, Vol. 5, No. 2, pp. 191–200.

Hofstede, G. (1980) *Culture's Consequences: International Differences in Work-related Values*, Beverly Hills, CA, Sage.

Hofstede, G. (1989) 'Organizing for cultural diversity', *European Management Journal*, Vol. 7, No. 4, pp. 390–7.

Holland, P. J., Hecker, R., and Sheen, J. (2002) 'Human resource strategies and organisational structures for managing gold-collar workers', *Journal of European Industrial Training*, Vol. 26, Nos. 2/3/4, pp. 72–80.

Hopkins, M. (1999) *The Planetary Bargain: Corporate Social Responsibility Comes of Age*. London, Macmillan.

Hopkins, N. (2012) 'G4S faces financial penalties over Olympic security failures', *Guardian*, 12 July. <http://www.guardian.co.uk/sport/2012/jul/12/g4s-financial-penalties-olympic-security>.

House, R. J. (1996) 'Path-goal theory of leadership: lessons, legacy and a reformulated theory', *Leadership Quarterly*, Vol. 7, No. 3, pp. 323–52.

Hsu, M. and Chiu, K. (2008) 'A comparison between I-Ching's early management decision-making model and Western management decision-making models', *Chinese Management Studies*, Vol. 2, No. 1, pp. 52–75.

Huczynski, A. and Buchanan, D. (2003) *Organisational Behaviour*, Harlow, Prentice-Hall.

Huczynski, A. A. and Buchanan, D. A. (2007) *Organizational Behavior* (6th edn), Harlow, Pearson Education.

Hughes, S. (2005) 'Competitive intelligence as competitive advantage: The theoretical link between competitive intelligence, strategy and firm performance', *Journal of Competitive Intelligence and Management*, Vol. 3, No. 2, pp. 3–18.

Human Resource Management International Digest (2012), 'Scottish semiconductor firm chips in with the skills that matter'. Award winning training promotes world class performance, *Human Resource Management International Digest*, Vol. 20, No. 5, pp. 10–12.

Hutton, W. (2002) *The World We're In*, New York, NY, Little, Brown & Company.

Ishikawa, K. (1985) *What is Total Quality Control? The Japanese Way*, New York, Prentice-Hall.

Jashapara, A. (2003) 'Cognition, culture and competition: an empirical test of the learning organization', *The Learning Organization*, Vol. 10, No. 1, pp. 31–50.

Jenkins, J, G. D., Mitra, A., Gupta, N., and Shaw, J. D. (1998) 'Are financial incentives related to performance? A meta-analytic review of empirical research', *Journal of Applied Psychology*, Vol. 83, pp. 777–87.

Johns, G., Xie, J. L., and Fang, Y. (1992) 'Mediating and moderating effects on job design', *Journal of Management*, Vol. 18, pp. 657–76.

Johnson, D. W. and Johnson, F. P. (2003) *Joining Together: Group theory and group skills* (8th edn), Boston, Allyn and Bacon.

Johnson, G., Whittington, R. and Scholes, K. (2011) *Exploring Strategy* (9th edn), Harlow, FT/Prentice-Hall.

Johnson, P. (2007) *20th Century Britain: Economic, Cultural and Social Change*, Harlow, Longman.

Jones, G. R. and George, J. M. (2007) *Contemporary Management* (5th edn), New York, McGraw-Hill.

Judge, T. A., Bono, J. E., Illes, R. and Gerhardt, M. W. (2002) 'Personality and leadership: A qualitative and quantitative review', *Journal of Applied Psychology*, August, pp. 765–80.

Jung, D. and Sosik, J. J. (2006) 'Who are the spell-binders? Identifying personal attributes of charismatic leaders', *Journal of Leadership and Organizational Studies*, Vol. 12, pp. 12–27.

Juran, J. M. (1974) *Juran's Quality Control Handbook*, New York, McGraw-Hill.

Kahneman, D. (19 October 2011) 'Don't Blink! The Hazards of Confidence', *New York Times*. <http://www.nytimes.com/2011/10/23/magazine/don't-blink-the-hazards-of-confidence.html?pagewanted=all&_r=0>.

Kain, E. (19 January 2012) How Technology Killed Kodak, Forbes.com <http://www.forbes.com/sites/erikkain/2012/01/19/how-technology-killed-kodak/>.

Kalleberg, A. L. (2001) 'Organizing flexibility: The flexible firm in a new century', *British Journal of Industrial Relations*, Vol. 39, No. 4, pp. 479–504.

Kassing, J. W. (2009) 'Breaking the chain of command: Making sense of employee circumvention', *Journal of Business Communication*, Vol. 43, No. 3), pp. 311–34.

Katz, D. and Khan R. L. (1978) *The Social Psychology of Organizations*, New York, NY, John Wiley & Sons.

Katz, R. L. (1974) 'Skills of an effective administrator', *Harvard Business Review*, Vol. 52, p. 94.

Katzenbach, J. R. and Smith, D. (1994) *The Wisdom of Teams: Creating the High Performance Organisation*, New York, Harper Business.

Kearney, C., Hisrich, R. D., and Roche, F. W. (2010) 'Change management through entrepreneurship in public sector enterprises', *Journal of Development Entrepreneurship*, Vol. 15, No. 4, pp. 415–37.

Kearns, P. (2007) *The Value Motive: The Only Alternative to the Profit Motive*, London, John Wiley & Sons.

Kelliher, C. and Anderson, D. (2010) 'Doing more for less? Flexible working practices and the intensification of work', *Human Relations*, 63, pp. 83–106.

Kettinger, W. J., Grover, V., Guha, S., and Segars, A. H. (1994) 'Strategic information systems revisited: A study in sustainability and performance', *MIS Quarterly*, Vol. 18, No. 1, pp. 31–58.

Keyton, J. (2005) *Communication and Organizational Culture: A key to understanding work experiences* (4th edn), Thousand Oaks, CA, Sage.

Kiang, M. Y. and Chi, R. T. (2001) 'A framework for analyzing the potential benefits of internet marketing', *Journal of Electronic Commerce Research*, Vol. 2, No. 4.

Kim, P. H., Dirks, K. T. and Cooper, C. D. (2009) 'The repair of trust: A dynamic bilateral perspective and multilevel conceptualization', *Academy of Management Review*, July, pp. 401–22.

King, N. and Anderson, N. R. (1995) *Innovation and Change in Organizations*, London, Routledge.

Kinicki, A. and Williams, B. K. (2010) *Management: A Practical Introduction* (5th edn), New York, McGraw-Hill Higher Education.

Kirkpatrick, S. A. and Locke, E. A. (1991) 'Leadership: do traits really matter', *Academy of Management Executive*, May, pp. 48–60.

Klein, K. J., Ziegert, J. C., Knight, A. P., and Xiao, Y. (2006) 'Dynamic delegation: Shared, hierarchical and deindividualised leadership in extreme action teams', *Administrative Science Quarterly*, Vol. 51, No. 4, pp. 590–612.

Klein, N. (2000) *No Logo: Taking Aim at the Brand Bullies*, London, Flamengo.

Kleinmuntz, B. (1990) 'Why we still use our heads instead of formulas: towards an integrative approach', *Psychological Bulletin*, Vol. 107, No. 3, pp. 296–310.

Koontz, H. and Weihrich, H. (2006) *Essentials of Management: An International Perspective* (3rd edn), New York, McGraw-Hill.

Kotler, P. and Lee, N. (2005) *Corporate Social Responsibility: Doing the Most Good for your Company and your Cause*, New York, John Wiley & Sons.

Kotter, J. P. (1990) *A Force for Change: How Leadership Differs from Management*, New York, The Free Press.

Kotter, J. P. and Schlesenger, L. (1979) 'Choosing strategies for change', *Harvard Business Review*, 57, pp. 106–14.

Kramer, R. M. (1989) 'When the going gets tough: The effects of resource scarcity on group conflict and cooperation', in Lawler, E.

and Markovsky, B. (eds), *Advances in Group Processes*, Vol. 7, Greenwich, CT, JAI Press, pp. 151–77.

Kramer, R. and Syed, J. (2012) *Human Resource Management in a Global Context: A Critical Approach*, Basingstoke, Palgrave Macmillan.

Laborde, G. Z. (1995) *Influencing With Integrity: Managament Skills for Communication and Negotiation*, Carmarthen, Crown House Publishing.

Lam, A. (2005) 'Organizational innovation', in Fagerberg, J., Mowery, D., and Nelson, R. (eds), *Handbook of Innovation*, Oxford, Oxford University Press.

Lampel, J., Mintzberg, H., Quinn, J. B., and Ghoshal, S. (2013) *The Strategy Process: Concepts, Contexts, Cases* (5th edn), Harlow, Pearson.

Lasalle, L. (27 January 2010) No dividend for CGI shareholders, *Globe and Mail*, Montreal. <http://www.theglobeandmail.com/globe-investor/no-dividend-for-cgi-shareholders/article4302863/>.

Laudon, K. C. and Laudon, J. P. (1998) *Management Information Systems: New Approaches to Organization and Technology*, Upper Saddle River, NJ, Prentice-Hall.

Lawrence, P. and Lorsch, J. W. (1967) *Organization and the Environment*, Boston, MA, Harvard Business School Press.

Leana, C. R. (1986) 'Predictors and consequences of delegation', *Academy of Management Journal*, Vol. 29, pp. 754–74.

Learned, E. P., Christensen, C. R., Andrews, K. R., and Guth, W. D. (1965) *Business Policy: Text and Cases*, Homewood, IL, Irwin.

Leavitt, H. J. and Lipman-Blumen, J. (1995) 'Hot Groups', *Harvard Business Review*, July. <http://hbr.org/1995/07/hot-groups/ar/1>.

Legerer, P., Pfeiffer, T., Schneider, G., and Wagner, J. (2009) 'Organizational structure and managerial decision', *International Journal of Economics and Business*, Vol. 16, No. 2, pp. 147–59.

The Leveson Inquiry (2012) *Culture, Practices and the Ethics of the Press*, London, The Stationery Office.

Levi, D. (2013) *Group Dynamics for Teams* (4th edn), London, Sage Publications.

Levinson, W. A. (2002) *Henry Ford's Lean Vision: Enduring Principles from the First Ford Motor Plant*, New York, Productivity Press.

Levitt, T. (1983) 'The globalisation of markets', *Harvard Business Review*, May/June.

Lewin, K. (1951) *Field Theory in Social Science, Selected Theoretical Papers*, New York, Harper & Row.

Lewin, K. (1952) *Field Theory in Social Science*, London, Tavistock/Routledge Paul.

Lewin, K. (1948) *Resolving Social Conflicts; Selected Papers on Group Dynamics*, New York, Harper & Row.

Lewin, K., Lippett, R., and White, R. (1939) 'Patterns of aggressive behavior in experimentally created social climates', *Journal of Social Psychology*, pp. 271–301.

Lewis, P. S., Goodman, S. H., and Fandt, P. M. (2000) *Management Challenges in the 21st Century* (3rd edn), Nashville, TN, SouthWestern Publishing.

Li, B. (2008) 'The classical model of decision making has been accepted as not providing an accurate account of how people typically make decisions', *International Journal of Business and Management*, Vol. 3, No. 6, pp. 151–4.

Ling, Y., Simsek, Z., Lubatkin, M. H. and Veiga, J. F. (2008) 'Transformational leadership's role in promoting corporate entrepreneurship: Examining the CEO-TMT interface', *Academy of Management Journal*, June, pp. 557–76.

Likert, R. (1961) *New Patterns of Management*, New York, McGraw-Hill.

Lindstrom, J., Samuelsson, S., and Hagerfors, A. (2010) 'Business contunuity planning methodology', *Disaster Prevention and Management*, Vol. 19, No. 2, pp. 243–55.

Lipnack, J. and Stamps, J. (2000) *Virtual Teams. People Working across Boundaries with Technology*, New York, John Wiley & Sons.

Litterick, D. (13 September 2002) The billionaire who broke the bank of England, *Telegraph*. <http://www.telegraph.co.uk/finance/2773265/Billionaire-who-broke-the-Bank-of-England.html>.

Lund, D. B. (2003) 'Organizational culture and job satisfaction', *Journal of Business and Industrial Marketing*, Vol. 18, No. 3, pp. 219–36.

Lunenburg, F. C. (2011) 'Understanding organizational culture: A key leadership asset', *National Forum of Educational Administration and Supervision Journal*, Vol. 29, No. 4, pp. 1–12.

Lussier, R. N. (2008) *Management Fundamentals: Concepts, Applications, Skill Development*, Mason, OH, South Western College.

Lustgarten, A. (2012) *Run to Failure: BP and the Making of the Deepwater Horizon Disaster*, London, W.W. Norton & Co.

Lykins, D. (2002) *Focus on Your Customers*, E-Business Advisor, Advisor Media, San Diego (August) pp. 10–3.

McAdam, R. and Henderson, J. (2004) 'Influencing the future of TQM: internal and external driving factors', *International Journal of Quality and Reliability Management*, Vol. 21, No. 1, pp. 51–71.

McCarthy, E. J. (1960) *Basic marketing: A Global-Managerial Approach* (13th edn), Homewood, IL, Irwin.

McClelland, D. C. (1988) *Human Motivation*, Cambridge, Cambridge University Press.

McCrea, R. R. (1992) 'Special Issue: the Five-Factor Model: Issues and applications', *Journal of Personality*, June.

McDonald, M. and Wilson, H. (2011) *Marketing Plans: How To Prepare Them, How To Use Them* (7th edn), Chichester, John Wiley & Sons.

McGrath, J. E. (1962) *Leadership Behavior: Some Requirements for Leadership Training*, Washington DC, US Civil Service Commission.

McGregor, D. (1960) *The Human Side of Enterprise*, New York, McGraw-Hill.

McIvor, R. (2005) *The Outsourcing Process: Strategies for Evaluation and Management*, Cambridge, Cambridge University Press.

McShane, S. and Travaglione, A. (2005) *Organisational Behaviour on the Pacific Rim*, Sydney, McGraw-Hill.

McWilliams, A. and Siegel, D. (2000) 'Corporate social responsibility and financial performance: correlation or misspecification?', *Strategic Management Journal*, Vol. 21, No. 5, pp. 603–9.

McWilliams, A. and Siegel, D. S. (2011) 'Creating and capturing value: Strategic corporate social responsibility, resource-based theory, and sustainable competitive advantage', *Journal of Management*, Vol. 37, pp. 1299–315.

Mallach, E. G. (2009) 'Information systems conversion strategies: A unified view', *International Journal of Enterprise Information Systems*, Vol. 5, No. 1, pp. 44–54.

Malone, T. W. (2004) *The Future of Work: How The New Order of Business Will Shape Your Organization, Your Managament Style, and Your Life*, Boston, MA, Harvard Business School Press.

Mann, L. (2005) *Leadership, Management and Innovation in R&D Project Teams*, Westwood, CT, Praeger.

March, J. G. (1988) *Decisions and Organizations*, London, Blackwell.

March, J. G. (1994) *A Primer on Decision Making*, New York, The Free Press.

Marshall, A. (1919) *Industry and Trade*, London, Macmillan.

Maslow, A. (1943) 'A theory of human motivation', *Psychological Review*, Vol. 50, No. 4, pp. 370–96.

Mason, E. S. (1939) 'Price and production policies of large scale enterprises', *American Economic Review*, Vol. 29.

Mata, J. F., Fuerst, W. L. and Barney, J. B. (1995) 'Information technology and sustained competitive advantage: A resource-based analysis', *MIS Quarterly*, Vol. 19, No. 4, pp. 487–505.

Mayer, R. C. and Gavin, M. B. (2005) 'Trust in management performance: Who minds the shop while the employees watch the boss?', *Academy of Management Journal*, Vol. 38, No. 1, pp. 24–59.

Mayo, E. (1933) *The Human Problems of an Industrialised Civilization*, New York, Macmillan.

Mayo, E. (1949) *Hawthorne and the Western Electric Company, The Social Problems of an Industrial Civilization*, New York, Routledge.

Mello, A. S. and Ruckes, M. E. (2006) 'Team composition', *Journal of Business*, Vol. 79, No. 3, pp. 1019–39.

Merchant, K. A. (1982) 'The Control Function of management', *Sloan Management Review*, Summer, pp. 43–55.

613

Merton, R. (1940), 'Bureaucratic structure and personality', *Social Forces*, Vol. 18, pp. 560–8.

Mietzner, D. and Reger, G. (2005) 'Advantages and disadvantages of scenario approaches for strategic insights', *International Journal of Technology Intelligence and Planning*, Vol. 1, No. 2, pp. 220–39.

Mill, J. S. (1861) *Utilitarianism*. 2007 edition. New York, Dover Publications Inc.

Miller, J. (14 June 2010) Toyota to Reduce Span of Control, gemba panta rei. <http://www.gembapantarei.com/2010/06/toyota_to_reduce_span_of_control_in_engineering_1.html>.

Milne, P. (2007) 'Motivation, incentives and organisational culture', *Journal of Knowledge Management*, Vol. 11, No. 6, pp. 28–38.

Mintzberg, H. (1978) 'Patterns of strategic formulation', *Management Science*, Vol. 24, pp. 934–48.

Mintzberg, H. (1979) *The Structuring of Organizations*, Englewood Cliffs, NJ, Prentice-Hall.

Mintzberg, H. (1983) *Power In and Around Organizations*, Englewood Cliffs, CA, Prentice-Hall.

Mintzberg, H. (1989) *Mintzberg on Management*, New York, Free Press.

Mintzberg, H. (1994a) 'The fall and rise of strategic planning'. *Harvard Business Review*, January–February, pp. 107–14.

Mintzberg, H. (1994b) *The Rise and Fall of Strategic Planning*, New York, NY, The Free Press.

Mintzberg, H. (2011) *Managing*, San Francisco, CA, Berrett-Koehler.

Mintzberg, H. and Quinn, J. B. (1988) *The Strategy Process*, Harlow, Prentice-Hall.

Moore, S. (2008) 'Business ethics? A global comparative study on corporate sustainability approaches', *Social Responsibility Journal*, Vol. 4, No. 1/1, pp. 172–84.

Morris, P. and Pinto, J. K. (2007) *The Wiley Guide to Project, Program, and Portfolio*, Hoboken, NJ, John Wiley & Sons.

Morris, W. (2005) A Survey of Organisational Creativity. <www.jpb.com/creative/OrganisationalCreativityMorris.pdf>.

Morse, N. C. and Reimer, E. (1956) 'The experimental change of a major organizational variable', *Journal of Abnormal and Social Psychology*, Vol. 52, No. 1, pp. 120–29.

Motwani, J., Levenburg, N. M., Schwarz, T. V., and Blankson, C. (2006) 'Succession Planning in SME's: An Empirical Analysis', *International Small Business Journal*, Vol. 24, No. 5, pp. 471–95.

Moustakas, C. (1990) *Heuristic Research: Design, Methodology, and Applications*, Newbury Park, CA, Sage Publications.

Mullin, R. (2008) 'Pfizer's stem cell research', *Chemical & Engineering News*, Vol. 86, No. 47, p. 11.

Myers, D. (2002) *Intuition: Its Powers and Perils*, New Haven, CT, Yale University Press.

Myers, I. (1962) *Introduction to Type: A Description of the Theory and Application of the Myers–Briggs Indicator*, Palo Alta, CA, Consulting and Psychologists Press.

Myers, I. B. and McCaulley, M. H. (1985) *Manual: A Guide to the Development and Use of the Myers–Briggs Type Indicator*, Palo Alto, CA, Consulting Psychologists Press.

Nadler, D. A. and Lawler, E. E. (1983) 'Motivation: A diagnostic approach', in Hackman, J. R., Lawler, E. E., and Porter, L. W. (eds) *Perspectives on Behavior in Organizations*, New York, McGraw-Hill.

National Cancer Action Team (2010) The Characteristics of an Effective Multidisciplinary Team (MDT), London, NHS.

Neisser, U. (1967) *Cognitive Psychology*, New York, NY, Appleton-Century-Crofts.

Nelson, B. (1 July 1999) Motivation Matters: Disney Magic? Recognition. Meetingsnet. <http://meetingsnet.com/corporate-meetings/motivation-matters-disneys-magic-recognition>.

Newall, S., Robertson, M., Scarbrough, H., and Swan, J. (2002) *Managing Knowledge Work*, Basingstoke, Palgrave.

Newby, L. and Howarth, C. (2012) 'How *Specsavers* attracts and nurtures outstanding talent', *Strategic HR Review*, Vol. 11, No. 4, pp. 193–8.

New York Times (1990) 'An Uneasy Alliance Is Born For Mitsubishi and Daimler', 20 September. <http://www.nytimes.com/1990/09/20/business/an-uneasy-alliance-is-born-for-mitsubishi-and-daimler.html?pagewanted=2&src=pm>.

Ngowi, A. B. (2000) 'Impact of culture on the application of TQM in the construction industry in Botswana', *International Journal of Quality and Reliability*, Vol. 17, No. 4/5, pp. 442–52.

Niles, R. (19 November 2009) Theme Park Insider, Las Vegas. <http://www.themeparkinsider.com/flume/200911/1551/>.

Noelle-Kimini, C. (2002) 'The Loya Jirga—An effective political tool? A historical overview', in Noelle-Kimini, C., Schetter, C., and Schlangenweit, R. (eds) *Afghanistan—A Country Without a State?* Frankfurt, IKO-Verlag fur Interkulturelle Kommunikation, pp. 37–52.

Nutt, P. C. (2004) 'Expanding the search for alternatives during strategic decision making', *Academy of Management Executive*, Vol. 18, No. 4, pp. 13–28.

O'Brien, J. A. (2002) *Managing Information Systems: Managing Information Technology in the eBusiness Enterprise* (5th edn), New York, McGraw-Hill.

Orlitzky, M., Schmidt, F. L. and Rynes, S. L. (2003) 'Corporate social and financial performance: A meta-analysis', *Organization Studies*, Vol. 24, No. 3, pp. 403–41.

Osterman, P. (2000) 'Work reorganization in an era of restructuring: Trends in diffusion and effects on employee welfare', *Industrial and Labor Relations Review*, Vol. 53, pp. 179–96.

Ouchi, W. (1979) 'A conceptual framework for the design of organizational control mechanisms', *Management Science*, Vol. 25, pp. 833–48.

Parikh, J. (1994) *Intuition: The New Frontier of Management*, Oxford, Blackwell Business.

Parker, S. and Wall, T. (1998) *Job and Work Design: Organizing Work to Promote Well-being and Effectiveness*, Sage, Thousand Oaks, CA.

Parsons, H. M. (1974) 'What Happened at Hawthorne? New evidence suggests the Hawthorne effect resulted from operant reinforcement contingencies', *Science*, Vol. 183, No. 4128, pp. 922–32.

Passmore, W., Francis, C., Haldeman, J., and Shani, A. (1982) 'Sociotechnical systems: A North American reflection on empirical studies of the seventies', *Human Relations*, Vol. 35, pp. 1179–204.

Paul, R. (11 March 2010) Controversial Amazon 1-Click patent survives review, Law & Disorder/Civilization & Discontents, arstechnica.com <http://arstechnica.com/tech-policy/2010/03/controversial-amazon-1-click-patent-survives-review/>.

Perkins, S. (2008) *Employee Reward: Contexts, Alternatives and Consequences*, London, CIPD.

Perrow, C. (1970) *Organizational Analysis: A Sociological View*, Belmont, CA, Wadsworth Publishing Co.

Perry, J. L., Mesch, D., and Paarlberg, L. (2006) 'Motivating employees in a new governance era: The performance paradigm revisited', *Public Administration Review*, Vol. 66, pp. 505–14.

Peters, T. J. and Waterman, R. H. (1982) *In Search of Excellence*, New York, Harper & Row.

Peterson, T. O. and Van Fleet, D. D. (2004) 'The on-going legacy of R. L. Katz: An updated typology of management skills', *Management Decision*, Vol. 42, No. 10, pp. 1297–308.

Pettinger, R. (2007) *Introduction to Management* (4th edn), Basingstoke, Palgrave Macmillan.

Pfeffer, J. and Salancik, G. R. (1974) 'Organizational decision making as a political process: The case of a university budget', *Administrative Science Quarterly*, Vol. 19, No. 2, pp. 135–51.

Pirson, M. and Malhorta, D. (2007) *What Matters to Whom? Managing Trust Across Multiple Stakeholder Groups*, Cambridge, MA, The Hauser Center for Non Profit Organizations, Harvard Univeristy.

Polak, P., Robertson, D. C. and Lind, M. (2011) 'The new role of the corporate treasurer: Emerging trends in response to financial crisis', *International Journal of Finance and Economics*, No. 78.

Pollitt, C. (1995) 'Justification by works or by faith? Evaluating the New Public Management', *Evaluation*, Vol. 1, No. 2, pp. 133–53.

Porter, M. E. (1979) 'How competitive forces shape strategy', *Harvard Business Review*, (March–April), pp. 137–45.

Porter, M. E. (1980) *Competitive Strategy*, New York, The Free Press.

Porter, M. E. (1985) *Competitive Advantage: Gaining and Sustaining Superior Performance*, New York, The Free Press.

Porter, M. E. (1996) 'What is Strategy?', *Harvard Business Review*, November–December, pp. 61–78.

Porter, M. E. (2001) 'Strategy and the internet', *Harvard Business Review*, March, pp. 63–78.

Porter, M. E. and Kramer, M. R. (2006) 'Strategy and society: The link between competitive advantage and corporate social responsibility', *Harvard Business Review*, December, pp. 78–92.

Porter, M. E. and Millar, V. A. (1995) 'How information gives you a competitive advantage', *Harvard Business Review*, Vol. 73, No. 4.

Potter, E. E. (2003) 'Telecommuting: The future of work, corporate culture, and American society', *Journal of Labor Research*, Vol. 24, No. 1, pp. 73–84.

Pradtare, M. T. (2011) *Strategic Managament: Concepts and Cases*, Delhi, PHI Learning.

Principles of The Sun, (March 2008) <www.thesun.co.uk/.../Sir-Alan-Sugar-The-Apprentice>.

Pritchard, C., Chumer, M., Willmott, H., and Hull, R. (2000) *Managing Knowledge: Critical Investigations of Work and Learning*, Basingstoke, Palgrave Macmillan.

Puddicombe, M. S. (2006) 'The limitations of planning: The importance of learning', *Journal of Construction Engineering and Management*, Vol. 132, No. 9, pp. 949–56.

Pugh, D. S., Hickson, D. J., Hinings, C. R. (1969), 'The context of organization structures', *Administrative Science Quarterly*, Vol. 14 No. 1, pp. 115–26.

Quah, T., Tan, C., The, H., and Srinivasan, B. (1994) 'Hedging strategies in international currencies options using neural network expert systems', *IBS Computing Quarterly*, Fall, pp. 29–36.

Quinn, J. and Ahmed, K. (11 August 2012) Sir David Walker: I will change Barclays, *Telegraph*. <http://www.telegraph.co.uk/finance/newsbysector/banksandfinance/9469221/Sir-David-Walker-I-will-change-Barclays.html>.

Quinn, R. E., Faerman, S. R., Thompson, M. P. and McGrath, M. R. (2003) *Becoming a Master Manager* (3rd edn), New York, Wiley.

Ray, G., Muhanna, W. A. and Barney, J. B. (2005) 'Information technology and the performance of the customer service process: A resource-based analysis', *MIS Quarterly*, Vol. 29, pp. 625–52.

Rayport, J. and Sviokla, J. (1995) 'Exploiting the virtual value chain', *Harvard Business Review*, Vol. 73, No. 6, pp. 75–85.

Reilly, P. (2011) 'HR's future in a global setting', *Human Resource Management International Digest*, Vol. 20, No. 3, pp. 3–5.

Ringland, G. (2006) *Scenario Planning* (2nd edn), Chichester, Wiley & Sons.

Riordan, C. M., Vandenberg, R. J., and Richardson, H. A. (2005) 'Employee involvement climate and organizational effectiveness', *Human Resource Management*, 44, pp. 471–88.

Ritzer, G. (2004) *The McDonaldisation of Society*, Thousand Oaks, CA, Forge Press.

Robbins, S. P. and Coulter, M. (2012) *Management* (11th edn), Harlow, Pearson.

Robbins, S. P., Millett, B., and Waters-Marsh, T. (2004) *Organizational Behavior* (4th edn), Harlow, Pearson Educational.

Robbins, S. P., Judge, T. A., and Campbell, T. T. (2010) *Organizational Behaviour*, Harlow, Pearson Education.

Robinson, B. (1 July 2002) Why Strategic Alliances Don't Work, Forbes.com <http://www.forbes.com/2002/07/01/0701alliances.html>.

Rowntree, B. S. (1901) *Poverty: A Study in Town Life*, London: Macmillan & Son.

Royal Academy of Arts (2013) The natural force of Tado Andro, London. <http://www.royalacademy.org.uk/architecture/architecture-resources/interviews/the-natural-force-of-tadao-ando,212,AR.html>.

Rumelt, R. P. (1991) 'How much does industry matter?' *Strategic Management Journal*, Vol. 12, No. 3.

Saee, J. (2005) 'Effective leadership for the global economy in the 21st century', *Journal of Business Economics and Management*, Vol. 6, Issue 1, pp 3–11.

Sanchez, P. (2004) 'Defining corporate culture', *Communications World*, Nov/Dec, International Association of Business Commmunication.

Sandino, T. (2007) 'Introducing the first management control systems: Evidence from the retail sector', *Accounting Review*, Vol. 82, No. 1, pp. 265–93.

Sandlund, C. (1 October 2002) Trust Is A Must, Entrepreneur. <http://www.entrepreneur.com/article/55354>.

Saunders, R. (1999) *Business the Amazon.com Way: Secrets of the World's Most Astonishing Web Business*, Washington DC, Capstone.

Saxton, J. L. (2007) Report on the Millaue Viaduct, Proceedings of Bridge Engineering 2 Conference, 27 April, University of Bath, Bath.

Scannell, M. and Scannell, E. (2009) *The Big Book of Team Motivating Games: Spirit Building, Problem Solving and Communication Games for Every Group* (Big Book Series), New York, McGraw-Hill.

Schein, E. H. (1985) *Organizational Culture and Leadership: A Dynamic View*, San Francisco, Jossey-Bass.

Schoemaker, P. J. H. (1991) 'When and how to use scenario planning', *Journal of Forecasting*, Vol. 10, pp. 549–64.

Schriesheim, C. M., Castro, S. L., Zhou, X., and DeChurch, L. A. (2006) 'An investigation of path-goal and transformational leadership theory predictions of the individual level of analysis', *Leadership Quarterly*, Vol. 17, pp. 21–38.

Schumpeter, J. A. (1949) *Economic Theory and Entrepreneurial History—Change and the Entrepreneur: Postulates and Patterns for Entrepreneurial History*, Cambridge, MA, Harvard University Press.

Scott, W. R. and Davis, G. F. (2006) *Organizations and Organizing: Rational, Natural, and Open Systems Perspectives*, Harlow, Pearson.

Sealy, P. (1999) 'How E-commerce will trump brand management', *Harvard Business Review*, July–August, pp. 171–6.

Secchi, D. (2010) *Extendable Rationality: Understanding Decision Making in Organizations*, New York, NY, Springer.

Selznick, P. (1957) *Leadership in Administration: A Sociological Interpretation*, Evanston, IL, Row, Peterson.

Semple, E. (2012) *Organizations Don't Tweet, People Do: A Manager's Guide to the Social Web*, Chichester, John Wiley & Sons.

Senge, P. (1990a) 'Building learning organisations', *Sloan Management Review*, Fall, pp. 7–23.

Senge, P. (1990b) *The Fifth Discipline: The Art and Practice of the Learning Organization*, London, Random House.

Shah, A. (28 May 2006) Corporations and Workers' Rights, Global Issues. <http://www.globalissues.org/article/57/corporations-and-workers-rights>.

Shaw, M. E. (1981) *Group Dynamics: The Psychology of Small Group Behaviour* (3rd edn), New York, McGraw-Hill.

Shipton, H. (2006) 'Cohesion or confusion? Towards a typology for organisational learning research', *International Journal of Management Reviews*, Vol. 8, No. 4, pp. 233–52.

Shreisheim, C. A., Cogliser, C. C., and Neider, L. L. (1995) 'Is it trustworthy? A multiple-levels-of-analysis reexamination of an Ohio State leadership study, with implications for future research', *The Leadership Quarterly*, Vol. 6, No. 2, pp. 111–45.

Simon, H. A. (1960) *The New Science of Management Decision*, New York, Harper & Row.

Simon, H. A. (1982) *Models of Bounded Rationality*, Cambridge, MA, MIT Press.

Simon, H. A. (1987) 'Making management decisions: The role of intuition and emotion', *Academy of Management Executive*, February, pp. 57–64.

Singai, M. and Sriram, R. (27 October 2012), How Richard Branson has emerged as a marketing asset for Virgin Group. *The Economic Times* <http://articles.economictimes.indiatimes.com/2012-10-27/news/34765201_1_richard-branson-mumbai-taxi-spaceport-america>.

Sinha, I. (2000). 'Cost transparency: The net's real threat to prices and brands', *Harvard Business Review*, Vol. 78, No. 2, pp. 43–50.

Sinofsky, S. and Iansiti, M. (2009), *One Strategy: Organizations, Planning and Decision Making*, Chichester, Wiley & Sons.

Sjoberg, L. (2007) 'The distortion of beliefs in the face of uncertainty', *International Journal of Management and Decision Making*, Vol. 8, No. 1, pp. 1–29.

Slack, N., Chambers, S., and Johnston, R. (2007) *Operations Management* (5th edn), Harlow, FT/Prentice-Hall.

Smith, A. (1776) *The Wealth of Nations*, ed. Andrew Skinner (1974) Harmondsworth, Penguin.

Smith, D. B., Hanges, P. J., and Dickson, M. W. (2001) 'Personnel selection and the five-factor model: reexamining the effects of applicant's frame of reference', *Journal of Applied Psychology*, February, pp. 100-12.

Smith, M. (2007) *Fundamentals of Management*, Maidenhead, McGraw-Hill.

Smith, V. (1997) 'New forms of work organization', *Annual Review of Sociology*, 23, pp. 315-39.

Soltani, E. (2007) *(Process) Control and Total Quality Management: A Qualitative Study of Three Manufacturing Organisations*, POMS 18th Annual Conference, Dallas TX, 4-7 May.

Soon, C. S., He, A. H., Bode, S., and Haynes, J. D. (2013) *Predicting Free Choices for Abstract Intentions*, Washington DC, National Academy of Sciences.

Sperandio, S. and Girard, P. (2010) 'Decision-making framework methodology: Risk assessment in strategic management', *International Journal of Management and Decision Making*, Vol. 11, No. 1, pp. 4-18.

Sreenivas, M. and Srinivas, T. (2008) 'Effectiveness of distribution network', *International Journal of Information Systems and Supply Chain Management*, Vol. 1, No. 1, pp. 80-6.

Starbucks (2013) Mission statement <http://stageaten.starbucks.com/about-us/company-information/mission-statement>.

Stevenson, H. H. and Jarillo, J. C. (1990) 'A paradigm of entrepreneurship: Entrepreneurial management', *Strategic Management Journal*, Vol. 11, pp. 17-27.

Stodgill, R. M. (1948) 'Personal factors associated with leadership: A survey of the literature', *Journal of Psychology*, Vol. 25, pp. 35-71.

Stonehouse, G., Campbell, D., Hamill, J., and Purdie, T. (2004) *Global and Transnational Business: Strategy and Management*, London, John Wiley & Sons.

Stricker, L. J. and Ross, J. (1962) *A Description and Evaluation of the Myers-Briggs Type Indicator* (Research Bulletin #RB-62-6), Princeton, NJ, Educational Testing Service.

Stum, D. L. (1999) 'Maslow revisited: Building the employee pyramid', *Strategy and Leadership*, Vol. 29, No. 4, pp. 4-9.

Surhone, L. M., Timpledon, M. T., and Marseken, S. F. (2010) *Quality Management System: Industrial Revolution, Frederick Winslow Taylor, Henri Ford, Quality (business), New Product Development, Standing Operating Procedure*, Beau Bassin, Mauritius, Betascript Publishing.

Surowiecki, J. (2004) *The Wisdom of Crowds. Why the many are smarter than the few*, London, Abacus.

Susanto, A. (2008) 'Organisational readiness for change: A case study on change readiness in a manufacturing company in Indonesia', *International Journal of Management Perspectives*, Vol. 2, No. 1, pp. 50-60.

Tatli, A., Mulholland, G., Ozbilgin, M., and Worman, D. (2007) *Managing Diversity in Practice: Supporting Business Goals*, London, CIPD.

Taylor, F. W. (1911) *The Principles of Scientific Management*, New York, Harper & Brothers.

Taylor, F. W. (2003) *The Principles of Scientific Management* (rev. edn), New York, Dover Publications Inc.

Taylor, R. (2002) *The Future of Employment Relations*, Swindon, ESRC.

Taylor, S. E. (2012) *How the Makers of Quicken Beat Microsoft and Revolutionised an Entire Industry*, Boston, MA, Harvard Business School Press.

Teale, M., Dispenza, V., Flynn, J., and Currie, D. (2003) *Management Decision Making: Towards an Integrative Approach*, Harlow, FT/Prentice Hall.

Teece, D. J. (1996) 'Firm organization, industrial structure, and technological innovation', *Journal of Economic Behavior & Organization*, Vol. 31, No. 2, pp. 193-224.

Teece, D. J., Pisano, G., and Shuen, A. (1997) 'Dynamic capabilities and strategic management', *Strategic Management Journal*, Vol. 18, No. 7, pp. 509-33.

Times 100 Business Case Studies (2013) 'Solving complex supply chain problems'. <http://

businesscasestudies.co.uk/dexion/solving-complex-supply-chain-problems/decision-making.html#axzz2WC2XIGbb>.

Thielen, D. (1999) *The 12 Simple Secrets of Microsoft Management*, New York, McGraw-Hill.

Thinkexist, com (2013) George Patton quotation <http://thinkexist.com/quotation/if_you_cant_get_them_to_salute_when_they_should/147747.html>.

Thomas, D. C. and Inkson, K. (2003) *Cultural Intelligence: People Skills for the Global Business*, San Francisco, Berret-Koehler.

Thorpe, R. and Homan, G. (2000) *Strategic Reward Systems*, Harlow, Financial Times/Prentice Hall.

Timmers, P. (1999) *Electronic Commerce: Strategies and models for business to business trading*, Chichester, John Wiley & Sons.

Tomkins, R. (2000) 'Revenge of the Proctoids', *Financial Times*, 12 June.

Trompenaars, F. and Hampden-Turner, C. (2006) *Riding the Waves of Culture: Understanding Cultural Diversity in Global Business*, Chicago, Irwin.

Tschappeler, R., Krogerus, M., and Piening, J. (2011) *The Decision Book: Fifty Models for Strategic Thinking*, London, Profile Books.

Tuckman, B. W. (1965) 'Developmental sequence in small groups', *Psychological Bulletin*, Vol. 63, pp. 384–99.

University of Kansas (2013) *The Community Toolbox: Documenting Health promotion Initiatives Using the PAHO Guide, Example 3: Azucarlito: A Company Free of Tobacco Smoke Workplace Initiative in Uruguay*, Kansas, KA, University of Kansas.

Upbin, B. (9 April 2010) Why Intuit Is More Innovative Than Your Company, Forbes.com <http://www.forbes.com/sites/bruceupbin/2012/09/04/intuit-the-30-year-old-startup/3/>.

Urwick, L. E. (1956) 'The manager's span of control', *Harvard Business Review*, May–June, pp. 39–47.

Van der Keij, R., Schraagen, M. T., Werkhoven, P., and Carsten, K. W. (2009) 'How conversations change over time in face-to-face and video-mediated communications', *Small Group Research*, Vol. 40, No. 4, pp. 55–381.

VanIngen, S. (2007) 'Leadership of project teams', *I*, Vol. 114, No. 1, pp. 55–8.

Veblen, T. (1919) *The Place of Science in Modern Civilisation and Other Essays*, New Brunswick, NJ, Transaction Publishers.

Vecchio, R. P., Hearn, G., and Southey, G. (2005) *Organisational Behaviour: Life at Work in Australia*, Marrickville, NSW, Harcourt, Brace & Co.

Vee Technologies (2013) <http://www.veetechnologies.com/services.htm>.

Verano-Tacoronte, D. and Melian-Gonzalez, S. (2008) 'Human resource control systems and performance: the role of uncertainty and risk propensity', *International Journal of Manpower*, Vol. 29, No. 2, pp. 161–87.

Vinas, T. and Jusko, J. (2004) 'Threats that could sink your company', *Industry Week*, September, pp. 52–61.

Volberd, H. W. (1998) 'Toward the flexible form: how to remain vital in hypercompetitive environments', in A. Y. Illinitch, A. Lewin and R. D. D'Aveni (eds), *Managing in Times of Disorder: Hypercompetitive Organizational Responses*, Thousand Oaks, CA, Sage, pp. 267–96.

Vos, D. and Meganck, A. (2009) 'What HR managers do versus what employees value: Exploring both parties' views on retention management from a psychological contract perspective', *Personnel Review*, Vol. 38, No. 1, pp. 45–60.

Vroom, V. H. (1964) *Work and Motivation*, New York, Wiley & Sons.

Wang, H. M. D. (2010) 'Corporate social performance and financial-based brand equity', *Journal of Product and Brand Management*, Vol. 19, No. 5, pp. 335–45.

Webb, T. (4 September 2009) 'More job losses expected in Shell restructuring', *Guardian*. <http://www.theguardian.com/business/2009/sep/04/shell-oil-job-losses>.

Weber, M. (1905) *The Protestant Ethic and the Spirit of Capitalism and Other Writings*, New York, Penguin Group.

Weber, M. (1947) *The Theory of Social and Economic Organisation*, New York, The Free Press.

Weber, L. and Mayer, K. L. (2010) Simon Says 'Expand the Definition of Bounded Rationality in Management Research, Atlanta Competitive Advantage Conference, Georgia State University, Atlanta, 15 February 15.

Wegg-Prosser, V. (1998) BBC Producer Choice and the management of organisational change, London, Brunel University Research Archive. <http://bura.brunel.ac.uk/handle/2438/4380>.

Weimer, G. (2001) Robots Take Over Automotive Plant Floors, Robotics Online, Penton Media Inc. <http://www.robotics.org/content-detail.cfm/Industrial-Robotics-Featured-Articles/Robots-Take-Over-Automotive-Plant-Floors/content_id/835>.

Weiss, J. W. (2008) *Business Ethics: A Stakeholder and Issues Management Approach* (5th edn), Cincinnati, South Western College Publishing.

Welsh, D. H. B., Luthans, F., and Sommer, S. M. (1993) 'Managing Russian factory workers: the impact of US-based behavoral and participative techniques', *Academy of Management Journal* (February), pp. 58–79.

Williamson, O. (2000) 'Strategy Research: Competence and Governance Perspectives', in Foss, N. and Mahnke, V. (eds), *Competence, Governance, and Entrepreneurship*, Oxford, Oxford University Press.

Wines of Chile (2012) Largest online marketing campaign aimed at Chinese market. <http://www.winesofchile.org/2012/10/wines-of-chiles-largest-online-marketing-campaign-aimed-at-chinese-market/>.

Wong, S.-Y. and Chin, K.-S. (2007) ' Organizational innovation management: An organization-wide perspective', *Industrial Management & Data Systems*, Vol. 107, No. 9, pp. 1290–315.

Wood, M. (2005) *In Search of the First Civilisation*, London, BBC Books.

Woodward, J. (1958) *Management and Technology*, London, HMSO.

Woodward, J. (1965) *Industrial Organization: Theory and Practice*, Oxford, Oxford University Press.

World Nuclear Association (2013) Fukushima Accident 2011, London, World Nuclear Association. <http://www.world-nuclear.org/info/Safety-and-Security/Safety-of-Plants/Fukushima-Accident-2011/>.

Wrege, C. D. and Greenwood, R. G. (1991) *Frederick W Taylor: The Father of Scientific Management, Myth and Reality*, New York, Irwin.

Wright, G. and Cairns, G. (2011) *Scenario Thinking: Practical Approaches to the Future*, Basingstoke, Palgrave Macmillan.

Wrzesniewski, A. and Dutton, J. E. (2001) 'Crafting a job: Revisioning employees as active crafters of their work', *Academy of Management Review*, Vol. 26, No. 2, pp. 179–201.

Yang, Y. (2011) 'Understanding diversity management practices: Implications of institutional theory and resource-based theory, *Group Organization Management*, Vol. 36, No. 1, pp. 6–38.

Yip, G. S. (1992) *Total Global Strategy: Managing for Worldwide Competitive Advantage*, Englewood Cliff, NJ, Prentice Hall.

Yukl, G. (1981) *Leadership in Organizations*, Englewood Cliffs, NJ, Prentice-Hall.

Yunus, M. and Jolis, A. (2003) *Banker to the Poor: The Story of the Grameen Bank*, London, Aurum Press.

Zabriskie, N. B. (1989) 'Involving the middle line managers in building strategic planning information', *Journal of Business & Industrial Marketing*, Vol. 4, No. 1, pp. 37–48.

Zacarro, S. J., Rittman, A. L., and Marks, M. A. (2001) 'Team leadership', *Leadership Quarterly*, Vol. 12, pp. 451–83.

Zacarro, S.J., Kemp, C., and Bader, P. (2004) 'Leader traits and attributes', in Antonakis, J., Cianciolo, A. T., and Sternberg, R. J. (eds), *The Nature of Leadership*, Thousand Oaks, CA, Sage, pp. 101–24.

Zsidisin, G. A. (2000) 'Purchasing organization involvement in risk assessments, contingency plans, and risk management: An exploratory study', *Supply Chain Management: An International Journal*, Vol. 5, No. 4, pp. 187–98.

Index